BOTSWANA
SAFARI GUIDE

OKAVANGO DELTA • CHOBE
NORTHERN KALAHARI

CHRIS McINTYRE
& SUSIE McINTYRE

www.bradtguides.com

Bradt Guides Ltd, UK
The Globe Pequot Press Inc, USA

Bradt GUIDES
TRAVEL TAKEN SERIOUSLY

ANGOLA

Okavango

Rundu

NAMIBIA

Caprivi Strip

Kwando

The Tsodilo Hills: A UNESCO-listed gallery of ancient Bushman art
page 425

Shakawe

Okavango Delta: Extraordinary wildlife-rich islands and waters
page 334

Okavango

Sepupa

Seronga

Tsodilo Hills

NAMIBIA

KEY

Main town or city	●
Other town	○
Airport	✈
Tarred road	▬
International boundary	—
National park/game reserve	– – –

Etsha 6

Etsha

Jao

Moremi Game Reserve

Gumare

Okavango Delta

Nokaneng

Boro

Aha Hills

Moremi Game Reserve: The oldest protected section of the Okavango Delta and a magnet for self-drivers
page 301

Tsau

✈ **Maun**

Motshabeng Flats

Toteng

Sehithwa

Lake Ngami

Khwebe Hills

BOTSWANA
map coverage

Tautsa Flats

Ngwanalekau Hills

Maun: Vibrant frontier town and gateway to the Okavango Delta
page 189

N

Bradt

0		50km
0		30 miles

Central Kalahari Game Reserve

Windhoek

Ghanzi

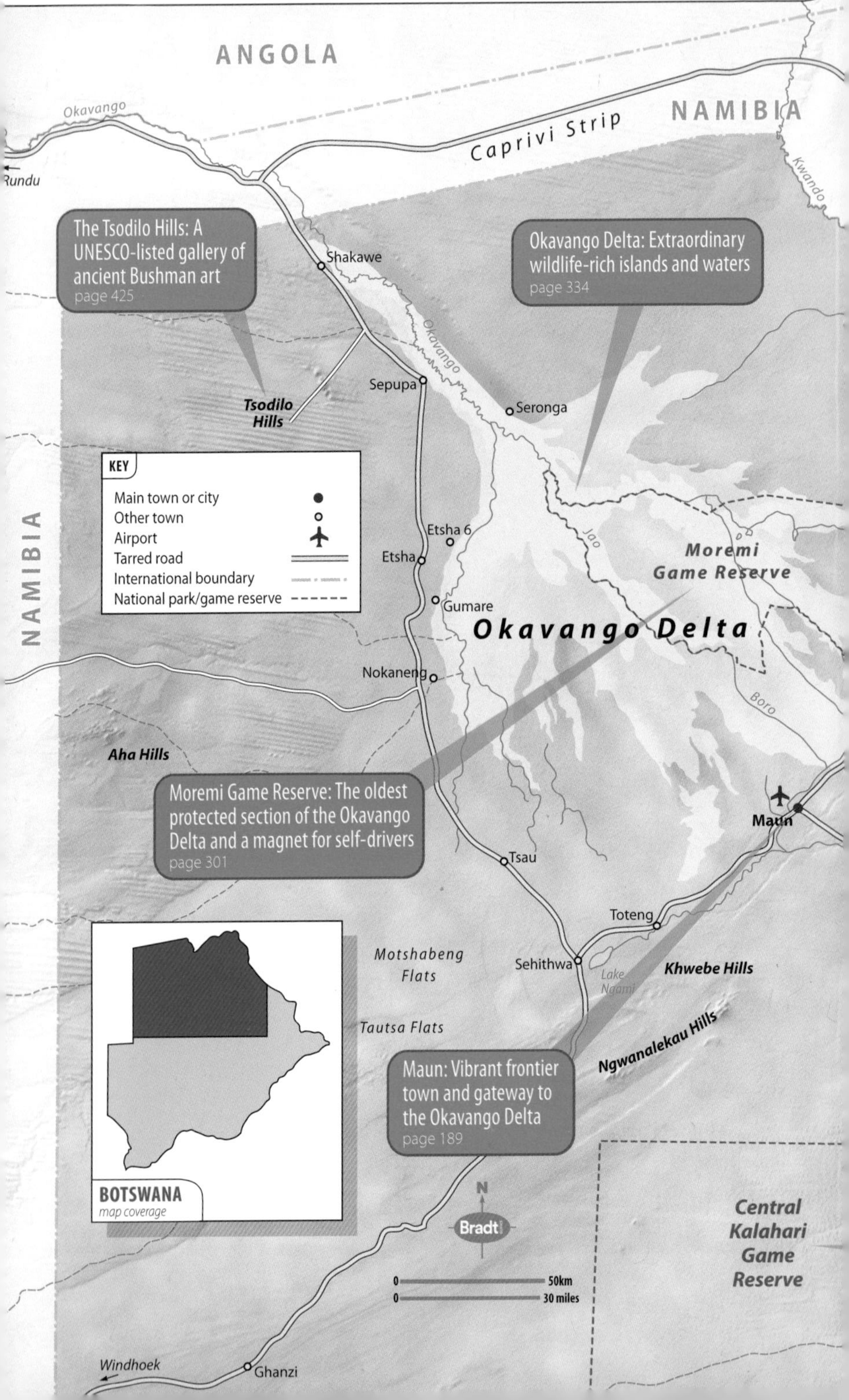

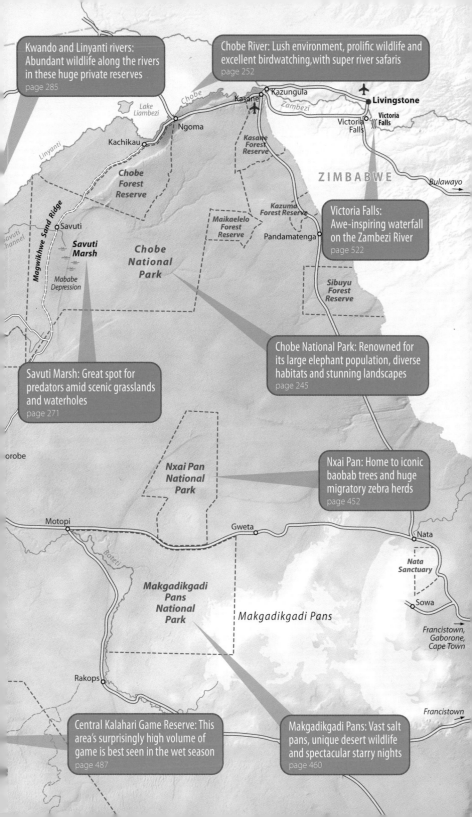

Kwando and Linyanti rivers: Abundant wildlife along the rivers in these huge private reserves
page 285

Chobe River: Lush environment, prolific wildlife and excellent birdwatching, with super river safaris
page 252

Victoria Falls: Awe-inspiring waterfall on the Zambezi River
page 522

Savuti Marsh: Great spot for predators amid scenic grasslands and waterholes
page 271

Chobe National Park: Renowned for its large elephant population, diverse habitats and stunning landscapes
page 245

Nxai Pan: Home to iconic baobab trees and huge migratory zebra herds
page 452

Central Kalahari Game Reserve: This area's surprisingly high volume of game is best seen in the wet season
page 487

Makgadikgadi Pans: Vast salt pans, unique desert wildlife and spectacular starry nights
page 460

Lake Liambezi

Chobe

Zambezi

Kasane

Kazungula

Livingstone

Victoria Falls

Victoria Falls

Ngoma

Kachikau

Linyanti

Savuti channel

Magwikhwe Sand Ridge

Savuti

Savuti Marsh

Mababe Depression

Kasane Forest Reserve

Chobe Forest Reserve

ZIMBABWE

Bulawayo

Maikaelelo Forest Reserve

Kazuma Forest Reserve

Pandamatenga

Chobe National Park

Sibuyu Forest Reserve

orobe

Nxai Pan National Park

Motopi

Gweta

Nata

Nata Sanctuary

Boteti

Makgadikgadi Pans National Park

Makgadikgadi Pans

Sowa

Francistown, Gaborone, Cape Town

Rakops

Francistown

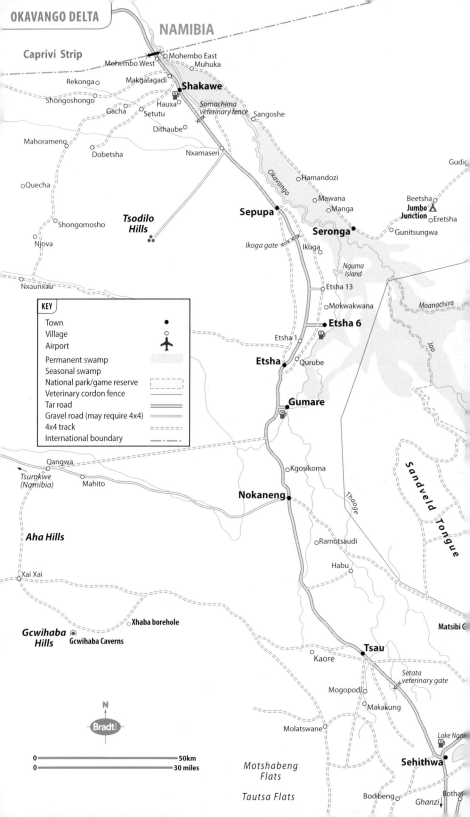

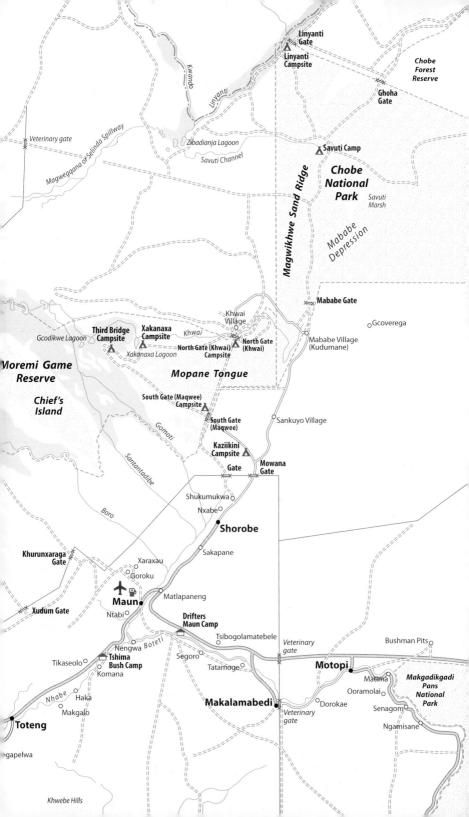

BOTSWANA
DON'T MISS...

THE OKAVANGO DELTA
Once a vast inland lake, the
Okavango Delta swells to three
times its size during the dry
months, creating Africa's biggest
oasis, a refuge for everything from
waterbirds to elephants
PAGE 334
(RH/S)

**THE KWANDO AND
LINYANTI RIVERS**
In wetter years this is a delta,
providing a refuge for a wide
range of wildlife such as lion
PAGE 285
(SS)

MAKGADIKGADI PANS
These fascinating dry salt pans
can be explored on foot, by 4x4
or on quad bikes PAGE 460
(JG)

MOREMI GAME RESERVE
With some of the richest
ecosystems in Africa, Moremi is
populated by a diverse range of
animals, including large numbers
of elephant PAGE 301
(OP/S)

CHOBE RIVERFRONT
This area is a magnet for wildlife,
including thirsty giraffe PAGE 252
(AVZ)

Chris McIntyre first visited Africa in 1987 after reading physics at The Queen's College, Oxford. He spent nearly three years teaching in Zimbabwe with VSO and travelled extensively across Africa. His experiences led him to write the UK's first guide to Namibia and Botswana, for Bradt Guides; since then he has continued to write and update Bradt Guides on Botswana, Namibia, Tanzania, Zambia and Zanzibar.

As the managing director of Expert Africa, a leading tour operator, Chris leads a talented team who design tailor-made holidays to southern and eastern Africa. They specialise in award-winning wildlife safaris, guided mobile expeditions and multi-generational family adventures. Chris is actively involved in development and conservation, advising various NGOs and projects associated with Africa, and occasionally writing for magazines and newspapers. A Fellow of the Royal Geographical Society, he lives with his wife Susie and their two bush-savvy children. He can be contacted via email at e chris.mcintyre@expert.africa or through the website below.

Susie McIntyre had an adventurous childhood in Zambia and Saudi Arabia, and has spent the last two decades promoting responsible global travel as a PR and marketing consultant, author and journalist. Susie has co-authored three Bradt guides: *Botswana Safari Guide, Zambia Safari Guide* and *Zanzibar*.

She is passionate about southern Africa: its people, wildlife and diversity. Her work spans Indian Ocean diving, conservation, community development and off-grid family adventures. Known for her thorough, on-the-ground research, and respected for her candid and enthusiastic approach to travel, she is dedicated to accurately representing the complexities of African countries.

When not traipsing around tropical isles and savannah, Susie lives in the British countryside with her husband and co-author, Chris, and their adventurous children. They usually spend significant time each year travelling and researching in Africa, to stay abreast of developments and continue to experience the continent they love.

Call the Author

Chris and his Expert Africa team are the best in the business at designing Botswana safaris. Call them now to help plan yours.

No bias, no hard sell: for real insight, contact the Experts.
UK: +44 203 405 6666   USA: 1-800-242-2434

www.expertafrica.com

We are extremely grateful to a few key contributors for their dedicated help in researching and writing sections within this guide.

Tom Morris first visited southern Africa in 2009, and since then has travelled the region extensively. He joined Expert Africa in 2015, where he not only spearheads the company's systems, but also creates bespoke itineraries to Botswana, Namibia and Zimbabwe. Tom did extensive research for this and the last edition; this time contributing to the chapters on the Kalahari Salt Pans, Moremi and some of the private reserves in the Okavango Delta.

Anton Walker grew up exploring Zimbabwe's national parks before travelling the world, training as a safari guide and working in some of southern Africa's premier camps. Now sharing his considerable passion and expertise as a specialist advisor at Expert Africa, Anton helped to update the Wildlife Guide and several private reserves in the Okavango Delta.

Mike Unwin is an award-winning freelance natural-history writer and illustrator, and author of Bradt's *Southern African Wildlife*. Mike contributed much expert natural-history information, and wrote most of the original chapter on the Kalahari's great salt pans. He now lives in England, having spent seven years in southern Africa pursuing wildlife around all corners of the region.

This guide has been built on the solid foundations laid by contributors to previous editions. Foremost among these are: Tricia and Bob Hayne, who worked on four previous editions of the book; African expert and fellow author Philip Briggs,

AUTHOR'S STORY *Chris McIntyre*

Botswana meant little to me at first; it was never in the news. Then, finding myself living in Zimbabwe, I remembered an old friend's enthusiasm for the Okavango Delta. So, in April 1988, I set off with two friends to Victoria Falls and hitched a lift in an open pick-up into Chobe. We were badly prepared, but even our lack of food and close encounters with hyenas added to the magic. No fences here; everything was so wild.

From Maun we splashed out on a few days' camping trip on a mokoro. While the boatman spoke little English, the Delta was magical, almost surreal – like floating on a tropical fish tank with animals everywhere around. The Okavango's lush greenery contrasted with the harsh dryness of the rest of the subcontinent. Iridescent birds flashed past, while terrapins sunbathed and otters played. All added to the feeling of paradise; we left entranced.

Thus started my love affair with the country. Since then I've been lucky enough to return many times. I've been guided by some of the best, learning more about the bush and its animals and plants. I've flown over the dry Kalahari and the verdant Delta, mesmerised by the ancient patterns of watercourses, islands and game trails. And I've walked and driven around, exploring for myself on the ground, exhilarated by the sense of freedom. Yet still I feel as if I've only scratched the surface of Botswana, and I always leave wanting to return.

who allowed us to build on his original text to create the Wildlife Guide; Octavia Kenny, who compiled the original history section; and my colleagues at Expert Africa, Maruska Adye-Rowe, Lucy Copson, Megan Green and Tracy Lederer, who are authorities on Botswana in their own right, and whose knowledge of safaris in Botswana contributes greatly to our understanding of travel here.

KEY TO SYMBOLS

-----	International boundary	⌂Λ	Accommodation covered in a different chapter or a more detailed map
=====	Tarred road	†	Church/cathedral
=====	Gravel road (may require 4x4)	》	Waterfall
=====	4x4 track	⌂	Cave/rock shelter
-----	Railway	⟡	Bird sanctuary
✈	Airport	♠	Isolated woodland feature
✛	Airstrip	✿	Notable baobab tree
⛴	Car ferry	○	Waterhole/borehole
🚍	Bus station	▲	Summit (height in metres)
⛽	Fuel station/garage	⊕	GPS location
P	Car park	⟷	Border post
ℹ	Tourist information	✕✕	Gate
⚱	Museum	●	Other place of interest
$	Bank		Marsh
✉	Post office		Salt pan
✚	Hospital/clinic		National park/reserve
✚	Pharmacy		Shopping centre/market
⌂	Hotel/lodge/guesthouse etc		Urban park
Λ	Campsite		

Contents

LIST OF MAPS

Introduction

Simply highlighting Botswana's incredible environmental diversity, region by region, would make an enticing introduction to this guide. It is easy to wax lyrical about the exclusivity of the Okavango Delta, the sheer scale of the private reserves around the Chobe, Kwando and Linyanti rivers, and the almost spiritual experience of lying under the Milky Way on the vast salt pans of Makgadikgadi. There are, however, reasons to visit Botswana that transcend its geography. We've travelled extensively across Africa, and Botswana has three overriding attractions as a world-class safari destination: stellar wildlife, seemingly endless space and the richest of histories.

Top of most visitors' lists is the wildlife. Whether this is your first safari or your 50th, Botswana will not disappoint. The sheer diversity of the country, from the arid Kalahari to lush, well-watered forest glades, ensures tremendous variety. Botswana is serious about its 'big game'. It has spectacular herds of elephants and buffalo, and prolific populations of predators. Off-roading on vast private reserves, safari enthusiasts can bounce across the bush in thrilling pursuit of a pack of wild dogs hunting; Botswana has probably the continent's best population of these highly endangered predators. Impressive prides of lions and coalitions of cheetah roam across much of the country's north. Yet often it's the country's smaller residents that captivate: tiny painted reed frogs on sedges, barking geckos and troops of habituated meerkats who'll balance on your head for a better view of their surroundings.

Second – and the underlying reason why many come here – is the feeling in Botswana that you're within an endless pristine wilderness, almost devoid of human imprint. For many of us, such space is the ultimate luxury. In Botswana, animals wander freely across vast reserves that are measured in thousands of square kilometres, not merely hectares. Exploring these wilder corners is invariably deeply liberating.

Third, and missed by some, is Botswana's rich history. It's often barely hinted at but, veiled and mysterious, it's all the more enticing. It reveals itself in the paintings at Tsodilo, and the magic that seems to surround those hills. You'll catch a glimpse of it as you search for Stone Age arrowheads on the Makgadikgadi Pans. And, standing on an ancient riverbed or the wave-washed hills around Savuti, it's hard not to look into the geology and wonder what forces shaped this country, long before you, or indeed any people, first set eyes on it.

Back in the present, the world is changing fast, and we'd be remiss not to observe that not all of those changes are positive. In the last edition of this guide, we touched on the impact of climate change in bringing record water levels to the Okavango Delta and Kwando–Linyanti river systems, filling many channels that had been dry for decades. As we have seen in other areas of the world too, the climate extremes are becoming more pronounced. And so it is that for the last few years, Botswana has received significantly lower levels of water flowing into its major watercourses. While there are some other factors that play into this, from tectonic plate movement to the volume of water used upriver in Angola, it is impossible not to observe the impact of less rainfall, especially on the Okavango, where the once-deep water channels and papyrus-lined lagoons that covered its eastern side have disappeared completely for now. These changes are too recent for us to make a definitive, sweeping judgement on their permanence and so, with that in mind, we've retained the regional vegetation details in areas where change may only be temporary. For now, we hope that these areas will be revitalised with returning water in the future.

As with most of the earth's great wilderness regions, Botswana's protected areas are under threat. There are numerous superb conservation organisations and proactive safari operators working across the country on myriad wildlife, environmental and community development projects to ensure pristine wilderness areas remain that way. However, the 21st century is an age when even the earth's wildest corners must earn their keep, adapt or change irrevocably.

Botswana's government has long been a beacon of prosperity and stability within an often-troubled continent. Financed largely by income from some of the world's largest diamond mines, it has set many good examples of how to run a country. However, Botswana's diamonds aren't forever. Current deposits are running out, and while production has increased, many expect the industry's output to be depleted by the end of this decade. When this happens, it will leave a gaping hole in the economy. Tourism is the obvious way to fill this, but exactly how is not obvious.

As it stands, Botswana's thriving safari industry is the envy of the continent: minimising impact by admitting only small numbers, who pay handsomely to rejuvenate themselves in its pristine environments. Some of this revenue is channelled back into development initiatives in the poorer communities surrounding these areas. This first-rate approach has been a very responsible one; it hasn't been a quick way for the country to get rich through tourism, but it has been sustainable.

Over the last few decades, we've seen the government flirt with the idea of higher-volume tourism in one or two areas, but only in recent years, under the current president, have we seen this become a reality. Although the original policy of high-cost, low-density tourism has not disappeared, it is being gradually eroded. Across the Okavango's private concessions, we've seen a move towards increasing the number of camps in each of the private concessions – in fact, this edition details 30% more camps here over the last five years. And while many of these areas are more than large enough to sustain the increase in visitors, some of these new camps will be occupying more marginal areas in terms of wildlife, and in other areas activities will be less exclusive. There has also been a move to encourage lower-cost properties along the Panhandle area, enabled in part by the completion of a bridge over the Okavango at Mohembo, which gives easier and cheaper access to an experience of the Okavango Delta from its western fringe, though whether this becomes a reality is yet to be seen.

Additionally, a whole new ring of concessions have been created around the existing reserves, and some of those allow hunting, which was reintroduced in Botswana by presidential decree in 2018 – a highly controversial decision. When viewed in conjunction with the shocking spike in poaching experienced in the country during the same period, we have found it hard not to view this decision, and the apparent political move away from conservation, with great sadness.

The majority of these steps to increase tourism revenue are moderate. However, as these moves progress, it remains to be seen if this pace of change will be enough to satisfy both the economic imperative for tourism to generate a larger slice of the national income and the populist elements of the government.

So our plea to you is twofold. First, go now and support Botswana's most responsible camps and operators; the country's people and conservation ventures need you. Second, having committed many of Botswana's secret corners to paper here, we ask you to use this guide with respect. Botswana's wild areas need great care to preserve them. Local people are easily offended, and their cultures eroded, by a visitor's lack of sensitivity. It's a magical country for a wild safari adventure: soak it all in, but be a thoughtful visitor as you do so.

AUTHORS' FAVOURITES Finding genuinely characterful accommodation or that unmissable off-the-beaten-track café can be difficult, so the authors have chosen a few of their favourite places throughout the country to point you in the right direction. These 'authors' favourites' are marked with a ✳.

PRICE CODES Throughout this guide we have used price codes to indicate the cost of those places to stay and eat listed in the guide. For a key to these price codes, see page 518 for accommodation and page 511 for restaurants.

MAPS

Keys and symbols Some maps include alphabetical keys covering the locations of those places to stay, eat or drink that are featured in the book. Note that regional maps may not show all hotels and restaurants in the area: other establishments may be located in towns shown on the map. Some lodges may appear on multiple maps with the accommodation symbol (⌂) where they serve as useful landmarks to aid navigation. On occasion, hotels that are not listed in the guide (but which might serve as alternative options if required or as landmarks) are also marked on the maps in this way.

Grids and grid references Several maps use gridlines to allow easy location of sites. Map grid references are listed in square brackets after the name of the place or site of interest in the text, with page number followed by grid number, eg: [188 B4]. Please note that, in order to keep the maps legible, not all sites have been pinpointed on the maps, but grid references have been supplied to highlight their general location.

NOTE ON DATUM FOR GPS CO-ORDINATES For all the GPS co-ordinates in this book, note that the datum used is WSG 84 – and you must set your receiver accordingly before copying in any of these co-ordinates.

All GPS co-ordinates in this book have been expressed as degrees, minutes and decimal fractions of a minute. Note that this now differs slightly from the format used by the Shell map, which uses degrees, minutes and seconds.

Note that Google Earth satellite images for some lodges, camps and key GPS locations in this book can be accessed directly at w expertafrica.com.

Part One

GENERAL INFORMATION

Location Southern Africa, between 20° and 30°E, and between 18° and 27°S

Size 581,730km²

Climate Subtropical. Summer (November–March): 14.6–35°C; winter (June–August): 2.9–28.9°C. Rainy season (December–March; highly localised) with annual rainfall of 650mm in northeast to less than 250mm in southwest.

Status Republic

Population 2,346,179 (2022 census, Statistics Botswana)

Population growth per year 1.66% (UN, 2024)

Life expectancy at birth 70 years (UN, 2024)

Infant mortality 34.9/1,000 live births (UNICEF, 2021)

Capital Gaborone; population 244,107 (2022 census, Statistics Botswana)

Other main towns Francistown, Lobatse, Selebi-Phikwe, Jwaneng, Orapa

Economy Major earners: diamonds, tourism, critical minerals, beef

GNI US$7,350 per capita (World Bank, 2022)

GDP growth rate 5.8% (World Bank and OECD, 2022)

Currency Pula (BWP, abbreviated to P)

Rate of exchange US$1 = P13.31, £1 = P17.50, €1 = P14.75 (September 2024)

Language English (official), Setswana (national), Shona & other local languages

Religion Christianity, traditional beliefs

International telephone code +267

Time GMT +2

Electricity 220 volts

Weights and measures Metric

Flag Broad, light-blue horizontal stripes, divided by black central stripe bordered by narrow white stripes

National anthem *Fatshe leno la rona*: 'Blessed be this noble land'

Public holidays 1–2 January, Good Friday, Holy Saturday, Easter Monday, 1 May (Labour Day), Ascension Day, 1 July (Sir Seretse Khama Day), third Monday and Tuesday in July (President's Day), 30 September (Independence Day), first Monday in October (Botswana Day), 25–26 December

Tourist board w botswanatourism.co.bw

1

The Natural Environment

PHYSICAL ENVIRONMENT

TOPOGRAPHY Botswana lies landlocked in the heart of southern Africa, straddling the Tropic of Capricorn and covering about 581,730km², of which about two-thirds is in the tropics. Most of the country is a gently undulating sandsheet with an altitude of between 900m and 1,300m. This is punctuated by occasional isolated rock outcrops, which are rarely more than 100m tall. Two major features stand out from this: the enormous salt pans and the huge inland delta of the Okavango River.

A relatively narrow corridor of land on the southeast side of Botswana is rockier and less flat than the rest, with sandstone and granite hills leading down to the Shashe, Limpopo and Marico rivers. This land is much more suitable for agriculture, and is where most of the country's population is concentrated.

Geological history Looking back into Botswana's geological history gives us insights to explain how the great salt pans and the Okavango Delta were formed. It's a long story though, of which we can give only a brief outline here. For a deeper and much more scholarly approach, seek out John Reader's *Africa: A Biography of a Continent* and especially Mike Main's *Kalahari: Life's Variety in Dune and Delta* (page 547). Both are excellent, giving much more comprehensive discussions of scientific thinking – the first in terms of Africa generally, and the second with immense detail specifically about Botswana.

Setting the scene To put discussions in perspective, and give our history a sense of scale, let me start at the beginning. Around 4,600 million years ago the earth's crust began to form and cool. A thousand million years later, fossils from South Africa's Barberton Mountain Land give us evidence of the first recorded, simple, single-celled bacteria.

By 3,300 million years ago more complex blue-green algae had appeared, though it took a further 2,300 million years for multi-cellular organisms to evolve. Palaeontologists say that around 600 million years ago there was an 'evolutionary explosion', when many different species evolved, including ancestors of most of the world's existing invertebrates.

About 230 million years ago the earth saw the emergence of both dinosaurs and the first mammals. For the next 165 million years the dinosaurs dominated the earth and the largest mammals that evolved were probably no bigger than present-day rabbits. Only around 65 million years ago, when some great calamity killed off most of the dinosaurs, did the mammals begin to rise to dominance and inherit the earth.

The supercontinent Meanwhile, somewhere between 135 and 10 million years ago the supercontinent, Gondwanaland, broke up and the continents started to move

3

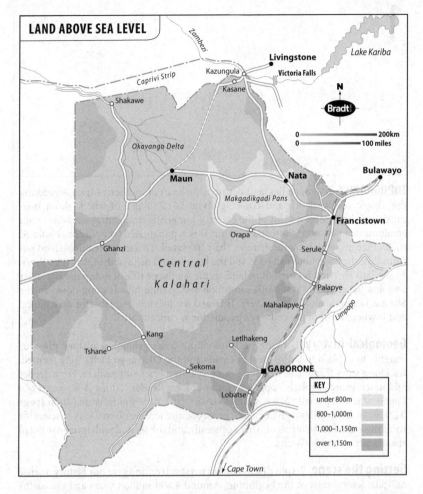

LAND ABOVE SEA LEVEL

Zambezi

Livingstone
Lake Kariba
Kazungula
Victoria Falls
Kasane
Caprivi Strip

Shakawe

N
Bradt

0 ———— 200km
0 ———— 100 miles

Okavango Delta

Bulawayo

Maun
Nata

Makgadikgadi Pans

Francistown

Orapa

Ghanzi
Serule

Central
Kalahari
Palapye

Mahalapye
Limpopo

Kang
Letlhakeng

Tshane
Sekoma
GABORONE

Lobatse
KEY

under 800m
800–1,000m
1,000–1,150m
over 1,150m

Cape Town

away from each other. By the time that the continents split from Gondwanaland, the basic rocks upon which southern Africa is built, the Karoo lavas, had been laid down. By about 65 million years ago – the end of the Cretaceous Period – most of the subcontinent's diamonds, gems and other mineral wealth had also been formed, and erosion was gradually wearing away at the land.

The world's earliest primate fossils are from Europe and North America, dating from around 65 million years ago, but it wasn't until about 4 million years ago that *Australopithecus* appeared in Africa – a prime candidate for being one of our earliest ancestors. This period, as our first ancestors were evolving, is about the time when we start looking at how Botswana's landforms were created.

The Kalahari's superlake During the Tertiary Period, which dates from about 65 million years ago, Botswana's climate was probably very arid, and as the region's rocks were gradually eroded, so the wind-blown sands accumulated and began to form what we now call the Kalahari.

Around 4–5 million years ago it's thought that the Okavango, Kwando and Zambezi rivers had completely different courses than they do today – probably all flowing into one channel which headed south through the Kalahari and into the Orange River and/or the Limpopo. (Different theories suggest different courses.)

Then, around 2–4 million years ago, it's thought that seismic shifts forced parts of southern and central Botswana upwards. Geologists identify the areas raised as the 'Zimbabwe–Kalahari Axis' and the 'Bakalahari Schwelle' – both of which are now watersheds in the region.

The net effect of these upward movements was to block the flow southwards of the rivers, and to form a superlake that had its deepest parts where the Makgadikgadi Pans are today. This greater Lake Makgadikgadi existed until very recently, though its extent varied greatly over the millennia, depending on the climate and inflows. It is thought that at its greatest, it covered an area of up to 80,000km², and that it probably only dried up in the last 10,000 years. At its largest it probably stretched as far as Lake Ngami in the west, what is now Chobe in the north, and beyond Nata to the edge of present-day Zimbabwe in the east.

Evidence suggesting the existence of this lake is dotted around its ancient shorelines. The great Magwikhwe Sand Ridge that you cross as you drive between Savuti and North Gate, probably defined one of its northwestern shorelines. Similarly, another is thought to have been the less obvious Gidikwe Sand Ridge, which lies just to the west of the Boteti River where it borders the present Makgadikgadi Pans National Park.

Look at the base of several of the Kalahari's isolated hills and you'll find rounded, water-washed pebbles and rocks worn smooth over the centuries by waves. The eastern side of the Ghoha Hills, north of Savuti, is a particularly clear example of this – though all of Savuti's hills show some of this history if you look carefully.

In some areas of the Makgadikgadi you can stroll around and find the flint arrowheads and other tools of Stone Age encampments, which must have sat beside the shores of this lake within the last few thousand years.

KIMBERLITE PIPES AND DIAMONDS

Diamond is a crystalline form of ordinary carbon formed under conditions of extreme pressure and temperature. In nature, such conditions are only found deep below the earth's surface, in the lower crust or upper mantle. Under specific circumstances, the rock matrix in which diamonds occur was subjected to such great pressure that it became fluid and punched its way up to the earth's surface in a volcanic pipe of liquid rock. This situation is similar to a conventional volcanic eruption, except that instead of basaltic magma being erupted through fissures in the crust, the volcanic material is a peculiar rock called kimberlite. This contains a wide assortment of minerals (including diamonds), often in addition to large chunks of other rocks that have been caught up in the whole process.

Although such kimberlite pipes occur throughout southern Africa, from the Cape to the DRC, only a small proportion of those discovered contain enough diamonds to be profitably worked. Among them are the Botswana mines at Orapa, Damtshaa, Letlhakane and Jwaneng. It's interesting to note that Botswana's western neighbour, Namibia, has diamond deposits along its Atlantic coast. These are 'secondary diamond deposits', because they do not come directly from kimberlite pipes. Instead, Namibia's diamonds are found in areas where ancient rivers have eroded kimberlite pipes in the interior, washing diamonds down to the sea, and depositing them in sediments there.

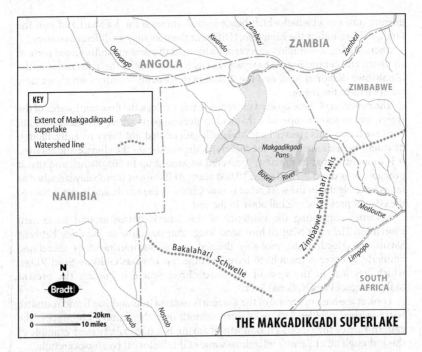

KEY

Extent of Makgadikgadi superlake

Watershed line

THE MAKGADIKGADI SUPERLAKE

From rifts to deltas At some time in the last million years (none of my sources seems to be sure exactly when), this water flow into the great Lake Makgadikgadi was gradually, probably quite slowly, cut off.

Northern Botswana has a series of deep, underlying faultlines running beneath its sands. These faults are thought to be the southernmost extensions of the same system of parallel faultlines that are pulling away from each other and have formed East Africa's Great Rift Valley. These extend south, forming the rift valleys of the Luangwa and Lower Zambezi, before cutting across the Zambezi at Victoria Falls. Here, amid the sands of the northern Kalahari, they are probably at their youngest and shallowest. In Botswana and Zimbabwe these two main faultlines run parallel to each other, from northeast to southwest.

Look at a map and you'll see the Zambezi flowing roughly south through western Zambia, until it reaches a point around Victoria Falls and what's known as the Middle Zambezi Valley (around where Lake Kariba is today). Effectively the Zambezi has been diverted, flowing into the Rift Valley and then northeast along it. This would have starved the great lake of its largest water supply, but clearer evidence of the faultlines can be seen in the present paths of two other rivers.

Look again at the map and you'll realise that the Kwando forms the Botswana–Namibia border, flowing southeast (roughly parallel to both the Zambezi and the Okavango). Then it clearly passes through an area where there's very little gradient, and forms a mini-delta, before abruptly changing direction to become the Linyanti River, and starting to flow northeast. (Note, in passing, the very clear parallels between the delta formations of the Okavango and Kwando/Linyanti rivers.)

This new course of the Linyanti River marks one faultline – known as the Linyanti–Gumare Fault. At Lake Liambezi, this river then seems to 'escape' from the confines of its fault to meander roughly southeast, until meeting another faultline parallel to the first. Here it is again renamed as the Chobe River, with a clearly defined course, flowing northeast and parallel to the Linyanti, along another faultline.

The Selinda (or Magweqgana) Spillway also flows roughly along the Linyanti–Gumare Fault, and further west the line cuts across the flow of the Okavango, just south of the base of the Panhandle. It effectively marks the start of the Delta proper. Parallel to this, but at the south end of the Delta, are the Kunyere and Thamalakane faults. The latter is clearly marked by the position of the Thamalakane River, which marks the most southerly extent of the Delta. Here the Thamalakane River collects the meagre outflow from the Okavango's Delta and diverts it southwest along the faultline, and ultimately into Lake Ngami and the Boteti. Maun sits in the narrow space between the Kunyere and Thamalakane faults.

Just like the parallel faults of the rift valleys further northeast, the Linyanti–Gumare Fault in the north, and the Kunyere and Thamalakane faultlines in the south are gradually pulling away from each other. Between them, the underlying base rock has dropped relative to the land outside the faults – some geologists say by

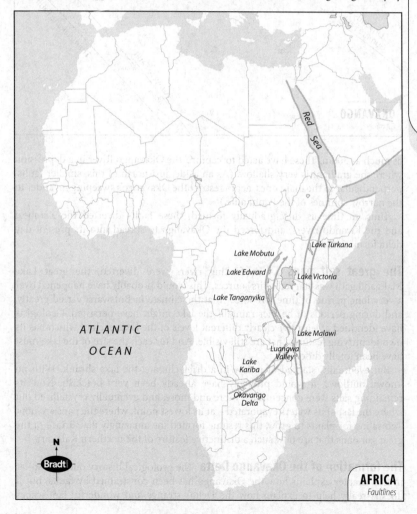

AFRICA
Faultlines

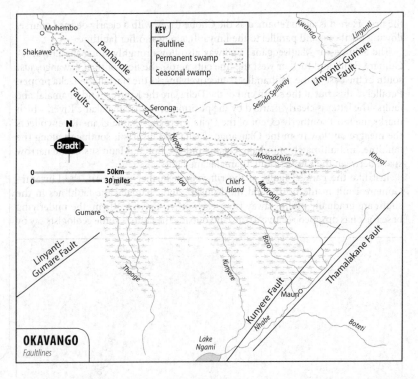

KEY
Faultline
Permanent swamp
Seasonal swamp

Mohembo
Shakawe
Panhandle
Faults
Seronga
N
Bradt
0   50km
0   30 miles
Gumare
Linyanti–Gumare Fault
Thaoge
Ngoga
Jao
Chief's Island
Kunyere
Kwando
Linyanti
Selinda Spillway
Linyanti–Gumare Fault
Moanachira
Khwai
Mboroga
Boro
Nhabe
Maun
Kunyere Fault
Thamalakane Fault
Boteti
Lake Ngami

OKAVANGO
Faultlines

as much as 300m. These have acted to 'capture' the Okavango River in a depression where the gradient is very shallow. (As an aside, just north of this, smaller faults, perpendicular to the main ones, act to restrict the Okavango's sweeping meander to the narrow confines of the Panhandle.)

Thus, in time as they gradually formed, these faults diverted the Zambezi and the Kwando rivers, and forced the Okavango to spread into its present-day delta formation.

The great salt pans As its feeding rivers were diverted, the great Lake Makgadikgadi was starved of its sources. This would probably have happened over a very long period of time. We know that the climate in Botswana varied greatly, and during periods of heavier rainfalls the lake might have persisted. Geologists have identified at least five clearly different levels of the lake, each of which has its own identifying features that are still visible. And for each the size of the lake must have been totally different.

But eventually, starved of inflow in a drier climate, the lake shrank. With no known outflows, it would probably have already been very brackish. Now its remaining salts were concentrated more and more, and eventually crystallised out where the last of its waters evaporated – at its lowest point, where the pans are now. Too saline for plants to grow, this residue formed the amazingly flat surface of the great salt pans that are now such a distinctive feature of the northern Kalahari.

The formation of the Okavango Delta The geological history outlined so far in this chapter explains how the Okavango has been constrained by faults, but it doesn't really help to explain how the Delta's strange and wonderful landscapes

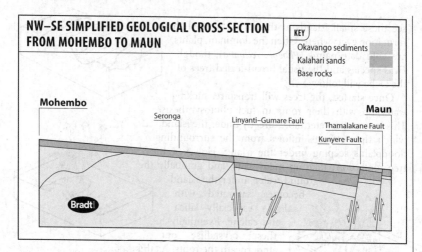

NW–SE SIMPLIFIED GEOLOGICAL CROSS-SECTION FROM MOHEMBO TO MAUN

KEY
Okavango sediments
Kalahari sands
Base rocks

Mohembo

Seronga

Linyanti–Gumare Fault

Maun

Thamalakane Fault

Kunyere Fault

Bradt

came about. That's really due to much more recent processes, of which we'll try to give a brief summary here.

From the air   Firstly, if you're flying over the Delta, note what you see. There are manmade tracks, like the straight lines of the buffalo fence, which surrounds part of the Delta. Or the close, parallel lines of bush tracks made by vehicles, sometimes curving, sometimes perfectly straight.

You'll also see more erratic, single tracks, often radiating from pans or waterholes; these are clear animal tracks. (Yes, animals have favourite paths that they like to use too.) Deeper in the Delta you'll find more and more winding drainage lines, of water channels which glint in the sun. Catch the light right and you'll realise that areas which you thought were thick, green vegetation are floodplains, which reflect the sky.

Look carefully at the 'browner' areas between these and you'll start to distinguish the dry land and the islands from the floodplains and the water. Look out for the small, round islands that often have a ring of palms around the outside of them. Note that some, at their centre, have barren patches of what looks like white salt.

Many islands will be longer. A few of these may look like a number of the small islands joined together. But many are long and narrow – we'll call them ribbon islands. Note how parallel their sides are, and how the vegetation on the edges looks that much more lush than the vegetation in the middle.

Building islands   The Okavango's an amazing sight from the air – and all the more incredible if you understand a little of how its features were formed. Here are the basics of the main methods.

Biological mechanism: round islands   The Okavango's floods are erratic and its water levels variable, sometimes giving the chance for small mounds to develop which, when flooding returns, are above the level of the flood. Often, but not always, these are termite mounds, made by the Macrotermes michaelseni termite.

Obtruding above the water level of the subsequent flood, the mound allows the termites to survive, and makes a handy perch for birds. Eventually seeds take hold, and grow into shrubs and trees, fertilised by the guano from the birds that rest there. In some areas of the Delta (the Jao flats stand out in my mind) you'll see these small islands at the early stages of their formation everywhere. Often the dominant plants are wild date palms (*Phoenix reclinata*), though *Ficus* species and the usual broad-leafed trees of the Delta will follow.

Once started, the trees will transpire, sucking water up with their roots to fuel photosynthesis. This lowers the water table directly under the island, which then attracts inflows from the surrounding floodplains seeping under the island. However, the tree roots don't take up many salts, and gradually the ground water under the island becomes saturated with salts – especially silica and calcite. Eventually these crystallise out underneath the roots. As this precipitate increases, the level of the ground around the edge of the island is raised.

This gradually acts to enlarge the island, raising it above the surrounding floodplains. However, as the island enlarges the groundwater that moves towards the centre of the island becomes increasingly saline – and eventually toxic to plants. The wild date palms die off first in the centre, as they are the least salt-tolerant, then the broadleaved trees, until finally the relatively salt-tolerant real fan palms (*Hyphaene petersiana*) will be the only trees in the centre. When the salt concentrations rise further they, too, die, leaving only salt-tolerant grasses like the spiky sporobolus (*Sporobolus spicatus*).

Capillary action and evaporation force the supersaturated water to the surface of the centre of the island, where salt deposits are now left and no plants can survive. This whole process is estimated to take at least a hundred years. The remaining crystalline salt deposits are known as 'trona' deposits, and are clearly visible as a white crystalline powder from the air or the ground.

Channel mechanism: linear islands The Okavango's water is at its richest in nutrients as it enters the Panhandle and the top of the Delta – as flowing over the nutrient-poor Kalahari sands of the Delta itself won't enrich it. In this Panhandle and upper Delta area, the deep waters are surrounded by the vigorous growth of papyrus (page 405).

These live and die fast, forming a mat of thick vegetal matter by the side of the channel. This builds up the sides of the channel, and gradually its deeper stems are compressed and start forming peat. Meanwhile, suspended sediments are deposited on the floor of the channel. Thus the whole channel,

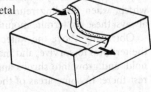

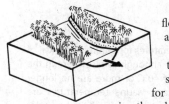

floor and papyrus surrounds, start to rise slightly above the surrounding floodplains.

Once this happens it only takes a hippo track, or some other leakage, for the water in the channel to cut through the peat sides of the channel and the papyrus beds find a completely alternative, lower path through the floodplains. This leaves behind a dry, slightly raised line of sandy deposits, lined on either side by high beds of peat. This higher land will encourage plants to grow, forming a long, narrow island, which can be enlarged by the biological mechanisms mentioned on page 405.

Once dry, the peat eventually burns down to a thin layer of nutrient-rich ash, which now lines this island, encouraging what biologists call 'sweet' floodplains. These support nutrient-rich grasses and other high-quality vegetation, and a rich growth of trees and bushes at the edge of these long islands.

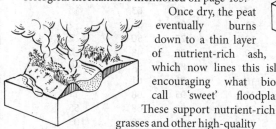

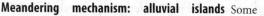

Meandering mechanism: alluvial islands Some islands in the Delta were probably built up first as sandy alluvial deposits during wetter periods in the Delta's history – as the banks beside meandering rivers. Then, when times became drier they were colonised by vegetation, and enlarged by the biological mechanisms mentioned above.

Geological mechanism: Chief's Island Chief's Island, the largest island in the Delta, is thought to have geological origins. Note that its western edge traces out a line which, if continued northwest, would coincide perfectly with the eastern faultline that constrains the Panhandle (a diagram shows this faultline on page 8).

Chief's Island was probably pushed up as higher land during the formative rifting/warping of the area, which fits with the observation that it is largely made up of uniform deposits of sand and clay.

CLIMATE Botswana is landlocked far from the coast and mostly in the tropics. It receives a lot of strong sunlight and most of the country is classed as either semi-arid or arid (the line being crossed when evaporation exceeds rainfall). In many respects, most of central and northern Botswana has a subtropical 'desert' climate, characterised by a wide range in temperature (from day to night and from summer to winter), and by low rainfall and humidity.

Botswana's climate follows a similar pattern to that found in most of southern Africa, with rainfall when the sun is near its zenith from December to March, and most areas receiving their heaviest rainfall in January and February. The rainfall is

The average maximum and minimum temperatures for Maun are typical of the pleasant climate in northern Botswana – although as elsewhere in the world, things are changing; temperatures of 40°C or more are no longer particularly unusual in October. Nevertheless, Maun's temperatures are slightly less extreme than you might expect in one of the Kalahari's drier environments. Similarly, expect the highs and lows in the heart of the Delta to be more moderate than this (lower highs, and higher lows!):

	Temp °C		Temp °F		Rainfall
	max	min	max	min	mm
January	31	20	88	68	150
February	30	20	86	68	110
March	30	19	86	66	72
April	29	17	84	63	18
May	28	13	82	55	2
June	25	10	77	50	2
July	24	9	75	48	0
August	28	12	82	54	0
September	33	16	91	61	3
October	35	20	95	68	11
November	34	20	93	68	55
December	32	21	90	70	103

heavier in the north and east, and lighter in the south and, especially, the southwest. The precise timing and duration of the rains is determined by the interplay of three airstreams: the moist 'Congo' air mass, the northeastern monsoon winds, and the southeastern trade winds. The water-bearing air is the Congo air mass, which normally brings rain when it moves south into Botswana from central Africa. Effectively a belt of rain works its way south across the continent, reaching its southernmost point around January or February. If you listen to any local weather forecasts, they'll probably refer to this as the intertropical convergence zone, or the ITCZ. As the sun's intensity reduces, the Congo air mass moves back north, leaving Botswana dry by around April.

January and February are the wettest months, with regular downpours in the late afternoon and temperatures reaching up to 40°C, though this is often moderated by afternoon cloud cover; daytime humidity ranges from 50% to 80%.

March sees decreasing rainfall but still some afternoon clouds, while **April and May** are lovely months, with only occasional April showers, and temperatures around 30°C – but be aware of occasional chilly Kalahari nights when temperatures just below freezing are possible.

June and July are the coolest months, with daytime highs around 25°C, and occasional cold snaps (down to -5°C at night) are common in the drier areas of the Kalahari. Warmer clothes are needed everywhere as soon as the sun disappears. **August** is similar but not as cold, and **September and October** mark the heart of the dry season, with low humidity and temperatures rising into the 30s Celsius as the months progress.

November brings unpredictable weather, with increasing humidity, gathering afternoon clouds and afternoon showers, while **December** sees temperatures between 20 and 33°C day and night, with regular afternoon rain and humidity around 50–60%.

HABITAT AND VEGETATION

In many ways a brief description of some of the main habitats for plants is really a step through the various types of environment that you'll encounter in Botswana.

As with animals, each species of plant has its favourite conditions. External factors determine where each species thrives, and where it will perish. These include temperature, light, water, soil type, nutrients, and what other species of plants and animals live in the same area. Species with similar needs are often found together, in communities which are characteristic of that particular environment. Botswana has a number of different such communities, or typical 'vegetation types', within its borders – each of which is distinct from the others. The more common include:

MOPANE WOODLAND The dominant tree here is the remarkably adaptable mopane (*Colophospermum mopane*), which is sometimes known as the butterfly tree because

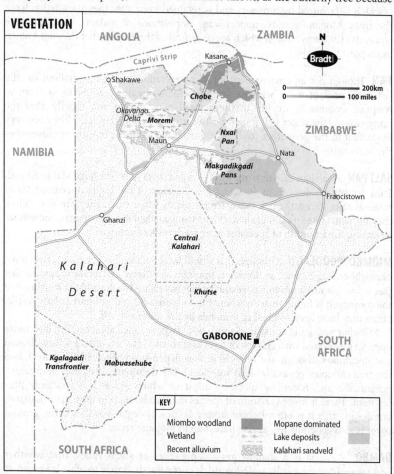

VEGETATION

ANGOLA

ZAMBIA

N

Bradt

Caprivi Strip

Kasane

Shakawe

0   200km
0   100 miles

Chobe

Okavango Delta   Moremi

ZIMBABWE

Nxai Pan

Maun

NAMIBIA

Nata

Makgadikgadi Pans

Francistown

Ghanzi

Central Kalahari

K a l a h a r i

D e s e r t

Khutse

GABORONE

SOUTH AFRICA

Kgalagadi Transfrontier   Mabuasehube

SOUTH AFRICA

KEY

Miombo woodland   Mopane dominated
Wetland   Lake deposits
Recent alluvium   Kalahari sandveld

of the shape of its leaves. Although it doesn't thrive on the Kalahari's sands, it is very tolerant of poorly drained or alkaline soils, and those with a high clay content. This tolerance results in the mopane having a wide range of distribution throughout southern Africa; in Botswana it occurs mainly in the Okavango–Linyanti region, and throughout the eastern side of the country.

Mopane trees can attain a maximum height of 25m when growing on rich, alluvial soils. These are then called cathedral mopane, for their height and the graceful arch of their branches. However, shorter trees are more common in areas that are poor in nutrients, or have suffered extensive fire damage. Stunted mopane will form a low scrub, perhaps only 5m tall. All mopane trees are deciduous, and the leaves turn beautiful shades of yellow and red before falling during the late dry season. Then, with the first rains, the trees become tinged with light-green young leaves. They flower around December and January, with clusters of small, yellow-green flowers.

Ground cover in mopane woodland is usually sparse; just thin grasses, herbs and the occasional bush. The trees themselves are an important source of food for game, as the leaves have a high nutritional value – rich in protein and phosphorus – which is favoured by browsers and is retained even after they have fallen from the trees. Mopane forests support large populations of rodents, including tree squirrels (*Paraxerus cepapi*), which are so typical of these areas that they are known as mopane squirrels.

PAN Though not an environment for rich vegetation, a pan is a shallow, usually seasonal, pool of water without any permanent streams leading to or from it. Mopane woodlands are full of these small pans during and shortly after the rainy season, the water being held on the surface by the clay soils. They are very important to the game that feeds here during the summer, but dry up soon after the rains cease.

SALT PAN A salt pan is, as its name implies, a pan that's salty. The huge Makgadikgadi Pans are the residues from ancient lakes. Because of the high concentrations of mineral salts found there – there are no plants there when they are dry. When they fill with water it's a slightly different story as algal blooms appear, sometimes attracting the attention of specialist filter-feeders like flamingos.

MIOMBO WOODLAND Although this would be the natural vegetation across most of neighbouring Zambia, in Botswana miombo woodland, and its associated *dambos* (see below), is uncommon. There are patches in central Chobe and the northeast of the country. It is found in areas where the soils are acid and not particularly fertile. Often they have been leached of minerals by the water run-off.

Miombo woodland consists of a mosaic of large wooded areas and smaller, more open spaces dotted with clumps of trees and shrubs. The woodland is broadleaved and deciduous (though just how deciduous depends on the available water), and the tree canopies generally don't interlock. The dominant trees are *Brachystegia*, *Julbernardia* and *Isoberlinia* species – most of which are at least partially fire-resistant. There is more variation of species in miombo than in mopane woodland, but despite this it is often known simply as 'brachystegia woodland'. The ground cover is also generally less sparse here than in mopane areas.

DAMBO A *dambo* is a shallow grass depression, or small valley, that is either permanently or seasonally waterlogged. It corresponds closely to what is known as a *vlei* in other parts of the subcontinent. These open, verdant dips in the landscape often appear in the midst of miombo woodlands and support no bushes or trees. In higher valleys among hills, they will sometimes form the sources of streams and rivers. Because of their permanent dampness, they are rich in species of grasses, herbs and flowering plants, like orchids – and are excellent grazing (if a little exposed) for antelope. Their margins are usually thickly vegetated by grasses, herbs and smaller shrubs.

TEAK FOREST In a few areas of the far north of Botswana, including the northern side of Chobe National Park, the Zambezi teak (*Baikiaea plurijuga*), also known as Rhodesian teak, forms dry semi-evergreen forests on Kalahari sand. Often these woodlands occur on fossil dune-crests. As this species is not fire-resistant, these stands are only found where fire is rare, and slash-and-burn-type cultivation methods have never been used. Below the tall teak is normally a dense, deciduous thicket of vegetation, interspersed with sparse grasses and herbs in the shadier spots of the forest floor.

The teak is a lovely strong wood, with an even texture and deep red-brown colour. It is expensive, often exported, and widely used – from furniture to classy wooden floors.

KALAHARI SANDVELD A number of trees and bushes thrive on Chobe's extensive areas of Kalahari sand, including various *Vachellia*, *Senegalia*, *Terminalia* and *Combretum* species. 'Kalahari sandveld' is a general term that we'll use to describe any of these plant communities based on sand.

In appearance they range from a very open savannah with a few tall trees separated only by low undergrowth, to quite dense tickets of (often thorny) shrubs which are difficult to even walk through. If you want to be a little more technical about this, then biologists will often divide this into distinctive subgroups, including:

Terminalia sericea sandveld occurs where you find deep, loose sand – these are unfertile areas which cover large areas of the Kalahari. The main species found here are the silver terminalia (*Terminalia sericea*), or silver cluster-leaf as it's sometimes called, and the Kalahari appleleaf (*Philenoptera nelsii*). These generally occur with wild seringa bushes (*Burkea africana*) and the bushwillow (*Combretum collinum*). Underneath these you'll often find the rather beautiful silky bushman grass (*Stipagrostis uniplumis*).

Vachellia erioloba woodlands also occur on sand, but often where there are fossil river valleys that have an underground supply of water throughout the year. Camelthorn trees (*Vachellia erioloba*) have exceedingly long taproots that reach this, sustaining large stands of these mature trees reaching an impressive 16–17m in height. They grow slowly but give good shade, so the bush cover beneath them is fairly sparse.

Vachellia tortilis woodlands are not found on such deep sand; instead they prefer the fine alluvium soils, which water has deposited over time. Although it forms homogenous stands less often than the camelthorns, a number of the very distinctive, flat-topped umbrella thorns (*Vachellia tortilis*) can often be seen together. Between these you'll find low grasses rather than much undergrowth. This results in a beautiful, quintessentially African scene which fits many first-time visitors' picture of the continent as gleaned from the blockbuster film *Out of Africa*.

MOIST EVERGREEN FOREST In the areas of higher rainfall and (as is more likely in Botswana) near rivers, streams, lakes and swamps, where a tree's roots will have

Conjure up an image of the African savannah and you could well be picturing a lone, flat-topped acacia breaking the horizon. Such is the iconic nature of this tree in the African landscape that discussions over changing the species name from *Acacia* have proved long and heated. In the end, though, the scientists have prevailed. With a view to differentiating the erstwhile African acacias from the native acacias of Australia, the former have been reclassified as *Vachellia* or *Senegalia* spp.

For the purposes of this guide, we have continued to use 'acacia' in a generic sense, but where we refer to individual species, we have corrected their names, as follows:

camelthorn (*Vachellia erioloba*)
candle-pod acacia (*Vachellia hebeclada*)
false umbrella thorn – aka Kalahari sand acacia or bastard umbrella thorn (*Vachellia luederitzii*)
umbrella thorn (*Vachellia tortilis*)
blackthorn (*Senegalia mellifera*)
bladethorn (*Senegalia fleckii*)
bluethorn (*Senegalia erubescens*)
knobthorn (*Senegalia nigrescens*)
monkey thorn (*Senegalia galpinii*)

Such recategorisation is not new, of course; these discussions are going on all the time. Another species name that has shifted allegiance is the *Lonchocarpus*, which is now known as *Philenoptera*:

Kalahari appleleaf (*Philenoptera nelsii* rather than *Lonchocarpus nelsii*)
raintree (*Philenoptera violacea* rather than *Lonchocarpus capassa*)

permanent access to water, dense evergreen forests are found. Many species occur, and this lush vegetation is characterised by having three levels: a canopy of tall trees, a sub-level of smaller trees and bushes, and a variety of ground-level vegetation. In effect, the environment is so good for plants that they have adapted to exploit the light from every sunbeam.

This type of forest is prevalent in the Okavango and Linyanti areas, and beside the country's larger rivers. It's perhaps worth distinguishing here between two very different types of this forest:

Riverine forests (occasionally called riparian forests) are very common. They line many of Botswana's major rivers and are found throughout the Okavango–Linyanti area. Typical trees and shrubs here include the jackalberry (*Diospyros mespiliformis*), African mangosteen (*Garcinia livingstonei*), sausage tree (*Kigelia africana*), large feverberry (*Croton megalobotrys*), knobthorn (*Senegalia nigrescens*), marula (*Sclerocarya birrea* ssp *caffra*), raintree (*Philenoptera violacea*) and various species of fig. Move away from the river and you'll find riparian species thinning out rapidly.

Swamp forest – or something very akin to it – occurs in tiny patches on small islands in permanently flooded areas of the Okavango. These islands, which will themselves occasionally be flooded, might include a mixture of fig and waterberry species, plus lots of wild date palms (*Phoenix reclinata*) and a few tall real fan palms (*Hyphaene petersiana*).

In the centre of slightly larger small islands, where the ground is salty from trona deposits (page 10), you will find only spiky sporobolus grassland (*Sporobolus spicatus*) – no trees at all!

FLOODPLAIN Floodplains are the low-lying grasslands on the edges of rivers, streams, lakes and swamps that are seasonally inundated by floods. The Okavango and, to a lesser extent, the Linyanti–Chobe region has some huge areas of floodplain. These often contain no trees or bushes, just a low carpet of grass species that can tolerate being submerged for part of the year. In the midst of most of the floodplains in the Okavango you'll find isolated small 'islands' slightly raised above the surrounding grasslands. These will often be fringed by swamp forest (page 16).

Sometimes the communities of vegetation will be 'zoned' to reflect the extent and frequency of the flooding. In areas that become submerged for long periods you'll find species like wild rice (*Oryza longistaminata*) and the sedge *Cyperus articulatus*.

KARIBA WEED

At several checkpoints in Botswana, particularly near rivers, notices are posted warning of the problems posed by the invasive waterweed, *Salvinia molesta*. Known locally as *mosthimbambo*, and more widely by its common names, giant salvinia or Kariba weed, it was first identified in the Zambezi River over 50 years ago. Since then it has become widespread throughout the southern part of the continent, migrating to the Chobe River in the 1980s.

A native of Brazil, Kariba weed is a water fern that was at one time sold for ornamental use in aquariums and garden ponds. With an exceptionally fast rate of reproduction, the plant spread rapidly from these relatively narrow confines into larger bodies of warm, relatively sluggish water. As the plant multiplies, its originally flat green leaves die back and fold together, forming an impenetrable mat that can be as much as a metre deep. The implications for waterways such as the rivers of Botswana are considerable. Not only do the matted plants create an obstruction, impacting on boat traffic and blocking irrigation pipes and water supplies, they also create an ideal breeding ground for mosquitoes and other insects. The impact on the environment is no less devastating, with indigenous plants affected by loss of light and oxygen, an effect that is compounded as decaying plants sink to the riverbed and adversely affect the development of fish and other river wildlife.

Control of such a virulent plant has proved extremely difficult. While it can be sprayed, this is rarely fully effective, and the chemicals used are in themselves harmful to the environment. Rather more successful has been the introduction of a weevil imported from Australia, *Cyrtobagus salviniae*, whose adults and larvae feed on and damage the plants under the right circumstances.

The problem is by no means confined to Africa. Kariba weed is on the environmental hit-list of countries across the globe, from New Zealand to the USA, where both sales and ownership of the plant are now banned. In Botswana, however, the challenge is to prevent serious damage to the country's aquatic ecosystem. With this in mind, the authorities have introduced strict measures, which include controlling the boats allowed on the country's waterways, and decontamination of those that are licensed.

Grasses such as *Imperata cylindrica* often dominate places that generally spend less time underwater.

CHANNELS Vegetation found in permanent channels includes the giant sedge or papyrus (*Cyperus papyrus*), which dominates large areas of the Okavango, plus species like the distinctive cylindrical hippo grass (*Vossia cuspidata*), the tall maize-like phragmites reed (*Phragmites australis*), used for thatching, and the unmistakable bulrush (*Typha capensis*).

LAGOONS Where the water is more still, in deep lagoons and side-channels where the surface is open but the water doesn't flow much, the bottom will often be covered with fairly stable peat deposits. This gives a stable base for many species of aquatic plants. Some are strictly submerged while others have floating leaves. An obvious indicator of this type of environment is the presence of waterlilies.

CONSERVATION

A great deal has been written about the conservation of animals in Africa; much of it is over-simplistic and intentionally emotive. As an informed visitor you are in the unique position of being able to see some of the issues at first hand, and to appreciate the perspectives of some of the local people. So abandon your preconceptions, and start by realising how complex the issues are.

A few ideas common to current thinking on conservation, and to many areas in the region, are outlined here and then framed in the context of Botswana.

BEING PRAGMATIC: CONSERVATION AND DEVELOPMENT Firstly, conservation must be taken within its widest sense if it is to have meaning. Saving animals is of minimal use if the whole environment is degraded, so we must consider conserving whole areas and ecosystems, not just the odd isolated species.

Observe that land is regarded as an asset by most societies, in Africa as it is elsewhere. (The San are a notable exception in this regard.) To 'save' the land for the animals, and use it merely for the recreation of a few privileged foreign tourists, is a recipe for huge social problems – especially if the local people remain excluded from benefit and in poverty. Local people have hunted animals for food for centuries. They have always killed game that threatened them or ruined their crops. If we now try to protect animals in populated areas without addressing the concerns of the people, then our efforts will fail.

The only pragmatic way to conserve Africa's wild areas is to see the *development* of the local people, and the *conservation* of the ecosystems, as interlinked goals. In the long term, one will not work without the other. Conservation without development leads to resentful local people who will happily, and frequently, shoot, trap and kill animals. Development without conservation will simply repeat the mistakes that most developed countries have already made: it will lay waste a beautiful land and kill off its natural heritage. Look at the tiny areas of undisturbed natural vegetation that survive in the UK, the USA or Japan. See how unsuccessful we in the northern hemisphere have been at long-term conservation over the past 500 years.

As an aside, the local people in Africa are sometimes wrongly accused of being the only agents of degradation. Many would like to see 'poachers' shot on sight, and slash-and-burn agriculture banned. But observe the importation of tropical hardwoods by the West to see the problems that our demands place on the natural environment in the developing world.

In conserving some of Africa's natural areas and assisting the development of its people, the international community has a vital role to play. It could effectively encourage African governments to practise sustainable long-term strategies, rather than grasping for the short-term fixes which politicians seem universally to prefer. But such solutions must have the backing of the people themselves, or they will fall apart when the foreign aid budgets eventually wane.

In practice, to get this backing from the local communities it is not enough for a conservation strategy to be compatible with development. Most rural Africans are more concerned about where they live, what they can eat, and how they will survive, than they are about the lives of small, obscure species of antelope that taste good when roasted.

To succeed in Africa, conservation must not only be *compatible* with development, it must actually *promote* it. Conservation efforts must also actively help the local people to improve their own standard of living. If that situation can be reached, then local communities can be mobilised behind long-term conservation initiatives.

Governments are the same. As the famous Zambian conservationist, Norman Carr, once commented, 'Governments won't conserve an impala just because it is pretty.' But they will work to save it *if* they can see that it is worth more to them alive than dead.

The continent's best current strategies involve trying to find lucrative and sustainable ways to use the land. They then plough much of the revenue back into the surrounding local communities. Once the local communities see revenue from conservation being used to help them improve their lives – to build houses, clinics and schools, and to offer paid employment – then such schemes rapidly get their backing and support.

Carefully planned, sustainable tourism is one solution that is working effectively. For success, local communities must see that visitors pay because they want the wildlife. Thus, they reason, the existence of wildlife directly improves their income, and they will strive to conserve it. It isn't enough for people to see that the wildlife helps the government to get richer; that won't dissuade a local hunter from shooting a duiker for dinner. However, if he is directly benefiting from visitors, who come to see the animals, then he has a vested interest in saving that duiker.

HIGH REVENUE, LOW VOLUME In the late 1980s Botswana's parks, and especially the Chobe riverfront area and Moremi, were being badly over-used. Many visitors were self-contained South Africans who would arrive with all their food and kit. They bought little in Botswana except their cheap park-entry tickets, and contributed little to the nation's economy.

In an effort to reduce numbers, and stave off serious environmental (and aesthetic) problems due to too many visitors, it was decided to increase the park fees by a factor of ten. This worked miraculously – reducing the number of visitors and their impact, but retaining the same level of revenue for the parks' authorities.

At the time this was revolutionary, even though now it seems obvious. Thus Botswana's policy of 'high-revenue, low-volume' tourism was born. Access to most of Botswana's wild areas is expensive in order to maximise revenues and keep environments pristine. The country is the envy of Africa for having a good, working system that is delivering increasing revenues as well as many local development initiatives.

This basic policy remained in place for about 30 years and indeed extended way beyond the national parks and game reserves to embrace virtually the whole of northern Botswana. In more recent years, perhaps the last decade, we've seen a steady softening of this approach: existing camps are often able to grow a little bigger than before; licences for more camps and lodges have been granted in existing concessions; and more lodges are springing up in the more marginal concessions surrounding the existing private reserves.

This isn't a radical departure from the 'high-revenue, low-volume' policy, but there is a gradual change. For the visitor, this means that even in private areas, you're likely to encounter a few more lodge vehicles than used to be the case.

NATIONAL PARKS AND RESERVES The national parks, like Chobe, and the game reserves, like Moremi, work on a simple system. Nobody lives in these (a handful of San in the Central Kalahari Game Reserve being the exception). Anyone can visit, provided they pay the fees. These are scaled to be cheapest for citizens of Botswana, reasonable for residents and more costly for visitors. (See page 127 for these charges.)

Private concessions or reserves Outside of the national parks and game reserves, northern Botswana has been divided up into a series of wildlife management areas (WMAs). See the map on page 335 for some of these. Those in northwestern Botswana, in Ngamiland, are numbered NG1, NG2, etc, up to NG51. These areas are normally referred to in Botswana as 'concessions' although in this guide we have used this term virtually interchangeably with the phrase 'private reserve' or simply just 'reserve'.

Within each of these, the government, via the local 'land board', has defined who owns the wildlife, and what can be done with it. Until January 2014, limited (controlled and sustainable) hunting was allowed in many of the concessions. This was outlawed throughout Botswana under Ian Khama's government, but reinstated in 2019 by the incoming president (see *Big-game hunting*, opposite).

Community concessions In most of these concessions, the approach taken centres around Community Based Natural Resource Management (CBNRM), a modern phrase for a strategy which tries to reconcile conflicts over resources between the people and the wildlife in its broadest sense.

CBNRM is based on the premise that the people living next to a resource are the ones best suited to protecting that resource, as they would lose most if that resource were lost, and gain most if it's managed well. There is also an ethical consideration: for example, the people who pay the costs of living near wildlife (destruction of crops and livestock, and loss of human life) should benefit from its conservation. Local people need to be involved in the decision-making process and to benefit from the areas around them, and CBNRM tries to make this possible.

Thus in most of Botswana's concessions, local communities now make decisions about how they are run, and they reap the rewards if they are run well and successfully. (NG22 and NG23 are an example of one such arrangement; page 350.)

TOURISM Botswana lies in the heart of sub-Saharan Africa – and its tourism is the envy of the continent in many ways. The country is regarded, quite rightly, as having some of the continent's best wildlife areas, which are still in generally pristine condition.

What's more, the expansion of tourism from the nucleus of the national parks to the areas around them has gradually increased the area effectively protected for wildlife since the 1980s. This is enlarging the contiguous area in northern Botswana available for wildlife, helping to ensure that game populations increase in size, and become more viable. In the words of the late Peter Sandenbergh, who ran safari camps and tourism operations in this area for longer than most, 'one of the greatest changes since coming to this area in 1983 has been the remarkable increase in animal numbers and species diversity.'

Tourism isn't yet as important to Botswana as diamonds or beef production, but it is increasing every year. By providing substantial employment and bringing foreign exchange into the country, it gives the politicians a reason to support conservation. When the diamonds run out – within the next few decades – Botswana needs to have an alternative, and renewable, source of income…and tourism is one of the most obvious contenders.

For the impact of tourism on the economy, see page 88. And for ways in which you can support both conservation initiatives and small local charities that directly help the people of Botswana, see page 154.

BIG-GAME HUNTING Big-game hunting, where visiting hunters pay large amounts to kill trophy animals, was for years practised on a number of private reserves and concessions. Just like photographic tourism, it was a valuable source of revenue in the long term for people living in the country's concessions.

In practical terms, there was room for both types of visitors in Botswana: the photographer and the hunter. The national parks, and some of the private reserves nearest the parks (eg: NG23, NG27A and NG27B), were designated for photographic visitors; here no hunting was allowed.

In many of the private reserves, controlled sustainable hunting was permitted, although a few (such as the concessions run by Wilderness Safaris, like NG15 and NG26) maintained a policy of no hunting. These concessions provide a buffer between the pristine national parks and the land around, a system designed to protect the national parks' animals from incursions by poachers, while the parks act as a large gene pool and species reservoir for the private concessions.

Despite this long-held policy, the government imposed a moratorium on commercial hunting, which includes trophy hunting, in January 2014. Effectively, this extended an earlier ban on lion hunting. The decision came as no surprise to many in Botswana, since it fulfilled a commitment to ban commercial hunting made by President Ian Khama prior to taking office in 2008.

With a change in political leadership, though, President Mokgweetsi Masisi lifted the hunting ban in 2019, citing growing human–wildlife conflicts and the potential economic benefits. It was argued that the hunting industry, including trophy hunting, had the potential to generate significant revenue for the country through hunting fees, licences and related tourism activities, which could be used for wildlife conservation efforts and rural community development.

Not surprisingly, the decision was met with both support and criticism, with some conservationists and animal welfare advocates expressing concerns about the potential impact on wildlife populations and the ethical aspects of trophy hunting. As a result, the issue remains a subject of debate and discussion both in Botswana and internationally.

POACHING Prior to the tumultuous years of the Covid-19 pandemic, Botswana generally had very little poaching. There had always been a bit of small-scale poaching of game 'for the pot' by local residents, but large-scale commercial poaching operations had been more or less stopped. The BDF (Botswana Defence Force) units based in strategic locations around the country's border, who were tasked with anti-poaching duties, certainly conducted some very effective

1

operations. Occasionally there was a complaint about poachers coming across the river from Namibia – putting the blame on people from other countries or communities for any issues is a very usual tactic, and one common the world over. But even this was usually small-scale.

However, the situation in recent years hasn't been quite so positive. In 2020, the Covid-19 pandemic disrupted normal wildlife conservation efforts and anti-poaching operations in various regions, and there was a shocking upsurge in poaching of rhinos and other endangered species; travel restrictions and lockdowns reduced surveillance, the economic downturn saw people seeking alternative sources of income and the lack of tourism affected conservation budgets. Meanwhile, the worldwide illegal wildlife trade continued to thrive, with demand for rhino horn in some markets providing a financial incentive for poachers.

As normality returned after the pandemic, the situation may have stabilised, at least for the rhino – although there are now very few free-roaming rhino left in northern Botswana (page 330). Anti-poaching work is being done in Botswana, but private-sector safari operators and conservation organisations are taking on more responsibility for this. Meanwhile, there is a widespread feeling that the strong political support that used to underpin Botswana's anti-poaching enforcement has diminished since around 2018.

Recent arrests of poachers entering Namibia, caught red-handed with ivory thought to be from Botswana, and an upsurge in reports of poached elephant ivory from Botswana, is worrying. Little concrete information about poaching in Botswana has been published by the authorities since 2019, which simply adds to levels of concern.

2

Botswana Wildlife Guide

This wildlife guide is designed to help you name most of the animals that you are likely to see in Botswana. Less common species are featured under the heading '*Similar species*' beneath the animal to which they are most closely allied or bear the strongest resemblance.

There are times, of course, when safari-goers are presented with a series of animal tracks rather than the animal itself. A good guide can make these come alive, helping you to make sense of what you see in the bush. They show you, for example, that cats' tracks have three lobes at the bottom, whereas dog and hyena tracks feature only two; point out the cheetah's claws, usually absent from other cat tracks; or the direction in which an elephant is walking from small scuff marks around its track. To help your interpretation, we have included some of the more widely seen tracks in *Appendix 1* (page 530); the more you learn, the more you'll enjoy about the bush.

For much more detailed information, see *Southern African Wildlife: A Visitor's Guide* by Mike Unwin, also published by Bradt Guides. There are also very comprehensive field guides to the flora and fauna of southern Africa, which usually cover Botswana, and several guides dedicated just to Botswana. See page 541 for my suggestions.

MAMMALS

Because the Okavango area is so well watered, its natural vegetation is very lush and capable of supporting a high density of game in the dry season. This spreads out to the

MM/S

surrounding areas during the earlier months of the year – accounting for the sheer volume of big game to be found in northern Botswana's parks and private reserves.

Overall, Botswana's large mammals are typical of the savannah areas of southern Africa. The large predators are here: lion, leopard, cheetah, wild dog and spotted hyena. Cheetah are found in higher densities here than in most other areas of the subcontinent, and northern Botswana has one of Africa's strongest populations of wild dogs.

Elephant and buffalo occur in large herds that roam throughout the areas where they can find water. Black and white rhino are native here, but waves of poaching have hugely impacted their numbers. At the time of writing, a handful of free-roaming white rhino remained in the Okavango, but were absent from most of the region (page 330).

Antelope are well represented, with impala, springbok, tsessebe and red lechwe each numerically dominant in different areas – depending on the environment. The sheer range of Botswana's ecosystems means that if you move about there is a really wide variety of species to be seen.

GAME MIGRATIONS: HISTORICAL FACTORS Like most of Africa's big game, some of Botswana's larger mammals undertake major seasonal migrations – or at least they did, until relatively recently. The 'big picture' was that large numbers of big herbivores put a great strain on the vegetation in any given locale, and so moving around gave the plants time to recover. Thus the basic pattern was for the game to move out into the Kalahari's drier areas during the rains, when they would have no difficulty finding small pools to drink from, and then gradually migrate back to sources of permanent water as the dry season progressed.

The main species involved were elephant, buffalo, zebra, wildebeest and hartebeest. These migrations still occur, and do affect the game densities in many areas, although they're much reduced due to two main factors.

First, competition for land from humans and their domestic stock, which has reduced the area over which the wildlife can range, and caused particular problems by monopolising some of the few areas of permanent water in the Kalahari.

Second, the erection of long, game-proof, disease-control fences, which have appeared across historical migration routes in the Kalahari. The first of these was in 1954, in response to insistence by European trading partners that, to import Botswana's beef, the country must have an effective strategy for containing and dealing with outbreaks of foot-and-mouth disease.

The relative damage done by these two factors is still a hotly debated issue in Botswana, but the results were serious. In some years tens and possibly hundreds of thousands of animals, mostly wildebeest, died of thirst or starvation, many in very close proximity to the fences. (See page 463 for further comments.) Some blamed the fences directly; others regarded them as a scapegoat for the real cause – the scale of human encroachment on the Kalahari. Whatever the cause, Botswana no longer has migrations of this scale.

See Mike Main's *Kalahari: Life's Variety in Dune and Delta* for a rational overview of this debate; various issues of *Botswana Notes and Records* (especially 1984) for more detailed partisan arguments; and Mark and Delia Owens' book *Cry of the Kalahari* for an impassioned but one-sided view of the people who observed it at first hand.

GAME MIGRATIONS: THE CURRENT STORY Mention the word 'migration' and there's a tendency to picture millions of wildebeest in the Serengeti, fording rivers of waiting crocodiles and filling endless flat plains. That's not what you get in Botswana, so forget those images.

What you do find is a modest but noticeable drift of game away from the main water points of the Chobe, Linyanti and Okavango around the start of the rains – usually some time during November – and a gradual return as the dry season progresses. However, the precise details vary with the species of game.

Elephant and **buffalo** make broadly similar movements. As the rains come, their large herds split into much smaller family groups, of which some move away from the Linyanti and Okavango systems. They spread out into the drier areas, especially the vast swathes of land dominated by mopane that lie between these areas (wildlife management areas NG14/15/16/18/20; see page 20 for an explanation of WMAs). Those from the Chobe riverfront areas similarly split, heading into the Chobe Forest Reserve and the rest of Chobe National Park, while some move east of Chobe National Park into Zimbabwe's Hwange National Park, and the Matetsi area between that and the Zambezi.

From around May the animals start to head back, and gradually join up into larger herds, until by September and October the riverfronts of the Chobe and Kwando–Linyanti have some of the most amazing densities of buffalo and (especially) elephants that you'll find anywhere in Africa.

The migrations of **zebra** are somewhat more complex, and still the topic of research, but it seems that during the rains large herds of zebra congregate on both Makgadikgadi and Nxai pans, forming an amazing spectacle (if you can find them). During the dry season these animals gather in numbers beside the Boteti River, the western boundary of Makgadikgadi National Park. Separate populations from the Okavango, Chobe and Linyanti areas move to more open parts of the Kalahari. Some of these groups always seem to pass through the sweet grass plains of the Savuti area around April–May, and often this coincides with their foaling season.

Wildebeest in the north of the country follow a similar pattern to the zebra, but those in the centre and south of the Kalahari are effectively now a separate population. It seems that numbers in the central area of the Kalahari have fluctuated wildly since records began; before the fences there was probably a big annual migration northeast in the dry season to Lake Xau – the nearest water point to the Central Kalahari Game Reserve (CKGR). Like **hartebeest** in the Central Kalahari, they move around with the season, but the details of their current migration patterns are unclear.

CATS

Lion (*Panthera leo*) Shoulder height 100–120cm; weight 150–260kg. Africa's largest predator, the lion, is the animal that everybody hopes to see on safari. It

Leopard

OP/S

Cheetah

L/S

is a sociable creature, living in prides of five to over 20 animals and defending a territory of 20–200km². Lions often hunt at night, and their favoured prey is large or medium-sized antelope such as wildebeest and impala – although they may take prey as large as buffalo or giraffe. Most hunting is done by females, but dominant males normally feed first after a kill. Rivalry between males is intense and takeover battles are frequently fought to the death, so two or more males often form a coalition. Young males are forced out of their home pride at three years of age, and cubs are usually killed after a successful takeover.

When not feeding or fighting, lions are remarkably indolent – they spend up to 23 hours of any given day at rest – so the anticipation of a lion sighting is often more exciting than the real thing. Lions naturally occur in any habitat, except desert or rainforest. They once ranged across much of the Old World, but these days they are all but restricted to the larger conservation areas in sub-Saharan Africa (with one residual population existing in India).

Lions occur throughout Botswana, and are very common in the main northern areas of Chobe, Linyanti–Kwando and the Okavango. They also range across the Kalahari, in the Nxai/Makgadikgadi areas and the CKGR, though the relative scarcity of prey leads to small, dissociated pride structures that have vast territories.

In the northern reserves, where food is plentiful, the converse is the case. Large prides are the norm and some, like those around North Gate and Savuti, have become so big that they make a speciality of killing young and juvenile elephants in order to have enough meat to go around. Even if visiting these prolific reserves for just a few days, you'd be unlikely not to see at least some lions.

Leopard (*Panthera pardus*) Shoulder height 70cm; weight 60–90kg. The leopard is the most solitary and secretive of Africa's big cats. It is an opportunistic hunter, using stealth and power, often getting to within 5m of its intended prey before pouncing. If there are hyenas and lions around then leopards habitually move their kills up into trees to safeguard them. This species can be distinguished from the cheetah by its rosette-like spots, lack of black 'tearmarks' and more compact, low-slung, powerful build.

The leopard is the most common of Africa's large felines. Some of Botswana's bush offers perfect habitat, with plenty of thickets, cover and big trees. The riverine woodlands found throughout the Chobe, Linyanti–Kwando and Okavango areas are firm favourites with them. Here they're quite often seen by sharp-eyed observers who scan low-hanging branches for these lounging felines. Meanwhile drives around dusk and early evening in the private concessions will sometimes yield good sightings of leopard going out on hunting forays as the light fades. Remarkably, leopard often seem unperturbed by the presence of a vehicle and spotlight, and will often continue whatever they are doing regardless of an audience; watching a leopard stalk is captivating viewing.

Leopards are very adaptable. There are many records of individuals living for years undetected in close proximity to humans, for example in the suburbs of major African cities like Nairobi, where they prey on domestic dogs. Given this, it's no surprise that they're also found throughout the Kalahari, though in lower densities commensurate with the relative lack of prey.

Cheetah (*Acinonyx jubatus*) Shoulder height 70–80cm; weight 50–60kg. This remarkable spotted cat has a greyhound-like build, and is capable of running at 70km/h in bursts, making it the world's fastest land animal. Despite superficial similarities, you can easily tell a cheetah from a leopard by the former's simple spots, disproportionately small head, streamlined build, diagnostic black tearmarks and preference for relatively open habitats. It is typically seen pacing the plains restlessly, either on its own or in a small family group consisting of a mother and her offspring. Diurnal hunters, cheetah favour the cooler hours of the day to hunt smaller antelope like springbok, steenbok and duiker, plus young wildebeest, tsessebe and zebra, and also warthog, large birds and small mammals such as scrub hares.

Given that cheetah never occur in high densities, Botswana is a better place than most to see them. In areas of plentiful game, they often lose their prey to lion or spotted hyena, so the relative scarcity of competition in areas like Nxai, Makgadikgadi and the Central Kalahari makes these locations ideal. These areas also harbour large populations of springbok – a cheetah's ideal prey – and their ability to go for long periods without water gives them flexibility to move far from waterholes. Although cheetah are often thought of as animals of the open savannah, they do need some cover from which to sprint – so the Kalahari's thin scrub is perfect for them.

Having said that, all of my sightings of cheetah in Botswana have been in some of the central Okavango's areas of densest game – on Mboma Island and in the Mombo Concession. Looking through the sightings records at the camps, it's certainly notable that many of these cats move further into the Delta as the waters recede, and then move back out into the surrounding Kalahari to avoid the floods.

Estimates suggest that there are about 4,500 cheetah left in southern Africa, plus 2,500 or so in East Africa, and a barely sustainable number in Iran. (They did occur throughout India and Pakistan, but were considered extinct until reintroduction from South Africa in 2023.) Scientists, noting a marked lack of genetic diversity among all living cheetah, have suggested that the species must have gone through a 'genetic bottleneck' in the past – thus perhaps all living cheetah are descended from one female. This goes some way to explaining why they are very susceptible to disease.

Caracal (*Caracal caracal*) Shoulder height 40cm; weight 7–20kg. Smaller but heavier than the serval, caracal resemble lynx, with their uniform tan coat, short tail and tufted ears. They are solitary, mainly nocturnal hunters that feed on birds, small antelope and young livestock. Caracal are remarkable hunters for their size, and will often take prey as large as, or even larger than, they are. Their style is very much like that of a leopard: they normally stalk their prey as closely as possible, before springing an ambush. They may also take many of the same species at once, even caching their prey in trees to return and feed later, and can be quite acrobatic hunters, known to bat birds out of the air.

Caracal occur throughout sub-Saharan Africa, easily adapting to a variety of environments. They're found throughout Botswana, but while game drives in the early evening provide your best chance of a glimpse of them, they're still very rarely seen.

Serval (*Leptailurus serval*) Shoulder height 60cm; weight 9–18kg. This long-legged cat is the tallest of Africa's 'small cats'. It has a slim build with a short tail and black-on-gold spots giving way to streaking near the head. Seldom seen, it is widespread and quite common in moist grassland, reedbeds and riverine habitats throughout Africa, including northern Botswana. It's largely absent from the drier areas of the Kalahari.

Caracal

OP/D

Serval

RH/S

Wild cat

IB/S

Spotted cat

B/S

Serval do particularly well in wetter areas where there is lots of long grass – and are common throughout the Okavango and Linyanti–Kwando areas, although they're relatively rarely seen. Serval prey on mice, rats, small mammals, birds, snakes and lizards and will sometimes even take fish or the young of small antelope. They use their big ears to locate their prey precisely by sound, and their long legs to see over tall grass, and to spring high as they pounce.

Similar species The smaller **African wildcat** (*Felis silvestris lybica*) ranges from the Mediterranean to the Cape of Good Hope, and is similar in appearance to the domestic tabby cat. It has a ringed tail, a reddish-brown tinge to the back of its ears and an unspotted torso – which should preclude confusion with the even smaller **small spotted cat** (*Felis nigripes*), a relatively rare resident of the central and southern Kalahari which has a more distinctively marked coat. Both species are generally solitary and nocturnal, often utilising burrows or termite mounds as daytime shelters. They prey upon reptiles, amphibians and birds as well as small mammals.

DOGS

Wild dog (*Lycaon pictus*) Shoulder height 70cm; weight 18–36kg. Also known as the painted hunting dog, the wild dog is distinguished from other African dogs by its large size and mottled black, brown and cream coat. Highly sociable, living in packs of up to 50 animals, wild dogs are ferocious hunters that literally tear apart their prey on the run. The most endangered of Africa's great predators, they are now threatened with extinction. This is the result both of relentless persecution by farmers, who often view the dogs as dangerous vermin, and of their susceptibility to diseases spread by domestic dogs; wild dogs are now extinct in many areas where they were formerly abundant, and they are common nowhere. The global population of fewer than 2,000 is concentrated in southern Tanzania, Zambia, Zimbabwe, Botswana, South Africa and Namibia.

Wild dogs prefer open savannah with only sparse tree cover and packs have enormous territories, typically covering 400km² or more. They travel huge distances in search of prey, so few parks are large enough to contain them. Northern Botswana has one of the healthiest and most prolific populations in Africa, and is probably the best place on the continent to see them. These range right across Chobe, the Kwando–Linyanti and Okavango areas, and spread out beyond these into Namibia and the northwest areas of the Kalahari.

Packs generally den around July to early October, and this is the only time when you can be fairly sure of seeing them. Sometimes they den in the same area for several years running, while at other times they'll change from year to year. For the best chances of a sighting – and a possibility of following a pack as they hunt (an amazing, exhilarating experience) – choose a mainly dry reserve with plenty of open ground. Make sure that off-road driving is permitted, or you'll never be able to follow them, and ideally night drives should be allowed. Selinda, Kwando, Kwara, Mapula, Chitabe and Vumbura would all currently be high on my list – and I've seen dogs in all of these. For up-to-date locations of wild dog sightings in Botswana, visit w expertafrica.com/wildlife/wild-dog/botswana.

Given that dogs will take most antelope and always run down their prey, the only strategy that their prey can adopt to avoid death is to run as far, and as fast, as they can. They will do this as soon as they realise that dogs are in the area. Thus if you ever see game seriously sprinting with a purpose, and just not stopping, then look hard: maybe there's a pack of dogs behind them!

Wild dog

Black-backed jackal

Side-striped jackal

Bat-eared fox

Cape fox

Black-backed jackal (*Canis mesomelas*) Shoulder height 35–45cm; weight 8–12kg. The black-backed jackal is an opportunistic feeder capable of adapting to most habitats. Most often seen singly or in pairs at dusk or dawn, it is ochre in colour with a prominent black saddle flecked by a varying amount of white or gold. Highly versatile and with a widespread distribution, the black-backed jackal is probably the most frequently observed small predator in Africa south of the Zambezi, and its eerie call is a characteristic sound of the bush at night. It is found throughout Botswana, with the exception of the far north of the country around the Chobe and Linyanti–Kwando areas, and is fairly common in the drier areas of the Kalahari.

Side-striped jackal (*Canis adustus*) Shoulder height 35–40cm; weight 8–12kg. Despite its prevalence in other areas of Africa, the side-striped jackal is common nowhere in Botswana. It occurs in the far north of the country, including Chobe, the Linyanti–Kwando area and the Okavango. It is about the same size as the previous species, but greyish in colour, with an indistinct pale horizontal stripe on each flank and often a white-tipped tail. These jackals are also usually seen singly or in pairs, at dusk or dawn. Both the side-striped and the black-backed jackals are opportunistic feeders, taking rats, mice, birds, insects, carrion, wild fruits and even termites.

Bat-eared fox (*Otocyon megalotis*) Shoulder height 30–35cm; weight 3–5kg. This endearing small, silver-grey insectivore is unmistakable, with its huge ears and black eye-mask. It can be found throughout Botswana, anywhere that the harvester termite (*Hodotermes mossambicus*) occurs. The best areas are usually short grass plains that receive relatively low rainfall – Savuti Marsh was a favourite habitat when the marsh was dry.

This canine is mostly nocturnal, but can sometimes be seen in pairs or small family groups during the cooler hours of the day, usually in dry open country. It digs well, and will often 'listen' to the ground (its ears operating like a radio-dish) while wandering around, before stopping to dig with its forepaws. As well as termites, bat-eared foxes will eat lizards, gerbils, small birds, scorpions, beetle larvae and other insects.

Insect populations vary with the seasons and bat-eared foxes will move with them. When conditions allow, some areas will have very high densities.

Similar species The **Cape fox** (*Vulpes chama*) is an infrequently seen dry-country predator which occurs throughout central and western Botswana, but is absent from Chobe and the north side of the Okavango. It lacks the prominent ears and mask of the bat-eared fox, and its coat is a uniform sandy-grey colour.

Spotted hyena (*Crocuta crocuta*) Shoulder height 85cm; weight 40–86kg. Hyenas are characterised by their bulky build, sloping back (lower hindquarters), coarse brownish coat, powerful jaws and dog-like expression. Sociable animals, hyenas live in loosely structured clans of about ten animals, led by females, who are stronger and larger than males, and live in a communal den. Contrary to popular myth, spotted hyenas are not exclusively scavengers; they are also adept hunters, which hunt in groups and kill animals as large as wildebeests. Nor are they hermaphroditic, an ancient belief that stems from the false scrotum and penis covering the female hyena's vagina.

Hyenas get more out of their kills than most other predators, digesting the bones, skin and even teeth of antelope. This results in the distinctive white colour attained by their faeces when dry – an easily identified sign of their presence in an area.

The spotted hyena is the largest hyena, identified by its light-brown, blotchily spotted coat. It is found throughout most of Botswana, only absent from the eastern areas around Ghanzi, and perhaps the country's furthest southern edge. These predators are common throughout the north, and will frequently scavenge around camps and campsites at night. Savuti's campsite was, for years, completely plagued by them, while few camps in the Delta are without a story of hyenas breaking into kitchens or eating their way through larders.

Although mainly nocturnal, spotted hyenas can often be seen around dusk and dawn, and their distinctive, whooping calls are one of the most wonderful, yet spine-chilling, sounds of the African night.

Brown hyena (*Hyaena brunnea*) Shoulder height 75–85cm; weight 40–55kg. Although rare (with only about 5,000–8,000 animals left in the wild), this secretive hyena occurs in the most arid parts of Namibia, and throughout Botswana, recently making appearances around Kwanda in the far north. It is unmistakable, with a shaggy, dark-brown coat – not unlike a large, long-haired German shepherd dog – with faint black stripes and a sloping back.

In contrast to the spotted hyena, brown hyenas do tend to scavenge rather than hunt, and are generally solitary while doing so. They are the dominant carnivore in the drier areas of the Namib and Kalahari, where clans (typically two to ten animals) will defend enormous territories against neighbouring clans. Individuals normally forage on their own and eat whatever they can, from small birds and mammals to the remains of kill, as well as fruit and vegetables. They have developed various adaptations to help them survive in arid environments. Their powerful jaws and strong teeth are capable of breaking through bones to access nutritious marrow. Additionally, their ability to extract moisture from their food, such as tsamma melons, reduces their dependency on water sources and means that they can survive for long periods in environments where water is scarce.

Brown hyenas are very rarely seen on game drives, although researchers based at Jack's Camp have habituated a small clan of hyenas to their presence – making this perhaps the best place in Africa to see them. For more information, see page 463.

Aardwolf (*Proteles cristata*) Shoulder height 45–50cm; weight 8–12kg. With a tawny brown coat and dark, vertical stripes, this insectivorous hyena is not much bigger than a jackal and occurs in low numbers in most parts of Botswana. It is active mainly at night, gathering harvester termites (specifically those of the genus *Trinervitermes*), its principal food, with its wide, sticky tongue. These termites live underground (not in castle-like termite mounds) and come out at night to cut grass and drag it back down with them. Occasionally the aardwolf will also take other insects, mice, birds and carrion.

Open grassland or lightly wooded areas form the typical habitat for aardwolf, which can sometimes be spotted around dusk, dawn or on very overcast days, especially during the colder months. The *Trinervitermes* termites often thrive on overgrazed land, which means that aardwolf are often more common on farmland than in national parks. There is nowhere that they are frequently sighted.

Spotted hyena

CS/S

Botswana Wildlife Guide   MAMMALS

2

Brown hyena

JG

Aardwolf

TF/S

Vervet monkey

SE/S

Lesser bushbaby

E/D

Chacma baboon

OP/S

PRIMATES

Chacma baboon (*Papio ursinus*) Shoulder height 50–75cm; weight 25–45kg. This powerful terrestrial primate, distinguished from any other monkey by its much larger size, inverted-U-shaped tail and distinctive dog-like head, is fascinating to watch from a behavioural perspective. It lives in large troops that boast a complex, rigid social structure characterised by a matriarchal lineage and plenty of inter-troop movement by males seeking social dominance. Omnivorous and at home in almost any habitat, the baboon is the most widespread primate in Africa, frequently seen in most of Botswana. The centre of the Kalahari (including the CKGR) is the only area from which it is absent.

There are three African races, regarded by some authorities as full species. The chacma baboon is grey, and confined largely to areas south of the Zambezi. The yellow baboon (*P. cynocephalus*) is the yellow-brown race occurring in Zambia, northern Mozambique, Malawi, southern and eastern Tanzania and eastern Kenya. The olive or anubis baboon (*P. anubis*) is a hairy green-to-brown baboon found in Ethiopia, Uganda, northern Tanzania and Kenya.

With a highly organised defence system, the only predator that seriously affects baboons is the leopard, which will try to pick them off at night while they are roosting in trees or cliffs. Campers in Chobe and Moremi should treat these animals with respect; long exposure to humans has taught them to steal, and not to be afraid.

Vervet monkey (*Cercopithecus aethiops*) Length (excluding tail) 40–55cm; weight 4–6kg. Also known as the green or grivet monkey, the vervet is probably the world's most numerous monkey and certainly the most common and widespread representative of the *Cercopithecus* guenons, a taxonomically controversial genus associated with arboreal living in African forests. Vervets are atypical in that they inhabit savannah and woodland rather than true forest, and spend a high proportion of their time on the ground. They occur throughout the northern and eastern parts of the country, but are absent from the drier areas of central, western and southern Botswana. Vervets like belts of tall trees with thick vegetation within easy reach of water, and much of northern Chobe, the Kwando–Linyanti area and the Okavango is ideal for them.

The vervet's light-grey coat, black face and white forehead band are distinctive – as are the male's garish blue genitals. Vervet monkeys live in troops averaging about 25 animals; they are active during the day and roost in trees at night. They eat mainly fruit and vegetables, though are opportunistic and will take insects and young birds, and even raid tents at campsites (usually where ill-informed visitors have previously tempted them into human contact by offering food).

Southern lesser bushbaby (*Galago moholi*) Length (without tail) 17cm; weight 142–250g. The lesser bushbaby is the most widespread and common member of a group of small and generally indistinguishable nocturnal primates, distantly related to the lemurs of Madagascar. In Botswana it occurs throughout the northern half of the country, including in Nxai and Makgadikgadi.

More often heard than seen, the lesser bushbaby can sometimes be picked out by tracing a cry to a tree and shining a torch into the branches; its eyes reflect as two red dots. These eyes are designed to function in what we would describe as total darkness. Lesser bushbabies feed on insects – some of which are caught in the air by jumping – and also on sap from trees, especially acacia gum.

Lesser bushbabies inhabit wooded areas, and in particular prefer acacia trees or riverine forests.

LARGE ANTELOPE

Sable antelope (*Hippotragus niger*) Shoulder height 135cm; weight 230kg. The striking male sable is jet black with a distinct white face, underbelly and rump, and long decurved horns – a strong contender for the title of Africa's most beautiful antelope. The female is chestnut brown and has shorter horns, while the young are a lighter red-brown colour. Sable are found throughout the wetter areas of southern and eastern Africa, but are common nowhere.

In Botswana they occur in the north, as far west as the central Okavango. The Chobe riverfront is a good place to look for them in the dry season, usually between Kasane and Chobe Game Lodge, where several herds frequent the valleys and come down to drink.

Similarly, sable are occasionally seen near the Kwando and Linyanti rivers. They're not common in the Delta region, but are seen periodically. Good sightings have been recorded around the Gomoti River, and in NG20 and NG21. The Vumbura Concession (NG22) probably offers the highest density of sable in the Delta, while they're generally absent from NG26, NG27, NG30 and further west.

Sable are normally seen in small herds: either bachelor herds of males, or breeding herds of females and young, which are often accompanied by the dominant bull in that territory. The breeding females give birth around February or March; the calves remain hidden, away from the herd, for their first few weeks. Sable are mostly grazers, though will browse, especially when food is scarce. They need to drink at least every other day, and seem especially fond of low-lying dewy vleis in wetter areas.

Roan antelope (*Hippotragus equinus*) Shoulder height 120–150cm; weight 250–300kg. This handsome horse-like antelope is uniform fawn-grey with a pale belly, large ears, short decurved horns and a light mane. It could be mistaken for the female sable antelope, but this has a well-defined white belly, and lacks the roan's distinctive black-and-white facial markings. The roan is relatively rare; common almost nowhere in Africa (Malawi's Nyika Plateau being the obvious exception to this rule). In Botswana, small groups are found in the Chobe and Kwando–Linyanti areas, and occasionally some will wander as far as the drier parts of the Okavango

Sable

Roan

Gemsbok

Delta – but they're always something of a rarity. Ngwezumba Pans is probably the best location to search for them, but they're not seen regularly even there.

Roan need lots of space if they are to thrive and breed; they don't generally do well where game densities are high. This alone precludes them from success in most of the Delta. Game farms prize them as one of the most valuable antelope. They need access to drinking water, but are well adapted to subsist on relatively high plateaux with poor soils.

Gemsbok (*Oryx gazella*) Shoulder height 120cm; weight 230kg. This is the quintessential desert antelope, unmistakable with its ash-grey coat, bold black facial marks and flank strip, and unique long, straight horns. Of the three races of oryx in Africa, the gemsbok is the largest and most striking. It occurs throughout the Kalahari and Namib and is widespread all over central and western Botswana. The dominant large antelope in the CKGR, it can be seen there in large numbers during the early months of the year.

As you might expect, gemsbok are very adaptable. They range widely and are found in areas of dunes, alkaline pans, open savannah and even woodlands. Along with the much smaller springbok, they can sometimes be seen tracking across open plains with only dust-devils and mirages for company. Gemsbok can endure extremes of temperature, helped by specially adapted blood capillaries in their nasal passages that can cool their blood before it reaches their brains. Thus, although their body temperature can rise by up to 6°C, their brains remain cool and they survive. They do not need drinking water and will eat wild melons and dig for roots, bulbs and tubers when grazing or browsing becomes difficult.

Waterbuck (*Kobus ellipsiprymnus*) Shoulder height 130cm; weight 250–270kg. The waterbuck is easily recognised by its shaggy brown coat and the male's large, lyre-shaped horns. The common race of southern Africa (*K. e. ellipsiprymnus*) and areas east of the Rift Valley has a distinctive white ring around its rump. The defassa race (known as *K. e. defassa* or *K. e. crawshayi*) of the Rift Valley and areas further west has a full white rump.

Only the common waterbuck occurs in Botswana, and it is restricted to the Chobe, Kwando–Linyanti and eastern sides of the Delta. Favourite areas include the northern side of the Linyanti Concession (NG15), and also Vumbura (NG22), but it is relatively uncommon elsewhere. Waterbuck certainly used to occur at Savuti when the channel flowed, but they deserted the area when the marsh dried up.

Red hartebeest

SWP/S

Blue wildebeest

OP/D

Waterbuck

E/D

Tsessebe

OP/S

Waterbuck need to drink very regularly, so usually stay within a few kilometres of water, where they like to graze on short, nutritious grasses. At night they may take cover in adjacent woodlands. It is often asserted that waterbuck flesh is oily and smelly, which may discourage predators.

Blue wildebeest (*Connochaetes taurinus*) Shoulder height 130–150cm; weight 180–250kg. This ungainly antelope, also called the brindled gnu, is easily identified by its dark coat and bovine appearance. The superficially similar buffalo is far more heavily built; when they have enough space and conditions are right, blue wildebeest can multiply rapidly and form immense herds – as perhaps a million do for their annual migration from Tanzania's Serengeti Plains into Kenya's Maasai Mara.

In Botswana during the middle of the 20th century wildebeest were probably the most numerous large herbivore, forming herds estimated at a quarter of a million individuals. Although they are still found throughout Botswana, these numbers have fallen drastically (page 463).

Wildebeest are best adapted to take large mouthfuls of short, nutritious grasses, and they need access to drinking water every two or three days. This limits them to remaining relatively close to a source of water, and if that dries up they will journey as far as necessary to find another.

Red hartebeest (*Alcelaphus buselaphus*) Shoulder height 125cm; weight 120–150kg. Hartebeests are ungainly antelope, readily identified by the combination of large shoulders, sloping back, glossy, red-brown coat and smallish horns in both sexes. Numerous subspecies are recognised, all of which are generally seen in small family groups in reasonably open country. Though once hartebeest were found from the Mediterranean to the Cape, only isolated populations still survive.

The only subspecies native to Botswana is the red hartebeest, which is found throughout the arid central, southern and western areas of the country. It can be seen in Nxai and Makgadikgadi, and is one of the more numerous large mammals in the CKGR. Hartebeest may occur in the drier, southwestern corners of the Delta, or in the drier parts of southern Chobe, but I've no records of them being seen in either location.

Hartebeests are more or less exclusively grazers, and although they like access to water they will eat melons, tubers and rhizomes when necessary. In the Central Kalahari they'll range widely, often with wildebeest, following thunderstorms in search of fresh, green shoots.

Tsessebe (*Damaliscus lunatus*) Shoulder height 120cm; weight 125–140kg. Tsessebe are basically a slightly smaller, darker version of hartebeest, coloured red-brown with an almost purple sheen, though their lower legs are distinctly paler. (A closely related subspecies is known as topi in East Africa.) The two look similar in profile or at a distance, although often in the field you can make a good guess from the environment which antelope you're looking at long before you're close enough to examine its colouring.

The tsessebe is found in northern Botswana, and is one of the most common antelope in some parts of the Okavango Delta. Its favourite habitat is open grassland, where it is a selective grazer, eating the younger, more nutritious grasses. This makes it efficient in pastures where some grasses are old and some fresh, or in more broken country, but less efficient than, say, wildebeest where the pasture is uniformly short, good grass. The tsessebe is one of the fastest antelope species, and jumps very well.

Kudu (*Tragelaphus strepsiceros*) Shoulder height 140–155cm; weight 180–250kg. The kudu (or, more properly, the greater kudu) is the largest member of the genus *Tragelaphus*. These medium-sized to large antelopes are characterised by their grey-brown coats with up to ten stripes on each flank. The male has magnificent double-spiralled corkscrew horns. Occurring throughout southern Africa, kudu are found all over Botswana.

These handsome antelope are particularly common in the well-wooded areas of Chobe, the Kwando–Linyanti region and the Okavango, though they also occur throughout the drier areas of the Kalahari. They are browsers that thrive in areas with mixed tree savannah and thickets, and the males will sometimes use their horns to pull down the lower branches of trees to eat.

Wherever they occur, kudu are normally seen in small herds, consisting of a couple of females and their offspring, usually accompanied by a male. Otherwise the males occur either singly or in small bachelor groups.

Eland (*Taurotragus oryx*) Shoulder height 150–175cm; weight 450–900kg. Africa's largest antelope, the eland is light brown in colour, sometimes with a few faint white vertical stripes. Relatively short horns and a large dewlap accentuate its somewhat bovine appearance. It was once widely distributed in eastern and southern Africa, though the population has now been severely depleted. Small herds of eland frequent grasslands and light woodlands, often fleeing at the slightest provocation. (They have long been hunted for their excellent meat, so perhaps this is not surprising.)

Eland are very rare in the Okavango area and although they do occur throughout Chobe, they are seldom seen. Better areas to see them are in the Kalahari's salt pans or, better still, the Central Kalahari. They are opportunist browsers and grazers, eating fruit, berries, seed pods and leaves as well as green grass after the rains, and roots and tubers when times are lean.

These large antelope run slowly, though can trot for great distances and jump exceedingly well. Eland have a very special significance for the San people – illustrated by the highlight of the famous 'van der Post panel' at the Tsodilo Hills (page 432), which is a painting of a particularly magnificent eland bull.

Kudu

Eland

OP/D

VS/S

MEDIUM AND SMALL ANTELOPE

Bushbuck (*Tragelaphus scriptus*) Shoulder height 70–80cm; weight 30–45kg. This attractive antelope, a member of the same genus as the kudu, is widespread throughout Africa and shows great regional variation in its colouring. (The animals found in sub-Saharan Africa are often claimed to be a subspecies, the 'Chobe bushbuck', though it seems likely that they're simply a colour variation of the main species.)

Bushbuck occur in forest and riverine woodland, where they are normally seen singly or in pairs. The male is dark brown or chestnut, while the much smaller female is generally a pale reddish brown. The male has relatively small horns that twist into a spiral at maturity. Both sexes are marked with white spots and sometimes stripes, though the stripes are often indistinct.

Bushbuck tend to be secretive and very skittish, except when used to people, when they relax and can become almost tame. They depend on cover and camouflage to avoid predators, and are often found in the thick, herby vegetation around rivers – and are the only solitary antelope in Africa that does not defend a territory. They will freeze if disturbed, before dashing off into the undergrowth. Bushbuck are both browsers and grazers, choosing the more succulent grass shoots, fruit and flowers. In Botswana they have a limited distribution around the Okavango, beside the Kwando–Linyanti and the Chobe. Look for them slowly picking their way through the thick bush near the water. (Serondela used to be a favourite spot, and Lebala Camp had a long-term resident male next to the dining area on our last visit.)

Impala (*Aepyceros melampus*) Shoulder height 90cm; weight 45kg. This slender, handsome antelope is superficially similar to the springbok, but in fact belongs to its own separate family. Tawny in colour, and lighter underneath than above, the impala has diagnostic black and white stripes running down its rump and tail, and the male has large lyre-shaped horns. The impala is one of the most widespread and successful antelope species in eastern and southern Africa. It is often the most common antelope in wooded savannah habitats, including most of Chobe and the drier, more forested parts of the Okavango Delta – though is rarely seen west of the Okavango, or south of Nxai Pan. Although they can survive without drinking, impala prefer to live near water and are largely absent from the Kalahari.

As you might expect of such a successful species, impala both graze and browse, depending on what fodder is available. Despite some people's tendency to overlook them as common, take a close look and you'll realise that they're exceptionally beautiful animals. Socially you'll normally see large herds of females and young, lorded over by a dominant male, and small bachelor groups of males.

Springbok (*Antidorcas marsupialis*) Shoulder height 60cm; weight 25–45kg. Springbok are graceful herbivores, similar in size to impala. Visitors from East Africa, noticing their passing resemblance to Thomson's gazelle (*Gazella thomsonii*), will not be surprised that they're southern Africa's only member of the gazelle family.

Even from a distance, springbok are unlikely to be confused with anything else; their finely marked short coats have fawn-brown upper parts and a white belly, separated by a dark brown band. Springbok generally occur in herds and favour dry, open country, preferring plains or savannah, and avoiding thick woodlands and mountains. They can subsist without water for long periods,

Bushbuck

CW/D

Impala

TW/S

Springbok

SE/S

Reedbuck

JG

Puku

OP/D

Red lechwe

SP/S

provided that there is moisture (minimum of 10%) in the vegetation that they graze or browse.

Since springbok are more dependent on food than water, they congregate in huge numbers during the rains on areas where they can find fresh, green shoots – such as the pans of the CKGR. In contrast, during the dry season they spread out across the vast arid parks of the Kalahari. This is exactly the opposite pattern to that followed by most water-dependent antelope, which typically congregate during the dry season (around rivers to remaining pans), while spreading out during the rains. This explains why the Kalahari's game is at its densest during the rains, whereas the game in Chobe and the Okavango is at its most prolific during the dry season.

Springbok occur throughout central and southern Botswana, where they are usually the most common small antelope by far; in Nxai, Makgadikgadi and the CKGR they number in the thousands.

Reedbuck (*Redunca arundinum*) Shoulder height 80–90cm; weight 45–65kg. Sometimes referred to as the southern reedbuck (as distinct from mountain and Bohor reedbucks, found further east), these slender antelope are uniformly fawn in colour, and lighter below than above. Only males have horns, but both sexes show a distinctive black glandular patch below each ear. They are generally found in reedbeds and tall grasslands, often beside rivers, and are easily identified by their loud, whistling alarm call and distinctive bounding running style.

In Botswana, reedbuck are found only where there is close access to water in the north: in northern Chobe, the Kwando–Linyanti region and throughout the Delta. They live in monogamous pairs that defend a territory.

Puku (*Kobus vardonii*) Shoulder height 80cm; weight 60–75kg. Easily confused with the red lechwe at a glance, the puku has an orange-tawny colour overall, which is lighter underneath than above. Its legs have no black markings, and its tail is a lighter yellow. Puku are smaller and slightly shaggier than lechwe, and the males have smaller, stouter horns than those of lechwe.

Puku are found all over eastern and central Africa, and are one of the most common antelopes in Zambia. Typically they inhabit open areas near rivers and marshes, though in Zambia are found in a wider variety of habitats. In Botswana their distribution is restricted to the floodplain areas of the Chobe riverfront, and often virtually the only place that you'll see them is around the aptly named Puku Flats, just west of Chobe Game Lodge.

Red lechwe (*Kobus leche*) Shoulder height 90–100cm; weight 80–100kg. Red lechwe are sturdy antelope with a chestnut-red coat, paler underneath than on top, and beautiful lyre-shaped horns. The males are generally larger and darker than the females. They need dry land on which to rest, but otherwise are adapted for life in the seasonal floodplains that border lakes and rivers. They will spend much of their time grazing on grasses and sedges, standing in water if necessary. Their hooves are splayed, adapted to bounding through their muddy environment when fleeing from the lions, hyenas and wild dogs that hunt them, making them the most aquatic of antelope after sitatunga.

Lechwe reach the southern limit of their distribution in the Okavango and Linyanti areas. They are also found in the DRC, Angola, Namibia's Zambezi Region (Caprivi Strip) and in Zambia, their stronghold. Given the right conditions, they can be found in huge numbers, and they are the most numerous antelope in the shallow-water environments of the Delta.

Sitatunga

RR/S

Steenbok

M/S

Klipspringer

SW/S

Sharpe's grysbok

ET/S

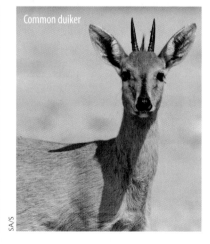

Common duiker

SA/S

Sitatunga (*Tragelaphus spekii*) Shoulder height 85–90cm; weight 105–115kg. This semi-aquatic antelope is a widespread but infrequently observed inhabitant of western and central African papyrus swamps, from the Okavango in Botswana to the Sudd in Sudan. In Botswana sitatunga are concentrated in the Okavango – which has a strong population – though they're also seen periodically in the Kwando–Linyanti and Chobe systems. The best places to spot them are deep-water areas with plenty of papyrus, including Moremi and in NG21, 22, 23, 24 and 25 concessions.

Because of their preferred habitat, sitatunga are elusive and seldom seen, even in areas where they are relatively common, and are exceedingly vulnerable to habitat destruction. Sitatunga are noted for an ability to submerse themselves completely, with just their nostrils showing, when pursued by a predator.

Klipspringer (*Oreotragus oreotragus*) Shoulder height 60cm; weight 13kg. The klipspringer is a strongly built little antelope, normally seen in pairs, and easily identified by its dark, bristly grey-yellow coat, slightly speckled appearance and unique habitat preference. Klipspringer means 'rockjumper' in Afrikaans and it is an apt name for an antelope that occurs exclusively in mountainous areas and rocky outcrops, from Cape Town to the Red Sea. Klipspringers are mainly browsers, though they do eat a little new grass; when spotted they will freeze, or bound at great speed across the steepest of slopes.

Though often thought to be absent from all but the extreme southeast corner of Botswana, over the years there has been a number of sightings in the hills around Savuti. Given that they only live in rocky hills and kopjes, and that most of Botswana is amazingly flat (or gently rolling at best), it's no surprise that only the odd isolated population exists. It's the same in other parts of their range. I've no reports of them at the Tsodilo Hills, but it would be a perfect habitat for them.

Steenbok (*Raphicerus campestris*) Shoulder height 50cm; weight 11kg. This rather nondescript small antelope has red-brown upper parts and clear white underparts, and the male has short straight horns. It is one of the most commonly observed small antelope, especially on farmland; if you see a small antelope fleeing from you across grassland, then it is likely to be a steenbok. Like most other small antelopes, the steenbok is normally encountered singly or in pairs and tends to 'freeze' when disturbed, before taking flight.

Similar species The **Oribi** (*Ourebia ourebi*) is a relatively widespread but generally uncommon antelope, which occurs in very localised areas throughout sub-Saharan Africa. It is usually found only in large, open stretches of dry grassland, where there are also patches of taller grass for cover. It looks much like a steenbok but stands about 10cm higher at the shoulder and has an altogether more upright bearing. In Botswana it is thought to occur in Chobe, and specifically in the Ngwezumba Pans area – although sightings of it even there are not common. **Sharpe's grysbok** (*Raphicerus sharpei*) is similar in size and appearance, though it has a distinctive white-flecked coat. It occurs alongside the steenbok in the far northeastern corner of Botswana, around northern Chobe and the Kasane area, but is almost entirely nocturnal in its habits and so very seldom seen.

Common duiker (*Sylvicapra grimmia*) Shoulder height 50cm; weight 20kg. This anomalous duiker holds itself more like a steenbok or grysbok and is the only member of its (large) family to occur outside of forests. Generally grey in colour, the common duiker can most easily be separated from other small antelopes by the black tuft of hair that sticks up between its horns. It occurs throughout Botswana, and across virtually the whole of southern Africa, with the exception of the Namib Desert. Common duikers tolerate most habitats except for true forest and very open country, and are tolerant of nearby human settlements. They are opportunist feeders, taking fruit, seeds and leaves, as well as crops, small reptiles and amphibians. Despite their widespread occurrence, duiker are relatively rarely seen.

OTHER LARGE HERBIVORES
African elephant (*Loxodonta africana*) Shoulder height 2.3–3.4m; weight up to 6,000kg. The world's largest land animal, the African elephant is intelligent, social and often very entertaining to watch. Females live in closely knit clans in which the eldest female plays matriarch over her sisters, daughters and granddaughters. Elephants' life spans are comparable with those of humans, and mother–daughter bonds are strong and may last for up to 50 years. Males, known as bulls, generally leave the family group at around 12 years to roam singly or form bachelor herds. Under normal circumstances, elephants range widely in search of food and water, but when concentrated populations are forced to live in conservation areas their habit of uprooting trees can cause serious environmental damage.

Botswana is home to more African elephants than any other country, with more than half the global population living in the Kavango Zambezi Transfrontier Conservation Area, a massive, international conservation area incorporating northern Botswana. Elephants are found in habitats ranging from deserts to rainforest; but they require trees and access to drinking water.

The Chobe, Kwando–Linyanti and Okavango areas have the greatest populations of elephants in Africa. During the rains, from December onwards, these disperse in the interior of the country, into the vast expanses of mopane forest and into the drier areas of the northern Kalahari. They split up into smaller family groups and spread out all over the place in order to find water (the clay pans of the mopane woodlands are especially valuable as sources).

Despite their range having become more restricted by human expansion over the years, individuals will often wander widely, turning up in locations from which they have been absent for years. However, as the dry season progresses and the waterholes dry up, small groups of elephants gradually coalesce into larger herds, and head for the permanent sources: the rivers and the Delta. Thus by September and October you can normally see huge herds of elephants along the Chobe, Kwando and Linyanti rivers. The number and size of herds in the Okavango increases too.

In many areas elephants have no natural predators (the huge prides of lion in the Savuti and North Gate areas are an exception to this rule); they are generally constrained by lack of suitable habitat (ie: trees and water), by man and by diseases such as anthrax. Thus in many confined national parks in southern Africa, there are programmes to cull elephants to restrict their numbers. This is controversial, even among ardent conservationists. Botswana has no such policy. The result, some argue, is an over-population of elephants here, and the severe environmental degradation to be seen around the riverfront in Chobe, where the riverine forests have been severely depleted; while not denying the observation, it's well worth remembering that there was a sawmill in this area, and extensive logging during the 1930s and early 1940s – so humans should take part of the blame for this.

T/S

Black rhinoceros (*Diceros bicornis*) Shoulder height 160cm; weight 1,000kg. This is the more widespread of Africa's two rhino species, an imposing and rather temperamental creature. Black rhino were once found all over northern Botswana, but were thought to have been poached to extinction here during the 1990s, while becoming highly endangered in many other countries within their range. Reintroduction efforts from 2003 were successful and saw numbers climb to an estimated 50 animals by the end of 2017. Sadly, resurgent poaching since 2018 seems to have largely wiped them out again (page 330).

Black rhino exploit a wide range of habitats, from dense woodlands and bush to arid semi-desert, and are generally solitary animals. They can survive without drinking for four to five days. However, their territorial behaviour and regular patterns of movement make them an easy target for poachers. Black rhino can be very aggressive when disturbed and will charge with minimal provocation. Their hearing and sense of smell are acute, while their eyesight is poor (so they often miss their target).

White rhinoceros (*Ceratotherium simum*) Shoulder height 180cm; weight 1,800–2,500kg. The white rhino is in fact no paler in colour than the black rhino: 'white' and 'black' are *not* literal descriptions. The description 'white' derives from the Afrikaans *weit* (wide) and refers to the animal's flattened mouth, an ideal shape for cropping grass. This is a good way to tell the two rhino species apart, since the mouth of the black rhino, a browser in most parts of its range, is more rounded with a hooked upper lip.

Unlike their smaller cousins, white rhino are generally placid grazing animals and are very rarely aggressive. They prefer open grassy plains and are often seen in small groups. In the accounts of the first trips across Africa by the early white explorers, white rhino were found (and shot) in huge numbers.

This species was almost extinct by the end of the 19th century, reduced to a tiny population in South Africa's Umfolozi and Hluhluwe reserves. Intensive conservation subsequently nurtured a recovery and gradually animals were reintroduced into selected locations across southern Africa. By the 1980s, it had become much more numerous than the black rhino, whose numbers were by then falling fast. Sadly, the early 21st century saw poaching resume, with South Africa's once-safe populations targeted ruthlessly. Prior to 2018, Botswana's wild areas were viewed as safe havens for rhino and many animals were relocated here from South Africa. Sadly since then, Botswana's reputation for rhino conservation has plummeted. At the time of writing, only a handful of white rhino remain in the Delta. See page 330 for a detailed summary of Botswana's rhino situation.

Hippopotamus (*Hippopotamus amphibius*) Shoulder height 150cm; weight 2,000kg. Characteristic of Africa's large rivers and lakes, this large, lumbering animal spends most of the day submerged but emerges at night to graze. Strongly territorial, herds of ten or more are presided over by a dominant male who will readily defend his patriarchy to the death. Hippos are abundant in most protected rivers and water bodies and are still quite common outside reserves.

Hippos are widely credited with killing more people than any other African mammal. They are clearly very, very dangerous – but we know of no statistics to support this claim, and many reliable sources suggest that elephant and lion kill just as many people. Crocodiles certainly kill more.

In Botswana you'll find hippo in good numbers in all of the major river systems: Chobe, Kwando–Linyanti and the Okavango. It would be difficult to go on safari in any of the wetter areas of northern Botswana without seeing large numbers.

Black rhino

26/S

White rhino

CM

Hippo

OP/D

Buffalo

JM

Giraffe

OP/D

Zebra

R/D

Buffalo (*Syncerus caffer*) Shoulder height 140cm; weight 700kg. Frequently and erroneously referred to as water buffalo (which is actually an Asian species), the Cape, or African, buffalo is a distinctive, highly social, ox-like animal that lives as part of a herd. It prefers well-watered savannah, though also occurs in forested areas. Buffalo are primarily grazers and need regular access to water, where they drink, wallow and swim readily if necessary. Lion often follow herds of buffalo, their favourite prey in some areas.

Huge herds are generally fairly peaceful. However, small bachelor herds, and especially single old bulls, can be very nervous and aggressive. They have a reputation for charging at the slightest provocation, often in the midst of thick bush, and are exceedingly dangerous when wounded.

Buffalo smell and hear well, but it's often claimed that they have poor eyesight. This isn't true, though when encountered during a walking safari, if you keep still and the wind is right they won't be able to discern your presence.

Common and widespread in sub-Saharan Africa, in Botswana the buffalo is limited to the north of the country, largely by the absence of sufficient water elsewhere. Their annual movements mirror those of elephants in general terms. During the rains, from December onwards, they disperse into the mopane forests and into the drier areas of the northern Kalahari, splitting up into smaller groups and spreading out. However, as the dry season progresses, they gather together into larger herds, and congregate near permanent sources of water: along the Chobe, Kwando and Linyanti rivers, and throughout the Okavango Delta. Then you'll see them in most reserves with water, though the open plains of NG23 (Duba Plains) seem to have particularly high concentrations of buffalo.

Giraffe (*Giraffa camelopardalis*) Shoulder height 250–350cm; weight 1,000–1,400kg. The world's tallest and longest-necked land animal, a fully grown giraffe can measure up to 5.5m high. Quite unmistakable, giraffe live in loosely structured herds of up to 15, though herd members often disperse, when they are seen singly or in smaller groups. Formerly distributed throughout eastern and southern Africa, in Botswana two subspecies of these great browsers are found largely in the centre and north of the country. The CKGR has a very healthy population of lighter-coloured Angolan giraffe (*G. c. angolensis*), as do Makgadikgadi and Nxai, while the South African giraffe (*G. c. giraffa*) is found through the Chobe, Kwando–Linyanti and Okavango areas.

Giraffe are adapted to browse vegetation that is beyond the reach of all the other large herbivores, with the exception of elephant. They prefer *Acacia* and *Combretum* species, and a 45cm tongue ensures they can pluck leaves from the thorniest branches. Images of giraffe feature in the Tsodilo Hills rock paintings (page 433).

Plains zebra (*Equus quagga*) Shoulder height 130cm; weight 300–340kg. Also known as common zebra, this attractive striped horse is common and widespread throughout most of eastern and southern Africa, where it is often seen in large herds alongside wildebeest. There are many subspecies of zebra in Africa, and most southern races, including those in Botswana, have paler brownish 'shadow stripes' between the bold black stripes (which are present in all races).

Zebra are common in most conservation areas, from northern South Africa and Namibia all the way up to the southeast of Ethiopia. In Botswana they occur in Makgadikgadi, Nxai and to the north – but we don't believe that they still occur within the CKGR. If the rains have been good in the Makgadikgadi Pans area, then during the first few months of the year you can witness huge herds of zebra roaming across the open plains in search of the freshest new grass.

Warthog (*Phacochoerus africanus*) Shoulder height 60–70cm; weight 45–150kg. This widespread and often conspicuously abundant resident of the African savannah is grey in colour with a thin covering of hairs, wart-like bumps on its face, and rather large, upward-curving tusks. Africa's only diurnal swine, the warthog is often seen in family groups, trotting around with its tail raised stiffly (a diagnostic trait) and a determinedly nonchalant air.

Warthog occur throughout Botswana, with the exception of the far south. Wherever they occur, you'll often see them grazing beside the road, on bended knees. Omnivorous eaters, they have adapted to eat grasses, roots, tubers and seeds in savannah areas.

Similar species Bulkier, hairier and browner, the **bushpig** (*Potamochoerus larvatus*) only occurs in the wetter areas of northern Botswana – northern Chobe, the Kwando–Linyanti and the Okavango. Like warthog, bushpig don't survive well near settlements: they damage crops and so are persistently hunted. That said, even where they do occur, they are rarely seen due to their nocturnal habits and preference for living in dense vegetation.

SMALL MAMMALS
African civet (*Civettictis civetta*) Shoulder height 40cm; weight 10–15kg. This bulky, long-haired, rather feline creature of the African night is omnivorous, feeding on small animals and carrion, though it will also eat fruit. It has a pale fawn coat, densely blotched with large black spots that merge into stripes towards the head. Civets are widespread and common throughout a band across northern Botswana, including Chobe, the Kwando–Linyanti and Okavango areas. They occur in many habitats, and make frequent cameo appearances on night drives.

Note that although they are occasionally referred to as 'civet cats', this is misleading. They are more closely related to the mongoose than the felines and belong in the same genus as genets.

Similar species Both the **small-spotted genet** (*Genetta genetta*) and the **large-spotted genet** (*Genetta tigrina*) are members of a big group of similar small predators found in Botswana. All the genets are slender and rather feline in appearance (though they are *not* cats), with a grey to gold-brown coat marked with black spots and bars, and a long ringed tail. Identification of genets is most easily done by looking at their distinguishing tail features: the smaller has a white-tipped tail and the larger a black-tipped tail.

You're most likely to see genets on nocturnal game drives or occasionally scavenging around game-reserve lodges. The small-spotted genet is found all over Botswana, whereas its larger cousin is thought to be restricted to the northern areas of Chobe, Kwando–Linyanti and Okavango. Genets are excellent climbers and opportunists, eating birds, small mammals and large insects.

Banded mongoose (*Mungos mungo*) Shoulder height 20cm; weight around 1–1.5kg. The banded mongoose is probably the most commonly observed member of a group of small, slender, terrestrial carnivores. Uniform dark grey-brown except for a dozen black stripes across its back, it is a diurnal mongoose occurring in playful family groups, or troops, in most habitats throughout northern and northwestern Botswana. These highly social, tight-knit groups (up to 80 individuals) are commonly seen in packs of 10–20, and are violently territorial if they encounter other packs. They feed on insects, scorpions, amphibians, reptiles and even carrion and birds' eggs, and troops can move through the bush at quite a pace.

Similar species Several other mongoose species occur in Botswana. Some are social and gather in troops; others are solitary. Several are too scarce and nocturnal to be seen by most visitors.

The water or **marsh mongoose** (*Atilax paludinosus*) is large, normally solitary and has a very scruffy brown coat; it is widespread in the Chobe, Kwando–Linyanti and Okavango regions, generally found near water.

The **white-tailed mongoose** (*Ichneumia albicauda*), or white-tailed ichneumon, is a solitary, large brown mongoose with long, coarse hair. It is nocturnal and easily identified by its bushy white tail if seen crossing roads at night. It occurs across northern Botswana and it can also be found in a few cattle-ranching areas, where it eats the beetle-grubs found in manure.

2

The **slender mongoose** (*Galerella sanguinea*) is also widespread throughout Botswana wherever it can find cover. It, too, is solitary, but it is very much smaller (shoulder height 10cm) and has a uniform brown or reddish coat and blackish tail tip. Its tail is held up when it runs.

The **large grey mongoose** (*Herpestes ichneumon*), also called the Egyptian mongoose, is a large mongoose with coarse, grey-speckled body hair, black lower legs and feet, and a black tip to its tail. It is found in the same northern areas of Botswana, but is common nowhere. It is generally diurnal, and is either solitary or lives in pairs. Large grey mongoose eat small rodents, reptiles, birds and also snakes, generally killing rather than scavenging.

Selous' mongoose (*Paracynictis selousi*) is smaller, with fine, speckled grey fur, and a white tip to its tail. It likes open country and woodlands, occurring in many northern and further eastern areas of Botswana. It is nocturnal and solitary, eating mainly insects, grubs, small reptiles and amphibians. It seems especially fond of the larvae of dung beetles, and so is sometimes found in cattle country.

The **yellow mongoose** (*Cynictis penicillata*) is a small, sociable mongoose with a tawny or yellow coat, and is commonly found across most of Botswana – even in the drier areas of the Central Kalahari. It normally forages alone and is easily identified by the white tip on its tail. This species often shares burrow systems with ground squirrels.

Finally, the **dwarf mongoose** (*Helogale parvula*) is a diminutive (shoulder height 7cm), highly sociable light-brown mongoose often seen in the vicinity of the termite mounds where it nests. This is Africa's smallest carnivore, and occurs in higher densities than any other. It is widespread throughout the Chobe, Kwando–Linyanti and Okavango areas, and is often seen. Groups of 20–30 are not unknown, consisting of a breeding pair and subordinate others. These inquisitive little animals can be very entertaining to watch.

Meerkat (*Suricata suricatta*) Shoulder height 25–35cm; weight 650–950g. Found throughout central and southwest Botswana, and much of neighbouring Namibia, meerkats, also known as suricates, are absent from the Chobe, Kwando–Linyanti and Okavango regions. The best places to see them are Makgadikgadi, the CKGR and further towards the southwest corner of Botswana (eg: the KD1 concession, south of Ghanzi, and the Kgalagadi Transfrontier Park).

Meerkats also belong to the mongoose family. These small animals are sandy to silvery-grey in colour, with dark bands running across their backs. They are exclusively diurnal and have a distinctive habit of sitting upright on their hind legs. They do this when they first emerge in the morning, to sun themselves, and throughout the day.

Living in complex social groups, meerkats are usually seen scratching around for insects, beetles and small reptiles in dry, open, grassy areas; while the rest forage, one or two of the group will use the highest mound around as a sentry-post – looking out for predators using their remarkable eyesight. Meerkats' social behaviour is very complex: they squeak constantly to communicate and even use different alarm calls for different types of predators. Because of their photogenic poses and fascinating social behaviour, they have been the subject of several successful television documentaries filmed in the southern Kalahari.

Honey badger (*Mellivora capensis*) Shoulder height 30cm; weight 12kg. Also known as the ratel, the honey badger is black with a puppyish face and grey-white back. It is an opportunistic feeder best known for its allegedly symbiotic relationship with a bird called the honeyguide which leads it to beehives, waits for it to tear them

Meercat

Honey badger

JC/S

Striped polecat

LR/S

SS

Spotted-necked otter

JPD/S

Clawless otter

SS

open, then feeds on the scraps. The honey badger is among the most widespread of African carnivores, and also among the most powerful and aggressive for its size. It occurs all over Botswana, but is thinly distributed and infrequently seen, except where it has lost its fear of people and started to scavenge from safari camps.

Similar species Other mustelids occurring in the region include the **striped polecat** (*Ictonyx striatus*), a common but rarely seen nocturnal creature with black underparts and a bushy white back.

Cape clawless otter (*Aonyx capensis*) Shoulder height 20–30cm; weight 10–21kg. This is the larger of the two species of otter that occur in southern Africa. It has a chocolate-brown coat with a pale cream-to-white chin and throat. In Botswana, it is restricted to the northern river systems of Chobe, Kwando–Linyanti and the Okavango (it's not found in broad, tropical rivers like the Zambezi), though will occasionally move away from there, across dry land, in search of other pools and waterways.

Cape clawless otters are active mostly around dusk and dawn, although they will sometimes be seen in broad daylight or at night. Rough skin on their paws gives excellent grip, and with this they prey mostly on frogs and fish. They'll also take freshwater mussels, and will use rocks to help them crack these open.

Although very shy (they'll usually flee when approached by a boat or people), these animals are delightful to watch, seeming very playful, with a variety of aquatic acrobatics, and cleaning their face and paws scrupulously after every meal. Visiting Botswana, you're most likely to see otters in the shallow floodplain areas of the Okavango when on a quiet mokoro trip.

Similar species The smaller **spotted-necked otter** (*Lutra maculicollis*) is darker with light white spots on its throat – though difficult to distinguish from its larger cousin unless you're familiar with them both. Its distribution and habits are similar to the Cape clawless, though it is more diurnal, and more tied to bodies of water.

Aardvark (*Orycteropus afer*) Shoulder height 60cm; weight 55–80kg. This singularly bizarre nocturnal insectivore is unmistakable with its long snout, huge ears and powerful legs, adapted to dig up the nests of termites on which it feeds. Aardvarks occur throughout southern Africa, except in the driest western areas of the Namib. Though their distinctive three-toed tracks are often seen, and they are not uncommon animals, sightings of them are rare.

Aardvarks prefer areas of grassland and sparse scrub, rather than dense woodlands, so much of Botswana's bush suits them well. You're most likely to see them on a late-night game drive, and many guides say that they are seen more often during the rainy season, from December to March.

Pangolin (*Manis temminckii*) Total length 70–100cm; weight 8–15kg. Sharing the aardvark's diet of termites and ants, the pangolin is another very unusual nocturnal insectivore, with distinctive armour plating and a tendency to roll up in a ball when disturbed. (Then it can swipe its tail from side to side, inflicting serious damage on its aggressor.) Sometimes known as Temminck's pangolins, or scaly anteaters, these strange animals walk on their hind legs, using their tail and front legs for balance. They are both nocturnal and rare, and their distribution is little known, although they are thought to occur throughout Botswana. Sightings are exceedingly rare; thus an average of three sightings of pangolin per year in NG31 Reserve counts as a remarkably prolific record by the standards of most areas in Africa!

Sadly, pangolins are the most trafficked animal in the world, which has caused great damage to their population.

Porcupine (*Hystrix africaeaustralis*) Total length 80–100cm; weight 15–25kg. This is the largest rodent found in the region, and occurs all over southern Africa, except for the western reaches of the Namib Desert. It is easily identified by its black-and-white-striped quills, generally black hair and shambolic gait. If heard in the dark, then the rustle of its foraging is augmented by the slight rattle of its quills. These fall out fairly regularly, and are often found in the bush.

Porcupines have a varied diet, and they are fairly opportunistic when it comes to food. Roots and tubers are favourites, as is the bark of certain trees; they will also

Aardvark

TR/S

Pangolin

W/D

Porcupine

RH/S

eat meat and small reptiles, or birds if they have the chance. You're most likely to see porcupines on night drives, as individuals, pairs or small family groups.

Similar species Also spiny, the **Southern African hedgehog** (*Erinaceus frontalis*) has been recorded in eastern and southeastern areas of Botswana, though it is small and nocturnal, so rarely seen even where it does occur. Hedgehogs are about 20cm long (much smaller than porcupines), omnivorous and uncommon.

Rock hyrax (*Procavia capensis*) Shoulder height 20–30cm; weight 4kg. Rodent-like in appearance, hyraxes (also known as dassies) share an ancient evolutionary lineage with elephants. This species and the similar **yellow-spotted rock hyrax** (*Heterohyrax brucei*) are often seen sunning themselves in rocky habitats, and become tame when used to people.

Hyraxes are social animals, living in large groups, and are largely herbivores, eating leaves, grasses and fruits; where you see large numbers, watch out for black eagles and other raptors, which prey extensively on them. In Botswana they're restricted to the southeast of the country, although places like the Tsodilo Hills would seem an ideal habitat for them.

Scrub hare (*Lepus saxatilis*) Shoulder height 45–60cm; weight 1–4.5kg. This is the largest and most common African hare or rabbit, occurring everywhere in Botswana. In some areas a short walk at dusk or after nightfall might reveal three or four scrub hares. They tend to freeze when disturbed.

Similar species Very similar, the **Cape hare** (*Lepus capensis*) has been recorded in Botswana, both in the southwest and in an area to the north of the great salt pans. However, distinguishing between these two similar species at night, when they are most likely to be seen, would be very difficult.

Ground squirrel (*Xerus inauris*) Shoulder height 20–30cm; weight 400–700g. This terrestrial rodent is common in the more arid parts of Botswana, including the Central Kalahari, and southeastern areas. It is grey to grey-brown with a prominent white eye ring and silver-black tail; within its range, it might be confused with the meerkat, which also spends much time on its hind legs. Unlike the meerkat, the ground squirrel has a characteristic squirrel mannerism of holding food in its forepaws.

The ground squirrel is a social animal; large groups share one communal burrow. It can often be spotted searching for vegetation, seeds, roots and small insects, while holding its tail aloft as a sunshade.

Bush squirrel (*Paraxerus cepapi*) Shoulder height 25–35cm; weight 100–250g. This common rodent is a uniform buff colour, with a long tail that is furry but not bushy. It is widely distributed all over southern and eastern Africa, and occurs throughout northern Botswana in most woodland habitats. Bush squirrels are so numerous in mopane woodlands that it can be difficult to avoid them, hence the species' other common names, the mopane or tree squirrel.

Bush squirrels live alone, in pairs or in small groups, usually nesting in a drey of dry leaves, in a hole in a tree. They are diurnal and venture to the ground to feed on seeds, fruit, nuts, vegetable matter and small insects; when alarmed they often bolt up the nearest tree, keeping on the side of the trunk away from the threat, out of sight as much as possible. If they can find a safe vantage point with a view of the threat, then they'll sometimes make a loud scolding alarm call.

Bush squirrel

OP/D

Rock hyrax

PC/D

Ground squirrel

Ro/D

Scrub hare

MAH/S

Nile crocodile

TO/S

Water monitor

RZ/D

Agama

GP/S

Skink

FK/S

Chameleon

SbG/S

Botswana's numerous ecosystems are home to more than 140 species of reptile – including the Nile crocodile.

NILE CROCODILE (*Crocodylus niloticus*) Length up to 5m; weight up to 1,000kg. Few visitors to Botswana will want to miss the opportunity to see this prehistoric apex predator. With its powerful serrated tail, horny plated skin and up to 100 peg-like teeth crammed into a long, sinister smile, the Nile crocodile is the stuff of nightmares and action movies. Contrary to the more lurid myths, crocodiles generally avoid people. Yet while they will not usually launch themselves into boats or come galloping after you on land, humans are still potential prey for a big crocodile, and tragedies do occasionally occur; when in crocodile country, it is sensible to keep your distance from the water's edge.

Crocodiles inhabit lakes, rivers and swamps. They can live up to 100, but reach sexual maturity at 12–15 years. Whereas youngsters are boldly marked in black and green, adults are generally a muddy grey-brown colour – usually lighter in rivers than in lagoons. Theirs is an amphibious life: basking on land, jaws agape to lose heat, or cruising the waters, raised eyes and nostrils allowing them to see and breathe undetected. As well as eating fish such as bream and barbel, adult crocs will ambush mammals up to the size of buffalo, grabbing them with an explosive sideways lunge from the water, before dragging them under to drown. Large numbers of crocodiles gather to scavenge big carcasses, churning up the water as they thrash and spin to dislodge chunks of flesh. They will even leave the water to steal a nearby lion kill.

LIZARDS The largest of the lizard species in Botswana are the monitor lizards, which can grow to over 2m in length, but there is also a large number of skinks, sand lizards, geckos, chameleons and agamas. With the arguable exception of the monitor lizards, which could in theory inflict a nasty bite if cornered, all are harmless to humans.

The **water monitor** (*Varanus niloticus*) is regularly observed by tourists, particularly on the banks of the Okavango's waterways, where you will often hear one splash into the water before seeing it. Size alone might make it possible to fleetingly mistake a monitor for a small crocodile, but the lizard's more colourful yellow-dappled skin and smaller head preclude sustained confusion. This species, and the less frequently seen **rock or white-throated monitor** (*Varanus albigularis*), are predatory omnivores, feeding on anything from birds' eggs to smaller reptiles and mammals, and occasionally carrion.

Also very common are various **agama** species, distinguished from other common lizards by their relatively large size of around 20–25cm, their large heads and their almost plastic-looking scaling. Depending on the species, this can be a combination of blue, purple, orange or red, with the flattened head generally a different colour from the torso. Another common family are the **skinks**: small, long-tailed lizards, most of which are quite dark and have a few thin black stripes running from head to tail. Botswana's only chameleon is the **flap-necked chameleon** (*Chamaeleo dilepis*), found throughout the Okavango Delta. During the day its excellent camouflage can make this lizard almost impossible to spot, as the light coming off the surrounding vegetation is picked up by cells in the chameleon's skin (chromatophores), which then replicate that colour. At night, however, chameleons are much more visible as they find it impossible to replicate the surrounding colours due to the lack of light.

SNAKES Of the 72 species of snake found in Botswana, roughly 80% are non venomous, and most are unlikely to be seen unless actively sought. The most frequently spotted non-venomous snake on safari is Africa's largest, the **rock python** (*Python sebae*), which has gold-on-black mottled skin and can grow to 5m or more. Pythons kill their prey – small antelopes, large rodents and similar animals – by strangulation, wrapping their muscular bodies around it until it cannot breathe, then swallowing it whole and dozing off for a couple of months while it is digested. Few are large or bold enough to tackle an adult human, but many could kill a small child. Much smaller but also frequently seen is the slender **stripe-bellied sand snake** (*Psammophis subtaeniatus)*, which grows up to 1m long and feeds on smaller reptiles, birds and rodents. It has large eyes and a yellow underside with stripes down either side, and is strictly diurnal.

One of the most commonly encountered venomous snakes is the **puff adder** (*Bitis arietans*), a large, thick-set resident that is rightly considered the most dangerous of African snakes – not because it is the most venomous or aggressive but because its notoriously sluggish disposition means it is more often disturbed than other snakes. Although it feeds mainly on rodents, it will strike when threatened, bending itself into a defensive S-shape.

Other venomous species, such as the **black mamba** (*Dendroaspis polylepis*), **boomslang** (*Dispholidus typus*) and **Mozambique spitting cobra** (*Naja mossambica*), are seldom seen and usually flee or go into cover way before you have a chance to observe them.

Stripe-bellied sand snake

W/D

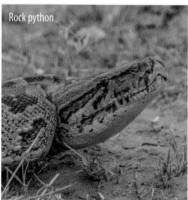
Rock python

LL/S

Puff adder

WF/A

Painted reed frog

Leopard tortoise

Marsh terrapin

TORTOISES AND TERRAPINS Tortoises and terrapins are unique in being protected by a prototypal suit of armour formed by their heavy exoskeleton.

The most common of the terrestrial tortoises is the **leopard tortoise** (*Stigmochelys pardalis*), which is named for its gold-and-black mottled shell, and can weigh up to 30kg. There's also the much smaller **Kalahari (serrated) tent tortoise** (*Psammobates oculifer*), found throughout Botswana, but much less common in the Delta.

Terrapins are essentially the freshwater equivalent of turtles. Somewhat flatter in shape than tortoises, they generally have a plainer brown shell. They might be seen sunning on rocks close to water or peering out from roadside puddles. Botswana's five species of terrapin are found largely around the Okavango swamps, along the Panhandle and in the Linyanti/Chobe region. These include the hinged terrapins and the **Okavango mud turtle** (*Pelusios bechuanicus*), which is one of the biggest of the species with quite a long, elongated, pronounced shell. The **marsh (or helmeted) terrapin** (*Pelomedusa subrufa*), however, is present throughout the country, even in the semi arid desert areas that include the Makgadikgadi and the Kalahari. During the drier months, it will dig deep underground to keep moist and cool, emerging as soon as the rains come.

FROGS The members of the frog family that are most frequently seen in Botswana are the **painted reed frogs**. Keep a close eye out when in a mokoro, and you'll spot these colourful little frogs folded up and stuck to the reeds with their sucker-pad toes. Up to about 40mm long, adults have extremely variable colours and patterns, from clear stripes through to dots, patches and vermiculations – and from bright green and yellow through to red and dark brown. Given the huge colour variability in these frogs, a precise identification will challenge many herpetologists, but the Angolan painted reed frog (*Hyperolius parallelus*) and the painted reed frog (*Hyperolius marmoratus*) are two key candidates. Listen at night beside water: the chorus of gentle individual notes, as if from tiny bells, is very distinctive: that's the frogs calling.

Large areas of Botswana are still covered by relatively undisturbed natural vegetation, and hunting is not a significant factor for most of Botswana's 597 recorded species of birds. Thus, with a range of natural habitats, Botswana is a superb birding destination.

There are fairly clear distinctions between the birds that you're likely to find in areas of swamp or open water, those that frequent riverine forest, and those found in the drier areas. None are endemic, though several have very restricted distributions. These include the slaty egret and the wattled crane, which are restricted to the Okavango, Linyanti and Chobe river systems, the brown firefinch, and the swamp nightjar. The Okavango Delta is a particularly good place for birdwatching as the habitats change from dry to flooded to deep water over very short distances.

MIGRANTS In addition to its resident bird species, Botswana receives many migrants. In September and October the Palaearctic migrants (ie: those that come from the northern hemisphere – normally Europe) appear, and they remain until around April or May. This is also the peak time to see the intra-African migrants, which come from further north in Africa. The rains from December to March see an explosion in the availability of most birds' food: seeds, fruits and insects. Hence this is the prime time for birds to nest, and the best season in which to observe them in their breeding plumage, even if it is also the most difficult time to visit the more remote areas of the country.

BIRDING HIGHLIGHTS Many of Botswana's birds are safari highlights in their own right, so even if you're intent on seeing the big five, be prepared to be entranced by some of the country's avifauna.

In wetland areas, look out for the delicate African jacana, also known as the Jesus bird for its apparent ability to walk on water. In the reeds above, the tiny malachite kingfisher is given away by its jewel-like colouring and bright orange beak, while the larger pied kingfisher is regularly seen hovering as it prepares to dive for its prey. Look higher, perhaps on a rock or a dead branch, to spot the sinuous African darter,

1. The striking **saddle-billed stork** (*Ephippiorhynchus senegalensis*) stands tall above the wetlands at a height of around 145cm, its wingspan stretching up to 2.7m. Females are smaller than males, and are distinguished by their yellow eyes. (W/D)
2. Also known as the lily-trotter or the Jesus bird, the **African jacana** (*Actophilornis africanus*) is unmistakable with its rich chestnut torso and wings. Exceptionally widely spread toes allow it to walk on lily pads and other light floating vegetation. (RZ/D)
3. Found in the shallow waters of the Okavango Delta, Linyanti and Chobe River areas, the **black heron** (*Egretta ardesiaca*) uses a distinctive 'canopy feeding' technique, creating umbrella-like shade with its wings to fish. it's fascinating to watch, and relatively easy to identify. (SP/D)
4. An endangered species, the massive **martial eagle** (*Polemaetus bellicosus*), with its pale spotted underparts, long feathered legs and piercing yellow eyes, is a ferocious predator. Hunting from a leafy perch or more often in flight, their keen eyesight allows them to locate prey from several kilometres away. The one photographed here had just polished off a passing guinea fowl in Selinda. (JM)
5. Conspicuous along the shores of most rivers and lakes, the **African fish eagle** (*Haliaeetus vocifer*) is a magnificent raptor with a chestnut belly and a yellow base to its large hooked bill. Its far-carrying banshee wail of a call – often heard as a duet – is one of the most evocative sounds of the African bush. (S/D)
6. Africa's heaviest flying bird, the **kori bustard** (*Ardeotis kori*) is a widespread resident of grassland habitats, and is especially common in areas like the dry Savuti Marsh. (OP/D)

then higher still for the distinct dark brown and white of the African fish eagle, which often perches on the tops of trees overlooking the river. Back in the treeline, a uniform tawny plumage may give away Pels' fishing owl, one of the Delta's most sought-after species that is notoriously difficult to spot.

Of the larger wetland inhabitants, top of the list is the extraordinary saddle-billed stork, a monogamous bird that is often seen in pairs. Around the edge of small pools and pans, spoonbills may jostle for position with storks – yellow-billed, marabou, open-billed and more – along with herons, egrets, pelicans, lapwings and ibis. But for a real spectacle, pay a visit to one of Botswana's heronries at Gcodikwe and Kanana, where thousands of birds congregate to breed towards the end of the dry season. This is also the time of year when a flash of crimson and turquoise signals the return of the carmine bee-eaters to nest in sandy riverbanks – though you may also see them on the wing after a fire, swooping on insects drawn out by the flames.

In drier areas, the lilac-breasted roller is no less dazzling for being relatively common. Equally spectacular, if far less common, is the African paradise whydah, which is in full breeding plumage between February and April. You'll find most of the hornbills here, too, along with Meyer's parrots and swallow-tailed bee-eaters.

The open plains are home to some of the larger birds, from ostriches to the kori bustard – Africa's largest flying bird, and claimed by Botswana as the national bird. High above, birds of prey range from the almost ubiquitous yellow-billed kite to the strongly marked bateleur, or short-tailed eagle, its chiselled head sometimes clear in silhouette against the sky. And then there are the vultures – many of them now endangered – who play a critical role in nutrient recycling and disease prevention within the ecosystem.

For more detail on the birdlife of Botswana's individual habitats, see their respective chapters.

1. Of the nine species of kingfisher that occur in Botswana, the gem-like **malachite kingfisher** (*Alcedo cristata*) most strongly resembles its European namesake. It is often observed perched motionless on reeds or shrubs alongside rivers and lakes, but is given away by its bright coloration. (CS/D)

2. A firm safari favourite, the insectivorous **lilac-breasted roller** (*Coracias caudatus*) prefers a woodland habitat, and will often perch conspicuously on a single branch, almost as if posing for photographs. (ChaM)

3. With stunning colouring, the **carmine bee-eater** (*Merops nubicoides*) is a welcome arrival in the summer months. The largest of the bee-eater family in southern Africa, it often congregates in colonies near rivers and marshes, where it nests in holes in steep sandy banks. (OP/D)

4. Nicknamed 'the flying banana', the **Southern yellow-billed hornbill** (*Tockus leucomelas*) is indeed aptly named and a common resident across Botswana. Foraging on the ground for insects, they are usually spotted in pairs or small groups moving from tree to tree across dry savannah and woodland areas. They have a distinctive, wavy flight path accompanied by a crescendo call, making them easy to identify. (L/D)

5. Gorgeous, emerald-green in colour and notable for its small size (17cm), the **little bee-eater** (*Merops pusillus*) is resident in Botswana all year. These delightful birds are commonly sighted in pairs or groups, perching on low branches, from where they hawk for flying insects before returning to the same spot. (OP/D)

6. With incredible bark-like plumage, the small **African scops owl** (*Otus senegalensis*) is beautifully camouflaged in its favoured perch close to the tree's trunk. Found in woodland, alone or in pairs, it's notable for its tufted ears, propensity to half-close its eyes and repetitive, frog-like call. (JM)

3

History, Politics and Economy

We can learn a lot about Botswana today by looking back into its history. Its far distant past, explaining some of the main features of its landscapes, is covered as part of *Physical environment*, from page 3. A potted overview of Botswana's more recent human history is given here, casting some light on its current politics and economics.

HISTORY

EARLY PEOPLES Read about the country's geological history and it's framed in terms of hundreds or at least tens of millions of years. Thus it's sobering to realise how relatively recent any human history is, and how much more compressed its timescales are.

Our knowledge about early human life in Botswana is derived from archaeology and from oral histories, which go back about 700 years. Written records date only from the arrival of Europeans in the 18th and 19th centuries. Most of these are personal accounts, which are interesting, but subjective. In many places the story is confused and incomplete, or even deliberately misleading.

However, archaeological evidence suggests that hunter-gatherer peoples have lived for about 60,000 years at sites like the Tsodilo Hills in the Kalahari. We know, too, that the ancestors of the Khoisan (comprising both the San and the Khoi people; page 72) were once widely dispersed throughout the continent, and probably had exclusive occupation of southern, central and eastern Africa from about 60,000 years ago up to the last 3,000 years.

Skeletons of a Khoisan-type people, dating back 15,000 years and more, are found throughout southern and eastern Africa. It is believed to be these people who made the rock paintings of people and animals that are found all over eastern and southern Africa and even in the Sahara Desert. The earliest paintings have been found in Namibia (the 'Apollo 11' cave) and are thought to date back 26,000 years.

Rock paintings found at the Tsodilo Hills are evidence that the living was good enough to allow the people to develop a vibrant artistic culture. Most experts believe that many of the paintings have deeper significance, probably connected with spiritual, religious or mythological beliefs. It is impossible to interpret them accurately without an in-depth knowledge of the culture and beliefs of those who created them. Unfortunately no group today claims historical responsibility. The local Zhu Bushmen claim that their god, Gaoxa, made the paintings.

The animals of Africa, such as antelope, eland, rhinos and giraffe, are the subject of many paintings. The images beautifully capture the form and the spirit of each animal. Humans also appear; one painting at the Tsodilo Hills shows a group of 15 men exhibiting the permanent erection, or semi-erection, which is a distinctive feature of San men from birth to death. Later paintings, featuring black men and sometimes war, are thought to depict the arrival of the Bantu farmers.

The San The San were perfectly adapted to their desert environment and had learned to survive its harsh extremes of climate – drought, unrelenting heat and sun in the winter, and heavy rains and floods in the summer.

Predominantly hunter-gatherers, it is thought that at various times, when the climate was more favourable, the San may also have owned and grazed stock. Several times in past millennia the climate of Botswana has been much wetter, and at others much drier than it is at the moment. Periodically the huge pans that are a distinctive feature of the landscape, such as at Makgadikgadi and Nxai, became great lakes, full of water and supplied by several rivers. Probably some San groups took advantage of plentiful supplies of water to acquire stock. Now the rivers have dried up and the Okavango Delta has receded, the pans are full of water only during the rainy season and the San are herders no longer. There are also more recent records of them owning and trading copper from secret mines in the Kalahari, and bartering it for iron.

The Khoi Around 3000BC, Late Stone Age hunter-gatherer groups in Ethiopia, and elsewhere in North and West Africa, started to keep domestic animals, sow seeds, and harvest the produce: they became the world's first farmers.

By around 1000BC these new pastoral practices had spread south into the equatorial forests of what is now the Democratic Republic of Congo, to around Lake Victoria, and into the northern area of the Great Rift Valley, in northern Tanzania. However, agriculture did not spread south into the rest of central/southern Africa immediately. Only when the technology, and the tools, of ironworking became known did these practices start their relentless expansion southwards.

It's thought that during the last centuries BC many Khoi-speaking peoples in northern Botswana converted their lifestyle to pastoralism – herding cattle and sheep on the rich pastures exposed by the retreating wetlands of the Okavango Delta and Lake Makgadikgadi.

It used to be thought that the Khoi acquired their stock during the (black) Iron Age, from Bantu-speaking farmers who are thought to have migrated into their area around 1,500 years ago. However, finds of sheep bone dating back 3,000 years now suggest that the Khoi had obtained stock long before the arrival of the Bantu, probably from East Africa where they had been herded for thousands of years. The Khoi spread, migrating with their livestock through central Namibia, as far south as the Cape of Good Hope, by about 70BC.

When the first Dutch settlers saw the Khoi in about AD1600 they lived in groups with a leader, but were split into smaller clans under their own headman. The clans came together only in times of stress or war. Because water was vital for the stock animals, the Khoi dug wells that were owned exclusively by the clan and group. In times of drought, when water was scarce, fights might erupt over these waterholes. Then each clan sent men to fight to protect the group's interests.

Each clan lived in a village, which was built inside a circular thorn hedge. In the centre were thorn enclosures to pen and protect the stock, surrounded by a circle of houses. Khoi houses are of a 'bender' or dome-tent construction type; that is, long flexible poles are bent to form arches and the ends stuck into the ground. They are then covered with mats. When the clan needed to move to find more water or grazing these huts were simply taken down and strapped on to the back of their animals.

Tlou and Campbell (page 544) describe one such village, which is known to have existed at Toromoja on the Boteti River (about 18km east of Rakops) around AD1200. A group of Khoi known as the Bateti lived there and kept long-horned cattle, sheep and goats, but they lived mainly on fish, zebra and other animals which they caught in the pits they dug by the river. They also ate plants, particularly waterlily roots. They had San servants who hunted and collected wild food for them. Sometimes they traded skins and ivory for iron tools, copper and tobacco, with the people living at Maun in the northwest, or the Toutswe people to the southeast.

Archaeologically speaking the Khoisan peoples were examples of Late Stone Age cultures; that is, their tools and weapons were made of wood, bone and stone. The Late Stone Age refers not to a period of time, but to a method and style of tool construction. Human beings had made stone tools for millennia and the name Late Stone Age refers to stylistic refinements and to the manufacture of tools developed for specific uses.

Specifically, experts define the transition from Early to Middle Stone Age technology as indicated by a larger range of stone tools often adapted for particular uses, and signs that these people had a greater mastery of their environment. This was probably in progress around 125,000 years ago in Botswana. They normally characterise the Late Stone Age by the use of composite tools, those made of wood and/or bone and/or stone used together, and by the presence of a revolutionary invention: the bow and arrow. This first appeared in southern Africa, and throughout the world, about 15,000 years ago. Skeletons of some of these Late Stone Age hunters had a close physical resemblance to the modern Khoisan people.

The Bantu-speaking farmers

The next people to arrive in Botswana were the Bantu-speakers. This collective term refers to a number of different tribes, from a related linguistic group, who over the course of thousands of years gradually migrated down into southern Africa from north of the Equator. The date of their arrival in Botswana is hard to pinpoint.

The Bantu were grain farmers (agriculturalists) as opposed to pastoralists or hunter-gatherers and they brought Iron Age technology with them; that is, their tools and weapons were made of iron. Physically these Iron Age farmers were much taller and heavier than the Khoisan, and they became the ancestors of the modern black Africans in southern Africa.

Crucial to the production of iron is a smelting furnace capable of reaching very high temperatures. Associated with the Iron Age is a new kind of pottery, which also had to be fired at high temperatures. Archaeologists use the finds of pottery and iron to date the arrival of the new people on the landscape of Botswana.

It is thought that the Bantu-speakers arrived in two main waves, bringing western and eastern Bantu languages. From West Africa, Late Stone Age farmers on the upper Zambezi were converted to the use of iron tools by about 300BC. From East Africa, Early Iron Age farming spread south along the east coast as far as the Zambezi by around 20BC.

By 200BC, in the Okavango–Makgadikgadi region, people were making a kind of pottery which archaeologists think was Khoi pottery influenced by western Iron Age (Bantu) styles, suggesting an initial contact between the two groups. The major Bantu influx probably occurred around the first few centuries AD, and the ancestors of the Khoisan people, with their simple Stone Age technology and hunter-gatherer existence, just could not compete. Since then the Khoisan have gradually been either assimilated into the migrant groups, or effectively pushed into the areas which could not be farmed. Thus the older Stone Age cultures persisted for much longer in the Kalahari (which is more difficult to cultivate) than in the rest of the country.

In theory, the stronger iron weapons of the Bantu should easily have made them the dominant culture. However, it took a very long time for Bantu language and culture to replace that of the Khoi; as late as the 19th century people were still speaking Khoi on the Boteti River. This supports a theory of communities living peacefully there, side by side, for a thousand years or more. In fact, there is some evidence of inter-marriage or inter-breeding between the two groups. The Batswana today have a mixture of Bantu and Khoisan features and they are noticeably lighter in skin colour than Bantu-speakers further north. They also tend to have the almond-shaped eyes, high cheekbones and thin lips of the Khoisan.

MORE IMMIGRANTS There are numerous problems with compiling a record of Bantu history in Botswana. We are dependent on oral history and archaeological records, and the two sometimes conflict with each other. The situation is very complex because of the number and mobility of the tribes involved.

The earliest dated Iron Age site in Botswana is an iron-smelting furnace in the Tswapong Hills, which is dated to around AD190. There is evidence of an early farming settlement of beehive huts made of grass matting, dating to around AD420 by the Molepolole River and a similar one has been found coexisting with Khoisan sites in the Tsodilo Hills, dating to around AD550.

By the 4th or 5th century AD, Iron Age farmers had certainly settled throughout much of southern Africa. As well as iron-working technology, they brought with them pottery, the remains of which are used by archaeologists to work out the migrations of various different groups of these Bantu settlers. These migrations continued, and the distribution of pottery styles suggests that the groups moved around within the subcontinent: this was much more complex than a simple north–south influx. Many of the tribes roamed over the whole of southern Africa, before various colonial authorities imposed artificial country borders in order to carve out territories for themselves.

This situation was complicated more recently by the prolonged and horrifically bloody tribal wars of the 19th century, known to historians as the Difaqane Wars.

BATSWANA HISTORY The Batswana rose to domination from among a number of powerful dynasties that spread out from the western Transvaal around AD1200–1400. During the period 1500–1600 the Phofu dynasty in western Transvaal disintegrated, with junior brothers forming breakaway, independent chiefdoms. Oral history traditions explain this as a response to drought. The archaeological record shows populations expanding into open country in small villages with cattle corrals, but by around 1700 the settlements were often larger towns built of stone and situated on hills, reflecting the growth of hostile states, and the need for a strong defence.

The Difaqane Wars The whole of southern Africa was subject to increasing disruption, migration and war from about 1750 onwards, as trading and raiding for ivory, cattle and slaves spread inland from the coasts of Mozambique, the Cape Colony and Angola. The tribes often captured opponents during battle and sold them to slave raiders. Some of the battles themselves may have been slave raids against an enemy tribe.

Paramount among the aggressors in these wars was an ambitious Zulu leader named Shaka, who controlled a large slice of Natal by around 1810. The Ngoni people, which includes the Zulu nation, refer to the wars which Shaka initiated as the Mfecane, or 'the crushing'. However, the Batswana people, who were among the victims of Shaka's wars of expansion, refer to them as the Difaqane, which means 'the scattering'. Because they scattered, so they dispersed others.

A good explanation of this period is covered in John Reader's excellent *Africa: A Biography of the Continent* (page 544). He summarises the root causes:

Thus they [the Zulus] were trapped in 'the trans-continental cross-fire of interrelated European plunder systems'. It was the unrelenting advance of settlers from the west, and the predacious demands of slavers in the east – exacerbated by intermittent drought – that set southern Africa in turmoil during the early eighteenth century. Not Shaka, not the Zulus, not the Mfecane.

Eventually, after the wars passed in the 1840s, the Batswana states of Ngwaketse, Kwena and the Ngwato rose to prosperity. They organised their people into wards with their own chiefs, but all paying tribute to the king. The states were in competition over trade benefits for ivory and ostrich feathers, down new roads, south to the Cape Colony. These roads also brought Boer trekkers and Christian missionaries to Botswana.

One of the Batswana kings, Sechele of the Kwena (1829–92), was baptised by David Livingstone (page 77), who passed through Botswana on his missionary travels. However, it was the Ngwato, who superseded the Kwena in trading supremacy, who produced the most remarkable and famous dynasty – and upon whom the following pages will concentrate.

Ngwato dynasty In *Serowe: Village of the Rain Wind* (page 544), Bessie Head describes this remarkable dynasty, beginning with the reign of Khama the Great. He was king when the capital of the Bamangwato (Ngwato) moved to Serowe in 1902. Previously the capital had been 115km away at Shoshong, and then at Palapye, but each time the tribe was forced to move on when water sources dried up. In 1902, two rivers, the Sepane and the Manonnye, flowed through Serowe, although both have subsequently dried up.

Khama the Great Khama was the eldest son of Sekgoma I, who was the chief when David Livingstone (page 77), the missionary explorer, first moved northwards through Botswana in the 1840s. While the capital had still been at Shoshong, Livingstone had converted Khama and his brothers to Christianity. Although their father had allowed the missionaries to stay with them, and was interested to talk to them, he had refused to give up the traditional ways.

Eventually this led to a war between father and son, which Khama won, becoming king of the Bamangwato. Khama was a poetic visionary who changed the customs of his people in line with his Christian beliefs, and who foresaw the need for strong protection in the colonial carve-up of Africa, and campaigned strongly for the British Protectorate of Bechuanaland (page 78).

Sekgoma II In 1916, Khama was kicked on the knee by a horse. At this time he invited his son Sekgoma II, who had been in exile for ten years governing his own branch of the Bamangwato, to come home and rule at Serowe. This he did, and subsequently ruled at Serowe for nine years, although for most of that time he remained in the shadow of King Khama. Most importantly Khama insisted that Sekgoma marry a woman given to him by the Bamangwato, and the heir from this marriage was Seretse, who would later become the first president of Botswana.

Tshekedi Khama Following the death of Khama, and shortly afterwards of Sekgoma II, Tshekedi Khama (Khama's son from a late second marriage) stepped in as regent until the four-year-old Seretse should come of age.

Where Khama was a visionary and politician, Tshekedi was full of pragmatic common sense and his rule, from 1926 to 1959, is marked by educational advances and self-help projects. When he first became leader there was only a primary school in Serowe. Then Tshekedi used his own money to send the young people of the village to South Africa for further education. From there they came home to teach in the village school. Later a secondary school and subsequently a college were built, using the voluntary labour of what were known as the age regiments (page 107). Also known as the *mephato*, these were groups of young men of about the same age, usually formed from those who had graduated from the tribal initiation ceremony (known as *bogwera*) at the same time. They could be called upon to carry out services for the good of the community, ranging from routine community tasks to helping out with emergencies.

Moeng College of Higher Education is exciting for the principles on which it was founded, which gave equal weight to traditional knowledge and craft skills alongside academic instruction. As an experiment in social relations the houses built for the teaching staff were the equivalent of houses for white government officials. It was the only college in southern Africa at the time where houses for white and black teachers were equal and where they lived together in the same hostel.

Seretse Khama During the reign of Tshekedi, a problem arose over the future of Seretse Khama. Seretse was educated abroad, in London, Fort Hare University in South Africa, and Oxford. In 1948, Seretse wrote to inform his uncle that he wanted to marry an Englishwoman, Ruth Williams. Tshekedi opposed the marriage on the grounds that a king or chief could not do as he pleased because he was the servant of the people, and an heir to the chieftaincy was at stake. Traditionally the chief's wife was chosen by the *morafe* or tribal group. Seretse insisted on his right to choose his own wife and married the Englishwoman.

They were still arguing when the British took matters into their own hands. In a case that created an international scandal, the British government barred Seretse from the chieftaincy of the Bamangwato, and exiled him for six years. They invited him to Britain, where they forced him to stay. They also banned Tshekedi Khama from entering the Bamangwato reserve.

Secret documents have since confirmed that this British intervention was in order to satisfy the South African government, which objected to Seretse Khama's marriage to a white woman at a time when the policy of racial segregation, apartheid, was being enforced in South Africa.

Seretse, Tshekedi and their people fought against this banishment. The Bamangwato refused to pay taxes, sent delegations to the British and led protests. They refused to accept a British-nominated chief, and many people, including women, were flogged for this refusal.

Finally Tshekedi visited Seretse in London and the two resolved their differences. Seretse returned to Botswana with Ruth. Although a condition of his return was that he remained barred from the chieftaincy, both he and Tshekedi continued to play an active role in the politics of Botswana, and were instrumental in the lead-up to independence.

Traders The earliest Europeans to come to Botswana were adventurers, explorers, hunters and missionaries. Travel in Botswana was very expensive, even then. A year's travel could cost up to US$600 – equivalent to what a soldier of the period might earn during 30 years in the army. So early travellers came to trade for ivory, which made them huge profits with which to finance their expeditions. They travelled in wooden wagons, drawn by oxen or horses, and brought guns, beads, clothing and other, less-valuable items, which they bartered for significant amounts of ivory.

One of the biggest problems on the journey was the lack of water. There were often stretches of 50km or more without any. Water would be carried on the wagons, but not enough for both men and beasts. Sometimes the oxen died of thirst. There are stories of the wagons being unhitched and the oxen led to the nearest water – which could be some kilometres distant – and then returning to pull the wagons further. Oxen often died from drinking bad water or from tsetse-fly bite, while horses died of tick bite. A distance of 20km per day was thought to be a good rate of travel.

However, a wagon that did make it could return with about 200 elephant tusks – worth around £1,200 when sold in Cape Town. As they heard tales of huge profits, more traders began to venture into the region and gradually introduced money, which had been unknown until then. Previously barter and exchange systems functioned in the village – one goat equals one woven grass basket, and so on. Subsequently money became important in trade and people were forced to either sell something, or sell their labour, to get money. Little paid work could be found in Botswana, so large numbers of people were forced to emigrate to find work, often in the mines in South Africa.

Meanwhile the traders began to settle in Botswana at Shoshong, though the Bamangwato chiefs, Sekgoma and Khama, were keen to prevent them from going further into the interior, so that they could maintain their trading supremacy.

Missionaries Following the traders came the missionaries, and missionary societies, who were already active in South Africa. Robert Moffat of the London Missionary Society (LMS) established a station at Kudumane, which brought Christianity to the Batswana and trained African evangelists to spread the word. It was to Kudumane that David Livingstone came in 1841. In 1845, he married Moffat's daughter, Mary, and they settled among the Bakwena.

DAVID LIVINGSTONE

David Livingstone's *Missionary Travels and Researches in South Africa* excited great interest in England. This account of his journeys across southern Africa in the 1840s and 50s had all the appeal that undersea or space exploration has for us now. Further, it captured the imagination of the British public, allowing them to take pride in their country's exploration of Africa, based on the exploits of an explorer who seemed to be the epitome of bravery and righteous religious zeal.

Livingstone had set out with the conviction that if Africans could see their material and physical well-being improved – probably by learning European ways, and earning a living from export crops – then they would be ripe for conversion to Christianity. He was strongly opposed to slavery, but sure that this would disappear when Africans became more self-sufficient through trade.

In fact Livingstone was almost totally unsuccessful in his own aims, failing to set up any successful trading missions, or even to convert many Africans permanently to Christianity. However, his travels opened up areas north of the Limpopo for later British missionaries, and by 1887 British mission stations were established in Zambia and southern Malawi.

Although ostensibly a missionary, Livingstone was primarily interested in exploration and in 1849 he and his party became the first whites to see Lake Ngami. He died in 1873 in Zambia, while looking for the source of the Nile.

Khama and his Bamangwato family at Shoshong were converted by the missionaries of a German Lutheran society, although he later joined the London Missionary Society Church. Most missionaries tried to change local Setswana customs, which they considered heathen and inferior to European Christian customs. Most of all they fought against the medicine men, who defended the old traditions. However, despite leaders like Khama who abolished male and female initiations, rain-making and beer drinking, some customs still flourish because people like them.

The early missionaries affected disinterest in politics, although they inevitably supported Christians against non-Christians. Their position was always precarious because they needed to retain the good will of the chiefs to remain in their mission posts. However, during the Protectorate, missionaries who knew they had the backing of the British government became quite cavalier, demanding the removal of chiefs who resisted Christianity.

Although the missionaries tried to destroy local cultures, they also provided education and established the first schools. They introduced useful tools such as the plough and the wagon, and taught gardening and crop irrigation. The missionaries' wives taught sewing and baking and helped to nurse the sick and deliver babies.

Botswana and the British British foreign policy in southern Africa had always revolved around the Cape Colony, which was seen as vital to British interests in India and the Indian Ocean. Africa to the north of the Cape Colony had largely been ignored. The Boers were on the whole left to their farming in the Transvaal area, since they posed no threat to the Cape Colony.

However, from the 1850s to the 1870s the Batswana leaders appealed to the British for protection against the Boers, who had formed their own free state ruling the Transvaal, but were continually threatening to take over Batswana lands in Botswana.

When Germany annexed South West Africa (now Namibia) in 1884, the British finally began to take those threats seriously. They became afraid that the Boers might link up with the Germans and prevent British access to the 'north road', leading to the interior of Africa – now Zambia and Zimbabwe. It was really to safeguard this road that the British finally granted Botswana protection in 1885. Significantly, the German government was told about the British Protectorate of Bechuanaland before the chiefs in Botswana.

Cecil John Rhodes Initially the British government had fully intended to hand the supervision of the Protectorate over to the government of the Cape Colony, but the Cape was unwilling to take on the responsibility and the potential expense.

In 1886, the Boers discovered large gold deposits in the Witwatersrand (around Johannesburg). The influx of money from this boosted the Boer farmers, who expanded their interests to the north, making a treaty with Khama's enemy to the east, the powerful Lobengula. This in turn prompted the British to look beyond the Limpopo, and to back the territorial aspirations of a millionaire British businessman and prominent Cape Colony politician, Cecil Rhodes. By 1888 Rhodes, a partner in the De Beers consortium, had control of the lucrative diamond-mining industry in Kimberley, South Africa. He was hungry for power, and dreamed of linking the Cape to Cairo with land under British control.

Rhodes was fuelled by the belief that other areas of Africa had great mineral wealth and he wanted to colonise them and reap that wealth. In order to do so he formed the British South Africa Company (BSAC) in 1889. At that time, if companies or individuals could obtain concessions to African land from the owners, they were able to colonise it for the Crown. The British government expected that these concessions would be obtained honestly. However, they were often gained fraudulently, by persuading illiterate African chiefs to sign (or put their mark on) documents which were presented to them as treaties, but which actually appropriated their lands.

The immediate reason for forming the BSAC was in order to colonise the land of the AmaNdebele and the Mashona (now Zimbabwe). In 1888, Rhodes's men had obtained, by trickery, a treaty known as the Rudd Concession from the King of the AmaNdebele, Lobengula. This granted Rhodes all mineral rights on the king's land. Although the king rejected the treaty when he discovered its real intention, Rhodes was nevertheless granted a royal charter by the British government.

The British also promised to transfer the Bechuanaland Protectorate to the BSAC, on condition that Rhodes first obtained the agreement of the Batswana rulers. Rhodes wanted the Protectorate, because he needed the right to build a railway across Bechuanaland. He further wanted to annex the Protectorate to Rhodesia (now Zimbabwe), and from there attack the Boer state of Transvaal from the north.

Rhodes and other British businessmen had stakes in the highly profitable gold mines at Witwatersrand (Johannesburg), but the state was controlled politically by the Boers. Rhodes wanted British rule in the Transvaal, to protect his profits from the gold mines.

The three chiefs In 1895, three Batswana chiefs, Khama, Bathoen and Sebele, travelled to London to plead a case against the British government handing over the Protectorate to Rhodes, whom they did not trust. Some Batswana chiefs had already signed concessions with the BSAC, but in nearly all cases they did not realise that they had given away their land. It was, in any case, against Setswana law to sell or give away land. Rhodes attempted to stop the kings in Cape Town and prevent them from going to Britain but he was unsuccessful.

In a meeting with Joseph Chamberlain, then the British Colonial Secretary, the three chiefs criticised the BSAC and asked that:

- Bechuanaland should remain a Protectorate directly under the Queen.
- Their independence should be preserved.
- Their lands should not be sold.
- Liquor drinking should be prohibited in their areas.

Chamberlain told them that the British government could not go back on its promise to transfer the Protectorate to the BSAC. However, he also said that the company would obey the Queen, so it was the same as being governed by her. Hence, the chiefs must reach an agreement with the BSAC. Then he went on holiday.

Instead the chiefs toured England, seeking the support of the British people against the company. Their campaign was organised by the London Missionary Society, and supported by temperance groups, anti-slavery and humanitarian groups and businesses that feared the effect of a costly war if the transfer went ahead. Chamberlain returned from holiday to find letters to this effect. Worried that the affair might become an election issue and lose the government votes, he agreed to the chiefs' demands, with the provisos that they must all cede the land which Rhodes required for the railway, and that taxation would be introduced to pay for the administration of the Protectorate.

The Jameson Raid A month later, in October 1895, Rhodes found a pretext for attacking the Transvaal. The raid was led by Dr S Jameson on behalf of the non-Boer whites or 'Uitlanders' in the Transvaal, who had complained of unequal treatment by the Boers. This famous raid, which came to be known as the Jameson Raid, was carried out from within the Bechuanaland Protectorate. However, it failed. The anticipated uprising of the Uitlanders never happened, so the raiders soon surrendered to the Boers.

The fact that Britain had allowed the Protectorate to be used to attack another country caused an international scandal. The British government, angered at being brought into disrepute by Rhodes, refused to transfer the Protectorate to the BSAC, and removed control of the Batswana lands that had been obtained for the raid.

It was the failure of the Jameson Raid, and Rhodes's subsequent – if temporary – disgrace, which protected the independent future of Botswana. Rhodes did later receive land for a railway strip and some blocks of 'Crown Land' – the Gaborone, Lobatse and Tuli blocks. These, together with the Tati Block and Ghanzi, which had been settled earlier, became the only European areas in Bechuanaland.

The Protectorate Britain continued to administer the Protectorate for 70 years, through the Anglo-Boer War (1899–1902) and two world wars. However, Britain disliked spending money on its colonies, and from the time the Union of South Africa was formed in 1910 it was always intended to transfer the Protectorate to the Union. The Batswana continued to fight against it, especially as they witnessed the poor treatment of black Africans in that country.

By 1955, the policy of the British government had changed. This was due in part to the problems with Seretse and Tshekedi Khama and the Bamangwato, and partly because of South Africa's gradual move towards apartheid and away from the more egalitarian values of the post-war society that was emerging in the UK and the rest of the West.

In 1956, Seretse, who was supported by many groups in Britain, including members of parliament, spoke strongly against the British government's intervention. Tshekedi also turned against the British, accepting Ruth as the rightful wife and demanding Seretse's return to Bechuanaland. He believed that the British wanted to use the problem to break his tribe, and as an excuse to transfer the Protectorate to South Africa.

However, by then the issue of transferring the Protectorate to South Africa's control was dead in the minds of the British government. Clearly Botswana would have to be diplomatically protected from South Africa's ambitions, but the British didn't seem to have a plan for it beyond that.

MODERN HISTORY
The dangerous decade The years between 1956 and 1966 were a dangerous, formative decade in Botswana's history. For a detailed, insider's view of it read *Botswana: The Road to Independence*, by Peter Fawcus and Alan Tilbury. The authors were two of Britain's most senior administrators who were at the sharp end of steering relations between Britain and the Protectorate during this period.

While the British government couldn't see into the future, supporters of Seretse Khama had organised political movements as early as 1952. Eventually a legislative council was set up in 1961, based on an interim constitution and limited national elections. Then Seretse Khama joined the legislative council, and the Protectorate's new executive council.

Meanwhile local politics was developing rapidly. The Bechuanaland People's Party (BPP) was founded in 1960, and later split into two factions, which were eventually to become the Botswana Independence Party (BIP) and the Botswana People's Party (BPP).

Both factions espoused a fairly radical agenda calling for immediate independence, the abolition of the chiefs, nationalisation of some lands and the removal of most whites from the civil service. With the material support of other nationalist movements in Ghana and Tanzania, 1960–61 saw support for the BPP grow rapidly in the townships of eastern Botswana.

From his position on the inside of government, Seretse Khama could see the danger that these parties posed to the constitution that was developing, and to the smooth running of the civil service after independence. Hence early in 1962, under a marula tree in Gaborone, he and five others (Ketumile Masire, A M Tsoebebe, Moutlakgola Nwako, Tsheko Tsheko and Goareng Mosinyi) formed the Botswana Democratic Party (BDP) to campaign for a more ordered transition to independence. All were experienced, educated men and between them had strong links throughout the country, in both the educated elites and the poorer rural communities.

In particular, Seretse Khama and Ketumile Masire, as president and general secretary of the party, formed a strong partnership, without any signs of the feuds and splits that had beset the opposition. One was from the north, the other from the south; one a chief, the other a commoner. Gradually their conservative message began to win over the electorate. This was helped by the fear that any radical new government could provoke problems with South Africa – which still apparently had an appetite for control of Bechuanaland.

Independence Fawcus and Tilbury observe that between 1956 and 1966, 'constitutional and political development far outstripped economic and social advance. The thought that independence might be at the end of the road only emerged in the early 1960s and was discounted by Lord Hailey as late as 1963.'

Fortunately since about 1956 there had been a slow build-up in Britain's financial grants to the Protectorate. By 1963, a £10 million plan was in place for development that covered the transition period around independence. This included the immediate start to constructing a new administrative capital, at Gaborone – as previously Bechuanaland had been administered from Mafikeng, over the border in South Africa.

During this time, Sir Ketumile Masire, Bechuanaland's first deputy prime minister and second president, commented that there was a high 'degree of consultation and co-operation between the local representatives of the British government and the people of Botswana' and that there was 'immense good will on both sides'. Perhaps this, more than anything else, explains how the transition was completed so peacefully.

On 1 March 1965, a remarkably peaceful election was held, with voters placing coloured symbols in envelopes to allow the largely illiterate electorate all to vote. This worked without problems. The BDP won 28 out of the 31 seats, and on 3 March 1965 Seretse Khama became the country's first prime minister. Within this new administration, a number of senior British public servants were kept on – including the minister of finance and the attorney general, and a senior civil servant in each of the ministries.

This clear victory for the BDP, and stable administration, gave the new government the platform from which to amend the constitution. The new Setswana name of the Republic of Botswana was chosen for the country, and on 30 September 1966, Sir Seretse Khama became the first president.

Politics since independence

1966–80: President Sir Seretse Khama Seretse Khama inherited a poor country. In 1965, the population stood at about 550,000 with a low level of literacy, and the country was gripped by a bad drought. Fortunately Britain was sympathetic to continuing to cover substantial costs of the new nation's administration, although with the discovery of diamonds at Orapa in 1967 by geologists from De Beers, and the subsequent mining operations which began in 1971, this assistance was only needed for six years after independence.

Botswana had long been in the Southern African Customs Union – and in 1969 it succeeded in renegotiating the terms of this, to become more financially independent. (Previously it had received a fixed percentage of total customs union income, rather than the income that was due directly from its own territory.)

During the 1970s Botswana's economy grew steadily, typically by around 12–13% per year, as Botswana extended its basic infrastructure for both mining development and basic social services for its population. Despite threats from, among others, the Marxist-leaning Botswana National Front (BNF), Sir Seretse Khama steered the country on a fairly moderate line – and the BDP was consistently re-elected in generally fair elections.

With civil war in Rhodesia throughout the 1970s, and apartheid regimes in South Africa and South West Africa (Namibia), Botswana's position was tricky. It accepted refugees from neighbouring countries, but refused to be used as a base for resistance organisations. Such neutrality was often severely tried, not least when, in February 1978, the Rhodesian army crossed the border and massacred 15 Botswana soldiers at Lesoma (page 242).

Zimbabwe gained independence in 1980, and the same year saw the foundation of the Southern African Development Coordination Conference (SADCC), with the aim of co-ordinating the region's disparate economies in the face of the huge economic muscle wielded by South Africa's apartheid regime.

Sir Seretse Khama died in July 1980 and, as envisaged by the constitution, was succeeded by his deputy, Sir Ketumile Masire. He left behind him an impressive legacy of a stable, prosperous country amid a changing subcontinent. He had skilfully steered Botswana, with foresight and prudence, during perhaps its most vulnerable period – leaving it with the firm foundations of a democratic tradition, and well-trained executive and administrative branches of government.

The 1980s: President Sir Ketumile Masire Masire's succession was mandated by another victory for the BDP in a general election to the National Assembly in 1984 – although at the same time they lost control of all the town councils except Selebi-Phikwe. This sign of discontent was widely ascribed to high levels of unemployment.

Just as the 1970s had witnessed upheavals in Rhodesia, so the 1980s saw the intensification of pressure on the white regime in South Africa to give way to majority rule.

Botswana continued to welcome refugees, but refused to harbour bases for the ANC's war on apartheid in South Africa. During this period Botswana had a delicate balancing act to play. Like most countries it was calling for an end to apartheid, and geographically it was one of the 'front-line' states in the battle against apartheid. However, Botswana's economy was so dependent on its southern neighbour that it couldn't afford to apply the sanctions that most countries were calling for.

In 1981, tensions arose with South Africa over the supply of military equipment from the USSR for the Botswana Defence Force (BDF), though by 1986 Britain and the USA were offering hardware to the BDF to deter South African incursions into Botswana.

Meanwhile on its eastern border, relations with Robert Mugabe's ZANU government were businesslike rather than terribly friendly. The early 1980s saw Mugabe's notoriously ruthless Fifth Brigade terrorising Matabeleland – the province adjacent to Botswana. Zimbabwean refugees flooded into Botswana including, in March 1983, the leader of ZAPU, Mugabe's opposition in the elections, Joshua Nkomo.

Nkomo left for London rapidly, but later allegations that the refugee camps were harbouring armed dissidents caused problems, culminating in a border skirmish in 1983 between the BDF and 'armed men wearing Zimbabwean military uniforms'. It wasn't until April 1989 that Botswana felt able to revoke the 'refugee' status for Zimbabwean nationals and, soon after, the refugees left – although Botswana continued to have many illegal migrants from Zimbabwe.

Internally, political tensions between the BDP and the BNF peaked in early 1987 with a referendum on constitutional amendments to the electoral system, which was boycotted by the BNF. However, by October 1989, the BDP demonstrated its substantial support by winning 65% of the votes in an election (a result which was again challenged by the BNF in several constituencies). In October the new National Assembly returned Masire to the president's office for a third term.

During this time there were several incursions into Botswana by South African troops – including two raids on alleged ANC offices in Gaborone in 1985 and 1986. But a few years later, tensions began to ease as South Africa's President De Klerk started to set his country on a course for majority rule. One of his first steps was independence for Namibia in 1990.

1990–98: President Sir Ketumile Masire The early 1990s saw several corruption scandals in which a number of ministers resigned – including, in March 1992, the vice president, Peter Mmusi. (Contrast these with the paucity of resignations that occur during corruption scandals in most governments and you'll realise this is a good sign, not a bad one, for the integrity of Botswana's government!)

The general election of October 1994 saw the BNF triumphing in the urban areas, winning 13 seats (37.7% of the vote), while the BDP, with 40 seats (53.1% of the vote), continued to command the support of the rural constituencies. The elections were peaceful, with around a 70% turnout, and at last Botswana had an opposition party capable of a serious challenge to the BDP.

During this time relations with Botswana's neighbours were generally good. However, in 1992, a border squabble arose between Botswana and Namibia over a tiny island (called Sedudu by Botswana, and Kasikili by Namibia) in the Chobe River. (For details of this argument, see page 240.) A potentially much more serious issue arose in 1996 when Namibia announced plans to construct a pipeline to take water from the Okavango River at Rundu. Given that this would impact directly on the Okavango Delta, the possibility of such a pipeline remains a source of great concern for Botswana.

Then, in 1998, an influx of refugees from Namibia's Caprivi Strip arrived, including Mishake Muyongo, who had been suspended as president of Namibia's

3

opposition party, the Democratic Turnhalle Alliance. He and other leading Caprivians had campaigned for independence for the province. By 1999, over 2,000 refugees were living near Gaborone. Namibia's extradition demands were refused, although eventually a settlement was brokered by the UNHCR whereby the most prominent refugees were granted asylum in Denmark, and the rest returned to Namibia under an amnesty.

Internal electoral reform had long been on the agenda in Botswana, with some consensus about the need for it from all the political parties. In 1997, various amendments to the constitution were passed, including a reduction in the voting age from 21 to 18 years old, the establishment of an electoral commission that is independent of the government, and a measure to restrict the president to a maximum of two terms in office.

When Masire retired in March 1998, it was at a time of infighting in the opposition, the BNF. This led to a split in the party, with dissident members forming the Botswana Congress Party (BCP). After 11 of the BNF's 13 deputies had defected, the BCP was declared the official opposition in July 1998.

1998–2008: President Festus Mogae
The day after Masire's retirement, his vice president, Festus G Mogae, head of the BDP, was inaugurated. Mogae was born in 1939 and trained at Oxford as an economist. He served as executive director at the IMF for anglophone Africa, and later in various senior government posts, including Governor of the Bank of Botswana. His new cabinet was virtually identical to the old one; the only new minister was Lt General Seretse Khama Ian Khama, son of Botswana's first president (the late Sir Seretse Khama), who in 1998 became vice president. Both men remained in office following elections in 1999 and 2004.

In 2003, Ian Khama became chairman of the BDP and five years later, when President Mogae stepped down at the end of his second term in office, he took on the presidency.

2008–18: Lt Gen Seretse Khama Ian Khama
Ian Khama – so known to differentiate him from his father – took office as president in April 2008, emphasising his commitment to democracy. Elections the following year returned the BDP with 53% of the votes, securing 45 seats in parliament, while their BNF and BCP rivals came away with just ten seats. Five years later, Khama remained in office for a second term, after the BDP was once again returned to government, despite garnering less than 50% of the votes. By contrast, the four opposition parties – the BNF and BCP, along with the Botswana Movement for Democracy and the Botswana People's Party – took 53% of the vote between them.

Ian Khama was born in the UK in 1953, and trained at Britain's Royal Military Academy in Sandhurst, before joining the newly formed Botswana Defence Force, rising to Commander in 1989. Known as an ardent conservationist, he was actively involved with environmental organisations, and in 2014 introduced a nationwide hunting ban. He promoted the importance of diversification within Botswana's economy, particularly in agriculture and tourism, with a view to lessening the country's dependence on diamond mining.

Khama was considered an assertive and autocratic leader, which rendered him unpopular in many quarters. Controversially, he introduced the Directorate of Internal Security, with its own powers, separate from the police force, with some observers concerned that the organisation could be used to punish or impede critics of the president or his administration.

On the international stage, Khama often took a hard line, sometimes finding himself a lone voice within the African Union. In 2011, he was one of the first to break off relations with Libya's Colonel Gaddafi; in 2016 he called for Zimbabwe's president Robert Mugabe to step down, and he condemned former Sudanese president Omar al-Bashir for his action in Darfur. He was vocal in condemning North Korea's human rights violations, and risked a backlash from the influential Chinese leadership, too, over a planned visit to Botswana by the Dalai Lama in 2017, although the Tibetan leader cancelled his trip.

As enshrined in the constitution, Ian Khama stepped down as president in April 2018, after two successive terms in office. Following bitter disagreement – personally and politically – with his successor, Mokgweetsi Masisi, Khama fled to South Africa, and switched his support to the Botswana Patriotic Front (BPF). An outspoken critic of his successor, Khama now lives in exile as tensions remain high. In January 2023, a Botswanan court issued an arrest warrant for Khama and the former heads of intelligence and police services, citing charges ranging from firearms possession to money laundering. Khama denied all charges, stating that they were fabricated as part of a political vendetta to harm him in advance of the 2024 national elections. It was thought that if Khama were able to campaign freely for these elections, the BDP would likely lose some of its strongholds, threatening the party's 57-year run of power.

In March 2021, the UN stated that intelligence agencies from three neighbouring countries had credible information on three separate assassination attempts on Khama. The Botswanan government has denied these accusations. There is little doubt that the serious nature of the current wranglings between Khama and Masisi have real potential to negatively impact Botswana's long-held reputation as a stable democracy.

Khama currently sits on the board of directors of the US-based organisation Conservation International.

2018–present: Dr Mokgweetsi Masisi

Botswana's fifth president Dr Mokgweetsi Masisi – a Florida State University science graduate, trained teacher and former UNICEF project officer – first became an MP and a government assistant minister in 2009, before rising to vice president under Ian Khama in 2014. Upon becoming president in 2018, Masisi sought to differentiate himself from his predecessor: he rowed back on key Khama policies, from the wildlife hunting ban to high alcohol levies, forged closer ties with China and purged the government of Khama's closest allies. He also vowed to fight corruption and open the economy. In his first election as president in 2019, he campaigned energetically and successfully. However, Masisi's popularity is facing significant challenges thanks to an increasingly confident opposition party (UDC), who had successful by-elections in 2022; his personal feud with Ian Khama; mounting concerns about transparency in government; allegations of judiciary interference; and increasing public concern about deteriorating public infrastructure and youth unemployment.

2024 elections

The next general election was scheduled to take place before October 2024 and was expected to see a major political shift in the country. The governing BDP faced considerable challenges in the run-up to the election, with corruption charges, 2022 by-election losses and criticism from Khama. Opinion polls at the time of writing showed a significant swing away from the BDP to the centre-left Umbrella for Democratic Change (UDC), a coalition of opposition parties under the leadership of Duma Boko. The UDC were polling at 41%, which

3

had the potential to lead them to power. However, with a significant 28% of voters still undecided, victory was far from certain for any party. Thanks to the general social and economic stability of the country as a whole, though, any political change was unlikely to bring real instability to the country.

GOVERNMENT AND ADMINISTRATION

Botswana's parliament is the supreme legislative body in the country. It plays a central role in the governance and decision-making processes of Botswana, shaping the country's laws and policies, and reflects the democratic principles and institutions that have been established in Botswana since independence in 1966. Parliamentary elections are held every five years.

The parliament consists of two houses: the National Assembly and the House of Chiefs. The National Assembly, the lower house, is composed of 57 members of parliament (MPs), who are directly elected through first-past-the-post voting. As a result, the electoral system affords little chance for minority parties to gain ground, and attempts by opposition parties to pool their resources against the might of the BDP have so far come to nothing, though the 2024 election may see the status quo challenged (page 85). The National Assembly is responsible for making and passing laws, debating policies and representing the interests of the people.

The House of Chiefs is the upper house, representing Botswana's traditional leadership and the interests of various ethnic communities. It is made up of chiefs and other traditional leaders, and while they do not have legislative powers, the House of Chiefs provides input and advice.

The president is appointed by parliament rather than directly elected by the population. This is a controversial issue, raising questions of limited voter influence and a lack of transparency and accountability; but in 2008 parliament rejected calls for the system to be changed to a popular vote, favouring the smooth transitions of power that the current system has afforded. Each president may serve for a maximum of two terms (ten years), after which the vice president automatically takes over. He or she is then given 18 months to prepare for a general election, with the country having a strong record of conducting peaceful, free and fair elections.

For administrative purposes, the country is divided into a mix of rural and urban districts.

ECONOMY

In economic terms, Botswana has long been one of Africa's success stories, reflecting both the country's natural mineral wealth and a political and social stability that far outweighs that of its neighbours. Underpinning this success has been the exploitation of Botswana's diamond mines, although other growth sectors have been in tourism, cattle farming and financial services.

In the 30-year period following independence in 1966, the economic growth rate averaged at just over 9% a year, marking the economy out as the fastest growing in the world, according to the World Bank. By the turn of the millennium, this stabilised at around 7% a year, although the country's heavy reliance on the mining sector has left it somewhat vulnerable to global shocks. This was seen dramatically in 2009 when the sector reeled from the effects of a worldwide recession and plummeted to –7%. The annual growth rate bounced back to 8% the following year, before the economy experienced something of a downturn in 2016, with high youth unemployment, and growth slowing to just 2.9% a year.

Economic growth reached 5.8% in 2022, but has since dropped again, largely as diamond production slowed, though this is likely to increase in the short-to-medium term as global demand for diamonds mined outside of sanction-restricted Russia has increased.

Inflation reduced in 2023 to 5.2% from 12.2% in 2022, and attempts to diversify the economy away from diamond mining and create employment opportunities are key focus areas to ensure a robust future economy.

ECONOMIC DEVELOPMENT Botswana's economy has undergone significant transformations since independence. While cattle farming played a crucial role in the country's early economy, the discovery and extraction of mineral resources, particularly diamonds, have become major drivers of growth and development.

Cattle raising remains an important economic activity in Botswana, with livestock farming contributing to both food security and export revenues. The significance of agriculture has decreased in relative terms compared with other sectors, although in January 2022, approximately 46% of Botswana's land area was still classified as permanent pasture.

The discovery of diamond deposits in the 1970s transformed the country's economy. Today, the mining sector, including diamond mining, contributes significantly to the country's wealth. Botswana is one of the world's leading producers of high-quality diamonds (see below), with record sales being reached in 2022, as the global market shunned Russian diamonds in favour of those from other countries.

However, recognising the finite nature of the country's diamond resources, Botswana has embarked on a strategy to diversify its economy and reduce its dependence on the gems. The government has identified several sectors for development, notably tourism (page 88) and the financial services sector, including efforts to establish Botswana as a regional financial, information technology and innovation hub.

INTERNATIONAL TRADE Total exports in 2022 were estimated at over US$8.28 billion, of which diamonds, insulated wire and copper ore accounted for 92%, with other export revenue sources including cattle, salt and soda ash. Significant revenue is also generated from tourism.

Major export markets are UAE (14%), Belgium (9%) and India (8%), with South Africa, Hong Kong, Namibia and Israel also significant.

In the same year, Botswana's imports were valued at around US$16.2 billion, with some 65% of these coming from South Africa, which supplies most of the country's electricity, as well as delivery trucks, fuel and non-industrial diamonds. The surprising import of diamonds reflects, in part, De Beers's international centre for diamond sales and sorting being located in Botswana's capital, Gaborone.

Botswana is a member of the Southern African Customs Union (SACU), an economic bloc also comprising South Africa, Namibia, Lesotho and Swaziland. Goods enter the markets of the other four member states free of import duty and other restrictions. Botswana is also an active member of the Southern African Development Community (SADC), a body that groups together 15 countries within the region and has its headquarters in Gaborone.

Diamonds Botswana's economic success is founded on its natural resources, particularly diamonds. Today, alongside Russia and Canada, it remains one of the leading producers of gem-quality diamonds in the world.

For over three decades after mining began in 1971, the industry catapulted Botswana's economy on to a course of sustained growth. Despite the 2008–09 global recession, a slump in sales in 2015, and the current global economic slowdown affecting demand for luxury items in the US and China, Botswana's diamond revenue remains strong. Approximately 30% of Botswana's current revenue, and 70% of its foreign exchange earnings, come from diamonds, with 2023 sales generating US$3.44 billion, albeit a drop from 2022's staggering US$4.59 billion.

Over the years, Botswana has certainly reaped the rewards of the success of the mining industry on its economy: its GDP per capita of US$7,738.90 in 2022 was among the highest rates in Africa.

Employment in the diamond industry – directly and indirectly – accounts for some 20% of the country's workforce, with a new ten-year deal signed with De Beers in 2023 promising 'tens of thousands of new jobs'. In an attempt to broaden the value of its diamond industry, the government has also encouraged the establishment of diamond-processing factories, luring them away from their stronghold in India.

Until 2011, most diamond mining was carried out by Debswana, a 50/50 partnership between De Beers and the Botswana government that was formed in 1969. Of the company's four large, open-cast operations, the first to be in production was at Orapa, west of Francistown. Opened in 1971, it was for many years the world's largest open-cast diamond mine. It was joined in 1975 by the nearby Letlhakane mine, and in 1982, by Jwaneng in the south of the country, which is still classed as the world's richest diamond mine, and is anticipated to remain in production until 2033. They are currently mining at a depth of 452m, with the expectation that this will reach a depth of 816m in the next decade. Debswana's fourth mine is the much smaller Damtshaa, near Orapa. With a written request to Debswana and ten days' notice, it's possible to visit any of their mines for a tour (☏ +267 361 4200; e corporateaffairs@debswana.bw).

Diamond mining has not been without controversy, though. In 2011, Gem Diamonds Botswana opened the Ghaghoo diamond mine within the Central Kalahari Game Reserve. The resulting displacement of San Bushmen communities for whom the area was home, and concerns for the environmental impact on a protected area, raised significant concerns and international discussion. While the mine had a potential yield of up to 20.5 million carats, the operation was eventually mothballed in early 2017 when faced with a downturn in the market for commercial diamonds. Similarly, Lerala mine, operated by Australian company Kimberley Diamonds in the Boteti region, closed for similar reasons, raising subsequent issues around the environmental responsibilities to rehabilitate natural surroundings following the closure of a mine.

Tourism Botswana is well known internationally for its pristine wilderness areas and wildlife, as highlighted in this guide, and tourism is a growing industry. The government's policy of encouraging small numbers of upmarket visitors to its pristine wilderness areas is proving successful within the overall aim of protecting the environment. Safaris have become important contributors to the economy: tourism accounted for 13% of GDP in 2019 and 9% of total employment, with significant numbers of low-income and female employees.

Needless to say, the Covid-19 pandemic had a massive impact on the tourism sector, with global travel largely grounded for 2020 and 2021. While 2022 started slowly, tourism rebounded rapidly in the latter part of the year and returned to pre-Covid levels in 2024.

The number of overseas tourists visiting the country had reached 1.830 million in 2018, with almost two-thirds coming from the USA, Germany and the UK. Although this is down from a peak of more than 2 million in 2008, the trend is now back on the upward trajectory that started in 1994, with visitor numbers projected to hit 2.73 million in 2027.

When the diamonds run out, Botswana needs to have an alternative, renewable source of income, and tourism is one of the most obvious contenders. The difficulty for the government will be trying to increase tourism's revenues while still keeping tourism a premium product, and hence at a low density. It is noticeable that when leases in the wildlife concessions come up for review, the operators are being allowed to construct additional camps, thus giving them the capacity for more visitors. While there is certainly space in some of the concessions for this, in others there is likely to be a knock-on effect in terms of exclusivity.

In the meantime, in order to increase the benefits from tourism without an adverse impact on the environment, attempts are being made to diversify into smaller 'ecotourism' projects that will benefit local communities at ground level, and to offset the negative effects of a clash between tourism projects and the needs of local people. Among these are community-based projects, such as that in Tsodilo Hills (page 425), aimed at boosting cultural tourism.

WORKFORCE Botswana has consistently made efforts to invest in education and skills development, with its education expenditure among the highest in the world (8.74% of GDP against a global average of 4.62%). As a result, the country has a relatively high literacy rate and a growing pool of skilled workers, particularly in fields like health care, education, engineering and information technology.

Employment opportunities focus on mining (especially diamond mining), manufacturing, agriculture and the services industry, especially government, retail and tourism. Industrial relations are generally good and Botswana has labour laws that govern employment relationships, including minimum wage regulations, working hours and worker protections.

However, a significant portion of the workforce operates in the informal economy, engaging in small-scale businesses and casual labour, which varies widely, from street vending to construction, agricultural labour and domestic-service roles.

The government has implemented initiatives to promote job creation and entrepreneurship, particularly among the youth and women, but like many countries, it faces significant challenges with youth unemployment. Despite having a well-educated, ambitious youth population, there can be limited opportunities for work, especially in rural areas. All of this leads to a broad social divide. Unemployment rose to 25.4% in 2022, with Covid significantly impacting employment in several sectors for the previous two years and increasing poverty rates significantly. Currently, 14.5% of the population are considered to be below the international poverty line, living on less than US$1.90 per day.

FOREIGN INVESTMENT The combination of political stability, low rates of taxation and the lack of exchange controls, which were abolished in 1999, has traditionally made Botswana attractive to investors. Key to any prospective investment is the Botswana Investment and Trade Centre (w bitc.co.bw), which is instrumental in pursuing government policies of privatisation and diversification, and facilitates direct foreign investment.

4

People and Culture

POPULATION OVERVIEW

Botswana remains one of the least densely populated countries in the world, currently making the top ten list, with only 4.23 people per km^2. The population was estimated at 2,346,179 following the 2022 census, reflecting a population growth per year of 1.4%, a slower rate than in previous decades. This growth rate is also low by African standards, and results from two conflicting issues. On one hand, 67% of fertile women use a modern method of contraception, which is exceptional for sub-Saharan Africa and reflects an educated people with a prosperous and generally developed economy. Conversely, while average life expectancy is currently estimated at 70 years, back to that of the mid-1990s, the intervening period saw it fall as low as 36 years, as the country battled with high levels of HIV/AIDS. Although some 20.7% of citizens are still living with HIV – consistently one of the highest rates in Africa – this is significantly lower than the peak of around 40%. Although the number of new infections has steadily decreased, down 34% since 2010, it is worth noting that 70% of new infections are in women aged 15–24. The government offers free antiretroviral therapy in response to the epidemic, with 84% of adults living with HIV receiving the medicine. It is hoped this will extend and improve recipients' quality of life, and reduce transmission of the virus.

UNICEF's statistics indicate that more than 96% of the population has access to safe water and 80% to adequate sanitation, while almost every child (98%) under one has been immunised against polio, diphtheria and BCG. These are very good levels by the continent's standards, and are no doubt helped by the government's policy of paying the full cost of all these vaccines.

However, these statistics say nothing of what Botswana's people are like. If you venture into the more rural areas, take a local bus, or try to hitchhike with the locals, you will often find that people are curious about you. Chat to them openly, as fellow travellers, and you will find most to be delightful. They will be pleased to assist you where they can, and as keen to help you learn about them and their country as they are interested in your lifestyle and what brings you to Botswana. That said, it's not uncommon, especially in the towns, to find people surly and largely uninterested sometimes…just as they are in London, or New York, or many other modern cities.

SOCIAL GROUPS OR 'TRIBES'

The people of Africa are often viewed, from abroad, as belonging to a multitude of culturally and linguistically distinct tribes – which are often portrayed as being at odds with each other. While there is certainly an enormous variety of different

Historians, anthropologists and social scientists are divided, and often perplexed, about what name to use for the people known as 'Bushmen'. The confusion is compounded by the mix of different tribal tags used in historical texts, often for reasons of political correctness.

San, Bushmen, San/Bushmen, Khoisan and Khoi are all used, often apparently randomly. In Botswana you'll also hear RAD (Remote Area Dweller) or Masarwa/Basarwa used, but the former is exceedingly vague and the latter (meaning 'people without cattle') often considered insulting. Equally insulting is the colonial term 'Hottentot'. Some avoid the term 'Bushmen', regarding it as debasing and sexist, often using 'San' in preference – which others claim to be a derogatory Nama word. Meanwhile 'Khoisan' is a language grouping, not a specific race or tribe, and also encompasses the Khoi (or Khoe or Khoi-Khoi or Khoi-khoin), and hence also Namibia's Damara and Nama people. All have similar 'click' languages, but they live very differently from many of the people who we think of as the Bushmen.

Ideally, we would use the term which these people use themselves, but there lies the rub. Ask villagers in the Kalahari and they will describe themselves as members of the Ju-/wasi, the !Kung, the Hai-//omn – or any one of a dozen other language groups. (See page 100 for an explanation of the !, / and // in these names.) If we used these much more precise linguistic terms (see page 538 for a few of the main ones), they would overly complicate our discussions and require an accuracy that is beyond me.

These people have no label for the broad racial category that we regard as 'the Bushmen'. They simply don't think of themselves as belonging to one race of people. Therefore, the concept of an overall grouping of people that we call 'Bushmen' must have originated from someone other than the people themselves. In truth, it is an invention of those who came to this corner of Africa later – a legacy of colonialism in its broadest sense.

Given the questionable validity of any term, I have used San throughout this book: not because I believe it to be more accurate than the alternatives, but simply because this is a term that is widely used in southern Africa, and widely understood elsewhere. It's also the term adopted by the Kalahari People's Fund (w kalaharipeoples.org), and agreed by various San communities in Namibia. That said, it's a vague term; just try to make it precise and you'll realise how inadequate it is. I apologise if it is, in any language, derogatory; it isn't meant to be.

ethnic groups in Africa, most are closely related to their neighbours in terms of language, beliefs and way of life. Modern historians eschew the simplistic tag of 'tribes', noting that such groupings change with time.

Sometimes the word 'tribe' is used to describe a group of people who all speak the same language; it may be used to mean those who follow a particular leader or to refer to all the inhabitants of a certain area at a given time. In any case, 'tribe' is a vague word that is used differently for different purposes. The term 'clan' (blood relations) is a smaller, more precisely defined, unit – though rather too precise for our broad discussions here.

Certainly, at any given time, groups of people or clans who share similar language and cultural beliefs do band together and often, in time, develop 'tribal' identities.

However, it is wrong to then extrapolate and assume that their ancestors will have had the same groupings and allegiances centuries ago.

In Africa, as elsewhere in the world, history is recorded by the winners. Here the winners, the ruling class, may be the descendants of a small group of immigrants who achieved dominance over a larger, long-established community. Over the years, the history of that ruling class (the winners) usually becomes regarded as the history of the whole community, or tribe. Two 'tribes' have thus become one, with one history – which will reflect the origins of that small group of immigrants, and not the ancestors of the majority of the current tribe.

Botswana is typical of many African countries. As you will see, there are cultural differences between the people in different parts of the country. However, in many ways these are no more pronounced than those between the states of the USA, or the different regions of the (relatively tiny) UK. There continues to be lots of inter-marriage and mixing of these peoples and cultures – perhaps more so than there has ever been, due to the efficiency of modern transport systems. Generally, though, there is very little friction between these communities (whose boundaries, as we have said, are indistinct), and Botswana's various peoples live peacefully together.

THE KHOISAN The Khoisan is a language grouping rather than a specific race or tribe, and includes the various peoples of both the San (page 72) and the Khoi (page 72). All have relatively light golden-brown skin, almond-shaped eyes and high cheekbones. Their stature is generally small and slight, and they are now found across southern Africa.

Our view of the San is partly informed by some basic anthropological and linguistic research, mostly applying to the Khoisan, which is worth outlining to set the scene.

Anthropology The first fossil records that we have of our human ancestors date back to at least 60,000 years ago in East Africa. These are likely to have been the ancestors of everyone living today. Archaeological finds from parts of the Kalahari show that human beings have lived here for at least 40,000 years. These are generally agreed to have been the ancestors of the modern Khoisan peoples living in Botswana today.

Language research Of the world's 20 linguistic 'families', four are very different from the rest. All these four are African families – and they include the Khoisan and the Niger–Congo (Bantu) languages. This is among the evidence that has led linguists to believe that human language evolved in Africa, and further analysis has suggested that this was probably among the ancestors of the Khoisan.

The Khoisan languages are distinguished by their wide repertoire of clicking sounds. These are very sophisticated. It was observed by Dunbar in 'Why gossip is good for you' (page 545) that, 'From the phonetic point of view these [the Khoisan languages] are the world's most complex languages. To speak one of them fluently is to exploit human phonetic ability to the full.'

At some point the Khoisan languages diverged from a common ancestor, and today three distinct groups exist: the northern, central and southern groups. Languages gradually evolve and change as different groups of people split up and move to new areas. Thus the evolution of each language is specific to each group, and reflected in the classifications described later in this chapter.

According to Mike Main in *The Visitor's Guide to Botswana* (now *The African Adventurer's Guide to Botswana*; page 546), the northern group are San and today they live west of the Okavango and north of Ghanzi, with representatives found as far afield as Angola. The southern group are also San, who live in the area between Kang and Bokspits in Botswana. The central group is Khoi, living in central Botswana, and extending north to the eastern Okavango and Kasane, and west into Namibia, where they are known as the Nama.

Each of these three Khoisan language groups has many dialects. These have some similarities, but they are not closely related, and some are different to the point where there is no mutual understanding. Certain dialects are so restricted that only a small family group speaks them.

This huge number of dialects, and variation in languages, reflects the relative isolation of the various speakers, most of whom now live in small family groups, as the Kalahari's arid environment cannot sustain large groups of people living together in one place as hunter-gatherers.

Genetic discoveries Most men have an X- and a Y-chromosome, while women have two X-chromosomes. All the information in a man's Y-chromosome will usually be passed on, without change, to all of his sons, but very rarely it alters slightly as it is being passed on, thus causing a permanent change in the chromosome's genetic sequence. This will then be the start of a new lineage of slightly different Y-chromosomes, which will be inherited by all future male descendants.

In November 2000, Professor Ronald Davis and a team of Stanford researchers (page 545) claimed to have traced back this lineage to a single individual man, and argued that a small group of East Africans (Sudanese and Ethiopians) and Khoisan are the closest present-day relatives of this original man – that is, their genetic make-up is closest to his. (It's a scientific indication of the biblical Adam, if you like.) This is still a very contentious finding, with subsequent researchers suggesting at least ten original male sources ('Adams') – and so, the jury remains out on the precise details of all these findings. If you're interested in the latest on this, you'll find a lot about it on the web; start searching with the keywords: 'Khoisan Y chromosome'.

The San There is not another social/language group on this planet that has been studied, written about, filmed and researched more than the San, or Bushmen, of the Kalahari. Despite this, or indeed because of it, popular conceptions about them, fed by their image in the media, are often strikingly out of step with the realities. Thus they warrant a separate section devoted to them.

The aim of these next few pages is to try and explain some of the roots of the misconceptions, to look at some of the realities, and to make you think. Even though I have spent a lot of time with San in the Kalahari, I find it difficult to separate fact from oft-repeated, glossy fiction. If parts of this discussion seem disparate, it's a reflection of this difficulty.

Historical views of the San Despite much evidence and research, our views of the San seem to have changed relatively little since both the Bantu groups and the first Europeans arrived in southern Africa.

When the first Bantu farmer migrated south through East Africa, the range of territory occupied by the foragers, whose Stone Age technology had dominated the continent, began to condense. By the time the first **white settlers** appeared in the Cape, the Khoisan people were already restricted to Africa's southwestern corners and the Kalahari.

All over the world, farmers occupy clearly demarcated areas of land, whereas foragers will move more and often leave less trace of their presence. In Africa, this

Looking at the lifestyle of the San who until recently remained in the more remote areas of the Kalahari, it's difficult not to lapse into a romantic view of ignoring present realities. There are too many cultural aspects to cover here, so instead we've just picked out a few that you may encounter.

NOMADS OF THE KALAHARI Perhaps the first idea to dispel is that the San are nomads. They're not. San family groups have clearly defined territories within which they forage, called a *n!ore* (in the Ju/'hoansi language). This is usually centred on a place where there is water, and contains food resources sufficient for the basic subsistence of the group.

Groups recognise rights to the *n!ore*, which is passed on from father to first-born son. Any visiting people would ask permission to remain in these. Researchers have mapped these areas, even in places like the Central Kalahari.

HUNTER-GATHERERS Any hunter-gatherer lifestyle entails a dependence on, and extensive knowledge of, the environment and the resident fauna and flora found there. In the Kalahari, water is the greatest need and the San know which roots and tubers provide liquid to quench thirst. They create sip wells in the desert, digging a hole, filling it with soft grass, then using a reed to suck water into the hole, and send it bubbling up the reed to fill an ostrich egg. Water-filled ostrich eggs are also buried at specific locations within the group's 'area'. When necessary the San will strain the liquid from the rumen of a herbivore and drink that.

Researchers have observed that any hunting is done by the men. When living a basic hunting and gathering lifestyle, with little external input, hunting provides only about 20% of their food. The remaining 80% is provided largely by the women, helped by the children, who forage and gather wild food from the bush. By the age of 12 a child might know about 200 plant species, and an adult more than 300.

HUNTING The San in the Kalahari are practised hunters. Their main weapon is a very light bow with a reed and metal arrow. The arrowhead is usually tipped with poison obtained from specific plants, snakes and beetles. (Today, the actual practice is increasingly uncommon when it's not done to earn money from observing visitors.)

All the community hunters may be involved in the capture of large game, which carries with it certain obligations. The whole group shares in the kill and each member is entitled to a certain portion of the meat.

made it easier for farmers, first black then white, to ignore any traditional land rights that belonged to foraging people.

Faced with the loss of territory for hunting and gathering, the foragers – who, by this time were already being called 'Bushmen' – made enemies of the farmers by killing cattle. They waged a guerrilla war, shooting poison arrows at parties of men who set out to massacre them. They were feared and loathed by the settlers, who, however, captured and valued their children as servants.

Some of the Khoisan retreated north from the Cape – like the ancestors of Namibia's Nama people. Others were forced to labour on the settlers' farms, or were thrown into prison for hunting animals that were their traditional prey, which were

There are various methods for hunting small game, from snaring to impaling, with specific techniques often shared within a family.

SOCIAL SYSTEM The survival of the San in the harsh environment of the Kalahari is evidence of the supreme adaptability of humans. It reflects their detailed knowledge of their environment, which provides them not only with food, but with materials for shelter and medicine in the form of plants.

Another important factor is the social system by which the San live. Social interaction is governed by unwritten rules that bind the people in friendship and harmony. One such mechanism is the obligation to lend such few things as are individually possessed, thereby incurring a debt of obligation from the borrower. The San also practise exogamy, which means they have an obligation to marry outside the group. Such ties bind the society inextricably together, as does the system of gift exchange between separate groups.

Owing to environmental constraints, a group will consist of between 80 and 120 people, living and moving together. In times of shortage the groups will be much smaller, sometimes consisting of only immediate family – parents, grandparents and children. They must be able to carry everything they possess. Their huts are light constructions of grass, and they have few possessions.

No-one owns property, no-one is richer or has more status than another. A group of San has a nominal leader, who might be a senior member of the group, an expert hunter, or the person who owns the water rights. The whole group takes decisions affecting them, often after vociferous discussions.

TRANCE DANCING Entertainment for the San, when things are good, usually involves dancing. During some dances, which may often have overtones of ritual or religion, the dancers may fall into a trance and collapse.

These trances are induced by a deliberate breathing technique, with a clear physiological explanation. Dances normally take place in the evening, around a fire. Then the women, children and old people will sit around and clap, while some of the younger men will dance around the circle in an energetic, rhythmic dance. Often this is all that happens, and after a while the excitement dies down and everyone goes to sleep.

However, on fairly rare occasions, the dancers will go into a trance. After several hours of constant exertion, they will shorten their breathing. This creates an oxygen deficiency, which leads to the heart pumping more strongly to compensate. Blood pressure to the brain increases; the dancer loses consciousness and collapses.

now designated property of the Crown. This story is told by Robert J Gordon in *The Bushman Myth: The Making of a Namibian Underclass* (page 544). The European settlers proved to be their most determined enemy, embarking on a programme of legislation and massacre. Many San died in prison, with many more shot as 'vermin'.

Thus the onslaught of farmers on the hunter-gatherers accelerated between the **1800s and the mid-1900s**. This helped to ensure that hunter-gathering as a lifestyle continued to be practical only in marginal areas that couldn't be economically farmed – like the Kalahari.

Throughout this period, a succession of Khoisan people were also effectively enslaved and brought to Europe and the US for exhibition. Sometimes this was under the guise of anthropology, but usually it didn't claim to be anything more than entertainment.

One of the first was the 'Hottentot Venus' – a woman who was probably of Khoisan extraction who was exhibited around London and Paris from 1810 to 1815, as an erotic curiosity for aristocrats. Others followed – for example, the six Khoisan people exhibited at the Coney Island Pleasure Resort, beside New York, and later in London in the 1880s, and billed as the 'missing link between apes and men'; or the 'wild dancing bushman' known as Franz, brought to England around 1913 by Paddy Hepston (see Q N Parsons's piece in *Botswana Notes and Records*; page 545).

In the **1950s**, a researcher from Harvard, John Marshall, came to the Kalahari to study the Kung! San. He described a peaceful people living in harmony with nature, amid a land that provided all their needs. The groups had a deep spirituality and no real hierarchy: it seemed like the picture of a modern Eden (especially when viewed through post-war eyes). Marshall was a natural cameraman and made a film that followed the hunt of a giraffe by four men over a five-day period. It swiftly became a classic, both in and outside of anthropological circles.

Other researchers agreed, noting a great surfeit of protein in the diet of the Kung! San and low birth rates akin to modern industrial societies.

The San were seen as photogenic and sources of good copy and good images. Their lives were portrayed in romantic, spiritual terms in the book and film *The Lost World of the Kalahari* by Laurens van der Post (page 540). This documentary really ignited the worldwide interest in the San and led to subsequent films such as *The Gods Must be Crazy*. All the images conveyed an idyllic view of the San as untainted by contact with the modern world.

The reality was much less rosy. Some of their major misconceptions have been outlined particularly clearly in chapter 13 of John Reader's *Africa: A Biography of the Continent* (page 544). He points out that, far from being an ideal diet, the nutrition of the San was often critically limited, lacking vitamins and fatty acids that would usually be associated with a lack of animal fat in their diet. Far from a stable population with a low birth rate, it seems likely that there had been a decline in the birth rate in the last few generations. The likely cause for this was periods of inadequate nourishment during the year when the San lost weight from lack of food, stress and the great exertions of their lifestyle.

In fact, it seems likely that the San are people who, over the last two millennia, have become relegated to an underclass by the relentless advance of both black and white farmers who did not recognise their original rights to their traditional land.

The San and the modern media Though scientific thought has moved on since the 1950s, much of the media has not. The San are still perceived to be hot news.

The outpost of Tsumkwe is the centre for many of the San communities in Namibia. It's a tiny crossroads with a school and a handful of buildings, in a remote corner of northeastern Namibia. Despite its isolation, film crews, journalists and photographers visit annually.

Talk to virtually any of the directors and you'll realise that they arrived with very clear ideas about the images that they wanted to capture. They all thought they were one of the first, and they wanted to return home with images that matched their pre-conceived ideas about the San as 'the last primitive hunter-gatherers'.

As an example, you'll often see pictures in the media of San hunters in traditional dress walking across a hot, barren salt pan. When asked to do these shoots the San's usual comment is, 'Why? There's no point. We'd never go looking for anything there.' But the shots look spectacular and win prizes…so the photographers keep asking for them. From the San's perspective, they get paid for the shots, so why not pose for the camera? I'd do the same! Thus, our image of the San is really one that *we* are constantly recreating. It's the one that we expect. But it doesn't necessarily conform to any reality. So on reflection, popular thinking hasn't moved on much from Marshall's first film in the 1950s.

Current issues for the San There are several issues affecting the rights of the San and their place in modern society. It's a fundamental tenet of the Botswanan government that it doesn't allow any of its policies to favour one ethnic group or another. This is generally held to be a very sensible approach, framed to avoid creating ethnic divisions and strife. However, the San are not recognised within the power structure accorded to the various chiefs of Botswana's other tribal groups; there's no San representation in the House of Chiefs (page 86), and no traditional land rights accorded to them. This puts them at a major political disadvantage. In addition, under Botswana law, hunting and gathering isn't recognised as a formal category of land use – so in local disputes the needs of the San are frequently subjugated to those of Botswana's farmers. All this serves to underpin their continuing fight for the right to live in the Central Kalahari Game Reserve.

Central Kalahari Game Reserve

We know this land belonged to our great-grandparents. But now, just because we are Bushmen, our land is being taken from us.

Bushman woman, Central Kalahari Game Reserve

One of the more contentious issues facing Botswana in recent years – with much rhetoric from all quarters – is whether or not the San have an ongoing right to live within the Central Kalahari Game Reserve (CKGR), continuing a presence that is estimated to date back some 20,000 years.

The CKGR was proclaimed in 1961 in the last days of the British Protectorate. Although for ease of administration it was designated as a game reserve, it was created with the intention of placating international concern over the well-being of the San, by safeguarding it for the San hunter-gatherers who were living there. Following independence, the rights of the San within the reserve were confirmed by Sir Seretse Khama (page 76). At that time, the population of the San within the CKGR was estimated at around 5,000 people.

It was an underlying assumption that the San would continue with their traditional lifestyle. So while hunting has always been banned within the game reserve, as it is in other Botswana reserves, hunting with bows and arrows was tacitly accepted. Similarly, the San's traditional means of sourcing and storing other food and water were in keeping with the sustainable approach to managing a game reserve.

Gradually, however, things started to change, as people from the San communities came into greater contact with modern society. Over several years, small homesteads were built within the reserve, crops were grown, and domestic animals introduced. When miners prospecting for minerals in the south of the reserve drilled a borehole for water, this was made available to the San community. Later, it is alleged that rifles were substituted for bows and arrows, and donkeys or horses introduced for transport. Government estimates suggested that if hunting within the reserve continued to grow, the wildlife would be decimated within decades. (That said, the dramatic loss of wildlife within the reserve over the last 30 years can also be laid at the foot of the cattle fences, which have served to prevent game from following their natural migration routes in search of water during the dry season.)

As early as 1986 a government white paper spelled out that the new policy was for the residents of the CKGR to be relocated outside the reserve, ostensibly so that they could access health, education and other facilities in common with other citizens. From then until 2002, the story was one of the government using carrots and sticks to attain this aim.

By 1996, the San population within the CKGR had been reduced to an estimated 1,482. At this stage, the largest settlement, a small village called Xade in the south of the reserve, had a borehole that supplied water and a few basic buildings. Just six years later, in 2002, only one extended family of 22 people remained – the only San people never to leave the reserve.

The San v the government Supporters of the San's right to remain alleged that from the mid-1990s until 2002, the government and its servants, including the park's game scouts, applied more and more pressure on the local people, forcing them to resettle outside the reserve. (The best known of these is named, with Orwellian flair, New Xade.) They alleged that San individuals were beaten and otherwise coerced into moving, and that even the water supply was stopped for those who elected to stay.

The government denied that they ever used force and insisted that any relocations were voluntary. Their view was that the water borehole – drilled by prospectors – was only ever intended to be temporary and that other services – such as mobile clinics – were withdrawn from Xade for reasons of practicality and cost.

Either way, it seemed likely that the government had, at best, been a little 'over-zealous' in its resettlement policy, and at worst may have committed serious injustices to the people in the reserve.

For me, the most pertinent question was 'Why bother?' The official line that the resettlement policy was to protect the game seemed implausible, given the bad press that this generated throughout the world. There were two obvious theories. One recognised that the government is putting an increasing emphasis on tourism, and was concerned that the presence of the San would detract from the tourist's experience. This really doesn't add up, as tourism could integrate well with the communities if given a chance, and provide a real income for them – and the whole process was started many years before tourism to the CKGR on any scale was viewed as a viable prospect. A second suggested that the government wanted to clear the way for the possibility of exploiting mineral claims in the area: diamond prospectors have long been looking for another find like Orapa beneath the Kalahari. This made little sense too; if an economic diamond pipe were found here – which has since proved to be the case – then no regulations would stand in the way of its exploitation. Implausible though it may seem, I believe that the government started by thinking, rather naively, that removal of the San from the CKGR was the 'best thing for all concerned' and were taken aback by the international campaign against it. Then they found themselves unable to backtrack without both losing face and making an exception for one ethnic group, which they didn't want to do.

In 2002, with the backing of the UK human rights organisation Survival International (w survival-international.org), 243 San people brought a case against the government, asserting their rights under the constitution to return to their ancestral lands. It was a long-running case, but finally, in December 2006, the three judges in the High Court ruled, by a majority of two to one, that the government's action was 'unlawful and unconstitutional', and 'failed to take account of the knowledge and culture' of the San. One judge added, 'In my view the simultaneous stoppage of the supply of food rations and the stoppage of hunting licences is tantamount to condemning the remaining residents of the Central Kalahari Game Reserve to death by starvation.'

The verdict was not the end of the dispute, however; there was no requirement for the government to provide services such as water for those electing to return to the reserve. On his inauguration in 2008, President Khama sought to find a way forward by calling a meeting between the San and the government (although he is quoted by Survival International as saying that the San's way of life was an 'archaic fantasy'). A draft management plan was circulated among cabinet ministers prior to discussion with local residents' groups and relevant non-governmental organisations (NGOs). Yet despite this initiative, little has changed. The government has provided a new borehole for the small San community. Diamond mining within the reserve was paused in 2017 as global demand fell.

Most of those who have 'returned' in fact come and go, spending weeks in the reserve, then leaving in order to collect benefits (known as 'destitute rations' – coupons that can be exchanged for eligible provisions such as oil or flour), or water, or food. They are not allowed to drill further boreholes, to build any permanent structure, to use any form of transport, or to take in any new domestic animals such as goats. Hunting continues to be banned inside the CKGR and, although the San people can apply for special game licences for hunting in the wildlife management areas that abut the reserve, their lawyers argue that they should not have to apply for what is theirs by right.

In a further blow to the San, in August 2013, their British lawyer was barred from the country, and a month later the High Court ruled that, for procedural reasons, they would not permit the San's latest legal attempt to gain free access to their ancestral land to proceed.

What next? For Survival International, the campaign goes on – as it has on and off for many decades. Meanwhile, the San living in the settlements outside the reserve face different challenges. In New Xade, where there is housing, water and government welfare agencies, the children benefit from both primary and secondary schools, and health needs are met by a modern hospital. Nevertheless, many complain that, with no opportunity to practise their traditional skills, the legacy of countless generations is being wiped out. And with no recent farming tradition, self-sufficiency is difficult. Some have found work on cattle farms or game farms and reserves, others in the tourist industry, but unemployment among the San is considerably higher than the national level of 18%. For many, the resulting disenfranchisement has led to situations of extreme poverty, with alcoholism a problem among some San populations.

Hope for the future? There are currently around 71,800 San living in Botswana. Perhaps one of the few rays of hope for these communities is that visitors really are willing to pay to see something of their 'traditional culture'. Hence the springing up of various traditional villages and tourism projects in both Botswana and neighbouring Namibia. These vary from really interesting, genuine insights into the people and their skills, to little more than curiosity shows put on for the benefit of visitors.

I'd probably argue that virtually all are worthwhile for the San – provided that they bring a substantial income into the community involved, and do so without actively harming the people's self-esteem. Meanwhile, from experience of the best,

Cultural sensitivity isn't something that a guidebook can teach you, though reading the section on cultural guidelines (page 152) may help. Being sensitive to the results of your actions and attitudes on others is especially important in this area.

The San are often a humble people, who regard arrogance as a vice. It is normal for them to be self-deprecating among themselves, to make sure that everyone is valued and nobody becomes too proud. So the less you are perceived as a loud, arrogant foreigner, the better.

Very few foreigners can pick up much of the local language without living here for a long time. (Readers may already realise that spellings of the same word can vary greatly.) However, if you want to try to pronounce the words then there are four main clicks to master. In the well-documented Ju/'hoansi language, these are:

/   a dental click, a sucking sound, made by putting the tongue just behind the front teeth.

//   a clucking sound, like that used in English to urge on a horse.

!   a sharp popping sound, like a cork coming out of a bottle, made by pulling the tongue down quickly from the roof of the mouth.

(a soft popping sound, made by putting your tongue just behind the ridge at the back of the front teeth (this is usually the hardest).

I know they can be absolutely fascinating personal interactions for the visitor, as well as acting to reinforce the community's own self-esteem and value in their own skills, while bringing much-needed money into the community.

What's become very, very clear is that making such a tourist–community interaction really successful for both parties needs the permanent commitment of someone on the ground who has been working with the community for a long period – and understands both the community and the tourists. Without this, such projects invariably fail.

The Khoi   The San are often described as hunter-gatherers and the Khoi as pastoralists. The distinction between the two Khoisan peoples is not quite so clear-cut, but it is generally useful. The Khoi, who live in central Botswana and Namibia, have herds of cattle, but continue to source some of their food from hunting and gathering, supplemented by milk products. Because of the intrinsic value of the animals, the Khoi milk their herds but do not kill them for food; stock animals are only killed to mark special occasions.

The ownership of property (stock) by the Khoi has created a more rigid and complex social structure than among the San. Property creates wealth, which can be inherited after the death of the owner, and so laws of inheritance have been developed, as well as laws to protect property. Wealth brings with it the power to control others, thus creating leaders. It also leads to a wealth-based economy that depends on the exchange of goods and work that have an economic value. What must be freely given among the San must be bought and paid for among the Khoi.

Little is known about the religious beliefs of the Khoi, though they believe in a Supreme Being and it is thought that some beliefs are similar to the San and can be traced back to a common source.

BANTU-SPEAKING PEOPLES After a complex history of conflict, a number of tribes of Bantu origin can now be found in Botswana. As discussed on page 90, today the word 'tribe' has colonial connotations, but unfortunately we do not have a suitable alternative. Likewise, definition by ethnic group is not considered politically correct in Botswana; all people are primarily Batswana (the people of Botswana), and only secondarily Bayei, Bakwena, European, etc. (Tribal names are frequently preceded by 'Ba', which means 'the people of...'.) Sometimes you'll also see the singular 'Motswana' or 'Matswana', used to mean a person from Botswana.

Batswana Although the same name applies to all the people of Botswana, the Batswana (or Tswana) are also the largest ethnic group in the country. (As an aside, colonial partitioning led to three-quarters of the Batswana actually living in South Africa.) The name embraces a number of different offshoots. The Batswana speak Setswana, which is the second language of Botswana, English being the official language.

The Bakalanga The Bakalanga are the country's second-largest population group after the Batswana, despite having been divided by colonial boundaries. Today over 80% of them live in Zimbabwe. Those in Botswana live mainly in the area around Francistown, although they are scattered as far afield as Maun, Palapye, Serowe, Mahalapye and Mochudi. Their origins are unclear, though some of them have probably lived in the region of the upper Shashe River for at least a thousand years. For the last 600 years they have been ruled by other peoples, but interestingly their conquerors have always ended by inter-marrying with the Bakalanga and adopting their customs and language.

The Bakalanga are primarily agriculturalists and this is reflected in their religion and culture, but cattle and goats are also kept, usually by the chief on behalf of his tribe. The chief would give cattle to people who had performed services to the tribe, or those who needed them in order to get married or to sacrifice to the ancestors. The primary importance of agriculture is shown by the traditional marital gifts of specially forged iron hoes that were given to the bride's parents to symbolise the continuity of her livelihood.

The Basubiya, the Bayei and the Hambukushu Around AD1600, these three groups of river-dwelling people all lived close together in the region to the south of the Chobe River. Their closeness is reflected in the similarity of their customs. Significantly, their system of inheritance meant that wealth and status were not passed to the first son, but through to the children of the father's eldest sister. So a man inherited the chieftaincy if his mother was the eldest sister of the chief.

The Basubiya According to tradition, after a fight over a lion skin the Bayei were defeated by the Basubiya. They moved away to the Linyanti River, but they still came under the rule of the Basubiya.

Meanwhile, the Hambukushu were driven from their homeland by the expansionist and tribute-seeking chief of the Balozi, whose capital used to be at Katima Mulilo (but is now in western Zambia). To avoid paying the tribute and escape his attentions, the Hambukushu left the Zambezi River and moved nearer to the Chobe and Linyanti rivers, into a region which was already occupied by the Bayei.

In time, the Basubiya grew very powerful and had a large state which stretched westwards from Luchindo on the Chobe River towards the Okavango. Eventually they were defeated by the Balozi and were incorporated into the Lozi empire until its

People and Culture SOCIAL GROUPS OR 'TRIBES'

4

collapse in 1865. According to Campbell, the Basubiya were mainly agriculturalists who also kept some cattle, sheep and goats. They cultivated the floodplains, which they prepared by hoeing in the autumn before the winter floods and planting crops such as millet, sweet reeds and melon when the floods had receded. Today they still live in the northwest and Chobe districts of the country.

The Bayei (and Banoka) In response to the Basubiya invasion, the Bayei moved away from the Chobe River, into the Okavango, and between 1750 and 1800 they firmly established themselves in the area of the Okavango Delta around Lake Ngami. This shallower, southern section of the Delta perfectly suited the Bayei, who lived mainly from fishing. They also kept cattle, but used them only as pack animals. In the Delta they encountered a group of Khoi called the Banoka (otherwise known as the River Bushmen), who had adapted their hunter-gatherer skills to the environment of the Delta.

The two peoples seem to have coexisted peacefully and even swapped skills. For example the Bayei taught the Banoka to fish with nets where before they had only used baskets. The Bayei made nets from the twisted fibres of succulent plants, which they then trawled behind their boats, called *mekoro*. A *mokoro* ('mekoro' is the plural form) is a dugout canoe that is poled from the rear. In return the Banoka taught the Bayei how to dig pits, filled with sharp pointed sticks, in the middle of a game trail, to trap unsuspecting animals on their way to the river.

A prize catch for the Bayei was the hippo, which is notoriously bad-tempered and dangerous and is liable to attack if surprised in the water. Sometimes it was hunted from the mekoro, when the Bayei's method, like that of the old whale hunters, was to harpoon the hippo from the boat. Instantly the animal would take flight, towing the mokoro in its wake. The hunters had to kill the hippo with their spears, before it either broke loose or killed them. This they did by attempting to reach the bank in their boats, tying the rope attached to the harpoon to a tree and waiting for the hippo to tire before approaching it with spears. Another favourite method of hippo hunting was to place a spear weighted with rocks suspended from a tree over a hippo trail. This capitalised on the fact that hippos live in the water during the day, but come out at night to graze, when they tend to keep to the same tracks.

While mekoro today are more likely to be transporting tourists for a spot of hippo watching, and may well be made of fibreglass instead of wood, they are still often poled by a Bayei man.

The Hambukushu Meanwhile the Hambukushu found that settling on the Chobe did not take them far enough from the Balozi tribute seekers, so they moved again and settled in the more northerly, upper reaches of the Okavango Delta. Being agriculturalists as well as hunters and fishermen, they preferred the deeper water there. Unlike the lower regions, this area did not flood when the rains came and so was more suitable for agriculture. They cleared the bush and planted crops along the river, such as millet, sugarcane, pumpkins and root crops.

Like the Bayei, the Hambukushu used mekoro, but instead of poling them standing up, they sat down and used paddles to propel them through the deeper water.

Alec Campbell's *The Guide to Botswana* (page 546) describes how the Hambukushu hunted for elephants:

They took the blade of a spear which had a barb in it and fixed this into a heavy piece of wood. They dug shallow holes on paths used by elephants and then set these spear blades facing upwards. The elephant stood on this, driving the blade deep into the bottom of its foot, after which it couldn't walk. When it was weak, men came with axes and slashed the tendons in its back legs so that it fell down and could be speared.

Today the Hambukushu are most famous for their beautiful hand-woven baskets, which are internationally recognised for their craftsmanship and design.

The wide variety of basket types reflects the numerous purposes for which they were traditionally used, ranging from enormous grain-storage baskets, to tightly woven beer baskets for holding the local brew. Unfortunately, the baskets are now being produced commercially, which enables the makers to earn a reasonable living, but has led to over-exploitation of the natural resources from which the baskets are made. The Hambukushu are also renowned as rain-makers, another skill which they have exploited commercially by selling their services to neighbouring tribes.

The Ovaherero and the Ovambanderu
The Ovaherero (or Herero) and their relatives the Ovambanderu are pastoralists, who keep large herds of sheep, goats, and especially cattle, which have a religious significance for them. According to their oral history tradition they seem to have moved southwest from central Africa, probably to escape the tsetse fly which spreads sleeping sickness and kills cattle and people.

The religious life of the tribe was of great importance. The tribe was divided into religious clans under a priest/chief. He owned the most cattle and he maintained a sacred herd on behalf of the tribe. On his death the priesthood and the care of the sacred herd passed to his son. The Ovaherero practised ancestor worship, and one of the priest's main religious duties was appeasing the dead relatives of the tribe.

As pastoralists, the clans led their herds in search of grazing but each clan had a designated area. Within this area the women built round huts from a framework of branches covered with mud. The huts were built in a circle around corrals for the animals. As well as tending the herds, the men hunted with wooden spears (their only iron came from trading with the Batswana). The women also collected wild food and made *omaere*, a kind of sour milk which was their staple food.

The presence of the Ovaherero people in Botswana dates back to the beginning of the 20th century, when they were living in what is now northern Namibia, but were becoming increasingly unhappy about their loss of land to the German colonists. In January 1904, their leader, Samuel Maherero, ordered a Herero uprising against the colonial forces. Initially the Hereros had success in taking many German farms and smaller outposts, and in severing the railway line between Swakopmund and Windhoek. However, later that year the German General von Trotha led a large German force including heavy artillery against the Hereros. By August the Hereros had been pushed back to their stronghold of Waterberg, with its permanent waterholes. On 11 August, the Germans attacked, and the battle raged all day. Though it was not decisive, the Hereros' spirit was beaten by the superior firepower and they fled east, into the Kalahari and towards Maun. Many perished; the rest settled in what is now northern Botswana. They had lost their cattle and were forced to work as servants to another tribe, the Batawana. However, they soon rebuilt their herds and also learned agriculture from the Batawana, which they used to supplement their traditional diet of soured milk.

Today, although most of the Ovaherero live in Namibia, some are still to be found in Botswana. The women are recognisable because they continue to dress in the clothes they were taught to wear by Victorian Christian missionaries, including long bulky dresses and elaborate headdresses.

4

The Kgalagadi This name (not to be confused with the name of the transfrontier park in Botswana and South Africa) is applied to different people of varied descent who currently live in the Kalahari Desert. There are five major groups who have settled in different areas of the Kalahari. They all have their own tribal names and customs and they speak a variety of languages – the combined form of which is a Sotho language, not a dialect of Setswana.

Of these groups, the Bakgwatheng remain in the east of the Kalahari on the fringes of the desert, which receives sufficient rainfall for their crops of sorghum, melons and beans. They also keep small herds of cattle, sheep and goats, and mine and work iron. As iron ore was not available in the heart of the Kalahari, these factors all restricted them to the desert's fringe.

The Bangologa and the Babolaongwe, on the other hand, are pastoralists with large herds of sheep and goats, and a few cattle. They obtain most of their food from hunting and gathering, so they are not reliant upon agriculture and they trade for iron, so they are able to live a nomadic existence within the desert. The other two groups are the Baphaleng and the Bashaga.

OTHER SOCIAL GROUPS

White Batswana The current white population of Botswana is much lower than that of its surrounding neighbours, and many are not permanent residents. This reflects the unusual history of Botswana: the fact that the country was a 'protectorate' rather than a colony.

Note that these small numbers of white Batswana are very different from the expatriate community (see below), who are often white but simply working in the country on a temporary basis. Many white Batswana will trace their families back to colonial immigrants who came over during British rule, but most are citizens of Botswana rather than, say, British. This is generally an affluent group of people, a number of whom own and run their own businesses.

Expatriates Totally distinct from the permanent population of white citizens of Botswana, there is also a significant 'expat' community in Botswana. These foreigners usually come to Botswana for two or three years to work on short-term contracts, often for multi-national companies in the mining, manufacture and agriculture sectors, or for aid agencies. Most are highly skilled individuals who come to share their knowledge with local colleagues – often teaching skills that are in short supply in Botswana.

There is also a significant number of foreigners working in the safari industry. These are often residents of other southern African nations who come to guide or manage camps for a few years, although as work permits become increasingly difficult to obtain and local training and empowerment initiatives grow, the number of expats in the safari business is slowly starting to fall.

LANGUAGE

Botswana's official languages are English and Setswana: 73% of the population speaks Setswana. Many people are at least bilingual, speaking English and their mother tongue, and possibly Setswana or Afrikaans, depending on what is locally required to get work.

According to data from 'Ethnologue: Languages of the World' (w ethnologue. com), there are at least 26 indigenous and three non-indigenous languages spoken in Botswana. For a scientific overview of these, see page 538.

It's worth reiterating here that all the world's languages have been grouped into around 14 major linguistic families (and 147 total groups in total), of which four are from continental Africa. These include the Khoisan and Niger–Congo language families, the former being among the world's most complex languages. For some hints on mastering its series of clicks, see page 100, and for a list of Botswana's main language groups, see page 538.

RELIGION

Religion in Botswana is characterised by a diversity of beliefs and practices. The country is known for its religious pluralism and tolerance, and people are generally free to practise the religion of their choice. Officially, Botswana is a Christian country, with almost two-thirds of the population claiming membership of a Christian group. These mostly belong to the Anglican, Methodist and United Congregational churches, but among several other denominations there are also Catholics, Lutherans and Zion Christians. (Members of this last are noted for the khaki dress worn when attending services.) Services are usually in Setswana, though the larger churches in the main towns also have English services, and the smaller, rural ones will sometimes use the local languages. Faith healing is often incorporated into services. Other religions, such as Islam, are represented only in the larger towns; their following is small, mainly among expat workers.

As usual in the subcontinent, many of Botswana's religions blend Christian beliefs with aspects of traditional beliefs. In times of crisis or ill health, most people are as likely to seek out a traditional healer as they are to visit a priest or a hospital. More often still, they will pursue both a traditional and a more Western approach at the same time. (From a medical standpoint, the best practices of traditional healers are increasingly lauded throughout southern Africa as holistic approaches, which can complement Western medicine.)

People's traditional beliefs depend largely on ancestry, differing widely from tribe to tribe, but generally incorporating a great respect for ancestors, a belief in their continued existence in the spirit world, and a certainty that their spirits affect everyone's day-to-day lives. Rituals and ceremonies are frequently conducted to honour and communicate with these ancestors and play an important role in the country's cultural calendar.

EDUCATION

The education system in Botswana is structured into levels, including pre-primary, primary, secondary and tertiary. The government has made significant investments in education to improve access and quality, allocating 25% (P15.04 billion) of government ministerial spending to education and skills development in 2023/24. Challenges, such as access to education in rural areas, teacher shortages and disparities in educational outcomes, still exist, but efforts are being made to tackle these problems.

Overall, the education system, which is taught in English from Grade 5 (age 10), follows a ten-year course focusing on both academic and practical skills. Children start in primary school at the age of six, moving on after Standard 7 and a further three years at junior secondary school, before sitting exams at age 15 to determine whether or not they may continue into senior secondary education, to study for the Botswana General Certificate of Education. Success in this opens up the option of attending a technical college or the University of Botswana.

Primary education is compulsory for all children and is free up to the age of 13, after which 95% of the cost is funded by the government. Primary school attendance is around 89/90% for boys/girls, falling at secondary level to around 85/82%. Adult literacy rates are 96/99% for men/women, comparable with the average rate for other upper middle-income countries.

The high levels of participation in education by girls is unusual in Africa, where sons are often favoured by their parents – but given women's pivotal role in bringing up children and running households in this traditional society, and their increasing role within the workforce, it bodes extremely well for Botswana's future.

Botswana has made efforts to improve access to education for students with disabilities, special educational needs and those considered disadvantaged or vulnerable. Under the country's Inclusive Education Policy, free diagnostic assessments and special education programmes and schools are available to support the educational needs of these students.

CULTURE

Botswana's diverse ethnic mix results in an equally diverse cultural heritage, although the importance of music and dance runs like a common thread throughout its people. Visitors to the country will often be treated to uplifting displays of traditional dancing and singing that will reflect in part the area in which they're based, and in part the traditions of those taking part. (For notes on San culture, see page 94.)

Bessie Head's book, *Serowe: Village of the Rain Wind* (page 544), offers an invaluable and very readable introduction to Batswana culture, Bamangwato style. (The Bamangwato tribe rose to ascendancy over the other tribes, following the Difaqane Wars. This was due partly to their prime location for trading contacts and partly to visionary leadership.)

The book gives a wonderful insight into an African village and the lives, knowledge and skills of the inhabitants. Writing in 1981, Head describes Serowe as a typical traditional village. Most people had three homes: one in the village, one at the lands where they ploughed, and one at the cattle post where they kept their cattle. The homes were all round, thatched mud huts and people moved from home to home all the time.

We learn how the homes were constructed – that the walls of the mud huts were built and externally decorated by the women, but were thatched by the men. The weaving of grass baskets was a woman's occupation, but tanning hide to make leather Batswana mats and blankets was a man's profession.

MUSIC Botswana's musical traditions are as varied as its culture. In traditional Batswana culture, the teaching of music and dance was incorporated into the initiation rites at puberty, and dancing, accompanied by the beat of drums, was once used to mark special occasions such as hunting or the annual harvest. Today, choral singing is particularly popular, with village choirs often coming together to celebrate national holidays – and guests at the safari lodges may well be regaled by staff with spontaneous and exceptionally harmonious singing.

With the policy of integration implemented at independence in the mid-1960s came a decline in individual cultural traditions. Since then, however, there has been a resurgence of interest. Traditional songs and dancing are widely taught in schools, and during the 1980s there was a revival of instruments such as the *segaba*, a simple violin used to accompany folk singing. Simpler still are the thumb pianos or *setinkane*, like miniature xylophones made with sheets of scrap metal on a small wooden base, and once widely played.

Recently, there has been an explosion of musical influence from overseas, resulting in a more modern culture of hip-hop artists and performers of *kwasa-kwasa* – a suggestive dance form akin to the rumba.

ARTS AND CRAFTS While the ancient rock art of the UNESCO World Heritage Site at Tsodilo Hills has gained international recognition, modern visual arts are much harder to find, at least outside of Gaborone, which is home to the National Museum and Art Gallery.

Visitors, however, should have no problem in finding examples of local crafts, especially beautiful basketry. The tradition stems from items woven for practical purposes such as storing or winnowing grain. Most of these are produced by women from the Bayei and Hambukushu groups in northwest Botswana, where the *mokolwane* palm – source of the fibres for basket weaving – is widely grown. Many are plain, but others have intricate patterns woven into their design. Now increasingly popular as souvenirs, these baskets can be deceptively complex in construction and time-consuming to craft, something that is rightly reflected in their costs.

Clay pots also have their place in traditional culture, being used both for storing water and for brewing beer, as well as for cooking. In rural villages, such pots were moulded from natural clays, then baked in the sun to dry, but today most potteries use kilns to fire their work. The pottery often features unique designs and symbols that carry cultural and spiritual significance, so be sure to ask the maker about these important details.

Artisans specialising in vibrant beadwork, woodcarving and leatherwork are also found throughout the country, with items for sale readily available in many safari camp shops and around the tourist centres of Maun and Kasane.

TRADITIONAL CULTURE AND CHANGE As a deeply committed Christian convert, Khama, the 19th-century leader of the Bamangwato (page 75), began to make changes to the traditional way of life. He reformed the *bogadi* tradition, under which a woman's children belonged to her husband, even if they were born after his death. Khama also laid down laws and regulations for his people to live by, including banning the consumption of alcohol.

One of his most significant changes was the abolition of the initiation ceremonies for men and women. One elderly man described the men's initiation ceremony or *bogwera*:

> Not only was the foreskin cut and the youths put through endurance tests, but one of us had to remain behind. He was killed in a painful way, in the secrecy of the bush. When we came home, it was made out that the youth had died because he could not stand up to the tests. Everyone knew the truth but it was treated as a deep secret. That was why Khama abolished bogwera.

However, the ritual was still important to mark the passing of boyhood into manhood, so Khama preserved the tradition of 'age regiments'. All young men had their coming of age marked by a gathering with prayers and lectures. Those who came of age at the same time formed an age regiment. From Khama's time on, the age regiments began to volunteer to work on community projects such as building schools or churches and many things were accomplished.

It was also largely due to the efforts of Khama that Botswana became a British Protectorate, known as the British Bechuanaland Protectorate. This probably saved the country from becoming another South Africa or Rhodesia (Zimbabwe) and resulted in Botswana's peaceful independence in 1966. When the Protectorate was finally granted, Khama expressed his gratitude and laid down the following principles of government, in a document which related primarily to the Bamangwato, but was later applied to the whole country:

> I am not baffled in the government of my town, or in deciding cases among my own people according to custom. I have to say that there are certain laws of my country which the Queen of England finds in operation, and which are advantageous to my people, and I wish these laws should be established and not taken away by the Government of England. I refer to our law concerning intoxicating drinks, that they should not enter the country of the Bamangwato, whether among black people or white people. I refer further to our law which declares that the lands of the Bamangwato are not saleable. I say this law is also good; let it be upheld and continue to be law among black people and white people.

The system of traditional law to which Khama referred in this document was well established. It centred upon the chief, whose position of prestige and power carried with it the obligation that the good of the tribe must be placed above personal desire. The chief held property and land on behalf of the tribe and had always to be available to his people to settle disputes and business affairs.

There was also a tribal court, known as a kgotla, to help him make decisions. This consisted of the headmen of the wards into which the village was divided, and of senior tribesmen. Disputes which could not be settled within the ward were brought to the kgotla. There was an obligation for people to be open in all their dealings with each other and to act in the best interests of the community.

5

Planning and Preparation

WHEN TO VISIT AND HIGHLIGHTS

There simply isn't one 'best time' to visit Botswana. Most tourists visit during the dry season, from around May to the end of October. Within that season, the period from mid-July to mid-October is definitely the busiest – although Botswana's small camps and vast private reserves ensure that it never feels busy, even when everywhere is full. In fact, the country's capacity for tourism remains tiny compared with that of South Africa, Kenya or Tanzania.

Most of those visiting outside of this season are safari cognoscenti, who visit early or late in the season – May to July or late October to November – when the camps are quieter. A much smaller number of visitors come during the rains, commonly referred to as the 'green season', between December and March. At this time, camps will frequently be quiet for days, which often means those in camp will receive an incredibly personal experience, with private game-drive vehicles and greater flexibility about bringing young children on safari. This is also the time of year when travellers can expect significant cost reductions for their trips.

Much of the blame for this 'glut or famine' of visitors lies with overseas tour operators. Many who advertise trips to Africa simply do not know Botswana well enough to plan safaris that work during the rainy season. It's much easier for them to make blanket generalisations, telling enquirers that it's 'not interesting' or that 'you won't see any game' if you visit in the wet season. Neither statement is true, as long as you choose your destinations carefully.

While the rains are not the ideal time for everybody's trip, they do make for a fascinating experience and should not be dismissed without serious thought.

What follows is some guidance on various issues to help you decide when the best time for your visit would be. It's perhaps worth mentioning also that one of the biggest reasons for coming to the Okavango – and you may only realise this once you've visited – is not the wildlife or the birds. It's simply the ambience that surrounds floating over lily-covered lagoons with the sun on your back and a gentle breeze in your hair. And this is certainly best when the skies are fairly clear of clouds – from April to November.

WEATHER For a detailed description of the weather that can be expected, see page 12, and note that Botswana's rainy season normally occurs between December and March, with January and February usually being the wettest months. Like everywhere, the weather in Botswana is less predictable than it once was, with greater extremes of temperature and rainfall.

Dry season April can be something of a transition month, with May to November being the easiest time to travel, as you are unlikely to meet rain and can expect clear blue skies. This is ideal for your first trip to Africa, or if seeing lots of big game is top of your wish-list.

Within this, you'll find June–August the coolest, when night temperatures in the Kalahari can drop below freezing. Then from September onwards the heat gradually builds up. The interior areas of the Kalahari, including central Chobe and the great salt pans, get very hot towards the end of October. Occasions when it reaches over 40°C in the shade have earned this the tag of 'suicide month'.

Everywhere November is a variable month. Some days will be hot. Some will be cooler, as gathering clouds shield the country from the sun. Sometimes these bring welcome showers; sometimes they simply build, and with them come tension and humidity.

Wet season Known in safari circles as the green season, from December to March, or sometimes April, the scenario is totally different, although the days can still vary enormously from one to the next. Even within a day, skies can change from sunny to cloudy within minutes and then back again. Downpours are usually heavy and short – and usually late in the afternoon – although there are often a few days when the sky remains grey and overcast. You will need a good waterproof, but I've always felt that the rains are seldom long enough to stop you doing anything.

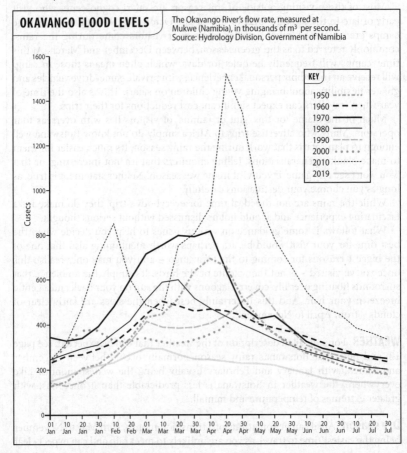

OKAVANGO FLOOD LEVELS The Okavango River's flow rate, measured at Mukwe (Namibia), in thousands of m³ per second. Source: Hydrology Division, Government of Namibia

KEY
1950
1960
1970
1980
1990
2000
2010
2019

Cusecs

THE OKAVANGO'S ANNUAL FLOOD

This very complex variable is really a minor point for most visitors – who will find the Okavango Delta enchanting whenever they visit. However, the flooding levels will have some influence on certain activities, and may even influence your choice of where you want to visit in the Delta.

The water levels at any point in the Okavango Delta depend mainly on three variables: first, the local rainfall in your location; second, the height of the seasonal flood of the Okavango; and third, your location within the Delta – the further north you are in the Okavango, the more water you're likely to have. The local summer rains and the arrival of the seasonal floods are generally out of sync by around two to six months, depending on exactly where you are within the Delta. This represents the time taken for the peak of the rains in the Okavango River's main catchment area – the Angolan highlands – to make it down the Okavango River and into the various areas of the Delta.

These annual floods have for years been monitored very carefully at Mukwe (Namibia), close to where the river enters Botswana – see the graph opposite. From this we know that the peak of the flood at this spot generally occurs between mid-March and mid-May – just after the local summer rains in the region of the Delta have come to an end. Given the tiny gradient and very slow flow rate, this surge of water from Angola can take up to six months to work its way from the Panhandle to the far extremities of the Delta's waterways.

Hence expect the highest water levels in most areas of the Delta to occur after the rains – from about May to August. After that, levels will generally fall until around February, when the local rains start to slowly raise water levels prior to the main flood.

Having said this, on one February visit, the rain didn't ever seem to end, and the skies remained grey for days – so I should perhaps recant this. In fact, I take the view that Africa's weather is just becoming harder to predict, and I was unlucky!

TRAVELLING CONDITIONS Travelling around Botswana in the dry season often has its challenges, but in some places in the wet season it's a totally different game. Then the areas of pure sand are still fine to drive on, and even a bit firmer than they are when it's hot and dry.

Driving yourself In some areas where the soil has a high clay content, the bush tracks become quagmires – the track from Rakops to the Central Kalahari Game Reserve's Matswere Gate near Kuke Corner is a fine example, as are most of the Makgadikgadi Pans. Some tracks, especially those in the Delta–Linyanti region, like the old route between Xakanaxa and North Gate, become submerged completely. Thus travel in Botswana during the wet season requires careful research, and scrupulous attention to your emergency precautions. If you're heading for somewhere remote in the wet season, then travelling with two or more vehicles is wise.

Flying around In contrast, the weather is seldom a problem if you're flying into one of Botswana's safari camps. All are used to the vagaries of the weather and the water levels, although they may affect your activities. Similarly, if you're heading out on a budget mokoro trip or safari, it shouldn't affect your trip significantly – though your vehicle may need the occasional push!

Ten years ago, taking children on safari in Botswana might have been considered unusual, but things are changing, and the country's lodges and camps haven't been slow to pick up on the trend.

The idea of taking a child on safari might at first seem obvious. You'll be out in a wilderness environment, with plenty of animals to watch, and seemingly non-stop entertainment. But that, of course, is part of the problem. The 'entertainment' cannot be guaranteed, so during a typical 3-hour game drive, there's often time when things that might fascinate you – colourful birds, the construction of a termite mound, last night's hyena tracks, even a(nother) herd of impala – will be of little interest to a child. And when big game is spotted, instead of being able to leap up and down with excitement, your child is expected to be absolutely quiet and still. Then there's the often unspoken concern of a sensitive child witnessing a kill.

Add to this the rather exclusive make-up of many safari camps, the safety issues within camp (dangerous wildlife, high walkways and unguarded pools being just a few), and the lack of opportunity for letting off steam, and the considerations mount up.

So how can it work? Although many lodges still maintain a very adult atmosphere, designating a high minimum age for children, several offer some form of 'family' accommodation. Sometimes that's simply a room with an extra bed or two, rather than anything particularly child-friendly; at others, it's a suite of rooms, either sharing a bathroom or with each of them en suite, and occasionally with their own lounge area. Several lodges, such as the Shinde Enclave (page 348), Linyanti Ebony (page 292) and the Selinda Explorers (page 296) camps, have a group of tents or chalets that are slightly separate from the main camp, so work particularly well for families. Some places, like Planet Baobab (page 484), are more laid-back, and more specifically, a handful of places – including Gomoti Plains (page 391), Khwai Lediba (page XX) and all of the Dhow suites at the Great Plains camps (page 214) – have built entirely separate houses that are exceptionally well suited to families, with space to play, and your own chef so that you can eat at times that suit your family rather than other guests. Mealtimes in many lodges can be a trial for children, though some will prepare meals early, so that you can dine with other guests while a member of staff (albeit not a qualified childminder) babysits for you. Another option is private family dining, at a time to suit you.

Even when lodges do accept families, many insist that those with children under, say, eight years old reserve a private vehicle and guide. If this at first seems draconian, consider too that this is for the benefit of the children, as well as for

Although there are fewer visitors during this period, Botswana's flight schedules don't change much, and only a few of its camps will close entirely. Many will close during this period for a few weeks of planned maintenance or any building work that's needed. Those that remain open are often very quiet – so if you've been to Africa before in the dry season, then this is a fascinating time to visit, like being introduced to a different side of an old friend.

VEGETATION During the wet season, the foliage runs wild. The Kalahari springs into life as the bush turns many shades of green. Open clay pans become small pools in the bush and it's a time of renewal, when a gentler light dapples Botswana's bush. When the rains end, the leaves in the Kalahari gradually dry and many

other guests. With your own guide, you select where you stop and spend time, and if your children want to ask questions, that's fine. Some camps, like Kwando (page 215), African Bush Camps (page 214) and Chitabe Lediba (page 387), can organise a specialist guide who will travel with your family and will even keep children occupied during siesta time – which can otherwise be particularly challenging. You'll need to book a private vehicle (from US$600–840 per day for a family of four), and a specialist guide will cost around a further US$310 per day, but your safari experience will be considerably enhanced.

Several camps accept quite young children but insist on a minimum age, for safety reasons, before a child can go on a mokoro trip or bush walk. The smaller camps can often be more flexible here, with guides who will assess the maturity of each child rather than applying a one-size-fits-all age limit. Other camps, such as those owned by Wilderness Safaris (page 216), tend to apply the 'rules' more strictly.

Putting children at the heart of safaris, Ker & Downey have a Young Explorers safari for children of seven or older. Based at Shinde Enclave (page 348) or Footsteps (page 349), a specially trained guide will be allocated to your family, focusing on the children both on safari and back in camp – though that doesn't include childminding. They can also accompany you to other Ker & Downey camps, including Okuti, thus broadening the experience for all. Depending on the ages of the children, activities might include making bows and arrows, fishing, bushcraft and quizzes – but the odd game of football or frisbee could also be thrown in. The key here is entertainment – bored children are the bane of everyone's life on safari, so be aware that if you opt for a conventional trip, you will need to take plenty to occupy your offspring when in camp.

A couple of other options can widen the choice. The first is to base yourself in a family-friendly hotel in Kasane, where you'll be rewarded with plenty of wildlife on game drives and boat trips into Chobe National Park without feeling cooped up the rest of the time. The other is to opt for a mobile safari, where children are less likely to feel restrained, and will probably relish the camping element. Four that spring to mind in Maun are Harkness Safaris and Barclay Stenner Safaris, both of whom are very child-friendly; Endeavour Safaris, which has no age restrictions; and Letaka Safaris, who have a special two-bedroom family tent with a lockable entrance, so you and your children will be secure under one roof – something that is particularly reassuring with younger age groups. Then, with your children both happy and safe, you can get on with enjoying a family safari.

eventually drop. More greys and browns appear, and good shade becomes harder to find. Eventually, by late September and October, most plants look dry and parched, coloured from straw yellow to shrivelled brown.

However, note that large areas of the Okavango have their own permanent water supply – regulated more by the annual floods than the rainfall – and so don't follow this pattern so clearly (page 111).

WILDLIFE From the point of view of most herbivores, the wet season is much more pleasant than the dry season. During the wet season, most animals live in enormous salad bowls, with convenient pools of water nearby. It's a good time to have their young and eat themselves into good condition.

Visitors who have been to Africa before will often find something special about being able to see all the animals when they aren't struggling with thirst and a lack of vegetation. It gives a sense of luxuriance and plenty, which isn't there in the dry season.

Migration patterns Before people started to have a big impact on Botswana's landscape (arguably, only in the last 150 years or so), many of the animals used to follow regular seasonal migration patterns, often over very large distances. It was the same throughout Africa originally; many species, especially the herding species of plains game, would move around to where the best food sources were to be found.

Despite the changes wreaked by man since then, the remnants of these migrations still happen. Understanding them will help you to work out what the best times are to visit the various parks.

The finer details of each area are covered under sections entitled 'When to visit', which are spread throughout the book. In very general terms they are:

Chobe Areas with riverfront are at their best during July–October. Traditionally, the Savuti Marsh area is totally different, with some good game all year, but probably at its best around March–May and (if the rains have arrived) November – when herds of zebra and plains game are passing through.

Kwando/Linyanti Follows the same basic pattern as Chobe's riverfronts – so it is best in the late dry season, when it's the only source of water for kilometres around.

Okavango/Moremi The central and northern areas of the Delta have permanent water all year, and equally permanent populations of animals. Thus many game species stay here all year, and densities of animals (excluding elephant and buffalo) don't change that much. However, in the dry season the permanent populations of game found on the edges of the Delta are swelled by an influx of animals from the parched Kalahari. Thus, the game densities on the accessible edges of the Delta often rise significantly as the dry season progresses.

Nxai Pan Can be erratic, but always used to be at its best when wet, from December to March – though often still very good into May and June. However, the artificial pumping of a waterhole a couple of kilometres north of the gate has changed this pattern. During the rest of the year, you'll find plains game staying here in numbers, often accompanied by a few lion.

Makgadikgadi Pans The pans themselves can be superb when wet, December to April; large herds of zebra and other plains grazers appear. On their western border, the Boteti River (or its channel) follows the opposite pattern, attracting game at the end of the dry season, around August to early November.

Central Kalahari Game congregates in the huge grassy valleys here, most famously in Deception Valley, when the vegetation is lush during and shortly after the rains, from about December to May.

Seasonal highlights If wildlife viewing is your overriding priority, or this is one of your first trips to Africa, then you'll be better visiting during the dry season. At this time, the animals are much easier to spot, as no thick vegetation obscures the view, and they are forced to congregate at well-known water points, like rivers, where they can be observed.

However, more experienced African travellers are missing out if they never travel during the rains – as it's completely different and can be superb. A few specific highlights of Botswana's animal calendar would include:

February–April	Most of the herbivores are in their best condition, having fed well on the lush vegetation. It's a perfect time to catch huge concentrations of springbok and oryx on the short grass plains of the Central Kalahari's fossil river valleys.
May–June	Probably my favourite time to be in Botswana (and most of southern Africa!). It's a great time to visit Savuti Marsh, and in the Okavango the floodwater moves down the Delta.
July–August	Leopard are generally easier to see, as they come out more during the twilight hours. Further into the year, they often wait until it is cool, only appearing later in the evening.
September–October	Elephant and buffalo tend to amalgamate into larger, more spectacular herds. (They splinter again just before the rains.) Lion sights become more frequent, as they spend more time near the limited remaining water sources.
November	Can be a great month as often the rains haven't arrived, leaving amazing game densities in the riverfront areas (yet visitors are thin on the ground and prices are low). However, too many cloudless days can mean high midday temperatures.
December–January	Crocodiles are nesting, and so found on or near exposed sandbanks. Various baby animals start to appear in November, followed by most of the mammals that calve sometime during the rainy season.

BIRDLIFE The birdlife in Botswana is certainly best when the foliage is most dense, and the insects are thriving, ie: in the wet season. Then many resident birds are nesting and in their bright, breeding plumage. This coincides to a large extent with the 'summer' period, from around October to March, when the Palaearctic migrants from the northern hemisphere are seen.

To give you an idea of the richness of the avifauna here, in the Okavango–Linyanti–Chobe areas during the rainy season it isn't difficult for competent ornithologists to record 100 different species between dawn and midday. Really energetic birdwatchers can notch up as many as 200 different species in a 24-hour period in somewhere as rich as the northern Chobe riverfront area. A real enthusiast might count about 320 species (out of the 550 or so which occur) during a two-week trip here.

Seasonal highlights The highlights of Botswana's birding calendar include:

February–April	Red bishop birds, yellow-billed storks and the spectacular paradise whydahs have their breeding plumage on display. If the rains have been good then the flamingos may be nesting on Sua Pan; ostriches gather in numbers on the pans of the Central Kalahari.

115

March–July	Wattled cranes and other opportunists follow the floods in the Okavango, snapping up drowning insects and reptiles.
April–June	Juvenile birds of many species abound as this season's young are fledged and leave their nests.
August–October	'Fishing parties' of herons, egrets and storks will arrive at pools as they dry up, to feed on the stranded fish.
September–November	Nesting carmine bee-eaters colonise soft vertical riverbanks, skimmers nest on exposed sandbanks, and large breeding colonies of storks and herons gather at places like the Kanana heronry and Gcodikwe Lagoon. Migrant waders appear beside the edge of most pans and lagoons.
November–April	Most of the weavers are in breeding plumage.

PHOTOGRAPHY I find the light clearest and most spectacular on bright days during the rainy season. Then the rains have washed the dust from the air, and the bright sunlight can contrast wonderfully with dark storm clouds. The vegetation's also greener and brighter, and the animals and birds often in better condition. However, it will rain occasionally when you're trying to take shots, and the long periods of flat, grey light through clouds can be very disappointing; you'll get few good shots then. Sometimes it can seem as if you're waiting for the gods to grant you just a few minutes of stunning light, between the clouds.

A much more practical time to visit is just after the rains, around April to June, when many of the advantages remain but you are less likely to be interrupted by a shower. (This is one of my reasons for being a fan of May as a great time to travel!)

The dry season's light is reliably good, if not quite as inspirational as that found during the rains. You are unlikely to encounter any clouds, and will get better sightings of game to photograph. Do try to shoot in the first and last few hours of the day, when the sun is low in the sky. During the rest of the day use a filter (perhaps a polariser) to guard against the sheer strength of the light leaving you with a memory card full of washed-out shots.

During the hotter months around October, you're also likely to encounter more bush fires than normal, which can leave a thin pall of smoke covering a large area. (This can especially be a problem near the border area with Namibia, when smoke from the many manmade fires there can drift across.)

WALKING SAFARIS For safe and interesting walking, you need the foliage to be low so that you can see through the surrounding bush as easily as possible. This means that the dry season is certainly the best time for walking – and even then I'd counsel you to choose where you visit very, very carefully as standards of walking guides can be highly variable. (See my comments on the safety of walking safaris on page 178.)

I wouldn't advise anyone looking for a serious walking trip to visit Botswana in the wet season. Walking through shoulder-high grass is nerve-racking with the best of walking guides, and only two or three operations in Botswana are really likely to have anything like that calibre of guide. The best months for walking are May to October, though away from the moderating influence of the Okavango's waters, October can be very hot for longer walks.

COSTS OF TRIPS Aside from the airfares to get here, which vary in their own way (page 131), some safari operators also lower their rates when business is quieter.

Generally June to October is the peak season when prices are highest; December to March is the green season when prices are lowest, and the rest of the year falls somewhere in between.

PUBLIC HOLIDAYS

1–2 January	New Year
March/April	Good Friday, Holy Saturday and
	Easter Monday
1 May	Labour Day
9 May	Ascension Day
1 July	Sir Seretse Khama Day
3rd Monday and Tuesday in July	President's Day
30 September	Independence Day
1st Monday in October	Botswana Day holiday
25 December	Christmas Day
26 December	Boxing Day

ORGANISING AND BOOKING YOUR TRIP

How you organise your holiday depends on what kind of a trip you're taking. Generally the more expensive the trip, the more organisation it needs.

ORGANISING A FLY-IN TRIP Most tourists who come to Botswana for a few weeks' safari fly between a series of remote safari camps; this is by far the easiest and most popular way to visit the country. Combinations of the Okavango Delta, and the Kwando–Linyanti and Chobe areas are most common, with relatively few people venturing further south or west into the Kalahari.

When to book? These trips are not difficult to arrange for a knowledgeable tour operator. If you have a favourite camp or operation, or will be running to a tight schedule, then book as far ahead as you can. Eight to ten months in advance is perfect. Bear in mind that most camps are small, and thus easily filled. They organise their logistics with military precision and so finding space at specific camps at short notice, especially in the busier months, can be tricky.

Unless you're lucky, or book very early, expect one or two of your chosen camps to be full. Usually there will be good alternatives available. That said, it's fairly rare for visitors to have a bad time in any of the upmarket camps in Botswana, as standards are generally high – so don't be put off just because your first choice isn't immediately available.

The exception to this is usually the rainy season – when camps often close for maintenance for a few weeks; those that do stay open, however, are seldom full.

How much? Safaris in Botswana are not cheap. The standards for an average fly-in safari camp are high, but so are the prices. For the most part, expect to pay around US$1,500–3,200 per person sharing per night in the high season, between June and October, but note that the very top camps will cost substantially more: US$4,000+ per person. This will include all meals, most drinks, laundry, activities and local drinks. Light aircraft transfers from Maun to the camps range from around US$200 to US$260 per person one-way.

All of the camps lower their rates outside the high season, often into multiple date bands. Generally, April to early June and November are considered 'shoulder seasons', and December to March typically sees lower green season prices: expect rates to drop to around US$800–2,000 per person sharing per night – which again includes everything except internal (and international) flights. Camps in the Kalahari will tend to have less variable rates than those in the Delta.

If you stay for a longer spell with some camps (and 'longer' can mean anything from three to seven nights), or groups of camps, then these rates will drop slightly; if you fly between camps every day or two, only spending one or two nights at each camp (not recommended) then they'll rise.

These trips are expensive, so you should expect a good level of service and knowledge from the operator who is arranging it for you. If you don't get it, go elsewhere.

How to book?

It's best to arrange everything at the same time, using a reliable, independent tour operator. Many operators sell trips to Botswana, but few know the country and the camps well. Insist on dealing directly with someone who does. Botswana's areas, camps and lodges do change, so up-to-date local knowledge is vital in putting together a trip that runs smoothly and suits you.

Most camps in Botswana are not standalone businesses, but are instead part of safari groups. These range from very small, three-camp operations to international corporations. It is, of course, possible to book directly with most of these companies, but it's worth bearing a few things in mind. Perhaps most importantly, these safari companies are primarily interested in selling space at their own camps and lodges – regardless of whether or not these are the best camps for you. They will not be interested in putting together itineraries in partnership with competitors' camps, even if this is your preference, so your travel options narrow considerably.

For the majority of travellers, it's wise to seek out an independent operator to help plan their perfect safari. Indeed, most of the larger groups of camps and lodges work largely with the overseas travel trade. And, as if to reinforce the point, some of these groups direct travellers to specialist travel agents and tour operators around the globe for their travel planning and booking.

The best way of booking a fly-in safari in Botswana is usually by arranging it many months in advance through a knowledgeable tour operator experienced in the kind of travel that interests you (page 119).

Which tour operator?

Many will include only camps from one local operator – perhaps using only Wilderness Safaris, or only &Beyond camps, or visiting nothing but Desert & Delta places. This is a really bad sign, as no one operator in Botswana has a monopoly of the best camps.

However, start asking detailed questions about the alternatives and you'll rapidly sort the best from the rest. Don't let anyone convince you that there are only half-a-dozen decent safari camps in Botswana; that's rubbish. If the person you're talking to hasn't been to the camps that you are interested in – or doesn't offer a genuinely wide choice to suit you – then find someone who does.

Here I must, as the author, admit a personal interest in the tour-operating business. I organise and personally run the UK operators Expert Africa (page 119). We are currently one of the leading tour operators to Botswana from around the world – based on my team's detailed personal knowledge of the country. We organise trips for travellers to Africa from all over the world, especially the UK and America. Our website has detailed original maps, extensive reviews from many of our travellers, and fully costed trips that include the widest choice of Botswana lodges and camps.

The best Botswana operators are specialists: their websites will have cliché-free, original text, and their staff will be able to talk to you from first-hand experience about the camps that interest you. You'll always get the best advice (and the best chance of problem-free trips) from people who have been to the places that you're thinking of going to personally. Do not settle for secondhand information; there are some excellent specialists available.

Perhaps because of the UK's historical links with Botswana, there seems to be more competition among UK tour operators than elsewhere. As a result, they are experienced in handling safari enquiries from around the world. They also have a reputation for being cheaper than US operators for the same trips – and certainly cheaper than similar trips booked directly with camps.

Whoever you ultimately book through, make sure first that the company has in place a 'bond' to protect your money in case they fail. In the UK, the most usual form of this is the ATOL licence; if a company doesn't have one of these, then question them very carefully indeed. All the following companies have good track records, and currently have ATOL bonds.

Reliable, international operators that specialise in Botswana, Africa and wildlife tours are detailed here. In addition, many global travel operators include trips to Botswana, including Abercrombie & Kent, Audley Travel, The Ultimate Travel Company and Scott Dunn. For companies specialising in self-drive tours, see page 125. Local tour operators can be found in individual chapters.

International tour operators

UK

Aardvark Safaris ☎ 01980 849160; e mail@ aardvarksafaris.com; w aardvarksafaris.com. Small upmarket operator with good knowledge of Botswana.

Botswana Specialists ☎ 01473 599083; e info@ botswanaspecialists.co.uk; w botswanaspecialists. co.uk. Tribes Travel offer a selection of trips worldwide based on strong fair-trade principles; this brand is an alternative way to book their Botswana trips.

Expert Africa ☎ 020 3405 6666; e info@expertafrica.com; w expertafrica.com. Award-winning operator with a team of enthusiastic Africa experts run by Chris McIntyre – one of this book's authors. I believe we have the best range of tailor-made fly-in & mobile-safari trips to Botswana!

The Explorations Company ☎ 01367 850566; e info@africanexplorations.com; w explorationscompany.com. Old-school operator, formerly known as African Explorations, now working worldwide.

Hartley's Safaris ☎ 01673 861600; e info@ hartleysgroup.com; w hartleys-safaris.co.uk. Established tailor-made specialists to East/ southern Africa & Indian Ocean islands, with close historical connections to Botswana.

Rainbow Tours ☎ 020 8131 9304; e info@ rainbowtours.co.uk; w rainbowtours.co.uk. Part of the Western & Oriental Group, with a varied Botswana programme.

Safari Consultants ☎ 01787 888590; e info@ safari-consultants.com; w safari-consultants.com. Very old-school tailor-made specialists to East/ southern Africa & Indian Ocean, with a competent Botswana programme.

Steppes Africa ☎ 01285 402139; e enquiry@ steppestravel.com; w steppestravel.com. Tailor-made specialist covering destinations including central, eastern & southern Africa.

Wildlife Worldwide ☎ 01962 302086; e reservations@wildlifeworldwide.com; w wildlifeworldwide.com. Worldwide operator which offers tailor-made & small-group wildlife holidays to all corners of the globe.

North America

The Africa Adventure Company 2601 E Oakland Park Bd, Suite 600, Fort Lauderdale, FL 33306; ☎ 0800 882 9453; e safari@ africanadventure.com; w africanadventure.com

Natural Habitat Adventures Bldg F, 833 W South Boulder Rd, Louisville, CO 80027; ☎ 0800 543 8917; w nathab.com

Overseas Adventure Travel 1 Mifflin Pl, Suite 400, Cambridge, MA 02138; 0800 955 1925; w oattravel.com. Members-only organisation who run group trips for 10–16 participants aged over 50.

Piper & Heath Travel e inquiry@piperandheath .com; w piperandheath.com. Small specialist operator led by former guide Chris Liebenberg.

Australasia

Bench Africa +61 2 9290 2877; e info@ benchafrica.com.au; w benchafrica.com. Owned by a Kenyan ground operator, this long-established, family-run company specialises in pan-African travel.

The Classic Safari Company +61 2 9327 0666; e info@classicsafaricompany.com.au; w classicsafaricompany.com.au. Tailor-made operator specialising in Africa & covering all of Botswana's safari areas.

Europe

Botswana Specialist +31 6 1366 3006; e info@botswanaspecialist.nl;

w botswanaspecialist.nl. Co-founded by a former Makgadikgadi guide, this small, new operator, with a Dutch- & English-language website, focuses on Botswana trips.

Makila Voyages +33 1 4296 8000; w makila. fr. Paris-based, tailor-made operator covering southern & East Africa.

South Africa

Go2Africa +27 21 481 4900; e contact@ go2africa.com; w go2africa.com. Large, web-based operator based in Cape Town.

Jenman African Safaris +27 21 683 7826; e info@jenmansafaris.com; w jenmansafaris.com. Family-run company with a wide range of options.

New African Safaris m +27 73 145 0932; e info@newafricansafaris.com; w newafricansafaris. com. Tailor-made safari and beach holidays, across southern and East Africa, are created by owner Pierre Burden from its Cape Town base.

Pulse Africa +27 11 325 2290; e info@ pulseafrica.com; w pulseafrica.com. Tailor-made trips to Africa & the Indian Ocean.

Suggested fly-in itineraries

Most fly-in trips to Botswana last between ten days and three weeks, and are often limited more by travellers' available budgets than anything else: trips here are expensive.

The Okavango Delta, Kwando–Linyanti and Chobe areas are the most common destinations, but the Central Kalahari, Nxai Pan and the Makgadikgadi Pans also have their own landing strips and are sometimes added on to the start or end of trips.

Less commonly, it's quite possible to plan a trip that's part mobile (fully guided and catered camping trips that move between wildlife areas) or self-drive, followed by a few days of relative luxury at a fly-in camp or two.

Concentrating on the fly-in element, the key to an interesting fly-in trip is variation: making sure that the different camps that you visit really are different. For me this means that they're in different environments and have different activities. So mix deep-water camps with shallow-water ones, and forested areas with open ones. That way you'll not only have the greatest variety of scenery, of which there's a lot in the Delta, but also see the widest variety of game.

I also prefer to mix camps run by different companies – one from Wilderness, one from &Beyond and one from Kwando, for example. I find that this makes a more interesting trip than staying at camps which are all run by the same company (sometimes in predictably similar styles).

When flying in, the costs of visiting the camps in the parks are very similar to the costs of those in the private concessions. Because of the ability to do night drives, to drive off-road, and (sometimes) to go walking, I generally prefer to use camps in private areas. Hence I've included relatively few of the camps which are inside the parks here.

For most trips, if you work on spending around three nights at each camp that you visit, that's ideal. Four would be lovely, though often visitors haven't got that much time (or money), whereas two nights is OK for some camps, but a fraction too short for most.

Here I'll give you a few ideas for combinations of areas that I think work well together, giving a real variation to trips. These are **not** lists of my all-time favourite camps; I have deliberately chosen not to pick out just my favourites (simply because the type of camps that I love – the simpler, smaller ones with their emphasis on guiding and wildlife – may not be so ideal for you). Instead, these are trips in which I think the various areas, camps and experiences go well together – and demonstrate what I mean about varying the areas that you stay in and the companies that you use.

Livingstone, Selinda and Okavango Delta: Ten nights/11 days
- Two nights Livingstone, a hotel or lodge
- Three nights Selinda Explorers, NG16 – balance of plains and forests with the option of guided walking safaris
- Two nights Kwara, NG20 – for deep-water motorboat trips plus some game viewing in areas of denser vegetation
- Three nights Kala, NG24 – for picturesque shallow-water mokoro trips, plus some game viewing in open floodplains

Livingstone, Kwando–Linyanti, Okavango and the Pans: 15 nights/16 days
- Two nights Livingstone, a hotel or lodge
- Three nights Lebala, NG14 – dry-land game viewing in mostly riverine forest
- Four nights Shinde Footsteps, NG21 – for shallow-water mokoro trips, walking and some game viewing in an open floodplain environment
- Three nights Sandibe, NG31 – for game viewing in a more forested environment
- Three nights Jack's Camp – something totally different on the great salt pans

Just the Okavango Delta: eight nights/nine days
- Three nights Machaba, NG19 – for dry-land game viewing in a forested, riverine environment
- Two nights Splash Camp, NG20 – active wildlife tracking in 4x4s and some water activities
- Three nights Setari, NG24 – for a deep-water island experience

After reading this book you'll realise there are so many possibilities that you'd be wise to talk through your wishes with someone who knows the camps and can work out what's best for you.

ORGANISING A BUDGET OR BACKPACKING TRIP If you're backpacking then usually you're more restricted by money than by time. Many of the side trips and safaris that you take will be organised at the time, on the ground – and trying to do too much in advance might be counterproductive.

So, read the book, and head off. Start by heading towards Maun or Kasane, keeping your eyes open and talking to people you meet to see what's going on. And enjoy! Much of the joy is the unpredictability of these trips; if you want everything fixed and arranged then backpacking isn't really for you!

In reality, none of Botswana's national parks or private reserves is suitable for anyone on a seriously restricted budget and without their own transportation. There are excellent hostels in Maun and Livingstone, but limited options elsewhere.

ORGANISING A MOBILE SAFARI Mobile trips in Botswana range from cheap-and-cheerful budget safaris to absolutely top-class operations running privately guided

Gordon Rattray (@gordonrattray) and Endeavour Safaris (w endeavour-safaris.com)
For people who use wheelchairs or have difficulties walking, Botswana is a relatively accessible safari destination. It is possible to book through a specialised operator and be sure that your needs are met, or to do enough preparation in advance and travel independently. Either way, with some endeavour, everybody can experience the unique highlights this country has to offer.

TRANSPORT

Air travel Most international travellers arrive via Johannesburg, where the services and facilities for those with disabilities rival and sometimes better those in Europe. Airlink connects Johannesburg and Cape Town with Maun, but limited cargo space on this route means that they do not always allow heavy, electric wheelchairs; it's important to notify them in advance of the dimensions and weight of your wheelchair to ensure that it will be loaded. In Maun, the airport terminal has an aisle chair, the staff are extremely efficient and there is a spacious accessible toilet.

The shorter flights from Maun into the Okavango Delta, Moremi Game Reserve, etc, are also quite possible; when I went, the pilot helped lift me first on to the plane floor and then on to my seat, and there was room to stow my wheelchair with the luggage. However, these planes are small and abide by strict weight limits, so a folding, lightweight wheelchair and soft baggage are essential. Also, do note that airfields in the Delta are usually just a landing strip with few other facilities, and if an aisle chair is needed in Kasane, this should be ordered from Gaborone in advance.

By road Safari vehicles in Botswana are often 4x4, and therefore higher than normal cars. This means that – unless you use a specialised operator with adapted cars and a hydraulic lift or manual ramps – wheelchair transfers may be more difficult. My advice is to thoroughly explain your needs and always stay in control of the situation.

It is possible to hire self-drive vehicles, but I know of no company providing cars that are adapted for drivers with disabilities.

Distances are large and roads are often bumpy, so if you are prone to skin damage you may need to take extra care. Place your own pressure-relieving cushion on top of (or instead of) the original car seat and, if necessary, pad around knees and elbows.

There is no effective legislation in Botswana to help facilitate journeys by bus for travellers with disabilities.

ACCOMMODATION In **Maun**, both Island Safari Lodge (page 197) and Thamalakane River Lodge (page 198) have two chalets with roll-in showers; Maun Lodge (page 197) has two rooms with roll-in shower but both have a 15cm step to enter the rooms; Cresta Riley's (page 196) has one step-free room with a bath, and Cresta Maun (page 196) has one room with a roll-in shower.

In **Kasane,** Mowana Safari Resort & Spa (page 229) and Chobe Marina Lodge (page 228) have adapted rooms; Chobe Bush Lodge (page 228) has two rooms with roll-in showers accessible by ramp, and Chobe Safari Lodge (page 229) has two rooms with roll-in showers; and Chobe Game Lodge (page 257) has two rooms with roll-in showers. Bakwena Lodge (page 226) also has two rooms with roll-in outside showers, but you'll need a plank to access the shower and the toilet space is very limited. Chobe River Lodge (page 229) has four yard rooms with no steps and roll-in showers.

There are several lodges and camps in the **Okavango Delta** that have a degree of accessibility, depending on your needs. Setari Camp (page 215) has a spacious tent designed for wheelchair users, with handles and a roll-in shower, but is accessible only by air in small Cessna or Caravan planes. Other camps are accessible by road: Savute Safari Lodge (page 278) has one tent with a ramp, roll-in shower and plenty of manoeuvring space; Okuti (page 318) is in general very accessible for wheelchair users, with very spacious rooms and level-entry showers, although the doors accessing the bathroom and shower room are quite tight; Camp Moremi (page 317) has ramps into the rooms and plenty of moving space, with roll-in showers; and Camp Xakanaxa (page 317) has ramps to access the main area and roll-in showers in the rooms, but no space next to the toilet for a wheelchair. In the Khwai area, Machaba Camp (page 312) has a spacious tent designed for wheelchair users, with handrails and a roll-in shower. **Outside the Delta**, Leroo La Tau Lodge (page 479) has a tent with a ramp, roll-in shower and plenty of manoeuvring space; and Dinaka Safari Lodge (page 501) has a tent with ramp and roll-in shower.

In Zambia's **Livingstone**, the Royal Livingstone and Avani Victoria Falls Resort hotels (page 514) each have two highly adapted rooms. In Zimbabwe's Victoria Falls Palm River Hotel, there are two accessible rooms with roll-in showers and handrails.

HEALTH AND SAFETY In general, doctors will know about 'everyday' illnesses, but you must understand and be able to explain your own particular medical requirements. Rural clinics are often basic so, if possible, take all necessary medication and equipment with you. It is advisable to pack this in your hand luggage during flights in case your main luggage is delayed.

It's well worth taking out membership of Okavango Air Rescue (w okavangorescue.com), which has a medically staffed and equipped helicopter with an emergency doctor for the Okavango Delta and the Kalahari.

Botswana can be extremely hot. If this is a problem for you, be careful to book accommodation with fans or air conditioning.

Security For anyone following the usual security precautions (page 166) the chances of robbery are greatly reduced. In fact, as a person with a disability I often feel more 'noticed', and therefore a less attractive target for thieves. But the opposite may also apply, so do stay aware of where your bags are and who is around you, especially during car transfers and similar activities.

SPECIALIST TOUR OPERATORS Endeavour Safaris (page 216) is the clear leader in disability travel in Botswana, with custom-designed mobile-camping equipment, several adapted vehicles and the option of boating safaris in the Delta.

FURTHER INFORMATION The UK's gov.uk website (w gov.uk/government/publications/disabled-travellers/disability-and-travel-abroad) gives general advice and practical information for travellers with a disability (and their companions) preparing for overseas travel. The Society for Accessible Travel and Hospitality (w sath.org) also provides some general information; Rolling Rains (w rollingrains.com) is a searchable website advocating disability travel.

5

trips for small family groups. Thus generalising among them is difficult, although levels of comfort vary. Typically, the cheapest are dubbed 'participation' safaris (where you pitch your own tent and muck in with all the chores). Then there's 'semi-participation', where you'll help – perhaps just pitching your own tent – but staff will be on hand; and 'non-participation' or 'fully serviced' – where the staff will do everything for you. As a general rule, the more they cost, the further in advance they should be booked. (For an indication of costs, see page 138.) The cheaper ones often survive on last-minute bookings from people who turn up; the more costly private ones can be booked up years in advance. Many safari companies are members of HATAB (Hospitality and Tourism Association of Botswana) and/or the Botswana Guides Association (BOGA), both of which have their own campsites that are reserved exclusively for tour operators.

Ideally, talk to someone who has been on safari with the mobile operator that you're considering before booking with them. If this isn't possible then don't hesitate to ask a lot of questions before you decide which trip is right for you. You'll be stuck with your guide and group for a week or more, so it's vital to make the right choice.

Most of these companies are based in Maun (page 213), with only a few elsewhere, in Kasane. The best often have overseas tour operators who know them well, and will sell their trips at around the same price (or even cheaper) than they do directly.

ORGANISING A SELF-DRIVE TRIP Describing the roads in Botswana is like describing Dr Jekyll and Mr Hyde. The tarred main routes, and most of the roads in the towns, can be beautifully smooth roads with excellent signposts. They're often delightfully free of traffic: a dream to drive on. They're eminently suitable to potter around in a normal 2WD such as a Toyota Corolla or VW Golf.

However, the tracks through the national parks and more remote areas can become nightmares. Inexperienced or badly prepared drivers will find themselves seriously challenged, with deep sand in the dry season, and glutinous mud when it's wet – often compounded by a complete lack of signposts or directions.

If you want to hire a self-drive vehicle for your trip, then you must treat Botswana's two personas very differently. Your biggest decision is your vehicle, as this will make or break the experience.

Hiring a 2WD If you are sticking to the towns and tar roads then hire a 2WD from one of the normal hire companies – Avis, Bidvest or Europcar would be the obvious three (see pages 193 and 225 for Maun and Kasane respectively). Contacting them directly, a medium-size saloon (Group C) for about two weeks will cost you around US$55 per day, including 'super' CDW (collision damage waiver; page 126) insurance cover and unlimited mileage, but excluding 12% VAT.

Hiring a 4x4 If you want to explore Botswana in your own 4x4, then you have three options: to hire locally; to rent a vehicle from a South African-based company; or to go with a UK specialist.

Whoever you choose to hire from, think carefully. What you need to drive into the bush in Botswana is a serious, fully equipped vehicle – and what you'd be hiring off-the-peg isn't always, in our view, up to the job. You need a vehicle that you can rely on, with long-range tanks, a high-lift jack, a spade and decent tow-rope, extra fuel cans if necessary and all the other bits and pieces that make all the difference. Perhaps most vitally, you need to have confidence that if anything goes wrong, there's a system in place to help you swiftly.

It is also worth noting that driving a 4x4 vehicle in Botswana demands a diverse set of skills and you should seriously consider your own competencies before embarking on this kind of travel. You will need to be proficient in off-road driving techniques, like navigating sand, mud and rocky terrain, and should have enough 4x4 knowledge to understand the capabilities and limitations of your vehicle. Navigation proficiency (you will not be able to rely on Google Maps) and basic mechanical know-how for maintenance and repairs are essential too. It's advisable to undergo training or gain experience prior to embarking on an African adventure if this is all new to you.

To **hire locally**, contact the hire companies directly (see the individual chapters); you'll find a twin-cab 4x4 hired for about two weeks will cost you upwards of about US$110 a day, including unlimited mileage, multiple drivers and standard insurance, but not CDW insurance cover, rising to at least US$260 a day with camping kit – and more for a Toyota Land Cruiser. For full insurance cover, you can expect to pay around US$40 a day. Most companies also charge a premium for the high-season months, usually July–October. Others may charge extra for VAT, a second driver, or indeed for mileage above a certain level.

Most of the **South African** companies simply deal with hiring out vehicles; they may make suggestions, but generally don't get involved with helping you plan your trip or give you any advice. A step up from this, in both price and completeness, are companies that provide not only a vehicle, but also put their expertise at your disposal and provide additional **back-up**. They cost more, but if you're not experienced in driving around southern Africa, then it's what you need. Neither of the operators listed below offers vehicle-only hire; to benefit from their knowledge and back-up you must arrange a whole trip through them.

South African 4x4s

Avis +267 686 0039 Maun, 625 0144 Kasane; e botswanares@avis.co.bw; w avis.co.za. For equipped rentals: e safarirental.reservations@avis. co.za; AvisSouthAfrica.

Britz 4x4 +27 11 230 5200; e bookings@britz. co.za; w britz.co.za. Range of 4x4s & camping kit options, with depots in Maun & Kasane.

Bushlore +27 11 312 8084; e info@ bushlore.com; w bushlore.com. Range of fully equipped & unequipped Toyota Land Cruisers & Hiluxes.

Bushtrackers Africa +27 11 465 2559; e info@bushtrackers.com; w bushtrackers.co.za. Fully equipped Toyota Land Cruisers & Hiluxes with pick-up/drop-off available in Maun, Cape Town & Johannesburg.

Kwenda Safari +49 8856 936 7720; e mail@ kwendasafari.com; w kwendasafari.co.za. Range of fully equipped Land Rovers & Toyota Land Cruisers. Also offers a 1-day, licensed Land Rover off-road training day (Johannesburg), covering theory & practical driving experiences – a great additional option if you're a novice.

4x4s with back-up

Drive Botswana 01614 084316/7 (UK), +267 492 1824 (Botswana); e info@drivebotswana. com; w drivebotswana.com. A self-drive safari specialist, with offices in both the UK & Botswana, offering trips in Botswana & across southern Africa. Their camping-equipped fleet of vehicles is made up of a range of sgl- & dbl-cab vehicles, each set up for 2–4 travellers. As well as camping equipment, Drive Botswana will also arrange satnavs & sat phones on request; for some areas they stipulate these as essential.

Safari Drive 01488 71140; e info@safaridrive. com; w safaridrive.com. Specialist African operators based out of the UK, with 1st-class knowledge of Botswana, concentrating on self-drive trips using their own well-equipped Land Rovers & Toyota Land Cruisers. They have vehicles & support based in Windhoek, Cape Town, Livingstone, Maun, Lilongwe & Arusha. Their fleet of Land Cruiser 79s are among the region's best-equipped vehicles & we have used them for many of our more adventurous research trips. As well as roof tents, cooking equipment, long-range fuel tanks, water tanks & camping equipment, each vehicle comes with a Garmin satnav loaded with Tracks4Africa & a sat phone. They can arrange lodge-to-lodge self-drive trips too, or a combination of camping & safari camps (the 14-night Classic Botswana trip costs from £4,267 pp).

Checking the fine print

The devil's in the detail, especially if you're looking at any of the cheaper options. You should check any rental agreement very carefully, so that you know your position. Preferably also discuss any questions or queries with someone within the company that is supplying you with the vehicle. A few specific pointers may help.

CDW insurance

The insurance and the collision damage waiver (CDW) clauses are worth studying particularly closely. These spell out the 'excess' that you will pay in the event of an accident. These CDW excesses vary widely, and often explain the difference between cheap rental deals and better, but more costly, options.

Some hire companies have very high excesses (ie: the amounts that you pay if you have a major accident). An 80% CDW is normal – which means that you will always pay 20% of the cost of any damage. However, look around and you should be able to reduce this to zero – although most hiring companies will still want a deposit, in case you damage or lose any of their vehicle's equipment.

Other fine print

Fortunately accidents are not common, but they do happen. When they do, it's very important to get the situation resolved swiftly and carry on with your trip. Some of the companies have quite onerous terms – so be aware of these before you agree to take the vehicle.

Driving in the national parks

Historically you could just arrive at any national park in Botswana and pay your park fees, but this is no longer the case. Currently, the official line is that entry fees for the national parks should be pre-paid in advance, as with the campsite reservations (page 128), unless you have your accommodation confirmation, in which case it should theoretically be possible to pay fees at the park entrance gates. However, do not rely on this; finding out which gates accept payment is next to impossible, and only a few of the wardens are authorised to accept payments (most are not allowed to issue permits or handle money, no matter how persuasive you try to be). So if you arrive at a gate when the appropriate wardens are not available, don't expect to be able to pass. The policy is strict: if you haven't got a paid permit, you won't be able to enter. That said, several experiences in recent years suggest that common sense applies where a genuine problem has arisen.

Bearing all this in mind, we recommend that you arrange park fees (page 127) in advance at one of the Department of Wildlife and National Parks (DWNP) offices, as it may well save you long delays and significant stress. For more information on driving once you get there, see page 169.

Park rules and regulations

Park entry and departure is only permitted through official gates (⊕ Apr–Sep 06.00–18.30 daily, Oct–Mar 05.30–19.00 daily). No driving is permitted in the parks outside these hours, so it is imperative to allow plenty of time for your journey, and to be at the gates or your campsite well before closing. Campers may only camp at designated sites, with prior reservation, and should leave the park before 11.00, or they will be liable for an additional day's park fees (which are payable to staff at the gates). The speed limit in all the national parks is 40km/h – though you'd be hard pressed to exceed this almost anywhere.

Both walking and swimming are prohibited within all Botswana's parks, as is the collection of firewood.

Park fees and permits Most organised trips will include park entry fees in their costs, but if you are travelling on your own then you must pay these directly to DWNP.

Park fees are usually made up of three components: for the people, for your vehicle and for a campsite. The amount payable will depend on your nationality/immigration status, and where your vehicle is registered. Campsite fees, however, are no longer fixed (see below).

There are offices in Gaborone, Tsabong, Ghanzi, Kang, Letlhakane, Maun, Kasane, Francistown and Two Rivers (Twee Rivieren Rest Camp and Kgalagadi Transfrontier Park), and they are usually open 07.30–16.30 Monday–Saturday and 07.30–noon Sunday, but do double-check these times before arrival. For self-drive visitors in northern Botswana, the most accessible of these are likely to be in Maun and Kasane, at the Sedudu Gate into Chobe National Park.

In theory, credit cards (Visa or Mastercard) can be used at the Sedudu and Ngoma gates, but it's as well to be prepared for the inevitable occasions when the card machines are not working. Cash payments should be made in pula; even where US dollars are accepted, the rate of exchange is not likely to be favourable; where possible it is best to have with you the correct change in pula.

At the time of writing, vehicle fees in Chobe were P115 per day for foreign-registered vehicles and P30 for local vehicles, and for all other national parks and reserves they were P75 per day for foreign vehicles and P20 for Botswanan ones.

Park entry fees (per person per day)

For Chobe and Moremi:

	Bots citizen	Bots resident	Non-resident
Adult (18+)	P30	P205	P270
Child (aged 8–17)	P20	P102.50	P135
Infant (7 and under)	free	free	free

For all other national parks and reserves:

	Bots citizen	Bots resident	Non-resident
Adult (18+)	P20	P145	P190
Child (aged 8–17)	P10	P72.50	P70
Infant (7 and under)	free	free	free

Booking accommodation If you're driving a 2WD on the tar, then you can afford to find a campsite in Maun or Kasane when you get there. If you need a room, then you only need to book one in advance during the busy season. For the rest of the year you shouldn't have a problem finding one.

Generally, finding a campsite outside the national parks is not a problem, though if you're not at a designated private site, you should always seek permission first (page 174). However, campsites within the national parks **must** be booked in advance and you should do this as far ahead as possible. Any lodges at which you plan to stay should also be reserved in advance, and notified that you are self-driving to get there.

National parks' campsites In line with Botswana's 'high-revenue, low-volume' policy (page 19), the number of campsite pitches in each national park is restricted. All campsites must be pre-booked; you cannot just turn up.

Sites are very, very limited and often booked out almost a year in advance, so if you're planning to camp inside the national parks, it is *essential* to book as early as you can. Reservations usually open 11 months in advance, and booking this far ahead is usually the ideal.

Privatisation of most of the campsites in recent years has fragmented an already challenging system, since – in theory at least – each of the operators only handles bookings for its own campsites. Thus, you will likely end up working with multiple operators in confirming your itinerary. It's possible that SKL and the Xomae Group will be prepared to help out with booking for other operators, though given the difficulty of communications, this isn't always as straightforward as it sounds, so it's crucial to allow plenty of time. Most sites in the northern parks are in the hands of four separate operators, with only a few still handled by the DWNP.

Once you have your campsites lined up, be sure to get written confirmation for each one stating not just the dates of your reservation, but also confirming the number of the pitch reserved. Only then will you be able to buy your park permits from the DWNP, as they will require written proof of your overnight accommodation booking before issuing a permit.

The system is not just unwieldy, it's also pretty costly. While the remaining DWNP sites still charge P30–60 pp (US$2–4.50), the privatised sites are significantly more for international visitors (page 127) – and that's exclusive of park fees and the P10 per-person bed levy.

On the plus side, many of these campsites and their ablution blocks do seem to be better maintained now, though inevitably some are better than others. This variation in standards runs through to the efficiency of the individual operators, too. While some seem to be very much on the ball, this is not always the case, so do double-check that all your paperwork is in order – do not assume.

All the campsite operators, except Bigfoot Tours, who are based in Gaborone, have offices in Maun, so are relatively easy for most overseas travellers to visit in person. That said, in reality you'll need to have confirmed everything months ahead of your arrival.

Campsite operators and fees (per person per night)

Bigfoot Tours +267 395 3360, 391 0927; m 7355 5573; e reservations@bigfoottours.co.bw; w bigfoottours.co.bw; P350/US$25. Runs a string of campsites in the CKGR (Lekhubu, Letiahau, Piper, Sunday, Passarge & Motopi).

DWNP Central booking, Gaborone +267 397 1405; e dwnp@gov.bw; Maun office +267 686 0368; ⏲ 07.30–16.30 Mon–Sat, 07.30–noon Sun; P30–60 pp/US$2–4.50, except Njuca Hills & Tree Island in Makgadikgadi Pans (P175/US$13).

Gaing-O Community Trust +267 297 9612; m +267 7310 9996; e kubu.island@btcmail.co.bw; w kubuisland.com; P150/US$11. The operator behind Kubu Island camping.

Kwalate Safaris Maun +267 686 5551; Sedudu Gate 625 0235; e kwalatesafari@gmail.

com; w kwalatesafaris.com; P500/US$36. Runs Ihaha Campsite in Chobe; & Xakanaxa & South Gate (Maqwee) sites in Moremi.

SKL Maun +267 686 5365/6; Sedudu Gate 625 0113; e reservations@sklcamps.co.bw; w sklcamps.com; P680/US$50. Runs Savuti & Linyanti campsites in Chobe; North Gate (Khwai) in Moremi; & Khumaga Campsite in Makgadikgadi Pans.

Xomae Group +267 686 2221; m 7320 4640; e bookings@xomaesites.com; w xomaesites.com. Runs Third Bridge (P680/US$50) & Gcodikwe & Gxhobega (P1,295/US$95) in Moremi, & South Camp (P517/US$38) & Baines' Baobab (P680/US$50) in Nxai Pan.

Campsite facilities Each campsite has a designated number of pitches. These are usually very large by European and American standards, and capable of taking several vehicles – perhaps a group of friends travelling together. However, if the campsite is busy, you can expect to share your site with one or even two other vehicles. Most of the campsites have relatively modern ablution facilities, though some – especially in the CKGR and Makgadikgadi – are more rudimentary, and hot water can be hit or miss. At the most basic sites you'll need to heat your water over a fire.

Most individual pitches have a firepit, and perhaps a barbecue (braai) stand. Regulations prohibit the collection of firewood within all Botswana's national parks and game reserves, so do make sure that you take sufficient with you, along with all the food, fuel and drinking water you will need for your trip. Although the occasional site, such as Savuti and Third Bridge, now has a small 'tuck' shop, don't rely on it.

Suggested self-drive itineraries
If you're driving yourself outside the national parks, and have lots of time, then you can afford to have total flexibility in your route, and plan very little.

However, if you're coming for a shorter time, and want to use any of the campsites in the national parks, then you would be wise to arrange your trip carefully beforehand; and since park accommodation must be booked in advance (page 128), this effectively commits you to a specific route and schedule.

Perhaps the most obvious and instantly rewarding trip for your first self-drive trip across Botswana would be between Livingstone and Maun. This is best done in the dry season.

Livingstone, Chobe, Moremi and Maun: 11 nights/12 days
This really is the fastest trip that you should consider through this area if you want to have time to enjoy the parks. Allowing more time would be better, and another three to four nights camping in the parks (including both Third Bridge and Xakanaxa for a few nights each) would improve it enormously. Since you're unlikely to need a vehicle in Livingstone, I suggest arranging a road transfer across the border and picking up your vehicle in Kasane. This will usually result in a better vehicle, better back-up and an easier trip.

- Two nights Livingstone – hotel/lodge (or campsite)
- Two nights Ihaha Campsite, Chobe
- Two nights Savuti Campsite, Chobe
- Two nights North Gate (Khwai) Campsite, Moremi
- Two nights Xakanaxa or Third Bridge Campsite, Moremi
- One night Maun – hotel/lodge (or campsite)

Of course it can easily be reversed. Some prefer Livingstone at the start, to relax after the flight; others prefer to leave it until the end, with the highlight of seeing Victoria Falls and buying quality curios before heading home.

We recommend that you use a hotel or lodge, rather than camp, for your first and last few days. We've learned that this base allows time and space to get organised more easily at the start and end of an overland adventure.

The Panhandle plus Tsodilo, Aha and Gcwihaba hills: 13 nights/14 days
To visit the hills of the northwest Kalahari, ideally consider a trip based out of Maun:

- One night Maun – hotel/lodge (or campsite)
- Two nights Guma Lagoon or Swamp Stop
- Two nights Tsodilo Hills – camping

- Three nights Nxamaseri Lodge or Shakawe River Lodge
- Two nights Aha Hills – basic camping
- One night Gcwihaba Caves – basic camping
- Two nights Maun – campsite or hotel/lodge

In the dry season, August or after, you might tag on a few days after Maun to visit the Boteti River area, where the game concentrations should then be good.

Whenever you go, I'd visit Tsodilo before Aha; it's considerably more accessible. Whatever route you take, don't try to get to Aha and Gcwihaba without sufficient fuel, food, water and a back-up plan. The roads in this remote area are neither well travelled nor well maintained, and getting stuck in deep sand is a real possibility. Do remember, too, to fill up with fuel wherever possible: Sehithwa, Shakawe and Gumare are the safest bets.

Nxai Pan and the Central Kalahari Game Reserve: 16 nights/17 days

If you're experienced in the African bush, feel a lot more adventurous, and don't mind the idea of spending hours digging yourself out of mud or sand, then consider a trip to Nxai and the northern part of the Central Kalahari Game Reserve. This would probably be at its best between April and July; if you're travelling earlier then getting around Makgadikgadi could be tricky so you might consider reducing your time there.

- One night Maun – hotel/lodge (or campsite)
- Three nights South Camp, Nxai Pan – camping
- Two nights Planet Baobab – campsite or lodge
- Two nights Khumaga Campsite Makgadikgadi Pans National Park
- Two nights Deception Valley, CKGR – campsite
- Two nights Sunday Pan, CKGR – campsite
- Two nights Passarge Pan or Phokoje Pan, CKGR – campsite
- One night Motopi Pan, CKGR – campsite
- One night Maun – hotel/lodge (or campsite)

As with any rainy-season trip or excursion into the Central Kalahari Game Reserve, you should be doing this with a minimum of two vehicles, and safety precautions like taking a satellite phone would be a good idea. You cannot rely on being able to restock on this trip, so you must ensure you take enough food, water and fuel with you from Maun.

RED TAPE

VISAS If you need a visa for Botswana, you must get one before you arrive. Currently, passport holders from over 100 countries **do not need a visa** and will be granted a 30-day entry permit on arrival. These countries are: the UK and most Commonwealth countries (except citizens from Cameroon, Ghana, Nigeria, Bangladesh, India, Pakistan and Sri Lanka who *do* currently need visas); most European Union countries (except citizens from Cyprus, Hungary, Lithuania and Malta); mainland USA and Canada; and South Africa.

The Botswana government's **e-visa website** (w evisa.gov.bw) has an up-to-date search facility to check individual countries' requirements, and an efficient application system. Alternatively, contact your local Botswana embassy or high commission (see opposite).

The prevailing attitude among both Botswana's government and its people is that visitors are generally good for the country as they spend valuable foreign currency – so if you look presentable, which is considered courteous in Botswana, and are respectful to immigration employees, then you should have no difficulty in entering Botswana.

Visa extensions If you want to stay longer than 30 days, then you must renew your permit at the nearest immigration office; a fee of P500 is payable. For a visa lasting longer than 90 days, you should apply to the appropriate Regional Immigration Officer (Gaborone department \ +267 361 1300, toll-free 0800 600777; ⊕ 07.30–12.45 & 13.45–16.30 Mon–Fri), preferably before entering Botswana; for details, see w gov.bw. Note that it's a serious offence to stay longer than 90 days in a 12-month period without permission.

Botswana is strict about **work permits**. These are now granted only for jobs for which a suitably qualified Botswana citizen is not available. Work permits can be obtained from the Ministry of Labour and Home Affairs (MLHA; \ 361 1100, toll-free 0800 600777).

TRAVELLING WITH CHILDREN If you're **travelling with children under 18 years**, Botswana's immigration rules state that you must provide a certified copy of their full, unabridged birth certificate, as well as a valid passport (an abridged birth certificate won't be accepted) to enter the country. If the child is travelling with one parent or with another adult, the parent or parents who aren't present will need to provide an affidavit giving their consent for the child to travel. There are no exceptions to this rule so do come prepared.

DIPLOMATIC MISSIONS A list of Botswana's embassies and high commissions abroad and within Botswana can be found at w gov.bw/ministries/ministry-foreign-affairs. Their full addresses are listed on w embassy-worldwide.com/country/botswana.

BOTSWANA TOURISM BOARD (\ +267 391 3111; e marketing@botswanatourism. co.bw; w botswanatourism.co.bw) In addition to a useful website, the tourist board is represented in most major towns in Botswana, including Maun and Kasane.

GETTING THERE AND AWAY

BY AIR The vast majority of visitors to northern Botswana fly via the gateways of Maun, which has an international airport, and Kasane, which is also effectively serviced by the nearby airports at Victoria Falls (in Zimbabwe) and Livingstone (in Zambia).

The national carrier, **Air Botswana** (\ +267 686 0391; e mubsales@airbotswana. co.bw, airportticketing@airbotswana.co.bw; w airbotswana.co.bw), does not fly outside southern Africa. Of the other airline links to Botswana, the most notable is **Airlink** (\ +267 686 5230; e customercare@flyairlink.com; w flyairlink. com). A popular routing for visitors to the region is to fly to Livingstone (airline code LVI) or Kasane (BBK) via Johannesburg (JNB), then leave from Maun (MUB), again routing via Johannesburg. There are also regular flights between Maun and Cape Town, and a new route launched between Maun and Addis Ababa, the hub of international carrier **Ethiopian Airlines** (\ +44 20 8987 2480, +267 311 1631; e RES@ethiopianairlines.com; w ethiopianairlines. com). Botswana's capital, Gaborone (GBE), is relatively rarely visited by safari travellers, although occasionally you might stop here as you fly between Maun and Johannesburg.

However you arrange your flights, remember some basic tips. First, make sure your purchase is protected. Always book through a company that is bonded for your protection – which in the UK means holding an Air Travel Organiser's Licence (ATOL) – or use a credit card.

Second, note that airlines don't always give the best deals direct. Often you'll do better through a discounted flight centre or a tour operator.

Third, book the main internal flights at the same time – with the same company – that you book your flights to/from Johannesburg. Often the airline taking you to Africa will have cheap deals for add-on regional flights within Africa. You should be able to get Johannesburg–Livingstone flights, or Maun–Johannesburg flights, at discounted rates provided that you book them at the same time as your return flights to Johannesburg. Further, if you book all your flights together with the same company, then you'll be sure to get connecting flights, and so have the best schedule possible. Don't be talked into getting an apparently cheap return to Johannesburg on the basis that you'll be able to then get a separate ticket to Maun; it'll cost you a lot more in the end.

From Europe Johannesburg has long been considered the best gateway to southern Africa, as it's widely served by many carriers. From Europe, several national carriers – British Airways, Lufthansa and Air France to name but a few – have regular **direct flights to Johannesburg**. Generally these are busy routes that fill up far in advance, so you're likely to get cheaper fares by booking well ahead rather than at the last minute; this is a virtual certainty during the busiest season from July to October, and in December–January around the Christmas period.

The last decade has seen a rise in the frequency and popularity of flights **via the Middle East**, using Emirates or Qatar Airlines. In 2019, Qatar partnered with Air Botswana to launch a Doha to Gabarone route (3 times a week), via Johannesburg, marking its first destination in Botswana.

Visitors are increasingly travelling via East Africa with the well-regarded Ethiopian Airlines, especially given its wide global network of connecting flights. From June 2024, it has been possible to fly directly from Addis to Maun, the Okavango Delta's gateway, three times a week. This route, operating at very sensible times, is a terrific way to connect straight into Botswana, on an airline offering reasonable rates. To fly **via East Africa**, consider Ethiopian Airlines routes, such as London Heathrow to Maun, via Addis, from US$1,500/£1,200 return (or, if you're connecting in Addis from another city: Addis to Maun US$680/1,000 one-way/return).

For a non-stop return from London to Johannesburg with a decent airline, expect to pay around US$1,500/£1,200 for most of the year, adding perhaps another US$190/£150 or so in school holidays, though for flights departing closer to Christmas, you'll be lucky to pay less than US$2,025/£1,600. Unless there's some major international upset, these flights become progressively more expensive as you get closer to the departure, climbing to several thousand dollars at short notice. So as with most long-haul destinations, book early for the cheapest flights.

One-way flights between Johannesburg and Maun, with **CemAir** (+27 (0)87 138 5203; e tickets@cemair.co.za; w flycemair.co.za) or Air Botswana should cost around US$230/£180, while Airlink should cost in the region of US$230/£200. Between Johannesburg and Livingstone, one-way economy flights with Airlink cost from US$75/£60 to US$290/£230, though most are around US$190/£150.

From North America If you are coming from the US, you will often pass through Johannesburg, and it's often easiest to route via London or another European capital as well. There isn't much of a discounted long-haul flight market in the US, so booking all your flights in the US will not always save you money.

In 2020, Delta Air Lines launched a new triangle route: Atlanta–Johannesburg–Cape Town–Atlanta. Onward connections to Maun make this a good option. South African Airways also fly direct from New York JFK and Washington Dulles to Johannesburg.

It is worth comparing these options with the cost of buying a US–London return in the US, and London–Botswana tickets from a good source in London. London is Europe's capital for cheap flights, and visitors from the US often discover that flights bought from the UK, as well as trips from UK tour operators, offer better value than those in America.

From Australasia Several airlines fly **from Australia** to South Africa: Qantas (direct, non-stop flights to Johannesburg and Cape Town from Sydney; flights from other Australian cities connect in Sydney); Emirates (from Sydney, Melbourne, Perth and Brisbane, via Dubai, to Johannesburg); Qatar Airways (from Sydney, Melbourne, Perth and Brisbane, via Doha, to Johannesburg); Cathay Pacific (from Sydney, Melbourne and Brisbane, via Hong Kong, to Johannesburg); and Singapore Airlines (from Sydney, Melbourne and Brisbane, via Singapore, to Johannesburg).

From New Zealand, there are five carriers operating from Auckland to Johannesburg: Qantas via Sydney, Emirates via Dubai, Qatar Airways via Doha, Singapore Airlines via Singapore and Cathay Pacific via Hong Kong. It is also possible to fly Air New Zealand and connect with one of its partners in Asia or Ethiopia.

From Namibia or Zambia It is possible, although rarely easier or cheaper, to approach Botswana from one of the region's other capitals, Windhoek (Namibia) or Lusaka (Zambia). There are certainly no direct flights to Maun, and all flights will necessitate a flight change in Johannesburg.

However, travel from Lusaka to Kasane is easier and more reliable. This journey is best thought of in two stages: Lusaka to Livingstone, then Livingstone to Kasane. Lusaka to Livingstone is a long 6-hour drive (though there are efficient and cheap coaches for the more adventurous), or a short 90-minute flight. There is a handful of good, small Zambian charter companies that will organise a charter flight on this route, or seats on a scheduled charter. Expect a cost of around US$220 per person with Proflight (w proflight-zambia.com).

It's very easy to arrange a transfer, by road or boat, between Livingstone and Kasane (page 223). The only downside of travelling via Zambia is that most visitors, including those just in transit, will be liable for visa fees.

OVERLAND Typically overland border posts open for about 8–12 hours a day, from between 06.00 and 08.00 in the morning. That said, some of the busier ones on main routes stay open considerably longer than this.

To/from Zambia Despite meeting Zambian territory only at a point in the Zambezi River, Botswana does have a border crossing with Zambia; the impressive Kazungula Bridge opened in 2021 with a modern, one-stop border post (ie: both Botswanan and Zambian customs and immigration are within the same building), which is open daily from 06.00 to 22.00. All payments can be made by bank card but there is an ATM outside the building and the process is fairly straightforward. This crossing is used by pedestrians, as well as for road and rail travel.

To/from Zimbabwe Botswana has several border posts with Zimbabwe, of which the two most important are the one on the road between Kasane and Victoria Falls (outside Kazungula village; ⊕ 06.00–20.00 daily; this is different to the Kazungula Bridge crossing into Zambia), and the one on the main road from Francistown to Plumtree (and hence Bulawayo), at Ramokgwebana (⊕ 06.00–22.00 daily).

A third, much smaller, post is at Pandamatenga (⊕ 08.00–17.00 daily). This is 100km south of Kasane, and sometimes used by visitors as a neat short cut into the back of Zimbabwe's Hwange National Park.

To/from Namibia Despite the long length of its border with Namibia, Botswana has very few border posts with its neighbour. The most important of these by far is the post on the Trans-Kalahari Highway, the route between the towns of Ghanzi and Gobabis. The border post is open 24 hours whether you approach from Mamuno post (Botswana) or Buitepos (Namibia).

The other two major crossings are at Mohembo (north of Shakawe and at the south end of Namibia's Mahango National Park; ⊕ 06.00–18.00) and across the Chobe River at Ngoma (⊕ 07.00–18.00).

Rather less well known are three other possible crossings into Namibia. The first is at the Dobe border post (⊕ 06.00–16.30 daily, Namibian time), on the road between Tsumkwe, in Namibia, and Nokaneng, on the west of the Delta. The other two, geared to those spending time in lodges right on the Namibian border, are between Kasane and both Impalila Island and Kasika (⊕ 07.30–16.30).

To/from South Africa South Africa has always been Botswana's most important neighbour politically and economically, and for many years (even before South Africa was welcome in the international fold) it was in a 'customs union' with South Africa and Namibia. Consequently, it's no surprise to find a range of border posts between Botswana and South Africa. In order, from northeast to southwest, with their daily opening hours, these are: Pontdrift (⊕ 08.00–16.00); Platjan (⊕ 06.00–18.00); Zanzibar (⊕ 08.00–16.00); Martin's Drift (⊕ 06.00–22.00) to Groblersburg; Parr's Halt (⊕ 06.00–18.00) to Stockpoort; Sikwane (⊕ 06.00–19.00) to Derdepoort; Tlokweng, near Gaborone (⊕ 06.00–midnight) to Kopfontein; Ramotswa (⊕ 07.00–19.00) to Swartkopfontein; Pioneer Gate, near Lobatse (⊕ 06.00–midnight) to Skilpadshek; Ramatlabama (⊕ 06.00–22.00); Phitshane Molopo (⊕ 07.30–16.30) to Makgobistad; Bray (⊕ 07.00–16.00); Makopong (⊕ 08.00–16.00); Tshabong (⊕ 06.00–18.00) to McCarthy's Rest; Middlepits (⊕ 07.30–16.00); Bokspits (⊕ 08.00–16.00); and Twee Rivieren (⊕ 07.30–16.00).

WHAT TO TAKE

This is an impossible question to answer fully, as it depends on how you intend to travel and exactly where you are going. If you are flying in for a short safari holiday then you need not pack too ruthlessly – provided that you stay within your weight allowance. However, note that smaller, privately chartered planes may specify a maximum weight of 10–12kg for hold luggage, which must be packed in a soft, squashable bag. Once you see the stowage spaces in a small charter plane, you'll understand the importance of not bringing along large or solid suitcases.

If you are backpacking then weight becomes much more important, and minimising it becomes an art form. Each extra item must be questioned: is its benefit worth its weight?

If you have your own vehicle then neither weight nor bulk will be so vital, and you will have a lot more freedom to bring what you like. Here are some general guidelines.

CLOTHING It's essential to dress appropriately for the environment and the activities you plan to take part in: items needed for a walking safari will clearly vary from those required for an elegant dinner at Victoria Falls. In general, safari requires casual, comfortable clothing, with warm layers, suitable footwear and some key accessories.

Remember to check the weather forecast for the time of year you're travelling and pack accordingly: don't assume that Botswana is always sunny and hot. Morning and evenings can be freezing on game drives if you're ill-equipped. Additionally, remember that most safari lodges and camps offer next-day laundry services, so you don't need to pack a different outfit for each day. And bear in mind the 15kg weight limit on small bush planes. Consider these guidelines when packing:

- **Lightweight, breathable fabrics:** Choose natural fabrics, such as cotton, bamboo or linen, or moisture-wicking, synthetic materials. These fabrics will keep you cool and comfortable in the heat of the day. If you're self-driving and camping, fast-drying fabrics are an advantage.
- **Neutral-coloured clothing:** Opt for neutral tones like khaki, beige or olive-green. These colours help you blend into the natural surroundings, and are critical if you intend on doing any walking. Avoiding white and vibrant colours is essential for walking safaris.
- **No camouflage clothing:** Avoid anything that looks military. Wearing camouflage is asking for trouble anywhere in Africa. You are very likely to be stopped and questioned by the genuine military, or at least by the police, who will assume that you are a member of some militia – and question exactly what you are doing in Botswana. Few will believe that this is a fashion statement elsewhere in the world.
- **Long-sleeved shirts and trousers:** Alongside some shorts and T-shirts for general wear, keep in mind that covering your skin gives protection from the sun, insects and thorny vegetation. Look for garments with UPF (Ultraviolet Protection Factor) for added sun protection. These items are equally useful after dark to protect from mosquitoes and ensure warmth after sunset.
- **Hat:** A wide-brimmed hat provides the best shade for your face, ears and neck, protecting you from the intense sun. Take a back-up cap as this is an essential piece of kit in avoiding sunstroke and burning.
- **Shoes:** Closed-toe shoes, trainers or lightweight boots with good tread are vital for walking safaris. Avoid open-toed shoes to protect your feet from thorns, insects and uneven terrain or bush walks. A pair of trekking or rafting sandals are cool and practical for around camp and on game drives.
- **Underwear and socks:** Some camps do not accept women's underwear in their laundry services due to cultural sensitivities (though in-room washing powder is provided). Women may wish to pack additional underwear though. Moisture-wicking socks will help to keep your feet dry and prevent blisters if you're walking.
- **Lightweight jacket and fleece:** Evenings and early mornings on safari can be cool (sometimes cold!), so pack a lightweight jacket and fleece for layering. If you're travelling in winter, bring gloves, a warm hat and scarf.

- **Rain gear:** Depending on the season and location of your safari, it's a good idea to pack a waterproof jacket.
- **Swimwear:** If your safari includes accommodation with swimming facilities, pack a swimsuit for relaxation and cooling off.
- **Sunglasses:** Take at least one decent pair of sunglasses, and a spare. A lack of sunglasses – because you lost or broke a pair along the way – can quickly ruin your overall experience.

CAMPING EQUIPMENT If you are coming on an organised safari, then even the most simple bush camp will mean tents with linen, mosquito nets and probably an en-suite shower and toilet. However, if you're planning on doing any camping by yourself, see page 175 for ideas of what you should bring, and note that equipment is easier to buy in Europe or North America.

ELECTRICAL APPLIANCES The local voltage is 220V, delivered at 50Hz. Sockets usually fit plugs with three square pins, like the current design in the UK, though plugs with three large round pins, like those in South Africa, are also widely in use. Ideally bring adapters for both.

When staying in bush lodges and even in the more upmarket camps, you are likely to have sockets in your room/tent, and increasingly a bank of international adapters and USB charging points. Even if these are not available in-room, it's usually easy to arrange to charge camera and phone batteries, as behind the scenes most camps run generators in order to power their kitchen and communications equipment. But, with the exception of the most lavish lodges, don't expect to be able to use a hairdryer out in the bush – few camps can cope with such a high-powered drain on their circuit. Any attempt to surreptitiously use one will usually result in the whole camp losing power!

OTHER USEFUL ITEMS Obviously no list is comprehensive, and only travelling can teach you what you need, and what you can do without. Here are a few of our own favourites and essentials. For visitors embarking on an organised safari, camps will have most things but useful items include:

- Sunblock and lipsalve – vital for protection from the sun
- Insect repellent
- Binoculars – essential for game viewing (one pair per traveller…You won't want to share when the action really starts!)
- A small pocket torch (page 176)
- 'Leatherman' or Swiss Army Knife multi-tool – never go into the bush without one
- A water bottle, especially on flights (page 176)
- Electrical insulating tape – remarkably useful for general repairs
- Camera – a long lens or decent zoom is vital for good wildlife shots
- Basic sewing kit – with some really strong thread for repairs
- Cheap waterproof watch (leave expensive ones, and jewellery, at home)
- Simple medical kit

And for those driving or backpacking, useful extras are:

- Concentrated, biodegradable washing powder or liquid
- Long-life candles – African candles are often soft, and burn quickly

- Nylon 'paracord' – at least 20m for emergencies and washing lines
- Back-up battery charger for phone
- Good compass and a whistle
- More comprehensive medical kit (page 157)

PHOTOGRAPHY AND OPTICS Outside of Gaborone, optical equipment isn't widely available in Botswana – so bring everything that you will need with you. Note that it is illegal to fly a drone over any national park or game reserve without a licence.

Pictures taken around dawn and dusk will have the richest, deepest colours, while those taken in the middle of the day, when the sun is high, will seem pale and washed-out by comparison. Beware of the very deep shadows and high contrast that are typical of tropical countries – cameras can struggle to capture the range of colours and shades that our eyes can. If you want to take pictures in full daylight, and capture details in the shadows, then you will need a good camera, and to spend some time learning how to use it fully. By restricting your photography to mornings, evenings and simple shots you will get better pictures and encounter fewer problems.

The bush is very dusty, so bring plenty of lens-cleaning cloths, and a blow-brush. Take great care not to get dust into the back of any camera, as a single grain on the back-plate can be enough to make a long scratch which ruins every frame taken.

BINOCULARS For a safari holiday, a good pair of binoculars is essential. They will bring you far more enjoyment than a camera, as they make the difference between merely seeing an animal or bird at a distance, and being able to observe its markings, movements and moods closely. Do bring one pair per person; one between two is just not enough.

There are two styles: the small 'compact' binoculars, perhaps 10–12cm long, which account for most popular modern sales, and the larger, heavier styles, double or triple that size, which have been manufactured for years.

Both vary widely in cost and quality. If you are buying a pair, then consider getting the larger style. The compact ones are fine for spotting animals; but are difficult to hold steady, and very tiring to use for extensive periods. You will only realise this when you are out on safari all day, by which time it is too late.

Around 8 x 32 or 8 x 42 is an ideal size for field observations, as most people need some form of rest, or tripod, to hold the larger 10 x 50 models steady. Get the best-quality ones you can for your money. A pair of decent budget binoculars, such as the Nikon Travelite Ex, will cost from around US$140/£100. In a different league entirely are top-of-the range binoculars manufactured by Leica and Swarovski. You will be able to see the difference instantly when you use them.

MONEY AND BUDGETING

Botswana has probably Africa's strongest and most stable currency, underpinned by the huge earnings of its diamond industry. The unit of currency is the pula – a word that also means 'rain' in Setswana, and hence tells you something about the importance of water in this country.

Theoretically, each pula is divided into 100 thebe, although one thebe isn't worth that much, so most prices are rounded to the nearest ten thebe. Notes come in denominations of 200, 100, 50, 20 and 10 pula, with coins of 5, 2 and 1 pula, and 50, 25, 10 and 5 thebe. Notes in circulation prior to 2009 are no longer valid.

The pula's exchange rate (page 2) is free-floating on the world market, so there is no black market for the currency. Thus don't expect to see any shady characters on the street hissing 'change money' as you pass; I never have. (If you do, then assume they're con men trying to dupe visitors who don't know any better!) As a result, US dollars, euros and UK pounds sterling are easily changed – and most of the more international businesses in the tourism sector set their prices in US dollars.

INFLATION Botswana generally maintains low and stable inflation rates (3.9% in January 2024) due to prudent economic management. Factors like global commodity prices, especially diamonds, influence inflation, with the government and Bank of Botswana regulating monetary policy to keep it under control.

BUDGETING Inevitably, the cost of visiting Botswana varies with the style in which you travel, and the places where you spend your time. However, Botswana's costs are relatively high and VAT (currently 14%) is charged on most transactions.

If you plan to get the most from what Botswana has to offer, you will probably need from US$700/£550 per person sharing per night for a good camp in a private concession in low season, rising to around double that in the high season. Put into context, this means that an eight-night/nine-day fly-in trip from the UK to good safari camps will start at about US$6,000/£4,500 per person sharing in low season, and rise to over double that in the high season, excluding flights to get to/from Botswana.

The top Okavango camps cost, in high season, in the range of US$2,500/£2,000 to US$4,400/£3,500 per person per night – making them only accessible for the most affluent of travellers.

This is high, even by African safari standards, but what you get for it is high quality, and includes everything: your accommodation, activities, food, most drinks (usually excluding spirits and non-house wines), and even the odd light aircraft (or helicopter) flight between camps. You'll stay at a handful of small safari camps, each of which is situated in a different, but often stunning, corner of a pristine wilderness. This is one of the world's top wildlife experiences – the kind of magical trip at which Botswana excels.

At the other end of the spectrum, if you travel through Botswana on local buses, camping and staying near the towns, then the country isn't too expensive. A budget of US$80–110/£60–80 per day for food, accommodation and transport would suffice. However, most backpackers who undertake trips on this sort of budget won't be able to afford to visit any of the camps or more remote wildlife locations – which means that they'll be missing out on a lot of what makes Botswana unique.

Somewhere in the middle, at around US$250–650/£200–500 per person per day, you'll find a real range of budget camping safaris run out of Maun, many between there and Victoria Falls, which will give you a real experience of Chobe and Moremi, and a taste of the Okavango Delta. They won't match what you'd find in the private concession areas, further into the wetter areas of the Delta, but they will make you glad you came to Botswana and probably harden your determination to return when you've a lot more money!

One mid-range option, which we'd recommend only for those with substantial African experience, is to hire a fully equipped 4x4. Such a choice enables you to camp, buy food, and drive yourself around. This requires driving ability and planning, and isn't something to undertake lightly. For costs, see the *Hiring a 4x4* section (page 124).

Budgeting for safaris Botswana isn't a cheap country to visit. This is due to a combination of the high costs of the logistics needed to operate in remote areas, plus the deliberate policy of the government to maximise revenues from tourism, while preserving the pristine nature of the country by using high costs to limit the number of visitors. That said, different kinds of trips need very different budgeting.

For self-drivers If you have your own rugged 4x4 with equipment and the experience to use it and survive safely in the bush, then you will be able to camp and cook for yourself. This is then an affordable way to travel and see those remote areas of Botswana which are open to the public.

Your largest expense will be the hire of a decent and well-equipped vehicle, as taking anything less into remote areas of wild bush is foolish. See *Hiring a 4x4* (page 124) for more comments on this, but expect it to cost from around US$300/£250 per day, including all your camping kit.

Your next largest expense will probably be park and camping fees in the national parks. These can be substantial, especially now that most of the campsites have been privatised. Rates vary, but with some of the more popular sites coming out at US$50/£40 per person per night, you'll need to budget around US$80/£64 per day, based on two people. Note, however, that there are still many interesting areas outside of the national parks – including parts of Makgadikgadi, the Tsodilo Hills, Aha Hills, Gcwihaba Caves and various offbeat areas of the Kalahari – where fees are considerably lower – or where no fees are payable.

The cost of food depends heavily on where you buy it, as well as what you buy – but most people will probably do one large shop in Maun or Kasane at the start of their trip, topping up on perishables as they progress. If you are sensible, US$15–25/£12–20 per day would provide good supplies.

For mobile safaris The question 'how much are mobile safaris?' is as tricky to answer as 'how long is a piece of string?' It depends on where your trip is visiting, what the equipment, staff and guides are like, and how big the group is. In short, these trips vary greatly. To choose you must carefully prioritise what you want, what will suit you, and what you can afford to pay. Note also that prices for higher-end trips are heavily dependent upon the time of year that you travel.

Backpackers looking for 'bargain-basement trips' are often happy to put up their own tents, do camp chores and supply their own kit. However, in practice the big costs for companies operating trips in these areas are not so much the tents and kit; but the vehicle maintenance, fuel, the guides and the park fees. Hence it's very hard to find trips around northern Botswana that are both good and cheap.

The cheapest trips tend to minimise their stays within the prime national parks where they can, perhaps by staying outside Chobe, which can be visited on a day trip, and even using the tarred road between Kasane and Maun via Nata rather than going through Chobe and Moremi. Some will also focus on Nxai and Makgadikgadi; others will include two–three days on a mokoro trip. Typical costs will be US$250–400/£200–300 per person sharing per day, based on a six-night trip with six participants.

By contrast, a luxurious mobile safari, visiting prime areas in the company of a small group with a good professional guide, might easily cost up to US$1,100/£850 per person sharing per day, including superb meals and all your drinks.

Between these two extremes, you ought to be able to get a trip of a decent quality as part of a small group for something around US$500–750/£400–600 per person per night sharing. Then expect to be camping in comfortable tents, with a small camp staff who will organise them, cook your meals and do all the chores.

As a final thought, if you really are seeking a great trip and great value, then travelling 'off season' makes a big difference. Costs in the green (rainy) season can be half what they are in the peak season – and you'll see far fewer other visitors while you're on safari.

For fly-in safaris to lodges and camps Again, the prices vary considerably. These are always at their highest between around July and October and at their lowest around November to April. You will find slightly less costly camps in more marginal areas outside of the parks.

Expect the simplest permanent camp within a national park or private reserve to cost US$500–600/£400–480 per person per night sharing during the green season – and for that to rise to at least US$750/£600 in the high season. This will almost always include all of your park fees, meals and activities, and usually most of your drinks.

Otherwise, a typical fly-in safari camp in a good area will cost around US$700–1,000/£550–800 per person per night sharing, all-inclusive in the green season, rising to US$1,200–2,400/£950–1,900 per person sharing in the high season.

If money really is no object, then there are a few really top-end places that cost up to about US$4,500/£3,570 in the high season. Having said this, there are three obvious caveats. First, none of the prices here includes flight transfers. These probably average out at about US$250/£200 per person per transfer, though working them out precisely is a complex business.

Second, you will almost always be quoted a rate for a 'package' of camps and flights; that's normal and often cannot be broken into its components.

And third, note that although the prices for camps given in this guide indicate what you can expect to pay (in 2024) if you book direct, this really should be a maximum figure. You will usually be able to get them a little cheaper if you book through a good tour operator – and this is especially true of the more costly lodges. See *Organising a fly-in trip*, page 117.

TIPPING Tipping can be a sensitive, and sometimes contentious, topic, and it's certainly one worth thinking about carefully. Read the section on local payments (page 184) and realise that thoughtlessly tipping too much is just as bad as tipping too little. Ask locally what's appropriate; here we can only give rough guidance.

Helpers with baggage might expect 10 pula, while sorting out a problem with a reservation would be P25–40 (US$2–3/£1.50–2.50). Restaurants often add an automatic service charge to the bill, in which case an additional tip is not usually given. If they do not do this, then 10% would certainly be appreciated if the service was good.

At safari camps, tipping is not obligatory – despite the assumption from some visitors that it is. If a guide has given you really good service then a tip of about US$10–15/£8–12 per person per day would be a generous reflection of this. If you have a private guide, consider increasing this to US$20/£16 per person per day. A similar bonus for a tracker or mokoro poler might be around US$5/£4 per person per day. And if you'd like to leave something in the communal tip box for distribution to the camp staff, then consider around US$5/£4 per person per day. Of course, if the service hasn't been that good, then don't tip.

Always tip at the end of your stay – not at the end of each day/activity. Do not tip after every game drive. This leads to the guides only trying hard when they know there's a tip at the end of the morning. Such camps aren't pleasant to visit and this isn't the way to encourage top-quality guiding. It's best to wait until the end of your stay, and then give what you feel is appropriate in one lump sum.

However, before you do this find out if tips go into one box for all of the camp staff, or if the guides are treated differently. Then ensure that your tip reflects this – with perhaps as much again divided between the rest of the staff.

To put our suggestions in perspective, it's perhaps worth bearing in mind that the Gross National Income (GNI) is about US$17.80 per person per day in Botswana. This is a reflection of the average income of Botswana's citizens. In contrast, the equivalent GNI in the UK is about US$55.20; in the United States about US$77.95; in New Zealand about US$50.90; and in Germany about US$65.99.

HOW TO TAKE YOUR MONEY Taking your money in the form of both cash (ideally US dollars, but pound sterling is a reasonable back-up) and credit cards is probably the ideal. Always bring a mixture of US$1, US$5, US$10 and US$20 notes (US$1 notes make useful, if generous, tips for porters). The risk of forgeries has understandably made people suspicious of larger denomination notes, and US$100 and even US$50 bills are often rejected in shops and even banks. South African rand are sometimes accepted, though not as widely as dollars or pounds – and they're not very popular.

While US dollars (and/or credit cards) are most useful for those staying in hotels and lodges, and are usually accepted in restaurants and tourist shops, elsewhere you will need to have some Botswanan pula, especially for smaller transactions and anything bought by the roadside. In more rural locations, nobody will accept anything else. Many fuel stations will accept only cash in pula; those that accept credit cards are still in the minority. It's advisable to make an ATM stop on arrival in Botswana to avoid being caught without local currency later in your trip.

Credit cards Cashpoint (ATM) machines that work with foreign credit cards can be found in most large towns, including Maun and Kasane, and some fuel stations. That said, you may need to try more than one bank before you find one that accepts your card.

Visa cards are more widely accepted than Mastercard, and generally cause fewer problems in shops too, so do bear this in mind when planning your trip. If necessary, you can obtain cash against a credit card inside the banks.

Most tourist lodges, hotels, restaurants and shops accept credit cards, with many now using contactless devices.

Banks If you need to change foreign currency, receive bank drafts, or do any other relatively complex financial transactions, then the banks are capable and efficient. Their opening times vary, but expect them to start around 08.30 and finish by 15.30 during the week. The bigger banks open on Saturday, too (typically 08.30–noon).

MAPS AND NAVIGATION

FINDING THE RIGHT MAP The best maps of northern Botswana for most visitors are those published in the Shell series, which stand head-and-shoulders above the rest. The first of these was the ground-breaking *Shell Tourist Guide to Botswana*, originally published in 1998, which incorporated a short but very informative 60-page booklet on the country – effectively an impressive mini-guidebook – and a serious, well-researched, original map. These were produced by Veronica Roodt, an expert on the flora and fauna of the area. What really made the difference was that, on the reverse, were smaller, inset maps of all the main parks, complete with a number of GPS waypoints. It was this information which revolutionised independent trips around Botswana, and effectively opened the doors for more travellers into some of the country's less-known areas like the Central Kalahari.

Since then Shell have also published more detailed *Chobe* and *Moremi* maps, as well as those covering the *Okavango Delta and Linyanti*, and the *Kgalagadi*. These have much more specific coverage of game-viewing tracks – utilising satellite images, and including bird and animal checklists. All are worth having, in addition to the main Botswana map, if you're visiting these areas.

South African publisher Tinkers (w tinkers.co.za) also covers three oft-visited areas: the *Chobe River Tourist Map*, *Chobe National Park Tourist Map*, and *Moremi Game Reserve Tourist Map* – each with game-drive loops and GPS co-ordinates. These and some of the Shell maps may be on sale at the park gates into Chobe and Moremi, but it makes more sense to buy them before you set off.

If you want more detailed, Ordnance Survey-type maps, then by far the best plan is to go directly to the offices of the Department for Surveys and Mapping, in either Maun (page 192) or Gaborone (+267 395 3251). Each of these two offices has roughly the same variety of excellent maps on offer, although some are always out of print. A particular favourite is the 1:350,000 map that covers the whole Okavango Delta area in detail. However, many of these maps were made several years ago; since then, tracks have changed, as has the location and number of safari camps. Therefore, unless you have plenty of time to interpret them, and can afford to carry around lots of maps, they're of limited use.

For something more up to date and altogether more useful you might consider visiting Ngami Data Services (page 192) in Maun, whose maps can be found hanging on the walls of many camps throughout Botswana. Their offerings range from historical souvenir prints to current maps with GPS co-ordinates. They even have a few helpful guides, of which the *Mobile Operators Campsite Guide* and the *Guide to the Tsodilo Hills World Heritage Site* are particularly good.

DIGITAL MAPPING Many overland travellers with a GPS would be lost – sometimes quite literally – without Tracks4Africa (w tracks4africa.co.za), a digital mapping software package that covers the whole continent. That said, it is only compatible with Garmin devices, and while the Tracks4Africa mobile app is often useful, it isn't as good as the real thing, being decidedly hit and miss in certain areas. I have also experimented with using the free maps.me app and have been surprised and very impressed. I wouldn't recommend that travellers rely on Google maps; it's not the right tool for driving in the bush.

For all of the above, you should certainly download any apps and maps that you need before you leave home, so you can use your device offline. Data roaming is prohibitively expensive, and even using a local SIM would leave you with a significant phone bill.

More general maps of Botswana, which you're most likely to find in bookshops and map stores outside Africa, are generally fine if you are visiting the towns and simply want to know roughly where the parks are. Among these is the expensive but tear-resistant Tracks4Africa map of *Botswana*, at 1:1m, with enlargements of eight key areas on the reverse, as well as an indication of driving times. Also tear-resistant is the double-sided offering from Reise Know-How at the same scale, with an indexed gazetteer – though the idea of using this to navigate anywhere off the tar is completely fanciful.

GPS systems If you are heading into one of the more remote parks in your own vehicle, then you really should invest in a decent GPS (global positioning system). These can fix your latitude, longitude and elevation to within about 10m, and are essential for travel in remote areas.

What to buy Commercial hand-held and car-mounted GPS units are readily available across the world, with prices from a few hundred dollars to many thousand. As is usual with high-tech equipment, their prices are falling and their features are ever expanding as time progresses.

We have used a variety of Garmin GPS receivers (w garmin.com) for years now and continue to rate their quality and reliability. Garmin GPS units are also compatible with the excellent Tracks4Africa mapping software (page 142). At the time of writing, Garmin GPS systems worth considering are the Montana, the Overlander preloaded with topographic maps of Africa, the GPSMAP series and the Zumo series designed specifically for motorcycles.

What a GPS can do A GPS should enable you to store 'waypoints' and build an electronic picture of an area, as well as working out basic latitude, longitude and elevation. So, for example, you can store the position of your campsite and the nearest road, making it much easier to be reasonably sure of navigating back without simply retracing your steps.

It will also enable you to programme in points, using the co-ordinates given throughout this book, and use these for navigation. (See page x for an important comment on datums.) Thus you should be able to get an idea of whether you're going in the right direction, and how far away your destination is.

When you return home, then knowing the GPS co-ordinates for a place will enable you to see satellite images of the place using programmes like Google Maps and Google Earth. See Expert Africa's website (w expertafrica.com) for a demonstration of the satellite images of lodges that are possible.

What a GPS can't do A GPS isn't a compass, and when you're standing still, it can't tell you which direction is which. It can only tell you a direction if you're moving. (A few of the most expensive GPS units do now incorporate electronic compasses.)

A GPS gives you a distance and a bearing for where you might want to go but it can't tell you how to get there. You'll still need to find a track. You should NEVER just set out across the bush following a bearing; that's a recipe for disaster.

Finally, not even top-of-the-range devices can replace a good navigator. You still need to be able to map-read, navigate and think to use a GPS effectively. If you're clueless on navigation then driving around the bush in Botswana will get you into a mess with or without a GPS.

Accessories Most GPS units use quite a lot of battery power so purchase an in-car (cigarette lighter) adapter for your GPS when you buy it. This will enable you to power it from the vehicle while you're driving. It's well worth taking a good supply of spare batteries too.

Warning Although a GPS may help you to recognise your minor errors before they are amplified into major problems, note that such a gadget is no substitute for good map work and navigation. They're great fun to use, but shouldn't be relied upon as a sole means of navigation. You MUST always have a back-up plan, including good paper maps, and an understanding of where you are – or you will be unable to cope if your GPS fails.

GETTING AROUND

BY AIR There are two ways to fly within Botswana: on scheduled airlines or using small charter flights.

Scheduled flights The national carrier, Air Botswana, operates the domestic scheduled network. This is limited in scope for most safari travellers, but generally very efficient and reliable. Air Botswana links Maun directly with Kasane, Gaborone and Johannesburg, while Kasane is linked to Gaborone, Francistown and Johannesburg.

Charter flights Small charter flights operate out of the hub of Maun, with Kasane as a secondary focus. They ferry travellers around the camps of northern Botswana like a fleet of air taxis. Predominantly using six to 12-seater planes, they criss-cross the region between a plethora of small bush runways. There's no other way to reach most camps, but flights are usually organised by the operator who arranges your camps as an integral part of your trip, so you'll never need to worry about arranging them for yourself.

You'll likely share with other travellers and camp staff on these small flights, with precise timings scheduled by the companies a few days beforehand. Expect flights to take anything from 10 minutes to under an hour, during which you may stop at one or two other airstrips before reaching your destination. (See page 9 to learn a little about the patterns that you'll be able to see in the landscapes below.)

DRIVING Driving in Botswana is on the left, as in the UK, and seatbelts must be worn. If you're planning to drive, you should have a photo driving licence.

The standard of driving is relatively good, but traffic – and accidents – are increasing, so remain alert, and avoid driving at night in any circumstances.

Speed limits are officially 120km/h (75mph) on major roads, decreasing to 80km/h (50mph) outside towns and on gravel roads, and 60km/h (37mph) in urban areas. Variations to these limits are generally signposted. That said, travelling at 120km/h on even the best of Botswana's tarmac roads is foolhardy, given the potential for animals such as goats and even elephants to wander across the road, or pot-holes to appear; stick to 80km/h. In national parks, there is a blanket limit of 40km/h – though you'll rarely be in a position to come close to this.

The police have radar equipment, and actively set up radar traps, especially just outside towns. Speeding tickets may sometimes be paid on the spot, against a signed receipt from the officer, but often you'll have to report to the nearest police station within 48 hours. Botswana's police are efficient; it'd be foolhardy not to obey such a summons.

At the time of research, in early 2024, the price of fuel in Botswana's main towns was around P17 (US$1.25) per litre for diesel, and P15 (US$1.10) for unleaded petrol. The further you travel away from the main centres, the more these prices are likely to increase.

Most roads in the towns, and the major arteries connecting these, are tarred and are usually in good condition, although traffic is increasing year on year. Away from these main arteries, though, and throughout virtually all of the wild areas covered by this guide, the roads are simply tracks through the bush made by whatever vehicles have passed that way. They are almost never maintained, and usually require at least a high-clearance vehicle – although often a high-clearance 4x4 is essential. During the wet season some of these tracks can be less forgiving, and become virtually impassable. Travelling on these bush tracks at any time of year is time-consuming – but very much one of the joys of an adventurous trip to Botswana. For more details, see page 169. For details of vehicle hire and maps, see pages 124 and 141.

BY RAIL There is a railway that links South Africa with Lobatse, Gaborone, Palapye, Francistown and Bulawayo (in Zimbabwe), but that's the only railway in the country – so is rarely used by travellers to northern Botswana.

BY BUS Botswana has a variety of local buses (detailed in individual chapters) that link the main towns together along the tarred roads. They're cheap, frequent and a good way to meet local people, although they can also be crowded, uncomfortable and noisy. In short, they are similar to any other local buses in Africa, and travel on them has both its joys and its frustrations.

There are two different kinds: the smaller minibuses, often VW combis, and the longer, larger, 'normal' buses. Both will serve the same destinations, but the larger ones tend to run to a timetable, go faster and stop less. Their smaller relatives usually wait to fill up before they leave the bus station, then go slower and stop at more places.

ACCOMMODATION

Although northern Botswana's accommodation is dominated by hotels, safari lodges and campsites aimed at visiting tourists, there is still a considerable variety in terms of both style and prices, with increasing numbers of new places opening since the last edition. Most establishments are graded nowadays, with between one and five stars awarded on the basis of 'furnishings, service and guest care', but inevitably this gives only part of the picture.

Prices quoted in this guide are usually international rates – those payable by visitors resident outside southern Africa. Some establishments – and especially the national parks' campsites – operate a two- or even three-tier pricing system, in favour of Botswana's citizens and southern African residents. All types of accommodation attract a tourism levy, or 'bed levy', of P10 per person per night. This is usually included in the rates, but in some of the cheaper establishments, or those where you pay per room rather than per person, it may be charged extra. Note that while rates were correct at the time of research in 2024, many will inevitably rise during the life of this guide.

ACCOMMODATION PRICES AND CODES Rates at most safari lodges in Botswana include full board and activities, whereas hotels and guesthouses are more usually priced for bed and breakfast. In both cases, we have coded prices in this guide to give an at-a-glance indication of relative costs. A few other establishments, however, fall outside this mould, and have not been allocated a code. These include campsites, and places where prices are based on dinner, bed and breakfast, or full board but without activities.

For urban establishments, and others offering **B&B accommodation**, rates are based on the cost of a double room with breakfast. Single supplements average around 20%, but may be absent in low season and significantly higher in peak season. VAT (14%) may be charged extra.

$$$$$	US$350+	£280+	P4,700+
$$$$	US$200–350	£160–280	P2,700–4,700
$$$	US$120–200	£95–160	P1,600–2,700
$$	US$60–120	£50–95	P800–1,600
$	up to US$60	up to £50	up to P800

For **all-inclusive** places, such as safari lodges and camps, rates are based on the cost of *one person sharing a room* per night. All safari lodge rates assume two adults in each room, and almost all will charge a single-person supplement. Unless stated in the listings, all-inclusive rates – marked as FBA (full board and activities) – also include local alcoholic drinks, laundry and park fees.

🐾🐾🐾🐾🐾	US$1,000+	£790+
🐾🐾🐾🐾	US$650–1,000	£515–790
🐾🐾🐾	US$300–650	£235–515
🐾🐾	US$125–300	£100–235
🐾	up to US$125	up to £100

HOTELS AND GUESTHOUSES Hotels in Botswana's towns tend to be aimed at visiting businesspeople, in which case they're functional but uninspiring, regardless of price level. That said, they're also generally clean and rarely unpleasant. Expect costs in Maun to start from around US$85/£67 for a double room per night, but in Kasane – which is more geared to international tourists – you'll find a mid-range room starting around US$120/£95 a night.

In recent years a few independent guesthouses have sprung up in Botswana's larger towns, including Maun and Kasane. They are often in suburban locations so they're really only practical if you've got your own vehicle. That said, a few are original in design and offer personal service with good local tips on offer. Expect to pay around US$125/£100 for a double room in these places.

LODGES AND CAMPS Botswana's safari camps vary from striking, decadent lodges, crafted by top international architects and designers, to simple spots with a few small tents, a campfire and a table under the shade of a tree. Increasingly, camps are creeping to the former category. But wherever you stay, the vast majority will have rooms that are at least as comfortable as a good hotel room, and most, even the tents, will far surpass this standard.

When the words 'tented camp' are mentioned in safari talk – and certainly in this book – banish any preconceptions of cramped scout tents, and think instead of designer chic under canvas. Comfortable beds, fine linen, en-suite flushing toilets, running hot and cold water for showers, solar-powered lights and thoughtful interior design are standard. Many tents will have electric fans, and an increasing number will have air conditioning. Traditional bucket showers, where a bucket is filled with hot water and raised on a pulley for you by camp staff, are exceptionally rare nowadays – and where they are present, they tend to rival hotel power-showers in water pressure and often have the most idyllic outdoor views.

Note that expensive does not always mean luxurious. Some of the top camps are very simply constructed. Equally, looking for basic, simple camps won't necessarily make your trip any cheaper. You're usually paying for virtually exclusive use of pristine wilderness areas, and will find little cost difference between a tiny bush camp and the largest lodge. In fact, if anything there's increasingly a premium on space in the smaller camps. These need booking earlier as many people find these friendlier and more intimate. A superlative guide or an exceptional environment and game will usually trump an impressive wine list or gym access for most safari enthusiasts.

EATING AND DRINKING

FOOD Camps, hotels and lodges that cater for overseas visitors serve a very international fare, and the quality of food prepared in the most remote camps is phenomenally high. When coming to Botswana on safari your biggest problem with food is likely to be the very real danger of putting on weight! Fresh fruit, home-grown vegetables and excellent Botswanan meat are whipped into a veritable feast for every meal and snack opportunity in the day. All of the safari camps have the skill and ability to cater for any dietary requirements, but it's important to let them know when booking so that they can be prepared – there's no last-minute popping out to the shops for specific ingredients in a remote camp.

Talking of any one 'local cuisine' in Botswana is misleading, as what a person eats is dependent on where they live and the ethnic group they belong to. In the Kalahari and Okavango there was relatively little agriculture until recently; there, gathering and fishing, supplemented by hunting, provided subsistence for the various groups.

In the kinder climes east of the Kalahari, where there is enough rain for crops, sorghum is probably the main crop. This is first pounded into meal before being mixed with boiling water or sour milk. It's then made into a paste *bogobe* – which is thin, perhaps with sugar like porridge, for breakfast, then eaten thicker, the consistency of mashed potatoes, for lunch and dinner. For these main meals it will normally be accompanied by some tasty relish, perhaps made of meat (*seswa*) and tomatoes (*moro*), or dried fish. Maize meal, or *papa* (often imported as it doesn't tolerate Botswana's dry climate that well), is now often used in place of this. (In Zimbabwe this same staple is known as *sadza*, in Zambia it's *nshima* and in South Africa *mealie-pap*.) You should taste this at some stage when visiting. Safari camps will often prepare it if requested, and it is always available in small restaurants in the towns.

Restaurant price codes Prices for restaurants listed in this guide have been coded as follows, based on the average cost of a main course.

$$$$$	US$15+	£12+	P205+
$$$$	US$12.50–15	£10–12	P170–205
$$$	US$10–12.50	£8–10	P135–170
$$	US$6–10	£4.75–8	P82–135
$	up to US$6	up to £4.75	up to P82

Self-catering If you are driving yourself around and plan to cook, stock up with food and supplies in Maun or Kasane before heading off. Both have several large, well-stocked supermarkets and a number of more specialist shops. Away from these main centres, the range will become sparser. Expect villages to have just a bottle stall, selling the most popular cool drinks (often this excludes 'diet' drinks), and a small shop selling staples like rice and (occasionally) bread, and perhaps a few tinned and packet foods. Don't expect anything refrigerated.

When stocking up, it is important to be aware that northern Botswana is effectively ringed by a veterinary fence – widely known as the vet fence or buffalo

5

fence – with regular checkpoints along the roads. The fence is in place to help protect the country's valuable cattle herds from infection with foot-and-mouth disease. For this reason, taking raw meat across the fence from a buffalo area into an area that is used for cattle farming is prohibited. The general rule of thumb (and there are a few quirky exceptions, so check your route) is that you are allowed to move meat from south to north and from east to west. However, you cannot move meat from north to south and from west to east past the vet lines as the northern regions are classified as foot-and-mouth-infected zones. If you are using the Tracks4Africa maps (paper or app) then the vet fence is shown as a clear red line. You can expect vehicle searches, including of fridges and cooler boxes, at these checkpoints, so do abide by the regulations.

DRINK

Alcohol Like most countries in the region, Botswana has two distinct beer types: clear and opaque. Most visitors and more affluent people in Botswana drink the **clear beers**, which are similar to European lagers and always served chilled. St Louis and Castle are the lagers brewed here by a subsidiary of South African Breweries. They are widely available and usually good. You'll also sometimes find Windhoek lager, from Namibia – which is similar and equally good. For **craft beers**, the excellent Okavango Craft Brewery in Maun (page 203) is worth a stop to sample their range of beers and Mowana cider and tour the micro-brewery. Self-drivers can stock up for sundowners too.

The less affluent residents will usually opt for some form of the **opaque beer** (sometimes called Chibuku, after the market-leading brand). This is a commercial version of traditional beer, usually brewed from maize and/or sorghum. It's a sour, porridge-like brew: an acquired taste, and it changes flavour as it ferments; you can often ask for 'fresh beer' or 'strong beer'. As a visitor you'll have to make a real effort to seek out opaque beer; most bars that tourists visit don't sell it. Locals will sometimes buy a bucket of it, and then pass it around a circle of drinkers. It would be unusual for a visitor to drink this, so try some and amuse your companions. If you aren't sure about the bar's hygiene standards, stick to the pre-packaged brands of opaque beer like Chibuku.

Soft drinks Soft drinks are available everywhere, which is fortunate when the temperatures are high. Choices are often limited, though the ubiquitous Coca-Cola and Fanta are usually available. Diet drinks are available in the towns, but rarely seen in the small bottle stores which pepper the rural areas – which is no surprise for a country where the rural population are poor and need all the energy their food and drink can give them.

Water Throughout the country, water in the main towns is purified and is generally safe to drink. Water quality is monitored by the Ministry of Health and the Water Utilities Corporation – a water supply authority. However, if you travel infrequently or know your stomach is particularly sensitive, it may be better to drink mineral water.

Out in the bush, most of the camps and lodges use water from boreholes. These underground sources vary in quality, but the water is usually perfectly safe to drink. Sometimes it is sweet, at other times a little alkaline or salty. The camps will usually advise you on the water quality: many will recommend that you brush your teeth and wash using the borehole water, but drink the filtered or mineral water provided.

There are excellent-value **handicrafts** available in Botswana. Look especially for the intricate, hand-woven baskets made from the fronds of the real fan palm (*Hyphaene petersiana*), and the many different handicrafts of the San, like jewellery made from ostrich eggshells.

There's usually a divide between the simpler outlets, perhaps direct from the producers, and the more stylish, well-located shops which often have the best pieces, but invariably charge the highest prices. There are plenty of these shops in Maun (page 205), and most safari lodges have small shops selling crafts and curios. Sometimes they stock items made by the staff or people in a local village; if that's the case, do buy something to support the initiative.

If you're starting or ending your trip in Livingstone, then don't miss the curio stalls near the border post to Victoria Falls, or those in Livingstone's Mukuni Park. These are among the region's best places for carvings (though expect to bargain hard). Other places to seek out would be the various curio shops in Maun and Kasane, for excellent baskets, and the small basket shops in towns west of the Delta.

MEDIA AND COMMUNICATIONS

POST BotswanaPost (w botswanapost.post), the government-owned postal service, is reliable, but often slow. They have post offices in all the larger towns, and a network of agencies in some of the larger villages. In northern Botswana, these include offices in Etsha 6, Ghanzi, Gumare, Gweta, Kasane, Kazungula, Maun, Nata, and Shakawe.

Letters are classified by size, with a 'standard' one being up to 120mm x 235mm x 20mm. For postcards and standard letters weighing less than 200g, stamps cost P8 to Botswana, P11–12 to the rest of Africa, P15 to Europe and P16 to the rest of the world. Parcel rates vary by destination and weight. Stamps are sometimes sold in curio shops, and most hotels and lodges will post letters on your behalf.

TELEPHONE Botswana's telephone system is very good, and you can dial some remarkably offbeat places from overseas. The presence of public phoneboxes on the streets is all but redundant nowadays, and mobile phones are as ubiquitous here as anywhere else in the world.

To dial into Botswana from abroad, the international access code is +267. From inside the country, dial 00 to get an international line, then the country's access code (eg: 44 for the UK, 1 for the USA), then omit the first 0 of the number you are calling.

Essential telephone numbers
Ambulance ☏997
Fire ☏998
Medical rescue ☏911
Medical air rescue ☏390 1601
Police ☏999

Mobile phones Mobile-phone coverage has increased rapidly in recent years, with reception found even in relatively small villages. Outside of these, though, and in the national parks, a mobile phone will be of no use at all.

Local, pre-paid SIM cards can be purchased in Kasane and Maun, significantly cutting the cost of calls from a mobile registered overseas. The major operators are Mascom (w mascom.bw) and Orange (w orange.co.bw), of which Mascom arguably has the better coverage, with BTC (w btc.bw) also available. Expect to pay about P10 for a SIM card, with top-up cards available in various denominations from P5. Consider buying a local eSIM before travelling from a company like SimOptions (w simoptions.com).

EMAIL AND THE INTERNET Most businesses in Botswana have access to the internet, though it can be slow. In general, it's best not to send large attachments via email until you're sure that the recipient can handle them, and if you don't get a reply from an email to Botswana within 48 hours, it's a good idea to resend it.

Contacting businesses, even small local operations, on WhatsApp is common practice and will often get the fastest response. Many small businesses have also created Facebook pages or Instagram accounts, which they use instead of creating a website.

MEDIA With a small population, many in rural locations, the press here is equally small, and partly relies on the larger South African media companies. However, Botswana has several newspapers, radio and television stations.

Independence issues Botswana's media is generally fairly free and expresses its opinions, even when it disagrees with government policy. Even media which are owned by the government are obliged by law to give basic coverage of opposition views as well as the official versions. That said, disagreements do occur on a fairly regular basis, and clearly the independent press here fights a continuing battle to remain independent.

The International Press Institute conducted an extensive investigation into the media environment in August 2022 and concluded that, while recent reforms in media laws have been positive, there are still areas requiring improvement to safeguard press freedom long-term.

Notably, the investigating team felt that there is a need for stronger protections for independent journalism to operate freely and a need for freedom-of-information legislation. There have been ongoing concerns over government influence on public media and misuse of advertising for many years, as well as increasing instances of strategic lawsuits against critical journalism, the unlawful seizure of journalists' phones and laptops, and concerns over the government's surveillance and intimidation.

The press Botswana's most widely read newspapers are the *Botswana Guardian* (w guardiansun.co.bw) and *Mmegi* ('The Reporter': w mmegi.bw), both published daily. *Mmegi* also has a sister publication, the *Monitor*, which comes out on a Monday. Other national papers include the *Botswana Gazette* (w thegazette.news), the *Midweek Sun* (w themidweeksun.co.bw), and the government's free weekday newspaper, the *Daily News* (w dailynews.gov.bw), while the Maun area has the weekly *Ngami Times* (w ngamitimes.co.bw).

Radio and television The government Department of Information and Broadcasting, based in Gaborone, runs both the national broadcast channel, Botswana Television (f), and Radio Botswana (w radiobotswana.gov.bw). There is also the privately run Gaborone Broadcasting Company (GBC), although the majority of people with televisions are connected to one of the large South African networks, such as the MultiChoice digital satellite service (DSTV), which is a pan-African, commercial broadcaster operating multiple channels.

The two state radio stations, Radio Botswana 1 (RB1) and Radio Botswana 2 (RB2), broadcast around the main towns, but away from these there's generally nothing but long-distance shortwave services. The non-commercial RB1 has no advertising and majors on news and current affairs, while the commercial station, RB2 – or 103 FM – features mainly popular music, from ballads, R&B, house, reggae, fusion and jazz to pop and disco. Within this you'll find the usual DJ banter, as well as news bulletins at regular intervals, in a mix of Setswana and English. Independent radio stations include Yarona FM (w yaronafm.co.bw; 106.6FM), Gabz FM (w gabzfm.com; 96.2FM) and Duma FM (w dumafm.co.bw; 93.0FM).

TRAVELLING POSITIVELY

Botswana is one of the richer of the developing nations, but despite this you may see scenes of poverty when you are visiting the country, especially in more rural areas. Beggars are fairly rare in the towns, but often the least able are dependent on charity. While giving a few coins to people is one way to put a sticking plaster over feeling guilty or sorry, this is not a long-term solution.

Similarly, although the visitor on an expensive safari is making a financial contribution to development and conservation in Botswana, he or she can do a lot more to help.

CONSERVATION The first thing to do if you want to help protect Botswana's wilder areas is to travel there, often; the income generated by tourism is the main hope to enable these areas to survive and thrive in the long term, and this in turn will make a positive contribution to conservation.

Most safari operators have programmes to help their local communities, having recognised that the mass of Botswana's people must benefit from tourism if conservation is going to succeed long term in Botswana. Thus, one very simple thing that you can do to help is to ask your tour operator and safari camp:

- Besides employment, how do local people benefit from this camp?
- How much of this camp's revenue goes directly back to the local people?
- What are you doing to help the people living near this reserve?
- How much control do the local people have in what goes on in the area in which these safaris are operated?
- Are there any projects that I can support?

If more visitors did this, it would make a huge difference in raising awareness of conservation and of the importance of local involvement in this sphere.

The second thing you can do is to support organisations (see below) that work in promoting knowledge of Botswana's wilder areas, in campaigning for environmental and social issues, and in research and conservation.

In addition, helping the country's poorer communities (page 154) will, ultimately, also help preserve the wildlife areas, as without sustainable economic development there's little long-term hope for the wildlife.

BirdLife Botswana ☎+267 319 0540; e blb@ birdlifebotswana.org.bw; w birdlifebotswana.org. bw; f. The local arm of BirdLife International has a bird population monitoring scheme that enables

Comments here are intended to be a general guide, just a few examples of how to travel more sensitively. They should not be viewed as blueprints for perfect Botswana etiquette. Cultural sensitivity is really a state of mind, not a checklist of behaviour – so here we can only hope to give the sensitive traveller a few pointers in the right direction.

When we travel, we are all in danger of leaving negative impressions with local people that we meet. It is easily done – by snapping that picture quickly, while the subject is not looking; by dressing scantily, offending local sensitivities; by just brushing aside the feelings of local people, with the high-handed superiority of a rich Westerner. These things are easy to do, in the click of a shutter, or flash of a dollar bill.

However, you will get the most representative view of Botswana if you cause as little disturbance to the local people as possible. You will never blend in perfectly when you travel – your mere presence there, as an observer, will always change the local events slightly. However, if you try to fit in and show respect for local culture and attitudes, then you may manage to leave positive feelings behind you.

One of the easiest, and most important, ways to do this is with **greetings**. African societies are rarely as rushed as Western ones. When you first talk to someone, you should greet them leisurely. So, for example, if you enter a bus station and want some help, do not just ask outright, 'Where is the bus to…?' That would be rude. Instead you will have a better reception (and a better chance of good advice) by saying:

Traveller:	'Good afternoon.'
Local:	'Good afternoon.'
Traveller:	'How are you?'
Local:	'I am fine, how are you?'
Traveller:	'I am fine, thank you. (pause) Do you know where the bus to…?'

This goes for approaching anyone – always greet them first. For a better reception still, learn the greetings in Setswana (page 536), or even the local language. While most people in Botswana understand English, a greeting in an appropriate local language will be received with delight.

Very rarely in one of the towns you may be approached by someone who doesn't greet you. Instead s/he tries immediately to sell you something, or even hassle you in some way. These people have learned that foreigners aren't used to greetings, and so have adapted their approach accordingly. A surprisingly effective way to dodge their attentions is to reply to their questions with a formal greeting, and then politely – but firmly – refuse their offer.

Another part of the normal greeting ritual is **handshaking**. As elsewhere, you would not normally shake a shop owner's hand, but you would shake hands with someone to whom you are introduced. Get some practice when you arrive, as there is a gentle, three-part handshake used in southern Africa which is easily

visitors as well as locals to contribute to data collection. Birders are asked to notify them about birds identified during Feb & Nov within a clearly defined area.

Botswana Predator Conservation +267 686 2363; e predatorconservation@gmail.com; w bpctrust.org. Fantastic, long-established organisation pioneering a raft of scientific research,

learned. It consists of taking each other's right hand, as for a normal handshake, but just shaking once, up and down. Then while leaving the thumbs linked, the grip is changed by both people raising their hands, until their arms make a right-angle. Each then grasps the other person's thumb and the top of their hand firmly. Then this is swiftly relaxed, with thumbs still interlinked, and the hands are dropped back into one last normal 'shake'.

Your **clothing** is an area that can easily give offence. Most people in Botswana frown upon skimpy or revealing clothing, especially when worn by women. Shorts are fine for walking safaris, but otherwise dress conservatively and avoid short shorts, especially in the more rural areas. Respectable locals will wear long trousers (men) or long skirts (women).

In 2021, Botswana's Court of Appeal upheld a decision to decriminalise **same-sex relationships**. LGBTQIA+ people applauded the court's commitment to equality and liberty, and heralded the judiciary's decision as an example for other African countries to repeal similar, often colonial-era, laws that have long criminalised gay sex. However, while it's not at all unusual in traditional societies to see two men or two women casually holding hands, public **displays of affection** between two people (LGBTQIA+ or heterosexual) may create tension and are best avoided.

Photography is a tricky business. Most people in Botswana will be only too happy to be photographed – provided you ask their permission first. The likelihood is that then everyone will smile for you, producing the type of 'posed' photograph that you may not want. However, stay around and chat for a while, and people will get used to your presence and stop posing; then you will get more natural shots (a camera with a quiet shutter is a help).

Note that special care is needed with photography near government buildings, bridges, mines, and similar sites of strategic importance. You must ask permission before photographing anything here, or you risk people thinking that you are a spy. (To be fair to the country, I've never come across such problems in Botswana, though I'd still exercise the same caution as in any other country.)

If you're seeking directions to somewhere, don't be afraid of **asking questions**. Most people will be polite and keen to help – so keen that some will answer 'yes' to questions if they think that this is what you want to hear. So try to avoid asking leading questions. For example, 'Yes' would often be the typical answer to the question, 'Does this road lead to…?' And in a sense the respondent is probably correct – it will get you there. It's just that it may not be the quickest or shortest way. To avoid misunderstandings, it is often better to ask open-ended questions like, 'Where does this road go to?' or 'How do I drive to…?'

The examples above are general by their very nature. But wherever you find yourself, if you are polite and considerate to the people of Botswana that you meet, then you will rarely encounter any cultural problems. Watch how they behave and, if you have any doubts about how you should act, then ask someone quietly. They will seldom tell you outright that you are being rude, but they will usually give you good advice on how to make your behaviour more acceptable.

local education & wildlife coexistence initiatives. Detailed website documents their current research projects & plans. Donate to their diverse initiatives & chart the progress in impressive reports.

Great Plains Foundation e info@ greatplainsfoundation.com; w greatplainsfoundation.com. Operating a number of excellent projects, including mobile school clinics; Solar Mamas, a scheme in which women are trained in installing & maintaining solar-powered home lighting systems in rural villages & helped to start their own solar businesses; & Conservation Roots, a land restoration project working with local communities to plant indigenous trees.

Kalahari Conservation Society +267 397 4557; e publicrelations@kcs.org.bw; TheKalahariConservationSociety. Environmental non-profit organisation working to protect Botswana's biodiversity & natural resources.

HELPING DISADVANTAGED COMMUNITIES There *are* ways in which you can make a positive contribution, but they require more effort than giving to someone on the street; perhaps this is the least you can do after an enjoyable trip to Botswana?

There is an established, trustworthy and reliable network of charities, churches and NGOs (non-governmental organisations). If you really want to help, then contact someone and make it happen!

Botswana has a whole range of good, small charities working at grassroots level to improve the lot of the poorest members of society here, and help them to develop economically. One good source of information is the website of the Ngamiland Council of Non-Governmental Organisations (NCONGO; +267 686 2851; e info@ncongo.org; w ncongo.org), which provides a brief synopsis of many of the groups doing valuable work in northern Botswana. It doesn't include all charities, but would be a good start to your research.

Another good port of call is Travel for Impact; also detailed below are a few individual charities concentrated on the north of the country.

Travel for Impact +267 686 4431; m 7230 7694; e tfibotswana@gmail.com; w travelforimpact.com. Established in Maun in 2013, TFI is a social enterprise linking the travel industry with a number of community initiatives in northern Botswana, most notably Bana Ba Letsatsi (see below), Women against Rape, AGLOW Polokong (helping disadvantaged elderly), Crafthood (empowering female weavers) & Maun Animal Welfare Society. Projects are detailed on their website & the team here is well placed to offer advice on where & how you can best help.
Bana Ba Letsatsi +267 686 4787; e info@ banabaletsatsi.org; w banabaletsatsi.org. A local charity helping vulnerable children in Maun (page 208).
The EcoExist Project +267 684 0290; m 7314 9517; e info@ecoexistproject.org;

w ecoexistproject.org. Looks for practical, effective ways for Okavango communities & elephants to coexist safely & for the benefit of both. From incentivising 'elephant aware' farming techniques & running the *Elephant Express* school bus, to supporting community-based tourism & tackling wildlife crime, they are a small but important group.
Love Botswana Outreach Mission +267 680 1114; e info@lovebotswana.org; w lovebotswana.org. Founded 35 years ago, this evangelical Christian organisation runs a number of community programmes alongside its faith-building mission, including 1 for young adults with hearing impairments seeking education & employment & a child welfare centre for vulnerable & orphaned children & those with disabilities.

VOLUNTEERING Botswana, like many African countries, hasn't been slow to take advantage of the upsurge in volunteering holidays. Despite this, there are many pitfalls for unwary volunteers, so be sure to do your homework – especially if you are trying to get involved with a local community.

Both Bana Ba Letsatsi and Love Botswana (pages 208 and above) have volunteer programmes, and it might well be worth contacting Travel for Impact (see above) for other ideas. Time in Botswana will do you lots of good; just make sure it's not to the detriment of your hosts; before you start your search, some of the many issues to consider include:

- For every bona fide organisation, there will be others who are willing to take your cash without delivering on their side of the deal.
- Try to be realistic about your skills; they will probably define what you can usefully contribute. Communities in Botswana don't need unskilled hobbyists; they need professionals. To teach skills properly takes years of volunteering or training, not weeks. (How long did *you* take to learn those skills?) So, for example, if you're not a qualified teacher or builder in your home country, then don't expect to be let loose to do any teaching or building in Botswana.
- Most volunteers will learn much more than the members of the communities that they come to 'help'; be aware of this when you describe who is helping whom.
- Make sure that what you are doing isn't effectively taking away a job from a local person.

WILDERNESS

MOKETE

"Nothing prepared me...

How raw and wild it is, it was like stepping back in time... some of the greatest density of wildlife one will ever see".

World-renowned wildlife cinematographer, Russell Maclaughlin

6

Health and Safety

There is always great danger in writing about health and safety for the uninitiated visitor. It is all too easy to become paranoid about exotic diseases that you may catch, and all too easy to start distrusting everybody you meet as a potential thief – falling into an unfounded us-and-them attitude towards the people of the country you are visiting.

As a comparison, imagine an equivalent section in a guidebook to a Western country – there would be a list of possible diseases and advice on the risk of theft and mugging. Many Western cities are very dangerous, but with time we learn how to assess the risks, accepting almost subconsciously what we can and cannot do.

It is important to strike the right balance: to avoid being excessively cautious or too relaxed about your health and your safety. With experience, you will find the balance that best fits you and the country you are visiting.

HEALTH *with Dr Daniel Campion*

PREPARATIONS
Travel insurance Visitors to Botswana should always take out a comprehensive **medical insurance policy** to cover them for emergencies, including the cost of evacuation to another country within the region. Such policies come with an emergency number (often on a reverse-charge/call-collect basis). It's a good idea to memorise this number or write it indelibly on your baggage, in case your internet access is patchy.

Immunisations Having a full set of immunisations takes time, ideally at least six weeks. Visit your doctor or travel clinic (see opposite) to discuss your requirements.

There is no risk of **yellow fever** in Botswana, but a certificate for yellow fever vaccine is required if you are arriving from a country with a risk of a yellow fever transmission or transiting for more than 12 hours through an airport of a country with a risk of yellow fever transmission. Take advice from a registered yellow fever centre.

It is wise to be up to date on **tetanus**, **polio** and **diphtheria** (usually available as an all-in-one vaccine), **typhoid** and **hepatitis A**. Immunisation against **hepatitis B** may also be recommended. Vaccination against **cholera** is not required for entry and the risk is generally low for travellers, apart from certain groups such as aid workers and those without access to clean water. Vaccination against **rabies** is a sensible precaution for all (page 161) and is particularly important if you intend to have contact with animals, or are likely to be 24 hours away from medical help. Ideally you should have three pre-exposure injections over a minimum of 21 days. Vaccination against **tuberculosis** (TB) is of limited value in adults, but may be recommended for a small number of travellers, eg: health workers planning to work in Botswana.

Malaria prevention Malaria is the greatest risk to travellers to Africa, and can be fatal. It occurs throughout northern Botswana, with the highest risk from November to June, so it is essential that you take all possible precautions against it. Key to these are the prevention of mosquito bites (page 159), and taking a suitable prophylactic agent; there is currently no malaria vaccine available for travellers.

The aim of taking this medication is to infuse your bloodstream with drugs that inhibit and kill the malaria parasites injected into you by a feeding mosquito. This is why you must start to take the drugs *before* you arrive in a malarial area – so that they are established in your bloodstream from day one. All also require time to kill the parasites – so unless there is a medical indication for stopping, it is important to complete the course after leaving the area as directed (usually one to four weeks depending on the medication). Unfortunately, malaria parasites continually adapt to the drugs used to combat them, so the recommended prophylaxis must adapt in order to remain effective. It is important to be aware that no anti-malarial drug is 100% protective, although those on prophylactics who are unlucky enough to catch malaria are less likely to get rapidly into serious trouble. In addition to taking anti-malarials, it is therefore important to avoid mosquito bites between dusk and dawn (page 158).

Seek advice from your GP or specialist travel clinic on the best anti-malarials to take; these currently include atovaquone/proguanil (often known by its trademark Malarone), doxycycline and mefloquine. The most suitable drug varies depending on the individual (their health and age) and the countries in which they are travelling. If you plan to spend a long time in Africa and visit remote areas, consider taking an emergency treatment kit in addition to prophylaxis.

It is also worth noting that no homeopathic prophylactic for malaria exists, nor can any traveller acquire effective 'natural immunity' to malaria after infection. Those who don't make use of preventative drugs are risking their lives.

Long-haul flights and DVT Prolonged immobility on long-haul flights can result in deep-vein thrombosis (DVT), which can be dangerous if the clot travels to the lungs to cause pulmonary embolus. The risk increases with age, and is higher in obese or pregnant travellers, heavy smokers, those taller than 6ft/1.8m, and anybody with a history of clots, recent major operation or varicose veins surgery, cancer, a stroke or heart disease. If any of these criteria apply, consult a doctor before you travel.

Travel clinics and health information A list of current travel clinic websites worldwide is available on w istm.org. For other journey preparation information, consult w travelhealthpro.org.uk (UK) or w wwwnc.cdc.gov/travel (USA). All advice found online should be used in conjunction with expert advice received prior to or during travel.

What to bring If you wear **glasses**, bring a spare pair. Those who wear contact lenses should bring spare ones, plus a pair of glasses in case the dust proves too much for the lenses. If you take regular **medication** (including contraceptive pills), ensure you bring enough with you. Pharmacies in Botswana's main towns, and in Livingstone, generally have good supplies of medicines, but away from these you will find very little. Hotels, lodges and safari camps, as well as providers of organised trips, usually have comprehensive emergency kits, but it is wise to bring a small personal **medical kit**, including:

- alcohol-based hand rub or bar of soap in plastic box
- antihistamine tablets
- antiseptic, eg: iodine or potassium permanganate
- blister plasters (if you plan any serious walking)
- condoms or femidoms and contraceptive pills
- impregnated bed-net or permethrin spray
- insect repellent
- lipsalve (ideally containing a sunscreen)
- malaria prophylaxis
- Micropore tape (for closing small cuts – and invaluable for blisters)
- paracetamol or aspirin (but note that aspirin should not be given in the event of snakebite, nor if you think you have dengue fever)
- sticking plaster (a roll is more versatile than pre-shaped plasters)
- suncream

If you are likely to end up in remote situations, you should also consider taking the following – and know how to use them:

- burns dressings (burns are a common problem for campers)
- malaria standby treatment (page 159)
- antibiotics such as azithromycin for severe diarrhoea
- antibiotic eye drops
- injection swabs, sterile needles and syringes

AVOIDING MOSQUITO AND INSECT BITES

The most dangerous biting insects in parts of Botswana are mosquitoes, because they can transmit malaria, dengue fever and a host of other diseases. The *Anopheles* mosquitoes that spread malaria are active at dusk and at night. Using a mosquito net over your bed and covering up exposed skin (by wearing long-sleeved shirts and tucking trousers into socks) in the evening are the most effective steps towards preventing bites. Bed-net treatment kits are available from travel clinics; these prevent mosquitoes biting through a net if you roll against it in your sleep, and also make old and holey nets protective. Mosquito coils and chemical insect repellents will help reduce your chances of being bitten, as will sleeping under a fan.

Mosquito repellent must be applied to all exposed skin. DEET (diethyltoluamide) is the active ingredient in many repellents, and has the most evidence to support its use: the optimum concentration is 50%. Icaridin at 20% is an effective alternative. Eucalyptus citriodora oil (or PMD) is the only 'natural' repellent with some evidence of effectiveness against mosquitoes, but it needs to be applied more frequently. Other remedies, such as eating garlic or taking vitamin B, are not evidence-based: never substitute these for an effective repellent.

Mosquitoes and many other insects are attracted to light. If you are camping, never put a lamp near the opening of your tent. In hotel rooms, be aware that the longer your light is on, the greater the number of insects that will be sharing your accommodation.

It is important to take precautions against other insect bites. During the day it is wise to wear long, loose (preferably 100%-cotton) clothes if you are pushing through scrubby country; this will keep off ticks (page 162) and also tsetse and day-biting *Aedes* mosquitoes, which may spread viral illnesses such as dengue

- lint, sterile bandage and safety pins
- oral rehydration sachets
- steristrips or butterfly closures
- strong painkiller (eg: codeine phosphate)
- tweezers
- water purification equipment (page 165)
- a good medical manual
- a digital thermometer

COMMON MEDICAL PROBLEMS

Malaria You can still catch malaria even if you are taking anti-malarial drugs, so you should do everything possible to avoid mosquito bites (see opposite). Malaria usually manifests within two weeks of transmission, but it can be as little as seven days and anything up to a year. The earlier it is detected, the better it usually responds to treatment. So, your immediate priority upon displaying possible malaria symptoms – including a rapid rise in temperature (over 38°C), and any combination of a headache, flu-like aches and pains, a general sense of disorientation, and possibly nausea and diarrhoea – is to visit a doctor or clinic (page 164); in the UK, go to your nearest hospital emergency department and say that you have been to Africa.

A simple test is usually adequate to determine whether you have malaria. You need three negative tests to be sure it is not malaria. While experts differ on the question of self-diagnosis and self-treatment, the reality is that if you think you

fever and zika virus. You can also treat natural-fibre clothing with clothing sprays that contain permethrin. The insecticide will kill mosquitoes on contact with the fabric; the clothes will survive a few washes and will still be effective.

Tsetse flies are now rare in the Okavango Delta thanks to a government initiative to eradicate them. The flies hurt when they bite and it is said that they are attracted to the colour blue; locals will advise if they are a problem and whether they transmit sleeping sickness.

Minute pestilential biting blackflies spread river blindness in some parts of Africa between 19°N and 17°S; the disease is caught close to fast-flowing rivers since flies breed there and the larvae live in rapids. The flies bite during the day but long trousers tucked into socks and DEET on exposed skin will help keep them off.

Tumbu flies or putsi, often called mango flies, are a problem where the climate is hot and humid. The adult fly lays her eggs on the soil or on drying laundry and when the eggs come into contact with human flesh (when you put on clothes or lie on a bed) they hatch and bury themselves under the skin. Here they form a crop of 'boils', each with a maggot inside. Smear a little Vaseline over the hole, and they will push their noses out to breathe. It may be possible to squeeze them out but it depends if they are ready to do so as the larvae have spines that help them to hold on. In putsi areas either dry your clothes and sheets within a screened house, dry them in direct sunshine until they are crisp, or iron them.

Jiggers, or sandfleas, are another flesh-feaster, which can be best avoided by wearing shoes. They latch on if you walk barefoot in contaminated places, and set up home under the skin of the foot, usually at the side of a toenail where they cause a painful, boil-like swelling. They need picking out by a local expert.

have malaria and are not within easy reach of a doctor, it would be wisest to start treatment. It's important to have clear written instructions from a travel clinic on the use of standby treatment. If you use a self-treatment kit, you should still seek medical assistance as soon as possible, for definitive diagnosis and treatment.

Travellers' diarrhoea Many visitors to unfamiliar destinations suffer a dose of travellers' diarrhoea, usually as a result of imbibing contaminated food or water. Rule one in avoiding diarrhoea and other sanitation-related diseases is arguably to wash your hands regularly, particularly before snacks and meals. As for what food you can safely eat, a useful maxim is: 'peel it, boil it, cook it, or forget it'. This means that fruit you have washed and peeled yourself should be safe, as should hot cooked foods. However, raw foods, cold cooked foods, salads, fruit salads prepared by others, ice cream and ice are all risky. See page 148 for details on safe water sources.

Resist the temptation to reach for the medical kit as soon as your stomach turns a little fluid. Most cases of travellers' diarrhoea will resolve themselves within 24–48 hours with no treatment at all. To speed up the process of acclimatisation, eat well but simply: avoid fats in favour of starches, and keep your fluid intake high. Bananas and papaya fruit are often claimed to be helpful. If you urgently need to stop the symptoms, for a long journey for example, then Imodium or another of the commercial anti-diarrhoea preparations will do the trick. They stop the symptoms by paralysing the bowel, but will not cure the problem. They should not be used if you have severe abdominal cramps with the diarrhoea. Travellers at high risk of complications may be advised to take a self-treatment kit containing an antibiotic (usually azithromycin) – this requires a prescription.

The most important treatment for diarrhoea, especially in Botswana's climate, is to avoid dehydration by drinking lots of water and other clear fluids. These can be infused with sachets of oral rehydration salts, though any dilute mixture of sugar and salt in water will do you good, for instance a bottled soda with a pinch of salt. If diarrhoea persists beyond a couple of days, it may be a symptom of a more serious sanitation-related illness (typhoid, cholera, hepatitis, dysentery, worms, etc), so see a doctor. You should also seek medical advice immediately if you develop a fever, notice blood or mucus in the stool or experience symptoms such as confusion, severe abdominal pain, jaundice or rash. If the diarrhoea is greasy and bulky, and is accompanied by sulphurous (eggy) burps, one likely cause is the parasite *Giardia*, which can cause persistent symptoms but is treatable. Again, seek medical advice if you suspect this.

Dengue fever This mosquito-borne disease – and other similar viruses – may mimic malaria, but there is no prophylactic medication available to deal with it. The mosquitoes that carry this virus bite during the daytime, so it is worth applying repellent if you see any mosquitoes around. Symptoms include strong headaches, rashes, excruciating joint and muscle pains and high fever. Dengue fever only lasts for a week or so and is not usually fatal. Complete rest and paracetamol are the usual treatment. Plenty of fluids also help. Some patients are given an intravenous drip to keep them from dehydrating. It is especially important to protect yourself if you have had dengue fever before: a second infection with a different strain can result in the potentially fatal dengue haemorrhagic fever. A vaccine against dengue is now available in the UK and Europe. Generally it is recommended only for those who have already had dengue, to prevent a severe second infection.

Sexually transmitted infections With an estimated adult HIV prevalence of over 20%, Botswana is ranked among the top four countries in the world most affected by HIV; other sexually transmitted infections are also common. About 40% of HIV infections in British heterosexuals are acquired abroad. Condoms or femidoms greatly reduce the risk of transmission. If you do have unprotected sex, visit a clinic as soon as possible; this should be within 24 hours, or no later than 72 hours, for post-exposure prophylaxis. And if you notice any genital ulcers or discharge, get treatment promptly.

Hepatitis This is a group of viral diseases which generally start with dark-coloured urine and light-coloured stools, progressing to fever, weakness, jaundice (yellow skin and eyeballs) and abdominal pains caused by a severe inflammation of the liver. **Hepatitis A** and **hepatitis E** are spread by ingesting food or drink contaminated by excrement. They are avoided in the same ways you normally avoid stomach problems – by careful preparation of food and by drinking only clean water – and you can be vaccinated against hepatitis A before you travel (page 156). Hepatitis B is spread in the same way as HIV (by blood or body secretions); there is also a vaccine (page 156), which is especially recommended for medical workers, those working closely with children and those travelling for six weeks or longer. There is no specific treatment for most forms of viral hepatitis, but with bed rest, a healthy diet and the complete avoidance of alcohol, most people recover within a few months. If you develop symptoms of hepatitis, contact your travel insurance and seek medical attention.

Rabies Rabies can be carried by any mammal (beware the village dogs and small monkeys that congregate around campsites in the parks) and is passed on to humans through a bite, a scratch or simply saliva on broken skin, or into your eyes, nose or mouth. You must always assume any animal is rabid as they can look well but still be infectious. Seek medical help as soon as possible after any potential exposure. Meanwhile scrub the wound with soap under a running tap, or while pouring water from a jug, for a good 10–15 minutes. Then pour on a disinfectant such as iodine or alcohol solution, which will guard against other infections and might reduce the risk of rabies.

Post-exposure prophylaxis should be given as soon as possible, though it is never too late to seek help, as the incubation period for rabies can be very long. Tell the doctor if you have had pre-exposure vaccine (page 156), as this will change the treatment you receive. Those who have not been immunised before will need four or five doses of vaccine and may also need a blood product called rabies immunoglobulin (RIG). This is expensive and is not usually readily available in Botswana, so it is important to insist on getting to a place that has it: this is another reason to have good insurance. And remember that, if you do contract rabies and don't receive prophylaxis, mortality is 100% and death from rabies is probably one of the worst ways to go.

Bilharzia or schistosomiasis Bilharzia is an unpleasant parasitic disease transmitted by freshwater snails most often associated with reedy shores. It cannot be caught in hotel swimming pools or the ocean, but should be assumed to be present in any freshwater river pond, lake or similar habitat, even those advertised as 'bilharzia free'. The most risky shores will be within 200m of villages or other places where infected people use water, wash clothes, etc. Ideally, however, you should avoid swimming in any fresh water other than an artificial pool. Topical application of insect repellent before exposure or drying off vigorously with a towel afterwards may help to prevent the *Schistosoma* parasite from penetrating the skin,

NATIONAL PARKS AND ANTHRAX

Outbreaks of anthrax are relatively common among the animals in Botswana's national parks, but the Botswana authorities monitor the situation very closely, putting affected areas off-limits to visitors for a considerable period of time.

To allay any fears, it's worth noting a few facts about anthrax. It is a bacterial disease caused by the spore-forming *Bacillus anthracis*, and is primarily contracted by herbivores such as cattle, goats or sheep; outbreaks among carnivores are rare. Humans can contract the disease only if they come into direct contact with infected animals, their carcasses or material, including soil; it cannot be passed from one human to another. Fortunately the risk for travellers is very low. Unless you're planning to eat the meat, or get close enough to touch any animal or part of an animal, you're not at risk – though remember to avoid buying souvenirs made from animal skin, however tempting. For the most part, the disease occurs in the dry season when animals graze closer to the soil, where the spores can survive for a considerable period of time – hence the recurrence of outbreaks year on year. For this reason, proper disposal of carcasses, usually by incineration, is a crucial part of anthrax control measures.

Symptoms of anthrax vary, but usually occur within seven days. Most infections result from a cut or graze coming into contact with the bacteria. In this instance, what appears to be an insect bite grows within a couple of days into a painless ulcer about 1–3cm across, with a black centre, and surrounding lymph glands may swell. This type of infection usually responds well to antibiotics. Rarely, as a result of inhalation of spores, the apparent symptoms of a common cold progress to severe breathing problems, with a bleak outlook. A third form of the disease, which may follow the consumption of contaminated meat, leads to inflammation of the intestine, with potentially fatal consequences. While an anthrax vaccine does exist, it is not normally recommended for visitors to Botswana.

but should not be relied upon. Bilharzia is often asymptomatic in its early stages, but some people experience an intense immune reaction, including fever, cough, abdominal pain and an itching rash, around four to six weeks after infection. Later symptoms vary but often include a general feeling of lethargy. Bilharzia can be tested for at specialist travel or tropical medicine clinics, ideally at least six weeks after likely exposure. Fortunately, it is easy to treat at present.

Tick-borne infections Ticks may spread tick bite fever and a few other dangerous rarities in Botswana. African tick bite fever (ATBF) is a bacterial illness with flu-like symptoms that can easily be treated with doxycycline, but as there can be some serious complications it is important to visit a doctor. It is most prevalent between November and January.

Ticks should ideally be removed complete, and as soon as possible, to reduce the chance of infection. You can use special tick tweezers, which can be bought in good travel shops; or failing this, with your fingernails, grasp the tick as close to your body as possible, and pull it away steadily and firmly at right angles to your skin without jerking or twisting. Applying irritants (eg: Olbas oil) or lit cigarettes is to be discouraged as a means of removal since they can cause the ticks to regurgitate and therefore increase the risk of disease. Once the tick is removed, if possible douse the wound with alcohol (any spirit will do), soap and water, or iodine. If you are travelling with small children, remember to check their heads, and particularly behind the ears, for ticks. Spreading redness around the bite and/ or fever and/or aching joints after a tick bite imply that you have an infection that requires antibiotic treatment. In this case seek medical advice.

Skin infections Any mosquito bite or small nick is an opportunity for a skin infection in warm, humid climates, so it is essential to clean and cover even the slightest wound in a quick-drying liquid antiseptic such as dilute iodine, potassium permanganate or crystal (or gentian) violet. One of these should be available in most towns. If the wound starts to throb, or becomes red and the redness starts to spread, or the wound oozes, and especially if you develop a fever, antibiotics will probably be needed.

Fungal infections also get a hold easily in hot, moist climates so wear 100%-cotton socks and underwear and shower frequently. An itchy rash in the groin or flaking between the toes is likely to be a fungal infection. This needs treatment with an antifungal cream such as Canesten (clotrimazole).

Heat and sun Heatstroke, heat exhaustion and sunburn are often problems for travellers to Botswana, despite being easy to prevent. First, take things gently; you are on holiday, after all. Next, keep your fluid and salt levels high: lots of water and soft drinks, but go easy on the caffeine and alcohol. Third, dress to keep cool with loose-fitting, thin garments – preferably of cotton, linen or silk. Finally, beware of the sun. Hats and long-sleeved shirts are essential. For any exposed skin, use high-factor suncream (at least SPF30 and a UVA of four or more stars), wear a T-shirt and waterproof suncream while swimming, and be especially careful of exposure in the middle of the day and of sun reflected off water. The glare and the dust can be hard on the eyes, too, so bring UV-protecting sunglasses and, perhaps, a soothing eyebath.

A fine pimply rash on the trunk is likely to be heat rash; cool showers, dabbing dry and talc will help. Treat the problem by slowing down to a relaxed schedule, wearing only loose cotton clothes and sleeping naked under a fan.

Eye problems Bacterial conjunctivitis (pink eye) is a common infection in Africa, particularly for contact lens wearers. Symptoms are sore, gritty eyelids that often stick closed in the mornings. They will need treatment with antibiotic drops or ointment. Lesser eye irritation should settle with bathing in salt water and keeping the eyes shaded. If an insect flies into your eye, extract it with great care, ensuring you do not crush or damage it, otherwise you may get a nastily inflamed eye from toxins secreted by the creature.

SNAKES, SPIDERS AND SCORPIONS With Marcel Van Driel, Helping Hands in Snake Safety (HHISS)

Encounters with aggressive snakes, spiders or scorpions are more common in horror films than in Botswana. If you are careful about where you place your hands and feet, especially after dark, in rocky areas or when gathering firewood, then there should be no problems. In all cases, the risk is minimised by wearing trousers and closed shoes. Simple precautions include shaking your boots empty before putting your feet inside, and always checking the back of your backpack before putting it on.

Snakes are very secretive and bites are a genuine rarity. Of Botswana's 58 different snakes, only nine (15%) have a type of venom strong enough to be life-threatening to people, so if bitten, *don't panic*: you are unlikely to have received deadly venom. It is important to keep the victim calm and inactive, and to seek urgent medical attention; head to the nearest farm, camp or town. Many 'traditional' first-aid techniques do more harm than good: tourniquets are dangerous; and suction and electrical inactivation devices do not work. The only treatment for a life-threatening snakebite is antivenom.

If you receive a bite that you fear may have been from a venomous snake:

- Call the Poison Information Centre on \+27 861 555 777 for immediate advice and evacuate to a hospital.
- Try to keep calm – it is likely that mild venom or no venom (a dry bite) has been dispensed.
- Stay very still – prevent movement of the bitten limb by applying a splint.
- Remove any jewellery or tight-fitting clothes from the bitten limb (most dangerous snakebites cause severe swelling).
- Do not attempt to dress or bandage the wound unless trained to do so. Most venomous bites cause localised tissue damage and swelling, and a dressing which becomes too tight could make matters worse. A pressure bandage is only advisable in the case of bites from mambas and non-spitting cobras, but they are complicated to apply and their correct use requires training.
- Never give aspirin or ibuprofen, which may exacerbate bleeding (paracetamol is safe).
- Never cut or suck the wound.
- Do not apply ice packs or electric current.
- Do not apply a tourniquet.
- Do not try to capture or kill the snake, as this may result in further bites.

If the offending snake *can* be captured without any risk of someone else being bitten, take it to show the doctor. But beware, since even a decapitated head is able to dispense venom in a reflex bite.

ASSISTANCE
Hospitals, dentists and pharmacies
Health care in Botswana is provided both by the government and on a private basis, with some facilities built and operated by mining companies. The UK Foreign Office has an online list of health facilities in Botswana: w gov.uk/government/publications/botswana-list-of-medical-facilities.

Botswana's main **hospitals**, in Maun (Letsholathebe II Memorial Hospital \0800 600897, +267 687 9000), Francistown (Nyangabgwe Referral Hospital \0800 600891, +267 241 1000) and Gaborone (Princess Marina Hospital \0800 600905, +267 362 1400), are capable of serious surgery and a good quality of care; they will also treat you first and ask for money later. However, the public health system is over-stretched and under-funded, so unless your illness is critical, it will take time for you to be attended to and treated at the public hospitals. Bear in mind, too, that a large number of patients in the public hospitals have serious infectious diseases, so there's a risk of coming away from these with something worse than you had when you arrived.

Assuming that you have comprehensive medical insurance as part of your travel cover – and you should check that you have – it is probably better to go to one of the better-funded **private clinics** found in each of the main towns. These cater for both affluent citizens of Botswana and expats/diplomatic staff/travellers. They will accept payment from travel health insurance schemes. For treatment of serious medical conditions, evacuation to South Africa may be necessary.

It's worth having a dental check-up before you go, as you could be several painful days from the nearest **dentist**.

Pharmacies in Botswana's main towns (as well as neighbouring Livingstone and Victoria Falls) generally have a good range of medicines, though specific brands are often unavailable. So bring with you all that you will need, as well as a repeat prescription for anything that you might run out of. Outside of the larger towns you probably won't be able to find anything other than very basic medical supplies. Thus you should carry a very comprehensive medical kit if you are planning to head off into the wilds (page 136).

In an emergency, contact:

Ambulance ❯997 (public hospital emergency service)
Medical Rescue International Emergency ❯992; international emergency number ❯+267 390 3066; helpdesk m 7132 2361; e enquiries@mri.co.bw; 🇫 @mribotswana. MRI organises 24hr medical evacuations from anywhere in Botswana. They insure individual travellers, & your own insurance company may pick up the bill if their services are needed, but many lodges are also members, covering you while you are staying there (though you will still need your own medical insurance).

Okavango Air Rescue Emergency ❯995, or ❯+267 686 1506 from a satellite phone; Maun office ❯+267 686 1616; Maun Airport m 7433 9743; e office@okavangorescue.com; w okavangorescue.com; 🇫. This fantastic, not-for-profit organisation is on call 24/7 & is most lodges' choice in an emergency. Using helicopters with a qualified doctor on board, they can airlift patients out of remote areas if necessary, as well as using fixed-wing, road and boat transfers for patients. Many tour operators include their services, but individual membership costs just P175/year – around US$13/£10.

STAYING HEALTHY Botswana is one of the healthiest countries in sub-Saharan Africa. It has a generally low population density, who are affluent by the region's standards, and a very dry climate, which means there are comparatively few problems likely to affect visitors. The risks are further minimised if you are staying in good hotels, lodges, camps and guest farms, where standards of hygiene are generally at least as good as you will find at home.

The major dangers in Botswana are car accidents (caused by driving too fast, or at night, on gravel roads) and sunburn (page 163). Both can be very serious, yet both are often within the power of the visitor to avoid.

The following is general advice, applicable to travelling anywhere, including Botswana.

Food and storage Throughout the world, most health problems encountered by travellers are contracted by eating contaminated food or drinking unclean water. If you are staying in safari camps or lodges, or eating in restaurants, you are unlikely to have problems in Botswana. However, if you are backpacking and cooking for yourself, or relying on local food, you need to take more care. Tins, packets and fresh green vegetables (when you can find them) are least likely to cause problems – provided that clean water has been used in preparing the meal. In Botswana's hot climate, keeping meat or other animal products unrefrigerated for more than a few hours is asking for trouble.

Water and purification Tap water in Botswana's major towns, and borehole water – which is used in most of the more remote locations – is safe for locals to drink, but may cause an upset stomach for an overseas visitor, so you would be wise to use bottled or treated water at all times – this includes cleaning your teeth. The majority of safari camps use borehole water that is extensively filtered, but increasingly they also have large containers of purified water, with which guests can fill their own water bottles (which are often supplied too). Bottled water is usually available as a back-up, too.

If you're going it alone, you might want to consider using a bottle with a built-in filter. Otherwise, to purify water yourself, first filter out any suspended solids, perhaps by passing the water through a piece of closely woven cloth. Then bring it to the boil, or sterilise it chemically. Boiling is much more effective, provided that you have the fuel available. Tablets sold for purification are based on chlorine dioxide. Iodine is no longer recommended for use and is not sold in the UK and the rest of Europe, since there have been concerns over its safety. Another, albeit expensive, alternative is to use an electronic sterilisation device, such as a SteriPen.

RETURNING HOME Many tropical diseases have a long incubation period, and it is possible to develop symptoms weeks after returning home (this is why it is important to keep taking anti-malaria prophylaxis for the prescribed duration after you leave a malarial zone; page 157). If you do get ill after you return home, be certain to tell your doctor where you have been.

SAFETY

Botswana is a safe country. If you are travelling on an all-inclusive trip and staying at lodges and hotels, then problems of personal safety are exceedingly rare. There

SAFETY FOR WOMEN TRAVELLERS   *Janice Booth*

When attention becomes intrusive, it can help if you are wearing a wedding ring and have photos of 'your' husband and children, even if they are someone else's. A good reason to give for not being with them is that you have to travel in connection with your job – biology, zoology, geography, or whatever. (But not journalism – that's risky.)

Pay attention to local etiquette, and to speaking, dressing and moving reasonably decorously. Look at how the local women dress, and try not to expose parts of yourself that they keep covered. Think about body language. In much of southern Africa direct eye contact with a man will be seen as a 'come-on'; sunglasses are helpful here.

Don't be afraid to explain clearly – but pleasantly rather than as a put-down – that you aren't in the market for whatever distractions are on offer. Remember that you are probably as much of a novelty to the local people as they are to you, and the fact that you are travelling abroad alone gives them the message that you are free and adventurous. But don't imagine that a Lothario lurks under every bush: many approaches stem from genuine friendliness or curiosity, and a brush-off in such cases doesn't do much for the image of travellers in general.

Take sensible precautions against theft and attack – try to cover all the risks before you encounter them – and then relax and enjoy your trip. You'll meet far more kindness than villainy.

will always be someone on hand to help you. Even if you are travelling on local transport, perhaps on a low budget, you will generally be perfectly safe if you exercise the usual precautions.

Outside of rougher parts of the main cities, crime against visitors, however minor, is rare. Even if you are travelling on local transport on a low budget, you are likely to experience numerous acts of random kindness, but not crime. It is certainly safer for visitors than the UK, USA or most of Europe.

To get into a difficult situation, you'll usually have to try hard. You need to make yourself an obvious target for thieves, perhaps by walking around at night, with showy valuables, in a less affluent area of a town or city. Provided you are sensible, you are most unlikely to ever see any crime here.

For women travellers, especially those travelling alone, it is doubly important to learn the local attitudes, and how to behave acceptably. This takes some practice, and a certain confidence. You will often be the centre of attention but, by developing conversational techniques to avert over-enthusiastic male attention, you should be perfectly safe. Making friends of the local women is one way to help avoid such problems.

THEFT Theft is not generally a problem in Botswana – which is surprising given the poverty levels among much of the population. The only real exception to this is theft from unattended vehicles, which is becoming more common in the larger towns. If you leave a vehicle with anything valuable on view, then you may return to find a window smashed and items stolen.

When staying at safari camps in the bush, you'll often find that there are no locks and keys on the doors and there is a tremendous amount of trust. Regardless of this, leaving cash or valuables lying around or easily accessible is both stupid and very unfair to the camp's staff. Your watch could easily be worth a year's salary to them; make sure you keep such items out of sight and out of the way of temptation. Most safari camps provide small safes in their rooms for such items.

Should you experience a theft in a camp, report it to the management immediately – but bear in mind that most such reports are solved with the realisation that the property's owner mislaid it themselves!

How to avoid it Like anywhere, thieves in the bigger cities here work in groups and choose their targets carefully. These targets will be people who look vulnerable and who have items worth stealing. To avoid being robbed, try not to look too vulnerable or too rich – and certainly not both. Observing a few basic rules, especially during your first few weeks in Botswana's cities, will drastically reduce your chances of becoming a target. After that you should have learned your own way of assessing the risks, and avoiding thefts. Until then:

- Try not to carry anything of value around with you.
- If you must carry cash, then use a concealed money-belt for your main supply – keeping smaller change separately and to hand.
- Try not to look too foreign. Blend into the local scene as well as you can. Act like a streetwise expat rather than a tourist, if possible. (Conspicuously carrying a local newspaper may help with this.)
- Rucksacks and large, new bags are bad. If you must carry a bag, choose an old battered one. Around town, a local plastic carrier bag is ideal.
- Move confidently and look as if you know exactly what you are doing, and where you are going. Lost foreigners make the easiest targets.

6

- Never walk around at night – that is asking for trouble.
- If you have a vehicle then don't leave anything in it, and avoid leaving it parked outside in a city.

Reporting thefts to the police If you are the victim of a theft then report it to the police. Also try to get a copy of the report, or at least a reference number on an official-looking piece of paper, as this will help you to claim on your travel insurance policy. Some insurance companies won't act without this reference. But remember that reporting anything in a police station can take a long time, and do not expect any speedy arrests for a case of pickpocketing.

ARREST To get arrested in Botswana, a foreigner will normally have to try quite hard. There's no paranoia about foreigners, who are generally seen as welcome tourists who bring money into the economy.

One simple precaution to avoid trouble is to ask for permission to photograph near bridges or military installations. This simple courtesy costs you nothing, and may avoid a problem later.

One excellent way to get arrested in Botswana is to try to smuggle drugs across its borders, or to try to buy them from 'pushers'. Drug offences carry penalties at least as stiff as those you will find at home – and the jails are a lot less pleasant. Botswana's police are not forbidden to use entrapment techniques or 'sting' operations to catch criminals. Buying, selling or using drugs in Botswana is just not worth the risk.

Failing this, arguing with any policeman or army official – and getting angry into the bargain – is a sure way to get arrested. It is essential to control your temper and stay relaxed when dealing with Botswana's officials. Not only will you gain respect, and hence help your cause, but you will also avoid being forced to cool off for a night in the cells.

If you are careless enough to be arrested, you will often be asked only a few questions. If the police are suspicious of you, then how you handle the situation will determine whether you are kept for a matter of hours or for days. Be patient, helpful, good-humoured, and as truthful as possible. Never lose your temper; it will only aggravate the situation. Avoid any hint of arrogance. If things are going badly after half a day or so, then start firmly, but politely, to insist on seeing someone in higher authority. As a last resort you do, at least in theory, have the right to contact your embassy or consulate, though the finer points of your civil liberties may be overlooked by an irate local police chief.

BRIBERY Bribery is not at all common in Botswana. Indeed, the country is widely regarded as one of the least corrupt countries in Africa, and the government takes a very strict anti-corruption stance and has established strong institutions. Certainly no safari visitor should ever be asked for, or offer, a bribe. It would be just as illegal as offering someone a bribe in their home country. Forget it.

7

Into the Wilds

DRIVING

Driving around Botswana is exceedingly easy if you stick to the network of first-class tarred roads between the towns, but heading into the bush is a completely different proposition, which usually requires a small expedition.

Botswana's bush tracks are maintained only by the passage of vehicles, and aren't for the novice, or the unprepared. However, if you've been to Africa at least once or twice before, perhaps including a driving trip around South Africa or Namibia, then such trips can be a lot of fun provided that you realise that you're embarking on an adventure as much as a holiday.

To explore the more rural areas and remote parks on your own you'll need a fully equipped 4x4 vehicle, stocked with food and water for your trip. Depending on where you are going, some form of back-up is often wise. This might be a reliable satellite phone, a radio (and the know-how to use it), someone tracking your schedule – with frequent call-in points so they can look for you if you don't turn up on time – or the security of travelling in convoy with at least one other vehicle.

Having assessed all the dangers, those who do this kind of trip often get addicted to the space and the freedom; it can be really rewarding and tremendous fun!

For general information on driving in Botswana, see page 144.

EQUIPMENT AND PREPARATIONS

Fuel Petrol and diesel are available in all of the larger towns, but supplies at fuel stations outside Maun and Kasane can be erratic, so it is wise to fill up frequently. For travel into the bush you will need long-range fuel tanks, and/or a large stock of filled jerrycans. (Only use metal jerrycans for fuel; plastic containers are highly dangerous.)

It is essential to plan your fuel requirements well in advance, and to carry more than you expect to need. Remember that using the vehicle's 4x4 capability, especially in low ratio gears, will significantly increase your fuel consumption. Similarly, the cool comfort of a vehicle's air conditioning will burn your fuel reserves swiftly.

Spares Botswana's garages generally have a comprehensive stock of vehicle spares – though bush mechanics can effect the most amazing short-term repairs, with remarkably basic tools and raw materials. Spares for the more common makes are easiest to find; most basic Land Rover and Toyota 4x4 parts are available. If you are arriving in Botswana with an unusual foreign vehicle, it is best to bring as many spares as you can.

Navigation See page 141 for detailed comments. There are several good maps designed for visitors that are widely available, while survey-style maps may be

169

obtained from the Department of Surveys and Mapping in Maun and Gaborone. For bespoke maps and while-you-wait printing, visit the excellent Ngami Data Services (page 192) close to Maun Airport or contact them beforehand with your requirements and then just collect your prints. It's wise to take a GPS (page 143) loaded with accurate, in-country information (we recommend Tracks4Africa). Do learn how to use it before you arrive, take an old-fashioned paper map as back-up, and never switch your brain off and rely totally on the technology.

BOTSWANA'S ROAD NETWORK Wherever you are driving in Botswana, no matter what the road surface, you should always be prepared for animals wandering on to the road and for pot-holes.

Tar roads Botswana's network of tar roads is gradually being extended. Although these roads are generally very good, don't be lulled into complacency; pot-holes do occur, with potentially devastating consequences if hit at speed.

Gravel roads There aren't many good gravel roads in Botswana – most are either good tar, or basic bush tracks. However, the few gravel sections can be very deceptive. Even when they appear smooth, flat and fast (which is not often), they still do not give vehicles much traction. You will frequently put the car into small skids, but with practice at slower speeds you will learn how to deal with them. Gravel is a less forgiving surface on which to drive than tar. The rules and techniques for driving well are the same for both, but on tar you can get away with sloppy braking and cornering which would prove fatal on gravel.

In addition to animals wandering on to the road and pot-holes, be prepared for sand-traps, or an unexpected corner. It is verging on insanity to drive over about 80km/h (50mph) on any of Botswana's gravel roads. Other basic driving hints include:

- **Slowing down** If in any doubt about what lies ahead, always slow down. Road surfaces can vary enormously, so keep a constant look-out for pot-holes, ruts or patches of soft sand that could put you into an unexpected slide.
- **Passing vehicles** When passing other vehicles travelling in the opposite direction, always slow down to minimise both the damage that stone chippings will do to your windscreen, and the danger in driving through the other vehicle's dust cloud.
- **Using your gears** In normal driving, a lower gear will give you more control over the car – so keep out of high 'cruising' gears. Rather stick with third or fourth, and accept that your revs will be slightly higher than they normally are.
- **Cornering and braking** Under ideal conditions, the brakes should only be applied when the car is travelling in a straight line. Braking while negotiating a corner is dangerous, so it is vital to slow down before you reach corners. Equally, it is better to slow down gradually, using a combination of gears and brakes, than to use the brakes alone. You are less likely to skid.

DRIVING AT NIGHT Outside of the main towns, never drive at night unless it's a matter of life and death. Both wild and domestic animals frequently spend the night by the side of busy roads, and will actually sleep on quieter ones. Tar roads are especially bad as the surface absorbs all the sun's heat by day, and then radiates it at night – making it a warm bed for passing animals. A collision with any animal at speed, even a small one like a goat, will not only kill the animal, but will cause very severe damage to a vehicle, with potentially fatal consequences for the driver and passengers. And in the bush, even on main roads, the danger of startling elephants is very real.

DRIVING TECHNIQUES You want a high-clearance 4x4 to get anywhere in Botswana that's away from the main arteries. However, no vehicle can make up for an inexperienced driver – so ensure that you are confident of your vehicle's capabilities before you venture into the wilds with it. You really need extensive practice, with an expert on hand to advise you, before you'll have the first idea how to handle such a vehicle in difficult terrain. Finally, driving in convoy is an essential precaution in the more remote areas, in case one vehicle gets stuck or breaks down. Some of the more relevant ideas and techniques include the following.

When and how to use a 4x4
Firstly, read your vehicle's manual. All makes are different, and have their quirks, and so you must read the manual before you set off. Note especially that you should never drive in 4x4 mode with fixed (or 'locked') differentials on tar roads. Doing this will cause permanent damage to the mechanics of your vehicle.

When you do encounter traction difficulties, stop when you can and put the vehicle into 4x4 – usually setting the second 'small' gearstick to '4x4 high' is fine for most situations.

If you're driving an older vehicle, check if the front two hubs of your vehicle have, at their centre, knobs to turn. (This is the case with many of the older Toyotas, though most newer vehicles have 'automatic' hubs.) If so, you'll need to turn these to the 'lock' position – a fact forgotten by many novices that causes untold trouble for them, and endless smug amusement for old Africa hands.

When you're past the problem, using 2WD will lower your fuel consumption, though many drivers will use 4x4 the whole time that they're in the bush. Remember to reset your hubs to 'free' before you drive on tar again.

Driving in sand
If you're in 4x4 and are really struggling in deep sand, then stop on the next fairly solid area that you come to. Lower your tyre pressure until there is a small bulge in the tyre walls (having first made sure that you have the means to reinflate them when you reach solid roads again). A lower pressure will help your traction greatly, but increase the wear on your tyres. Pump them up again before you drive on a hard surface at speed, or the tyres will be badly damaged.

If you have your own vehicle, and thus have a choice, there are tyres designed specifically for driving in sand, so it may be worth considering these – although bear in mind that the sides will bend more easily than those designed for tarmac surfaces, so you'll not want to use these for long distances on the tar.

Where there are clear, deep-rutted tracks in the sand, don't fight the steering wheel – just relax and let your vehicle steer itself. Driving in the cool of the morning is easier than later in the day because when sand is cool it compacts better and is firmer. (When hot, the pockets of air between the sand grains expand and the sand becomes looser.)

If you do get stuck, despite these precautions, don't panic. Don't just rev the engine and spin the wheels – you'll only dig deeper. Instead stop. Relax and assess the situation. Now dig shallow ramps in front of all the wheels, reinforcing them with pieces of wood, vegetation, stones, material or anything else which will give the wheels better traction. Clear sand from beneath the chassis as, even on high-clearance vehicles, this could be the root of the problem. Then lighten the vehicle load (passengers out) and – if possible – push. Don't let the engine revs die as you engage your lowest ratio gear. That probably means using '4x4 low' rather than '4x4 high'. Use the clutch to ensure that the wheels don't spin wildly and dig themselves further into the sand.

Sometimes rocking the vehicle backwards and forwards will build up momentum to break you free. This can be done by the driver intermittently applying the clutch and/or by getting helpers who can push and pull the vehicle at the same frequency. Once the vehicle is moving, the golden rule of sand driving is to keep up the momentum: if you pause, you will sink and stop.

Grass seeds in the Kalahari After the rains, the Kalahari's tracks are often knee-high in seeding grass. As your vehicle drives through, stems and especially seeds can build up in front of and inside the radiator, and get trapped in crevices underneath the chassis. This is a major problem in the less-visited areas of the Kalahari. It's at its worst from March to June, after the rains, and in the areas of the great salt pans, the CKGR, and the tracks around Tsodilo and the Aha Hills. The main tracks around Chobe and Moremi are used relatively frequently, and so present less of a problem.

The presence of long grass on the tracks causes a real danger of overheating (see below) and fire. First, the build-up of seeds and stems over the radiator insulates it. Thus, if you aren't watching your gauges, the engine's temperature can rocket. It will swiftly seize up and catch fire. Second, the grass build-up itself, if allowed to become too big, can catch fire due to its contact with the hot exhaust system underneath the vehicle.

There are several strategies to minimise these dangers; best apply them all. First, before you set out, buy a few square metres of the tightly woven window-meshing gauze material used in the windows of safari tents. Fix one large panel of this on the vehicle's bull-bars, well in front of the radiator grill. Fix another much closer to it, but still outside of the engine compartment. Hopefully this will reduce vastly the number of seeds reaching your radiator.

Second, watch your vehicle's engine-temperature gauge like a hawk when you're travelling through areas of grassland.

Third, stop every 10km or so (yes, really, that often) and check the radiator and the undercarriage for pockets of stems and seeds. Pay special attention to the hot areas of the exhaust pipe; you should not allow a build-up of flammable material there. Use a stick or piece of wire to clean out any seeds and stems before you set off again.

Overheating If the engine has overheated then the only option is to stop and turn it off. Stop, have a drink under a tree, and let it cool. Don't open the radiator cap to refill it until the radiator is no longer hot to the touch. Even then, keep the engine running and the water circulating while you refill the radiator – otherwise you run the risk of cracking the hot metal by suddenly cooling it. Flicking droplets of water on to the outside of a running engine will cool it.

When driving away, switch off any air conditioning (as it puts more strain on the engine). Open your windows and turn your heater and fan full on. This may not seem pleasant in the midday heat – but it'll help to cool the engine. Keep watching that engine-temperature gauge.

Driving in mud This is difficult, though the theory is the same rule as for sand: keep going and don't stop. That said, even the most experienced drivers get stuck. A few areas of Botswana have very fine soil known as 'black-cotton' soil, which becomes impassable when wet (the road from Rakops to the CKGR's main gate is legendary in this respect).

Push-starting when stuck
If you are unlucky enough to need to push-start your vehicle while it is stuck in sand or mud, there is a remedy. Raise up the drive wheels, and take off one of the tyres. You should have a hi-lift jack with you, and know how to use it.

Then wrap a length of rope around the hub and treat it like a spinning top: one person (or more) pulls the rope to make the axle spin, while the driver lifts the clutch, turns the ignition on, and engages a low gear to turn the engine over. This is a very difficult equivalent of a push-start, but it may be your only option.

Rocky terrain
There's not much of this in northern Botswana – but you will find some in the southeast. Have your tyre pressure higher than normal and move very slowly. If necessary, passengers should get out and guide you along the track to avoid scraping the undercarriage on the ground. This can be a very slow business.

Crossing rivers and other stretches of water
The first thing to do is to stop and check the river. You must assess its depth, the type of riverbed and its current flow; and determine the best route to drive across it. This is best done by wading across the river (though in an area frequented by hippos and crocodiles this is not advisable – err on the side of caution if you are unsure). Beware of water that's too deep for your vehicle, or the very real possibility of being swept away by a fast current and a slippery riverbed.

If everything is OK then select your lowest gear ratio and drive through the water at a slow but steady rate. Your vehicle's air intake must be above the level of the water to avoid your engine filling with water. It's not worth taking risks, so remember that a flooded river may subside to safer levels by the next morning.

Driving near big game
The only animals which are likely to pose a threat to vehicles are elephants – and generally only elephants which are familiar with vehicles. So, treat them with the greatest respect and don't 'push' them by trying to move ever closer. Letting them approach you is much safer, and they will feel far less threatened and more relaxed. Then, if the animals are calm, you can safely turn the engine off, sit quietly, and watch as they pass you by.

If you are unlucky, or foolish, enough to unexpectedly drive into the middle of a herd, then don't panic. Keep your movements, and those of the vehicle, slow and measured. Back off steadily. Don't be panicked, or overly intimidated, by a mock charge – this is just their way of frightening you away. For detailed comments, see page 266.

BUSH CAMPING

Many 'boy scout' type manuals have been written on survival in the bush, usually by military veterans. If you are stranded with a convenient multi-purpose knife, then these useful tomes will describe how you can build a shelter from branches, catch passing animals for food, and signal to the inevitable rescue planes which are combing the globe looking for you – while avoiding the attentions of hostile forces.

In Africa, bush camping is usually less about survival than comfort. You're likely to have much more than the knife: probably at least a bulging backpack, if not a fully loaded 4x4. Thus the challenge is not to camp and survive, it is to camp and be as comfortable as possible. With practice you'll learn how, but a few hints might be useful for the less experienced.

WHERE YOU CAN CAMP In national parks, there are strictly designated campsites that you should use, as directed by the local wildlife officers. These must be pre-booked or you are unlikely to be allowed entrance.

Outside of the parks, if no campsites are designated, you should ask the local landowner, or village head, if they are happy for you to camp on their property. If you explain patiently and politely what you want, then you are unlikely to meet anything but hospitality in most areas of rural Botswana.

CHOOSING A SITE Only experience will teach you how to choose a good site for pitching a tent, but a few general points, applicable to any wild areas of Africa, may help you avoid problems:

- Avoid camping on what looks like a path through the bush, however indistinct. It may be a well-used game trail.
- Beware of camping in dry riverbeds: dangerous flash floods can arrive with little or no warning.
- In marshy areas camp on higher ground to avoid cold, damp mists in the morning and evening.
- Camp a reasonable distance from water: near enough to walk to it, but far enough to avoid animals which arrive to drink.
- Give yourself plenty of time before it gets dark to familiarise yourself with your surroundings.
- If a lightning storm is likely, make sure that your tent is not the highest thing around.
- Finally, choose a site which is as flat as possible – you will find sleeping much easier.

CAMPFIRES Campfires can create a great atmosphere and warm you on a cold evening, but they can also be damaging to the environment and leave unsightly piles of ash and blackened stones. Deforestation is a major concern in much of the developing world, including parts of Botswana, so if you do light a fire then use wood as the locals do: sparingly. If you have a vehicle, consider buying firewood in advance from people who sell it at the roadside – or collect it in areas where there's more wood around.

If you collect it yourself, then take only dead wood, nothing living. Never just pick up a log: always roll it over first, checking carefully for snakes or scorpions.

Experienced campers build small, highly efficient fires by using a few large stones to absorb, contain and reflect the heat, and gradually feeding just a few thick logs into the centre to burn. Cooking pots can be balanced on the stones, or the point where the logs meet and burn. Others will use a small trench, lined with rocks, to similar effect. Either technique takes practice, but is worth perfecting. Whichever you do, bury the ashes, take any rubbish with you when you leave, and make the site look as if you had never been there. (See page 546 for details of Christina Dodwell's excellent *An Explorer's Handbook: Travel, Survival and Bush Cookery*.)

Don't expect an unattended fire to frighten away wild animals – that works in Hollywood, but not in Africa. A campfire may help your feelings of insecurity, but lion and hyena will disregard it with stupefying nonchalance.

Finally, do be hospitable to any locals who appear. Despite your efforts to seek permission for your camp, you may effectively be staying in their back gardens.

USING A TENT Whether to use a tent or to sleep in the open is a personal choice, dependent upon where you are. In an area where there are predators around (specifically lion and hyena) then you *must* use a tent – and sleep completely inside it, as a protruding leg may seem like a tasty take-away to a hungry hyena. This is especially true at organised campsites, where the local animals are so used to humans that they have lost much of their inherent fear of man.

Outside wildlife areas, you will usually be fine sleeping in the open, or preferably under a mosquito net, with just the stars of the African sky above you. On the practical side, sleeping under a tree will reduce the morning dew that settles on your sleeping bag. If your vehicle has a large, flat roof then sleeping on this will provide you with peace of mind, and a star-filled outlook. Hiring a vehicle with a built-in roof-tent is a perfect solution for many, though it can take time to pack when wanting to rush off on an early-morning game drive.

CAMPING EQUIPMENT FOR BACKPACKERS If you are taking an organised safari, you will not need any camping equipment at all. If you're hiring a 4x4, then it's best to hire one here with all the kit. However, for those backpacking, there is very little lightweight kit available in Botswana. Most of the equipment is designed to be sturdy, long-lasting and carried around in vehicles. So buy any lightweight kit before you leave home, as it will save you a lot of time and trouble once you arrive. Here are a few comments on various essentials.

Tent During the rains a good tent is essential in order to stay dry. Even during the dry season one is useful if there are lion or hyena around. If backpacking, invest in a high-quality, lightweight tent. Mosquito-netting ventilation panels, allowing a good flow of air, are essential. (Just a corner of mesh at the top of the tent is *not* enough for comfort.) Don't go for a tent that's small; it may feel cosy at home, but will be hot and claustrophobic in the heat.

A dome tent with fine mesh doors on either side that allow a through draught makes all the difference when temperatures are high. The alternative to a good tent is a mosquito net, which is fine unless it is raining or you are in a big-game area.

Sleeping bag A lightweight, three-season sleeping bag is ideal for Botswana most of the time, though probably not quite warm enough for the very coldest nights in the Kalahari. Down is preferable to synthetic fillings for most of the year, as it packs smaller, is lighter, and feels more luxurious to sleep in. That said, when down gets wet it loses its efficiency, so bring a good synthetic bag if you are likely to encounter much rain.

Ground mat A ground mat of some sort is essential. It keeps you warm and comfortable, and it protects the tent's groundsheet from rough or stony ground (do put it underneath the tent!). Closed-cell foam mats are widely available outside Botswana, so buy one before you arrive. The better mats cost double or treble the cheaper ones, but are stronger, thicker and warmer – well worth the investment.

Therm-a-Rests, the combination air-mattress and foam mat, are strong, durable and also worth the investment – but take a puncture repair kit with you just in case of problems. Do watch carefully where you site your tent, and try to make camp before dark. My trusty Therm-a-Rest deflated badly one night in the Kalahari, sleeping near the Mamuno–Buitepos border. Breaking camp the next morning, I lifted the mat to find a large scorpion in its burrow immediately beneath the mat.

Sheet sleeping bag Thin, pure-cotton or silk sheet sleeping bags (or sleeping bag liners) are small, light and very useful. They are easily washed and so are normally used like a sheet, inside a sleeping bag, to keep it clean. They can, of course, be used on their own when your main sleeping bag is too hot.

Stove When choosing a camping stove, consider factors such as fuel availability, ease of use, portability and your specific cooking needs. Whatever you choose, make sure to follow safety guidelines when using any camping stove, and always have a back-up plan for cooking in case your primary stove fails or runs out of fuel in a remote spot.

Some stoves come with a complete set of lightweight pans and a very useful all-purpose handle. Often you'll be able to cook on a fire with the pans, but it's nice to have the option of making a hot drink in a few minutes while you set up camp.

Multi-fuel stoves are excellent for remote areas where different fuel sources might be available. They can run on various liquid fuels, including white gas, kerosene and even unleaded petrol. Brands like MSR WhisperLite and Primus OmniFuel are known for their durability and versatility. Do bring a tough (purpose-made) fuel container with you as the bottles in which fuel is sold will soon crack and spill all over your belongings.

Gas canister stoves use pressurised canisters, and are popular for their ease of use and maintenance. It's best to look for models that can run on more readily available butane or propane canisters. Note that gas canisters are not allowed on aircraft, though these stoves can be purchased in major towns.

Rocket stoves are designed for efficient wood- or biomass-burning. They are ideal for areas with limited fuel resources and are known for their fuel efficiency and reduced smoke production. Brands like EcoZoom and Solo Stove offer good options.

Torch (flashlight) This should be on every visitor's packing list – whether you're staying in upmarket camps or backpacking. Find one that's small and tough, and preferably water- and dust-proof. Headtorches leave your hands free (useful when cooking or mending the car) and the latest designs are relatively light and comfortable to wear. Consider one of the new generation of super-bright LED torches; the LED Lenser range is excellent.

Those with vehicles will find that a strong spotlight, powered by the car's battery (perhaps through the socket for the cigarette lighter), is invaluable for impromptu lighting.

Water containers For everyday use, a small two-litre water bottle is invaluable, however you are travelling. If you're thinking of camping, you should also consider a strong, collapsible water bag – perhaps 5–10 litres in size – which will reduce the number of trips that you need to make from your camp to the water source (ten litres of water weighs 10kg). And to be sure of safe drinking water, consider taking a bottle with a filter (page 165).

Drivers will want to be self-sufficient for water when venturing into the bush, and so carry several large, sturdy containers of water. If you're driving a vehicle specially kitted out for camping, ensure that the water tank is full at the outset.

See page 134 for a memory-jogging list of other useful items to pack.

ANIMAL DANGERS FOR CAMPERS Camping in Africa is really very safe, though you may not think so from reading this. If you have a major problem while camping, it will probably be because you did something stupid, or because you forgot to take a few simple precautions. Here are a few general basics, applicable to anywhere in Africa and not just Botswana.

Large animals As a general rule, big game will usually not bother you if you are in a tent – provided that you do not attract its attention, or panic it. Elephants will gently tiptoe through your guy ropes while you sleep, without even nudging your tent. However, if you wake up and make a noise, startling them, they are far more likely to panic and step on your tent. Similarly, scavengers will quietly wander round, smelling your evening meal in the air, without any intention of harming you.

- Remember to use the toilet before going to bed, and avoid getting up in the night if at all possible.
- Scrupulously clean everything used for food that might smell good to scavengers. Put these utensils in a vehicle if possible; if not, suspend them from a tree, or pack them away in a rucksack inside the tent.
- Do not keep any foodstuffs in your tent, especially those with a strong smell like meat or citrus fruit. Their smells may well attract unwanted attention.
- Do not leave anything outside that could be picked up – like bags, pots, pans, etc. Hyenas, among others, will take anything, potentially harming them and definitely upsetting you. They have been known to crunch a camera's lens, and eat it…
- If you are likely to wake in the night, then leave the tent's zips a few centimetres open at the top, enabling you to take a quiet peek outside.

Creepy crawlies As you set up camp, clear stones or logs out of your way with great caution: they make great hiding places for snakes, spiders and scorpions. Long moist grass is ideal territory for snakes, and dry, dusty, rocky places are classic sites for scorpions.

If you are sleeping in the open, it is not unknown to wake and find a snake lying next to you in the morning. Don't panic; your warmth has just attracted it to you. You will not be bitten if you gently edge away without making any sudden movements. (This is one good argument for using at least a mosquito net!)

Before you put on your shoes, shake them out. Similarly, check the back of your backpack before you slip it on. Just a curious spider, in either, could inflict a painful bite.

WALKING IN THE BUSH

Walking in the African bush is a totally different sensation from driving through it. You may start off a little sleepy for a daybreak walk – but swiftly your mind will wake. There are no noises except the wildlife and you. So every noise that isn't caused by you must be an animal; or a bird; or an insect. Every smell and every rustle has a story to tell, if you can understand it.

With time, patience and a good guide you can learn to smell the presence of elephants, and hear when a predator alarms impala. You can use ox-peckers to lead you to buffalo, or vultures to help you locate a kill. Tracks will record the passage of animals in the sand, telling what passed by, how long ago, and in which direction.

Eventually your gaze becomes alert to the slightest movement; your ears aware of every sound. This is safari at its best: a live, sharp, spine-tingling experience that's hard to beat and very addictive. Be careful: watching game from a vehicle will never be the same again for you.

WALKING TRAILS AND SAFARIS One of Africa's biggest attractions is its walking safaris – which bring people back year after year. However, because of the danger involved, the calibre and experience of guides when walking is far more important than when driving. Anyone with a little experience can drive you around fairly safely in a large metal vehicle, but when you're faced with a charging elephant you need to be standing behind a real expert to have much chance of survival.

Even if you're on safari with an armed guide who is experienced with dangerous big game, walking will always present more danger than driving. This is simply because humans are more vulnerable on foot than they are when encased by a vehicle. However, major problems and injuries are few and far between – well within the limits accepted by most travellers who opt for 'adventurous' holidays across the world.

Walking guides I am still not confident that Botswana has progressed well towards the implementation of rigorous minimum standards for guides who lead walking safaris. Zimbabwe has for many years led the field, with a really tough training course leading to the exalted status of 'pro guide'; in many ways this is Africa's 'gold standard' of guiding.

Zambia has adopted an alternative, but also very safe, system requiring an armed scout and an experienced walking guide to accompany every walk. The scout controls the problem animal, the guide controls the group of people. It's rarely necessary to fire even a warning shot, and injuries are exceedingly rare.

However, Botswana, like South Africa, has minimum standards which I think are too low for walking guides. Thus, in my opinion, the term 'qualified guide' in Botswana doesn't mean that I should necessarily feel safe going walking with them. Thus it's mostly up to the individual safari operation to make sure its guides are experienced.

These days there are a number of very good operations that take walking safaris seriously, understand the issues and put safety at the top of their agenda. I'm confident to go walking with such operations.

The rest are a mixed bag; some use good guides, others I've been out with I felt were actually dangerous. One good rule of thumb is the presence of a rifle. If your guide *doesn't* carry one, then I certainly wouldn't walk with them to anywhere where we were likely to see any dangerous game. (The converse doesn't apply though; carrying a rifle does not make an inexperienced guide safe.)

Often you'll see advertising for camps in the Okavango with comments along the lines that your guide is 'a man of the swamps, completely at one with his environment'. This is doubtless true, but doesn't imply that this same guide automatically has the foresight, command and communication skills to look after frightened foreigners while avoiding game in a dangerous situation. Knowing how to save himself is different from controlling a small group, and saving *them* from a nasty end.

Thus my advice is that if you want to do much walking in Botswana, go to one of the places that really concentrate on walking safaris. The rest of the time, stick to boats and driving. Only go walking with guides who are armed, know how to use their guns, and you have discussed the issues with and satisfied yourself that they have sufficient experience for you to be safe.

Etiquette for walking safaris If you plan to walk then avoid wearing any bright, unnatural colours, especially white. Dark, muted shades are best; greens, browns and khaki are ideal. Dark blue tends to attract tsetse flies in areas where they are found, so best to avoid that if you can. Hats are essential, as is sunblock. Even a short walk will last for 2 hours, and there's no vehicle to which you can retreat if you get too hot.

Binoculars should be immediately accessible – one pair per person – ideally in dust-proof cases. Cameras too, if you decide to bring any, as they are of little use buried at the bottom of a camera bag. Heavy tripods or long lenses are a nightmare to lug around, so leave them behind (and accept, philosophically, that you may miss some shots).

Walkers see the most when walking in silent single file. This doesn't mean that you can't stop to whisper a question to the guide; just that idle chatter will reduce your powers of observation, and make you even more visible to the animals, who will usually flee when they sense you.

With regard to safety, your guide should always brief you in detail before you set off. S/he will outline possible dangers, and what to do in the unlikely event of them materialising. Listen carefully: this is vital.

Face-to-face animal encounters Whether you are on an organised walking safari, on your own hike, or just walking from the car to your tent in the bush, it is not unlikely that you will come across some of Africa's larger animals at close quarters. Invariably, the danger is less than you imagine, and a few basic guidelines will enable you to cope effectively with most situations.

First, don't panic. Console yourself with the fact that animals are not normally interested in people. You are not their normal food, or their predator. If you do not annoy or threaten them, you will be left alone. No matter how frightened you are, you'll probably run slower than whatever is worrying you. So don't try to run; think your way out of the tight spot.

If you are walking to look for animals, then remember that this is their environment, not yours. Animals have evolved within the bush, and their senses are far better attuned to it than yours. To be on less unequal terms, remain alert and try to spot them from a distance. This gives you the option of approaching carefully, or staying well clear.

Animals, like people, are all different. So while we can generalise here and say how the 'average' animal will behave, the one that's glaring at you over a small bush may have had a really bad day, and be feeling much grumpier than normal.

Finally, the advice of a good guide is far more valuable than the simplistic comments noted here – though a few general comments on some potentially dangerous situations might be of use. Animals here are listed alphabetically.

Black rhino While black rhino sightings are exceptionally rare these days, if you are both lucky enough to find one, and then unlucky enough to be charged by it, climb the nearest tree or side-step at the last second. (It is amazing how even the least athletic walker will swiftly scale the nearest tree when faced with a charging rhino.)

Buffalo This is probably the continent's most dangerous animal to hikers, but there is a difference between the old males, often encountered on their own or in small groups, and large breeding herds.

The former are easily surprised. If they hear or smell something amiss, they will charge without provocation – motivated by a fear that something is sneaking up on them. Buffalo have an excellent sense of smell, but fortunately they are also short-sighted. As with rhino, avoid a charge by quickly climbing the nearest tree, or by sidestepping at the last minute. If adopting the latter, riskier, technique then stand motionless until the last possible moment, as the buffalo may well miss you anyhow.

The large breeding herds can be treated in a totally different manner. If you approach them in the open, they will often flee. Sometimes though, in areas often used for walking safaris, they will stand and watch, moving aside to allow you to pass through the middle of the herd.

Neither encounter is for the faint-hearted or inexperienced, so steer clear of these dangerous animals wherever possible.

Elephant Normally elephants are only a problem if you disturb a mother with a calf, or approach a male in *musth* (state of arousal), so keep well away from these. In some areas of Africa, lone bulls can be approached quite closely when feeding, but in Botswana this usually results in problems. If you get too close to any elephant it will scare you off with a 'mock charge': head up, perhaps shaking – ears flapping – and trumpeting. Lots of sound and fury. This is intended to be frightening, and it is. But it is just a warning and no cause for panic. You should just freeze to assess the elephant's intentions. When it's stopped making a fuss, back off slowly. Don't run. There is no easy way to avoid the charge of an angry elephant, so take a hint from this warning and move away.

When an elephant really means business, it will usually put its ears back, lower its head, and charge directly at you. This is known as a 'full charge' and they don't stop. It is one of the most dangerous situations in Africa. Then you probably have to run – but elephants are much faster than you, so think while you run. Aim to get behind an anthill, up a tall tree, or out of the way somehow.

See also page 266 for details on how to manage this behaviour if you are in a vehicle.

Hippo Hippo are fabled to account for more deaths in Africa than any other animal (ignoring the mosquito). Having been attacked and capsized by a hippo while in a mokoro, I find this very easy to believe. Visitors are most likely to encounter hippo in the water (page 50), when in a boat or mokoro.

However, as hippos spend half their time grazing, they will sometimes be encountered on land. Away from the water, out of their comforting lagoons, hippos are even more dangerous. If they see you, they will probably flee towards the water – so the golden rule is never to get between a hippo and its escape route to deep water. Given that a hippo will outrun you on land, standing motionless is probably your best line of defence; if you must run, then head away from water or try to put a large, solid obstacle between you and the animal.

Leopard Leopard are seldom seen by those on foot, and would normally flee from the most timid of lone hikers. However, if injured, or surprised, then they are very powerful, dangerous cats. Conventional wisdom is scarce, but never stare straight into the leopard's eyes, or it will regard this as a threat display. (The same is said, by some, to be true with lion.) Better to look away slightly, at a nearby bush, or even at its tail. Then back off slowly, facing the direction of the cat and showing as little terror as you can. Loud, deep, confident noises are a last line of defence. Never run from a leopard.

Lion Tracking lion with a top guide can be one of the most exhilarating parts of a walking safari. Sadly, they will normally flee before you even get close to them.

However, it can be a problem if you come across a large pride unexpectedly. Lions are well camouflaged; it is easy to find yourself next to one before you realise it. If you had been listening, you would probably have heard a warning growl about 20m ago. Now it is too late.

The best plan is to stop, and back off slowly, but confidently. If you are in a small group, then stick together. Never run from a big cat. First, they are always faster than you are. Second, running will just convince them that you are frightened prey, and worth chasing. As a last resort, if they seem too inquisitive and follow as you back off, then stop. Call their bluff. Pretend that you are not afraid and make loud, deep, confident noises: shout at them, bang something. But do not run.

John Coppinger, one of Africa's most experienced guides, adds that every single compromising experience that he has had with lion on foot has been either with a female with cubs, or with a mating pair, when the males can get very aggressive. You have been warned.

Snakes Most snakes are really not the great danger that people imagine, and will flee when they feel the vibrations of footsteps; only a few will stay still. The puff adder is probably responsible for more cases of snakebite than any other venomous snake in Botswana because, when approached, it will simply puff itself up and hiss as a warning, rather than slither away. This makes it essential always to watch where you place your feet when walking in the bush.

Similarly, there are a couple of arboreal (tree-dwelling) species which may be taken by surprise if you carelessly grab vegetation as you walk: so don't!

Spitting cobras are also encountered occasionally; they will aim for your eyes and spit with accuracy. If one of these rears up in front of you, then turn away and avert your eyes. If the spittle reaches your eyes, you must wash them out immediately and thoroughly with whatever liquid comes to hand: water, milk or even urine if that's the only liquid that can be quickly produced. See also page 163.

Black mambas are another particularly dangerous snake, and although they will usually flee from people, there are occasional reports of large individuals being very aggressive.

BOATING

Trips on motorboats and mekoro are very much an integral part of a safari trip to northern Botswana – they're both very different, and both a lot of fun. Almost no operators use the paddle-yourself Canadian-style canoes that are popular elsewhere in Africa.

BY MOKORO In *Lake Ngami and the River Okavango* (page 543), the explorer Charles John Andersson describes a mokoro used by him on Lake Ngami in the early 1850s:

> The canoe in which I embarked (and they are all somewhat similarly constructed) was but a miserable craft. It consisted of the trunk of a tree, about 20 feet long, pointed at both ends, and hollowed out by means of fire and a small hatchet. The natives are not at all particular as to the shape of the canoe. The after part of some that have come to my notice, would form an angle of near 45 degrees with their stem! Nevertheless, they were propelled through the water by the Bayeye (my boatmen were of that nation) with considerable speed and skill.

The 'appointments' of the canoe, consist of a paddle and a pole, ten to twelve feet in length. The paddle-man sits well in the stern, and attends mostly to the steering; while his comrade, posted at the head of the canoe, sends her along, by means of the pole, with great force and skill.

The natives, however, rarely venture any distance from the shore in their frail skiffs.

Local inhabitants of the Okavango still use mekoro like this, but for visitors it's more usual to have simply a single poler standing up at the stern and propelling the craft with a long pole. It's very like the punting done at some universities in Britain; a gentle form of locomotion best suited to shallow waters.

Only certain trees are suitable for making mekoro; they must usually be old, straight and strong. Jackalberries (*Diospyros mespiliformis*), sausage trees (*Kigelia africana*) and kiats (*Pterocarpus angolensis*) are favourites, while occasionally African mangosteens (*Garcinia livingstonei*) and rain trees (*Lonchocarpus capassa*) are also used. The wood used to make the poles to propel them is less crucial, though these are often made from silver-leaf terminalia trees (*Terminalia sericea*).

The last few decades have seen a mushrooming demand for mekoro, which began to deplete the older specimens of these species in some areas. Fortunately, fibreglass mekoro, that look very similar, are now being made, and are used by almost all safari camps today. If you are given a wooden craft, check with your camp that when it's no longer usable, they intend to replace it with a fibreglass version. The Delta can't afford to lose more of its oldest trees!

BY MOTORBOAT Motorboats are used on the rivers, and in the deeper channels and lagoons of the Okavango. They can be a lot of fun, although – used carelessly – their noise and (especially) their wake can do a lot of damage, so be sensitive to the dangers and don't encourage your guide to speed. (It can be a good idea to state this from the outset.) You'll often see much more by going slowly anyhow.

Interesting variations on this theme include the small, double-decker boats that afford views out over the top of the papyrus beds and make for idyllic sundowner cruises.

THE MAIN DANGERS It's tempting to fret about dangerous animals in Africa, but it's foolish to get paranoid: animal injuries on safari are rare. With common sense and a little knowledge, boat and mokoro trips are generally very safe, although nobody should discount the very real dangers posed by hippos and crocodiles. Canoes and mekoro are more vulnerable than chunky aluminium motorboats – just as walkers take slightly more risks than those on safari in robust 4x4 vehicles.

Hippo are strictly vegetarians, and will usually attack a mokoro only if they feel threatened. Your poler is usually standing up, so he has the best vantage point for spotting potential dangers ahead. It's helpful if you're either silent, or making so much noise that every animal in the bush can hear you approaching!

During the day, hippopotami will usually congregate in deeper water. The odd ones in shallow water, where they feel less secure, will usually head for the deeper places as soon as they are aware of a nearby mokoro. Avoiding hippos is then generally a case of steering around the deeper areas, and sticking to the shallows. This is where the poler's experience, knowing every waterway in the area, is invaluable.

Really large and deep channels and waterways are seldom a problem, as the hippos can avoid you provided that you make enough noise so that they know you are around. Shallow floodplains are also fairly safe, as you'll see the hippo in advance, and avoid them.

Problems usually occur when mekoro use relatively small and narrow 'hippo trails', where hippos can submerge but can't get far enough away. Then there's a danger of accidentally approaching too close, inadvertently surprising a hippo, and/or cutting it off from its path of retreat to deeper water. Then the hippo feels cornered and threatened, and may even attack. Occasionally camps will send mekoro out in small groups, with an armed guide in the lead mokoro; though this is the exception rather than the rule. In practice, incidents happen so rarely, and yet so fast, that I'm unsure if this would really give much real protection.

Hippo attacks are not common, but do happen and can have very serious consequences. An angry hippo can overturn a mokoro without a second thought, biting at it and/or its occupants. Once in this situation, there are no easy remedies.

Crocodiles may have sharp teeth and look prehistoric, but are of little danger to you…unless you are in the water – or very close to the edge. Then the more you struggle and the more waves you create, the more you will attract their unwelcome attentions. Very occasionally this could become an issue when a mokoro is overturned by a hippo; you must get out of the water as soon as possible, either into another canoe or on to the bank.

When a crocodile attacks an animal, it will try to disable it, normally by getting a firm, biting grip, submerging, and performing a long, fast barrel-roll. This will disorient the prey, drown it, and probably twist off the limb that has been bitten. In this dire situation, your best line of defence is probably to stab the reptile in its eyes with anything sharp that you have. Alternatively, if you can lift up its tongue and let the water into its lungs while it is underwater, then a crocodile will start to drown and will release its prey.

I have had reliable reports of a man surviving an attack in the Zambezi when a crocodile grabbed his arm and started to spin backwards into deep water. The man wrapped his legs around the crocodile, to spin with it and avoid having his arm twisted off. As this happened, he tried to poke his thumb into its eyes, but with no effect. Finally he put his free arm into the crocodile's mouth, and opened up the beast's throat. This worked. The crocodile left him and he survived with only a damaged arm. Understandably, anecdotes like this about tried and tested methods of escape are rare.

MINIMUM IMPACT

When you visit, drive through, or camp in an area and have 'minimum impact' upon it, this means that the area is left in the same condition as – or better than – when you entered it. While most visitors view minimum impact as being desirable, do spend time to consider the ways in which we contribute to environmental degradation, and how these can be avoided. Most of these points apply to any areas of rural Africa.

DRIVING Use your vehicle responsibly. If there's a road, or a track, then don't go off it – the environment will suffer. Driving off-road can leave a multitude of tracks that detract from the 'wilderness' feeling for subsequent visitors. Equally, don't speed through towns or villages: remember the danger to local children, and the amount of dust you'll cause.

HYGIENE Use toilets if they are provided, even if they are basic long-drop loos with questionable cleanliness. If there are no toilets, then human excrement should always be buried well away from paths, or groundwater, and any tissue used should be burned and then buried with it.

If you use rivers or lakes to wash, then soap yourself near the bank, using a pan for scooping water from the river – making sure that no soap finds its way back into the water. Use biodegradable soap. Sand makes an excellent pan-scrub, even if you have no water to spare.

RUBBISH Biodegradable rubbish can be burned and buried with the campfire ashes. Don't leave it lying around: it will look very unsightly and spoil the place for those who come after you.

Bring along some plastic bags with which to remove the rest of your rubbish, and dispose of it appropriately at the next large town. Items that will not burn, like tin cans, are best cleaned and squashed for easy carrying. If there are bins, then use them, but also consider when they will next be emptied, and whether local animals will rummage through them first. For this reason, it's probably best not to use the bins at most national parks' campsites; better to carry out all your own rubbish to the nearest town.

HOST COMMUNITIES While the rules for reducing impact on the environment have been understood and followed by responsible travellers for years, the effects of tourism on local people have only recently been considered. Many tourists believe it is their right, for example, to take intrusive photos of local people – and even become angry if the local people object. They refer to higher prices being charged to tourists as a rip-off, without considering the hand-to-mouth existence of those selling these products or services. They deplore child beggars, then hand out sweets or pens to local children with outstretched hands.

Our behaviour towards 'the locals' needs to be considered in terms of their culture, with the knowledge that we are the uninvited visitors. We visit to enjoy ourselves, but this should not be at the expense of local people. Read the section on cultural guidelines (page 152) and aim to leave the local communities better off after your visit.

LOCAL PAYMENTS If you spend time with any of Botswana's more rural communities, perhaps camping in the bush or getting involved with one of the community-run projects, then take great care with any payments that you make.

First, note that most people like to spend their earnings on what they choose. This means that trying to pay for services with beads, food, old clothes or anything else instead of money isn't appreciated. Ask yourself how you'd like to be paid, and you'll understand this point.

Second, find out the normal cost of what you are buying. For example, most community campsites will have a standard price for a pitch. Find out this price before you sleep there. It is then important that you pay about that amount for the pitch – not less, and not too much more.

As most people realise, if you try to pay less you'll get into trouble – as you would at home. However, many do not realise that if they generously pay a lot *more*, this can be equally damaging. Local rates of pay in rural areas can be very low, and a careless visitor can easily pay disproportionately large sums. Where this happens, local jobs can lose their value overnight. (Imagine working hard to become a game scout, only to learn that a tourist has given your friend the equivalent of your whole month's wages for just a few hours' guiding. What incentive is there for you to carry on with your regular job?)

If you want to give more – for good service, a super guide, or just because you want to help – then either buy some locally made produce (at the going rate), or donate money to one of the organisations working to improve the lot of Botswana's most disadvantaged. See page 154 for ideas, but also consider asking around locally; you'll often find projects that need your support.

Many lodges and camps assist with excellent, well-managed community projects, and will be able to suggest a good use for donations. Increasingly they're becoming more involved in the welfare of their surrounding communities, which is something you can also encourage.

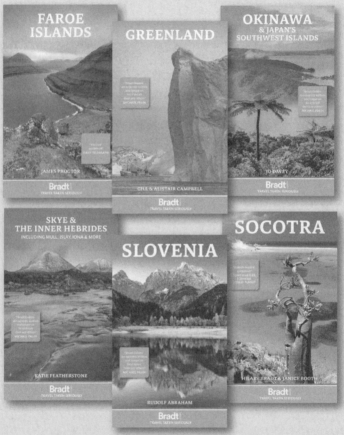

Part Two

THE GUIDE

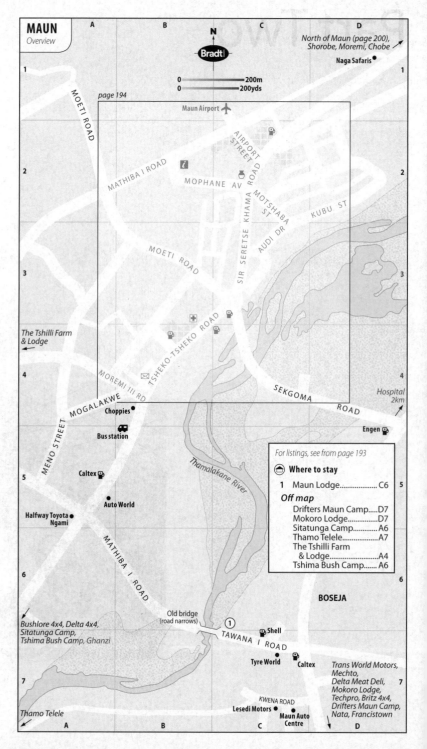

MAUN
Overview

N

Bradt

0 ——————— 200m
0 ——————— 200yds

page 194

North of Maun (page 200),
Shorobe, Moremi, Chobe →

Naga Safaris ●

Maun Airport ✈

MOETI ROAD

MATHIBA I ROAD

AIRPORT STREET

MOPHANE AV

MOTSHABA ST

SIR SERETSE KHAMA ROAD

KUBU ST

AUDI DR

MOETI ROAD

The Tshilli Farm
& Lodge
←

TSHEKO-TSHEKO ROAD

SEKGOMA ROAD

Hospital
2km
→

MOREMI III RD

MOGALAKWE

MENO STREET

Choppies ●

Bus station

Caltex

Auto World ●

Halfway Toyota
Ngami ●

Thamalakane River

Engen

MATHIBA I ROAD

BOSEJA

Old bridge
(road narrows)

Bushlore 4x4, Delta 4x4,
Sitatunga Camp,
Tshima Bush Camp, Ghanzi
←

① TAWANA I ROAD

Shell 🛢

Tyre World

Caltex

Trans World Motors,
Mechto,
Delta Meat Deli,
Mokoro Lodge,
Techpro, Britz 4x4,
Drifters Maun Camp,
Nata, Francistown
↓

KWENA ROAD

Lesedi Motors ●

Maun Auto
Centre ●

Thamo Telele
←

8

Maun

Founded in 1915, this once-dusty, sprawling town has been the start of expeditions into Botswana's wilds ever since. Today, Maun is unquestionably the safari capital of the country. Its elongated centre is dotted with shops and offices, and its suburbs – until relatively recently dominated by traditionally built, thatched rondavels – glint in the sun reflecting off tin-roofed houses.

In the 1980s, everywhere and everything here seemed geared towards the tourism bonanza. Maun had a rough-and-ready, frontier feel, as contemporary cowboys rode into town from the bush in battered 4x4s. Its focal points were the camps north of town – Island Safari Lodge and Crocodile Camp – and the old Duck Inn opposite the airport.

Then, as Maun became the administrative centre for the northern and western parts of Botswana, government departments moved here en masse. The town's roads became sealed tar, rather than pot-holed gravel tracks, which opened the door to an influx of saloon cars from the rest of the country. Finally, the tourism product itself changed. The pendulum swung away from last-minute budget trips bought in Maun, to upmarket safaris booked in advance from overseas. The new breed of visitors just change planes here; they seldom spend more than a few hours at Maun Airport.

However, for those who are driving themselves, Maun remains a centre from which to get organised, and perhaps a place to look at what cheaper safari options are available. It also offers an increasing number of pleasant places to stay, original cafés and restaurants, and activities to interest those who may find themselves with time on their hands between flights, or who are stopping over here before or after a safari.

GETTING THERE AND AWAY

Maun is 950m (3,100ft) above sea level, and however you are travelling, it is fairly easy to reach.

BY AIR
Scheduled services Maun is well connected by scheduled international and domestic flights, although timetable changes can be frequent with some operators.

Air Botswana [194 E2] (page 131) connects with Johannesburg daily and five times a week to Gaborone. Their hour-long service to Kasane is limited to Monday, Tuesday, Thursday and Saturday.

Flights with **Airlink** (page 131) between Maun, Johannesburg and Cape Town operate daily in each direction, and another South African carrier, **CemAir** (\+27 87 138 5203; e tickets@cemair.co.za; w flycemair.co.za), flies daily each way between Maun and Johannesburg.

Mack Air (page 190), a reliable and well-established charter airline in the country, has launched scheduled services between Botswana, Namibia and Zimbabwe, including daily scheduled services between Kasane and Victoria Falls (US$225 pp).

And most recently, in 2024, **Ethiopian Airlines** (page 131) launched a direct service between Maun and their hub in Addis Ababa, which allows travellers to connect on to their extensive global network. There are currently three scheduled flights a week, with the outbound flight from Maun touching down in Ndola, Zambia en route.

Charter airlines
Maun has a number of air charter companies, where you can hire light aircraft for private flights and transfers. These can sometimes be economical if you have four or five people travelling together. Unless otherwise stated, the following companies operate from Maun Airport. We include their contact details here not because you ever need to book your own flights between the camps; you don't: that's always done for you by the camps concerned, or your tour operator back home, and is invariably cheaper than chartering them directly with the airlines. However, you may want to contact them in case of emergency, or to organise a pleasure flight over the Delta, or even to charter a plane somewhere fairly unusual for the day – like the Tsodilo Hills. For details of scenic flights, see page 210.

Boro Air m +267 7180 0612; e reservations@ flyboro.com; f flyboro. Fixed-wing scenic flights over the Delta (20–60mins).

Delta Air \ 686 0044; e res1@footsteps-in-africa.com; w footsteps-in-africa.com/collections/delta-air. With 25 years' experience, Delta Air has a close association with many Lodges of Botswana camps & does not usually deal directly with the public.

Helicopter Horizons Apollo Hse [194 C2], Mophane Av; \ 680 1186; m 7133 0969; e res7@ helicopterhorizons.com; w helicopterhorizons. com. The only company operating scenic helicopter flights & transfers over the Okavango Delta, as well as trips to Tsodilo Hills & Makgadikgadi Pans.

Kavango Air \ 686 0323; m 7130 5112; e info@kavangoair.com; w kavangoair.com. Scenic flights & transfers in a fleet of Cessnas.

Mack Air \ 686 0675; e reservations@ flymackair.com; w flymackair.com. Operating for over 25 years, Mack Air maintains an excellent reputation as a reliable, high-quality air charter company that doesn't have ties

to any camps. It has 24 planes with 6–14 seats; the smaller ones (which allow everyone a window seat) are also used for scenic flights.

Major Blue Air \ 686 5671; e info@ majorblueair.com; w majorblueair.com. Has operated camp transfers & scenic flights in 3-, 5- & 7-seater planes since 2010.

Moremi Air \ 686 3632; e info@moremiair. com. Linked with Kwando Safaris, this is another charter specialist. Their fleet of aircraft is geared to both passenger transfers & scenic flights.

Safari Air \ 686 0022/680 1494; e info@ desertdelta.com, reservations@safariair.co.bw; w desertdelta.com. The company operates transfers to the lodges associated with Desert & Delta Safaris.

Wilderness Air \ 686 0086; e info@ wilderness-air.com; w wildernessdestinations.com. Owned by Wilderness Safaris, Wilderness Air organises virtually all the flights in Botswana for clients to Wilderness camps, making them the biggest 'small' airline here.

Maun Airport
[194 D1] On the north side of town, Maun's airport (code MUB) is just a stone's throw from many of the local safari operators, and equally close to a number of bars, restaurants, shops and other facilities. In spite of the town's small

size, the airport is one of southern Africa's busiest thanks to the stream of small planes flitting to and from Okavango lodges from this hub.

Maun's modernised terminal building opened in January 2023, following construction of a longer runway and the arrival of larger planes (Boeing 737 and Airbus A320s can land here).

Increased check-in counters, separate screening for international and domestic passengers, larger departure halls and better flight display boards have all improved a previously cramped and chaotic airport.

There are several **car hire companies** based in and around the airport terminal; see *Getting Around* (page 192). **Botswana Tourism** (airport office ☏ 686 3093) where various leaflets are on display, DHL couriers (⊕ 08.00–17.00 Mon–Fri), and Okavango Air Rescue (page 165) also have bases in the main foyer.

There is a café inside the terminal but some of the better options sit immediately across the road from the airport, notably the terrific Duck Café Bar (page 203) and Dusty Donkey Café (page 203) – both of which offer super barista coffees, freshly prepared, deliciously healthy food and indulgent treats, and helpful staff.

The airport itself has no reliable left-luggage facility, but if you're passing through to visit camps in the region by light aircraft, most safari companies will collect any spare baggage from you, store it off-site and return it to you as you leave.

BY CAR Ignoring the odd tiny bush track, there are only three significant roads linking Maun with the rest of the country:

Northeast towards Kasane: Routing right through Chobe National Park, it's about 360km of bush and thick sand (accessible only by 4x4) northeast to Kasane. For details of this track, through Shorobe to Moremi and Chobe, see *The road north of Maun: to Moremi and Chobe*, page 218.

Southwest towards Ghanzi and Namibia: It's about 285km of well-maintained tar road to Ghanzi and around 210km further to the Namibian border at Mamuno.

East towards Nata and Francistown: Nata is about 305km due east along the tarred A3, which divides Nxai Pan and Makgadikgadi Pans national parks. The road crosses the 24-hour police and veterinary control post north of Makalamabedi. Note that you cannot take any red meat through this checkpoint if you're heading east.

BY BUS Maun's smart bus station on Tsheko-Tsheko Road [188 B5] replaced its chaotic predecessor close to the local market a few years ago. Street vendors were quick to take advantage of the concrete shelters, selling drinks from colourful coolboxes to thirsty travellers, but otherwise there are few amenities.

There are regular departures for the major destinations, stopping at most of the larger towns on the way. The first buses leave at around 05.30, then regularly through the morning, but do check times beforehand, and arrive early. These destinations include: **Francistown** (5½hrs, P145 one-way); **Gaborone** (10½hrs, P135–170 one-way); **Ghanzi** (3–4hrs, P82–120 one-way); **Nata** (3½hrs, P95 one-way); and **Shakawe** (7hrs, around P110 one-way).

To reach **Kasane** (8hrs, P180 one-way), hop on a bus towards Francistown and change at Nata. There is also an overnight LAWA bus (m 7351 2751), which departs around 21.00 (7hrs, P165 one-way). As always, travelling on unlit roads in the dark – by car or bus – is not generally recommended on road safety grounds: pot-holes, wandering animals and other drivers are very real hazards.

The larger bus companies include: **AT&T Monnakgotla Travel & Tours** (☏ 399 5913, 393 9788; m 7211 1250; w monnakgotla.co.bw); **Gibfly Enterprises** (m 7468 8155); **Golden Bridge Express** (m 7130 2017; f); **JNG Express** (☏ 391 6629;

m 7474 5195; e jngexpress1@yahoo.com; f jngexpress1); **LAWA** (✆ 240 1832; m 7351 2751; e info@lawaholdings.co.bw; w lawaholdings.co.bw); and **Seabelo Express** (✆ 395 7078; e subots@botsnet.bw).

If you are **connecting to South Africa**, Seabelo sell Greyhound tickets for when you reach SA, and in late 2023, AT&T launched a direct Gaborone–Johannesburg service (four times a week; P400).

ORIENTATION

Finding your way around Maun is relatively simple. Though the town straddles the Thamalakane River, most places of interest are on the northern side. Here, there are two real focal points: the airport area, and the area around Riley's Garage. For the purposes of distances in this guide, we have taken Riley's Garage as the centre of Maun.

MAPS If you want to head anywhere 'off-piste' in Botswana's bush, then there are several options. The Shell maps, by Veronica Roodt, have long been the standard references for most travellers, and are sold in some curio shops and garages in Maun, though more recently the Tracks4Africa Botswana Traveller's Paper Map (4th Edition), which can be purchased online (w tracks4africa.co.za) in advance of travel, has become a great (and recommended) back-up to their excellent navigation app.

In Maun, maps can be purchased at **Ngami Data Services** [194 C2] (Mathiba I Rd; ✆ 686 0581; m 7285 7306; e colm@ngami.net; w nds-printingbotswana.com; ⊕ 09.00–17.00 Mon–Fri) which offers an impressive and detailed range of maps and guides of Botswana's towns, national parks and areas of interest, which can be printed to order on site and in the size you require. They also have prints of historical maps, the earliest of which is from the 1500s, which make for a great souvenir. The **Department of Surveys and Mapping** [194 E2] (Airport Av; ✆ 686 0272; e imauano@gov.bw; ⊕ 07.30–12.45 & 13.45–16.30 Mon–Fri) sells more traditional survey maps at a range of scales, all of which can also be ordered in advance by email.

GETTING AROUND

If you're staying around the centre, between the airport and Riley's, then **walking** is feasible, though it can be hot. Otherwise, you'll need some form of transport, most of which operates out of the **bus** station [188 B5] on Tsheko-Tsheko Road. All public transport vehicles, including taxis, have blue number plates.

A **taxi** out to one of the camps to the north of town will cost P70–90 (or more if there's a long sand track involved), depending on your negotiating powers. If it's a shared taxi – when the driver stops to take another lift at the same time – you can expect to pay considerably less, though not as little as one of the locals. Taxis have their telephone numbers displayed on the doors, and can be pre-booked. Ask at your accommodation in Maun for a reliable contact number, as these tend to change all too frequently.

Small **combis** ply frequently between the back of the bus station and the outlying suburbs. Typically, vehicles leave only when full, but they will drop you on request and fares are fixed at just a few pula.

In theory there are ten clearly defined routes, with numbers painted on the front of the vehicles, but some have not been operational for many years. For the visitor, the most useful routes are as follows:

Route 1	Airport, & north as far as Audi Camp
Route 5	Maun Lodge
Route 7	Letsholathebe II Memorial Hospital

VEHICLE HIRE

Avis/Budget [194 C2] Mathiba 1 St; 686 0039; m 7583 6018; e avismun@botsnet.bw, botswanares@avis.co.za; w avis.com; 08.00–13.00 & 14.00–17.00 Mon–Fri, 08.00–14.00 Sat, noon–18.00 Sun. For a fully equipped 4x4, contact Avis Safari Rental (+27 11 392 5202; e safarirental. reservations@avis.co.za; w avis.co.za/safari-rental). Office in terminal & another immediately opposite (Budget).

Britz [188 D7] Matshwane Industrial Site, Unit 1; 686 1190; w britz.co.za; 08.00–17.00 Mon–Fri, 08.00–14.00 Sat. Established 4x4 rental company operating in South Africa, Namibia & Botswana, letting a range of fully equipped Toyota Land Cruisers.

Bushlore [188 A6] Thuso Rehability Centre Rd; 625 1359; e info@bushlore.com; w bushlore. com 08.00–17.00 Mon–Fri, 08.00–13.00 Sat. Fully equipped 4x4 Toyota Land Cruisers – including some with roof tents – for 2–4 travellers.

Europcar [194 D1] Mathiba I Rd; 686 3366; w europcar.co.za; 08.00–17.00 Mon–Thu, 08.00–19.30 Fri, 08.00–13.00 Sat–Sun

Hertz [194 D1] Mathiba 1 St; +266 861186; e res@hertz.co.za; w hertz.co.za; 08.00–19.00 Mon–Fri, 08.00–13.00 Sat

Techpro Safari [188 D7] 592 Boseja; m 7326 8590; w techprosafari.com. Fully kitted-out Toyota Land Cruisers, including several equipped with camera mounts, gimbals & electronic roof hatches for photographers. One-way rentals between the company's bases in Maun, Cape Town & Windhoek are available at no extra cost.

Travel Adventures Botswana [194 F1] Sir Seretse Khama Rd; 684 0351; m 7636 7205; e reservations@traveladventuresbotswana.com; w traveladventuresbotswana.com; 08.00–17.00 Mon–Sat, 08.00–noon Sun. Toyota Hilux twin cabs or Land Cruisers can be rented as they are, or kitted out with everything you'll need for a camping safari into the national parks. Can also help with national park campsite bookings.

TOURIST INFORMATION

Botswana Tourism [194 C2] (246 Apollo Hse, Mophane Av; 686 1056, airport 686 3093; e maun@botswanatourism.co.bw; 07.30–18.00 Mon–Fri, 09.00–14.00 Sat) has an office close to the airport, and another within the airport building.

The local newspaper, *The Ngami Times* (w ngamitimes.co.bw), is published weekly on Fridays; it is useful for details of local sports and entertainment, and offers an insight into Botswana's political situation and news scene. It's available online and from outlets across town, including the shop at Riley's Garage.

WHERE TO STAY

Just as Maun has evolved in recent decades, so have the places to stay. In the 1980s, the few camps on the northern side of town felt like outposts in the wilderness. Places like Crocodile Camp and Island Safari Lodge had the atmosphere of oases of comfort. They seemed like remote lodges and often, when the water was high enough, mokoro trips would start from the banks of the Thamalakane River beside the lodge, to pole adventurers into the Delta.

Now, although many visitors are still drawn to the riverside establishments, times have changed. Better roads and more neighbours have made these camps feel less isolated and more a part of Maun. Less water in the river over many years put an end to mokoro trips starting in Maun. And while visitors, especially backpackers,

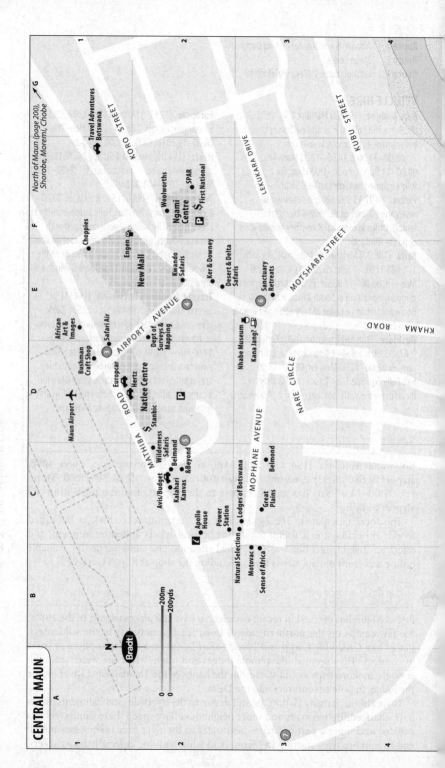

CENTRAL MAUN

North of Maun (page 200),
Shorobe, Moremi, Chobe

Travel Adventures Botswana

KORO STREET

Choppies

Woolworths

Ngami Centre   SPAR
First National

Engen

New Mall

Kwando Safaris

Ker & Downey

Desert & Delta Safaris

LEKUKARA DRIVE

African Art & Images

Bushman Craft Shop

Safari Air

Europcar

Hertz

AIRPORT AVENUE

Dept of Surveys & Mapping

Sanctuary Retreats

MOTSHABA STREET

Maun Airport

Natlee Centre

Stanbic

Nhabe Museum

Kana Jang?

KHAMA ROAD

MATHIBA I ROAD

Wilderness Safaris

Belmond

Avis/Budget

Kalahari Kanvas

&Beyond

NARE CIRCLE

MOPHANE AVENUE

Apollo House

Power Station

Lodges of Botswana

Great Plains

Belmond

Natural Selection

Motovac

Sense of Africa

Bradt

N

0   200m
0   200yds

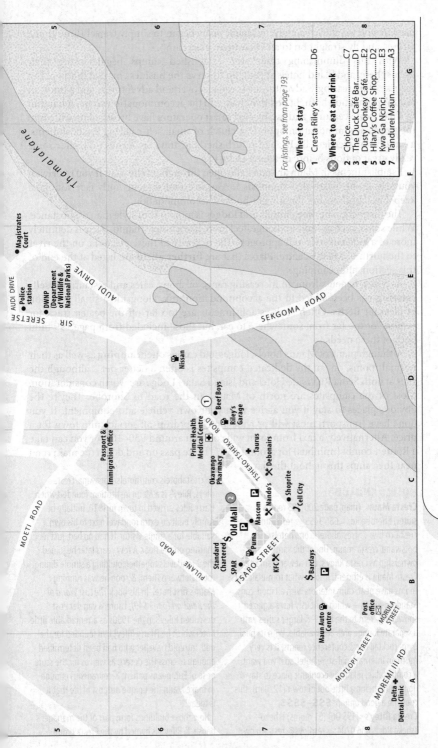

Maun WHERE TO STAY **8**

Thamalakane

Magistrates Court
Police station
DWNP (Department of Wildlife & National Parks)

AUDI DRIVE
SIR SERETSE
AUDI DRIVE

SEKGOMA ROAD

Passport & Immigration Office

MOETI ROAD

Nissan

Beet Boys

Prime Health Medical Centre

Okavango Pharmacy

Riley's Garage

TSHEKO-TSHEKO ROAD

Taurus

Debonairs

Shoprite

Cell City

Nando's

Mascom

Old Mall

Standard Chartered

SPAR

Puma

Maun Auto Centre

PULANE ROAD

TSARO STREET

KFC

Barclays

Post office

MORULA STREET

MOTLOPI STREET

MOREMI III RD

Delta Dental Clinic

For listings, see from page 193

Where to stay
1 Cresta Riley's D6

Where to eat and drink
2 Choice C7
3 The Duck Café Bar D1
4 Dusty Donkey Café E2
5 Hilary's Coffee Shop D2
6 Kwa Ga Ncinci E3
7 Tandurei Maun A3

195

used to stop for at least a night in Maun, many began to simply transit through the airport and fly straight on to an Okavango safari camp.

With this diminishing trade, the established camps began losing their atmosphere, and bland hotels sprung up to serve the business market in town. But the rise of increasingly adventurous travellers, overland adventurers and a boost in Maun's population brought positive change to the accommodation scene. A handful of small-scale ventures and established safari operators have breathed new life into the town's accommodation options: a clutch of small self-catering establishments, a handful of excellent B&Bs, and refurbished old-time favourites now offer some really great options before or after a Delta trip.

Establishments in Maun are normally open throughout the year. If you're driving yourself, do be aware that signposts for some establishments only face south, so keep a watchful eye out for any pre-booked accommodation.

The distinction between **hotels and lodges** is more one of style than of substance. While some, such as Mokoro Lodge, feel more like a hotel, Thamo Telele is definitely more of a lodge in style and approach. The majority of these places lie on the river to the north of Maun's centre. Places that are **further afield** are listed at the end of this section, after camping.

As Maun benefits from an increasing range of shops, cafés and restaurants, **self-catering** has been added to the accommodation mix, alongside a small selection of pleasant **B&Bs**. Often such establishments are too far off the beaten track for visitors, or too far from somewhere to eat, but those included from page 199 fulfil both of these needs.

Although many of Maun's hotels, lodges and camps offer **camping** as well as their normal rooms, one of the dedicated campsites is often a better bet – although the sites at both Sedia Riverside Hotel and Island Safari Lodge are worth consideration. Most of the campsites are north of Maun, on the road to Shorobe. They're the obvious places to stay if you arrive with your own vehicle and equipment. If you don't have transport, most will provide a pick-up/drop-off service into town for a price. Alternatively, a taxi from town will cost you around P50–100, or you can take a Route 1 combi (minibus) for around P5–7. These pass up and down the main road near the camps throughout the day.

HOTELS AND LODGES

Cresta Maun [map, page 200] (83 rooms & suites) Shorobe Rd; 686 3455; e resmaun@ cresta.co.bw; w crestahotels.com/hotels/ botswana/cresta-maun. Under the same ownership as Cresta Riley's, but newer & smarter, Cresta Maun is efficient, if somewhat formulaic. All rooms have neat, calm interiors with all mod-cons. Standard rooms – which curiously have a glazed shower adjacent to the bed – & larger suites with a separate lounge area are available. With its pool, gym, cocktail bar & conference rooms, it is very much an international-style hotel, so if you want a comfortable, relatively economic place to stay & don't mind being a little out of town (12.5km), this could be a good option. $$$–$$$$

Cresta Riley's [195 D6] (51 rooms) Tsheko-Tsheko Rd; 686 0204; e resrileys@cresta.co.bw;

w crestahotels.com/hotels/botswana/cresta-rileys. Riley's is a Maun institution, founded when Harry Riley arrived in town in 1910. Initially he simply built an extra rondavel next to his own, suitable for a single visitor. It had no bed, just reed matting on the floor. A few years later he joined the 2 rondavels together, building a simple dining room between them, & soon he was running Maun's first hotel. In his book *The Lost World of the Kalahari (page 540)*, Laurens van der Post described Riley's in the 1950s as a 'remarkable little hotel which he [Harry Riley] had founded for the odd, intrepid traveller who had been determined enough to cross the desert, as well as for the score or so of Europeans patient & courageous enough to make Maun the unique outpost of life that it is today'.

Now those buildings form part of the manager's house, & Riley's is owned by the Cresta group.

Today's visitors will benefit from a central location on the main street & clean & reliable en-suite rooms (including 10 suites with a balcony & lounge); best are those upstairs, whose high thatched ceilings go a long way to keeping them cool. There's also a pool & pool bar, surrounded by lawns with tables under thatched umbrellas, a children's play area & a gym. The modern restaurant is a tad soulless, but service & food are good, & you can opt to eat outside where you'll be entertained after dark by an orchestra of frogs in the nearby Thamalakane River. **$$$**

Crocodile Camp Safari & Spa [map, page 200] (15 chalets, camping) Shorobe Rd; 684 0830; m 7560 6864; e croccamp.res@sklcamps.co.bw; reservations@sklcamps.co.bw; w sklcamps.com/lodge/crocodile-camp. On a site sloping down to the Thamalakane River 15km north of town, Croc Camp is an old Maun institution. The neat, en-suite chalets (ranging from standard rooms overlooking the gardens to 'presidential' with river-view decks & plunge pools) have a modern look with comfortable beds. Near the car park, a separate campsite, with a modern ablution block, is divided into 10 large pitches under a few shady camelthorn trees. Some pitches benefit from individual water & power supplies, & overland trucks have their own discrete area.

Cantilevered over the river, the thatched Croc Rock Bar is a great place for sundowners, while families especially enjoy the palm-shaded swimming pool & its wide deck dotted with loungers under umbrellas. Receiving mixed reviews, the restaurant is open for all meals, with dining spread between tables on the lawns & the open-sided dining room. There's also a conference centre, on-site Marulana Spa & a range of activities available, including motorboat & mokoro trips starting from the camp. **$$–$$$**

Grays Eden Sanctuary [map, page 200] (12 rooms) 1566 Matlapaneng; m 7528 7273; e sandrine@grayseden.com; w grayseden.com. Created by husband & wife team Sam & Sandrine, Grays Eden opened in 2024 as an elegant boutique hotel on the banks of the Thamalakane River, a super addition to the Maun hotel scene. Just 15mins from the airport, its 5 thatched villas & 7 fishermen's cottages are light, bright & immaculately finished. Whitewashed buildings & cool, calm, contemporary interiors have been crafted with immense care & attention to detail.

If you can bring yourself to leave the comfort of your room, laze on the plush, pole-shaded veranda, relax under the fringed umbrellas on loungers by the pool, book a treatment in the spa, & look forward to the home-cooked meals served in the Eden Kitchen & wine tastings on offer in the Wine Cave or by one of the lovely fires. It's a beautiful spot to recoup from a long flight before safari. Children of all ages welcome. *Fisherman cottage: US$200 pp Jan–Mar, US$250 pp Apr–Dec, B&B inc airport transfers, 1 boma sundowner experience & 1 spa treatment. Villa: US$350 pp Jan–Mar, US$425 pp Apr–Dec, B&B inc airport transfers, 1 boma sundowner experience & 1 spa treatment.* **$$$$–$$$$$**

Island Safari Lodge [map, page 200] (12 chalets, 6 rooms, camping) Sir Seretse Khama Rd; 686 0300; e enquire@africansecrets.net; f; w islmaun.com. When I first visited Maun in 1988, Island Safari Lodge was already a well-established hub. Set in 116ha beside the western bank of the Thamalakane River, about 12km north of Maun, it has a pretty location under a forest canopy dominated by tall sycamore figs.

Accommodation is in twin-bedded, en-suite thatched chalets, set among lawns & indigenous vegetation close to the river. Further back is a terrace of 6 'heritage rooms', some of which connect & include bunk beds for families. Recently, there have been reports that maintenance is sometimes lacking. If you're self-sufficient, the shady campsite (US$14 pp) has 2 toilet blocks and a shower block, & there are 10 dedicated spaces for overland trucks around the perimeter, catering for up to 100 campers.

Landscaped gardens lead down to the river, where meals are served in the long bar/restaurant (⊕ 06.00–22.00 daily) with sports TV & Wi-Fi. Cooling off is easy, with a small pool close to the restaurant & a larger one by the campsite. The lodge can organise day trips to Chief's Island or Moremi (US$275 pp; min 2 people), mokoro excursions (US$108 pp) & packed lunches (P200 pp). **$$$**

Maun Lodge [188 C6] (140 rooms, 12 chalets) 459 Boseja; 686 3939; e bookings@maunlodge.co.bw; w maunlodge.com. On the banks of the Thamalakane River, Maun Lodge is the town's largest hotel & a reliable stopover, popular with overland groups & independent travellers alike. The en-suite rooms are neat & simple, if a little dated, but the main areas are pleasant & the staff are welcoming. The thatch-&-brick chalets are particularly good value, & each has its own parking space, while more expensive options overlook the river, including 2 family chalets.

The open-air Boma restaurant & Riverview bar are nice spots to spend an evening, with the bonus of live music some days. As well as a range of light meals, there's an extensive buffet that includes grills, vegetarian options & some local dishes: perfect if you don't want to venture out. To keep you cool, there are 2 separate swimming pools, for adults & children, & a gym. $$$–$$$$

Mokoro Lodge [188 D7] (36 rooms) ✆ 680 0551; e mokororeservations@maunlodge. co.bw; w mokorolodge.com; f; ⊕ MOKLOD 20°01.646'S, 23°26.255'E. Out of town on the Nata road, 3.4km from central Maun, this simple, clean motel is set back from the road, with good security. Twin & dbl en-suite rooms are fairly basic but have all the essentials, plus AC, sat TV, a kitchenette & a no-nonsense bathroom. This is perhaps more geared towards local business travel but would make a reasonable & economic place to spend the night if you're passing through, & self-drivers will appreciate the covered parking space next to the room. There's a restaurant serving simple meals of pizzas & burgers. Rate is exc b/fast. $

Sedia Riverside Hotel [map, page 200] (40 rooms, 5 cottages, camping) 305 Sir Seretse Khama Rd; ✆ 686 0177; m 7341 7978; e info@sediahotel. com; w sedia-hotel.com. The wide-fronted hotel occupies extensive grounds just 6km from the airport, & is well signposted from the main road. Although not quite as costly as Riley's or Maun Lodge, it has a livelier, more colourful atmosphere.

In the foyer, which is adorned with traditional African wall-hangings & large wooden animal carvings, you will find a couple of soft chairs & cool drinks to welcome you on arrival. Most of the rooms are laid out along 2 wings facing into the hotel's gardens, each with its own outside entrance. Bright colours adorn twin or dbl beds; en-suite bathrooms incorporate a bath with shower; & each room has AC, ceiling fan, tea/coffee station, TV & phone. Closer to the river, larger 1- & 2-bedroom cottages boast a fridge & kettle, AC, lounge with TV & a shady veranda.

At the back of the hotel, set among lawns, is a large swimming pool, for use by hotel & campsite guests. The surrounding terrace is a popular venue

for casual dining, while the more formal restaurant comes into its own in the winter & if you're looking for Wi-Fi. There is also a bar with a pool table, & a separate children's playground.

Beyond the lawns, a large & sprawling campsite (P135 pp) leads down to the Thamalakane River, where campers share well-kept hot showers & toilets. There is plenty of tree shade for your own tent, or with advance booking, you can organise a pre-erected dome tent. The option to park next to your tent is particularly useful.

The hotel is the base for Afro Trek (page 217), who operate a variety of budget safaris & mokoro trips, & is a 20min walk to Okavango Craft Brewery (page 203) if you fancy sampling the excellent local beer or are looking for a nearby dining alternative. $$–$$$

Thamalakane River Lodge [map, page 200] (34 chalets, 2 family rooms) Shorobe Rd; ✆ 686 4313; m 7531 6585; e res1@botswanabooking. com; w trlmaun.com; ⊕ THAMAL 19°53.362'S, 23°33.412'E. This riverside hotel, 19km (20mins) north of the town, has one of the most attractive settings in Maun. Paths wind through the gently sloping site to the neat chalets (2 Kingfisher units have 2 bedrooms for families), all set in well-tended gardens & facing the Thamalakane River. Stone walls, steeply thatched roofs, tiled floors, ceiling fans & pole-shaded terraces help to mitigate the sun's rays, & each chalet is clean & thoughtfully decorated with traditional touches. All guests may use the pool, which is set in a grassy clearing & shaded by large trees, & in-room massages can be organised, as well as activities in & around Maun.

Popular locally is the restaurant, an open-sided thatched building, surrounded in part by a large, looping water-lily pond and a tree-shaded terrace with view towards the river. With options from steak & seafood to pizzas & vegetarian dishes, or plated 3-course, à la carte meals (US$47 pp), there's plenty of choice, but if you are not staying at the lodge you will need to make a reservation.

Mokoro trips, from 1hr (US$30 pp) to overnight camping (US$400 pp), full-day (US$325 pp; min 2 people) and sunset boat cruises (US$28 pp), Moremi day trips (US$325 pp) and other excursions are available. *Babbler chalets US$155 pp sharing, B&B; Kingfisher chalets US$225 pp sharing, B&B.* $$$$–$$$$$

Thamo Telele [188 A7] (9 tents, 2 chalets) Contact Natural Selection (page 215); ⊕ TREELO 20°03.896'S, 23°22.881'E. Previously Royal Tree Lodge, Thamo Telele sits within a 2km² private game reserve, about 20mins southwest of Maun (or 5mins by helicopter). Refurbished in 2022 & now part of the Natural Selection group, the lodge feels more remote than it is thanks to the tall trees, thick bush & presence of wildlife – making it an ideal spot to begin a Botswana safari after a long-haul flight.

Winding sandy paths lead through the bush to the 9 spacious, air-conditioned Meru tents, which are raised on wooden platforms surrounded by mature trees. For each, a private deck with a couple of chairs leads into an airy bedroom with wooden floors, bold giraffe-pattern artwork & brightly coloured chairs. To the back, there's an en suite with a bath, large mirror & twin basins on a feature wall of colourful wallpaper. 2 separate doors lead to a well-screened outdoor shower & separate toilet cubicle.

In the lodge's 2 thatched chalets, often used for honeymooners, the structure is more substantial & spacious but the décor is similar, & the feeling more intimate. The bathrooms, with a deep bath & outdoor shower, are modern yet entirely in keeping, & sliding patio doors lead to a small veranda at the back.

The main communal area is a large, semi-circular building with a tall thatched roof. At one end of the open-plan space is a dining area & at the other a large lounge with an honesty bar. Oriental rugs, teal-blue chairs & an eclectic mix of furniture lend a comfortable, relaxed feel, and the woven giraffe murals & the lodge's name (translation: 'long neck') are a nod to Thamo Telele's connection with the Giraffe Conservation Foundation. Large, bi-fold glass doors lead from the main area to an extensive teak deck, which has been built around an enormous leadwood tree, and serves as the venue for shady alfresco meals. There's a lap pool with sunloungers under a shady pergola, & a spa in the making. Activities here include the popular 'Giraffe Experience' (US$150 pp) – an escorted waterhole trip with a naturalist to observe the reserve's herd & learn about the individuals & the organisation's work to protect this surprisingly threatened species. Do ask questions to get the most from this experience. There are also well-marked, self-guided walking trails around the reserve

(30mins to 1½hrs), & with no large predators, this is a relatively safe way to stretch your legs after a long flight. These trails also provide a great opportunity to spot plains game – giraffe, zebra, kudu, springbok, impala, oryx, eland & ostrich – & offer great birdwatching opportunities (over 300 species recorded here). You can take a guide with you for US$40 pp. There are also a few fat bikes if you're keen to cover more ground, although the wildlife viewing will be easier on foot. Horseriding (US$122 pp; all abilities; advance booking necessary) is also available. *US$425–600 pp, FB inc transfers from Maun.* **$$$$$**

B&BS AND SELF-CATERING

Discovery Bed & Breakfast [map, page 200] (9 chalets) Shorobe Rd; m 7244 8298, 7436 0198; e discoverybookings@gmail.com; w discoverybnb.com. A taste of Botswana's culture comes to life in this quiet, attractively planted complex, about 15km north of the airport down a 300m track to the west of the main road. Neat, timber-framed rondavels, painted inside & out in zigzag patterns of browns, ochres, deep reds & greens, are set on a sandy plot around a firepit, in the form of a traditional village. Inside are rustic twin or dbl wooden-framed beds swathed in mosquito netting, with bedside lights, ceiling & free-standing fans, a toilet & basin behind a reed screen, & private showers under the stars; some also have a small veranda. A family chalet has a dbl bed & a set of bunks, ideal for 2 (young) children. The reception area doubles as a homely b/fast room, & there's a small pool in the deck at the back. Carol's Coffee Shop (⊕ 13.00–18.00 most days) serves cappuccinos, iced coffees & freshly baked cakes. During high season, set evening meals (P220 pp) are available on request, but there are several dining options nearby, & restaurants & activities are happily arranged by the friendly Dutch owners & their team. **$$–$$$**

The Maun Studios [map, page 200] (3 studios, 1 tent) Sedia Ward; ✆ 686 0254; m 7418 9266; e themaunstudios@gmail.com; w themaunstudios.com. Situated in picturesque gardens on the banks of the Thamalakane River, 7km from the airport, this is a great option for those who would prefer not to stay in a traditional hotel or lodge. 3 large studio bungalows & a riverfront Meru tent are spread around the grounds that surround the owners' home. Each is comfortably furnished & has its own kitchenette & en-suite bathroom. Although primarily a self-catering option, b/fast is included & is served on a terrace overlooking the gardens & river. For other meals & activities, helpful owners Margaret, Rocky & Sarah are happy to assist with suggestions, reservations for restaurants & excursions around Maun. It all feels more like a holiday home than a B&B, & with secure parking, an inviting plunge pool, river walks & a firepit for sundowners (all of which, like the gardens, are shared with the owners), guests could easily spend more than the customary overnight stopover here. **$$$**

Queness Inn [map, below] (8 rooms) Disaneng Rd; 684 1000; m 7441 4337; e quenessinnmaun@gmail.com; w quenessinn. com. On the southern side of the Thamalakane River, this self-catering option with large rooms can feel a little out of the way, despite being only

6km from Riley's. The en-suite dbl rooms, organised around a courtyard garden, have sat TV, Wi-Fi, a well-equipped kitchenette & AC; 2 family rooms have a separate lounge with sofa bed. There is also an outdoor braai area & secure on-site parking. **$$**

CAMPING AND BACKPACKING

Audi Camp [map, below] (camping, 10-bed house) Shorobe Rd; 686 0599; m 7532 3065; e info@audisafaris.com, info@okavangocamp. com; w okavangocamp.com. While standards elsewhere tend to fluctuate, Audi Camp remains one of Maun's constants. It's clean, friendly & well cared for, with the whole multi-level site securely fenced & patrolled at night by guards. The camp, about 12km from Maun centre on the road north to Moremi & Chobe, is well signposted. It's worth noting that its name is entirely unrelated to cars, but is instead Setswana for fish eagle.

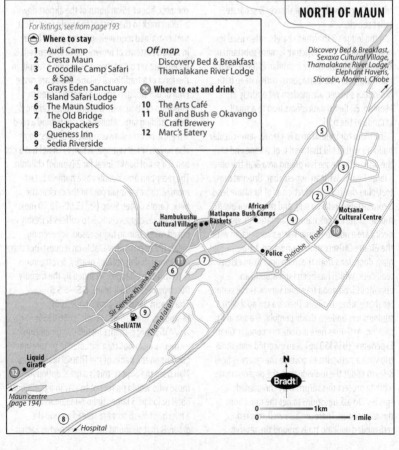

NORTH OF MAUN

Discovery Bed & Breakfast, Sexaxa Cultural Village, Thamalakane River Lodge, Elephant Havens, Shorobe, Moremi, Chobe

Motsana Cultural Centre

African Bush Camps

Matlapana Baskets

Hambukushu Cultural Village

Police

Shorobe Road

Sir Seretse Khama Road

Thamalakane

Shell/ATM

Liquid Giraffe

Maun centre (page 194)

Hospital

N

Bradt

0 ——————— 1km
0 ——————— 1 mile

At the top of the complex is a sandy campsite under mopane trees, with a basic, shared camp kitchen, & ablutions in a large, ochre rondavel that has open-air showers & hot water. Pitches with power have their own braai & water supply. Bring your own tent, or rent one of their pre-erected, en-suite Meru tents. These tents come with comfortable beds & linen, as well as electric lights & fans, & are available in the campsite or on decks overlooking the river, where they also have their own firepits & braai. Firewood & ice are available, as is a laundry service. If you don't fancy sleeping under canvas, try a room in the 4-bedroom riverside house, which has its own kitchen & bathroom.

The camp has a large thatched bar & a restaurant area on a lower level that serves meals & snacks (⏱ 07.00–22.00 daily), from toasted sandwiches to steaks & vegetarian options. Down again, & near the river, is a large & very popular swimming pool. A great little shop sells a range of curios, while almost opposite is Motsana Cultural Centre, which incorporates a café & puts on occasional cultural events. The camp itself is also the base for Audi Safaris (page 217). *Camping: P140/70 adult/child; power point P80/night. Meru tent: P590/825 sgl/ dbl, B&B. Tents on decks: P780/920 sgl/dbl, B&B. House P3,850 (max 10) or P800 dbl. Transfer from town P300/vehicle, up to 9 people.*

The Old Bridge Backpackers [map, opposite] (camping, 8 dorm beds, 8 tents) Off Sir Seretse Khama Rd; ☏ 686 2406; m 7317 7260; e info@ maun-backpackers.com; w maun-backpackers. com. 10km north of town & tucked down a well-signposted but rather pot-holed lane beside the bridge over the river, 'The Bridge' was once Maun's best backpacker hang-out. Sadly, some recent traveller reports have been far less positive, with issues over poor maintenance, general cleanliness & a seemingly unreliable booking system. It may be wise to check recent reviews for an update before committing to stay here. Given its prime location, we hope the situation improves.

If you do decide to go, there is space for independent campers, as well as pre-erected tents (5 of which are en suite & overlook the river), some simple dome tents & a block of 'dorm' beds. All share toilets & open-air showers, as well as a basic self-catering kitchen. There's a large, thatched central area, with a TV for sports' matches, pool table, a small swimming pool, & tables & chairs set

out under the trees for meals of pizzas & burgers. Activities are run by their own in-house operator, Old Bridge Tours & Safaris. *Camping P110 pp; pre-erected tent P440/550 sgl/dbl; en-suite tent P660/770 sgl/dbl.*

FURTHER AFIELD
Drifters Maun Camp [188 D7] (10 tents, camping) Chanoga; m 7230 4472; e drifters@ drifters.co.za; w drifters.co.za. Some 32km south of Maun, towards Nata, the local base of South African overland safari company Drifters has 5 camping pitches & 10 Meru tents with twin beds, including 4 that are en suite. If you're heading south, & driving a high-clearance 4x4, it's well worth considering a night here. Down a 1km sandy track just beyond the village of Chanoga, you'll find a wide riverfront location with grassy lawns, where the thatched bar & restaurant, exclusive to those staying on site, are attractively decorated with wall hangings & baskets. There is a volleyball court & a small pool, but the greatest attraction is the Boteti River, which, when flowing attracts numerous waterbirds – including flamingos, pelicans & knob-billed ducks. Camping is on a small, tree-shaded site, with an ablution block & hot water. *Camping US$10 pp; tent US$35 pp inc b/fast.*

Sitatunga Camp [188 A6] (12 chalets, 10 tents, camping) ☏ 680 0380; m 7250 6420; e bookings@deltarain.com; w deltarain.com; ⨐ deltarainsafaris; ✪ SITAT 20°04.476'S, 23°21.296'[E]. Within a secure complex, Sitatunga remains a popular choice for overlanders, but for independent campers pre-booking is almost essential. To get there, head southwest from Maun towards Ghanzi, before turning off the main road about 12km from Riley's Garage. The lodge is about 2km from the main road down a sandy track, although it is accessible by 2WD.

The large campsite lies under trees, with pitches well spread out; each has a standpipe & power point & shares basic but clean ablutions. Best of the accommodation are the 10 en-suite Meru tents. These are quite spacious, with mosquito nets over twin beds, a tea station, an electric fan & outdoor showers. Brick-walled, canvas-roofed chalets feel a little dark & cramped by comparison, albeit with AC, a ceiling fan & access to a swimming pool, shared exclusively by chalet guests. There's a handy laundry service, Wi-Fi, firewood & ice.

Maun WHERE TO STAY

8

There's no self-catering kitchen, but braai facilities are available with reservation in a large, airy bar area. There's a larger pool by the bar & a volleyball court. *Camping P140/105 adult/child. Tent P780 dbl; chalet P840 dbl (both max 2 people).*

The Tshilli Farm & Lodge [188 A4] (5 chalets) m 7140 7379; e tshillifarm@gmail.com; tshillifarm; ✆ 19°54.021S, 23°23.092E. A brilliantly original addition to the accommodation scene, Tshilli Farm is a great farm-stay about 45mins from Maun, where you can relax & experience rural, agricultural Africa in comfort & good company. Owned & run by Maun local & former safari guide Adi, this laid-back lodge is part of his working farm, where the focus is on natural, regenerative practices & growing much, much more than just chillies, as the tasty, farm-fresh produce served in the restaurant will attest. The farm's commitment to sustainability is reflected in its dedication to a raft of environmentally conscious practices in evidence across the property.

Set on an island in the floodplains, Tshilli's 5 chalets are raised on simple wooden decks, tucked into the bush. Inside, mesh windows allow for a breeze over comfortable beds. There's an en-suite bathroom at the back of each chalet, partially open to the trees, with a timber floor, great shower, sink & toilet. It's a simple & rustic spot but perfectly comfortable.

At the centre of the lodge, in an open-sided barn building, is the farm's well-known kitchen & restaurant, a homely lounge with deep-cushioned sofas, cow hide rugs, stacks of coffee-table books & arguably some of Botswana's best pizzas fresh from the wood-fired oven. There's also a small thatched bar under the leadwood trees for evening socialising, with a campfire. Darts & table tennis are on offer & there's an inviting pool, complete with hammocks & shady loungers to take in the serenity of the surroundings. & if you find you don't want to leave, there are voluntourism opportunities so you can get involved with farm life over longer stays. $$–$$$

✳ **Tshima Bush Camp** [188 A6] (4 tents) m 7484 2079, 7534 2225; e info@ tshimabushcamp.com; w tshimabushcamp.com; ✆ TSHIMA 20°11.449'S, 23°14.430'E. Also on the Ghanzi road, some 30km southwest of Maun, Tshima is run by a hospitable couple, Verena & Russell. It's a friendly, low-key spot in 30ha of land bordering the Nhabe River, where marked walking trails make exploring easy. The occasional elephant crosses through camp, but for many birding is the draw: around 350 species have been identified here.

Facing into the bush, Tshima's smart walk-in tents have twin beds under mosquito nets, & modern en-suite bathrooms. Each has a table & chairs on the veranda, plus its own picnic bench, so b/fast – brought to your tent in a basket each morning – can be both relaxed & private. In the evening guests can enjoy a 3-course dinner (P350) under the stars, with travellers raving about the home-cooked meals. The team here are adept at organising excursions into the Delta, Moremi Game Reserve, Nxai Pan National Park & elsewhere. With easy 2WD access from the tarred road, Tshima is a tranquil place for a spot of R&R, but note that you cannot just drop in: reservations are essential. $$$

✗ WHERE TO EAT AND DRINK

As a small town, Maun might not be a fine-dining hotspot, but there are increasingly some great places serving tasty, home-grown favourites in pleasant surroundings. Everywhere is informal and relaxed, but their laid-back vibe does not mean Maun's dining options are lacking in style or flavour; far from it.

Quirky, owner-run restaurants offer good-value meals from breakfast to dinner, alongside several great 'coffee and cake' cafés, and even a few cocktail and live music venues. Several are within walking distance of the airport, most are licensed, and vegetarians are extremely well catered for almost everywhere.

In addition to those listed here, several **hotels and camps** have restaurants open to the public; the riverside terrace at Thamalakane River Lodge (page 198) is probably the pick of the bunch.

For **traditional food**, try Choice or Kwa Ga Ncinci for a genuinely local hangout. Or close to the airport, pop out at lunchtime to one of the street stalls for a cheap and satisfying serving of pap and stew.

There are also numerous **fast-food** places, including KFC [195 B7], Nando's [195 C7], Debonairs [195 C7] and Wimpy at the Engen fuel station [194 F1].

The Arts Café [map, page 200] In the Motsana Cultural Centre, Shorobe Rd; m 7847 1624; ⏰ 08.00–16.00 daily. 10mins from the centre of Maun (en route to Moremi), this licensed café in the cool, covered courtyard of a relaxed arts' centre is a quirky spot for b/fast or lunch, or even just an ice cream. Good coffee, fresh bread, fluffy American pancakes & wraps on the menu, with free Wi-Fi, some small craft shops, a travel agency & a beauty salon to add to the attraction. The local farmers' market is held here on the last Sun of the month (⏰ 09.00–noon). $–$$

Bull and Bush @ Okavango Craft Brewery [map, page 200] Sir Seretse Khama Rd; ☎ 686 0017; e sales@okavangocraftbrewery. com, director@bullbus.com; ☐ okavangobrewery, bullandbushbotswana; w okavangocraftbrewery. com; ⏰ noon–22.00 Tue-Thu, noon–midnight Fri–Sat, noon–21.00 Sun. Opened in 2019 as northern Botswana's 1st licensed micro-brewery – the Okavango Craft Brewery – in 2024, the brewery announced a collaboration with Bull and Bush, a much-loved pub from Gaborone, and changed its name accordingly. Offering great ambience, decent burgers, BBQ ribs, wood-fired pizza & award-winning local beers – all with the brewery backdrop behind the bar – it continues to be a success. From live music nights to international rugby, Happy Hour to Conservation on Tap speaker events, there's invariably something happening here. And if beer isn't your tipple, try the Mowana Cider – an apple and baobab special also made on site. Brewery tours are also available, offering insight into the company's partnership with local NGO Ecoexist, whose farmers produce the millet for the brewers while using sustainable agricultural practices designed to improve peaceful coexistence with elephants. $–$$$

Choice [195 C7] Old Mall, Tsheko-Tsheko Rd; m 7583 5434; ⏰ 09.00–21.00 daily. For a hearty helping of traditional food, join the lunchtime queues at Choice. It feels rather like a fast-food joint, with wooden tables & benches, but the buffet features a range of Botswana specials, including oxtail, rice & greens. $

The Duck Café Bar [195 D1] Mathiba I Rd; m 7701 2978; ☐ theduckmaun; ⏰ 07.00–17.00 daily. Under pole shading and white umbrellas opposite the airport terminal, The Duck is a great café offering everything from fresh filter coffee & sugar-dusted almond croissants to homemade quiche, delicious salads & steak frites. You can even pick up some great souvenirs here before flying home. Occasionally open in the evening for live music & dinner, the café also hosts art exhibitions for local creatives & operates a book exchange. $–$$

Dusty Donkey Café [194 E2] 1 Airport Av; m 7615 7105; e dustydonkeycafe@gmail.com; w dustydonkeycafe.com; ☐; ⏰ 07.30–16.00 Tue–Fri, 08.00–16.00 Sat, 08.00–15.00 Sun. Just a few mins' walk from the airport terminal, Dusty Donkey's wide roadside terrace attracts locals & travellers alike, & it's easy to see why. From refreshing iced teas to milkshakes & juices, & a wooden table laden with delicious cakes under glass domes, it's a great place for b/fast or a tasty snack. Daily blackboards show tempting lunch specials such as Buddha bowls loaded with roasted veg couscous, capers & feta; Asian wraps; smashed avocado drizzled with chilli oil on sourdough; & impressive burgers stacked with onion rings & homemade slaw. If you're hitting the road, order a delicious packed lunch to go. A small shop sells handmade local crafts & accessories. $–$$

Hilary's Coffee Shop [194 D2] Off Mathiba I Rd; ☎ 686 1610; e hilary@calitzsafaris. com; w hilaryscoffeeshop.wordpress.com; ⏰ 08.30–16.00 Mon–Fri, 08.30–noon Sat. On a quiet cul-de-sac, close to the airport, Hilary's has been serving since about 1995, & remains one of the more interesting & reliable places to eat during the day in Maun, with well-shaded tables set outside among pot plants. Hilary & her staff make everything on the premises, from mayonnaise & salad dressing to bran muffins; the home-baked wholewheat bread is sublime, & with a little advance notice can be made to order for a camping trip. Expect superb home-cooked b/fasts, tasty wholesome lunches – Hilary's Jumbo Sandwich is always on the menu – tasty salads, daily specials & delicious desserts & cakes. Vegan, vegetarian & gluten-free dishes available. $$

Kwa Ga Ncinci [194 E3] 361 Sir Seretse Khama Rd; m 7710 6757; e kgsnsocials@gmail.com; ☐ KwaGaNcinciBW; ⏰ 07.00–22.00 Mon–Sat, 07.00–21.00 Sun. Owned by the engaging Ncinci, this welcoming place serves up sandwiches, pasta & traditional specials at feet-in-the-sand wooden tables. 'Braaiday Friday' sees steak & sausage with pap (a local, smooth maize porridge) & a cocktail hour. $-$$

✳ **Marc's Eatery** [map, page 200] Nunga Conservation, Sir Seretse Khama Rd; \684 0883; m 7400 2955; e info@marcseatery. com; w marcseatery.com; f; ⏰ 10.30–15.00 &17.00–late Mon–Fri, kitchen closes 20.30). Set in a neatly tended garden just outside of town, with an eclectic, mouth-watering menu of fresh flavours & global influences, Marc's is justifiably a local dining highlight. The food is consistently excellent, the ambience buzzing & the team, led by Marc himself, are dedicated to raising the bar for food in Maun. They serve an à la carte menu of 'designer sandwiches', original salads, fresh pasta dishes & a host of burger options. There's an ever-changing specials board, a dedicated vegetarian & vegan

menu, children's specials & a licensed bar. Be sure to book in advance.

Alongside the restaurant, The Deli sells a fabulous range of homemade sauces, soups, stews & sausages, as well as freshly baked breads & cakes, perfect if you're heading on a self-drive camping trip & fancy some treats. You can also order a take-away b/fast & packed lunch. $-$$

Tandurei Maun [194 A3] Village Complex, 448 Moeti Rd; \680 0227; f tandureimaun; ⏰ 10.30–22.30 daily. Under open-sided thatch, close to the airport, this pleasant, owner-run establishment (with a sister restaurant in Francistown) is a local favourite. Quirky in design, with an old, red air-rescue plane mounted on the roof, it offers authentic Indian food, with butter masalas, seekh kebabs & rotis perennially popular. Open from b/fast, they also serve coffees, homemade cakes & toasted sandwiches, & now Chinese noodles too. Food is tasty. $-$$

ENTERTAINMENT AND NIGHTLIFE

Maun's nightlife is fairly limited. The lively bar at The Old Bridge Backpackers (page 201) has long done its best to fill the void, and is a good spot to unwind after time in the bush. More recently, the arrival of the Okavango Craft Brewery (page 148), which occasionally hosts live music nights, has become a popular hang-out for locals and visitors.

For something different and a little more cultural, the Kana Jang? Café at the Nhabe Museum (page 209) occasionally hosts poetry evenings; find out more from Poetavango (m 7294 7614; e info@poetavango.org.bw; f).

SHOPPING

Most shops are open Monday to Friday from around 08.00 until 17.00, and Saturday to noon or thereabouts, with supermarket hours considerably longer.

FOOD AND DRINK You can buy most things here that you'll find in a supermarket in Europe or North America, although you may need to look around and brand names may be different. The choice (especially of fresh fruit and vegetables) may not be as varied and it is always worth bringing items linked to specific dietary requirements with you. Several of the **supermarkets** are on Tsheko-Tsheko Road to the south of Riley's Garage. These include Maun's oldest, Shoprite [195 C7] (Tsheko-Tsheko Rd), and its more recent rivals: SPAR, with branches at the Old Mall [195 B7] and in the Ngami Centre [194 F2]; Choppies, near the bus station [188 B4] and a smaller branch in New Mall [194 E1]; and Woolworths on Koro [194 F2]. Most are open daily from 08.00 until about 19.00 or 20.00 on weekdays, but close at around 17.00 on Saturdays and 15.00 on Sundays.

If you're after fresh **bread**, from ciabatta rolls to tasty topped pissaladière, you can email an order or visit the bakery at **Marc's Eatery** (see above), where you'll also pick up handmade sausages, sauces and myriad edible treats. If you're self-catering in Maun or heading off on a self-drive safari, do consider a trip to the excellent **Delta Meat Deli** [188 D7] (Lion's Gate, Sekgome Rd; ☎ 686 1419; e deltadeli@ yahoo.com; ⓕ deltameatdeli; ⏰ 07.30–17.30 Mon–Fri, 07.30–13.30 Sat) where the team will portion, vacuum-pack and freeze meat for you, as well as selling an array of produce from chorizo to Danish pastries. It can be ordered in advance for collection and the quality is excellent. **Beef Boys** [195 D7] (☎686 4771; e rizanie4@ gmail.com; ⓕ Beef-Boys-Meat-Market; ⏰ 09.00–18.00 Mon–Fri, 09.00–15.00 Sat), on Tsheko-Tsheko Road beside Riley's Garage, offers a similar packing service, alongside their imported cheeses and fresh fruit and vegetables.

Supermarkets don't sell **alcohol**. To purchase beer, visit the Okavango Craft Brewery (page 148) for some quality, local options or head to TOPS at SPAR (Koro) or one of the branches of Liquorama, where wine and spirits are available.

You'll find lots of small stalls and local sellers around Maun, including near the bus station. They're certainly worth checking out for the odd pile of fruit and vegetables, but also for more offbeat foods, like mopane worms in season, and secondhand items.

SOUVENIRS, CRAFTS, BOOKS AND CURIOS
There's no shortage of places that sell curios in Maun, and virtually every camp in Botswana has a small curio shop, so it pays to shop around. It's also well worth seeking out individual workshops, or places where the work of local craftspeople is available. For several things under one roof, try Motsana Cultural Centre [map, page 200], where there's a curio shop, Textures and a gallery of local art and photographs.

African Art & Images [194 E1] Maun Airport; ☎ 686 3584, 686 0825. This upmarket gift-shop-cum-gallery inside the airport compound gates sells high-quality African art, carvings, baskets, jewellery & some beautiful photographs & prints.

Bailey's Art Centre [194 E3] Inside the Nhabe Museum, Sir Seretse Khama St; m 7314 7446. The shop at this community-based cultural museum allows local artisans to showcase & sell their pottery, basketry, woodwork & paintings.

Bushman Craft Shop [194 D1] Maun Airport; ☎ 686 0025, 686 0339; e gentrade@info.bw; ⏰ 08.00–17.00 daily. Just inside the airport gates, this tangerine-coloured shop sells a good range of books & maps, postcards, crafts, curios, safari clothes & all-important hats. Barely a min's walk from the check-in desks, it's perfectly situated to dash out to while you're waiting for a plane.

The Craft Centre Power Station [194 C2], Mophane Av; ☎ 686 3391, 686 0220. In the jazzy, multicoloured Power Station, about 5–10mins' walk from the airport, the Craft Centre is a small studio selling local ware including pottery, textiles, paper products & paintings – much of it handmade on the premises. They also run workshops if you're in town for longer.

Jazella's Natlee Centre [194 D2], Airport Av; ☎ 686 1900; ⓕ jazellas.thecraftmarket; ⏰ 07.00–18.00 daily. Jam-packed full of jewellery, bags, women's clothes, wall hangings, books & much, much more.

Matlapana Baskets (aka Botswana Quality Baskets & Hambukushu Baskets) [map, page 200] Sir Seretse Khama Rd; ☎ 680 1255; m 7227 1422, 7191 3303; e tkushonya@gmail.com. Award-winning master weaver Mma Thitaku Kushonya sells baskets from her workshop about 8km north of Maun Airport. This site showcases not only her work but that of women whom she has empowered by teaching them basket weaving. Look for it on the right-hand side as you head north on Sir Seretse Khama Rd, just behind a small general store; if you reach the bridge you have gone too far. Do pay her a visit: her work is excellent &, whether you are looking for a souvenir or to learn a little more about basket weaving, you'll be glad you went. To have a go at basket weaving yourself & to learn more about the Hambukushu tribe, consider a visit next door to Hambukushu Cultural Village (page 209).

Textures Motsana Cultural Centre [map, page 200], Shorobe Rd; m 7144 6036. This is an Aladdin's cave of curios, jewellery & women's clothes, well sited next to a popular café.

CAMPING EQUIPMENT Most visitors bring their own camping equipment, or are booked on trips which include it, be that fully kitted-out 4x4s or safari camps. For those on budget trips, some of the tour operators hire out their kit for the duration of your trip. However, if you need to buy anything, or you need some of your own kit repaired, then there are a few specialist options.

Kalahari Kanvas [194 C2] Mathiba I Rd; 686 0568; e info@kalahari-kanvas.com; w kalahari-kanvas.com; ⊕ 09.00–17.00 Mon–Fri, 09.00–noon public hols. From its beginnings in 1986 as a tiny tent-repair company, Kalahari Kanvas has burgeoned into a major manufacturer of tents & equipment for the safari industry, with another office in Kasane. They still offer a tent-repair service & also hire out an amazing range of kit by the day, from a knife, fork & spoon set to a 2-person dome tent, & everything in between.

It's best to book equipment in advance via email/web form, & deposits are required, proportional to the items hired. Note that all kit must be returned to this office & they are closed at w/ends.
Riley's Garage [195 D7] See opposite; ⊕ 24hrs daily; vehicle spare parts 08.00–17.00 Mon–Fri, 08.00–13.00 Sat. Selling a huge range of quality camping kit, from Tentco dome & Meru tents to chairs, beds, lanterns, solar showers, freezer packs & Leatherman or Opinel knives.

CLOTHES Several of the camping equipment outlets also stock safari gear, and for last-minute safari purchases you could try the Bushman Craft Shop (page 205), but for basic tops and trousers, you'd probably do better at one of the more general clothing stores: Ackermans at Old Mall [195 B7], PEP at Engen Centre next to Shoprite [195 C7], JB Sports in New Mall [194 E2], Mr Price in Old Mall [194 B7] or Woolworth's in the Ngami Centre [194 F2]. More specialist than any of these, with a good range of safari clothes, sports clothing and boots, is West Sports at Riley's Garage [195 D7] (Tsheko-Tsheko Rd; 686 0483).

OTHER PRACTICALITIES

For most visitors these days, Maun is above all a place to restock, refuel and get organised.

BANKS AND MONEY The main **banks** – Stanbic [194 D2] (Natlee Centre, Mathiba I Rd), First National Bank [194 F2] (Ngami Centre), Barclays [195 B7] (Tsheko-Tsheko Rd) and Standard Chartered [195 B7] (Old Mall) – have ATM machines that accept Visa and, less frequently, Mastercard, so this is usually the easiest, quickest and cheapest way to get pula. It's worth noting that not all Visa cards will work in all ATMs, so if one fails it is worth trying another before contacting your bank. Alternatively, with your passport and a little time spent in queues, you can cash travellers' cheques or obtain a manual cash advance on a credit card at any of these three.

Bureaux de change generally offer a quicker service and longer hours than the banks. **Unimoni** is located inside Choppies supermarket in New Mall [194 E1] (⊕ 08.30–19.30 Mon–Sat, 09.30–13.30 Sun) and **Open Door** is by Riley's Garage [195 D7] (686 3150; ⊕ 08.00–17.30 Mon–Fri, 09.00–13.00 Sat–Sun). It's a good idea to check commission rates at both and do your sums before exchanging. There is also a small kiosk in the airport building which, although convenient, may not offer the best rates.

For travel in Botswana, as elsewhere in the world, it's well worth considering the use of a **currency converter debit card**, such as those available from Wise, Revolut or Monza, which allow you to minimise currency conversion charges and ATM fees.

COMMUNICATIONS Local SIM cards and various pre-paid plans for one to 30 days can be purchased at various outlets along Tsheko-Tsheko Road, including the Mascom office [195 C7] in Old Mall, Orange in the Agora Projects building at Old Mall [195 B7], and Cell City near Shoprite [195 C7]. It's also possible to buy an **eSIM card** (a virtual SIM) for Botswana in advance of travel from various online suppliers.

POST The **post office** [195 B8] (⊕ 08.00–19.00 Mon–Fri, 08.30–noon Sat) is on Tsheko-Tsheko Road, south of Barclays Bank, and there's a **DHL** in the airport terminal foyer [194 D1] (✆ 686 1207, 370 5700; ⊕ 08.00–17.00 Mon–Fri).

CAR REPAIRS AND SPARES Should the worst happen, and you **break down** in the bush without back-up, then help is at hand from Mechto [188 D7] (16 Nkwe Street, Boseja; ✆ 686 3913; m 7130 3788, 7236 8888; e info@mckenzie4x4.com; w mckenzie4x4.com). You could also try Trans World Motors and Delta 4x4 (see below), who both offer recovery and breakdown services.

There are several reliable **fuel stations** in Maun. If you're self-driving into the bush, Maun is the best place to make sure your 4x4 is in tip-top condition, with plenty of spares. Places that may be able to help are usually open Monday to Friday and Saturday morning, and include:

Auto World [188 A5] Tsheko-Tsheko Rd; ✆ 686 3890; m 7157 9222; ⊕ 08.00–17.00 Mon–Fri, 08.30–14.00 Sat, 09.00–13.00 Sun. Spares for most major makes of vehicle.

Delta 4x4 [188 A6] ✆ 686 4572; ⊕ 07.30–17.30 Mon–Thu, 08.00–17.00 Fri, 08.00–13.00 Sat. Just south of Maun Sports Complex on the Ghanzi road, Delta offers vehicle repairs, 4x4 hire & vehicle recovery in the Delta & Kgalagadi.

Halfway Toyota Ngami [188 A5] 17 Tsheko-Tsheko Rd; ✆ 686 0252; ⊕ 07.30–17.30 Mon–Fri, 08.00–13.00 Sat. Maun's Toyota dealer also has spares & a body shop. They will repair all makes of vehicle, not just Toyotas.

Maun Auto Centre [188 C7] 1997 Matshwane Industrial Estate; m 7350 5158; e maunautocentre@yahoo.com; ⊕ 08.00–17.00 Mon–Fri. Reliable, experienced mechanics, Martin and Wouter, are well regarded by self-drive overlanders & experienced with both Toyota and Land Rover vehicles.

Motovac [194 B3] 521 Mophane Av; ✆ 686 0872; also at 5 Boseja; ⊕ 08.00–17.00 Mon–Fri, 09.00–13.00 Sat–Sun. Local branches of the national spares & accessories chain.

Riley's Garage (Shell) [195 D7] Tsheko-Tsheko Rd; ✆ 686 0203; e parts@rileys.co.bw; ⊕ 24hrs. In the centre of town, Riley's has a fuel station, as well as a workshop, & a shop (Autozone) carrying a wide range of spares, tyres & batteries. Also sells camping equipment (see opposite).

Trans World Motors [188 D7] Boseja Industrial; m 7130 2729, 7211 6010; e transworldmotors@gmail.com; w transworldmotorsbotswana.com; ⊕ 07.30–17.30 Mon–Fri, 08.00–13.00 Sat. About 1km beyond Caltex. Offers spares, mechanical repairs & a 24hr breakdown service.

TyreWorld [188 C7] Boseja; ✆ 686 0107; ⊕ 07.30–17.30 Mon–Fri, 07.30–13.00 Sat. New tyres and repairs.

HEALTH Maun's modern **Letsholathebe II Memorial Hospital** [188 D5] (Disaneng Rd; ✆ 687 9000) is located to the east of the town. If you're coming from Shorobe or one of the lodges to the north, then continue straight over at the roundabout before the bridge rather than heading into town; it's clearly signposted.

There are also a couple of good **private clinics** and a **dentist**. **Pharmacies** are usually open normal shopping hours, but most have an emergency number for calls out of hours. It makes sense to bring spare glasses and contact lenses with you, but if you do need an **optician**, try Opticals Botswana in Old

Mall [195 C7] (Tsheko-Tsheko Rd; 686 1742; e sales@opticalsbotswana.com; w opticalsbotswana.com).

Delta Dental Clinic [195 A8] Moremi III Rd; 686 1023, 686 4224
Okavango Pharmacy [195 C7] Old Mall, Tsheko-Tsheko Rd; emergency 686 0043, 7170 6435

Prime Health Medical Centre [195 C6] Old Mall, Tsheko-Tsheko Rd; 686 1411, 686 2999; m 7131 4224
Taurus Pharmacy [195 C7] Tsheko-Tsheko Rd; 686 3340

WHAT TO SEE AND DO

Maun is really much more of a place to get organised than a destination in its own right. Those visitors who do stay for more than one night tend to use the town as a launching point for day trips (to book these, see the operators listed on page 213) and aren't generally looking for activities in or around the town. If you do have time to kill, here are a few suggestions, which include the opportunity to try your hand at basket weaving.

IN AND AROUND MAUN There's little in town to delay most safari visitors, bar a couple of low-key cultural attractions, though exploring the river is a pleasant way

---

BANA BA LETSATSI   *Tricia Hayne*

To the casual observer, Botswana's society appears to retain much of its traditional, close-knit fabric based on strong family and community ties. Yet currently one in five children are orphans, and because of HIV/AIDS the number of orphaned and vulnerable children in Botswana continues to rise.

When Emily Cusack was working as a nurse in Maun in 2002, she noticed small numbers of children begging on the streets rather than being in school or at home. From her own resources, she set about entertaining them, collecting them up in a borrowed pick-up truck for a couple of hours' activities. Today, the organisation that she founded, Bana Ba Letsatsi ('The Sunshine Children'), has more than 200 children on its register, aged from four to 21, with myriad success stories, including the recent university graduation of a boy who's been with the group from a young age. In May 2023, under the guidance of the organisation's dynamic director Taboka Rotsi, the charity moved into a new, purpose-built centre, with classrooms, accommodation for 40 children, counselling rooms, a library and computer room.

The children at Bana Ba Letsatsi have often never been to school, or have dropped out, and the charity focuses strongly on education as a means of rehabilitating them. Most of them are orphaned and left in the care of relatives who in turn neglect them and deprive them of basic needs such as education, food, clothing, care and support. This leads to them finding other means of surviving such as begging and searching for food from rubbish bins. As a result of neglect, many are victims of sexual or physical abuse at home or on the streets; they abuse drugs and alcohol, and they beg.

The day begins at 08.00 with the youngest children being picked up, while the others walk to the centre. Here, preparations are made for showers, breakfast, packed lunches and uniforms. Non-formal education begins, children go to school, and at lunchtime a meal is served to all the children. Afternoons are spent doing homework with the teachers, in sessions with the counsellors, playing football,

to spend an afternoon, and horseriding is an added option. If you've time on your hands, you could check out what's on at the large **Maun Sports Complex**, which lies about 2.5km southwest of Riley's Garage on the road towards Ghanzi. It's used for political rallies as well as sports matches, with details published in the local newspaper, *The Ngami Times*.

Nhabe Museum [194 E3] (Sir Seretse Khama Rd)
More of a gallery than a museum, this small venue has periodically changing exhibits that often showcase the art of local students. A small collection of artefacts includes musical instruments and hunting tools. '*Nhabe*', incidentally, is from the Bushman word for the sound of cattle pulling their feet out of the mud, now more usually rendered as '*ngami*'.

Hambukushu Cultural Village [map, page 200] (Sir Seretse Khama Rd; 680 1255; m 7227 1422, 7191 3303; e tkushonya@gmail.com; P300/3hrs)
Next door to Matlapana Baskets (page 205) and under the same ownership, this is a great place to spend an afternoon. Thitaku Kushonya will take you on a 3-hour journey around a replica of a traditional Hambukushu village. Among other things you get to try your hand at basket weaving and to take home what you produce; to play traditional Hambukushu games; to learn how food was traditionally sourced and grown; and

receiving medical attention, washing clothes, or doing creative activities. As few of the children have an evening meal at home, a snack is served before they leave.

During the school holidays the centre tries to introduce the children to new experiences, such as going into the Delta to see the wildlife or going on camping trips into the pans. In a country whose major attraction is its wildlife, most of these youngsters have never seen an elephant, or indeed been near the national parks. There are also life-skills sessions, when agencies such as the police, government social workers and NGOs dealing with child-related issues address adolescents on comprehensive sexuality education, juvenile delinquency, drugs and alcohol abuse.

As well as working with the younger children, Bana Ba Letsatsi also runs a successful youth programme for those over 18, offering technical skills training in plumbing, carpentry, hospitality or cooking. On completion, the charity works hard to gain them work experience and ultimately employment.

Bana Ba Letsatsi receives no funding from the government, so donations and sponsorship are much appreciated (and can be made through the website). So, too, are offers of help: the charity welcomes skilled volunteers, preferably for at least six months, but all expenses need to be covered by the volunteer. And if you find yourself with room in your luggage, perhaps you could take something for the Sunshine Children: they would welcome the normal family basics, such as underwear, T-shirts or shorts; plasters and hygiene materials; footballs; pens and pencils. Just phone ahead or email to arrange collection (686 4787; e info@banabaletsatsi.org; w banabaletsatsi.org) – or if time isn't on your side, you could contact the charity's long-term partner, Ker & Downey (page 214) or Travel for Impact (686 4431; m 7437 9830; e tfibotswana@gmail.com, info@ travelforimpact.com; w travelforimpact.com), who will arrange for the items to be collected from you at the airport.

even to try on some traditional clothing. It is certainly worth ringing ahead or dropping in the day before to pre-book a tour.

Sexaxa Cultural Village [map, page 200] (Shorobe Rd; contact Lesego on m 7502 5870; w sexaxa-village.com; ☉ daily; US$20/10 adult/child) For a hint of Botswana's traditional way of life, pay a visit to this cultural village, 18km north of Maun on the Shorobe road; it's clearly signposted to the left. The village is designed to give visitors an idea of Bayei culture, urban style – as opposed to the rural culture depicted at Shandereka Cultural Village near Moremi (page 219). If you're just dropping in, don't hold your breath; it's far better to book ahead. Generally visits are around 2½ hours but additional time and even a traditional meal can be negotiated.

Thamalakane River Boat trips along the Thamalakane River are a great way to while away an hour or two, keeping an eye out for birds. Costs vary, but US$60 an hour for a four-seater boat is a good indication. Contact Afro Trek (page 217) or Thamalakane River Lodge (page 198). If birding is the primary appeal, it may be worth contacting the local branch of BirdLife Botswana (☏ 686 5618; m 7465 4464; e birdlifemaun@botsnet.bw; w birdlifebotswana.org.bw) to see if one of their members would be prepared to guide you along the river for an hour or two.

Horseriding Riding for all levels can be organised through Jen Weimann at African Animal Adventure Safaris (page 218). Typically rides are along (and sometimes in!) the Thamalakane and Boro rivers. Hard hats are available. All abilities of rider are also welcome by Ride Botswana (page 218) at Thamo Telele (page 199), where you could find yourself riding among zebra, giraffe and other wildlife.

FURTHER AFIELD
Elephant Havens (Mirapene; m 7636 7532, 7380 9428; e info@elephanthavens. com; w elephanthavens.org; ☉ 09.00–10.00 & 16.00–17.00 daily; advance booking essential) About an hour's drive northeast of Maun (45km), Elephant Havens is a sanctuary for orphaned elephants. The 140-acre site, on the banks of the Gomoti River, provides young elephants with daily care and companionship, with the ultimate goal of reintroducing them to the wild. Founded in 2017, Elephant Havens works to protect African elephants and provide education to reduce conflicts between humans and elephants in the area. The charity of the same name provides financial and technical resources to the orphanage, which is operated in partnership with the Botswana Government's Department of Wildlife and National Parks.

For US$100 per person, visitors can spend an hour interacting with and photographing the young elephants up close, as well as meeting the elephant handlers and hearing about their conservation education initiatives. Alternatively, for US$500 per person, you can visit Elephant Havens in combination with a 60-minute scenic helicopter trip over the Delta with Helicopter Horizons (page 190).

Scenic flights Short flights over the Delta in light aircraft or helicopters are offered by several companies (page 190). Most people tend to book for 45 minutes then regret it; an hour is a better bet. Rates are usually quoted per person, and vary depending on the company, fuel costs and the number of people in the aircraft. As an indication, you can expect to pay from around US$300 per person for a five-seater. Helicopter trips are more expensive at around US$280/380 per person for

45 minutes/1 hour, for up to three people, with each person having a window seat and their own headset.

Mokoro trips Perennially popular are mokoro trips into the Delta, lasting from one to three days. Typically you'll leave Maun by motorboat between 07.30 and 08.30, depending on where you are staying, reaching the launch site 15km upstream in about 45 minutes, and returning in the evening by about 17.00. When the river was dry, and vehicle transfers took around 2 hours each way, a single-day trip hardly seemed worth the effort, but a shorter boat transfer changes the dynamics considerably.

Almost all these trips are run by the same community trust, the OKMCT (see below), but can be booked only through an affiliated tour operator; you cannot book direct or drive yourself in. However, although the polers, mekoro and areas being offered by the various competing companies in Maun are all exactly the same, prices vary according to the individual company. As an indication, Audi Camp charges P2,700 (US$197) per person for a day trip including lunch, with a single supplement of P250 (US$18) per day. For an overnight trip, with two days on the water, expect to pay around P7,000 (US$510) including all concession fees, food and camping equipment. On a similar basis, the three-day two-night trip costs P8,800 per person. A trip very like this was my first view of the Okavango and, while it has its limitations, I'd still regard it as remarkably good value.

Moremi Game Reserve Several tour operators offer trips into Moremi, costing from around US$270 per person for a day trip (minimum two people), to US$900 per person for a three-night all-inclusive trip for four people travelling together. Typically such trips include a guide, park fees, camping equipment, meals and transfers, but most exclude drinks.

Lake Ngami About 90km west of Maun, Lake Ngami is very accessible as a half- or full-day trip from Maun if you have your own transport – but do ascertain first whether or not there's water in the lake. For details, see page 422.

African Guide Academy (AGA) (1 Rodeo Drive; ↘ 680 0115; e info@ guidetrainingcourses.com; w guidetrainingcourses.com) Travellers or safari enthusiasts looking for a wildlife experience with a difference and to gain a recognised qualification in guiding can join one of the formal courses offered by the African Guide Academy, which vary in length from one to four weeks. Set up as the Okavango Guiding School in 2003, and run by the Reed family, the AGA trains guides in wildlife and ecology. It is based at Kwapa Camp in the Okavango Delta, with students staying in en-suite 3m x 4m Meru tents with flush toilets and bucket showers, and attending classes under canvas or out in the wilderness.

Courses are varied, from tracking to nature guiding and specialist birding. Skills include poling a mokoro, tracking wildlife, rifle handling and safely approaching big game on foot. All courses are taught by licensed guide trainers and qualifications are formally recognised within the industry.

A shorter one-week Track and Sign Course, which is tailored to international travellers, could easily be incorporated into a self-drive or lodge experience. Although you do not gain a qualification, you are likely to take away many skills and a deeper understanding of the bush, as this course includes many of the practical and theoretical highlights from the lengthier Nature Guide and Trails Guide courses. Participants also help to benefit one aspiring local guide, who receives sponsorship from the school and joins students for the duration of the course.

BEYOND MAUN: GETTING ORGANISED

Although the majority of those passing through Maun are pre-booked on an all-inclusive trip, this is also the best place for independent travellers and those without plans to get organised. If it all seems rather overwhelming, there are just a few points to remember.

ORGANISING A TRIP INTO THE NATIONAL PARKS If you are organising your own trip, note that you can no longer go into the national parks without proof of a confirmed reservation for your campsites or other accommodation (unless you plan just a day trip). Theoretically, provided that you have this confirmation, it is possible to pay entrance fees on the gate, but it is best not to rely on this and instead organise and pay for these in advance at one of the Department of Wildlife and National Parks (DWNP) offices (see opposite). For details of the system, see page

127. If you'd rather have some help, then contact one of the travel agents, who can act as a sort of one-stop shop, arranging anything from a scenic flight to setting up your whole trip, including national parks, transport and accommodation. Finally, there are the tour operators and safari companies, whose role is to organise your whole safari, usually using their own suppliers – which may include their own lodges and aircraft.

National parks campsite operators
Most of the campsite operators have offices in Maun, and unless you have everything in writing beforehand, you may need to visit more than one of them to confirm your bookings, so do allow plenty of time. That said, both SKL and the Xomae Group are in theory prepared to do the legwork for you – though it's wise not to bank on it. For a list of which campsites each operator runs, see page 128.

Department of Wildlife & National Parks (DWNP) [195 E5] Sir Seretse Khama Rd (next to police station); 686 0368, 686 1265; e dwnp@gov.bw; ⏰ 07.30–16.30 Mon–Sat, 07.30–noon Sun
Kwalate Safaris New Mall [194 E2], Sir Seretse Khama Rd; 686 5551; e kwalatesafari@gmail.com; w kwalatesafaris.com; ⏰ 08.00–16.30 Mon–Fri, 08.00–14.00 Sat

SKL Group [195 E5] Apollo House, 246 Mophane Street; 686 5365/6; e reservations@sklcamps.co.bw; w sklcamps.com; ⏰ 08.00–17.00 Mon–Fri, 08.00–13.00 Sat
Xomae Group New Mall [194 E2], Sir Seretse Khama Rd; 686 2221; m 7386 2221; e xomaesites@bctmail.co.bw; w xomaesites.com; ⏰ 07.30–17.00 Mon–Fri, 08.00–13.00 Sat

Travel agents
Maun may appear to be full of travel agents, but many of the companies you see are in fact tour operators (page 213) who own and run camps and safari companies. However, if you look hard there is a handful of normal travel agents who (generally) know the local safari industry well, and can help you choose a trip. They are especially useful if you arrive in Maun without any arrangements and want to book a budget trip immediately. In such cases, booking through one of these agents will cost you exactly the same as booking directly with the camp or safari company.

The caveats to this are, firstly, that none is well prepared for booking a range of the top-end lodges at short notice; there's very little demand for this. Secondly, some will have their own favourite camps or operators – so do ask them to be exhaustive about researching the options for you before you make a decision. Also ask them to make very clear if anyone associated with them has any links with the camps or trips that they're suggesting to you. (This shouldn't necessarily put you off booking – but you ought to know!)

Liquid Giraffe [map, page 200] Nunga Conservation, Sir Seretse Khama Rd; +27 66 046 1572; e info@liquidgiraffe.com; w liquidgiraffe.com
Safari Essence 686 1344; m 7230 9099; e passion@safari-essence.com; w safari-essence.com. Sister company to Endeavour Safaris (page 216).

Sense of Africa [194 C3] Eagle Hse, Mophane Av; 686 0822/3; e info@senseofafrica-botswana.com; w senseofafrica.com. This very good, independent travel agent, previously called Travel Wild, is a friendly, helpful & efficient one-stop shop for what to do in & around Maun, short trips into the Delta, & longer holidays in Botswana. They also have offices in Namibia, Kenya, Uganda & Tanzania.

Tour operators and safari companies
Looking at the length of this list – which is by no means comprehensive – you'll realise that Maun is the safari capital of

Botswana. Listed below alphabetically, followed by specialist mobile, horseriding and camping/canoeing operators, these safari companies range from large operators with many camps through to tiny outfits that are little more than a guide and a vehicle. Since prices change regularly, these have not been included – although for an indication of the costs of, say, a mobile safari, see page 139.

While many of the larger operators have staff in Maun, as well as booking offices overseas, the smaller operations may take days, or even weeks, to answer communications – sometimes because the whole team is out of the office on a mobile safari.

For the sake of completeness, also included here are a few larger companies that operate from towns other than Maun, but very much focus on safaris that originate here. International tour operators are listed from page 119.

Larger safari groups

&Beyond [194 C2] off Mathiba I Rd; ☏ 686 1979, reservations +27 11 809 4300 (South Africa), +44 1527 962339 (UK), +1 619 598 1199 (USA); e contactus@andbeyond.com; w andbeyond. com. Formerly Conservation Corporation Africa, &Beyond is a leading company committed to high quality, including good food & impressive standards of guiding, with a tracker & guide on every vehicle. Of 25 lodges throughout East & southern Africa, they have 4 in Botswana's Okavango Delta: Nxabega, Sandibe, Xudum & Xaranna. They also offer 2 semi-permanent tented camps – Savute Under Canvas & Chobe Under Canvas – & itineraries focusing on families with teenagers, specialist birders & a Chobe–Okavango combination trip.

African Bush Camps [map, page 200] Sir Seretse Khama Rd; ☏ +27 21 701 0270 (South Africa), +44 800 041 8187 (UK), +1 888 344 1126 (USA); e contact@africanbushcamps.com; w africanbushcamps.com. A conservation- & community-minded operator, ABC has been steadily expanding its camp portfolio in southern Africa. They have both established luxury camps & a couple of simple bush camps across Botswana – Linyanti Bush Camp, Linyanti Ebony & Linyanti Expeditions, as well as Khwai Lediba, Khwai Leadwood & Migration Expeditions in Nxai Pan – & a new camp, Atzaró Okavango, offering 'boutique in the bush' from late 2023, plus the Thorntree River Lodge over the border near Livingstone. They operate a dedicated training programme for female guides & accommodate families well.

Belmond [194 C3] Mophane Av; ☏ 686 0302, reservations +27 21 483 1600 (South Africa), +44 845 077 2222 (UK); e safaris@belmond.com; w belmond.com. Part of the global group that runs hotels & lodges around the world, including the famous Venice–Simplon *Orient Express* train, Belmond have 2 upmarket lodges in Botswana: Savute Elephant Lodge & Eagle Island Lodge. Specifications in each are comparable to top hotels, very much belying their 'tent' status.

Desert & Delta Safaris [194 E2] Sir Seretse Khama Rd; ☏ 680 1494; e info@desertdelta.com; w desertdelta.com. This established operator, which recommends that their lodges be booked through a tour operator, runs Chobe Game Lodge, Chobe Savanna Lodge, Savute Safari Lodge, Camp Moremi, Camp Okavango, Xugana Island Lodge, Camp Xakanaxa, Nxamaseri Island Lodge & Leroo La Tau. A sister company, Safari Air, operates a charter air service, enabling integrated access to each lodge.

Great Plains Conservation [194 C3] Mophane Av; ☏ +27 87 354 6591 (South Africa), +44 20 3150 1062 (UK), +1 347 305 4201 (USA), emergency +27 79 284 5945; e info@greatplainsconservation. com; w greatplainsconservation.com. Great Plains operates Okavango Explorers Camp, Selinda Camp, Selinda Explorers Camp, Zarafa Camp, Duba Plains Camp, Duba Explorers Camp & Sitatunga Private Island Camp. The company is very focused on raising the bar in standards of environmental & social responsibility. Their camps & vehicles all cater extremely well to photographers, on top of the impressive levels of service & comfort.

Ker & Downey Botswana [194 E2] Cnr Airport Av & Sir Seretse Khama Rd; ☏ 686 1282, 686 1418; m 7577 5300; e info@kerdowney.bw; w kerdowneybotswana.com. Born out of Kenya & operating in Botswana since 1962, Ker & Downey have a long pedigree in Delta safaris. From the purchase of Khwai River Lodge in 1979 to the excellent collection of camps it runs today – Okuti,

Many of the camps in northern Botswana benefit from cool waterside locations above (BSN/S)

Camping in Botswana's national parks can feel exceptionally remote PAGE 173 right (BH)

The best of Botswana's safari lodges boast a very high level of luxury below (SS)

above
(MM/S)

A walking safari provides the ultimate adrenalin rush, but it's important to stay safe PAGE 177

left
(SS)

Riding safaris are a great, non-intrusive way to see the Okavango's resident wildlife PAGES 365 & 380

below
(r/S)

Game drives in the Okavango Delta give visitors an exceptional view of wildlife, including lion prides

Travelling by mokoro is a relaxed way to explore the
tranquil waters of the Okavango PAGE 181

above
(H/D)

A scenic flight gives an entirely different perspective
on migrating buffalo PAGE 210

below
(BM/D)

top
(M/D)
The iconic baobab – here in the Makgadikgadi Pans – is known as the 'tree of life' PAGE 462

above left
(TH)
Waterlily (*Nymphaea nouchali caerulea*) PAGE 343

above right
(KP/D)
Wild dagga plant (*Leonotis nepetifolia*) PAGE 360

below
(JG)
During the rains the desolate Makgadikgadi Pans come to life, with migrating herds of zebra and wildebeest PAGE 463

The Central Kalahari Game Reserve is Africa at its most remote PAGE 487
above left
(JG)

Considered to be the highest point in the Kalahari, the Tsodilo Hills rise above the surrounding desert PAGE 425
above right
(JP/D)

The rarely visited Gcwihaba Caves are part of a labyrinth of underground passages PAGE 434
right
(SS)

above (DT/D) Guiding visitors around the Kalahari helps the San retain the hunting and gathering skills that have been honed over millennia PAGE 94

below left (RI/D) Baskets are hand woven for use in the home, as well as for decorative purposes PAGE 107

below right (LC/S) Traditionally Botswana's main carbohydrate, sorghum is pounded and then made into porridge of different consistencies PAGE 147

Performed as social rituals, for healing and to encourage rainfall, San dances are accommpanied by rhythmic clapping and singing, and build to a dramatic crescendo PAGE 95

above (AVZ)

Colourful fabrics hang from a roadside stall in Kasane

right (TH)

Sporadically inhabited for about 60,000 years, the Tsodilo Hills feature some of the world's most impressive rock art PAGE 425

below (RB/S)

above
(LBP/S)

Breathtakingly beautiful vistas and misted cloud forest make for a magical walk at Victoria Falls, over the border in Zambia or Zimbabwe PAGE 522

below
(AM/S)

Adrenalin-infused activities abound at Victoria Falls, from bungee-jumping to giant gorge-swings and world-class white-water rafting PAGE 524

Kanana, Shinde, Shinde Enclave, Shinde Footsteps & Dinaka – Ker & Downey has consistently & positively evolved. Spanning the Delta, Moremi & Kalahari, its camps each offer a different safari experience, while retaining great staff, comfort levels & good value. Alongside camp conservation initiatives, Ker & Downey actively support underprivileged children through Maun-based NGO Bana Ba Letsatsi (page 208).

Kwando Safaris [194 E2] Airport Av; `686 1449; e info@kwando.co.bw; w kwando.co.bw. Kwando is an independent operator running first-class camps in Botswana. Lagoon & Lebala are primarily dry-land camps beside the Kwando River in NG14, while Kwara, Splash & 4 Rivers have a full range of dry & wet activities in the Kwara Concession, on the north side of the Delta, as well as Mma & Rra Diare, Pom Pom, Moremi Crossing & Gunn's Camp. Further south are Nxai Pan Lodge, within the national park of the same name, & Tau Pan Lodge, in the Central Kalahari Game Reserve. The camps are all different, but all operate game drives with both a tracker & a guide – a real advantage when it comes to tracking predators. Their focus is on enthusiastic wildlife spotting rather than excessive frills in camp, although their camps are of a high standard.

Lodges of Botswana [194 C3] 537 Mophane Av; `686 0220; e info@lodgesofbotswana.com; w lodgesofbotswana.com. This Maun-based company owns & runs 3 low-impact camps in NG27B: Delta Camp, Oddballs' Camp & Oddballs' Enclave. They have particularly close links with both Delta Air & the Bushman Craft Shop.

Machaba Safaris `686 2281; e info@ machabasafaris.com; w machabasafaris.com. Machaba Safaris was founded in 2012 by a trio of safari aficionados keen on reviving the classic safari experience: tented camps with great guiding working under the motto 'People first. Planet first'. In Botswana, Machaba operates 6 terrific camps: Machaba Camp, Little Machaba, Gomoti Plains Camp, Gomoti Private & Kiri Camp in the Okavango, & Ngoma Safari Lodge in Chobe Forest. They also operate 4 camps in Zimbabwe. Camp teams are consistently first-class in knowledge & service, & the commitment to community-driven conservation initiatives is evident through the Machaba Foundation.

Natural Selection [194 C3] The Power Station, Mophane Av; `684 0931, reservations +27 21

001 1574; e reservations@naturalselection. travel; w naturalselection.travel. Founded in 2016 by a dedicated group of conservation-minded safari operators, each with considerable experience, Natural Selection operate an ever-increasing number of highly individual camps in Botswana: 5 in Makgadikgadi (Jack's, San Camp, Meno A Kwena, Camp Kalahari & Planet Baobab); Tawana in Moremi; Thamo Telele near Maun; & 10 around the Okavango Delta (Mapula Lodge, Mokolwane, Hyena Pan, Sable Alley, Little Sable, Sky Beds, Tuludi, Duke's Camp, Duke's East & their magical latest opening, North Island Okavango). Natural Selection handles sales & marketing while allowing these camps to keep their individuality.

Okavango Hidden Gems `+27 86 165 2826; m 7169 8168; e maunres@okavangohiddengems. com, reservations@okavangohiddengems.com; w okavangohiddengems.com. Operating in NG32, this newer safari company currently has 2 intimate camps: Amber River Camp & Camp Maru. One to watch given the traveller reviews thus far.

Sanctuary Retreats [194 E3] Motshaba St; reservations `+27 11 438 4650; e reservations.safrica@sanctuaryretreats.com; w sanctuaryretreats.com. Part of the Abercrombie & Kent group, Sanctuary Retreats operates 4 lodges in Botswana: Chobe Chilwero, Chief's Camp, Stanley's Camp & Baines' Camp, as well as Sussi & Chuma in Livingstone.

Setari m +44 7725 138637; e kate@ setaricamp.com; w setaricamp.com. Founded in 2017, Setari may be a relatively new operator, but its owners are steeped in Botswana's safari industry & are highly knowledgeable. Its 3 island camps are at the base of the Panhandle in the far north of the Delta – Setari Camp, Kala Camp & Kala Treehouse.

Singita `+27 21 683 3424; e enquiries@ singita.com; w singita.com. Based in South Africa, this highly regarded, luxury ecotourism company is expected to assume the management of Abu Camp & Seba Camp.

Stars of Africa `+27 21 035 1410; e book@ starsofafrica.travel; w starsofbotswana.travel. Handling the marketing & reservations for a collection of locally owned camps in the Delta, Chobe & Moremi National Park: Mogogelo Camp, Xaro Lodge, Camp Savuti & Camp Linyanti.

Wilderness Safaris [194 C2] Mathiba
I Rd; ☎ 686 0086, reservations +27 11
257 500, emergency +27 82 576 9171;
e enquiry@wildernessdestinations.com;
w wildernessdestinations.com. Started by safari
guides Colin Bell, Chris MacIntyre (not this book's
author!) & Russel Friedman in Botswana in 1983,
this has since grown into one of the subcontinent's
leading safari operators, working throughout
southern Africa. From their office in Maun, they
also market Botswana's largest selection of safari
camps – 22 in total. These are mostly in private
reserves & include DumaTau, Little DumaTau,
King's Pool, Linyanti Tented Camp & Savuti Camp
in NG15; Vumbura Plains & Little Vumbura in
NG22; Kwetsani, Jacana, Jao, Tubu Tree, Little
Tubu & Pelo in NG25; Chitabe & Chitabe Lediba
in NG31; Qorokwe in NG32; Mokete in NG41;
Mombo Camp & Little Mombo in Moremi Game
Reserve; & Kalahari Plains in the CKGR. Marketed
as 'adventures', 'classic', or 'premier', their style,
standard & prices vary, yet Wilderness effectively
sets the baseline for high-quality camps in
Botswana, by which other operators tend to be
measured. Wilderness advises travellers to book
their camps through a tour operator.

Wilderness also owns the flight company
Wilderness Air, & offers non-participatory mobile
safaris, which aim to recreate the atmosphere
of an unhurried exploratory journey, operating
primarily in private concession areas. Departures
are guaranteed with a min of 2 guests (max 8).

Mobile safari specialists

Barclay Stenner Safaris 148 Matlapaneng
Rd; m 7389 3375; e john@barclaystenner.com,
james@barclaystenner.com; w barclaystenner.
com. John Barclay & James Stenner have been
running tailor-made mobile safaris all over
Botswana for a number of years & they accompany
every trip. Their fun & informative safaris
usually head into the Okavango Delta, Chobe,
Makgadikgadi Pans & Central Kalahari, & also visit
the Ju/'hoansi Bushmen of the Kalahari. Options
range from basic mobile camping to luxurious
offerings with Persian carpets, Egyptian cotton
sheets & fine cuisine.
Beagle Expeditions (Page 364) Very unusually
for a mobile operator, Beagle operates in one
of the Delta's private concessions: Abu (NG26).
Owned and run by an experienced husband-and-

wife team, Simon & Marleen Byron, their trips
focus on the Kweene River region.
Bush Ways Safaris ☎ 686 3685; e safari-res@
bushways.com; w bushways.com. Established
in 1996, Bush Ways operates scheduled mobile
safaris lasting 7–18 days, as well as tailor-made
tours. Itineraries cover Chobe, Moremi, Nxai,
Makgadikgadi & the CKGR, as well as Victoria Falls,
the Zambezi Region (Caprivi Strip) & some parts of
Zambia. Travellers can opt for semi-participation
or fully serviced camping trips, which are run even
with just 1 participant, or lodge-based safaris,
with no hidden costs or 'kitty' requirements. French
& German translators are provided on selected
safaris. Bush Ways also owns Sango Safari Camp &
Khwai Guest House in Moremi, & Chobe Elephant
Camp, Boteti River Camp, Deception Valley Lodge &
The Dune Camp.
Capture Africa ☎ 686 1200; m 7173 1356;
e info@captureafrica.net; w captureafrica.com.
Brian & Hildrene Gibson founded their mobile-
safari operation in 1997. Theirs is a flexible
approach, with different styles of tents to cater
for a variety of travellers, including children of all
ages. They specialise in private tailor-made luxury
safaris with specialist guides.
Drumbeat Safaris ☎ 686 3096;
m 7141 9684; e drumbeat@drumbeatsafaris.
com, drumbeatsafarismaun@gmail.com;
f drumbeatsafaris. Established in 1996,
Drumbeat is still run by its Dutch co-founder
Annelies Zonjee, who organises fully inclusive
comfortable & luxury mobile safaris throughout
northern Botswana, as well as lodge-based
safaris & helicopter trips. Mobile safaris are
always private (min 2 people) so you won't be
sharing – a real plus for families. Guests stay
in walk-in tents, usually in private campsites
within the parks, & travel in game vehicles, with
the equipment & staff either trailed behind or
transported separately.
Endeavour Safaris ☎ 686 0887; m 7176
9099; e info@endeavour-safaris.com;
w endeavour-safaris.com. Based on the premise
that everyone should have the chance to visit &
experience Botswana's wilderness, Mike & Silvia
Hill's safari operation caters for a range of budgets,
from privately guided mobile safaris to luxury fly-
in lodge options & boat safaris in the Delta. Where
Endeavour really scores, however, is in its safaris for
families (no age restrictions); & for senior travellers

& those with disabilities, including guests with mobility issues & those who have hearing & visual impairments – just be sure to let them know your needs & the extent of your disability. The company's modified Land Cruiser & mobile camp are maintained & operated by specially trained staff too.

Harkness Safaris m 7289 3736/26; e enquiries@harkness-safaris.com; w harkness-safaris.com. Founded in 2008, Andrew Harkness's family-run safari operation caters for up to 12 guests, including families, in dome or walk-in tents, with en-suite long-drop toilets & bucket showers. Trips are tailor-made but usually start in Maun & finish in Kasane or Victoria Falls, taking in Moremi, Khwai, & the Savuti & Chobe River areas of Chobe National Park. The CKGR can be included in any itinerary.

Letaka Safaris ✎ 680 0363; e info@ letakasafaris.com; w letakasafaris.com. Brothers Brent & Grant Reed, of the 6-part Nat Geo *Safari Brothers* television series, set up Letaka in 2000, focusing on set-departure trips in Moremi & Chobe, as well as to Makgadikgadi & Nxai pans. These, including specialist birding & photography trips, are all led by a team of high-quality guides. You'll stay in walk-in tents with gauze windows, solar-powered lights & an en-suite long-drop loo & bucket shower – with hot water brought to your tent on request.

Masson Safaris ✎ 686 2442; e massonsafaris@ gmail.com; w massonsafaris.net. This small, family-run operation runs mobile photographic safaris, both scheduled & tailor-made, concentrating on game & birdlife, with a general appreciation of Botswana's more remote areas (they're especially keen on the great salt pans, Tsodilo & the Central Kalahari). Ewan Masson, who has been guiding in Botswana for 30 years, leads most trips. Expect walk-in dome tents, complete with linen, washstand, reading light & a private chemical flush loo. Game drives are taken in open safari vehicles (max 8 guests).

Penduka Safaris ✎ 686 4539; m 7130 0215; e info@pendukasafaris.com; w pendukasafaris. com. Started in 1963 by Izak Barnard, Penduka is one of the oldest mobile operators in southern Africa. Today it's run by Izak's son Willem & his wife Sallie, who offer both scheduled & tailor-made safaris throughout Botswana, Zambia & Namibia. All are fully inclusive & fully serviced, using

spacious tents with open-air, en-suite bathrooms, complete with a chemical toilet and bucket shower, & custom-built vehicles to maximise game viewing & to suit the tough road conditions.

Roger Dugmore Safaris ✎ 686 2427; e rdsafaris@ngami.net; w rogerdugmoresafaris. com. Owned & run by Roger Dugmore, this small company runs private mobile tented safaris & specialised photographic expeditions around Botswana's national parks & wilder areas of the desert & Okavango Delta, including quad-bike expeditions to Makgadikgadi Pans. Roger has over 30 years' wilderness-guiding experience & likes to take time for guests to get to know each area.

Wilderness Dawning Safaris m 7389 3671; e reservations@wildernessdawning.com; w wildernessdawning.com. This reliable small operator offers scheduled camping safaris of 10, 11 & 14 days with experienced Batswana guides. Hosted trips, for 4–10 guests, are spent entirely in the national parks, with the exception of Victoria Falls, & (for 1 trip) a couple of nights on the *Okavango Spirit* houseboat in the Okavango Panhandle. The houseboat can also be booked independently of a safari tour.

Camping, boating, canoeing and budget safaris

Afro Trek Safaris m 7414 5628, 7123 7478; e afrotreksafaris@gmail.com; w afrotreksafaris. com. Based at the Sedia Riverside Hotel (page 198), Afro Trek offers 1–3-day mokoro trips, 4x4 game safaris, birdwatching excursions & short trips in & around Maun & Moremi. There are also 7–18-day mobile safari options.

Audi Safaris ✎ 686 0599; m 7532 3065; e info@ okavangocamp.com, info@audisafaris.com; w audisafaris.com. Operating for over 20 years, the safari operation based out of Audi Camp (page 200) organises budget trips into the Delta, Moremi, Nxai Pan & the Central Kalahari. From mobile camping safaris to drive-in mokoro trips, their trips typically require min 2 people & include meals, park fees, vehicle, guide & camping equipment, with travellers expected to bring their own drinks & sleeping bags, & muck in with all camp chores. Your own luggage can be stored at base.

Khwai Development Trust Apollo Hse [194 C2], off Mathiba I Rd; ✎ 686 2365, 680 1211; e khwai@ btcmail.co.bw; ⏱ 07.30–16.30 Mon–Fri, 08.00–12.30 Sat. This is where you book the

Trust-run campsites in NG19. They can also organise an escort guide for mokoro trips, bush walks & to accompany night driving.

Naga Safaris [188 D1] The Pumpkin Patch, Shorobe Rd; ✆ 686 2353; m 7163 7250, 7182 5999; e info@nagasafaris.com; w nagasafaris. com; ⏰ 08.00–17.00 Mon–Sat. Owned & run by local Batswana, this friendly outfit offers mobile camping safaris, either with their own guides & cooks or fully self-catered, into various Botswana parks, as well as Victoria Falls. Camping equipment is available for hire.

Pride of Africa m 7230 2590; e reservations@ prideofafrica-safaris.com; w prideofafrica-safaris. com. 4-day camping trips across the Delta, moving between island campsites on motorboats.

Horseriding specialists

African Animal Adventure Safaris m 7336 6461; e jen@africananimaladventures.com;

f adventuresandgetaways. In addition to local rides, Jen Weimann offers overnight horseriding trips in the Ngamiland region, perhaps along the Boro River or on the edge of the Delta, as well as further afield to the Makgadikgadi Pans.

African Horseback Safaris ✆ 686 1523; e reservations@africanhorseback.com; w africanhorseback.com. Specialist horseriding safaris based out of Macatoo Camp (page 366) on the western side of the Delta, in NG26.

Okavango Horse Safaris ✆ 686 1671; e safaris@okavangohorse.com; w okavangohorse. com; f . For details, see page 365.

Ride Botswana m 7248 4354, 7348 3710; e info@ridebotswana.com; w ridebotswana. com. Extremely experienced, family-run company offering riding for all levels at their Maun base at Thamo Telele (page 199), Ride Botswana offers horseriding safaris for experienced riders in the Makgadikgadi Pans & Okavango Delta.

THE ROAD NORTH OF MAUN: TO MOREMI AND CHOBE

FROM MAUN TO MOREMI GAME RESERVE The journey from Maun to Moremi's South Gate entrance takes around 2 hours. Head northeast out of Maun, past the airport turn-off, towards the hospital. After about 10km, turn left at the roundabout towards Shorobe. It's a good tar road, passing Crocodile Camp, but beware of travelling too fast as you'll find domestic animals on many stretches.

Just under 40km out of Maun you'll pass through the sizeable village of **Shorobe**. The village is 53km south of Moremi Game Reserve's South Gate, and marks the northern limit of the tar road between Maun and Moremi or Kasane. Drive slowly through here as you can usually expect plenty of goats and people wandering on the road. Dotted through the village are a few small shops which sell soft drinks and very basic supplies. Do take time to check out the excellent craftsmanship of the women at the **Shorobe Basket Co-operative**, housed in a neat thatched building at the northern edge of the village. Established in 1995, the co-operative's 30 expert weavers have recently received a significant government grant to establish an agro-forestry scheme to sustainably grow trees like the mokolwane, whose bark they use for weaving, and establish a vegetable garden alongside their business.

From Shorobe, a wide gravel road leads to the veterinary control fence (vet fence), or the 'buffalo fence' as it's locally known. Constructed to protect the all-important cattle industry from disease that may be transmitted from wildlife north of this point, the road from the fence is a deep sand track, making 4x4 travel essential. This stretch of the road is very slow going and it's important to drive with care.

Just 2km after the vet fence, a left-hand turning is signposted to Moremi Game Reserve, bringing you after a further 32km through mopane and acacia woodland to the reserve's South Gate. For comments on this road, see page 325.

⌂ **Where to stay** *Map, page 336*
There's a national park campsite at South Gate (Maqwee) itself (page 324) and the Kaziikini Community Campsite (page 398) – and a couple of camps around

Shorobe (NG35), which make it possible to break the journey overnight or for a meal.

Mochaba Crossing (7 chalets, 9 tents, 10 camp pitches) `\`686 4087; m 7763 2072, 7601 9825; e reservations@mochabacrossing. com; w mochabacrossing.com; ⊕ MOCHCR 19°46.883'S, 23°38.550'E. Some 30km north of Maun, 3km south of Shorobe village, Mochaba makes a useful stopover – for a drink, a meal or overnight. Facing across the bush towards the Thamalakane River, neat ochre-painted, en-suite chalets under thatch are set in well-maintained lawns. Furnished with twin or dbl beds (or 4 beds), all rooms have a tiled shower & toilet, a fridge, kettle & AC. Spotless if cramped en-suite tents line the edge of the dusty campsite, while smaller tents – still with fans & electric lights – share the open site & (clean) ablutions with other campers. There's a pool & barn-like restaurant (⊕ 07.30–18.00; $–$$) serving à la carte meals all day. *Camping US$20 pp.* **$$$–$$$$**

CONTINUING TO CHOBE If you're heading straight to Chobe, follow the directions on opposite page for Moremi, but after the buffalo fence continue straight ahead instead of turning left for South Gate. This leads, after about 24km, to the village of **Sankuyo**. There's little to delay the passing motorist here, beyond a shop, a couple of bars and a school, but the village is the base for the Sankuyo Tshwaragano Management Trust, which operates in the small NG33 Concession. As well as Kaziikini Campsite and Shandereka Cultural Village, the trust owns Santawani Lodge (page 398).

Continuing north from Sankuyo, you'll reach a slightly obscure left turn after 13km. Ignore this and after a total of 30km, you'll come to Mababe Village. From the village, where the road bears northwest, continue for another 3km to a junction. Turning right here will lead after a final 7km to Chobe's Mababe Gate (⊕ MABGAT 19°06.182'S, 23°59.119'[E]).

Had you taken the obscure left turning after Sankuyo (at ⊕ MORCUT 19°29.050'S, 23°55.111'E), you would be driving due west along the Moremi cutline before it joins up with the road between Moremi's South and North gates. We understand that it is a legitimate way to access North Gate, but it is not a route that we have driven, so we would welcome any feedback from readers.

Where to stay A number of lodges lie close to the road leading north to Chobe. There's one in the drier NG43, which lies to the east of Sankuyo: Mankwe Tented Retreat (2hr drive from Maun; page 401). There's another in the neighbouring NG41, which shares its northern and western boundaries with Chobe National Park: Mogotlho Safari Lodge (a further 20km north of Mankwe; page 400). For details of both the lodges and the reserves, see page 398.

8

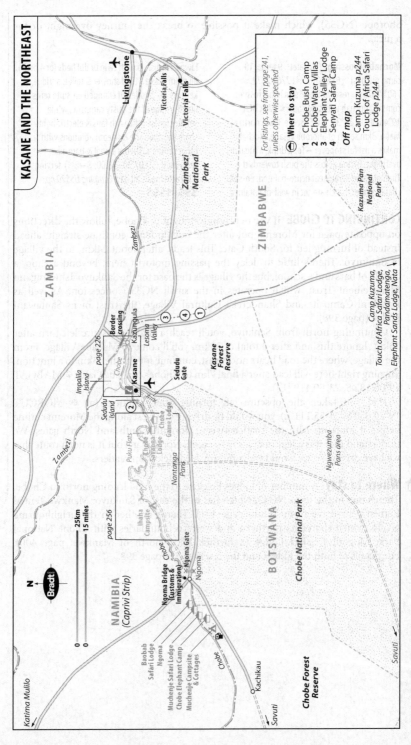

KASANE AND THE NORTHEAST

ZAMBIA

ZIMBABWE

BOTSWANA

NAMIBIA (Caprivi Strip)

Livingstone

Victoria Falls

Victoria Falls

Zambezi National Park

Kazuma Pan National Park

Border crossing

Kazungula

Lesoma Valley

Kasane

Sedudu Gate

Kasane Forest Reserve

Sedudu Island

Impalila Island

Zambezi

Chobe

Zambezi

page 226

page 256

Chobe Safari Lodge

Chobe Game Lodge

Puku Flats

Nantanga Pans

Ihaha Campsite

Chobe National Park

Ngwezumba Pans area

Ngoma Gate

Chobe

Ngoma Bridge (Customs & Immigration)

Ngoma

Baobab Safari Lodge

Ngoma

Muchenje Safari Lodge

Chobe Elephant Camp

Muchenje Campsite & Cottages

Chobe

Kachikau

Chobe Forest Reserve

Savuti

Savuti

Katima Mulilo

Camp Kuzuma, Touch of Africa Safari Lodge, Pandamatenga, Elephant Sands Lodge, Nata

N Bradt

0   25km
0   15 miles

For listings, see from page 241, unless otherwise specified

Where to stay
1 Chobe Bush Camp
2 Chobe Water Villas
3 Elephant Valley Lodge
4 Senyati Safari Camp

Off map
Camp Kuzuma p244
Touch of Africa Safari Lodge p244

9

Kasane and the Northeast

KASANE

The administrative centre of Chobe District, Kasane is on the surface just a small town in the northeast corner of Botswana. It lies on the southern bank of the Chobe River, a few kilometres from its confluence with the Zambezi – where the borders of Zambia, Zimbabwe, Namibia and Botswana meet at a point. Thus, while the town is of limited interest in itself, it is an important gateway: to the Chobe National Park; to Victoria Falls in Zimbabwe and Livingstone in Zambia; to the road across Namibia's Zambezi Region (Caprivi Strip); and to the small charter flights which ferry visitors between the various lodges in northern Botswana.

With the opening of the impressive Kazungula Bridge over the Zambezi River in 2021 and a great new airport, Kasane and the neighbouring town of Kazungula have the air of border settlements geared to travellers refuelling, refreshing and moving on. Multiple fuel stations, small shopping malls and a well-stocked Shoprite supermarket meet the needs of pan-African self-drivers and truckers, while small guesthouses and family-run restaurants cater to those pausing en route to national parks within Botswana and beyond.

For many people, Kasane is a relaxing place to stay for a couple of days and to take advantage of its proximity to Chobe National Park, and the opportunities for scenic boat cruises and game drives.

GETTING THERE AND AWAY

By air Kasane (airline code BBK) is a busy gateway for the light aircraft that taxi visitors around the camps of northern Botswana, and its scheduled traffic is gradually beginning to pick up, too, with regular international as well as domestic flights.

Direct flights between Kasane and Johannesburg are operated daily by Airlink (\ 625 2354). Air Botswana (Hunters Africa Mall; \ 625 0161) operates on the same route three times a week, albeit two of those days via Gaborone and Francistown. Most travellers coming through Kasane will also pass through Victoria Falls or Livingstone, whose airports have frequent flights to/from Nairobi, Harare and Johannesburg. Do note, however, that depending on your nationality you may need to pay US$30–75 for a visa. In theory, there is also the option to buy a KAZA Univisa in Lusaka, Livingstone and Victoria Falls, at US$50 per person, which covers you for travel in both Zambia and Zimbabwe, along with day trips to Botswana, but in practice these are not always available. Currently, British, US, Canadian, many European and Australasian travellers do not need a visa to enter Zambia, but they do require one for Zimbabwe, although this can be arranged on arrival. The 90-minute road transfer between Kasane and Victoria Falls or

Livingstone costs around US$75 per person, or you could charter a plane – albeit at exceptionally high cost.

Kasane Airport Bright, efficient and modern, Kasane International Airport is set on a ridge just a couple of kilometres west of the town. A taxi to or from town should cost between P50 and P150 (US$4.50–15) depending on exact location and number of passengers.

There are desks at the airport for Air Botswana, Airlink and Botswana Tourism (\ 625 0424) as well as several car-rental agencies. There's also a bureau de change, and even a VIP lounge, basic curio and snack shop and a café.

By car
To/from Nata and Francistown From Kasane it is about 316km of tarred road to Nata, and 506km to Francistown. For details of the drive between Kasane and Nata, see page 243.

To/from Zimbabwe
Kazungula There is an excellent tarred road from Zimbabwe to the Kazungula border (⊕ 06.00–20.00) and across into Botswana. This means that one of Africa's biggest attractions for visitors, Victoria Falls, is only an hour's drive away, making it an easy day trip from Kasane – and, more notably, allowing Chobe to be visited as a day trip from the Falls.

About 2km after entering Botswana at the substantial immigration office, there's a T-junction. The right turn heads to the Kazungula Bridge and Zambia; the left leads you through a quick disease-control post. Here your vehicle will be driven through a pool of insecticide and you'll be asked to stamp your shoes on a soaked mat. You may also be checked to make sure that you're not importing banned animal products – like fresh meat, milk, bones or skins (all part of Botswana's zealous efforts to protect their national herd from diseases) and more recently, fruit and vegetables. Less than 2km later there's a right turn to Kasane, while straight on leads to Nata and Francistown. From here, it's about 12km east of Kasane town.

If you're on an organised trip, it's very easy to have an efficient road transfer arranged for you between Kasane and Victoria Falls town or the airport. It'll take about 2 hours, cost US$45–70 per person, one-way and the driver will direct you at the border crossing. At the time of writing, single-entry visa charges were US$30/55 (US/UK citizens) for Zimbabwe and US$30 for Botswana. It's worth noting that the KAZA Univisa is a great option if you can get one – though it does rely on the Wi-Fi for the printer to be working and the holographic paper to be in stock on the day you arrive, neither of which is guaranteed! The Univisa is valid for travel between Zimbabwe and Zambia and day trips into Botswana; it costs US$50 and it is valid for 30 days.

If you're **travelling with children under 18 years**, bear in mind Botswana's strict immigration requirements (page 131).

Pandamatenga About 93km south of Kasane and 223km from Nata, 'Panda', as it's locally known, is one of the country's few arable-farming areas. Its small centre is distinguished by the prominent grain silos, which tower over the surrounding sorghum, sunflower and maize fields. The small border post with Zimbabwe (Mpandamatenga border; ⊕ 08.00–17.00 daily) is less than 50km from Robins Camp, deep in the heart of Zimbabwe's Hwange National Park, so it can be a convenient way to drive between Chobe and Hwange. If you do need to eat or rest here, **Panda Lodge and Camp** (6 rondavels, camping; ☏ 624 0129; m 7229 6068; e pandalodge@yahoo.com; f pandalodgecamp; **$–$$**) offers neat, en-suite rondavels in shady gardens (US$110/dbl) and 8 camping pitches (US$5 pp) with ablutions, braai facilities, a good restaurant, Wi-Fi in the main area and a lovely pool. **Touch of Africa Safari Lodge** (page 244), 5km north of the village, and **Wildtrack Safaris Eco Lodge** are on the border. On a practical note, there's an Engen petrol station with a handy ATM, and a reasonably well-stocked little shop for cold drinks and basic supplies.

To/from Zambia While transfers from Livingstone Airport are easily arranged and relatively inexpensive (about US$45–70 pp one-way), the Zambian government charges US$50 per person for a KAZA Univisa. Thus, unless you're rushing through, it's well worth an overnight stop in Livingstone, giving you the opportunity to visit Victoria Falls before heading on to Kasane. The journey from Livingstone to the border takes about 50 minutes along a straight, tarred road of about 65km, running parallel to the Zambezi. The excellent new bridge at Kazungula and its one-stop border post make this an extremely efficient crossing point.

Kazungula The much anticipated, US$259 million **Kazungula Bridge** is a road, rail and pedestrian bridge that opened in May 2021 to relieve pressure from the old pontoon ferry and enhance trade routes in the region. At just under 1km in span and with a curious curve to avoid crossing into Namibia or Zimbabwe at this border quadripoint, the bridge and improved border-crossing facilities have transformed this once chaotic and slow crossing point.

Foot passengers can get to the border by minibus or taxi from near the bus station in Kasane. It's currently P300 to cross the bridge as a pedestrian.

If you are crossing the border here with a **vehicle**, there is a raft of paperwork (and payment) required – insurance, immigration, car import permit, carbon and road tax and police levy. It's often worth enlisting the help of one of the many 'agents' who are likely to hassle you at the border. Come prepared with plenty of cash (US dollars and kwacha) and a good deal of patience. As is often the case at busy border crossings, it's worth keeping a close eye on your belongings, ideally leaving someone with your vehicle while another deals with the paperwork. Fees vary by vehicle size but expect to pay around US$15 for a car and US$20 for a 4x4 vehicle.

If you're relying on **public transport** to get to Botswana from Livingstone, there's a regular bus service to Sesheke run by Mazhandu Family Bus, which stops at Kazungula (Zambian side).

Sesheke Heading west from Kazungula, on the Zambian side, it's about 130km to the small town of Sesheke, the gateway to Zambia's Western Province and Namibia. Heavy traffic has left the section of road from Kazungula to Sesheke in very poor condition, with frequent and sizeable pot-holes making the road slow going. Sesheke itself (✣ 17°28.599'S, 24°17.208'E) is an underwhelming, if strategically important, border village, linked by an excellent 900m bridge to a smaller town on the other side, known locally as Katima Zambia. The bridge, financed largely by Germany, was opened in 2004 by the presidents of Zambia and Namibia. It lies about 5km inside Zambian territory, and was only the fifth bridge constructed to span the width of the Zambezi. Although Sesheke does have a few stores, a small branch of Finance Bank, a few small guesthouses and a fuel station, if you're self-driving to Namibia, it's worth noting that fuel is considerably cheaper across the border in Katima Mulilo and supplies more plentiful.

To/from Namibia Ngoma (page 255) is the location for a bridge across the Chobe, and a border with Namibia (✆ 623 6002; ⏰ 07.00–18.00). It's about 51km from the centre of Kasane by good tar road, or rather more if you take the scenic riverside route (4x4 essential) through Chobe National Park. From Ngoma, it's a further 69km of good tar road to the main town of Namibia's Zambezi Region (Caprivi Strip), Katima Mulilo. To cross between Katima Mulilo and Zambia see page 510.

By bus Kasane's bus station [226 C3] is on Chilwero Road, behind the Shell garage in the centre of town. Buses operated by LAWA (✆ 240 1832; m 7351 2751; e info@ lawaholdings.co.bw; w lawaholdings.co.uk) leave Kasane for Francistown (5hrs), Maun (8hrs, P225), Nata (3–4hrs, P120) and Gaborone (10hrs, P290) every day in the morning and evening. There are real risks to travelling on dark roads at night, so consider your departure time carefully. If you want to get to Maun, there are two choices. Either take the slow overnight bus, leaving at 21.00 and arriving in Maun at around 05.00 the following morning, or take the Francistown bus and change at Nata (page 481). There is also a twice-weekly bus service to Zambia's capital, Lusaka. Whatever your destination, arrive at least half an hour early to purchase tickets or book by telephone in advance.

Regular minibuses also ply between Kasane and Nata, linking on to both Francistown and Maun, with fares on a par with the larger buses.

To get to Kazungula for the ferry across to Zambia, or to cross into Zimbabwe, take a minibus from the roadside just up the hill from the bus rank. Alternatively, take a taxi from the same point.

ORIENTATION Kasane is largely a linear town, spread out along President Avenue, which shadows the Chobe River as it meanders from east to west, forming Botswana's boundary with Namibia. Most of the visitors' lodges stand on the river's southern bank, accessed by short side roads, but others are further downstream, in the Kazungula area.

A second tar road runs parallel to the town and the river to reach the border with Namibia at Ngoma. This actually cuts inland through the Chobe National Park, though isn't usually of interest for game viewing. Another tar road, which offers the only 2WD access to the rest of Botswana, heads southwards towards Nata and the rest of the Eastern Corridor area.

Maps There are few good maps of Kasane or its environs, perhaps because it's relatively easy to find your way around, especially with the advent of smartphone maps.

For Chobe National Park, you need a good paper map though – phone and apps can and do fail on occasion! The Shell map by Veronica Roodt is very good and is usually available from the shop at Chobe Safari Lodge, as is the Chobe National Park map/souvenir guide published by Tinkers. The most up-to-date map is the Tracks4Africa Botswana Traveller's Paper Map (4th Edition), which can be purchased online (w tracks4africa.co.za) in advance of travel.

GETTING AROUND Most visitors to the Kasane area will either have their own transport, or be visiting as part of an organised trip with an all-inclusive package – so the general lack of transport won't be a problem. If you're backpacking or want to explore alone on a budget, you'll find a few minibuses that ply up and down the main road from behind the bus station. These are particularly useful for those staying at the eastern end of the town or in Kazungula. There are also several taxis, labelled Kasane Taxi Services, which tend to congregate near the supermarkets and uphill from the bus station. If you'd prefer to book ahead, try Uncle George (m 7144 0055).

Many hotels will arrange transfers or trips to Kasane from Victoria Falls or Livingstone, or vice versa. You can expect to pay US$40–100 per person, excluding any visa costs, depending on numbers and whether or not you want a guide.

Car hire For self-drive car hire the options are increasing, with major companies now based at the airport and open for both incoming and outgoing flights. Note that it'll usually be cheaper to make a reservation in advance, rather than turn up and take the rate at the counter. For an indication of rates, see page 139. There are a couple of reliable 4x4 rental companies in Kasane, offering fully equipped vehicles for self-drive safaris. These will invariably need booking a reasonable amount in advance.

For fuel, there are three 24-hour garages: the Shell garage in the centre of town [226 C3], Puma at Tlou Safari Mall [227 E2], next to Shoprite, and Engen at Kazungula Junction [227 G3]; all three accept credit cards.

At Kasane Airport
AT&T Rentals m 7700 7584;
🕐 08.00–17.00 Mon–Fri
AVIS 625 0144; w avis.co.za; 🕐 08.00–13.00 & 14.00–17.00 Mon–Fri
Europcar 625 0730; w europcar.com; 🕐 08.00–17.00 Mon–Fri, 08.00–13.00 Sat–Sun
Hertz 397 1099; w hertz.co.za; 🕐 08.00–19.00 Mon–Fri, 08.00–noon Sat

Specialist 4x4 rental companies
Bushlore 38 Teemane Road, Kazungula; 625 1359; m 7247 9737; e info@bushlore.com; w bushlore.com; 🕐 08.00–17.00 Mon–Fri, 08.30–13.00 Sat. Fully equipped 4x4 Toyota Land Cruisers – inc some with roof tents – for 2–4 travellers.
Chobe 4x4 Kasane Airport; m 7173 8458, 7164 7740; e info@chobe4x4.com; w chobe4x4.com; 🕐 08.00–18.00 Mon–Sat. Fully equipped 2- & 4-door Toyota Land Cruisers, with roof tent options.

TOURIST INFORMATION Botswana Tourism [226 B3] has an office near the bus station in Kasane (Madiba Shopping Centre; 625 0555; e kasane@ botswanatourism.co.bw; 🕐 07.30–18.00 Mon–Fri, 09.00–14.00 Sat). There's plenty of scope for browsing along shelves packed with leaflets and brochures, but don't expect detailed planning assistance.

WHERE TO STAY For a small town, Kasane – and the neighbouring Kazungula – has a good array of accommodation options, from top-class hotels to small lodges, B&Bs and a range of campsites. Almost all offer that all-important Zambezi riverside location, and unless otherwise stated, are open year-round.

When planning where to stay in this area, do consider all the options. If you're just passing through Kasane, it might make sense to stay outside the national park, since accommodation here tends to be a little cheaper than those in the park, and you may also save a few days' park fees. Be aware, though, that the further they are from the park entrance, the longer it will take before you are in a wildlife environment. If you're visiting the Kasane area specifically to see northern Chobe, and can afford one of the lodges in the park or near Ngoma (page 255), then you might be better there. For those with their own transport, or seeking more of a bush feel with a lower price tag, a third option could be the Lesoma Valley (page 241).

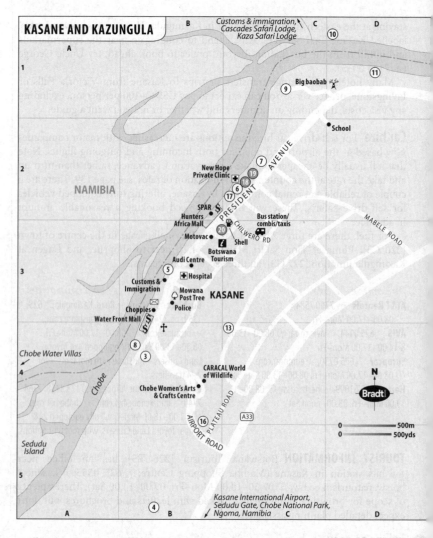

KASANE AND KAZUNGULA

Customs & immigration,
Cascades Safari Lodge,
Kaza Safari Lodge

Big baobab

School

New Hope
Private Clinic

NAMIBIA

SPAR
Hunters
Africa Mall

Motovac

Bus station/
combis/taxis

Shell

Botswana
Tourism

Audi Centre

Customs &
Immigration

Mowana
Post Tree

Police

KASANE

Choppies
Water Front Mall

Chobe Water Villas

CARACAL World
of Wildlife

Chobe Women's Arts
& Crafts Centre

Chobe

Sedudu
Island

N

Bradt

0 _____ 500m
0 _____ 500yds

Kasane International Airport,
Sedudu Gate, Chobe National Park,
Ngoma, Namibia

PRESIDENT AVENUE

CHILWERO RD

MABELE ROAD

PLATEAU ROAD

AIRPORT ROAD

A33

There are some excellent campsites around town, all sharing facilities with lodges. Worth checking out are Big Five Chobe Lodge, Chobe Safari Lodge, Kubu Lodge and Thebe River Lodge. Note that some of the campsites in Kasane will not accept advance bookings from individual campers (against overland groups), so in high season it's a good idea to arrive early.

Hotels, lodges and chalets

Bakwena Lodge [227 G2] (15 rooms) 625 2812; m 7842 8873; e reservations@chobebakwena. com; w chobebakwena.com. Opened in 2013, Bakwena has an immediate sense of tranquillity. Nestled in a heavily wooded site, right on the Chobe River, it has genuine eco-credentials & a calming atmosphere. It's all very understated & natural. The thatched lounge, dining & bar area is styled with cane & wooden furniture, softened by pale fabrics & lampshades made from traditional fish traps. There's an enticing eco-pool, naturally filtered by plants, & a firepit by the river, while higher up, a peaceful viewing area looks across to Impalila Island. Accommodation is split between rooms along the river, & others built on high stilts among the trees.

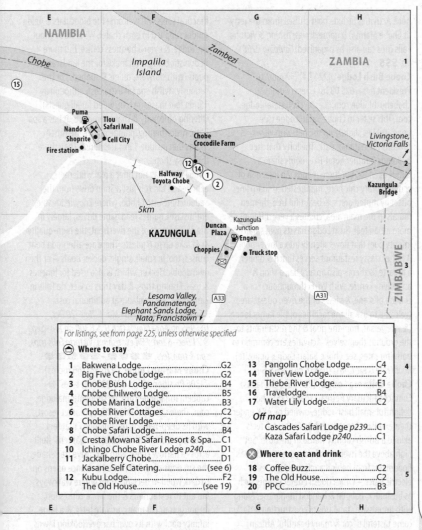

For listings, see from page 225, unless otherwise specified

Where to stay

1	Bakwena Lodge...................................G2		13	Pangolin Chobe Lodge..............C4
2	Big Five Chobe Lodge.........................G2		14	River View Lodge...........................F2
3	Chobe Bush Lodge..............................B4		15	Thebe River Lodge........................E1
4	Chobe Chilwero Lodge.......................B5		16	Travelodge.......................................B4
5	Chobe Marina Lodge..........................B3		17	Water Lily Lodge...........................C2
6	Chobe River Cottages.........................C2			
7	Chobe River Lodge..............................C2			*Off map*
8	Chobe Safari Lodge.............................B4			Cascades Safari Lodge *p239*.....C1
9	Cresta Mowana Safari Resort & Spa..C1			Kaza Safari Lodge *p240*..............C1
10	Ichingo Chobe River Lodge *p240*........D1			
11	Jackalberry Chobe..............................D1			**Where to eat and drink**
	Kasane Self Catering...........................(see 6)		18	Coffee Buzz.....................................C2
12	Kubu Lodge..F2		19	The Old House................................C2
	The Old House.....................................(see 19)		20	PPCC..B3

All have both indoor & outdoor showers, & a private veranda, with AC in the treetop houses, but just fans in the river rooms, which benefit from a cooling breeze. There are guided bicycle tours & village walks from the lodge, sundowner cruises & excursions into Chobe National Park, using their own vehicles & boats; allow extra time for the 25min journey so you'll still enjoy a full 3hrs in the park. *US$633/859 pp/sgl May–Oct, US$540/723 pp/sgl Nov–Apr. FBA inc local transfers.* 🛏🛏🛏

Big Five Chobe Lodge (aka Big Five Toro Lodge) [227 G2] (38 chalets, camping) ☏ 625 2272; m 7652 7355; e reservations@chobebig5.com; w chobebig5.com. Just 600m from the turn-off

towards Kasane from Kazungula, Big Five has a riverside location & neat rows of small, square chalets – those at the front are nicely placed with a river view, while rooms in the 'enclave' are slightly larger & cooler. Screened doors from a brick veranda lead into each of the thatched chalets, which have tiled floors, fans, AC, TVs, kettles & en-suite showers. Behind these, a level, grassy campsite hosts both overland groups (on a separate site) & independent campers, who benefit from 22 neat pitches with power points, a fireplace & private (hot water) ablution facilities. There's a wide, central lounge/dining area, open to the river, a separate riverside bar & a secluded pool. Activities include boat cruises (from the jetty at Chobe Marina) & game drives; fishing & Victoria Falls trips can also be organised. *Camping P200 pp.* **$$$**

Chobe Bush Lodge [226 B4] (42 rooms) President Av; 625 0336; e reservations@ chobebushlodge.com; f; w chobesafarilodge. com. This sister to Chobe Safari Lodge (see opposite) lies slightly up the hill, with views towards the national park. The lofty thatched buildings & rather hotel-like rooms share a family likeness, but there it ends. An injection of contemporary chic here, manifested in sharp lines offset by muted greys, & beautiful tree-themed murals in the main area, creates a very different, more urban feel. Bush Lodge has its own small infinity pool that flows silently into a lower pool. A rather classy restaurant serves lunch & dinner à la carte, & there's also an airy bar, a shop & an activity centre, with Wi-Fi throughout. For a change of scene, & views of the river, guests are welcome to use all the facilities of the larger lodge (& vice versa), from the pool & the restaurants to the grounds themselves. Activities are common to both (for rates, see Chobe Safari Lodge, opposite). *Room rate is exc b/fast (US$35 pp).* **$$$$**

Chobe Chilwero Lodge [226 B5] (15 chalets) Contact Sanctuary Retreats (page 215). This delightful small bush lodge, owned by A&K under their exclusive Sanctuary Retreats brand, feels akin to a British country house in the bush. Set high above the river, it looks out over the Chobe's floodplains from behind a relatively discreet electric fence – which doesn't deter visitors such as bushbuck, baboon & banded mongoose. Along with impressive standards of construction & design come tasteful décor & many beautiful African artefacts that create something of the feel of an ethnological museum.

An imposing entrance hall leads through to the elegant lounge, where a small ante-room has an excellent selection of books, magazines & games, & a discreetly covered TV. Great effort goes into the food here & the service is impeccable but friendly. Large, solidly built guest 'cottages' topped with thatch & cooled by AC are inviting in their own right, each with a canopied bed, free-standing bath, indoor & outdoor showers & an individual table & chairs set in lawns dotted with mature trees. Even more substantial is the Pool Suite, where privacy runs to its own plunge pool.

Practical souls will welcome the binoculars & field guides supplied in each chalet, Wi-Fi throughout the lodge, & even a business centre, but more hedonistic beings will make for the landscaped pools (with showers, toilets & sunbeds) or the seriously stylish spa (at extra cost, although a 15min foot massage is included for all guests). Offering Africology & Thalgo products, it has a spa bath, hydrotherapy, plunge pool, & treatment rooms that include 1 in a treehouse. Then there's the classy shop…

The lodge may not offer a real wilderness experience, but it is just a 5min drive from the Sedudu Gate into Chobe, where knowledgeable, enthusiastic guides lead game drives, largely in the eastern part of the riverfront; the high-quality 4x4s take up to 6 guests. There are afternoon boat cruises, too, in small, single-decker boats – or their own double decker, which is also used for lunches & teas. Fishing trips, & day trips to Victoria Falls in Zimbabwe, are available at additional cost.

Suite US$775 pp 6 Jan–Mar & Nov–20 Dec, US$965 pp Apr–May & Oct, US$1,300 pp Jun–Sep & 21 Dec–6 Jan. FBA exc fishing, Victoria Falls trips, spa & transfers. 🐘🐘🐘🐘–🐘🐘🐘🐘🐘

Chobe Marina Lodge [226 B3] (66 rooms) 21306 President Av; 625 2220/1; e res1@ chobemarinalodge.com; w chobemarinalodge. com. There's no mistaking this upmarket resort, with its deep-red & ochre buildings that feel instantly at one with its luxuriant gardens. Built across a narrow creek, with extensive tree shade, the spacious tiled & thatched entrance opens on to dark wooden decking, from where walkways fan out to restaurants & the bar, a curio shop, in-house tour company, private jetty, & a large infinity pool with its own bar overlooking lawns along the river.

Rooms, including 1 adapted for those with mobility issues, range from the Tlou Luxury Suites to the Puku Honeymoon Suite, & surprisingly spacious Nare Studios, which can be interconnecting for families. All overlook the Chobe River & have tiled floors, TV, AC, fan & safe, a bath & separate shower, & a private balcony.

The hotel has 2 dining options: informal buffet-style at the Mokoros Family Restaurant above the pool, or the 1st-floor Commissioners Restaurant, where à la carte meals are served in AC comfort or on a balcony overlooking the river. There's free Wi-Fi & a 100-seat conference room, but if relaxation is more your thing, try a massage in the Kwa Maningi Spa.

Activities, here as elsewhere, focus on the river, with well-guided river cruises in intimate 16-seater boats, fishing trips, & of course game drives. Returning by river to the rhythm & vitality of traditional dancers performing above the jetty is an occasional highlight not to be missed. $$$$$

Chobe River Lodge [226 C2] (12 rooms) 714 President Av; m 7164 6064; e res@ botswanabooking.com; w choberiverlodge. com. This small, friendly lodge, 5km from the national park, is relaxed, personal & well designed: a welcome change from the more corporate style of the larger lodges. Unobtrusively tucked behind secure gates, it has a tranquil setting with attractive gardens, currently home to a trio of warthogs, a huge troop of curious banded mongooses & some lovely birdlife (look out for woodland kingfishers & iridescent sunbirds). At the heart of the lodge, the airy central area is set under a soaring thatch & black steel structure. Its deep leather sofas, enormous banqueting table (albeit set with spaces to allow for private dining) & decorative metalwork, with designs including huge monstera leaves climbing the walls & latticework lights, all have a modern feel, while a small, zen-like cascading pool provides a peaceful backdrop. Adjacent to this, a shaded terrace, complete with sunloungers, overlooks an expanse of neat lawn leading to the river.

The rooms – 7 of which face the garden, while 5 are tucked around a small courtyard – are spacious & neat, kitted out in natural fabrics, with AC, ceiling fans & a modern en-suite shower room. The lodge offers game drives, fishing & boat cruises from its own jetty at the end of the garden, using its own vehicles, boats & guides, & can arrange trips to Victoria Falls on request. *US$300 pp dinner, B&B. Chobe game drive US$65 pp exc park fees; Chobe boat cruise US$55 pp exc park fees. Children all ages, 6+ for activities.* $$$$

Chobe Safari Lodge [226 B4] (90 rooms, camping) President Av; 625 0336; e reservations@chobesafarilodge.com; w chobesafarilodge.com. On a spacious site overlooking the river, on the western fringes of town, Chobe Safari Lodge is the oldest of Kasane's camps. Its wide lawns, well shaded by mature trees, attract warthogs, families of banded mongoose & numerous birds. Although it is the closest lodge to the national park for boat trips, this makes little difference if you're driving, since the entrance to the park is several kilometres by road.

The impressive reception, lobby, lounge, activity centre & restaurant shelter under a huge, open-sided thatched structure whose heavy rafters are an occasional playground for vervet monkeys. In front, a sparkling crescent-shaped pool is surrounded by loungers & tables beneath the trees, making this an attractive lunch venue; the burgers are said to be excellent & buffets at lunch & dinner (US$35/45) are very popular. Other facilities include a very well-stocked shop, a proper spa that's open to all, Wi-Fi access throughout, & 2 bars, with the Sedudu bar at the campsite a favourite place for sundowners.

There's a good choice of accommodation, in 2 price bands. At the top end, the modern 'river' rooms & slightly larger, predominantly dark-wood 'safari' rooms have twin or dbl beds, en-suite shower & bath, AC/fan, TV, safe, kettle & phone, plus a balcony or veranda overlooking lawns to the river. 'Standard' rooms, & the lodge's original rondavels, now have AC, TV & safes, as well as braai stands. For a party of 4, the family rooms are particularly good value. Meanwhile, the neat, well-tended campsite by the river offers shaded, level sites & a trio of clean ablution blocks. A few pre-erected tents are available, & it's popular with organised overlander groups & independent campers alike.

Game drives (US$50 pp exc park fees) depart at 06.00, 08.00 & 15.00 daily, while well-guided boat cruises (US$50 pp) leave at 15.00. For something a little more intimate you can explore the river between 07.00 & 14.00 in a small motorboat with a driver (US$65/hr), or go fishing (US$50 pp/2hrs inc tackle). Other excursions include a guided Victoria Falls day trip (US$260 pp exc visa) & a Namibian village walk on Impalila Island (US$50 pp; no visa necessary as a 1-day visitor's permit is granted en route). *Room rate is exc b/fast (US$35 pp). Camping US$20 pp. Children all ages.* $$$–$$$$

Cresta Mowana Safari Resort & Spa [226 C1] (108 rooms) 625 0300; e resmowana@ cresta.co.bw; w mowanasafarilodge.net. The Botswana flagship of the Cresta group, Mowana was conceived on a grand scale. Well designed, airy & spacious, it makes imaginative use of wooden decking, with an old baobab tree at its heart. Dbl & twin en-suite rooms, along with 8 suites, 12 family rooms & 2 rooms for travellers with disabilities, are attractively finished with river views, & offer everything that you'd expect from a top international hotel, including remote-control AC, fan, phone, fridge, TV & safe.

Overlooking the river are 2 restaurants & a cocktail bar. The main restaurant has both an à la carte menu & a set-price buffet. Above it, the open-sided upstairs bar/lounge catches the breeze, with a warming wood fire for winter evenings. Less formal is the outside bar & restaurant located above a large, modern pool with separate children's pool. Guests will also appreciate the smart curio shop, an internet room & free Wi-Fi throughout. But talk of the town is the extensive riverside spa, whose treatment rooms, sauna, jacuzzi & pool share a lovely setting; even the gym has a certain appeal!

For the business visitor, there are conference facilities for up to 100 people, but most guests are more interested in the game drives & boat cruises that venture into Chobe National Park from the hotel's own jetty. In case that's not enough, there's also a tennis court & a 9-hole golf course, as well as African cultural evenings. **$$$$$**

Jackalberry Chobe [226 D1] (16 tents) 706 President Av; 625 1272, 625 0995; e reservations@theberiversafaris.com; w jackalberrychobe.com. Part of the Thebe River Safaris portfolio (page 238), this pleasant riverfront lodge has 16 luxury tents, broad decks for river views & a thatched, open, safari-style central lounge/dining area. Comfortable leather sofas, a classic bar area, tables dotted around the terrace for alfresco dining, an elevated firepit & an adjacent infinity pool all overlook the wide Chobe River. It's a tranquil spot from which to visit the national park, enjoy local river activities & regroup before or after safari. Raised on timber decks, the classic safari tents either overlook the river or bush, but all have comfortable interiors, with nicely furnished beds, a large en-suite bathroom with both a claw-foot bath & shower, & a small terrace. Activities on land & water can be arranged, with 3hr game drives into the national park on offer in the morning, followed by sunset boat cruises. Guided day trips to Victoria Falls (US$180 pp) & transfers (US$64 pp) are also available. *River*

View Tent from US$421 pp Nov–Apr to US$495 pp May–Oct, FBA; Bushveld View Tent from US$383 pp Nov–Apr to US$451 pp May–Oct, FBA. **$$$**

Kubu Lodge [227 F2] (11 chalets, camping) Kubu Rd, Kazungula; 625 0312; m 7126 5000; e reservations@kubulodge.net; w kubulodge. net. Situated 10km from the centre of Kasane & 7km from the Zimbabwean border, Kubu stands on a 30ha sloping site beside the Chobe River, clearly signposted from the main road. Proudly owner-run, the lodge has been part of Kasane for many years & remains friendly, personable, & immaculately kept.

Kubu's square thatched chalets are substantial wooden buildings with steps up to a veranda at the front, set under shady trees in lush green lawns sloping down to the river. Recently rebuilt & upgraded, each is well furnished with timber & metal furniture, mosquito nets, screened windows, ceiling & standing fans, tea/coffee facilities, Wi-Fi & dbl/twin or trpl beds. There's a compact en-suite bathroom with hairdryer & amenities.

Overlooking the river, the restaurant offers indoor & outdoor seating for meals on the 2-tier veranda & braai area. B/fast is included daily, with the option of lunch & a 4-course dinner; the menu changes daily. A bar, small boma for special occasion dinners, swimming pool down by the river (chalet guests only), reading lounge & curios shop make up the lodge facilities.

A few mins' walk from the lodge, Kubu's campsite is popular with private campers. There are 7 sand pitches with trees (limited shade at the end of the dry season), each with a braai stand & security lights, & there are 2 water standpipes & 5 plug points. Toilets & hot showers are clean & functional, & there's a small plunge pool for campers. Part of the campsite slopes down to the river so, though the road is lit, it's wise to take a torch if you plan to eat at the restaurant in the evening (booking required).

Game drives & boat cruises into Chobe National Park operate morning & afternoon, & fishing trips can be organised too. While the jetty at the lodge is used for cruises to the confluence of the Chobe & Zambezi rivers, guests going on a boat trip into Chobe National Park are transferred by road to a jetty in Kasane. The extensive grounds feature a marked nature trail, with helpful notes & a map on hand. *Camping US$24 pp. Children 4+ allowed in* chalets. ⊙ *Closed mid-Jan–Feb. US$365 dbl, B&B; US$958 dbl, FBA inc airport transfers.* **$$$$$**

Pangolin Chobe Lodge [226 C4] (14 rooms) Contact Pangolin Photo Safaris (page 238). This contemporary lodge sits above the town, just a short drive from the airport & close to Chobe park gate for an early start. Given its ownership, it comes as no surprise that it is geared to the needs of photographers – who can start with the sunset view from the lodge towards the Chobe floodplains, & draw inspiration from the wildlife photography adorning the walls. The facilities include an editing area & excursions in Pangolin's customised boats & 4x4 vehicles – though for non-photographic guests there are also more conventional means of transport.

Back at the lodge, the en-suite bedrooms are built on 2 storeys & come with AC, twin or dbl beds, & a balcony sharing the view, along with a large desk & lots of space for camera gear. Balancing the rooms, & featuring the same clean design lines, the main area incorporates a dining room & pool terrace at ground level, with a bar & editing space above. *US$595 pp Jan–Mar & Oct–Dec, FBA; US$750 pp Apr–Sep, FBA. Set-departure guided wildlife photography itineraries cost from US$4,595 pp Apr–Sep for 7 days, FBA.* **$$$–$$$$**

River View Lodge [227 F2] (11 chalets, 1 house) 625 0967; e info@riverviewlodgechobe.com; w riverviewlodgechobe.com. In spite of an uninspiring entrance & rather utilitarian, painted brick chalets, this is a friendly, well-organised & intimate lodge with an enviable riverside location. There are plenty of trees, too, to the delight of the local bushbaby population, but hippos & crocs are deterred by a discreet electric fence. Twin, dbl & family chalets benefit from AC & fans, tea & coffee stations & fresh, contemporary décor. There's also an attractively laid-out self-catering private home for up to 4 people, though most guests dine in the central area (dinner US$32 pp). A lounge, bar, firepit & swimming pool complete the picture, & there's Wi-Fi throughout. As well as the standard boat cruises & game drives into the park (US$39 pp exc park fees), the lodge offers activities including cultural excursions & day trips to Victoria Falls. For self-drivers, secure parking is a bonus. *US$270 dbl, B&B.* **$$$$**

Thebe River Lodge [227 E1] (31 rooms, camping) President Av; 625 0995;

e reservations@theberiversafaris.com; w theberiversafaris.com. This long-established, family-owned site is about 5km from the centre of town, by the Puma fuel station. The base for Thebe River Safaris (page 238), it is well run & retains something of the feel of a popular backpackers' lodge. Simple, clean, modern rooms are built in a thatched block around a courtyard. All are en suite, with twin beds (plus 1 family room), mosquito nets, tea & coffee facilities, & ceiling fan.

The campsite is usually occupied by overlanders or travellers taking a trip with Thebe – whose activities are some of the most affordable in Kasane. That said, Thebe do also accept bookings from independent campers. Each of the campsite pitches has access to power supply, water & a braai stand. There's a restaurant, bar & a small pool nearer the river. Transfers & day trips can be arranged to & from Victoria Falls & Livingstone (day trip P960 pp). *P876 pp, B&B; camping P129 pp, exc government bed levy.* **$–$$**

Travelodge [226 B4] (66 rooms) Plateau Rd; 625 0625; e gm.kasane@travelodge.co.bw; w travelodgekasane.co.bw. There's no missing the corporate lime green & grey of this hotel, which is geared largely to the conference market. That said, it's pretty close to the airport, so could offer a practical bed for the night if you arrive late or are leaving early. Small but innocuous rooms have the standard hotel fittings, including a TV, safe, kettle & fridge, & there's a pool in neat lawned gardens. **$$$**

Water Lily Lodge [226 C2] (10 rooms) President Av; 625 1775; e reservations@waterlilylodge-botswana.com, reservations@janalatours-botswana.com; w waterlilylodge-botswana.com. Water Lily Lodge looks like a giant, cream-washed rondavel built around a central fountain. Nicely presented en-suite rooms overlook the river, with doors on to the garden or a small balcony. Inside are twin beds & mosquito nets, plus AC, TV, safe, desk, fridge & kettle.

Meals can be taken in the attractive restaurant or outside on a thatched terrace alongside a convivial bar & a small, kidney-shaped pool. The à la carte menu ($$) focuses on fresh fish (including excellent bream), steaks & chicken dishes & local cuisine, as well as lighter lunches. Boat cruises, game drives & day trips to Victoria Falls are on offer through their own tour company, Janala Tours (page 238). **$$$**

B&Bs and self-catering

Chobe River Cottages [226 C2] (6 rooms) President Av; 625 2863; m 7553 2117; e bookings@choberivercottages.com; w choberivercottages.com. This secure set-up is smart & airy, with modern apartment-style rooms adorned with evocative aerial photographs. Stroll past the small free-form pool (with separate baby pool), & the warthogs pulling at the grass beyond, & you'll come to a high viewing deck above the river.

From the large kitchenette off the lounge area to the bedrooms with AC & ceiling fans, it's all exceptionally well equipped. There's a sofa bed in the lounge for an extra couple of guests, & the veranda even has a giant mosquito-net curtain so you can sit out in privacy & comfort after dinner cooked on your own barbecue. If you don't fancy self-catering (SPAR is just a short walk away for supplies), then Coffee Buzz is on hand for b/fast & lunch, with the Old House for an evening meal. *Rate is exc b/fast.* **$$$**

Kasane Self Catering [226 C2] (2 cottages, family room) President Av; 625 0114; m 7553 2117; e trish@chobeselfcatering. com; w chobeselfcatering.com. Under the same ownership as Chobe River Cottages, & almost adjacent, these 2 cottages have an entirely different style & atmosphere. Each has a leafy porch & chairs

looking out to the tranquil, verdant gardens of Trish Williams's home, a haven for birds (including several endemics) that showcases her profession as a landscape gardener. In the bedrooms – a twin & a dbl – handmade patchwork quilts lend a homely touch to dark-wood traditional furniture, yet there's AC to keep the temperature down, a kitchenette with all that you could need for self-catering, & a private barbecue area. There is also a family room, suitable for 2 adults & 2 children, with a dbl bed & sofa bed, & a small private garden & braai. Here, as at Chobe River Cottages, there are safes, secure parking & free Wi-Fi, & guests are welcome to use the neighbouring pool & riverside viewing deck. *Rate is exc b/fast.* **$$**

The Old House [226 C2] (10 rooms) Same contact details as the restaurant (see below). This popular, family-run restaurant offers B&B in clean, comfortable, unpretentious rooms, decorated by a local artist. All have AC & en-suite showers. The complex is wheelchair-accessible, as is 1 of the rooms. There's free Wi-Fi, secure parking, a plunge pool & a very good gift shop – & of course the relaxed, pub-style bar & restaurant. The normal range of activities can be organised, including morning 4x4 game viewing, sunset river cruises & full-day safaris into Chobe National Park (10mins away). *US$95 pp, B&B.* **$$$**

✕ WHERE TO EAT AND DRINK Between them, Kasane's hotels and lodges offer a range of restaurants, some of them very good, and most visitors choose to eat in their place of accommodation.

For something more relaxed, seek out the Old House, or PPCC next to the fuel station, which majors on good Indian cuisine. For a more local flavour, there's the restaurant at Water Lily Lodge (page 231). And if you're craving fast food, Kasane can oblige in the form of Nando's in Tlou Safari Mall [227 E2], next to the Puma garage.

Coffee Buzz [226 C2] 721 President Av; m 7127 5509; ⏲ 07.00–16.00 daily. Bettina Kelly's pleasant, fan-cooled café does a good b/fast, as well as coffee & cakes, fresh juices, milkshakes & a range of lunch dishes. The menu, dubbed 'German-African' cuisine, includes 2 daily specials, 1 of which is vegetarian, alongside burgers, Chobe fish & chips, & serious sandwiches. Relax in the garden around the small pool or on cushion-clad benches at wooden tables inside. **$$**

The Old House [226 C2] 718 President Av; 625 2562; e reservations@oldhousekasane. com; w oldhousekasane.com; ⏲ 06.30–21.30 daily. This relaxed old favourite is a popular

place, with wooden tables & sports TV for the latest on the rugby field. Food – focusing on burgers, steaks, salads & pizzas – is served under cover or on a wooden poolside deck facing the garden, where you can wander down to the river. If you're coming in the evening, it's best to book. **$$–$$$**

PPCC [226 B3] 81 President Av; 625 2237; ⏲ 10.00–22.00 daily. Opposite Hunters Africa Mall, PPCC (Pizza Plus Coffee & Curry) is a central spot, popularly known as 'The Indian', with a great reputation & good vegetarian options. Eat inside or out on the small, shaded terrace set back from the road; take-away available. **$$**

SHOPPING
Food and drink The town's reliable **supermarkets** are the most accessible for travellers: SPAR [226 B2] (⏱ 07.30–19.00 Mon–Fri, 08.00–18.00 Sat, 08.00–17.00 Sun), opposite the Shell garage, Choppies at both Water Front Mall [226 B3] (⏱ 07.30–19.00 Mon–Fri, 07.00–18.00 Sat, 08.00–17.00 Sun) and Kazungula Junction [227 G3] (⏱ 08.30–19.30 Mon–Sat, 14.00–19.30 Sun), and Shoprite in Tlou Safari Mall [227 E2] at the Kasane turn-off. These are well stocked with fresh produce, meat and bakery items, alongside a wide selection of dried and tinned items and just about everything you'd need for a camping trip, from matches and thermos flasks to foldaway chairs.

While supermarkets themselves are not licensed to sell **alcohol**, SPAR has its own off-licence, Tops (Hunters Africa Mall; ⏱ 10.00–19.00 Mon–Fri, 10.00–18.00 Sat), on the parade in front of the supermarket.

Crafts, gifts and books These are the domain of the gift shops at the various hotels along the river, with Chobe Safari Lodge [226 B4] among the best.

It's also worth checking out the various craft shops in the parade behind SPAR [226 B2], and the mosaics at Coffee Buzz [226 C2]. For locally made baskets and other crafts, venture up to the Chobe Women's Arts and Crafts Centre (see below) and browse the market stalls around the Shell garage area for wooden curios and lengths of colourful local fabric to jazz up your table.

Buzzadi Trading [226 C2] Coffee Buzz, President Av; m 7131 8956; ⏱ 08.00–16.00 Mon–Sat. An eclectic little gift shop at Coffee Buzz, featuring an array of locally handmade items: Bettina Kelly's mosaic mirror frames, colourful paintings, kitenge soft toys, basketry & much more.

Chobe Women's Arts & Crafts Centre [226 B4] Airport Rd; ⏱ 10.00–16.30 daily, but hours can vary. Based next to the CARACAL World of Wildlife, this is a co-operative of 16 or so women who get together to make traditional baskets & to teach their skills to others. In theory, the women

work in situ, so that visitors can watch them dye the palm leaves, weave, & meet the person who created 'their' basket; in practice, opening hours are a little erratic & there are often only a couple of women here at a time. They are gentle, kind-hearted & delighted to talk about their craft, so it's well worth taking time to visit & chat…& source a personal souvenir.

Gecko Gift Shop [226 C2] At the Old House (see opposite); ⏱ 08.00–17.00 daily. This colourful Aladdin's cave of gifts, jewellery & textiles is found at the Old House – so you can combine browsing with a spot of lunch or a drink.

Clothes and equipment Kasane is a small town with limited shopping options beyond essentials. **PEP** and **Dunns** [226 B2] (both Hunters Africa Mall; ⏱ 08.30–17.30 Mon–Fri, 09.00–13.00 Sat–Sun) sell everyday tops, trousers and shoes in an emergency. For items of safari clothing, you'll probably do better at the shops in the larger hotels. For other essentials, the supermarkets are well stocked.

OTHER PRACTICALITIES Kasane is an obvious spot for changing money, with a couple of **banks** plus several ATMs, including at the Puma and Engen fuel stations. If you're planning to change currency, it's normally quicker to go to one of the town's **bureaux de change**, where rates are only slightly lower than at the bank, queues are shorter, and opening hours are considerably longer. While working out how much cash to change, note that park fees are best paid in pula, so bear this in mind if you're intending to drive yourself through the national parks.

Local **SIM cards** can be purchased at many outlets, including Orange at the SPAR [226 B2], Cell City [226 F2] beside Tlou Safari Mall and Cell World at

Kazungula Junction [227 G3]. Particularly efficient is the Mascom office tucked almost out of sight next to Choppies at Water Front Mall [226 B3] (⏰ normal shopping hours).

Kasane's main **post office** [227 G3] (⏰ 08.00–16.00 Mon–Fri, 08.30–noon Sat) is at Kazungula Junction. A second, smaller office [226 B3] (⏰ 08.00–16.00 Mon–Fri, 08.00–11.00 Sat) remains in the town, just down from Water Front Mall. You can also get stamps in the larger hotels.

If you're unlucky enough to **break down**, Kasane's not a bad place to do so, as it's used as a supply base by some of the safari operators. Certainly if you're heading across Chobe and Moremi you should make sure your vehicle's in tip-top shape before you head off.

Kasane's **hospital** [226 B3] (📞 0800 600898) is on the main road towards Chobe Safari Lodge. The town also offers a couple of private clinics along with a dentist and a pharmacy.

Banks

ABSA [226 B2] By the SPAR; 📞 625 0221; ⏰ 08.30–15.30 Mon–Fri, 08.15–10.45 Sat. ATMs at SPAR & Choppies supermarket [226 B3].

B&BS Bank [226 B3] Water Front Mall; 📞 625 2460; ⏰ 08.30–15.30 Mon–Fri, 08.15–10.45 Sat

First National Bank [226 B4] Water Front Mall; 📞 625 2414; ⏰ 09.00–15.00 Mon–Fri, 09.00–11.00 Sat. Outside ATMs & full bank services.

Bureaux de change

Open Door Bureau de Change [226 B2] SPAR; 📞 625 2088; w foreignexchangebotswana.com; ⏰ 08.00–18.00 Mon–Fri, 08.30–16.00 Sat, 09.00–16.00 Sun. Other branches at Hunters Africa Mall [226 B2] & Kazungula Junction [227 G3].

Unimoni Exchange m 7236 4397; w unimoni. com; ⏰ 08.00–19.00 Mon–Sat, 14.00–19.00 Sun. Branches inside Choppies stores at both Water Front Mall [226 B3] & Kazungula Junction [227 G3].

IT and photography

Kasane Computers [226 B3] Audi Centre; 📞 625 2312; m 7520 7936; e info@kasanecomputers.com; w kasanecomputers.com; ⏰ 08.00–17.00 Mon–Fri, 08.00–13.00 Sat. Selling memory sticks, camera memory cards, batteries & even cheap cameras, as well as IT & office supplies. They'll also download your digital photos on to a memory stick – a great back-up in case of memory-card disasters – or print them.

Vehicle repairs and equipment

Halfway Toyota Chobe [227 F2] 152 Upper Rd; 📞 625 0772; w halfwaychobe.com; ⏰ 07.30–17.30 Mon–Fri, 08.00–13.00 Sat. Official Toyota dealership with a dedicated workshop for servicing and repairs.

Motovac [226 B3] Close to the Shell garage in Kasane & [227 G3] at Kazungula Junction; 📞 625 0848; ⏰ 08.00–17.00 Mon–Fri, 08.00–13.00 Sat, 09.00–13.00 Sun. Sells spares for most major makes, including Land Rover, Nissan & Toyota.

Health

New Hope Private Clinic [226 C2] 720 President Av; 📞 625 1733; m 7199 3199; e newhopeprivateclinic@gmail.com; f newhopeprivateclinic; ⏰ 08.00–17.00 Mon–Fri, 08.00–14.00 Sat. General medical consultancy.

Pharma Africa [226 B3] Audi Centre; 📞 625 1502; m 7120 7667, emergency 7322 8502; ⏰ 09.00–18.00 Mon–Fri, 08.00–14.00 Sat, 10.00–noon Sun. Good consulting pharmacy.

Poly Clinic [227 G3] Kazungula Junction; 📞 625 1548; m 7267 2140; ⏰ 07.00–18.00 Mon–Fri, 09.00–15.00 Sat, 11.00–13.00 Sun. Small pharmacy with a polyclinic offering X-ray & laboratory facilities, & links to a doctor, paramedic & MRI.

Smiles Dental Clinic [227 G3] Kazungula Junction; 📞 680 0090; m 7410 4383; e info@ smilesdental.co.bw, ⏰ 08.00–17.00 Mon–Fri, 09.00–13.00 Sat

WHAT TO SEE AND DO Attractions in Kasane itself are limited to a handful of relatively low-key wildlife and recreational operations. There is, though, the rather quirky **Mowana Post Tree** [226 B3], in the grounds of the police station, but still accessible to the public. Over the years, this venerable old baobab, with its capacious hollow trunk, has served variously as a jail, a mail collection point and – in the 1960s – as a recruitment station for men going to work in the South African mines. The connection was one of logistics, since the mail, the prisoners and the miners were all transported in the same vehicles.

CARACAL World of Wildlife [226 B4] (3102 Airport Rd; ✆ 625 2392; e admin@caracal.info; w caracal.info; ⏰ 10.00–16.00 daily; standard tour P95; behind scenes tour P150) This is a great place to see some of Botswana's smaller indigenous fauna. From mambas, cobras and boomslangs you'll move on to other, harmless snakes, along with bushbabies, chameleons, raptors, vultures and banded mongooses. These last are the subject of a research project by CARACAL (the Centre for Conservation of African Resources: Animals, Communities and Land use) into why the animals are contracting a new strain of (non-human) TB.

A standard tour, lasting between 45 minutes and an hour, introduces visitors to the diet, physical characteristics and habits of the various inhabitants of the centre. More hands-on is the 'behind the scenes' tour, lasting an extra half an hour or so, when you also get to hold some of the more benign snakes. A visit here is worth combining with a stop at the low-key Chobe Women's Arts and Crafts Centre (page 233), which occupies a thatched building at the entrance.

Chobe Crocodile Farm [227 F2] (✆ 625 0430; e crocsue@gmail.com; ▪ chobecrocfarm; ⏰ 08.00–12.30 & 14.00–16.30 Mon–Fri, 08.00–13.00 Sat, open public holidays; P100/40–60 adult/child) A long-running family business, Kasane's crocodile farm, down a quiet lane close to Kubu Lodge, is a particularly good place to take children, with tours during which you can see the eggs, hatchlings and larger creatures. Do phone ahead, though; opening hours can change.

Spa treatments Kasane isn't bad on the pampering front. Though spas at the likes of Chobe Chilwero are exclusive to lodge guests, those at some of the bigger hotels are open to non-residents as well. At Chobe Safari Lodge (page 229) you'll find **Spa Kwa Maningi** [226 B3] (m 7155 9522; e kwamaningi@gmail.com; w chobesafarilodge.com; ⏰ 09.00–17.00 daily); options at this small spa range from exfoliations, pedicures and manicures to waxing and tinting, and their 'signature' treatments: a traditional African foot wash (US$85) and the 60-minute Hakuna Matata (US$85), combining massage, facial cleansing and sun protection. There's also the **Cresta Mowana Safari Resort & Spa** [226 C1] (page 229); with four treatment rooms, a sauna, steam room, hot tub and serene infinity pool, this is a place for serious self-indulgence, backed by Clarins products. There's the option of open-air sessions, too, overlooking the river, and a double treatment room for couples.

Other activities In Kasane, Cresta Mowana Safari Resort & Spa [226 C1] (page 229) has a **tennis** court, **gym** and nine-hole **golf** course that are open to all. Although the local branch of Birdlife Botswana does not currently organise **birdwatching** excursions, recommended birding guides in Kasane include Spokes Ntswabi at Classified Safaris (m 7142 1153; ▪ ClassiSafaris) and Peace Shamuka at Last Eden Safaris (m 7177 0324, 7123 3235; e p.shamuka@last-eden.com;

w last-edensafaris.com). In town, look out around dusk for **bat hawks** hunting above residential areas for Mozambique free-tailed bats on the wing.

Several tour operators run **fishing** trips on the Chobe and Zambezi rivers, in search of bream and tigerfish, and **canoeing and mokoro** trips on the Chobe River can be organised from the western side of the park (page 261).

AROUND KASANE

CHOBE NATIONAL PARK (NORTHERN AREA) (⊕ Apr–Sep 06.00–18.30 daily, Oct–Mar 05.30–19.00 daily; P190 pp with Botswana tour operator, P270 pp & P30–115/vehicle for self-drivers) The Sedudu Gate entrance to Chobe National Park is a 10-minute drive from Kasane, so visitors to the town can easily explore the park's northern area from a game-drive vehicle or from the river – the latter being one of the region's top attractions. Excursions can be organised either through your lodge, or directly with one of a handful of small local safari operators (see opposite), while 4x4 self-drivers can explore themselves. Costs for boat cruises and game drives vary considerably according to the operator, the style and the number of participants, but average around US$40 per person for 3 hours for each activity, plus park fees.

River trips Boat cruises range from ten-seater motorboats to double-storey boats taking large groups on a champagne breakfast. Most trips last around 3 hours (from US$32), but local operator Flame of Africa (see opposite) – veterans of the river for 25 years – have a triple-decker boat, the *Chobe Explorer*, which operates full-day excursions (from US$127 pp inc lunch & bar drinks; ⊕ 11.00–sunset) around Impalila Island and into the national park for up to 26 passengers. Up top there are shaded sunloungers, with more seating on the middle deck, and a restaurant, which serves a buffet barbecue lunch.

The game viewing from the river can be surprisingly good, especially in the later afternoon during the latter half of the dry season. Large numbers of elephants are virtually guaranteed, and often whole herds will cross the river from one side to the other.

Some of the lodges/operators will send you out on a private little boat with a driver and a coolbox. The small boats give you a lot more flexibility in what you concentrate on, and how long you stop somewhere, as it's just a question of requesting what you want to do from your boat captain. It's certainly our favourite way to see the Chobe riverfront area, and probably remains one of our favourite safari experiences in Africa. It can be magical.

Given the number of lodges in the area, the river can become quite full of boats at times, so if you want a quieter, all-day experience, try and arrange for a boat to depart as early as possible. Most of the cruises don't leave until after 09.00, so you'll have the river almost to yourself for a few hours – apart from the occasional Namibian fisherman in a mokoro (there's no fishing allowed in the national park from Botswana).

With the 2021 opening of the impressive Kazungula Bridge, several operators now also offer 2-hour boat trips (US$59) to see the bridge and visit the world's only 'quadripoint' – the meeting of four countries at a single spot – in the Zambezi.

Game drives Organised game drives generally head west straight into the national park, and then cover the game-drive roads and loops around the riverfront area (see from page 252 for more details of these areas). If you're organising a trip with a local company, remember to compare the various options available, asking how long the drive is, and how much of that time it takes to get to the park gate and back. Typically trips last about 3 hours (from US$32), with some operators offering a 5-hour trip including a bush lunch (check out Flame of Africa's 'Chobe Chow' from US$110), and a few whole-day excursions (from US$102), either all by 4x4 or divided between vehicle and boat cruise.

Naturally, the lodges further east will spend more of this getting to and from the park than those further west, but in some cases they build in extra time to allow for the longer journey. Either way you're going to find yourself mostly around the eastern side of the riverfront area, where traffic densities are relatively high.

The national park allows driving only in daylight hours, so lodges that advertise night drives are conducting these outside the park, in areas where big game is much more limited.

National park permits Self-drivers should note that the Sedudu Gate into Chobe National Park (625 0235) is one of the busiest of the national-park gates, and hefty queues can be anticipated, especially between June and October. Thus do allow plenty of time, or – if an early start is important – pay your fees the night before. Although technically these can be paid in pula, US dollars, sterling, rand or by Visa or Mastercard, in reality it's best to stick to pula or – if the machines are working – a bank card. There is some discrepancy about other currencies, and even when they are accepted, the rate of exchange can be very poor. For those planning to camp, there is a handy kiosk here manned by staff from SKL (625 0113; ⏰ 08.30–17.00 daily), who run the Savute and Linyanti campsites within Chobe National Park, and Kwalate Safaris, who operate Ihaha Campsite, also in Chobe, along with Xakanaxa and South Gate (Maqwe) in Moremi. For more details, see page 213.

Technically, independent drivers are not allowed into the park until after 10.00, allowing the tour operators to get in first, though it's hard to ascertain if this is enforced. In practice, access times probably depend on how busy the gate is on a given morning.

Tour operators, safari companies and travel agents Because overland truck companies that are not officially registered in Botswana can't use their own vehicles in the park, there's a strong market in Kasane for day trips into Chobe. Most of the hotels and lodges organise these for their own guests, but some welcome outsiders too, and there are also several independent companies. There is also a handful of mobile safari operators based in Kasane.

For those all-important national park bookings, make your way to Chobe National Park's Sedudu Gate (page 236).

African Odyssey [226 B3] Chobe Marina Lodge; 625 0500; m 7354 9482; e botsreservations@bots.wildhorizons.co.zw; w wildhorizons.co.za. Offers game drives, river cruises, fishing, various guided trips & walks in the Kasane area. Partners with Wild Horizons in Zimbabwe for seamless border transfers & Victoria Falls activities.

Big Sam Hubber [226 C2] President Av, nr the Old House; 625 0947; m 7355 0441; e info@ bigsamhubber.co.bw; w bigsamhubber.co.bw; ⓕ bigsamhubberbotswana. Recommended locally, Big Sam offers reliable & affordable boat cruises (3hrs, US$25 pp), game drives (3hrs, US$35 pp) & Victoria Falls trips (US$45 pp), as well as Falls transfers (US$10 one-way) & camping trips (US$220–415 pp, 1–3 nights).

Flame of Africa [226 B2] 22 Hunters Africa Mall, President Av; 625 2248; m 7375 0380; e kasane@flameofafrica.com; w flameofafrica. com. Experienced company offering most excursions in the Kasane area, including full-day trips on their triple-decker boat, the *Chobe Explorer* (from US$127 pp), Kazungula Bridge tour (US$34 pp) & Chobe 4x4 day trips (from US$106 pp).

Janala Tours & Safaris [226 C2] Water Lily Lodge, President Av; 625 1775; m 7127 8288; e reservations@janalatours-botswana.com; w janalatours-botswana.com. This tour company linked to Water Lily Lodge offers some of the more affordable trips into the national park (3/day; US$37 pp), as well as boat cruises & mobile safaris further afield.

Kalahari Tours & Safaris [226 C2] 721 President Av, next to Coffee Buzz; 625 0880; m 7389 7596; e info@kalahari-tours.net; w kalaharichobe.com. This is the place for day trips & a range of simple, short camping safaris into Chobe National Park.

Malachite Safaris m 7354 9482; e malachitesafaris@gmail.com. Reggie specialises in canoe trips on the Chobe River (page 252). He also offers game drives & boat trips.

Pangolin Photo Safaris 625 1945; m 7642 9758; e info@pangolinphoto.com; w pangolinphoto.com. The ultimate tour company for photographers – from beginners to experienced – Pangolin uses custom-built vehicles & boats with swivelling tripods, & DSLR cameras & telephoto lenses supplied. Operating set-departure, multi-day trips from their Kasane base, with experienced photo guides & a firm focus on delivering super wildlife photography opportunities. Small-group trips (max 8), combining Botswana's Ker & Downey properties & Pangolin Chobe Hotel are an excellent option.

Thebe River Safaris [227 E1] 625 1272; e reservations@theberiversafaris.com; w theberiversafaris.com. As well as running a popular campsite & lodge (page 231), Thebe organises its own realistically priced game drives & boat cruises into the national park. It is also the base for a mobile-safari operation, with tailor-made & set trips around northern Botswana. Run by the whole van Wyk family, trips are graded 'budget, middle or luxury' depending on how much effort & money you are willing to expend.

Further afield Most of the lodges and tour operators in Kasane can organise trips further afield, including mokoro trips close to Ngoma, village walks across the river in Namibia, and excursions to Victoria Falls in Zambia or Zimbabwe – the last with or without a guide.

ON THE NAMIBIAN BORDER Although technically on Namibian soil, there are several lodges on the northern side of the Chobe River that use Kasane as a base. Many of their visitors come through Kasane, and their activities feature trips on the river beside the park.

One of these – Chobe Savanna Lodge – stands on land directly opposite the national park, and is covered, along with various riverboats, on page 258. Three others lie northeast of Kasane, on Impalila Island, and a fourth, Chobe Water Villas, is just north of Sedudu Island, and are listed on page 241. For more extensive detail on the Impalila area, and the rest of Namibia's Zambezi Region (Caprivi Strip), see one of my other guidebooks: *Namibia: The Bradt Guide*.

Impalila Island area Around Kazungula is the confluence of the Chobe and the Zambezi. The Zambezi flows relentlessly to the sea but, depending on their relative heights, the Chobe either contributes to that, or (occasionally) reverses its flow and draws water from the Zambezi. Trapped between the two rivers is a triangle of land, of about 700km², which is a mixture of floodplains, islands and channels that link the two rivers. This swampy, riverine area is home to several thousand people of Namibian nationality, mostly members of Zambia's Lozi tribe. (The main local languages here are Lozi and Subiya.) Most have a seasonal lifestyle, living next to the river channels, fishing and farming maize, sorghum, pumpkins and keeping cattle. They move with the water levels to higher, drier ground as the waters rise.

The largest island in this area, Impalila Island, is at the far eastern tip of Namibia, home to around 2,000 people living in some 43 small villages. It gained notoriety during the 1980s as a military base for the South African Defence Forces (SADF), as it was strategically positioned within sight of Botswana, Zambia and Zimbabwe. It still boasts a 1,300m-long runway (✪ 17°46.48'S, 025°11.23'[E]) of compressed gravel, used today by charter airlines to bring visitors to the lodges, but the barracks are now a school, serving most of the older children in the area.

If you transfer to the island from Kasane, you'll have to clear customs and immigration for both Botswana and Namibia on arrival and departure. Fortunately, as borders go, the **customs and immigration post** on the island (⊕ 07.30–16.30) is fairly laid-back and informal.

Flora and fauna Impalila Island, along with the channels and floodplains to its west, is part of a 73km² conservancy, created in 2005 and locally managed by the community to sustainably use the natural resources, protect wildlife and empower the local community.

The area's **ecosystems** are similar to those in the upper reaches of the Okavango Delta: deep-water channels lined by wide reedbeds and rafts of papyrus. Some of the larger islands are still forested with baobabs, water figs, knobthorn, umbrella thorn, mopane, pod mahogany, star chestnut and sickle-leaved albizia, while jackalberry and Chobe waterberry overhang the rivers, festooned with creepers and vines.

With the exception of small populations of bushbuck, warthog and common impala in the island's woodlands, **large mammals** are scarce around Impalila itself, and those that do occur swim over from Chobe. Elephants and buffalo sometimes swim over to Namibia, and even lions have been known to take to the river in search of the tasty-but-dim domestic cattle kept there. For wildlife viewing, most visitors here will head on water safaris along the Chobe River.

Even with few large mammals here, the **birdlife** is spectacular, with over 450 recorded species in the area. For many birdwatchers, the prime time to visit begins with the arrival of the summer migrants in September, when the local bird population rises by up to 20%, and extends through to March. From December to March, the birds are in full breeding plumage, making for spectacular sightings and great photographic opportunities. Year-round, the river is home to myriad birds though: large flocks of white-faced ducks congregate on islands in the rivers, African skimmers nest on exposed sandbanks, and both reed cormorants and darters are seen fishing or perching while they dry their feathers. Kingfishers are numerous, from the giant to the tiny pygmy, as are herons, egrets and open-billed storks. However, the area's most unusual bird is the unassuming rock pratincole with its black, white and grey body, which perches on rocks within the rapids and hawks for insects in the spray.

Where to stay Visitors to the island arrive either by air at the small airstrip or by boat from Kasane. The island location means that none of the lodges here operate their own game drives to Chobe; they're limited to water-based safaris.

Cascades Safari Lodge [226 C1] (8 chalets) Ntwala Island; w croisieurope.travel/lodge/cascade-lodge. As with Kaza Safari Lodge (page 240), Cascade is now owned by river cruise company, CroisiEurope, & generally only hosts travellers on their set itinerary trips. The location is beautifully secluded: a cluster of islands within the Mambova Rapids, reached from a natural reed-fringed harbour. Long wooden walkways lead to the main area, facing the rapids, & on to the chalets. The large dining area & comfortable lounge are smartly decorated with large black-&-white photographs, white beaded chandeliers & leather sofas. Both open on to a wide tiered terrace with a great view across the river.

Each of the wooden chalets has sliding glass doors on to a wooden veranda, overlooking the rapids. Inside, gleaming timber floors & traditionally styled furniture sit alongside AC, Wi-Fi & TV. The en-suite bathrooms are large, with moulded concrete baths, twin sinks & a separate shower & toilet. Outside, the well-screened private terrace & palm-shaded plunge pool are both perfect spots to soak up the riverfront views. A fleet of aluminium boats is at the ready for guests to explore the quiet backwaters, indulge in a spot of fishing, or take in a sunset cruise. ☉ *All year.* 😺😺😺

Ichingo Chobe River Lodge [226 D1] (8 Meru tents) ✆ +44 808 189 0987 (UK), +1 800 865 1547 (US); e enquiry@zqcollection.com; w ichingochoberiverlodge.com. Ichingo occupies a secluded site on the south of Impalila Island, overlooking the quiet backwaters of some of the Chobe River's rapids, a world away from busy Kasane just across the water. In same fold as the *Zambezi Queen* & *Chobe Princess* riverboats (page 258), Ichingo retains the warm atmosphere of a lovely old lodge, enhanced over recent years with increased creature comforts: AC, king-size beds (or large twins) & larger bathrooms in the walk-in tents, colourful cushions in the lounge area, & a smart plunge pool overlooking the rapids.

Each of the classic Meru safari tents is set high above the flood levels – important in a location where the rise & fall of water is up to 2m. Simply but comfortably decorated with tiled, en-suite shower rooms at the back & a shaded deck at the front, with views of the Chobe River through the vegetation, dominated by the water-tolerant waterberry trees & the orange-fruited mangosteen. Meals are taken around a large wooden table in the thatched central area that fronts on to the river, or under the stars on the riverbank.

The lodge is a super base for birdwatching, fishing (popular with families & fly-fishermen – who bring their own equipment – on the rapids) & wildlife viewing from their fleet of little boats along the Chobe River, some of which are customised for photographers. There are also visits to a local Namibian village & walks to a giant, 2,000-year-old baobab, the 'Tree of Life'. *SA Rand 8,562 pp (US$445) Mar–Nov, SA Rand 7,922 pp (US$412) Dec–Feb, FBA inc road transfer (from Kasane airport/border) & boat transfer to Namibian immigration, exc Chobe National Park game drives. Children all ages.* ☉ *All year.* 😺😺😺

Kaza Safari Lodge [226 C1] (8 chalets) w croisieurope.co.uk/lodge/kaza-lodge. Situated on the northwest of Impalila Island, overlooking the Zambezi's Mambova Rapids, the former Impalila Island Lodge served in many ways to bring the island to people's attention. Now owned by river cruise company CroisiEurope, it is primarily used by guests on its southern African itineraries. Kaza has a peaceful location, about 45mins by boat from Kasane (or a shorter boat trip to the south of Impalila Island followed by a 10min drive). The large thatched bar/dining area, with a comfortable lounge, built beside a huge 700-year-old baobab, opens on to the elevated, riverside terrace. Adjacent to this, the lovely infinity pool, & its umbrella-shaded reclining loungers, also have terrific views across the river.

Set in lush lawns & accessed by timber boardwalks, each of the pale, painted chalets has sliding glass doors on to a small veranda with a plunge pool overlooking the river through palm fronds. Inside, furniture is made from local mukwa wood, with its warm yellow hue, & there are comfortable king-size beds, wicker armchairs & new, modern en suites with freestanding bath & shower.

There are boat cruises, sunset cruises & fishing excursions, while back on land, you can walk to a local village from the lodge, take an ox-cart to the 2,000-year-old 'Tree of Life' baobab or explore by bike with a guide. ☉ *All year.* 😺😺😺

Sedudu Island area The precise boundary between Namibia and Botswana in this area has been defined to follow the deepest channel of the Chobe River – a definition that works well for most river boundaries. However, the Chobe splits into many streams, whose strengths and depths seem to gradually alter over the years.

Sedudu Island (or Kasikili Island, as it's called in Namibia) is a very low, flat island which covers about 3.5km² when the waters are low, but shrinks to a much smaller size when it is flooded. It's used mainly for grazing cattle.

Both Botswana and Namibia have claimed that the island belongs to them. In the 1990s, it was occupied by the Botswana Defence Force (BDF) who built several watchtowers on it – chunky structures towering over the island's grassy plains, and cunningly disguised with variegated military-pattern netting. In early 1995, both

Botswana and Namibia agreed to put the issue before the International Court of Justice (ICJ) in The Hague, and in 1996 they both agreed to abide by its eventual judgement.

Botswana argued that the northern channel was the main river channel, while Namibia maintained that the southern channel was the larger one. Finally, in December 1999, the ICJ pronounced that the border should 'follow the line of the deepest soundings in the northern channel of the Chobe River around Kasikili-Sedudu Island'.

That said, the court also diplomatically ruled that 'in the two channels around Kasikili-Sedudu Island, the nationals of, and vessels flying the flags of, the Republic of Botswana and the Republic of Namibia shall enjoy equal national treatment'.

For visitors, this means that game-viewing boats from both countries are allowed on both sides of this tiny, troublesome patch of floodplain!

Where to stay Map, page 220

There's just one lodge in this area, on the northern banks of the Chobe River as it skirts Sedudu Island.

Chobe Water Villas (16 chalets) +264 81 122 7991; e chobe.res@ol.na; w chobewatervillas.com. Looking across to Sedudu Island from Namibia's Kasika Conservancy, & nearer to the park than any of Impalila Island's lodges, Chobe Water Villas exude contemporary chic. A clean-lines design, natural colour palette & details inspired by aspects of Namibian culture & environment lend a modern twist to African style: 'rain chimes' in the elegant restaurant mimic thunder when stirred by the breeze, woven bird's-nest lampshades hover over the bar & striking wildlife photography inspires. The library & the cleverly screened buffet area are thoughtful touches, & for the warmer months, there's an infinity pool mirroring the Chobe River, & a drinks table set in a shallow pool of water for cocktails with cool toes. For cooler evenings, firepits materialise riverside, or you can snuggle in the cosy sunken seating areas. With Wi-Fi throughout & sports TV in a small meeting room, the outside world isn't far away though.

The impressive thatched chalets stand on stilts at the water's edge, their decks, complete with telescopes, offering almost unbroken views from wooden sunloungers, as if from the prow of a ship. For extra seclusion, 4 of them are on 'honeymoon island', reached across a bouncy suspension bridge. Inside, all is calm & orderly, with the same contemporary styling, a king-size bed & comfortable sofa, ceiling fan (no AC), Nespresso machine, complimentary minibar, & a great big bathroom with a separate shower & bath. Power is supplied by a combination of solar panels & generator, with inverters for lights at night.

Game drives & river cruises in & around Chobe National Park are included in the rates; other options, such as village tours & trips to Victoria Falls, can be organised at extra cost. Guests usually arrive by boat from Kasane, clearing Namibian immigration at Kasika.

At the time of finalising this guide, Chobe Water Villas were undergoing renovations & we were informed that 'significant changes' with the business were afoot, so do double-check the latest information if you're considering visiting. ☾ *All year.* ♕♕♕–♕♕♕♕

LESOMA VALLEY Some 20km from Kasane, the tranquil Lesoma Valley (also spelled Lehsoma or Lisoma) lies to the east of the main Kasane–Nata road, in the Kasane Forest Reserve. It also sees a reasonable amount of wildlife, especially in the dry season when elephant are regular visitors to the camps' waterholes, along with various antelope and the occasional predator. For those seeking a more affordable option away from the bustle of Kasane, this area could be worth considering.

Where to stay Map, page 220

Chobe Bush Camp (9 chalets) m 7567 0336; e reservations@chobebushcamp-botswana.com; w chobebushcamp-botswana.com; ◈ WLB&BC 17°52.770'S, 25°14.114'E. Just south of Senyati, this laid-back bush camp is under the same ownership as Water Lily Lodge (page 231) in Kasane. 5 thatched, en-suite, khaki canvas chalets are built on high stilts overlooking a waterhole, & 4 dbl chalets are grouped together in a block with travelling groups in mind. The accommodation here is separated from the waterhole by a fence. It's a solar camp, with generator power only in the

evening, & no Wi-Fi, so arrive with your tech & cameras well charged. There's a photography hide beside the waterhole & excursions are operated by Water Lily's own tour company (page 231): 3hr Chobe game drive or boat cruise (both from US$37 pp). *US$140 pp, B&B; US$165 pp, FB.* **$$$$**
Elephant Valley Lodge (20 tents) +27 11 568 4264; m 7301 4359; e res@anthology.co.za;

BOTSWANA DEFENCE FORCE   *Tricia Hayne*

Many, if not most, young boys in Botswana, when asked what they'd like to do when they grow up, will respond that they'd like to join the army. If that shows the esteem in which the Botswana Defence Force is held, it gives no indication of the short history that underpins the organisation.

In 1966, when Botswana gained independence from Britain, the country had no military presence. Money was tight, and the best that the government could muster was a paramilitary unit within the police force. At the time, this seemed all that was necessary.

However, despite Botswana's stability, the capacity of this small force was soon swamped by the knock-on effect of anti-colonial struggles along its eastern, southern and western borders. The increasingly violent conflict in Rhodesia saw both refugees and freedom fighters seeking a safe haven in Botswana, but the Rhodesian security forces were swift to follow their dissident population, and the fighting spilled indiscriminately on to Botswana's soil. At the same time, the country's western borders were threatened by similar cross-border skirmishes from South West Africa (now Namibia), then suffering under the apartheid regime of South Africa. To compound the problem, security forces in South Africa itself were crossing into Botswana in their hunt for anti-apartheid activists. Thus, Botswana – and its citizens – were threatened on every side, and the police force was increasingly unable to cope.

It was against this background in 1977 that the Botswana Defence Force was formed. Initially a body of just 600 men, incorporating the police paramilitary unit, it fell under the command of the deputy police commissioner, with Seretse Khama Ian Khama (later Botswana's president) as his deputy.

The new force was soon to come under intense pressure. Only a few months later, on 27 February 1978, reports were received of a Rhodesian military presence just inside Botswana's northeastern border, near Kasane, apparently intent on flushing out anti-government guerrillas from Rhodesia. The BDF responded, only to drive straight into an ambush. In total, 15 members of the force were killed in the incident – the first of the BDF's soldiers to die in action. A memorial to the men who died lies on the road leading down to Lesoma Village (⊕ LESOMA 17°54.528'S, 25°13.470'E).

By the end of the 1980s, Khama himself was in command of the army. Today the BDF is over 12,000 strong, with many of its officers trained in the USA. In addition to internal responsibilities, which include vital anti-poaching patrols in Botswana's national parks, the force is involved in international peacekeeping duties as part of SADC and UN forces.

w elephantvalleylodge.co.za; ⊕ ELEVAL
17°51.193'S, 25°14.585'E. Sister camp to
Kazidora in the Delta, Elephant Valley Lodge is
set in secluded surroundings some 7km south
of Kazungula Junction on Hunters Rd. The final
1.8km to the lodge is a sand track but guests
without a 4x4 can arrange to be picked up at
the junction.

With gnarled tree trunks supporting the low,
thatched entrance, the lodge is traditionally
styled with umber concrete, polished stonework
& heavy wooden furniture. Stepping down into
the main bar, lounge & separate restaurant, the
view opens out & Elephant Valley really comes
into its own. Comfortable seating, raised up
on wooden decking under thatch, overlooks a
good-size, floodlit waterhole, which regularly
attracts elephant & buffalo. There's also an
adjacent infinity pool, surrounded by hanging
chairs & wicker loungers. At the back, classic
walk-in safari tents, on concrete plinths, are
arranged on a shaded grassy site, some around
a 2nd organically shaped pool. Interiors are
comfortable & unpretentious, with an en suite
at the rear of the tent & a few soft chairs on
the porch. While the location is an attraction
in itself, game drives & boat cruises can be
organised in Chobe National Park too, a drive
of about ½hr. *From US$460–480 pp Nov–Apr
to US$589–616 pp May–Oct, FBA.* ⊕ *All
year.* 🦏🦏🦏-🦏🦏🦏🦏

Senyati Safari Camp (8 chalets, camping)
m 7188 1306, 7531 5288; e senyatisafaricamp@
gmail.com; w senyatisafaricampbotswana.
com; ⊕ SENYAT 17°52.331'S, 25°14.167'E. Some
10km from the Engen garage at Kazungula, &
well signposted from the tar road down a 1.8km
sandy track (there's separate 2WD access too),
Senyati has something of a backpackers' vibe.
The place is predominantly self-catering, though
they do sell meat, ice & firewood, & there's a big
bar (⊕ 17.00 daily) & a new restaurant (pre-
book meals before 17.00) looking down on to
the camp's waterhole. Rustic chalets with AC,
simple kitchens & barbecues are dotted around
the site, some attractively thatched, others (more
spacious) built of brick under tin roofs. These
sleep 4–10 people, with bedding supplied. For
the 19 private camping pitches, each with its
own toilet, shower, braai & power point, you'll
need to bring all your own kit, including tents.
Don't miss the subterranean bunker positioned
by the waterhole, offering some great ground-
level photo opportunities of wildlife coming
down to drink. There's also a small pool at the
back surrounded by an electric fence to protect
from elephants, free Wi-Fi in the evenings, & a
laundry service. Game drives, fishing & Victoria
Falls trips can be organised, the last in Senyati's
own 23-seater bus. *Chalet P2,471/dbl; camping
P295/158 adult/child aged 4–11.* ⊕ *All year.*
$$–$$$

HEADING SOUTH FROM KASANE

Kasane is ideally situated for those driving into Botswana's national parks. The road
south to Maun via Chobe and Moremi is covered on page 279. For Kasane to Savuti,
see page 263. For Kasane to Nata, read on.

KASANE TO NATA The long, straight, tarred A3 road from Kasane to Nata covers
some 316km. For self-drivers it is effectively the gateway from Kasane to the
Makgadikgadi Pans and the Central Kalahari Game Reserve, as well as south
to Francistown and Gaborone. It's also increasingly popular with truck drivers
heading to the border, particularly at night, so try to avoid travelling after dark.

Between Kasane and Pandamatenga it's generally a good road surface. That said,
aside from the occasional stopping area, the road is relatively narrow, so it's not
ideal if you're looking for a picnic spot.

Though the journey is not terribly interesting scenically, the road forms a
corridor between the unfenced Chobe National Park and Hwange National Park
over the border in Zimbabwe. As a result, the area sees a fair amount of wildlife,
especially elephants, throughout the year – which for drivers means exercising
considerable caution. As with most roads in rural Africa, driving at night is

asking for trouble – especially as grey elephants are well camouflaged against the grey tarmac.

At the Ngwasha veterinary checkpoint, about 64km north of Nata, you can expect stringent checks for prohibited goods, specifically any form of red meat. Staff regularly confiscate meat from self-drive vehicles, so unless you're prepared to cook it at the roadside, it's not worth taking the risk. The system is there to protect the country's vital cattle industry from the disastrous consequences of foot-and-mouth disease, which can be spread over long distances through contaminated meat, among other things. You may also be asked to get out of your vehicle and sanitise not only the shoes you're wearing but also those in your luggage in a foot trough, so it makes sense to keep all footwear easily accessible.

Where to stay
Places to stay along this road are listed below from north to south. Most are geared to those stopping overnight rather than being destinations in their own right, and some have camping facilities. As the northern part of the road is sandwiched between Chobe and Hwange national parks, the area benefits from the wildlife that roams freely between the two. Thus, at least during the dry season, you could see a fair amount of game, including elephant, giraffe, zebra, tsessebe, sable and possibly wild dog.

For details of places to stay in Nata, see page 481.

Camp Kuzuma [map, page 220] (7 suites) \+27 2 1671 7729; m 7581 7311; e info@campkuzuma. com; w campkuzuma.com; ✪ CAMKUZ 18°20.409'S, 25°29.203'E. Founded in 2011, Camp Kuzuma looks & feels more like a lodge in the Delta. It lies in its own concession just inside the Kazuma Forest Reserve. To find it, turn left off the main road about 65km from Kazungula, on to the cutline towards the Zimbabwean border, then it's a further 3km to the camp.

The elevated main area overlooks a large waterhole frequented by elephant; there's a pool & deck at the front; & inside are a well-stocked bar, coffee machines, open-plan lounge & dining area. It's all very light, stylish & breezy. Well-spaced canvas suites, including a family suite, are accessed along elevated wooden walkways. King-size beds (or twins) form the centrepiece, with bedside tables & 2 chairs. A stone partition at the head of the bed separates the bedroom from the bathroom, with twin basins, twin indoor showers, an outdoor shower, a claw-foot Victorian bathtub – & of course a flush toilet.

An open-sided spa, with a private area for massages overlooking the bush, will appeal to those looking for a little pampering, while activities include morning, evening & night game drives & guided walks. Further afield, sunset cruises & day trips to Chobe National Park &

Victoria Falls can be arranged at extra cost. US$425 pp Apr & Nov, US$620 pp May–Oct, FBA. US$50 pp transfer from Kazungula (one-way). No children under 7. ⊙ Apr–Nov. 🐾🐾🐾–🐾🐾🐾🐾

Elephant Sands Lodge [447 G2] This simple but welcoming spot is clearly signposted 7km south of the vet fence, or 53km north of Nata, & is well known for its busy elephant waterhole. For details, see page 483.

Touch of Africa Safari Lodge [map, page 220] (7 chalets, camping) m 7156 6029; e touchofafricabotswana@gmail.com; ⬛ TouchofAfricaBW; ✪ TOASL 18°30.163'S, 25°36.256'E. Some 100km south of Kazungula, & 5km north of the turning to Pandamatenga, this family-run lodge to the east of the road makes a good stopover. Lawns dotted with lemon trees surround the buildings & a small pool. Comfortable en-suite thatched chalets, each painted a deep orange, are simply furnished with a ceiling fan & shaded veranda. Power is supplied by a generator. B/fast (P40–75) & dinner (P80–130) from an à la carte menu are served in a central dining area, which encompasses a bar & lounge. Guided game drives & guided walks (both P300 pp, min 2 people) can be organised, & there's a waterhole – watch out for herds of sable & giraffe – for evening viewing after a long drive. ⊙ All year. **$$$**

10

Chobe National Park and Forest Reserve

Chobe National Park takes its name from the Chobe River, which forms its northern boundary, and protects about 10,700km² of the northern Kalahari. Its vegetation varies from the lush floodplains beside the Chobe River to the scorched area around the Ghoha Hills, dense forests of cathedral mopane to endless kilometres of mixed, broadleaf woodlands. And then there's the beauty of the newly flowing Savuti Marsh. This is classic big-game country, where herds of buffalo and elephant attain legendary proportions, matched only by some exceptionally large prides of lion.

Much of the park is devoid of water in the dry season, and most of it is inaccessible, so this chapter concentrates on the four main areas of Chobe that are accessible: the Chobe riverfront, Ngwezumba Pans, Savuti and the Linyanti. It also covers the Chobe Forest Reserve, a populated enclave almost surrounded by the park.

BACKGROUND INFORMATION

HISTORY The Chobe's original inhabitants were the Bushmen, followed by the Hambukushu, Bayei and Basubiya. The 1850s saw David Livingstone pass through the area, on his way to seeing Victoria Falls, and a succession of big-game hunters seeking trophies and ivory. The area was first protected as a game reserve in 1961, and then proclaimed a national park in 1968, which was none too early.

Despite this distant trophy-hunting past, the game density in some areas of the park remains remarkable, ensuring the park's continued popularity. Simply driving a few kilometres along the Chobe riverfront in the dry season is demonstration enough, as you'll be forced to halt frequently to allow game to wander slowly across the road, or to watch herds coming down to drink from the river.

However, perhaps more than any of Botswana's parks, Chobe has felt the impact of tourism. In the 1980s, park fees were low and the few basic campsites were full. Rubbish became a problem, solitary game viewing was almost impossible and the animals became habituated to people. While Chobe has never been busy by East African standards, its three or four basic public campsites and simple network of game-viewing roads couldn't cope with so many visitors.

Fortunately, around 1987, the government started to implement a policy of 'high-cost, low-density' tourism. Park fees went up and the numbers of visitors dropped. With regular increases in these park fees the flood of visitors through the park has become more of a moderate flow. These days, most of the park feels like a wilderness area and even the 'honey pot' of the northern Chobe riverfront area isn't

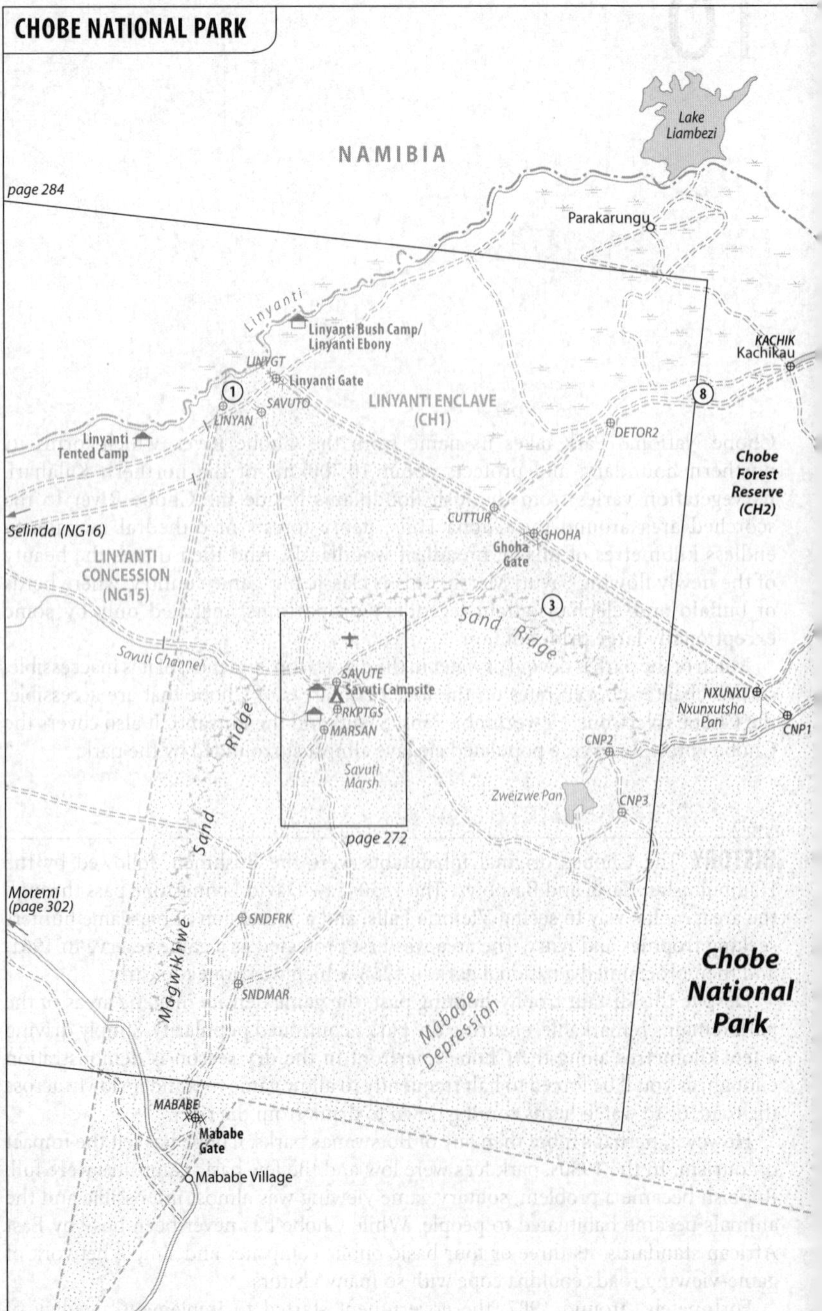

NAMIBIA

Lake
Liambezi

page 284

Parakarungu

Linyanti

Linyanti Bush Camp/
Linyanti Ebony

LINYGT

Linyanti Gate

SAVUTO

LINYANTI ENCLAVE
(CH1)

KACHIK
Kachikau

(1)

LINYAN

Linyanti
Tented Camp

DETOR2

(8)

*Chobe
Forest
Reserve
(CH2)*

CUTTUR

Selinda (NG16)

LINYANTI
CONCESSION
(NG15)

GHOHA

Ghoha
Gate

Sand Ridge

(3)

Savuti Channel

+

SAVUTE
Savuti Campsite

RKPTGS
MARSAN

*Sand
Ridge*

*Savuti
Marsh*

NXUNXU
Nxunxutsha
Pan

CNP1

CNP2

Zweizwe Pan

CNP3

page 272

*Moremi
(page 302)*

SNDFRK

Magwikhwe

*Sand
Ridge*

SNDMAR

*Mababe
Depression*

*Chobe
National
Park*

MABABE

Mababe
Gate

Mababe Village

Maun

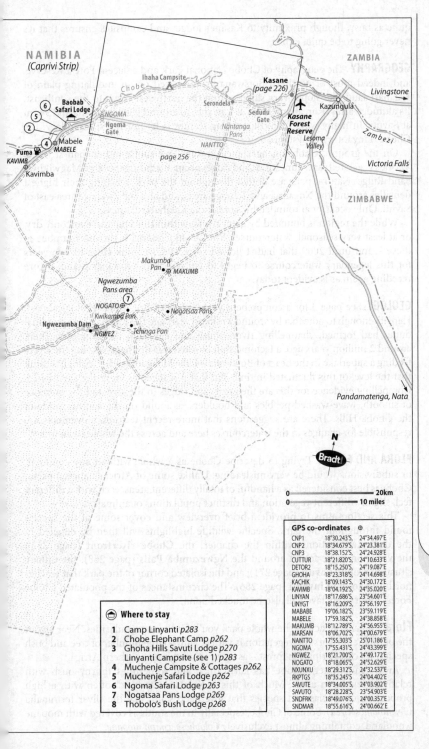

NAMIBIA
(Caprivi Strip)

ZAMBIA

ZIMBABWE

Ihaha Campsite

Chobe

Kasane *(page 226)*

Kazungula

Livingstone

Serondela

Sedudu Gate

Kasane Forest Reserve

Baobab Safari Lodge

6
5
2

NGOMA

Ngoma Gate

Nantanga Pans

Lesoma Valley

Zambezi

Victoria Falls

4 Mabele
MABELE

Puma
KAVIMB

Kavimba

NANTTO

page 256

Pandamatenga, Nata

Makumba Pan
MAKUMB

Ngwezumba Pans area

NOGATO **7**

Kwikamba Pan

Nogatsaa Pans

Ngwezumba Dam
NGWEZ

Tchinga Pan

N

Bradt

0 ———————— 20km
0 ———— 10 miles

Where to stay
1 Camp Linyanti *p283*
2 Chobe Elephant Camp *p262*
3 Ghoha Hills Savuti Lodge *p270*
Linyanti Campsite (see 1) *p283*
4 Muchenje Campsite & Cottages *p262*
5 Muchenje Safari Lodge *p262*
6 Ngoma Safari Lodge *p263*
7 Nogatsaa Pans Lodge *p269*
8 Thobolo's Bush Lodge *p268*

GPS co-ordinates	⊕	
CNP1	18°30.243'S,	24°34.497'E
CNP2	18°34.679'S,	24°23.381'E
CNP3	18°38.152'S,	24°24.928'E
CUTTUR	18°21.820'S,	24°10.633'E
DETOR2	18°15.250'S,	24°19.087'E
GHOHA	18°23.318'S,	24°14.698'E
KACHIK	18°09.143'S,	24°30.172'E
KAVIMB	18°04.192'S,	24°35.020'E
LINYAN	18°17.686'S,	23°54.601'E
LINYGT	18°16.209'S,	23°56.197'E
MABABE	19°06.182'S,	23°59.119'E
MABELE	17°59.182'S,	24°38.858'E
MAKUMB	18°12.789'S,	24°56.955'E
MARSAN	18°06.702'S,	24°00.679'E
NANTTO	17°55.303'S,	25°01.186'E
NGOMA	17°55.431'S,	24°43.399'E
NGWEZ	18°21.700'S,	24°49.172'E
NOGATO	18°18.065'S,	24°52.629'E
NXUNXU	18°29.312'S,	24°32.537'E
RKPTGS	18°35.245'S,	24°04.402'E
SAVUTE	18°34.005'S,	24°03.902'E
SAVUTO	18°28.228'S,	23°54.903'E
SNDFRK	18°49.076'S,	24°00.357'E
SNDMAR	18°55.616'S,	24°00.662'E

quite as busy, though proximity to Kasane's lodges and campsites ensures that it's never going to be quiet either.

GEOGRAPHY The geography of Chobe National Park and adjacent Forest Reserve, and indeed most of northern Botswana, is one based on an undulating plain of Kalahari sand that slopes very slightly from the northwest down to the southeast. Its altitude varies from about 950m at Linyanti, to around 930m at Ihaha and 942m at Savuti. In many ways its most defining feature is its northwest boundary: the Chobe–Linyanti river system.

On the ground, Chobe's geographical features are subtle rather than striking. Various vegetated sand dunes and sand ridges occur, including the large Magwikhwe Sand Ridge. Natural pans are dotted throughout the park, reaching their highest densities around the Nogatsaa and Tchinga areas, and also the Zweizwe area east of Savuti. Only occasional rounded hills break the Kalahari's flatness.

While the region is bounded by great rivers, within this area there are only dry, or at least very seasonal, watercourses. The Savuti Channel is the most famous of these – and until 2009 that hadn't flowed since 1982! It took close to two years for this legendary watercourse to begin to fan out across the marshland, before receding again as is evident today.

GEOLOGY See page 3 for a comprehensive overview of Botswana's geological past. Here it's enough to note that by around 3 million years ago the Kalahari's longitudinal dunes had formed, channelling rivers south and east into the Limpopo. Then, around 2 million years ago, a tectonic shift blocked this drainage, leaving the rivers feeding a superlake in the heart of Botswana – Lake Makgadikgadi. Geologists think that the level of this fluctuated in time, but that it reached as far as the Savuti area. Compelling evidence for this are the great sand ridges in the area and the presence of smooth, wave-washed pebbles and boulders, as found on the southern side of the Ghoha Hills. There are suggestions that more recent tectonic movements are responsible for changes in the watercourses here and across the whole Delta today.

FLORA AND FAUNA Trying to describe Chobe as a whole without any comment or subdivisions would be very misleading. Unlike some of Africa's national parks, Chobe is best considered as a handful of totally different areas, each with a different feel, slightly different vegetation and distinct populations of animals.

This section aims to provide a brief overview and cover some of the species found throughout the park. Specific wildlife highlights will then be detailed in the dedicated sections within the chapter: the **Chobe riverfront** (page 252); the variation to be found around the **Ngwezumba Pans** (page 268); the unique situation around **Savuti** (page 271); and the isolated corner of the park that reaches northwest to the **Linyanti** (page 286). The circumstances of the populated Chobe Forest Reserve enclave will also be touched upon.

Flora In general, across the whole park you'll find many similarities. Near any of the permanent rivers the vegetation is varied, with a large number of tree and bush species. It's classic riparian forest – as occurs throughout southern Africa.

Away from water, Chobe has fairly thick and sometimes thorny bush with relatively few open areas. Much of this is Kalahari sandveld, often with a high proportion of acacias and species that love deep sand, like the silver terminalia (*Terminalia sericea*). Some of Chobe, especially in the south, is covered with mopane woodland, containing almost exclusively *Colophospermum mopane*.

The main exceptions to this are a few areas of (geologically) recent alluvial deposits, like Savuti Marsh, which look totally different. Here you'll find the skeletons of various acacias and leadwoods (*Combretum imberbe*) on open plains covered in couch grass (*Cynodon dactylon*) – the latter being the principal attraction to the area for zebra.

Fauna Most of Chobe's wildlife is found across the whole park. Occasional elephants and buffalo are seen everywhere, but the large herds generally follow a highly seasonal pattern of migrations. These are principally dictated by the availability of water.

As the dry season progresses, all the small clay pans in the bush (and particularly the mopane woodlands) dry up. Then the elephants and buffalo start to form larger herds and migrate to the permanent waters of the Chobe and Linyanti rivers. These gather in their thousands by the rivers, having come from as far away as Zimbabwe's Hwange National Park. Then, as soon as it rains and the small pans in the bush start to fill with rainwater, the animals move away again and disperse.

Many of the park's animals will follow a smaller-scale, less noticeable version of this type of seasonal migration to the water, and this is what makes the game viewing in Chobe so remarkable towards the middle and end of the dry season.

At any time of year, Chobe's big game includes blue wildebeest, Burchell's zebra, impala, kudu, tsessebe, giraffe, impala, common duiker, steenbok, warthog, baboon and vervet monkey throughout the park. Eland, sable and roan antelope also range across the park, but are relatively scarce, just as they are elsewhere in southern Africa.

Lion and spotted hyena are very common, and are generally the dominant predators, while leopard, cheetah and wild dog all occur, though are seen much less frequently. Both side-striped and black-backed jackal are present – though the former are found more in the north of the park, and the latter in the south. Brown hyena probably occur, though rarely, in the drier parts of the south, though they don't seem to coexist happily with a high density of lion or spotted hyena.

Cape and bat-eared fox are found here, though again the Cape fox prefers the drier south. I once had a particularly good sighting of a whole family of bat-eared foxes in the middle of the open plains on Savuti Marsh, early in the morning on a cold September day. There are a variety of mongooses found here; the most often seen of these are probably the banded and dwarf species, both of which are social, and very entertaining to watch.

FOLLOW THE HONEYGUIDE...

Co-operative relationships between mammals and birds are unusual, but the honey badger enjoys two. Its association with the greater honeyguide is well known. This small bird uses a distinctive song to lure the honey badger to a bees' nest, whereupon it feasts on the grubs after the badger has ransacked the nest and had its fill of honey.

Less well known is the honey badger's association with the pale chanting goshawk. This relationship is of no benefit to the badger, since the goshawk – or sometimes a pair of them – simply follows the bigger predator around as it digs and forages for prey, and pounces on any rodent or reptile that slips past. The badger may have the last laugh, though, since goshawk eggs and nestlings are among its 59 different prey species that have been recorded in the Kalahari.

Serval, caracal, aardwolf and aardvark are found all over the park, though are only occasionally seen due to their largely nocturnal habits. Pangolin are found here too, though they're very rarely seen.

If you have the chance to take any night drives in areas adjoining the park (no night drives are allowed inside the park), then you've a good chance to spot scrub hares, spring hares, lesser bushbabies, porcupines, genets (small-spotted and large-spotted), civets, African wildcats and honey badgers.

Though white and black rhino would occur here naturally, as they should throughout northern Botswana, populations were decimated by poaching and all but wiped out by the early 1990s. Both species were reintroduced into Moremi in the early 2000s, with wandering rhinos occasionally turning up in Chobe. However, an upsurge in poaching since 2018 has meant that visitors here are, once again, exceedingly unlikely to see these animals.

Birdlife More than 450 species of birds have been seen in Chobe – too many to even try to list here. Therefore I'll cover the birding highlights in the separate sections concerning the specific areas within the park. Note that the summer migrants generally arrive around October and leave again in March.

PRACTICAL INFORMATION

WHEN TO VISIT Noting the general comments made on page 109, you'll generally find a wider variety of bird species here in the wet season, many of which will be in their breeding plumage.

The movement of the animals is rather more complex. Most of Chobe's larger herbivores migrate with the seasons, to find water to drink and pastures new. These movements are, to a large extent, predictable, so bear them in mind as you plan your trip to maximise your chances of good game viewing.

Like most of Africa's game migrations, the principle is simple. The animals stay close to the permanent sources of water during the driest months, then they disperse into the forests and open grasslands at the start of the rains to take advantage of the fresh grazing and browsing. In northern Botswana, this means that game becomes more and more prolific near the permanent watercourses – the Chobe, the Linyanti, and the edges of the Okavango – as the dry season wears on. Then, as soon as the rains come, many animals head south and east into the interior's forests and plains, especially the Makgadikgadi area and Nxai Pan. This gives the vegetation beside the rivers a little time to recover, so that when the dry season returns the animals will again find some grazing near the water.

The finer details of this are more complex, and slightly different for each species. Zebra, for example, have been the focus of a research project which tracked them using radio transmitters and a microlight aircraft, based in Savuti. This study suggested that they spend the rainy summer, from November to about February, in the Mababe Depression – venturing south to Nxai Pan, and then following the Boteti River down to around Tsoe, before heading across to the Gweta area and back north to Nxai Pan.

In March and April they pass through Savuti for a few months, where they foal. This makes a particularly good foaling ground as rich alluvial deposits from the old Savuti Channel have left the area with mineral-rich soil supporting particularly nutritious grasses. A few months later, as dryness begins to bite around July, they move again towards the Linyanti for the dry season. Finally in late October and November, they return to the Mababe area as the rains begin and the grasses start to sprout.

Similarly, Sommerlatte (page 545) studied elephant movements in the park in the mid-1970s. Though clearly movements have changed since then, he found that the highest wet-season concentrations were around the Ghoha Hills, the eastern side of the Mababe Depression, and the mouth of the Ngwezumba River (the Nogatsaa/Tchinga pans area).

For the visitor, this means that the game in the dry season is best in the river areas. In the wet season, and just afterwards, the interior pans are definitely worth a visit. Savuti is unusual in that, remarkably, it has good game all year, but is especially interesting around April/May and November.

ORIENTATION Though the maps make Chobe National Park look complex, it's really very simple. In the northeast corner is Kasane, and in the southwest corner the road leaves for Maun and Moremi. Most visitors drive in on one side, and exit the other – and in the middle all roads lead to Savuti. There are concessions and camps around the national park, particularly along the Linyanti River, but in terms of orientation, work on this basis!

North of Savuti there's a 'direct' road that links it to Kasane via the Chobe Forest Reserve and the Chobe riverfront area. Then there's an indirect route that travels to Kasane via the Nogatsaa Pans area in the forested heart of the park. Most visitors choose one of these routes; see page 263 for a discussion of their relative merits in various seasons. In all the above I use the word 'road' loosely – to mean two adjacent tyre tracks in the sand. You need a high-clearance 4x4 for a trip to Chobe, and plenty of time.

Maps Aside from the ubiquitous Tracks4Africa map and app (page 142), there is really only one other map of Chobe that is worthwhile for normal navigation: the Shell map of Chobe National Park by Veronica Roodt. The main map itself is fairly small, but it has a good inset of the game-viewing tracks of the Chobe riverfront area, and also aerial photograph backdrops for first-rate insets of the area around Savuti and Nogatsaa.

GETTING ORGANISED As with most of Botswana's wilder areas, there are basically three ways to visit Chobe: on a fly-in trip, staying at the lodges and camps; on a mobile-safari trip, organised by a local safari operator; and on a self-drive trip with all your own equipment and food.

Only self-drive visitors really need to do much of their own planning, and they should take absolutely everything they'll need to live on between Maun and Kasane, including generous supplies of water. Chobe is often combined with Moremi on such a trip – which, taken at a relaxed pace, typically takes about ten days. You should stock up on food, fuel and supplies before you leave. There are a few small local shops in the villages of the Chobe Forest Reserve, but otherwise there's nothing available on the whole route, and certainly no fuel.

Although it's only about 300km between Maun and Kasane across Chobe, a lot of the driving is in second gear and permanent 4x4, so prepare for fuel consumption that's perhaps two or three times your normal tar-road consumption. In addition to long-range fuel tanks, it's wise to carry at least one if not two additional jerrycans of fuel.

The park entrance gates are open 06.00–18.30 from April to September, and 05.30–19.00 from October to March. Park rules prohibit cars on the roads between sunset and sunrise, and it would be extremely foolish to attempt to drive after dark anyway, so be careful to plan your journey to give plenty of time. The speed limit in the park is 40km/h, though you'll be very unlikely ever to get near this on the deep sand tracks which are the park's roads.

Booking and park fees If you're flying into organised camps, then your park fees will probably already be included in the price of your safari. If you're driving into Chobe, you'll need to have booked all your campsites in advance. You'll then need to present confirmation of your campsite bookings at the park gates before you can purchase your permit to enter. See page 127 for details of how this works, and a scale of the fees.

CHOBE RIVERFRONT

Perhaps the park's greatest attraction is its northern boundary, the Chobe River. In the dry season animals converge on this stretch of water from the whole of northern Botswana. Elephant and buffalo, especially, form into huge herds for which the park is famous. In November 1853, David Livingstone passed through the area and described the river:

> though the river is from thirteen to fifteen feet in depth at its lowest ebb, and broad enough to allow a steamer to ply upon it, the suddenness of the bending would prevent navigation; but should the country ever become civilised, the Chobe would be a convenient natural canal.

Fortunately that kind of civilisation hasn't reached the Chobe yet – there are certainly no canal boats to be seen – and today's traveller must make do with 4x4s or the small motorboats that weave along the river, among channels still ruled by hippos.

FLORA AND FAUNA The Chobe River meanders through occasional low, flat islands and floating mats of papyrus and reeds. These islands, and beside the river, are always lush and green – and hence attract high densities of game. Beside this the bleached-white riverbank rises up just a few metres, and instantly becomes dry and dusty. Standing on top of this are skeletons of dead trees, sometimes draped by a covering of woolly caper-bushes.

In several areas this bank has been eroded away, perhaps originally where small seasonal streams have joined the main river or hippo tracks out of the water have become widened by general animal use to access the floodplains. Here there are often mineral licks, and you'll see herds of animals in the dry season coming down to eat the soil and drink from the river.

Flora On the bank beside the river the vegetation contains many of the usual plants found in riparian forest in the subcontinent. Yet despite this it has a very distinctive appearance, different from that of any other African river – and this difference is perhaps largely due to the sheer volumes of game, and especially elephants, that visit it during the dry season.

The main tree species found in this riverine forest include Natal mahogany (*Trichilia emetica*) – which isn't found in the rest of Botswana – plus Rhodesian teak (*Baikiaea plurijuga*), large feverberry (*Croton megalobotrys*), umbrella thorn (*Vachellia tortilis*), knobthorn (*Senegalia nigrescens*), raintree (*Philenoptera violacea*), African mangosteen (*Garcinia livingstonei*), bird plum (*Berchemia discolor*), jackalberry (*Diospyros mespiliformis*) and the odd sausage tree (*Kigelia africana*).

Because of the intense pressure from elephants, you'll often see the still-standing remains of dead trees which have been ring-barked by elephants, with the termite-resistant skeletons, probably leadwoods (*Combretum imberbe*), being particularly noticeable.

These riverside forests can seem quite denuded towards the end of the dry season, which many naturally blame on heavy grazing by the game. Clearly this has an impact here, but commercial logging took place along this riverside before and during World War II and also took its toll of some of the larger trees.

Despite this, several different types of bushes thrive here. Buffalo thorn (*Ziziphus mucronata*) and knobbly combretum (*Combretum mossambicense*) are common, though Chobe's most distinctive bush must be the remarkably successful woolly caper-bush (*Capparis tomentosa*). This sometimes grows into a dense, tangled shrub, but equally often you'll find it as a creeper which forms an untidy mantle covering an old termite mound. Sometimes you'll even find it covering the crown of dead trees, or draped continuously over a series of bushes.

If you're out game viewing with a local guide, then ask him or her if they know of any local medicinal uses for the woolly caper-bush. The plant has very strong antiseptic qualities, and both Palgrave and Roodt (page 542) report that this is one of the trees most widely used in Africa for its magico-medicinal properties.

Fauna The game densities along the Chobe riverfront vary greatly with the seasons, but towards the end of the dry season it is certainly one of Africa's most prolific areas for game. It is an ideal destination for visitors seeking big game. Elsewhere in the dry season you'll find fascination in termites or ground squirrels, but here you can find huge herds of buffalo, relaxed prides of lion, and perhaps Africa's highest concentration of elephant – huge herds which are the hallmark of the area.

One of the main attractions of the boat trips on the Chobe is that large family groups of elephants will troop down to the river to drink and bathe, affording spectacular viewing and photography. You'll find these here at any time of day, but they're especially common in the late afternoon, just before sunset.

When it's very dry you'll also find elephants swimming across the river at night to raid the relatively verdant crops and farms on the Namibian side, often coming back to Botswana during the day when the villagers feel more confident to emerge and scare them.

If you are not floating but driving, then be careful. Read my specific comments on driving near elephants (pages 266) and err on the side of caution. Most of Chobe's elephants are in family groups containing mothers with calves. They can be sensitive to any perceived threat, so keep a respectful distance from them. This can be especially difficult when you see licensed guides driving closer, but you should still keep your distance. Their experience, and general coolness in case of elephant aggression, will allow them to do relatively safely what would be dangerous for you to attempt.

If you find your car surrounded by elephants, then try to relax. Virtually all of Chobe's elephants have seen lots of vehicles before, and so are unlikely to get too upset. Don't panic or rev your engine; just sit quiet and still until the animals have passed. Ideally switch off your engine – but this is not for the faint-hearted.

The riverfront itself offers the best chance in Chobe to see hippos, crocodiles and the odd sunbathing leguvaan (water monitor). While there, also look out for the delightful Cape clawless and spotted-necked otters, which make their homes in the riverbank.

Perhaps the riverfront's most talked-about antelope is the Chobe bushbuck. This is a localised race, or perhaps a subspecies, of the bushbuck (*Tragelaphus scriptus*) which has wide distribution within sub-Saharan Africa, from the edge of rainforests to the edges of the Kalahari and throughout the eastern side of southern Africa. Their coloration exhibits a lot of regional variation, and there is certainly a distinctive race that occurs only in this Chobe riverfront area – with brighter coloration and clearer markings than are found in the rest of southern Africa.

Bushbuck are small, attractive antelope which usually occur singly or in pairs. Only the males have horns, which are short and spiralled. They are well camouflaged, with a red-brown coloration, like the soil, and a covering of white spots that blend into the shadows of the riverside's thick vegetation. They will freeze if disturbed, and there are reliable reports of lions and hyena passing within 10m of a plainly visible bushbuck and not noticing it. Only if disturbed will they bolt for cover as a last resort.

Another antelope often noted here is the puku (*Kobus vardonii*) – which some sources claim is rarely seen. This is true, but only if you've never been to Zambia, where puku are arguably the most common antelope. South of the Chobe they probably occur only in this Chobe riverfront area, and especially around the aptly named 'Puku Flats' peninsula of the floodplain.

The red lechwe (*Kobus leche*) is another water-loving antelope that is resident here, and is easily confused with the puku at first glance. Look closely and you'll see that the lechwe's underparts are much lighter, their coats seem less shaggy, and the males' horns larger. Also notice that when they run, lechwe tend to hold their heads close to the ground, while puku normally run with their heads held much higher. This makes identifying them from a distance easier – and soon you'll realise that red lechwe are usually the most common antelope on Chobe's floodplains.

Waterbuck and reedbuck are also usually found in wetter areas, and so are seen around Chobe riverfront and Linyanti but not elsewhere in Chobe. Roan are also found here, but are fairly scarce, as befits an antelope that is sought after by private game areas and is expensive to buy. Finally, the beautiful sable antelope are common nowhere, but I've seen large and relaxed herds here on several occasions. Being specialist grazers, they are more commonly found in the wooded south of the riverfront, though as sable and roan usually drink during the middle of the day, you will quite often see a small herd near the riverfront road, between Ngoma and Kasane.

Birdlife From a boat on the main river in the park you're likely to spot numerous beautiful kingfishers (pied, giant, some malachite and the occasional half-collared), with the pied seeming to be particularly numerous, perching on reeds by the river, or hovering to hold their eyes static above the river's surface. You'll also see plenty of reed cormorants and darters, various bee-eaters, hamerkops, wire-tailed swallows, a high density of fish eagles and even African skimmers (November–March only; the best place to see them is probably near Hippo Pools, beside Watercart Drive).

The fringes of the islands and floodplain are particularly good for birding, being home to many storks, herons, geese, egrets and a wide variety of lapwings (blacksmith, long-toed, crowned, wattled and, of special interest, white-crowned). Particularly unusual and worth seeking are rufous-bellied and white-backed night herons, slaty egrets, brown firefinches and wattled cranes. On the Puku Flats, look out for rosy-throated longclaw, black coucal and coppery sunbirds.

For a totally distinct environment attracting several different species, head downstream and out of the park, to the shallow rapids dotted with rocks, which are adjacent to Impalila Island on the Chobe and Zambezi rivers. (The Chobe's are the Kasane Rapids, while those on the Zambezi are known as the Mambova Rapids.)

In the dense waterside vegetation before the rapids look out for the shy finfoot, while around the rapids themselves there's a thriving population of rock pratincoles.

If you have the chance to explore the Kasai Channel (which connects the Zambezi and Chobe rivers), then do so. Technically you'll need to cross into Namibia, so this trip is probably easiest to undertake from one of the lodges on Impalila Island (page 239). Here you'll find small lagoons beside the main channel covered in waterlilies, and bird species that include the uncommon lesser and purple gallinules, lesser jacanas and moorhens, pygmy geese and African rails. On the edge of these, in the adjacent reeds and papyrus beds you'll probably hear (if not see) chirping cisticolas, greater swamp warblers and swamp boubous.

Back inside the park, in the band of forest back from the river, you'll find many drier-country species, including coucals (Senegal and coppery-tailed), oxpeckers, sunbirds (you can find coppery sunbirds here, too), rollers (look out for the racket-tailed), hornbills, flycatchers, weavers, shrikes, spurfowl and francolins. Large flocks of helmeted guineafowl seem particularly visible, and are especially fond of loitering along the tracks in front of vehicles. Or so it seems! Even the main tar road throws up interesting sightings; look out for ground hornbills and red-crested korhaans.

There's a tremendously wide range of raptors here, from the ubiquitous fish eagles perching on dead trees overlooking the river, through to the huge martial eagles patrolling the drier woodlands. Other resident eagles include the uncommon western banded snake eagle, black-breasted and brown snake eagles, bateleur (also known as short-tailed eagle), tawny, long-crested, Ayres' and African hawk eagle. These are joined in the summer by migrant eagles, including steppe and Wahlberg's eagles, and all year by many species of falcons, goshawks, harriers, kites and even the rarely seen bat hawk. The area has good numbers of white-backed vultures, often seen around a kill, but the vulnerable lappet-faced, white-headed and hooded vultures are also present.

ORIENTATION The southern bank of the Chobe River is slightly raised above the river, perhaps 3–4m high. Below this is a fairly level floodplain of short green grass and reeds, through which the river follows a very meandering course, roughly west to east, with many switchbacks, loops and adjacent old lagoons.

High on the bank is the main riverfront track, which is wide but for the most part sandy. This leads from Kasane to the Ngoma Gate fairly directly. Looping off from this are game-viewing tracks. Most of those on the north side drop down to the floodplains, and then loop around by the river. Those few heading off south usually follow straight firebreaks into the dry woodlands that make up the bulk of Chobe behind the thin band of riparian forest.

You can't get lost, provided that you don't cross to the south of the main road. Head east and you'll reach Kasane; west and you'll find Ngoma.

The game densities are generally at their best between Kasane and Ihaha, although the density of vehicles is also high here. When you head west past Ihaha, towards Ngoma, you'll find an increasing number of Namibians herding cattle on the floodplain areas across the Chobe River. Game densities in the forest reserve are significantly lower than those in the park, but you do have better chances of spotting some less common species like sable and roan antelope.

For details of the roads between Kasane and Savuti, see page 263.

Ngoma border post (🕐 06.00–18.00) At the westernmost point of the Chobe riverfront is the Ngoma Gate (✪ NGOMA 17°55.719'S, 24°43.665'E), which marks the boundary between Chobe National Park and Chobe Forest Reserve. Turning

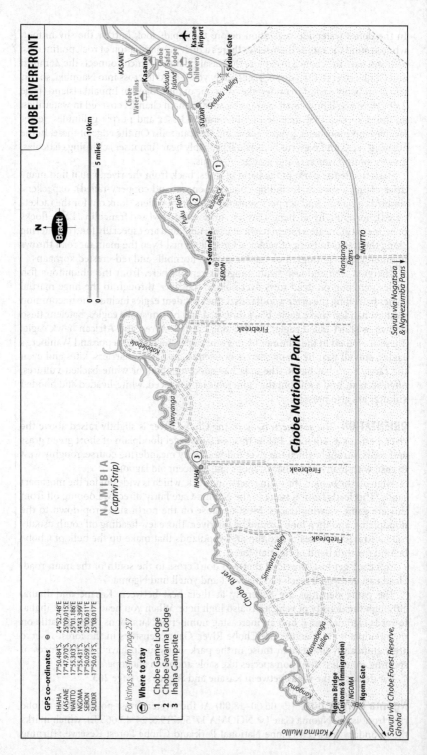

CHOBE RIVERFRONT

GPS co-ordinates ⊕

IHAHA	17°50.484'S,	24°52.748'E
KASANE	17°47.970'S,	25°09.015'E
NANITO	17°55.303'S,	25°01.186'E
SERON	17°55.431'S,	24°43.399'E
SUDXR	17°50.059'S,	25°00.611'E
	17°50.613'S,	25°08.017'E

For listings, see from page 257

⊕ **Where to stay**
1 Chobe Game Lodge
2 Chobe Savanna Lodge
3 Ihaha Campsite

KASANE

Chobe Water Villas

Kasane

Sedudu Island

Chobe Chilwero

Kasane Airport

Sedudu Gate

Chobe Safari Lodge

SUDXR

Sedudu Valley

Puku Flats

BUSHBUCK DRIVE

Serondela

SERON

Kaboolebole

Nanyanga

Firebreak

Chobe National Park

Firebreak

Firebreak

Simwanza Valley

Chobe River

Kaswabenga Valley

Kangomo

IHAHA

NAMIBIA
(Caprivi Strip)

Nantanga Pans

NANTTO

Savuti via Nogatsaa & Ngwezumba Pans

Ngoma Bridge
(Customs & immigration)
NGOMA
Ngoma Gate

Katima Mulilo

Savuti via Chobe Forest Reserve, Ghoha

N
Bradt

0   5 miles
0   10km

northwest towards the river at this point brings you to the border post at Ngoma, where on the Botswana side is a mid-1990s building perched high above the river by a venerable old baobab, complete with picnic benches. On the other side of the river, Namibia has a more imposing office next to the tarred bridge, about 2km further on. Both are efficient, pleasant and generally quiet. As with many borders, don't be alarmed if you see the odd soldier wandering around with a gun, and don't even think about taking any pictures near the bridge without permission.

From the border, it's signposted 57km to Kasane, 65km to Kazungula, 115km to Savuti and 362km to Nata. Over in Namibia, the completion of the 69km stretch of gravel road between the Ngoma border and Katima Mulilo means that you can now drive from Kasane into Namibia and right across the Zambezi Region (Caprivi Strip) on a good tar road.

WHERE TO STAY *Map, opposite*

Many people visit the Chobe riverfront while staying in or around Kasane (pages 225 and 239), or possibly from a base at Ngoma (page 255). Generally the options inside Botswana's parks are more expensive, but they have better locations. Within northern Chobe, there are only two permanent choices: the basic public campsite at Ihaha or the stylish Chobe Game Lodge. There is also a semi-mobile operation, Chobe Under Canvas, while several safari boats cruise on the Zambezi and Chobe rivers, as well as into the contiguous wetlands of Namibia's Zambezi Region (Caprivi Strip). As Namibian-registered vessels, they are permitted to cruise the waters of the Chobe when the national park is closed and all Botswana-registered vessels must leave, so offer a unique opportunity to watch game and experience the tranquillity of the river after dark and at sunrise. On the opposite side – technically in Namibia – there is another lodge, which we've included here as it is directly opposite Chobe, and is primarily used to visit the park, though you need to clear customs (⊕ 07.30–16.30) in each direction. All these options must be pre-booked; you cannot just turn up, even at the campsite. For other lodges on the Namibian side of the river, but closer to Kasane, see page 238.

Lodges

Chobe Game Lodge (40 rooms, 4 suites)
Contact Desert & Delta Safaris (page 214); lodge \ 625 0340; w chobegamelodge.com; ⊕ CHOBGL 17°50.850'S, 25°05.083'E. Opened in 1973, about 9km from the park's Sedudu Gate, this is the largest lodge in any of Botswana's national parks. Occupying a sloping site above the river, it offers luxury hotel service & style, with unusual design features: tribal antiques, arches in warm tones, North African styling & exotic surroundings.

Each of the comfortable rooms is set slightly into the bank with a barrel-vaulted ceiling & French windows on to a balcony or small veranda overlooking the river, about 60m away. The style is cool yet colonial: cream-screed floors are dotted with Persian-style rugs, the furniture is solid Rhodesian teak with comfortable chairs, & punkah-punkah ceiling fans (as well as AC)

combine with Indian marquetry to add a touch of the Orient. Smart en-suite bathrooms have a curvaceous bath, separate rain shower & twin basins beneath Indian-framed mirrors. Large suites come equally well furnished but with a 2nd bedroom, & the honeymoon suite boasts a small, private infinity pool. When Elizabeth Taylor & Richard Burton chose this as a romantic place in which to be remarried & spend their honeymoon in 1975, it was something of a PR coup!

An extensive wide riverside walkway, entirely accessible by wheelchair, makes it possible to take a stroll, then enjoy a drink or a meal at one of several intimate seating areas along the way, with one eye on the plains below. The food is good, with a buffet for b/fast & lunch, & a more leisurely à la carte dinner served by candlelight. In the main building, a rather womblike bar downstairs contrasts with the more masculine upstairs bar, complete with full-size billiard table

& a terrace overlooking the river. A library with TV & computers (there's free Wi-Fi throughout), an attractive pool, a gym (fortunately with AC), a small treatment room, & a big, colourful curio shop add to the facilities.

Activities, led by an all-female guiding team, comprise morning & evening game drives, mid-morning boat cruises, & a sunset cruise on arrival. These are taken in newly acquired vehicles & boats that are largely electric powered, lowering the impact of activities on the environment. Guests may also tour behind the scenes & discover other ways in which the lodge gained its high-level eco-credentials; it's fascinating! *Std room from US$942 pp Jan–Mar & Dec to US$1,406 pp Jun–Oct, FBA exc spa & premium drinks. Sgl supplement US$406/ night. Children all ages.* ⊕ *All year.* 🛏🛏🛏🛏

Chobe Savanna Lodge (13 chalets) Contact Desert & Delta Safaris (page 214); w chobesavannalodge.com; ✪ CHOBSL 17°49.838'S, 25°03.198'E. The smaller sister lodge of Chobe Game Lodge, Chobe Savanna is tastefully traditional in style. It stands in the private Kasika concession on the Namibian side of the river, facing west over the Puku Flats, with superb views across a quiet stretch of the river & its floodplains. The main building, a 2-storey, thatched, open-sided structure, houses a lounge, library & dining room, & provides 270-degree views over the Chobe River & national park. Outside, there's a plunge pool, a wooden sundeck & an open boma for evening fires. The lodge's relaxed & informal atmosphere creates a welcoming environment to enjoy the surroundings.

The brick-&-thatch suites each have a simple, African-inspired décor with a spacious en-suite bathroom. There's AC, overhead fans, minibars & tea/coffee-making facilities, & narrow balconies that overlook the river. Activities major on game viewing & fishing by motorboat, as well as sunset cruises. There are also nature walks along the river & trips to one of the local villages. *From US$490 pp Jan–Mar to US$630 pp Jun–Oct, FBA. Children all ages.* ⊕ *All year.* 🛏🛏🛏

Mobile camps and camping

⁎ **Chobe Under Canvas** [not mapped] (5 tents) Contact &Beyond (page 214). Like its sibling Savute Under Canvas (page 278), this is effectively a mobile camp that moves every 5 days between private campsites along the Chobe

riverfront (although never with guests on site). Guests are collected from Kasane Airport, with a 1hr game-drive transfer to the camp. No self-drivers are allowed into camp, so those with their own vehicle should leave it in Kasane & transfer from there.

Accommodation is in simple, en-suite twin or dbl tents, with battery-powered lamps, an open-air bucket shower (hot water on request) & a separate flushing toilet. A communal tent offers shelter for drinks, dining or just relaxing with a book. With game drives in the morning & afternoon, & boat cruises along the river, there's plenty to keep guests occupied until a traditional bush dinner, served under the stars. It's a rustic camping experience with high levels of service. *From US$650 pp Feb–Mar to US$1,090 Jul–Oct, FBA inc 1 photographic boat excursion with Pangolin Photo Safaris (page 238). No children under 12.* ⊕ *mid-Feb–Dec.* 🛏🛏🛏–🛏🛏🛏🛏

Ihaha Campsite (10 pitches) Contact Kwalate Safaris (page 213); ✪ IHAHA 17°50.484'S, 24°52.748'E. About 35km west of the Sedudu Gate, Ihaha is the only campsite for private visitors within northern Chobe. If you're taking the riverfront road from Kasane you'll come to a signpost close to 3 sharp turns in the road, which effectively form a square around the gate.

Large pitches run parallel to the river, some with almost unlimited views across to the Namibian plains, though not all have good tree shade. It's not terribly pretty, but the ground is firm & sandy underfoot, & it's a great spot to while away the hours watching the abundance of waterbirds by the river, or herds of elephants, impala & zebra grazing among the cattle on the other side. Ihaha is unfenced & campers have reported lions in camp on more than one occasion, & have even witnessed a wildlife kill here. 2 ablution blocks, with warm water courtesy of solar panels, are reasonably clean, & each pitch comes with a water supply, firepit, bin & braai. The camp manager may be able to arrange a boat trip & laundry. *P265 pp (US$20) exc park fees & bed levy. Firewood bundle P50.* ⊕ *All year.*

Safari boats [not mapped]

***Chobe Princess* boats** (4–5 cabins) 📞+27 21 715 2412, +44 808 189 0987 (UK),+1 800 865 1547 (USA); e enquiry@zqcollection.com;

More intimate & more wide-ranging than the *Zambezi Queen*, the 3 *Chobe Princess* boats – with 4 or 5 cabins – cruise some 50km of the Chobe River, mooring at points as far west as Serondela over 2–3 nights. The modern, en-suite cabins are smaller than on the *Zambezi Queen*, but similarly well appointed, with AC & large picture windows, so you can sit & watch wildlife from your bed, as well as on deck. This is the chance for total relaxation with a drink, a book or a dip in the on-board plunge pool – or indeed all 3 together! For more action, tender boats are available for fishing, game viewing or birdwatching with an experienced guide, & there is also the opportunity to visit a Namibian village. *Trips depart from Kasane on Mon, Wed & Fri. SA Rand 9,518–10,850 pp (US$506–577) sharing Dec–Feb, SA Rand 11,733–13,441 pp (US$623–714) sharing Mar–Nov, FBA inc transfer from Kasane Airport/Immigration Office; exc community development levy SA Rand 100 pp/ night. Sgl supplement 30%. Children 7+.* ⊕ *All year.* 😊😊😊–😊😊😊😊

Pangolin Voyager (5 cabins) Contact Pangolin Photo Safaris (page 238). Launched in 2015, this is the ideal boat for keen photographers, who will appreciate the specialist tender boat that comes complete with rotating chairs & swivelling tripods. For less-dedicated photographers in the group, there are 3 other small boats to enable concurrent trips for fishing, birdwatching or simply enjoying the river.

En-suite cabins, on the lower deck, have twin beds (or a dbl), fans & gauzed windows that allow the breeze to circulate. Above you'll find a lounge, communal dining table & braai area, while up top is largely open to the elements, giving great views over the river & national park. An experienced photographic host can be booked in advance (US$850/night) to accompany your group. On 7–10-day set-departure workshops, cameras & lenses are also available. *Exclusive-use charter US$2,995 Jan–Mar & Nov–Dec, US$5,995 Apr–Oct, FBA inc transfers from Kasane.* ⊕ *All year.* 😊😊😊–😊😊😊

Zambezi Queen (14 suites) ☏ +27 21 715 2412, +44 808 189 0987 (UK), +1 800 865 1547 (USA); e enquiry@zqcollection.com; w zqcollection. com/zambezi-queen. The *grande dame* of Chobe's riverboats, the *Zambezi Queen* is a luxury houseboat that offers a relaxing safari experience as it moves slowly between 2 mooring points on the Chobe River over 2–4 nights. On deck there's a pool & various areas for relaxing in the shade or

SERONDELA

For years the only campsite in northern Chobe was at Serondela (⊕ SERON 17°50.059'S, 25°00.611'E), sprawling along the riverside about 17km west of Kasane. The local animals had lost their fear of man, and all the dangerous big game seemed to make a point of regularly sauntering through camp. Over the years, ignorant tourists had taken to feeding some of the animals and the baboons, particularly, became a menace – aggressive, adept at stealing food if you turned your back for a second, and even able to open zips on unguarded tents.

On one occasion a lone male bounded on to the tailgate of my 4x4, snatching a packet of biscuits in its jaws from a food box, and sprinted off – all in a matter of seconds while I and a companion were a few steps away at the front of the vehicle. Before leaping up into the back it knew that we'd seen it and were coming back to chase it, but also knew that it was faster and so continued. It was obviously very well practised at this sort of smash-and-grab raid.

Further, Serondela was relatively close to the eastern side of the park, so it added considerably to the density of traffic in the peak times for game viewing: dawn and dusk. So for several reasons the site was closed in the late 1990s and superseded by the new Ihaha site. Today it is used by safari groups and self-drivers as a tranquil riverside picnic site, complete with benches and tables, and even toilets.

soaking up the sun, & at night a telescope beckons guests to explore the heavens. In the lounge areas, AC assures cool comfort, & you can spot animals as they approach the water from the adjacent restaurant & well-stocked bar. There's mosquito screening throughout, including in the individual suites which feature sliding doors to private balconies & river views from the comfortable beds. Modern amenities (AC inc) & en-suite bathrooms with showers ensure a comfortable stay.

The houseboat also offers tender-boat excursions, allowing passengers to explore the wildlife of the national park & try activities such as fishing for tigerfish or bream (in season). Cultural experiences, such as visits to Namibian villages, can also be arranged. *Trips depart from Kasane on Mon, Wed & Fri. SA Rand 13,325–15,719 pp (US$708–835) sharing Dec–Feb, SA Rand 14,800–17,469 pp (US$796–928) sharing Mar–Nov, FBA inc transfer from Kasane Airport/Immigration Office; exc community development levy SA Rand 130 pp/ night; sgl supplement 30%. Children 13+.* ⊙ *All year.* 👑👑👑👑

THE ZAMBEZI REGION (CAPRIVI STRIP)

As you look across the Chobe River – and indeed the Linyanti – from Botswana you're looking into Namibia's Zambezi Region, also known as 'The Caprivi Strip'. But how did the land come to belong to Namibia in the first place? On the map, the Zambezi Region appears to be a strange appendage of Namibia rather than a part of it. It forms a strategic corridor of land, linking Namibia to Zimbabwe and Zambia, but seems somehow detached from the rest of the country. The region's history explains why.

When Germany annexed South West Africa (now Namibia) in 1884, it prompted British fears that they might try to link up with the Boers, in the Transvaal, thus driving a wedge between these territories and cutting off the Cape from Rhodesia. Out of fear, the British negotiated an alliance with Khama, a powerful Tswana king, and proclaimed the Protectorate of Bechuanaland – the forerunner of modern Botswana. At that time, this included the present-day Caprivi Strip. Geographically this made sense if the main reason for Britain's claim was to block Germany's expansion into central Africa.

Meanwhile, off Africa's east coast, Germany laid claim to Zanzibar. This was the end game of the colonial 'scramble for Africa', which set the stage for the Berlin Conference of July 1890. Then these two colonial powers sat down in Europe to reorganise their African possessions with strokes of a pen.

Britain agreed to sever this Zambezi Region from Bechuanaland and give control of it to Germany, to add to their province of South West Africa. Germany hoped to use it to access the Zambezi's trade routes to the east, and named it after the German chancellor of the time, Count George Leo von Caprivi. In return for this (and also the territory of Heligoland in the North Sea), Germany ceded control of Zanzibar to Britain, and agreed to redefine South West Africa's eastern border with Britain's Bechuanaland.

At the end of World War I, the Caprivi was reincorporated into Bechuanaland; however, in 1929, it was returned to South West Africa, then under South African rule, and once again became part of Namibia.

In more recent times, on 9 August 2013, the Caprivi Strip was formally renamed the Zambezi Region. The Namibian government made this decision as part of an effort to eradicate the colonial history associated with the area and to recognise the cultural and land rights of the local people. Both names, however, remain in common usage.

WHAT TO SEE AND DO Game viewing and birdwatching are the main activities on the Chobe riverfront; walking and night drives are not allowed. Most visitors explore along the floodplains beside the river, which offers relatively easy game viewing, even without a guide.

If you're driving yourself and have a little time to spare, don't ignore the roads away from the river on the western side of this riverfront section, particularly the Kaswabenga and Simwanza Valley roads, as well as the firebreaks marked on Veronica Roodt's maps of Chobe. The landscape here is broken country with rocky hillsides and gullies: classic leopard country and very different from anything else you're likely to see in Chobe. You'll often find surprisingly good concentrations of game here in October, despite its apparent distance from the river, because the game tends to rest in the shade of the forest on its way to and from the water.

Canoeing and mokoro trips are also conducted on the river along the western fringes of the park, near Ngoma, but participants may be collected from Kasane, as well as from lodges within and to the west of the park. Do remember that you'll be sharing your space with both hippos and crocodiles, so make sure that you and your guide have given serious thought to the safety aspects of such a trip.

If your accommodation doesn't include activities, try **Malachite Safaris** (m 625 1537; m 7468 5154; e malachitesafaris@gmail.com; w malachite-safaris.com) or **Thaoge Safaris** (m 7142 4372; e bookings@thaogesafaris.com; w thaogesafaris.com).

CHOBE FOREST RESERVE

Chobe Forest Reserve is an enclave largely surrounded by Chobe National Park. To the northwest of it are seasonal marshes, Lake Liambezi and, eventually, Namibia.

The reserve, and the area to the northwest of it – concessions known as CH1 and CH2 – were long designated respectively for photographic safaris and community-managed hunting, but since the ban on commercial hunting in January 2014, this has changed.

The traditional photographic area in CH1, beside the Linyanti River, is the location of Linyanti Bush Camp and its sister camp. However, as the flora and fauna here are essentially the same as in the Linyanti Concession, we have included these camps in the Linyanti chapter (page 285).

Most visitors simply pass through the southern corner of CH2 between Kasane and Savuti (see *Western route: via the riverfront*, page 265, for details of this drive). Yet for those visiting the riverfront, the lodges near Ngoma are well worth consideration, not least as Chobe's game-drive loops become quieter as you move west from the Kasane area to Ngoma.

 WHERE TO STAY *Map, page 246*

There are now four lodges here in the forest reserve, although the fourth – Baobab Safari Lodge – is run for the exclusive use of groups. All are worth considering as alternatives to those in the Kasane area, as well as potentially convenient stopovers. The lodges are set high on a ridge overlooking the Chobe River floodplain and are normally reached by road from Kasane, taking about an hour for the transfer. The newer campsite is lower down the hill, so closer to the Chobe floodplain. In 2018, a boat jetty was opened in the park, upstream from the Ihaha Campsite so away from the busy Kasane area. This is for the exclusive use of Ngoma Safari Lodge, Muchenje Safari Lodge and Chobe Elephant Camp, each of which has a light, pontoon-style boat for seasonal sunset cruises, breakfast or lunch on the river, and birding.

Chobe Elephant Camp (18 chalets) 686 3763; e reservations@chobeelephantcamp. com; w chobeelephantcamp.com; ✆ CHOBEC 17°56.840'S, 24°42.055'E. It celebrated its 10th birthday in 2023, but Chobe Elephant Camp remains the newest lodge in the Chobe Forest Reserve, with a tranquil location & magnificent views across the Chobe floodplains from its high, rocky site. Its turning off the tar road is at the same point as Muchenje Safari Lodge (see right), from where it's signposted down a 600m sand track.

With a view to mitigating the effects of a harsh climate & the impact on the environment, the entire lodge has been constructed of Kalahari filled sandbags – while a pool helps guests to cool off in the heat. It's an understated, relaxed place, focusing on the setting & friendly service rather than the frills, though with AC, inside & outside showers & king-size beds in the rather rustic chalets (4 of them suited to families with a shared central lounge), creature comforts are not lacking. The cavernous lounge, dining & bar area, reached from the chalets along gravel paths, is open on 3 sides, its few walls whitewashed to create something of a farmhouse feel. Meals, though, are often taken outside, where there's a warming firepit that's lit in the evenings. Staff are friendly & welcoming, & the guiding – on game drives, boat cruises & sunset cruises on their own boat – is good. Guests may also explore the river from a mokoro or canoe, or take part in cultural visits to a local village. *From US$400 pp Jan–Mar & Dec to US$590 Jul–Oct pp, FBA inc local drinks, activities, park fees, laundry & transfer from Kasane. Self-drive US$315–440 pp, FBA exc activities.* ⊕ *All year.* ♨♨♨

Muchenje Campsite & Cottages (3 cottages, 3 tents, camping) m 7500 7327; e bookings@ muchenjecampsite.com; w muchenjecampsite. com; ✆ MUCHCC 17°57.261'S, 24°40.658'E. This family-owned-&-run spot is particularly well placed for those heading to or from Savuti (there's even a fuel station almost adjacent!), as well as those looking to explore the western side of the riverfront on a budget. Some 7.2km from the Ngoma border post, & just off the tar road, it's geared entirely to self-catering travellers, with home-grown vegetables for sale, bread to order, & a small shop selling meat, firewood & ice. There's Wi-Fi reception here, too, & a small pool nearby. The cottages, each with a dbl bed & a sleeper

couch, can sleep up to 4, & have tiled patios with table & chairs & a braai, proper kitchenettes, AC, & outside showers. For campers, there are 10 individual & very separate pitches – some looking across the floodplains – sharing 6 private (& spotless) showers & toilets. Backed by a beautiful baobab tree, there are also 3 permanent walk-in tents, which share ablutions with other campers but have their own small kitchenette, braai facilities & private verandas, with twin beds & electric lights inside. It's a well-thought-out place with a real understanding of travellers' needs. Activities can be organised on request. *Cottage from P1,195/night; camping P470 for 2 adults/ night; both exc bed levy.* **$–$$**

Muchenje Safari Lodge (10 chalets) m 7320 1489; e info@muchenje.com; w muchenje.com; ✆ MUCHEN 17°57.115'S, 24°42.361'E. Perched on the escarpment overlooking the Chobe River & floodplain, Muchenje was built in 1996 by Matt & Lorna Smith, who have owned & run it ever since. It's a comfortable, traditional lodge with a strong sense of hospitality & a good team of staff. To get there, follow the signs from the T-junction at Ngoma towards Mabele & Savuti; the turning to Muchenje is just 3km along on your right.

Well-spaced thatched chalets are comfortably furnished with a dbl or twin beds surrounded by a walk-in mosquito net. Each has a modern en-suite shower & toilet, AC & ceiling fan, electric lights, & a veranda with a view. Discreetly tucked away is a honeymoon (or family) chalet – it sleeps up to 4 – with a 2nd storey, a large bathtub, & an absolutely private veranda set to one side.

At the heart of the lodge, a wide, solid, stone building under a high thatched roof forms a crescent above the plain, making the most of the setting. Here you'll find a large table for communal dining, a lovely curved central bar with plenty of seating, & a small clothes/curio shop. Above the bar is a game-viewing platform which, along with a big pool, shares that impressive view. & in the evening, bush dinners can be arranged in their private boma.

Activities at Muchenje are many & varied; if you want to be busy all day, you can be! Game drives into the national park use an area that tends to be more private than around Kasane, as less traffic reaches this far west. Bush walks (with armed guides) in the forest reserve are also offered, as is birdwatching on the river. Those staying 2 nights or more – which includes most guests – can opt for a full-day safari taking in a midday boat cruise along the Chobe (thus avoiding the afternoon 'boat rush'), followed by a picnic lunch in the bush & a game drive back through the park. Their boat will allow a more open & convivial style of boat trip, too, & if you'd like to visit a local village school, your guide may introduce you to his family & show you round. *From US$510 pp Jan–Mar & Dec to US$835 pp Jul–Oct, FBA inc Kasane transfers. US$450/day for private vehicle. Children 8+; younger on request in low season.* ⏱ *All year.* 🛏🛏🛏–🛏🛏🛏🛏

Ngoma Safari Lodge (8 chalets) Contact Machaba Safaris (page 215); ⊕ NGOMSL 17°56.513'S, 24°42.558'E. More or less adjacent to Muchenje, Ngoma perches on a high ridge overlooking the Chobe River & its tree-dotted floodplains. The heart of the lodge is strategically multi-tier, topped with its open-fronted, thatched lounge, dining area & bar, which spills out on to the umbrella-shaded terrace & down towards the natural rock-hewn pool – complete with its own waterfall – & firepit area. Wherever you sit, the panoramic views over the floodplain below are superb. The whole lodge is rustically elegant (don't miss the beaded chandeliers!), grounded in its sense of place & with more than a hint of tradition. There's Wi-Fi throughout, & a spotting scope to help you to keep an eye on wildlife in the distance.

Well spaced along the ridge, the high-thatched, split-level chalets soak up the view from individual patios with sunloungers & tiny plunge pools – the envy of the local elephant population. There are outside showers, too, while inside are raised bathrooms with twin basins, a bath & separate toilet. On a lower level, the comfortable beds – lit by good lights, cooled by AC & enveloped by mosquito nets – face the plains through full-height glazed windows, & cool drinks, tea & coffee & biscotti are on hand to help while away the afternoon. 2 rooms can be converted to trpls. The room nearest the central area has no steps, so is more suitable for those with limited mobility.

Typically, guests spend their 1st day on a short game drive either to the river below the lodge or into Chobe National Park, with their 2nd full-day trip taking in a game drive through the park, lunch & a cruise on the Chobe River. Walks & night drives in the forest reserve, leisurely cruises on their own boat, & mokoro trips are further options. You could even do a (very long) day trip into Savuti. *From US$650 pp Jan–Mar to US$1,190 pp Jun–Oct, FBA inc Kasane transfers. Children 10+.* ⏱ *All year.* 🛏🛏🛏–🛏🛏🛏🛏

LAKE LIAMBEZI AREA

This large, shallow, ephemeral lake is located between the Linyanti and Chobe rivers. When full, it covers some 10,000ha, although since 1985 it has been much drier, and frequently something of a dustbowl – with the exception of the rains of 2009. Thus for many years, people and cattle have populated its bed rather than hippos and crocodile.

Lake Liambezi's main source of water used to be the Linyanti River. However, even in recent years of good rain it failed to fill the lake after filtering through the Linyanti Swamps (which themselves are very dry). Even despite good water levels in the Kwando–Linyanti system in the 2011–12 rainy season, it didn't break through as far as Liambezi. As a result there has been a trend towards less and less water in the lake and the marshes around it, and more villages. By 2014, however, for the first time in many years Lake Liambezi had a few inches of water in it, due to good rains, a recovery of the Bukalo Channel from the northeast, and possibly some flow-back from the Chobe River. In 2020, the waters of the Zambezi River caused the Chobe to reverse its flow and Liambezi once again began to fill.

DRIVING FROM KASANE TO SAVUTI

There are two routes through Chobe National Park between Kasane (⊕ KASANE 17°47.970'S, 25°09.015'E) and Savuti. Certainly the shorter is the western route, which is about 172km from Kasane to Savuti, via the Chobe Forest Reserve, and can take in the Chobe riverfront drive (see opposite) if you have time. The alternative is the eastern route, which is about 207km long. This stays within the park and passes through the Nogatsaa Pans area. Both have their own appeal – and their own challenges.

The western route is arguably the more beautiful, especially if you drive along the riverfront, but the eastern route is generally quieter, and has a particularly scenic stretch running parallel to the Ngwezumba River. Note that in the wet season, you're recommended to use the western route. Firstly, it's probably slightly more frequented by vehicles. Secondly, you'll find it particularly easy to get stuck in the clay soils found around the pans (both Nogatsaa/Tchinga and further south at Zweizwe). That said, if you do brave the pans route, the birding can be particularly good at that time of year.

Don't imagine that the western route is always easy at that time. Most of this is fairly thick sand and you'll often be crossing fossil dunes with woodland on the crests and scrub or grasslands in the valleys. There's a section where water sometimes gathers just south of the Ghoha Hills, so beware of problems there after heavy rains.

EASTERN ROUTE: VIA THE PANS For the eastern route, you need to take the tar road from Kasane towards Ngoma, away from the river. About 18km beyond the Sedudu Gate into the park, you'll reach a crossroads (⊕ NANTTO 17°55.303'S, 25°01.186'E). A right turn, north, would take you to the riverfront road in the Serondela area. Left, signposted to Nogatsaa 50km, and Photha 78km, leads you to the Nantanga Pans (1km), and on to the only road south through Chobe National Park.

About 23km from the tar road you'll come to a fork. Here you can take either route, as they join up at a clear junction by Makumba Pan (⊕ MAKUMB 18°12.789'S, 24°56.955'E) about 12–14km further on. If you bear right at the fork, then you'll need to turn right at this junction; if you've taken the left fork, then continue straight on at the junction. Some 13km from the junction (at ⊕ NOGATO 18°18.065'S, 24°52.629'E), there's a left turn towards the Nogatsaa Pans Lodge, which is actually on the edge of Kwikamba Pan.

For Savuti, continue straight on here, skirting the complex of roads around Nogatsaa and Tchinga pans towards a crossroads close to Ngwezumba Dam (⊕ NGWEZ 18°21.700'S, 24°49.172'E). At this point, follow the signpost straight on to Savuti, following the dry bed of the Ngwezumba River, with occasional vistas opening up through the trees. After about 31km you pass some solar panels on the left, then a further 2km brings you to a small track on the right (at ⊕ CNP1 18°30.243'S, 24°34.497'E), which leads after almost 4km to Nxunxutsha Pan (⊕ NXUNXU 18°29.312'S, 24°32.537'E), at the southernmost point of the Chobe Forest Reserve. If you were to take this track, and bear left around the edge of the pan, you'd find yourself on a track going uphill towards two beautiful baobab trees. This leads almost immediately on to the cutline between Chobe Forest Reserve and Chobe National Park, and after another 33km of relatively straightforward driving to the Ghoha Gate into the park (⊕ GHOHA 18°23.025'S, 24°14.732'E).

To continue to Savuti, however, ignore the turning towards Nxunxutsha Pan, and continue broadly southwest (to ⊕ CNP2 18°34.679'S, 24°23.381'E). From here the road takes a more southerly direction, leaving the riverbed behind. About 7km later, where the road splits (⊕ CNP3 18°38.152'S, 24°24.928'E), take the right turn leading southwest through the pans. After a further 11km the road turns west and finally northwest towards Savuti. This track enters Savuti by the south side of Qumxhwaa Hill (Quarry Hill) and joins the western route from Kasane just north of the channel.

The total distance from Kasane to Savuti along the eastern route is about 207km, and it takes 5 or 6 hours to drive in the dry season. An advantage is the possibility of a midway stop at the Ngwezumba Pans (page 268), although scenically this route lacks the beauty of the Chobe River.

WESTERN ROUTE: VIA THE RIVERFRONT Taking the western route you have a choice of ways to start. If you're in a hurry, or starting late in the day, then drive the 57km to Ngoma from Kasane on the tar. Alternatively, and much more enjoyably, meander along the riverfront road, which passes Serondela and Ihaha before joining up with the end of the tar road at Ngoma near the border post (page 255). Both routes are a little over 50km, but whereas the tar road will take about an hour (the speed limit is 80km/h), the river route will take several, depending on how much you stop to watch animals or take photographs.

Whichever route you take, you'll reach the park gate at Ngoma, where you may be required to sign the register and possibly also to walk across a disinfectant mat while the wheels of your vehicle are sprayed to prevent the spread of any disease. Then you should take a left turn, heading roughly southwest, and signposted as the B334 to Mabele (12km), Kachikau (37km), Parakarungu (67km) and Savuti (110km). This is now tarred all the way to Kachikau, making the first part of the journey – through the **Chobe Forest Reserve** (page 261) – very straightforward. On a practical note, there's a fuel station 7km south of Ngoma, a boon for anyone heading into or out of Savuti.

About 11.5km from the border post, you'll pass a big baobab and a large sign proclaiming **Mabele**. You'll still be able to see the Chobe floodplain off to the right, but with little game on it. There's a small, basic shop, Mabele General Dealer (⊕ MABELE 17°59.182'S, 24°38.858'E), on the right before the football pitch, and basket weaving co-operative, Vuche Vuche. The vegetation is mostly acacia species here, with lots of umbrella thorn (*Vachellia tortilis*), but the scenery becomes less inspiring.

Some 25km from Ngoma you come to **Kavimba**, whose landmark two baobabs stand guard on each side of the road (⊕ KAVIMB 18°04.192'S, 24°35.020'E). This is the location of the Kachempati Basket Weavers Co-operative (☎ 625 0339; ⊕ 08.00–17.00 daily) – so if you're interested, it may be worth asking around for their craft shop. Then a little over 10km later you'll reach the sprawling town of **Kachikau** (marked on some maps as Kachekabwe), where you can buy a limited range of drinks and foodstuffs. There's also a forestry camp here, and the well-built Liswaani Community School. In the centre of town (⊕ KACHIK 18°09.143'S, 24°30.172'E) there's a right turning signposted to Setau, a small settlement in the communal area to the north of the forest reserve, near Lake Liambezi.

Just beyond Kachikau, some 92km from Kasane, the tar road comes to an abrupt halt, reverting almost instantly to deep, sandy tracks. Having passed a bottle store and Chobe Craft Centre on the left, this leads after some 10km to the turn-off point for those driving themselves to **Thobolo's Bush Lodge**, about 3km west of this road (for details, see page 268). The country around here is rolling vegetated dunes, which means lots of corrugations and deep, deep sand. Plenty of leadwood trees are around, so beware of punctures (especially if you've reduced the pressure in your tyres for the sand). The long, strong, leadwood spines will cause punctures in even the sturdiest of 4x4 tyres.

AVOIDING PROBLEMS Elephants are the only animals that pose a real danger to vehicles. Everything else will get out of your way, or at least not actively go after you, but if you mistreat or misjudge elephants, there's a chance that you might have problems. Most drivers who are new to Africa will naturally (and wisely) treat elephants with enormous respect, keeping their distance out of fear.

In the more popular areas of Chobe or Moremi, where the elephants are habituated to vehicles, you'd have to really annoy an already grumpy elephant for it to give you any trouble. However, a few basics are worth noting, with the caveat that every animal is an individual with unique moods and experiences.

Firstly, **keep your eyes open and don't drive too fast**. Surprising an elephant on the road is utterly terrifying, and dangerous for both you and the elephant. Always drive slowly in the bush!

Secondly, **think of each animal as having an invisible 'comfort zone'** around it. Some experts talk of three concentric zones: the fright, flight, and fight zones – each with a smaller radius, and each more dangerous. If you actively approach then you breach that zone, and will upset it. So don't approach too closely: keep your distance. How close is 'too close' depends entirely on the elephants and the area. You can often approach more closely in open areas than in thick bush though. That said, if your vehicle is stationary and a relaxed, peaceful elephant approaches you, then you should not have problems if you simply stay still.

Thirdly, **never beep your horn or flash your lights** at an elephant: either is guaranteed to annoy it. If there's an elephant in your way, just sit back, relax and wait; elephants always have right of way in Africa!

If you are unexpectedly surrounded by peaceful elephants when your vehicle is switched off, don't panic. Don't start the engine, as that will startle them. Just sit there and enjoy it. Only when they are a distance away should you start up. When you do decide to move, never start and move off simultaneously, which will be interpreted as the vehicle being aggressive. Instead start up quietly, wait a little and then move.

Finally, **look carefully at the elephant(s)** and consider:

- Are there any calves around in the herd? If so, expect the older females to be very protective and easily annoyed – keep your distance.
- Are there any males in musth around? These are fairly easy to spot because of a heavy secretion from penis and temporal glands and a very musty smell. Generally these will be on their own, unless they are with a cow on heat. Such males will be excitable; you must give them a wide berth.

Continuing southwest, the next 40km towards the national park are, quite simply, challenging. The final 16km or so can be particularly hard going, with many a vehicle getting bogged down in the sand. To avoid this, you can take a right fork towards Linyanti, as indicated by the signpost at ⊕ DETOR2 18°15.250'S, 24°19.087'E, rather than the left fork (signposted to Savuti). This leads to a point on the cutline (⊕ CUTTUR 18°21.82'S, 24°10.633'E) which is about 7.7km northwest of the gate. Thus you just need to turn left along the cutline to return to the main track, and turn right to the gate. Although you'll still encounter plenty of sand on this route, it's not as thick as the more direct alternative. (For anyone heading in the opposite direction, from Savuti to Kasane, you would simply turn left up the

- Are there any elephants with a lot of seepage from their temporal glands, on the sides of their heads? If so, expect them to be stressed and irritable. This is likely to have a long-term cause – perhaps lack of good water, predator pressure or pain – but whatever the cause, that animal is under stress, and so should be given an extra-wide berth.

FACING A CHARGE If you get into a hair-raising situation with elephants, **you must keep cool**. This is extremely serious and your logic must rule your fear.

Most often a situation occurs when one of the herd is upset with you. It's most likely that you've approached too closely or quickly. An annoyed elephant will usually first **mock charge**. This normally involves a lot of ear flapping, head shaking and loud trumpeting. The individual then runs towards you with ears spread wide, head held high, and trumpeting loudly. This can be terrifying, especially if you're not used to it. But be impressed, not surprised; elephants weigh up to 6,000kg and have had several million years to refine this into a really frightening spectacle.

However shocking, if you stand your ground then almost all such encounters will end with the elephant stopping in its tracks. It will then move away at an angle, with its head held high and turned, its back arched, its tail raised, and the occasional head-shake. Often you'll find the 'teenagers' of the herd doing this – testing you and showing off a bit.

In response, if you flee or back off rapidly during a mock charge, the elephant will probably chase your vehicle, perhaps turning a mock charge into a full charge. So, *before* you move, make very certain that you have a swift escape route, that you won't run out of road, and that you can drive faster than the elephant can run. (In deep sand, you can forget this.)

If the elephant is really getting too close, then increasing the revs of your engine – commensurate with the threat – may encourage the animal to stop and back down. Steadily press your accelerator further down as the elephant gets closer; do not use the horn.

A **full charge** is quite different, and fortunately rare – expected only from injured or traumatised elephants, cows protecting calves and males in musth. In this scenario, the individual will fold its ears back, put its head down, and run full speed, bulldozer-like, at your vehicle. Your only option is to drive as fast as you can. If you can't get away then try revving your engine, matching its threat with your engine's noise. I'd also start praying – this is a *seriously* dangerous situation to be in!

cutline immediately after exiting the gate, and then take a right turn (⊕ CUTTUR) just after the end of a band of mopane trees.)

Either way, about 80km from Ngoma you'll arrive at the impressive **Ghoha Gate** (⊕ GHOHA 18°23.025'S, 24°14.732'E), which marks the end of the forest reserve, and the start of Chobe National Park. If you were to turn right here, then this very rough and sandy cutline would lead you to the **Linyanti Gate**, on the Linyanti River just east of Linyanti Campsite, and to the camps run by African Bush Camps.

Savuti, however, is a further 28km to the southwest, so you'll need to sign in at the gate, produce your camp reservations and pay your park fees.

As you enter the national park you'll see the Ghoha Hills on your left in the distance. A few kilometres later you'll pass the first of the hills, which is dotted with baobab trees, and now topped by Ghoha Hills Savuti Lodge. The road inside the park is generally a little less sandy than that outside, although it does cross the northern edge of the Magwikhwe Sand Ridge just south of the hills.

About 25km after the entrance gate you'll pass a sharp-angled right turn, which leads to Savuti airstrip, and a couple of kilometres further on you'll reach a bridge over the usually dry Savuti Channel, almost next to Savuti Campsite. Although this route is shorter (about 172km in total) and the first part at least is more spectacular than the eastern route described on page 264, the southern section is generally more difficult and time-consuming to drive.

Where to stay   Map, page 246

Thobolo's Bush Lodge   (12 chalets, camping)
m 7441 2251; e thobolosbushlodge@gmail.com; w thobolosbushlodge.com; ✛ THOBOL 18°12.273'S, 24°23.519'E. Thobolo's is well placed to explore the upper section of the Chobe riverfront, Savuti Marsh & the Linyanti River, & a convenient stop for self-drivers travelling between Kasane/Ngoma & Savuti. You'll find it signposted from both Kachikau – where you go to the end of the tar road, then turn off for a further 10km to the lodge - & from Ghoha Gate, where you turn north for 19.6km from the cutline (at ✛ CUTTUR 18°21.82'S, 24°10.633'E).

The man behind the lodge, Mike Gunn, has been influential in Botswana's tourist industry since the early 1980s. Having founded, & sold, camps on the Khwai River & in the Delta, he turned his attention to restoring & reviving this old hunting concession, & Thobolo is the result. An eco-conscious lodge through & through, it has sun-tracking solar panels providing energy, a light-gauge steel construction to avoid the use of indigenous timber, high quality insulation, & solar-operated boreholes to replenish the water in Barangwe Pan daily, thus attracting good numbers of wildlife back to the area's largest natural pan.

Constructed over 2 storeys, the main area has a traditionally styled bar & lounge overlooking Barangwe Pan & its regular stream of animals quenching their thirst. There's also a shop for basic necessities geared towards campers & self-caterers & a reception area where maps & local information are available. B/fast & dinner options can be booked in advance & are served in the boma or on the viewing deck, though each well-screened chalet also has its own fully equipped kitchen with table & chairs. 9 of the chalets have 2 pleasant en-suite, twin bedrooms, with an upstairs viewing area for sundowners, while 3 chalets cater for families with 3 dbl rooms, but no upstairs deck. There are ceiling fans & screen windows for a breeze but no AC here. A separate campsite, with dotted acacias for shade & an ablution block with hot water showers, toilets & a washing-up area, shares the views over the waterhole.

Daily game drives (US$225 pp for 2 people) are available, departing at 08.00 & including a picnic lunch before returning to camp for sunset by the waterhole. *Chalet US$295 pp dinner, B&B; or US$250 pp self-catering; camping US$40 pp. Children all ages.* ☺ *All year.* **$$$$**

NGWEZUMBA PANS

About 70km south of the Chobe River, and reached along the eastern route described on page 264, lies a large complex of clay pans surrounded by grassland plains, mopane woodlands and combretum thickets. There are well over a dozen individual pans: Nogatsaa, Gxlaigxlarara, Tutlha, Tambiko, Kabunga, Kwikamba and Phoha, to name but a few, and all hold water after the rains. This makes them a natural focus during the first few months of the year, when the animals tend to stay away from the permanent waters of the Linyanti and Chobe rivers.

If any of the water pumps here are working consistently then the pans are likely to attract wildlife during the dry season too. Should you be planning to head this way in the heart of the dry season, it's worth asking first at one of the gates into the park if the pumps are working. Do also ensure that you over-cater on all essentials, have familiarity in driving on loose sand, carry a satellite phone, share your route plan, and ideally travel in convoy. This is a less-frequented area of the park and travellers have been known to get lost here, with sadly fatal consequences for at least one man in the last decade.

FLORA AND FAUNA With water there, the pans are excellent in the dry season. Early in the dry season they're quite likely to hold water anyway – so taking the eastern route certainly makes sense around May–August. Once the natural water dries up, the pumps are vital. With water in the late dry season you can expect herds of Chobe's game interacting; it's a place to just sit and watch for hours.

Curiously, perhaps the area's most notable game doesn't need permanent water and so is found here all year. This area is perhaps the only place in Botswana where **oribi** antelope occur naturally. These small, elegant grazers are orange-red above, white underneath, have a dark circular scent gland under their ears and a short bush tail with a black tip. Only the males, which are very territorial, have short, straight horns. They are usually seen in pairs, or small groups, feeding in the open grasslands during the morning or late afternoon. If startled they will often emit a shrill whistle before bounding off at a rapid rate with a very jerky motion.

This is also the only area of Chobe where you've any real chance of spotting **gemsbok** (or oryx). This is the dominant large antelope species in the parks south of here, but it's relatively unusual to see them in Chobe. These pans, together with the complex around Zweizwe, are also probably the park's best place to spot roan antelope, which never thrive in areas of dense game but seem to do well around here.

For **birdwatchers**, the pans, and especially the larger ones like Kwikamba Pan, can be superb during the rains. Expect a whole variety of aquatic birds passing through including Egyptian and spur-winged geese, lesser moorhen, red-knobbed coot, red-billed and Hottentot teal, African pochard, dabchick and even the occasional dwarf bittern or whiskered tern. The large grassland plains here also attract grassland species such as yellow-throated sandgrouse, harlequin quail, croaking cisticola and, occasionally, Stanley's bustard.

WHERE TO STAY *Map, page 246*
There used to be two DNPW campsites at Nogatsaa – which was a great place for watching the game coming to bathe and drink, and still has a tall hide, and the very basic Tchinga (alias 'Tshinga' and 'Tjinga'). These have long been closed, but the arrival of Nogatsaa Pans Lodge in 2017 reopened this little-visited area of Chobe to independent exploration with a safari lodge, chalets and a nearby campsite for self-drivers.

Nogatsaa Pans Lodge (12 chalets, camping) +27 63 613 9144; e reservations@ghohahills. com; w ghohahills.com/nogatsaa-pans; ⊕ NOGATP 18°19.324'S, 24°53.207'E. The sister lodge to Ghoha Hills Savuti Lodge (page 270), Nogatsaa Pans Lodge has a stunning location, right on the edge of the large, open Kwikamba Pan, which is pumped to retain water all year round – to the relief of the resident wildlife, from elephant & hippo to sable antelope & lion.

About 2hrs 4x4 travel from Kasane (80km), or a 10min transfer from the airstrip (15min flight to Kasane, 50min to Maun; helicopter transfers available), the lodge itself is smart, almost minimalist, with muted khaki tones in its thatched main area & tented chalets to blend with the surrounding environment. Arranged around the pan, the chalets are huge, though some are more private than others. They're entered through sliding glass doors off a wide veranda, with large gauze windows & a fan. Inside, the design lines are simple, with cream canvas walls, whitewashed wooden floors, black-metal-framed furniture & thoughtfully placed rugs & cushions. A king-size bed (or twins) takes centre stage, backed by a desk, affording wide views across the waterhole. To one side of the tent are twin sinks & a storage area, with both inside & outside showers & the toilet tucked out of sight. In the family suite, 2 bedrooms are separated by a lounge area with a sofa bed to take an extra child, & a bathroom at the back. By day, you can stroll to the main area along the sand path behind the chalets, but after dark you will be driven to & from your room; wildlife in this completely open camp is ever-present.

In the comfortable main area, the open-plan lounge is dotted with cowhides on teak floors, leather sofas, kubu-cloth cushions & timber tables, opening on to a wide, pole-shaded deck with loungers, an infinity pool, hanging cushioned chairs, a lovely little bar & a raised viewing platform for idyllic sunsets, wildlife viewing & stargazing. Delicious meals are taken either individually or as a group, as you prefer, & the staff here are incredibly friendly & accommodating.

Activities follow a typical safari day, with morning & afternoon game drives to explore the nearby pans & around the dry bed of the Ngwezumba River.

About 200m from the lodge, 8 shady, forest pitches all have a firepit & lockable rubbish bin, with access to a shared ablution block & a basic but clean washing-up area. There are waterhole views & an adjacent hide for game viewing. The site is unfenced & guests here are advised to drive to the lodge for activities, meals (on request) & spa treatments. *From US$578 pp Apr–Jun & Nov–Dec to US$788 pp Jul–Oct, FBA exc road transfers. Campsite US$85 pp. Children 6+.* ⊕ *Apr–Dec.* 🛏🛏🛏–🛏🛏🛏🛏

GHOHA HILLS

Most people pass through the Ghoha Gate on their way to Savuti with scarcely a glance at the two hills that give this area its name. That's not unreasonable given the game-rich areas further south, yet the hills are notable for providing the only high ground for some distance. They also afford the only lodge a super vantage point.

Many years ago the area was inhabited by the Basubiya, and rocks by the turning to the lodge indicate that there was once a well here. The predominant vegetation is Zambezi teak, scattered across deep tracts of Kalahari sand. The thickets provide a perfect hiding place for steenbok, and offer good camouflage for giraffe, which in turn are stalked by waiting lion, but the game is very skittish.

GETTING THERE AND AWAY Most visitors fly in to Savuti airstrip by small plane (35min from Kasane; 50min from Maun) followed by a 40-minute road transfer to the lodge, though a helicopter ride directly to the lodge is also possible (48min from Kasane). The other option is to transfer by road from Kasane through parts of Chobe (150km; 3hrs).

For self-drivers, the turning is signposted to the left just 7km from the Ghoha Gate, then it's a further 1.8km to the lodge, culminating in an unexpectedly steep and rocky track.

 WHERE TO STAY *Map, page 246*
Ghoha Hills Savuti Lodge (11 chalets) 319 0662, 620 0001, +27 63 613 9144; e reservations@ghohahills.com; w ghohahills. com; ⊕ GHOHAL 18°26.175'S, 24°13.122'E. This smart lodge is perched on a granite hill above the plains, facing east to catch the sunrise. Entirely Batswana owned, it is set in its own private concession within the national park, with an exclusive 60km network of game-viewing tracks. From a viewing deck at the lodge, you can observe 2 waterholes, one of them overlooked by a well-shaded hide which makes a perfect spot for a sundowner. While pre-booked helicopter trips over Savuti can be organised, most guests spend their time on a full-day game drive to the Savuti Marsh, taking in some rock paintings en route. The journey

takes at least an hour each way, so exploring the area around camp is often restricted to the evening of arrival or the early morning. Thus, while the lodge is quite a way from Savuti, it may best be considered as a satellite from there, rather than as a destination in its own right.

High standards have been set for the buildings here. As if marching up the hill, huge en-suite tented chalets, including 2 family suites, have either twin beds or a king-size dbl. In front, a giant gauze panel feels like a living cinema screen with the plains as backdrop, & at the back are a separate toilet & shower. Higher again, you'll come to an extensive central area, like a large, thatched tithe barn, stylishly set on several levels with apron decks looking over the plains. Well-prepared meals are usually served at private tables, but if guests wish to eat together, or with their guide, this can be arranged. There's the option of private dinners on the deck below, where a pool is set among the rocks & there's a warming firepit for winter evenings – or stargazing with the lodge's telescope. Crowning the hill is a gym, its panoramic view shared by the picture window from the spa treatment room. *From US$636 pp Jan–Mar & Dec to US$1,109 pp Jul–Oct, FBA exc Kasane road transfers. Campsite US$85 pp. Children all ages.* ⊕ *All year.* 😋😋😋–😋😋😋😋

SAVUTI

Unlike most game-viewing areas, Savuti isn't just about animals. Its game can be great, but that's only half the story. To understand the rest, and discover some of its spirit, you must dig into its history – from the geological past, to the first humans and then the European hunters, 'explorers' and conservationists – and learn of the reputation of some of its famous characters. Savuti appears in more stories than all the other game areas in Botswana combined. So seek these out before you come, as only then will you really appreciate why Savuti has a legendary quality about it.

HISTORY The key to the area's attraction is the mysterious Savuti Channel, which is often dry (as it has been for a large part of the last 40 years) but sometimes, inexplicably, flows. Its journey starts in a lagoon at the southern tip of the Linyanti Swamps, and when it flows, it meanders a little south and then eastwards until it enters the national park.

Continuing east, it flows through a wide gap in the Magwikhwe Sand Ridge (in former times, its flow probably formed this gap); this is the place usually referred to as Savuti. From here the channel turns abruptly south, and spills out into the Mababe Depression, a huge flat area which was once the bed of an ancient lake (page 4), and formed the flat expanse of the Savuti Marsh.

At its peak, with the channel and marsh full, it must have been like a vast drinking trough over 100km long, penetrating the heart of the dust-dry northern Kalahari. It's no surprise that it attracted huge quantities of game and, in turn, whatever people were around at the time.

Beverly and Dereck Joubert's National Geographic documentary, 'Africa's Stolen River,' charts the drying up of the Savuti Channel over seven years, and the impact on the area's wildlife as competition for water intensified.

San/Bushmen The early hunter-gatherers certainly had settlements here, evidenced by at least five sites in the hills around Savuti containing rock art. Archaeologists link these paintings with those in the Tsodilo Hills, and with the traditions of people of the Okavango.

A few of these sites are known to the guides at some of the lodges here, so if you are staying at one then request for your guide to take you to see them. Despite park regulations about walking, at least one of these sites now has a clear signpost to it. However, you need to think *very* carefully before trying this on your own – given

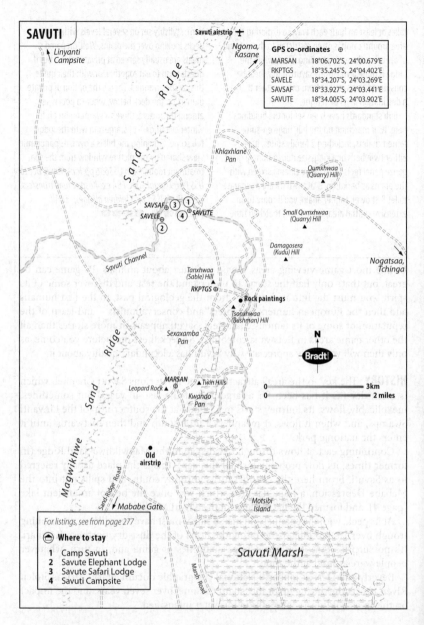

SAVUTI

Savuti airstrip ✈

↗ Linyanti
Campsite

Ngoma,
Kasane

Sand Ridge

Khlaxhlane
Pan

Qumxhwaa
(Quarry) Hill ▲

SAVSAF ⊕ ③ ①
SAVELE ⊕ ④ SAVUTE
② ⊕

Small Qumxhwaa
(Quarry) Hill ▲

Damagosera
(Kudu) Hill ▲

Nogatsaa,
Tchinga ↘

Savuti Channel

Tanxhwaa
(Sable) Hill ▲
RKPTGS ⊕

● Rock paintings

Tsonxhwaa
(Bushman) Hill ▲

Sexaxamba
Pan

N

Bradt

MARSAN ⊕
Leopard Rock ▲   ▲ Twin Hills
Kwando
Pan

0 _____ 3km
0 _____ 2 miles

Sand Ridge

Magwikhwe Sand Ridge

● Old
airstrip

Sand-Ridge Road

↙ Mababe Gate

Motsibi
Island

Marsh Road

Savuti Marsh

For listings, see from page 277

☻ **Where to stay**
1 Camp Savuti
2 Savute Elephant Lodge
3 Savute Safari Lodge
4 Savuti Campsite

GPS co-ordinates ⊕	
MARSAN	18°06.702'S, 24°00.679'E
RKPTGS	18°35.245'S, 24°04.402'E
SAVELE	18°34.207'S, 24°03.269'E
SAVSAF	18°33.927'S, 24°03.441'E
SAVUTE	18°34.005'S, 24°03.902'E

not only the park's rules, but also the high density of lion, leopard, buffalo and elephant in the area.

Early explorers There are many reports of this area from the early European explorers – fascinating if only to look back and see what they recorded of Savuti. In June 1851, when Livingstone passed through here, the marsh was a 'dismal swamp' some 16km long, fed by both the Mababe (now called Khwai) River, which spilled over from the Okavango system, and also by the 'strongly flowing' Savuti Channel.

Chapman also crossed the channel around 1853, when he recorded it as dry. When the great white hunter, Frederick Courtney Selous, came in 1874, the channel was full and flowing into the marsh. However, when Selous came back in 1879 he noted that the channel had partially dried out, and no longer fed the marsh. Mike Main, in his excellent book on the Kalahari (page 547), concludes that sometime in the 1880s the channel dried up.

Modern history The channel seems to have remained dry until a heavy rainy season, 1957–58, when it began to flow strongly once again. This continued until 1966, when it dried up once more. It then flowed from 1967 to 1981, when it seemed permanent and enhanced the area's reputation as a top game destination.

In the 1970s, Lloyd Wilmot started a camp here, Lloyd's Camp, which was to put both Lloyd and Savuti on the map. Lloyd is, in fact, the son of one of the Okavango's famous crocodile hunters, Bobby Wilmot, and has many sisters, most with strong connections in the area. A safari here was always offbeat. Lloyd built up a reputation for empathy with the game, and a total lack of fear for his own safety when dealing with it. Everyone who visited came away with stories of remarkable animal encounters, and Savuti's reputation grew.

However, the channel's flow was gradually reducing and, in 1982, it ceased to flow completely. Gradually the water shrank into a few remaining pools, and then they dried up too. With them went the fish, hippos, crocodiles and all the other creatures that had lived there. During this time Lloyd was frequently photographed kneeling or lying in front of a thirsty elephant, excavating sand from a hole in the bottom of the channel until he reached water. This sad time was well chronicled in a film, *The Stolen River*, by Dereck and Beverly Joubert. It's also one of the main subjects of Clive Walker's book, *Savuti: the Vanishing River* (page 541).

Nobody really knows why it stopped, as nobody understood why it started again after almost 80 years of dryness. Explanations range from changes in the paths used by the Linyanti's hippos to tectonic shifts; see Mike Main's book, *Kalahari*, for a more detailed discussion. That the channel flowed once more between 2009 and 2014 is thus of considerable note.

Even with the channel dry, Savuti remains a classic area for game. Experts observe that the soil here is especially good, and the grazing particularly rich. Furthermore, there are now several permanent waterholes in the area. The oldest, near the centre of Savuti, is pumped by the national park, while two others are in front of the two lodges in the area. A further two are towards the bottom of the marsh, on opposite sides of it – and these try to attract the game, and especially the elephants, away from the centre of Savuti which has been so heavily impacted by game over the years.

FLORA AND FAUNA

Flora Savuti's habitat is a mostly undistinguished thick thorny scrub, with camelthorn (*Vachellia erioloba*) and silver terminalia (*Terminalia sericea*) making up much of it, though there are also large areas of mopane (*Colophospermum mopane*). You'll also find substantial stands of shaving-brush combretum (*Combretum mossambicense*) and Kalahari appleleaf (*Philenoptera nelsii*), and it's perhaps the most westerly area where you can find the lovely paper-bark albizia (*Albizia tanganyicensis*). Dotted all over the drier parts of the area are landmark baobab trees (*Adansonia digitata*); their ability to survive being ring-barked is essential to survival here.

The main contrast to these wooded areas is the Savuti Marsh. Here, the dry areas of the marsh are covered with a variety of perennial grasses that stand above the (geologically) recent alluvial deposits of the channel. These grasses are tolerant of the slightly higher salinity levels present, and some are particularly nutritious and a great attraction for the game when there's moisture about.

Here you'll also see the skeletons of dead trees, still standing in the flat grasslands and newly flooded marsh areas. These were mostly camelthorns, umbrella thorns (*Vachellia tortilis*) and leadwoods (*Combretum imberbe*) which are thought to have seeded and grown up between the 1880s and the 1950s, when the marsh was dry. Then when it flooded in the late 1950s they were drowned – though the hard, termite-resistant wood still stands.

On the southern side of the marsh you can see the bush gradually starting to invade the grasslands again, with the distinctive, low 'round mounds' of candle-pod acacia (*Vachellia hebeclada*) leading the aggressors.

Fauna   At the heart of the park, Savuti sees most of the park's species (page 248), with the normal exception of the Chobe bushbuck and the water-loving species. If you visit when there's water, the reedbuck and waterbuck may well have made their way back.

Whereas when the channel is dry, much of the interest is concentrated around the three remaining waterholes, where there is plenty of water to be found. Either way, there is invariably a lot of game. Lion are frequently found lying around, and big herds will pause as they approach, or wait until their thirst overcomes their fear.

Savuti's elephants are notable for a number of old bulls that live in the area permanently, and are often individuals known to guides who have spent a lot of time in the area. These are augmented by large breeding herds which pass through. Whenever it's dry you can be sure that there's action and jostling for drinking positions at waterholes and along the channel.

In recent years, at least one local lion pride has grown so large that they will kill elephants to satisfy their hunger – traumatising the local elephants in the process. (The Khwai River area in Moremi has a similar phenomenon.)

Spotted hyena have always been numerous and very noticeable at Savuti. In the late 1980s and early 90s they would appear at the campsite, skulking around the bins, as soon as the sun set. After dark, and when people had gone to sleep, they'd pick up anything that they could carry, and eat anything small enough to crunch up – including, I was once assured, a glass lens from a 35mm camera! My aluminium camping cooker was stolen by a hyena once at Savuti, and still bears the scars of its strong jaw.

S M Cooper (page 544) studied the clan sizes here in 1986–88, and found that there were five territorial clans in the area, and a number of transient animals passing through. The clans each averaged about 18 adult females, six males, five of unknown sex and ten cubs under two years of age – so around 39 members of each clan. They tend to prey on reliable, low-density resident game species like impala and warthog throughout the year, and augment this by feasting on the herds as they pass through the area, especially the newborn zebra foals.

Despite the presence of so many lion and hyena, leopards also do well here, perhaps helped by the presence of the rocky kopjes which make a perfect habitat for them. Daryl and Sharna Balfour have some lovely shots of leopard at Savuti in their book on Chobe (page 541).

Once, when driving with one of Lloyd's guides (who shall remain nameless), we realised that there was an early-morning commotion in the air, and followed this to a young female leopard that had *just* killed an impala. The guide knew that she had a cub nearby to feed. However, our vehicle's approach had, unwittingly, frightened the leopard off her kill, and soon after we arrived so did a hyena – which proceeded to claim the prize.

Such was the maverick nature of Lloyd's Camp that this guide simply jumped out of the cab, grabbed the hindquarters of the impala, and started upon a tug of war with the hyena for the carcass. Spurred on by this, and the realisation that the cub would otherwise miss a meal, I joined in. Eventually we won the carcass and hauled it up on to a low branch hoping that the leopard would reclaim it.

But nature, once upset, isn't so easily put right. As we pulled back from the scene the hyena returned, stretched up on its hind legs, and plucked the impala from the branch with ease. Others swiftly joined it, devouring it within minutes. The leopard had already given up and disappeared, perhaps in disgust.

In the wet season there are still movements of buffalo, zebra and wildebeest which come on to the marsh to graze, though the huge herds of buffalo that used to come when the channel last flowed have now stopped coming. In his guide to Botswana (page 546) in 1968, Alec Campbell describes the scene on the marsh at that time:

Here the Savuti Channel carries water from the Linyanti…forming a marsh about a meter deep. From June to December huge herds of buffalo visit the marsh to feed in the surrounding scrub mopane and one can see as many as 6,000 daily. Out on the flats which surround it on the southern and western sides are herds of bull elephants, wildebeest, impala, giraffe, tsessebe and sometimes large numbers of zebra. Lion are also quite common.

Cow elephants with their young spend much time in the taller mopane to the east of the marsh but come down to drink in the afternoon. Hippopotami and waterbuck are to be seen in the Channel especially near the mouth where it enters the marsh.

Numbers now probably don't match what was seen then, though April–May is still the prime time for zebra and wildebeest herds to pass through, usually foaling as they go. The precise timing of this is heavily dependent upon the local rainfall patterns.

The dry season can witness large numbers of tsessebe move on to the marsh area to graze. Occasionally, at the end of the dry season, oryx have been known to appear at the south end of the marsh, but they are very uncommon this far north.

OH, HUEY!

One of Savuti's more famous residents was an elephant named Baby Huey, who had become very relaxed around people. He'd also picked up a liking for oranges, after foolish visitors fed him. Gradually he came to associate people with food. When I first visited Savuti in 1998, this was a problem.

Nobody drives around at night, but on that trip we were woken one morning at 05.00 by a vehicle driving up to our tent. The couple inside it had seen our fire burning, and come to seek sanctuary. It seems that they, and their small son, had been sleeping in the back (the pick-up section) of their 4x4 when Baby Huey had passed by. Smelling oranges, he'd used his tusk on the front cab like a can-opener on a tin, and then delved inside for a snack.

The couple were completely traumatised, and left Chobe at first light. Two days later Baby Huey was shot – and camping visitors are still banned from bringing citrus fruit into the park. And all because people were naive enough to feed the animals.

The kori bustard (*Ardeotis kori*) is one of the world's heaviest flying birds, weighing up to 17kg, and – despite a wingspan of 2.8m – it is a reluctant flyer, needing a good run-up to get airborne. On the ground, these stately birds are conspicuous figures, and are often seen around the pans, either picking their way hesitantly across the grassland in pairs, at least 100m from each other, or resting in the midday shade of an acacia.

Kori bustards often associate with game herds, whose trampling hooves disturb the locusts, beetles, reptiles and other small creatures on which they feed. In turn, they sometimes provide a similar service for the carmine bee-eater (*Merops nubicoides*). This dazzling bird arrives from central Africa in October and spreads out across the grassland in large flocks. Its usual hunting technique is to hawk for insects – particularly bees – in acrobatic sorties from a fixed perch, such as an anthill or bush, and return to the perch to dispatch and swallow the catch. In open grassland, where fixed perches are in short supply, a kori bustard provides an ideal mobile alternative.

In fact, the bustard goes one better than a bush by actively stirring up food for the bee-eater, which snaps up whatever it can catch around the bigger bird's feet before settling again on its back. Bee-eaters are not known to try this trick from the backs of mammals, yet the bustard remains surprisingly tolerant of its passengers, and sometimes two or more of them will hitch a ride.

Always you'll find groups of giraffe in the acacia woodlands on the edge of the marsh and all over the area.

Finally, if you're anywhere around the hills in the area, then P C Viljoen (page 545) notes that several klipspringer were spotted here on the Qumxhwaa Hill (Quarry Hill) in 1978 and 1979. This has since been confirmed by several reliable sources. Their existence here is remarkable, as the nearest other significant klipspringer population is probably in Zimbabwe's Hwange National Park, about 130km to the east.

Birdlife The list of bird species found in Savuti runs to over 450 species, but some of the more unusual include the Marico flycatcher, crimson boubou, capped wheatears, pennant-winged nightjars (stunning, but only during the summer, October–January; look especially on the roads at dusk) and Bradfield's hornbill.

In addition, when you're in areas of acacia woodland then keep a look-out for racket-tailed rollers and the spectacular displays of the male broad-tailed paradise whydahs in breeding plumage (February–April).

On Savuti's open areas you'll find the occasional secretary birds, Stanley's bustard, and plenty of the larger kori bustards. The Balfours' coffee-table book on Chobe (page 541) has a wonderful picture of a carmine bee-eater using the back of a kori bustard as a perch from which to hawk around for insects. Kori bustards are Africa's heaviest flying birds, but heavier still is the flightless ostrich, which can sometimes be seen here. During the summer, Abdim's and white storks congregate in numbers on the marsh.

GETTING THERE AND AWAY It's a day's drive from either Kasane or Maun to Savuti, so most guests at the lodges fly in to Savuti's airstrip (which can take planes as large as a DC3) or come by helicopter right into camp.

Visitors to the campsite usually arrive driving their own fully equipped 4x4s, complete with all their supplies. For driving details, see pages 218 and 263.

ORIENTATION The (normally dry) Savuti Channel starts from the Zibadianja Lagoon, at the southern tip of the Linyanti Swamps, and flows through the Linyanti Reserve, before entering the national park about 35km away. Heading east, it cuts through a wide gap in the Magwikhwe Sand Ridge, around which are a number of low, rounded hills – the Gubatsaa Hills. This area, about 54km due east of the lagoon, is known as Savuti – and aside from the years between 2009 and 2014 – has been dry for much of the past 35 years. From here, the channel spreads out into the Mababe Depression, forming a large marshy area covering about 110km², and known as the Savuti Marsh.

Maps There are numerous small, winding sand roads around Savuti, relatively few landmarks and very few signs on the tracks. It's easy to become disoriented. If you want to explore the area in detail, you should have with you Veronica Roodt's excellent Chobe map, the Tracks4Africa map (page 142), and preferably also their app downloaded on to your GPS. Some maps are often available at the park gates, but it's wise not to rely on this. Good advice on current conditions for self-drivers can be gained from online community forums such as w 4x4community.co.za and w ioverlander.com.

WHERE TO STAY *Map, page 272*
Savuti's two luxury camps, its campsite and mid-range lodge are all close to each other. All face on to the Savuti Channel and are near the bridge over the channel, just to the north of the marsh. Note that the small Savuti Camp (page 290), though on the Savuti Channel, is in the private Linyanti Concession west of Savuti: nowhere near the marsh, nor in the area that has, historically, been known as 'Savuti'.

Stay in the area for long and you'll hear of the legendary Lloyd Wilmot and his Lloyd's Camp; this became something of an institution here, but has sadly now closed.

Because they are in the national park, the lodges here are not permitted to conduct night drives, or to drive off-road, so all activities concentrate on 4x4 game drives during the day – usually with the option to visit local Bushmen paintings on request.

Camp Savuti (5 tents) Contact SKL or Stars of Africa (page 215). This relatively traditional camp is a large, sandy site next to the main Savuti Campsite (page 279). Set up on wooden platforms, its Meru-style tents have verandas overlooking the (usually dry) Savuti Channel. With twin/dbl beds, AC, en-suite corner baths, flush toilets & open-air showers, they're fairly large & well finished, if a little dated. Do be aware that one of the chalets is literally adjacent to one of the campsite pitches, so is not as private as you might expect. You may also share your early-morning & afternoon game drives with campers, with up to 8 people on a vehicle. Steps lead up to the chalets & to the open-fronted central area, whose pole-walled sides under a thatched roof help to keep it airy & cool.

With leather chairs, cowhide rugs & handmade baskets, it's a simply furnished area, combining a lounge, large bar & dining area. By the channel, a simple wooden platform provides the option for dining under the stars. *From US$630 pp Dec–Mar to US$870 pp Jul–Oct, FBA inc airstrip transfer. Children 6+.* ☺ *All year.* 🛏🛏🛏🛏

Savute Elephant Lodge (12 chalets) Contact Belmond (page 214); ⊕ SAVELE 18°34.207'S, 24°03.269'E. Close to Savute Safari Lodge (page 278), Elephant Lodge is elegantly styled, with spacious, thatched, tented chalets facing west across the Savuti Channel, with safari chairs & a relaxing day bed on the veranda from which to watch the wildlife at leisure. The well-insulated tents are lined with cream canvas & feature polished timber floors

& chic interiors, with a lovely duvet-covered four-poster bed, smart furniture & stylish batik-&-indigo fabrics adding a modern pop of colour. The AC/heating units & ceiling fan can, like the room's lights, be used day & night; there's an intercom system in case of emergency & a minibar for refreshments. Behind the wooden headboard are twin basins, a bath, large mirrors & plenty of storage space, with polished hardwood doors opening on to a separate flush toilet, & a secluded rain shower.

Paved paths under acacia trees link the rooms with the camp's bar, lounge & dining room, a large, light area filled with woven sofas, giant gourd light-fittings & slow whirring fans. It's a calm, contemporary space that leads out to a wide terrace & a lovely lap pool on a lower deck, all overlooking the channel. When it's dry, a waterhole is pumped here, attracting elephants to jostle in the water in front, & guests can witness these interactions up close from a low-level hide. The lodge emphasises the quality of its à la carte meals, served on the terrace, in the smart dining area or at traditional barbecue evenings held in Mothupi's Boma. With a spotting scope on the terrace, Wi-Fi throughout, a discreet library with a guest computer & sat TV, & an open-sided, African Botanicals spa tent, Elephant Lodge is filled with 21st-century mod cons & amenities. It's very similar to its sister camp, Eagle Island Lodge (page 375) in the Delta, with which it shares a professionalism marked by friendly service.

Activities here focus on game drives, with opportunities to visit the impressive baobab grove & Bushmen paintings. There is also a hide overlooking the waterhole for watching wildlife closer to home. Birdwatching, especially in Dec–Mar, is popular too. *From US$792 pp Jan–Mar & mid-Nov–23 Dec to US$1,848 pp Jun–Sep & festive period, FBA. Children 6+.* ⊕ *All year.* 👑👑👑👑–👑👑👑👑👑

✳ **Savute Safari Lodge** (12 chalets) Contact Desert & Delta Safaris (page 214); ⊕ SAVSAF 18°33.927'S, 24°03.441'E. Savute Safari Lodge opened in 1999, right next to the site of the old Lloyd's Camp, so the local wildlife is exceptionally relaxed with people – to the point that lions have occasionally been found sleeping on the paths between rooms. (There's a discreet electric fence around the lodge &, as with most wildlife camps in Botswana, guests are always escorted by the staff if walking around the camp after dark.) Here, as at the Elephant Lodge, most visitors arrive by plane.

Reopened in Jun 2024 after a complete rebuild, this excellent lodge has always been warm in atmosphere, welcoming & very professional, with perhaps a small-hotel feel. While its sophistication & luxury levels have certainly increased, its essence remains.

On arrival, the stripped-timber & thatch central area is immediately appealing, with a smart, formal lounge & beautiful gift shop. Sliding doors open on to a wide, elevated deck where pole-shading covers casual seating areas & a welcoming bar, & from where a lovely pool, surrounded by sunloungers with umbrellas, offers respite from the midday sun. A circular firepit extends out from the main area, with a sunken hide affording eye-level contact with the prolific animals who visit the lodge's waterhole. Water is pumped here in the dry season, & as a result, elephants regularly congregate here, especially in the afternoons, & you may well spot lions or even giraffe coming to drink too.

Dotted among tall trees, the 12 rooms, one of which is designed for families, are a fusion of classic safari style – traditional thatching, khaki canvas & enormous gauze picture windows – with luxurious, contemporary interiors. Each offering excellent views of the Savuti Channel, these rooms are beautifully designed, with clean lines, pale timber furniture, a muted Kalahari colour palette & a raft of amenities, from private outdoor showers to in-room temperature control. Centred on a huge bed, with armchairs to the front of the tent & a well-equipped en suite to the back, they're serene & sophisticated spaces.

Activities focus on game drives in the Savuti area, including the Savuti Marsh, & trips to see the San rock paintings at Gubatsa Hills are easily arranged. When we've visited, the guides were keen & enthusiastic about finding the wildlife, with elephants, wild dogs & hyenas in evidence, & the zebra migration (around Nov–Dec & Feb–Apr). With notice at the time of booking, private guides (US$500) can be arranged for a whole day. *From US$645 pp Jan–Mar & Dec to US$1,160 pp Jun–Oct, FBA. Children 6+.* ⊕ *All year.* 👑👑👑–👑👑👑👑

Savute Under Canvas [not mapped] (5 tents) Contact &Beyond (page 214). The khaki canvas of this mobile camp may not look inspiring, but this operation takes glamping to a whole new level. These semi-mobile, tented camps are based at private campsites within the Savuti area, in the same way that Chobe Under Canvas (page 258) operates within Chobe. Most guests stay for 2 or 3 nights, but the max is 5; in order to protect the environment from damage, the entire camp is moved every 5 days to a new site. Thus, the large en-suite tents, proper twin or dbl beds with truly comfortable bedding & good bedside lights, hot bucket showers & flushing toilets are packed up, along with the central 'mess tent', which serves as a dining area & bar, & the selection of field guides that are on hand for you to peruse. 2 game drives a day enable you to explore the area, returning in time for brunch or a starlit dinner. The food, from the most basic of kitchens, is extremely good (do ask to look 'backstage'), & the service is excellent. *From US$540 pp Feb–Mar to US$870 pp Jul–Oct & festive season, FBA. Children 12+. ⏲ Open Feb–Dec.* 🐾🐾🐾–🐾🐾🐾🐾

Savuti Campsite (14 pitches) \ 620 0218; contact SKL (page 213); ⊕ SAVUTE 18°34.005'S, 24°03.902'E. Savuti's newly privatised campsite is now fronted by an impressive DWNP office & entrance gate, but remains a wonderful place to camp for wildlife. The site is unfenced, but an ingenious circular wall surrounding the ablution block is designed to be elephant-proof. Smaller animals like cats can easily get out over the wall, but not easily get in. Here there are toilets, showers & a laundry area, with solar-heated water & electric light.

Many of the numbered pitches sit under old camelthorn trees (with pitch No 1 being particularly good), but shade is very limited in the wet season, when the trees have no leaves. Each has its own braai stand, & a water tap ingeniously encased in concrete to prevent elephants from pulling the pipes to access the clean water (they would often make such an effort for clean water, rather than drinking from the dirty waterhole!). The size of the site, & the distance between the pitches, is such that some campers even drive to the ablution block after dark. Others opt for the proximity & shade offered by the reserve pitches closer to the block. Visibility is good, with not too much undergrowth, though it can be very dusty & there may be the low whine of a generator in the background.

A very limited shop (⏲ 11.00–noon & 15.00–19.00) stocks a small selection of biscuits, tinned goods, beer, wine, basic toiletries & sometimes firewood – oh, & boot polish! – but don't rely on any particular item being available; you should still aim to bring in everything you need. Game drives can be organised through Camp Savuti (page 277), depending on the season.

Alongside the elephants for which Savuti is famed, the camp has almost nightly visits from spotted hyenas which, I once discovered, can carry away a full rucksack at high speed, despite being pursued. They will steal & eat anything, from a camera lens to a bar of soap, so leave nothing outside. Then sit back after dinner, turn off your lights, & shield your eyes from the fire. Now, when your vision has adjusted to the dark, shine around a powerful torch. With a little patience you should be able to pick out the ghostly green eyes of hyena, just beyond your firelight. (But beware of shining a torch accidentally at a passing elephant. They don't like this at all!) If you do have any hyena problems, remember that they will push their luck, but are essentially cowardly animals. Chase them & they will run, sometimes dropping their spoils. Just be very careful of what else you might run into during the chase! *US$50 pp, exc park fees.* ⏲ *All year.*

WHAT TO SEE AND DO Game viewing and birdwatching are the main activities at Savuti, and there's always something going on – though you might have to look quite hard for it at the end of the dry season. It's always worth talking to the rangers at the gate, and any safari guides you meet there, for their latest sightings – they are usually very helpful. Driving at night is not allowed, but often the wildlife will come quite close enough if you just stay in your campsite/lodge and keep looking around you. There are also some interesting rock paintings on Tsonxhwaa (Bushman) Hill, signposted from the road at ⊕ RKPTGS 18°35.245'S, 24°04.402'E.

DRIVING SOUTH FROM SAVUTI

TO THE MABABE GATE From the DWNP office at Savuti Campsite, it's a drive of about 66km along the direct route south to the Mababe Gate, though you can add another 7km if you take the scenic marsh road. About 5km south of the campsite, just before the hill known as Leopard Rock, the track splits two ways. This junction (⊕ MARSAN 18°06.702'S, 24°00.679'E) is shown very clearly on Veronica Roodt's Chobe map. Along this short stretch, you'll see a couple of signs pointing to the left stating 'rock paintings'.

At the junction, the left-hand track is the **marsh road**, signposted to Savuti Marsh and following its western side. More scenic than the sand-ridge road, it's often a particularly good area for giraffe due to the high number of acacia trees around. In the dry season, it's also a much easier drive, albeit very rutted in parts, but it's a bad route to choose during the rainy season, as you will almost certainly get stuck.

The right fork is the **sand-ridge road**, which heads west of the marsh, and is the more direct route towards the Mababe Gate and Maun. Taking this you will come to another fork after about 25km (⊕ SNDFRK 18°49.076'S, 24°00.357'E), where you bear left for the old sand-ridge road, or right for a dull but relatively straight transit road which now bears the 'sand-ridge' name, and eventually bears left before reaching the gate. The old sand-ridge road is named for the Magwikhwe Sand Ridge, which you'll cross about 26km south of Savuti. Don't expect this to be too obvious, as the ridge is little more than a wide, vegetated sand dune. You will climb slightly to get on to it, and drop slightly to come off – and in between the driving is more difficult than normal as your vehicle's tyres will sink deeper into the sand.

Both the marsh road and the old sand-ridge road meet up again at ⊕ SNDMAR 18°55.616'S, 24°00.662'E, about 20km north of the Mababe Gate: the old sand-ridge road takes 37km to reach this from the junction, and the marsh road about 44km. A sign here reads: Khwai 45km, North Gate 54km and Maun 133km. Around here the road becomes more difficult during the rains. In contrast to Savuti's relatively lush vegetation, there is little ground cover, and only low stunted mopane trees to protect the soil from the extremes of the elements. The road's fine earth is hard-baked when dry, and very slippery when wet.

On reaching the Mababe Gate (⊕ MABABE 19°06.182'S, 23°59.119'E; ☏ 620 0219), you sign out of (or into) Chobe National Park, by presenting your park permit.

CONTINUING TO MOREMI GAME RESERVE AND NORTH GATE
From the Mababe Gate, a wide gravel road leads all the way to North Gate, passing through Khwai Village on the way. While this is much faster than the old route, it misses out on the stunningly beautiful valley of the Khwai River (page 307) where, after the unrelenting dryness of southern Chobe in the dry season, the lily-covered waterways and shady glades under huge spreading umbrella thorns (*Vachellia tortilis*) are completely magical.

The road is not difficult to find, but there are a couple of junctions that can be confusing. Almost immediately south of the Mababe Gate, the road forks, with a green block indicating Moremi to the right; straight on is for Maun directly. Continuing towards Moremi, you'll come after 4km to another green block (⊕ TOKHW 19°07.719'S, 23°58.078'E). Ignore the signpost right to Khwai, but continue straight ahead for a further 3.5km. At the T-junction, turn right on to the transit road between Mababe Village and North Gate.

The road crosses NG18, the Khwai Community Development Trust concession, so you cannot drive off route without a permit. Close to the board proclaiming the trust's ownership, you'll see a signpost to the left to their two Magotho campsites, but otherwise it's an uneventful drive to the Khwai River. You will, though, come to a turning north along this road (at ⊕ SEROTO 19°04.317'S, 23°50.071'E), signposted to Seronga. Beware of this, as it would lead you astray through private concessions towards Selinda.

Continuing to North Gate, the road turns sharply to the left then comes to a bridge. From here, it's a further 6.5km to North Gate (⊕ NOGATE 19°10.394'S, 23°45.092'E). First, though, you'll go across (or around) another river, pass through Khwai Village, and finally cross a pole bridge over the Khwai River. On occasion, heavy flooding has made the river crossing almost impassable. In these instances, detours will usually be signposted around this to the east. If warning logs are laid across the road, do not be foolhardy and pass; the river is deceptively deep even for large 4x4s.

CONTINUING TO MAUN Going straight on at the Mababe Gate fork will lead you much more directly and quickly to Maun, reaching Mababe Village (also known as Kudumane) on the gravel road, after about 10km. Here you'll take a right turn, passing through Sankuyo, the veterinary fence, and then Shorobe, before a final stretch on the tar to Maun. (See page 218 for the latter part of this route – and if you have a GPS then set it for ⊕ MAUN at 19°58.508'S, 23°25.647'E to keep you in roughly the right direction!)

If your destination is Maun, then don't imagine that travelling through the edge of Moremi (on the direct road from North Gate to South Gate) is a quick option. It'll take a good 6 or 7 hours to reach Maun this way. You'll have some slow, heavy driving across the sand ridge, and will be liable for an extra set of park fees for Moremi (even if you have already paid some for the same day in Chobe). However, if you have pre-arranged a few nights in Moremi, then do take this road and don't miss the chance to stop off. It offers a completely different experience.

Where to stay There are several accommodation options, both lodges and campsites, along the route towards Maun. Wilderness Safaris' new camp, **Mokete** (page 400), lies to the east of Mababe Gate and self-drivers can park their vehicles securely in Mababe village before transferring there. Only 5 minutes' drive from the village are **Nokanyana** (page 401), **Mogotlho Safari Lodge** (page 400) and **Tshaa Campsite** (page 400) close to Mababe Village, then a little over 20km further south there's a right turn to **Mankwe Tented Retreat** (page 401). Further south again is **Kaziikini Campsite** (page 398).

LINYANTI

The Linyanti River acts as a magnet for game during the dry season, just as its continuation, the Chobe, does further north. Only a few kilometres of the river fall within Chobe National Park, and this section tends to be dominated by some very thick reedbeds and vegetation, so can be a disappointing area for wildlife. In addition, reaching this area requires a considerable side-track from the established Moremi–Savuti–Ihaha route across Chobe, so it has tended to get few visitors in the past.

East of the park's short river section is the Linyanti Enclave (CH1) photographic concession. This is the location of Linyanti Bush Camp and Linyanti Ebony, which are covered in the next chapter, dedicated to the area's private reserves (page 291). To the west is NG15, the Linyanti Concession (page 286), which has several good camps, the nearest of which is Linyanti Tented Camp. Between these two private areas, within the national park, are the similarly named Linyanti Campsite and Camp Linyanti. Visitors driving themselves are restricted to the national park area and CH1; access to the camps within the Linyanti Concession is permitted only on a fly-in safari.

Note that despite there being a track marked on the maps from Seronga towards the Linyanti, this is not a practical one to use to get here from the west. First, neither private self-drive vehicles nor mobile operators are allowed to drive through the private concessions between the Linyanti and Okavango. Secondly, even if you were permitted to travel this route and had a good GPS, navigation would be a complete nightmare!

FLORA AND FAUNA This area has a very similar ecosystem to that of the Chobe riverfront (page 252), although the vegetation beside the water here seems to have many more large trees and to be in a more natural state. As Chobe's Linyanti riverfront is sandwiched between two private concession areas, it's a relatively limited size for game driving. You'll usually see large numbers of elephant at the end of the dry season, but this small stretch of the park is seldom quite as rewarding as the Chobe riverfront area, where the wildlife is much more relaxed. The presence to the east of an area where hunting was still practised relatively recently explains some of the animals' skittish behaviour, although things have improved considerably. West of Linyanti is the private Linyanti Reserve, which is an excellent area with a long stretch of beautiful riverfront and some very good wildlife (page 286).

GETTING THERE AND AWAY Linyanti Campsite and Camp Linyanti (and therefore Linyanti Bush Camp and Linyanti Ebony; page 292) can be approached along deep, sandy tracks either on the transit road direct from Savuti (about 40km) or along the cutline from the Ghoha Gate (totalling 43km). Whichever route you take, you will need solid 4x4 driving experience and good concentration to undertake the drive: the sand is very deep, and tyre-track channels are deep and bumpy from previous vehicles. As always on these sandy routes, ensure your tyre pressure is reduced.

If you're coming from Kasane, follow the directions for Savuti (page 263) until you reach the cutline, where instead of turning left for the Ghoha Gate, you turn right towards the Linyanti River. From here it's a slow-going 28km to the Linyanti Gate (✪ LINYGT 18°16.209'S, 23°56.197'E), where you'll need to present your permit before proceeding to the campsite or lodge, just 5km to the southwest.

From Savuti, drive over the bridge across the Savuti Channel and on to its north bank, and then turn left, heading northwest. Within 1km or so, you'll approach a T-junction, and take a left heading westwards. This crosses the sand ridge (though you may not notice this!) and about 3km later there are two left turnings. Ignore these. Follow the road around to the right, heading in a more northerly direction.

The first few kilometres of this drive are relatively easy, but after this there's about 30km of trickier driving – very deep sand and tougher going, especially one 3km stretch that will test your driving skills (and your vehicle) to the maximum. The scenery is gently rolling dunes, with many flatter areas of low mopane. Visiting one October, I found large numbers of elephants on the road north. Towards the river there was also a pall of dust and woodsmoke hanging over the woods, which was clearly coming from fires raging across the river in Namibia, though in the same month a few years later, the air was clear.

For those doing this journey in reverse, the transit road is signposted from just inside the gate. Note, however, that the roads around Linyanti Campsite are confusing to navigate, so be particularly vigilant in finding the right track south from here. The correct turning is at ✪ SAVUTO 18°18.228'S, 23°54.903'E, where there's a motley collection of signs at a clear crossroads. Having once inadvertently taken the cutline road south from Linyanti, ending up at the (then flowing) Savuti Channel before realising our mistake, you have been warned to keep a close eye on your navigation!

⬆ WHERE TO STAY   *Map, page 246*

Fully equipped self-drivers can stay at the national parks' Linyanti Campsite or Camp Linyanti. Just outside the park, some 10km to the north, are the camps run by African Bush Camps. As these share much of the same landscape as those in the Linyanti Concession, they are detailed in the relevant private concessions' chapter (page 285).

Camp Linyanti   (5 tents) Contact SKL or Stars of Africa (page 215). Under the same management as the campsite, Camp Linyanti is a simple, tented camp. Its main lounge–dining area, right on the river, is complemented by expanses of wooden decking & a campfire, both of which are well positioned to make the most of the picturesque setting across the floodplains to Namibia's Zambezi Region (Caprivi Strip). The 5 Meru-style tented chalets are simple, spacious & comfortable, with polished timber furniture, river views through large, mesh picture windows, a small deck with chairs, AC, & an en-suite bathroom, complete with outdoor showers. Game drives & boat cruises can be arranged, though riverfront drives are obviously limited by the proximity of private reserves on either side of the park

here. *From US$598 pp Jan–Mar to US$838 pp Jul–Oct, FBA exc transfers. Children all ages.* ⊕ *All year.* 🛏🛏🛏🛏

Linyanti Campsite   (5 pitches) Contact SKL (page 213); ✪ LINYAN 18°17.686'S, 23°54.601'E. About 40km from Savuti, this is a beautiful little site, close to the river with some tree shade & a very quiet setting – a relief after the deep sand drive to get here! Its pitches each have a brick firepit & braai stand & they all share a small but new ablution block, with hot showers & flushing toilets. There's no drinking water available – although filtering & treating river water would be possible in an emergency. Elephants & hippos frequently pass through camp, so do be aware. Safari activities can be organised through Camp Linyanti (see left). *US$50 pp, exc park fees.* ⊕ *All year.*

WHAT TO SEE AND DO   Game drives, walks, mokoro excursions and boat trips (water levels permitting) can be organised at Camp Linyanti for all visitors – campers and lodge guests alike. There are 7km of accessible riverfront in this corner of the park, with new game-drive routes opened. Next to the riverbank, there are plenty of reedbeds, which can be a delight for birdwatchers, and the water is home to countless hippo. I've come across the occasional person who absolutely adores this section of the park.

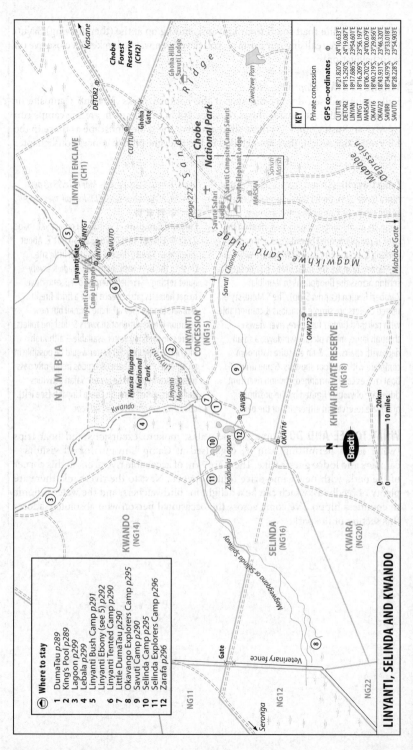

Where to stay

1. DumaTau p289
2. King's Pool p289
3. Lagoon p299
4. Lebala p299
5. Linyanti Bush Camp p291
6. Linyanti Ebony (see 5) p292
7. Linyanti Tented Camp p290
7. Little DumaTau p290
8. Okavango Explorers Camp p295
9. Savuti Camp p290
10. Selinda Camp p295
11. Selinda Explorers Camp p296
12. Zarafa p296

KEY

Private concession

GPS co-ordinates ⊕

CUTTUR	18°21.820'S,	24°10.633'E
DETOR2	18°15.250'S,	24°19.087'E
LINYAN	18°17.686'S,	23°54.601'E
LINYGT	18°16.209'S,	23°56.197'E
MARSAN	18°06.702'S,	24°00.679'E
OKAV16	18°40.219'S,	23°29.856'E
OKAV22	18°43.931'S,	23°46.320'E
SAVBRI	18°34.979'S,	23°33.018'E
SAVUTO	18°28.228'S,	23°54.903'E

LINYANTI, SELINDA AND KWANDO

11

Linyanti, Selinda and Kwando Reserves

Almost parallel to the Okavango, the Kwando River flows south from Angola across Namibia's Zambezi Region (Caprivi Strip) and into Botswana. Like the Okavango, it starts spreading out over the Kalahari's sands, forming the Linyanti Swamps. Also like the Okavango, in wetter years this is a delta, complete with myriad waterways linking lagoons: a refuge for much wildlife. It's a wild area, much of which is on the Namibian side of the border, in the Nkasa Rupara National Park (formerly Mamili National Park), where it's difficult to access. A faultline channels the outflow from these swamps into the Linyanti River, which flows northeast into Lake Liambezi, and thence into Chobe.

Both the Kwando and the Linyanti rivers are permanent, so for the animals in Chobe and northern Botswana they are valuable sources of water. Like the Chobe and Okavango, they have become the ultimate destination for migrations from the drier areas across northern Botswana – and also sought-after safari destinations, especially in the dry season.

This area, between the Chobe National Park and the Okavango Delta, has been split into three large concessions – Kwando in the north, Linyanti in the east, and Selinda in the middle. In some ways these are similar, as each encompasses a large area of mopane woodlands and smaller, more prized sections of riparian forest and open floodplains on old river channels. Look at the locations of the camps and you'll realise that much of the interest lies in these floodplains and riparian forests – diverse habitats rich in species.

Away from the actual water, two fossil channels are also worthy of attention: the Savuti Channel and the Selinda Spillway, which intermittently flow with water. Both areas, however, offer contrasting and interesting wildlife spectacles.

BACKGROUND INFORMATION

HISTORY The Kwando River has its headwaters in Angola, from where it flows south across Namibia's Zambezi Region (Caprivi Strip), forming one boundary between Namibia and Botswana. Progressing over the Kalahari's sands, it is thought that once – around 1–2 million years ago – it continued southeast, probably through the course of the present-day Savuti Channel, into the Mababe Depression to swell the vast Lake Makgadikgadi (see page 4 for more on the geological history of the region). Then, at some point in the last million years, tectonic shifts raised up a faultline running northwest which effectively 'captured' this river, and diverted it along the fault to flow into the Chobe and Zambezi rivers, thus creating what we now call the Linyanti River.

Around the same time, a parallel fault – the Thamalakane Fault – is also thought to have halted the Okavango's course, trapping it and ultimately silting it up to form an inland delta. As the gradients in this part of the northern Kalahari are very small indeed (1:4,000 is typical of the gradient in the Okavango Delta) the routes taken by these watercourses are very susceptible to the tiniest tilts in the earth's surface. As an aside, these faults probably mark the most southerly extent of Africa's Great Rift Valley.

Like the trapped Okavango, silting gradually allowed the Kwando/Linyanti river to spread out into a small inland delta, forming what we call the Linyanti Marshes today.

There is one further geographical feature of note in this area: an ancient river course known as the Magweqgana (spelled in various ways) or Selinda Spillway. This splits off from around the Okavango's Panhandle area, and heads northeast, entering the Linyanti River system just north of the Zibadianja Lagoon. This doesn't seem to be the obvious product of any local faultlines – although it does roughly follow the line of the Linyanti–Gumare Fault. It's either some form of overflow from the Okavango Delta, or perhaps an ancient river course, or both. Either way it's highly visible from the air, and on the ground offers a rich and open environment for game.

GEOGRAPHY The geography of the various parts of this area follows on directly from its geological history, and can easily be divided into four types of environment.

Firstly, there are the Linyanti Swamps, composed of river channels, lagoons, reedbeds and banks of papyrus. Secondly, adjacent to these is a narrow belt of riparian forest that lines these waterways – on the northern edge of the Linyanti Reserve, and the eastern edge of Kwando.

Thirdly there are two intermittent rivers, the Selinda Spillway and the Savuti Channel. Although both were dry for a number of years, both have flooded annually since 2009. There are similarities as well as differences between them, most notably the sheer width of the Selinda Spillway as it approaches the Linyanti Swamp compared with the relatively narrow Savuti Channel.

Finally, and common to all the concessions, are large areas of dry woodland dominated by large stands of mopane trees, which cover most of the three areas but are usually of least interest to the visitor on safari.

LINYANTI CONCESSION (NG15)

The Linyanti Concession covers 1,250km² of the northern Kalahari, dominated by large areas of mopane woodlands. However, its northern and western edges are bounded by the waters of the Linyanti River, complete with a string of lagoons and marshes. Adjacent to this is a narrow band of highly varied riparian forest which is the focus of most safari activities.

Cutting from west to east, through the southern part of the concession, is the bed of the Savuti Channel. This was a dry sand river during the 1990s and early 2000s, where a number of waterholes would attract game during the dry season. The channel started flowing once again in 2008, and has flowed intermittently through the concession ever since, reviving the lush, riverine woodland along its banks, which in turn attracts a range of wildlife.

FLORA AND FAUNA Until commercial hunting was outlawed throughout Botswana in 2014, the Linyanti Reserve was technically a 'multi-purpose concession', where both photographic safaris and hunting were allowed. Regardless of the country's legalisation of hunting again in 2019, Wilderness Safaris – who have been running the reserve for more than 20 years – have always focused exclusively on photographic tourism, thus reducing any negative impacts of hunting on the animal populations.

Flora As with the animals, in many ways the vegetation here is very similar to that of the Chobe riverfront area, though it generally seems in much better condition. It's thicker, older and more lush – though perhaps that is simply the result of much less logging by humans and slightly less pressure from the animals.

In the dry season there is usually at least 1km of open ground between the slightly raised riverbank, dotted with mature riparian forest, and the actual waters of the Linyanti. Most of this is open grassland, which will flood occasionally at times of very high water in the river system. In this area you'll find some smaller bushes, like russet bush-willows (*Combretum hereroense*) and Kalahari star apples (*Diospyros lycioides*) – the latter also known as toothbrush bushes after a surprisingly effective use for their thinner branches. (You may also hear this called the blue bush.)

Beyond the floodplain, and up the riverbank, you'll find classic riparian forest with plenty of tall species like knobthorn (*Senegalia nigrescens*), raintree (*Philenoptera violacea*), leadwood (*Combretum imberbe*), jackalberry (*Diospyros mespiliformis*), African mangosteen (*Garcinia livingstonei*) and some marvellous spreading sycamore figs (*Ficus sycomorus*). There are some woolly caper-bushes (*Capparis tomentosa*) in the lower vegetation, but fewer of them than you'll notice beside the Chobe.

Inland, far from the river, is dominated by mopane (*Colophospermum mopane*), though there are also mixed areas, notable for their Kalahari appleleaf (*Philenoptera nelsii*), wild seringa (*Burkea africana*), and others in the areas of deeper sand, like old watercourses. Baobabs (*Adansonia digitata*) are dotted around sporadically.

The area around Savuti Camp is very much like this dry woodland, interlaced with sandy fossil riverbeds, while along the narrow Savuti Channel itself you'll find more open grassland.

Fauna All year round you're likely to see impala, kudu, giraffe, reedbuck, steenbok, warthog, baboon and vervet monkeys throughout the area. Lion and spotted hyena are common, and generally the dominant predators, while leopard are often seen in the riparian forest and can be the highlight of night drives.

Cheetah occur, but not very frequently, and may have moved out of the area. Wild dog usually stay near their dens from around June to September (with July and August being the most reliable time), and then range widely over most of northern Botswana. Wild dog sightings on the reserve were reportedly consistent in 2023, with three packs being spotted regularly: the impressive 17-strong Zibadianja group and two smaller packs. (As an aside, dens in wild areas like this are not easily located, even when wild dogs have a presence in the vicinity.)

Blue wildebeest and Burchell's zebra are present all year, although around May they arrive in larger numbers, remaining within reach of the water until just before the rains begin in around November–December, when they normally head southeast towards Savuti Marsh. Elephants and buffalo follow a similar pattern, with small groups around all year, often only bulls, but with much larger breeding herds arriving in June–July and staying until December. During this time you'll regularly find very large herds of both buffalo and elephant, hundreds strong. Sable and roan antelope are regularly seen from June to December, congregating at waterholes around midday in herds up to 25 strong. Tsessebe occur, but are uncommon. Eland are very rare here, and gemsbok don't occur this far north.

Waterbuck are permanent residents, especially towards the northeast of the concession. This is one of relatively few areas of Botswana where they're found. Keep a look-out around King's Pool and Linyanti Tented Camp, particularly at the interface between the mopane woodlands of the interior and the riparian forest by the river. Sitatunga are occasionally sighted from boat trips on the river and from the deck of Linyanti Tented Camp.

Side-striped and black-backed jackal are around, the latter reaching the extreme northern edge of its distribution here (so it isn't common). Bat-eared fox are regularly seen; the area around King's Pool airstrip seems to be a particular favourite. Mongooses, especially banded and dwarf, are always around, and even bushpig are resident at DumaTau.

Serval, caracal, African wildcat and aardwolf all occur. Aardvark are occasionally seen, with one local expert reporting that they used to be spotted frequently in the riverine forest near the Zibadianja Lagoon.

When you're out on night drives, you've also got a chance to see scrub hares, spring hares, lesser bushbabies, porcupines, genets (small-spotted and large-spotted), civets and honey badgers.

Birdlife In the riparian woodlands, birds of particular interest include wood owls, swamp boubous, brown firefinches, white-rumped babblers and collared sunbirds. Of particular note is the beautiful Schalow's lourie, a local race of the Knysna lourie found in this region.

There are numerous summer migrants, including carmine bee-eaters that nest here in their hundreds. There are several colonies in the area, including one between King's Pool and DumaTau, where there used to be a hide. Carmines tend to arrive around September and leave by March–April. Some appear to have learned to follow vehicles down the Savuti Channel, catching the crickets that jump away from the moving wheels. Others use the kori bustards, which frequent the channel, as moving perches. Other summer visitors include the thick-billed cuckoo and the narina trogon.

The raptors are well represented. Bateleur and fish eagles are probably the most numerous, but you're also likely to spot African hawk, and tawny, martial and black-breasted snake eagles. Gymnogenes are relatively common. When the first rains come in December, migrants like Wahlberg's and steppe eagles seem notably attracted to the first flush of green in the Savuti Channel – hence December to February can be a particularly good time here.

Throughout the year, western banded snake eagles are also sometimes seen, though they're not common, along with giant eagle owls, bat hawks (look out on the edge of the forest, by the river, in the evening) and the occasional Pel's fishing owl.

On the water there's a host of different species, though some of the marshes and lagoons within the Linyanti Concession can be difficult to access. Some of the more unusual residents include slaty and black egret, rufous-bellied heron, painted snipe, long-toed lapwing, African rail and wattled crane. African skimmers usually nest here in September, with Zibadianja Lagoon, among others, being a favourite spot for them.

WHEN TO VISIT Note the general comments made on page 109, and then also the specific comments made for the Chobe riverfront on page 114 – because the Linyanti's riverfront has broadly the same kind of game movements as that area. In short: game concentrates around here when it needs the water, and spreads out when it can easily drink elsewhere.

This means that the game will be better when it's drier, although you'll find a wider variety of bird species here in the wet season, many of them in their breeding plumage.

GETTING THERE AND AWAY Getting to any of the camps in the Linyanti Concession is simple: you fly. Wilderness Safaris (who run all four camps) include light-aircraft flights in their trips into these camps, and it's very easy to fly here from Maun, Kasane, or another camp in northern Botswana. The airstrip ✈ DUMAIR 18°31.948'S, 23°39.264'E) is equidistant between DumaTau and Savuti Camp.

Logistics at all these camps are worked out well in advance, and everybody who arrives must have a prior reservation (most made months earlier). No self-driving visitors are allowed into the area, even those with reservations. So if you drive in, you can expect to be escorted off the property and pointed in the direction of a public road!

WHERE TO STAY *Map, page 284*
All five camps within the Linyanti Reserve are owned by **Wilderness Safaris** (page 216). They range from the substantial comfort of King's Pool to the much simpler bush-camp style of Linyanti Tented Camp, and are listed here from north to south. All cater exclusively for fly-in visitors and none will accept visitors who want to drive in.

King's Pool (8 suites) ✈ KINGSP 18°26.276'S, 23°42.415'E. Named after the Swedish royalty who honeymooned in Linyanti in 2010, this luxurious lodge is indeed fit for a king. One of Wilderness's flagship safari camps, luxurious accommodation, super service & good food are on offer. Sited under the shade of leadwoods & jackalberries, it overlooks an oxbow lagoon on the Linyanti River & the swamps beyond from a position in the very heart of the reserve, almost 18km northeast of DumaTau & a similar distance from Linyanti Tented Camp.

Each of the well-spaced suites, including 2 bedrooms, are on high wooden decking under a traditional thatched roof. Accessed through ornate doors, the interiors are extensive & stylish, with safari-style canvas-&-gauze wall panels paired with contemporary hotel-standard bathrooms. Four-poster beds swathed in mosquito netting, leather armchairs & teak furniture with rich fabrics give a classic feel. Large folding doors lead to a wide deck with a small plunge pool, shower & a sala – think exclusive thatched gazebo with day bed – overlooking the Linyanti River.

You could justifiably just relax here & watch wildlife on the river – & many visitors do – though for the energetic, each room comes with a yoga mat & mini weights. The minimalist, open-fronted

central area is equally well appointed, with leather chairs & extensive decking: a great place to watch elephants coming down to the water. There's also an open-air boma for meals under the stars, a swimming pool &, separately, a couple of hides, including one for eye-level wildlife viewing along the lagoon. Both double as a lovely setting for lunch, with one a great option for dinner *à deux*, though it's questionable if this offers better game viewing or birdwatching than is already possible from the balconies of the chalets.

Activities are mainly 4x4 game drives, day & night. These concentrate on the riverine forest areas beside the water &, when dry, the wide grassy floodplains between the river's water & the high bank. Short walks are also possible, & when the water levels are high enough (around Apr–Aug, though increasingly difficult to predict) there's a double-decker boat, the *Queen Sylvia*, for gentle sundowner cruises – with sleepouts on board a further option. *From US$1,420 pp Jan–Mar to US$3,410 pp Jun–Oct, FBA exc transfers.* ⊕ *All year.* 👑👑👑👑👑

DumaTau (8 tents) ✈ DUMATA 18°32.217'S, 23°33.917'E. At the western end of the Linyanti, overlooking the Osprey Lagoon from its southeastern shore, DumaTau is east of the source of the Savuti Channel. Its location between

11

2 elephant corridors means that pachyderm sightings are almost guaranteed, especially in the dry season between Jun & Oct, & the camp's elevated design permits elephants to get very close without any awareness of spellbound spectators just metres away.

Rebuilt & relocated several times over the years, DumaTau's latest reinvention reopened in 2021 with 8 luxurious suites, 1 specifically designed for families, all overlooking the lagoon & marshes either side of the main area. Under peaked, beige canvas, their spacious interiors are warm & contemporary, with retracting mosquito nets affording broad vistas through panoramic gauze picture windows from the comfortable beds. En-suite bathrooms are modern with shiny copper sinks. There are 'curiosity boxes' tucked in the rooms to uncover artefacts & local wildlife facts, & a broad deck for whiling away siesta times by the waterfront plunge pool.

There is a tiered central area, complete with dining room, bar & lounge, & steps down to a splendid, circular boma set out into the lily-strewn lagoon. In addition, shared with neighbouring Little DumaTau, Osprey Retreat is a wellness centre with a beautiful lap pool, modern moulded sunloungers on a shaded deck, souvenir shop, spa & deli kitchen for healthy snacks & fresh juices. Activities focus on 4x4 game drives, day & night, which visit the riverine forest beside the Linyanti, as well as the drier areas along the upper reaches of the Savuti Channel & the mopane forest between. Short walks are sometimes possible, & when water levels are high, a boat can be used on the lagoon & in nearby waterways. Guests staying 3 nights or more may pre-book (at no additional cost) a sleepout on the reserve's covered star deck at the source of the Savuti Channel (with a guide in a tent not too far away). *From US$1,560 pp mid-Jan–Mar to US$3,750 pp Jun–Oct, FBA exc transfers.* ⊕ *All year.* 😋😋😋😋😋

Little DumaTau (4 tents) Adjacent to DumaTau (page 289), this elegant little camp is the 2021 offshoot of its well-known sister camp next door. There are just 4 tented suites here, each with large, gauze picture windows, linear decks inset with a plunge pool overlooking the water, & contemporary interiors of woven leather, acacia-wood mosaic & dusky pink linen. An intimate central area offers an open-fronted lounge, bar, individual dining, a swimming pool overlooking

the hippo-filled lagoon & a sandy, circular firepit for after-dinner drinks & stargazing. The camp is connected by a raised walkway to Osprey Retreat, where it shares leisure facilities with DumaTau. *From US$1,560 pp mid-Jan–Mar to US$3,750 pp Jun–Oct, FBA exc transfers.* ⊕ *All year.* 😋😋😋😋😋

Savuti Camp (6 tents) ⊕ SAVUTI 18°35.834'S, 23°40.412'E. Savuti Camp stands beside the Savuti Channel, about 42km due west of the Savuti Marsh – the area within the Chobe National Park that's commonly known as 'Savuti'. It's about 13km as the eagle flies from Zibadianja Lagoon.

The camp's classic Meru-style safari tents, 1 designed for families, are raised up on individual wooden decks with a veranda, under the cool shade of a large thatched roof. All have en-suite showers, toilets & washbasins with hot & cold water.

There's an open-fronted dining room, bar & lounge area under a thatched roof, with a star deck, campfire & small pool overlooking the water. Activities concentrate on 4x4 game drives by day & night, although walks are also possible, & there are several elevated hides to visit. For 30 years, until the heavy rainfall of 2008–09, the waterhole in front of the camp was the only source of water in the dry season for kilometres around, giving the camp a justified reputation for great lion & elephant sightings. Now, as it appears that the dry periods are back, the few kilometres of water here continue to attract large herds of game & their attendant predators. *From US$930 pp/ sharing mid-Jan–Mar to US$1,940 pp/ sharing Jun–Oct, FBA exc transfers.* ⊕ *All year.* 😋😋😋😋–😋😋😋😋😋

Linyanti Tented Camp (4 tents) About 10km southwest of Chobe's Linyanti Campsite (page 283), & not to be confused with Linyanti Bush Camp (see opposite), this is an old-style safari camp, far from the plush, interior-designer chic found in many of Wilderness's camps. Wood-framed, canvas-walled chalets are comfortable & well appointed with explorer trunks for storage, directors' chairs & an en-suite shower. Like the slightly elevated timber-&-canvas, open-fronted dining & bar area, they all overlook the Linyanti Marshes & floodplains. There's a pool & a log-pile hide close to an elephant path, with views over the river. Activities are limited to day & night game drives in the camp's concession & day trips further afield. Rates quoted only as part of a group trip. With a max of 8 guests, it is often used by set-departure fly-in groups & families or small groups of friends. *From US$530 pp mid-Jan–Mar* to US$1,000 pp Jun–Oct, FBA exc transfers. ⏱ *All year.* 🛏🛏🛏–🛏🛏🛏🛏

LINYANTI ENCLAVE (CH1)

Just to the east of Chobe National Park's Linyanti Gate, this concession shares a very similar environment to that of the Linyanti Reserve (page 286), although the riverside camps here offer water-based activities, as well as game drives. Note that Linyanti Campsite and Camp Linyanti lie within Chobe National Park, so are covered in that chapter (page 245).

GETTING THERE AND AWAY Whereas camps within the Linyanti Reserve (NG15; page 286) are exclusively for fly-in guests, those in CH1 can also be accessed by self-drivers – although all guests must have a prior reservation; you cannot just turn up here.

By air Guests arriving by air at one of African Bush Camps' properties are flown to Saile airstrip, from where it's a pleasant half-hour game drive to Linyanti Bush Camp and Linyanti Ebony.

By car Self-drivers can approach the Linyanti River camps from one of two directions, both involving significant stretches of deep sand. From Kasane, the best option is to drive towards Chobe National Park's Ghoha Gate (as described under *Driving from Kasane to Savuti*, page 263), but then to turn right along the cutline; this is outside the park, so you don't need to pay park fees. Some 36km from the Ghoha Gate you'll reach the Linyanti Gate, where you turn right. From here, it's just over 4km northeast along the river to Linyanti Bush Camp. Approaching from Savuti, you could either head north to the Ghoha Gate, then continue along the cutline as page 264, or take the direct if little-used route to the Linyanti Gate as described on page 265, then continue north for a further 4km or so to the camps.

🛖 **WHERE TO STAY** *Map, page 284*

African Bush Camps (page 214) operates three camps here: Linyanti Bush Camp, the adjacent Linyanti Ebony and the most recent 'expedition-style' camp, Linyanti Expeditions. For every guest, a daily levy (included in rates) is made to the African Bush Camps Foundation. This in turn ploughs the money back into the fields of education, conservation, community infrastructure and empowerment, so your visit is having a direct benefit on the wider community.

For the simpler and unrelated Linyanti Campsite and Camp Linyanti, both sharing a river frontage but within Chobe National Park, see page 283.

✳ **Linyanti Bush Camp** (6 tents) ⊕ LINYBC 18°14.804′S, 23°57.514′E. From its position on the forest's edge, Linyanti Bush Camp offers sweeping views across the seemingly boundless Linyanti Marshes. You can take in the unobstructed panorama from various vantage points: the elevated central area, the swimming pool, or the veranda of the generous wood-framed tents. The cosy central area encompasses a dining area & comfortable lounge & acts as a friendly, social gathering point. Check out the collection of local artefacts, grab a book & a drink from the little bar, or sit out on the wooden deck, overlooking the firepit & its circle of inviting chairs. There's also a quirky curio shop where baskets made by a women's co-operative make great souvenirs.

Sandy pathways meander from this area to the 6 en-suite tents, each sitting on a shaded wooden deck. The tent interiors exude an old-world charm, with polished furniture, natural fabrics & traditional wooden chests. Gauze windows afford a refreshing breeze & great vistas, which are also on offer from the rain shower. It's understated comfort in a classic safari style, but far from outdated.

Linyanti Bush Camp offers flexible activities, with 4x4 game drives, both day & night, guided walks &, when water levels permit (usually Dec– Aug) boat & mokoro trips. For those staying for 3+ nights in Apr–Nov, there's an unforgettable 30min helicopter flight across the marshes & wooded hinterland. *US$748 pp Jan–Mar & Dec, US$881 pp Apr–May & Nov, US$1,270 pp Jun–Oct, FBA inc conservation/community fee. Children 12+.* ☉ *All year.* 👑👑👑👑–👑👑👑👑👑

Linyanti Ebony (4 tents) Adjacent to Linyanti Bush Camp, & very similar in style, but with only 4 tents, Ebony is ideal for small groups or families looking for an exclusive-use safari camp. With this in mind, there are child-specialist guides on hand & 1 elevated family tent, sleeping up to 5 in 2 interconnecting, en-suite rooms (1 even has a claw-foot bath with a view). The other 2-person tents are set on low wooden decking & are not unlike those at Bush Camp: simple, comfortable furnishing set on polished wooden floors & maximising the view with gauze windows.

The central lounge/dining tent is open to the front, with its deck shaded beneath a mature ebony tree & with a traditional firepit facing the marsh. Activities follow an identical format to those at its sister camp, with the same vehicles & guides. *Rates as Linyanti Bush Camp (page 291). Children all ages.* ☉ *All year.* 👑👑👑👑– 👑👑👑👑👑

Linyanti Expeditions (6 tents) [not mapped] With only 6 classic safari tents, Linyanti Expeditions has an authentic, intimate atmosphere, reminiscent of traditional bush camps. The simple tents are not lacking in 'wow factor', though, as each room features a 'star suite' – a secure, mesh-covered space that allows guests to relocate their beds beneath the Milky Way for a special sleeping experience. All tents have en-suite bathrooms, with copper sinks, canvas shelves, eco-friendly toilets & open-air showers. The tented main area features a communal dining spot, with an open kitchen, a separate lounge & a central campfire. Activities such as walking safaris, river mokoro trips & day/night game drives are available. Linyanti Expeditions also offers great opportunities for birdwatching, with a chance to observe carmine bee-eaters nesting along the banks of the river in season (Sep–Dec). It's a good spot for more adventurous, back-to-basics safari travellers. *US$640 pp May, US$915 pp Jun–Oct, FBA inc conservation/community fee. Children 16+.* ☉ *May–Oct.* 👑👑👑–👑👑👑👑

SELINDA CONCESSION (NG16)

Selinda covers a long swathe of 1,350km², including a large section of the Magweqgana or Selinda Spillway, the often-dry waterway that links the Okavango to the Linyanti Swamps. However, after a period of close on 30 years, the Spillway is again flowing all the way from the Okavango Delta to the marshes of the Kwando and Linyanti, transforming the landscape into a mosaic of savannah and wetland.

Most of the reserve's camps are in the far east of the concession, in a very open area where small tree-islands stand amid large dry plains. The western side of the concession is largely thick combretum and mopane forest.

FLORA AND FAUNA
Flora Like many Delta areas, different vegetation types in the Selinda Concession create a diverse and dynamic ecosystem, supporting a wide array of wildlife species. The availability of water in the area, particularly along the Selinda Spillway and the seasonal floodplains, is a key factor influencing the distribution of flora and fauna in the area.

The area around Selinda and Zarafa camps is the wide mouth of the Magweqgana or Selinda Spillway. This area primarily consists of expansive floodplains, dotted with small palm islands. On rare occasions, the Spillway experiences flooding, causing temporary water retention. This phenomenon leads to the demise of numerous small trees and shrubs across the plains, ultimately transforming the landscape into only vast marshes and grasslands.

Until 2009, these cleared areas had been gradually colonised by 'pioneer species' of invading bushes, among them the wild sage (*Pechuel-loeschea leubnitziae*), which covered large areas of the Spillway with its aromatic grey-green foliage, and the candle-pod acacia (*Vachellia hebeclada*). The subsequent return of water removed these young acacia trees from the floodplains, though fortunately for the large giraffe population, plenty exist elsewhere.

Dotted around this area are small, slightly raised 'islands' of trees. These have been here for decades, and can survive the periodic flooding – though see the comments on page 9 if you're curious as to how such 'islands' are formed. The trees found on these tree-islands are typical in many ways of those in the riparian forests, though with the addition of lots of real fan palms (*Hyphaene petersiana*), thanks to the palm nuts deposited and germinated in elephant dung. Some are tall trees, many are only bush-size, but all help to make Selinda's environment a particularly attractive one. Among the other tree species here, African mangosteens (*Garcinia livingstonei*) seem particularly common and lush, their branches all apparently flung outwards, as if a green bomb had exploded inside.

To the north of the concession, along the Kwando border, and west towards the Okavango Delta, mopane forest dominates.

Fauna As in the Linyanti and Kwando reserves, there's a population of resident game here, which is swelled from about June onwards by the arrival of large numbers of game which move into the reserve for its proximity to the permanent waters of Zibadianja Lagoon and the Kwando–Linyanti river system. Wildlife viewing on the Selinda Reserve is particularly good during the dry period from June to around late October/early November, although we have also had phenomenal game viewing in the off season.

Permanent game includes impala, red lechwe (on the east side near the lagoon, with a resident population that rises and falls in accordance with the water levels), kudu, tsessebe, giraffe, reedbuck, steenbok, warthog, baboon and vervet monkeys. There is an extremely healthy **lion** population in Selinda. In 2023, over 30 lions, across two prides, were resident in the concession: the well-known Selinda Pride, who had ten infant cubs on our last visit, and the impressive coalition of six males, known as The Army Boys. In addition, 25 individual lions are known to move between here and Kwando, making for consistently excellent 'big cat' sightings and often plenty of playful cubs.

Spotted hyena are also common, and there are often good sightings of **leopard**, thanks to the three females and five males patrolling the area, several of whom appear very relaxed.

Selinda's very open country should make this an excellent environment for **cheetah**, and although not currently resident in the concession, cheetah are seen in the area. A coalition of two brothers were frequently moving between the Kwando and Selinda concessions in 2023, hunting and patrolling their expansive territory.

Once one of Botswana's better reserves for **wild dog**, Selinda's last resident pack disappeared in 2019. Now, with only occasional visitors passing through the concession, it's likely that the current strength and numbers of the lion population has informed the wild dogs' decision to den and hunt elsewhere. At the time of writing, six adult dogs were roaming in and out of the concession from Kwando. Although wild dog do range over the whole of northern Botswana, if you want any chance of seeing them then you'll need a place where your guide can drive off-road, to stick with them as they hunt, and where there's lots of dry, open grassland with not too many trees, so that the driving is relatively free of obstacles. This narrows the choice down to a few of the private reserves, but would include Selinda, Mombo, Vumbura, Kwara, Linyanti, the area around the Khwai River, and the southern side of Kwando. This doesn't mean you won't see wild dogs elsewhere; you will. However, if you're going out specifically to look for dogs, start in these areas.

Herds of **wildebeest**, albeit in declining numbers, and **zebra** arrive around May, staying here until just around November–December, when the majority move south towards the Makgadikgadi Pans. Elephants and buffalo follow a similar pattern with individuals being seen all year, and larger breeding herds arriving around June–July and staying until December. **Eland** appear from the northwest and are most likely to be seen in October to November, while **sable** and **roan** are best around the Spillway at Selinda Explorers, though none of these antelope species is common.

Black-backed and side-striped **jackal**, **bat-eared fox** and various **mongooses** are resident, as are the more nocturnal **serval**, **African wildcat** and **aardwolf**, though spotting the latter in the vegetation is extremely difficult. The illusive caracal has now not been spotted in the concession since 2015. Night drives will often locate scrub hares, spring hares, lesser bushbabies, genets (small-spotted and large-spotted), civets, sometimes honey badgers or porcupines, and – rarely – aardvark.

Birdlife The combination of wet and dry habitats attracts a wide range of bird species. Virtually all of the birds typical of riparian woodlands in the neighbouring Linyanti and Kwando reserves (pages 286 and 297) also occur in the tree-islands of Selinda. In addition to this, the reserve is noted for good sightings of collared palm thrush, plus species of open grasslands like ostriches, secretary birds, kori bustards, red-crested korhaans, various sandgrouse and both common and (from November to March) harlequin quails. The family of coursers is well represented here – with the uncommon bronze-winged and three-banded varieties occurring, as well as the more widespread Temminck's and double-banded coursers.

During Botswana's summer months the birding is at its best, with all the European and central African migrants in residence. At this time, black coucal, coppery-tailed coucal, colonies of carmine bee-eaters, who nest along the Kwando and Linyanti rivers, and flocks of Abdim's and white storks can be seen, along with African skimmers fishing on the surface of the lagoons. Sightings of wattled cranes have improved and families of endangered ground hornbills are in evidence. Raptor concentrations are always good, with eagles aplenty (steppe, Wahlberg's, short-tailed/bateleur, hawk and fish eagles), lappet-faced and white-backed vultures scouring the plains, and ospreys frequenting the area.

GETTING THERE AND AWAY With the Spillway flowing, the Selinda Reserve is effectively cut off from Maun and Kasane by rivers, so all visitors arrive by air. The flight takes about an hour from Maun or Kasane, and is very easily organised by the camp or your tour operator. There's an airstrip situated halfway between the Selinda and Zarafa camps, less than 5km from either of them.

 WHERE TO STAY *Map, page 284*
All the camps in the Selinda Concession are now run by **Great Plains Conservation** (page 214), but the pioneer here was Linyanti Explorations.

Linyanti Explorations started in Botswana in 1976 as the small, owner-run operation that founded Chobe Chilwero (selling it in 1999), and they solidified their reputation with the superb, simple camps of the Selinda Reserve. Over the years, as ownership of Botswana's safari camps became concentrated into fewer companies, and many of those camps have opted to prioritise luxury, Linyanti Explorations dared to be different. It stayed simple, concentrating on its wildlife and guiding – and hence was always a personal favourite!

In 2006, the company was bought by Great Plains Conservation, which is backed by Dereck and Beverly Joubert, notable wildlife film-makers and photographers. They stopped the (controlled) hunting that took place in the west of the reserve, and spent a great deal of money upgrading and rebuilding the camps, including the transformation of a former hunting camp, Motswiri, into Okavango Explorers, which stands in a lovely spot beside the Selinda Spillway in the far west of the concession.

Like most of Botswana's high-quality camps, bookings for all these must be made well in advance and virtually everyone flies in. Great Plains encourages travellers to book through good overseas tour operators that specialise in Africa.

Okavango Explorers Camp (6 tents)
⊕ MOTSWI 18°46.00'S, 23°02.05'E. On the banks of the Selinda Spillway, Okavango Explorers Camp opened in Jul 2022, as the most recent addition to the Great Plains group of camps. As with the others, this is a stylish, early-explorer tented camp with an equally relaxed atmosphere & an experienced, friendly team. Slightly elevated, the main area is an elegant, open-fronted tent with a communal dining table, bar & comfortable lounge, all overlooking the sandy firepit & seasonal Spillway beyond. It's a relaxed, social space, with meals often taken under the stars or, occasionally, surrounded by lanterns with your feet in the clear water.

With only 6 Meru tents, this is an intimate camp offering a highly personal service. The tents are spacious, & all can be made up as comfortable dbls or twins. Expedition-style dark-wood furniture, from free-standing fans to travelling trunks, sit alongside soft East African furnishings, crisp white bed linen & thoughtful mod-cons, including solar-powered lighting. Each tent has a canvas-walled open-air bathroom with a flush toilet & an impressive 200-litre bucket shower, which rivals most hotel showers. Décor is decadent but practical & the essence of a classic, wildlife-focused camp is retained.

Guiding is good & activities include game drives (day & night), alongside a strong focus on delightful walks through the woodland on the edge of the Spillway, & mokoro excursions (water levels permitting; usually May–Sep). We've seen good populations of zebra, impala, giraffe, elephant & buffalo here, as well as great

sightings of roan antelope. A past highlight in the exact location of this camp was witnessing 2 wild dog kills in as many days. *From US$1,200 pp mid-Jan–Mar to US$2,010 pp mid-Jun–Oct, FBA inc conservation fees. Children 6+.* ⊕ *All year.* 👑👑👑👑

Selinda Camp (3 tents, 1 exclusive-use suite)
⊕ SELIND 18°31.897'S, 23°31.354'E. Standing on the edge of the Selinda Spillway, Selinda Camp is a long-time favourite & now one of Botswana's smallest & most exclusive camps, spectacular in both style & service.

The 3 substantial tented guest suites, each with a lavish en-suite bathroom, private veranda & plunge pool, are on raised wooden decks under thatched canopies. Entered through ornate, studded Zanzibari doors, the space is elegant & thoughtfully curated, with tactile textures, furniture & objets d'art from all over Africa, & modern-day conveniences, from ultrasound insect repellent to solar-power AC. Beds are exceptionally comfortable, Chesterfield sofas & hammocks are inviting & the shiniest copper baths are indulgent. If exercise is preferred, a yoga mat, weights & an exercise bike are on hand in each room, as are complimentary camera kit & Swarovski binoculars.

The camp's main building is a towering A-frame thatched structure, complete with burnished copper lights, intricate carved columns & art by wildlife artist Keith Joubert. High-backed leather chairs sit at the immaculately laid banqueting table overlooking the reed-edged Spillway, deep-cushioned sofas invite relaxation & there's a self-service bar in a scarlet kitchen dresser. Meals are served both indoors & under the shade of a beautiful Natal mahogany, where the candlelit dinners are marvellously atmospheric. There's also a spa with a resident therapist, a stylish boutique & a well-stocked wine cellar.

The team are enthusiastic about their activities, which concentrate on 4x4 game drives in the morning & afternoon/evening. The former can start very early (a good sign of commitment to their game spotting!), while the latter eventually become spotlit night drives. Short walks can be organised, often as part of a drive, & during the winter months canoeing & boating are on offer, which depart from the jetty right at the front of camp. Hides across the reserve also offer good spots to relax during an afternoon siesta.

In addition to the 3 tents around camp, the separate 2-bedroom Selinda Suite, akin to its counterparts, the Dhow Suite at Zarafa, & the Duba Plains Suite, comprises a large tented suite with 2 bedrooms. The Selinda Suite operates exclusively, with guests having access to their own private vehicle, safari guide, chef & manager.

Selinda Camp: US$1,935 pp mid-Jan–Mar, US$2,460 pp Apr–mid-Jun & Nov–mid-Dec, US$3,665 pp, sharing mid-Jun–Oct & festive season, FBA inc park fees & laundry; exc transfers. Selinda Suite: US$9,290–17,590 for 4, FBA inc conservation fees & transfers. ⊕ *All year.* 😀😀😀😀😀

✱ **Selinda Explorers Camp** (4 tents) ⊗ SELEXP 18°30.686'S, 23° 25.913'E. About 90mins' drive west of Selinda & Zarafa, on the banks of the Selinda Spillway, Selinda Explorers is designed in the style of a traditional early-explorer-style tented camp, albeit a luxurious, permanent one. Modest in scale compared with Selinda Camp, & significantly less lavish than the opulent Zarafa Camp, Selinda Explorers still radiates style & its curated aesthetic makes it as elegant as many of Botswana's high-end lodges. Soft furnishings hail from Zanzibar & East Africa, a subtle Middle Eastern influence is detected in the cushioned tea-tent vibe, & its staff are uniformly engaging & attentive. Everything, in fact, exudes a quiet confidence. The results are a camp that presents a wilderness experience without compromising on luxury or service.

Beside an enormous mopane tree, the central area consists of 2 elegant open-fronted tents: 1 a dining area & bar, & the other a lounge adorned with overlapping rich red Persian rugs, leather furniture, Omani floor cushions, Zanzibari chests & beaten metal lanterns, creating a distinctly Arabian twist. Low, cushion-covered timber sofas encourage guests to put their feet up, flick through one of the owner's coffee table wildlife books & indulge in the moment. Or simply sit in a hammock by the small plunge pool & see what wanders by in this wildlife-rich area. The camp atmosphere really comes to life as the sun goes down, when it is lit entirely by paraffin lanterns & a central campfire glows beside an active, ever-growing termite mount.

There are 4 generous pale-canvas tents, 1 of which is geared to families or friends with 2 linked en-suite tents & a shared shaded veranda. The beds are extremely comfortable, the expedition-style furniture continues & the en-suites are spacious.

When it comes to activities, flexibility is the buzzword here: take b/fast to enjoy at a scenic bush stop, enjoy lunch any time you return to camp, take game drives along the river or head into the bush on foot accompanied by experienced armed guides. When there's water (May–Sep in a good year), explore the Spillway by mokoro from right in front of the main area. *From US$1,200 pp mid-Jan–Mar to US$2,010 pp mid-Jun–Oct, FBA inc transfers & conservation fees. Children 6+.* ⊕ *All year.* 😀😀😀😀😀

✱ **Zarafa** (4 tents, 1 exclusive-use suite) ⊗ ZARAFA 18°35.17.5'S, 23°31.544'E. Zarafa is the very definition of refined African adventure. On a naturally raised bank overlooking the lagoons, reedbeds & floodplains that stem from the Zibadianja Lagoon, it is unquestionably one of Botswana's most exclusive, most beautiful & most costly camps. It's a Relais & Châteaux property, owned & created by renowned wildlife filmmaker Dereck Joubert & his wife, photographer Beverly Joubert, & their passions are evident throughout the camp: the distinctive décor & original monochrome photography; the low environmental footprint & in-room portfolio explaining the work of the Great Plains Foundation; & the Swarovski binoculars, digital SLR cameras & memory cards provided for guests' use.

Zarafa's luxurious tented suites are raised on decks constructed from reclaimed railway sleepers, & accessed through ornate Zanzibari doors. Inside, the early-settler aesthetic is paired with contemporary photography & first-class amenities. There are inviting leather sofas on claret-coloured rugs, heavy, brass-trimmed trunks, a crystal decanter, & in the open-plan bedroom/bathroom area, a deep copper bath sits alongside a spherical suspended gas fire, a rain shower & the most comfortable of beds. Effective AC & heating are both discreetly hidden. On the terrace, there's a plunge pool & alfresco shower, with everything from watercolour sets to yoga mats & weights on hand for in-room entertainment.

Under giant jackalberry trees, Zarafa's equally stylish tented lounge, dining room, bar & library are intimate spaces, all leading out on to decked areas overlooking the floodplains. Wildlife, particularly elephant & hippo, is a common sight here. On separate visits, we've been lucky enough to see both a 16-strong pack of wild dogs & herds of elephants playing near the water's edge directly in front of the camp! Most meals – from stone-baked pizzas to hearty 3-course dinners – take advantage of the vista & are served outside as small, social gatherings (private dining on request) & are accompanied by wine from the temperature-controlled cellar.

Activities are very flexible: day & night game drives (full day on request) are in custom-built Toyota Land Cruisers, with bucket seats & photographic aids as standard; they can also arrange walks, catch-&-release fishing trips (exc Jan–Feb) & idyllic trips on the pontoon boat at Zibadianja Lagoon. There's also a gym & in-room massage is available, while one of the most tasteful camp gift shops in Botswana stocks locally made gifts & stylish safari clothes.

Adjacent to Zarafa main camp, Zarafa Dhow Suite is a very special, exclusive-use, 2-bedroom private villa. Operating completely independently of the main camp, with its own dedicated team – manager, guide, chef & staff – Dhow Suite is the ultimate spot for a secluded safari escape with family or friends. In keeping with the exploration-style décor of main camp, the heavy Zanzibari doors open on to a central area complete with Chesterfield sofas, leather-buckled trunks & crystal decanters. But beyond is the real draw: an enticing, tiered deck with sweeping views across the reedbeds & water. Hippos munch the short grass below the firepit, vervet monkeys snatch a drink from the pool & elephants parade past en route to the water. Use the spotting scope to seek out lions, burn some calories on the exercise bike or just pull up a chair & soak it all up. The expansive bedroom suites are either side of the main area, with enormous picture windows, huge beds swathed in mosquito netting & concealed AC/heating in the headboards. Lattice screens hide copper baths & rain showers, there's ample storage, good charging facilities (inc USB) & thoughtful home comforts aplenty. A metal globe containing the glowing gas fire is a lovely winter touch! Zarafa is certainly indulgent, but the camp is beautiful, service impeccable, wildlife good & eco-credentials strong (100% solar with a biogas system to produce cooking gas). *Zarafa Camp: US$1,935 pp mid-Jan– Mar, US$2,460 pp Apr–mid-Jun & Nov–mid-Dec, US$3,665 pp mid-Jun–Oct & festive season, FBA exc transfers. Zarafa Dhow Suite: US$9,290–17,590 for 4, FBA inc conservation fees & transfers.* ⊕ *All year.* 🏵🏵🏵🏵🏵

KWANDO CONCESSION (NG14)

On the northern edge of Botswana, bordering Namibia across the Kwando River, the Kwando Concession covers an enormous 2,320km² of very wild bush. It's one of Botswana's larger wildlife concessions. Beside its eastern boundary, formed by the river, is a narrow belt of riverine forest. In the south this opens out into some large tree-islands and open, grassy floodplains. There are two photographic camps on this productive eastern side: Lagoon and Lebala.

The vast western part of the concession includes huge tracts of thick mopane woodland.

FLORA AND FAUNA

Flora   Kwando's environment and ecosystems are similar to those of the Linyanti and Selinda reserves. The north of the reserve is most like the Linyanti Reserve, in that it's dominated by the presence of the river, which runs on its eastern border in a roughly straight line. Adjacent to this is a band of riverine forest, characteristically rich in its variety of trees. These include African mangosteen (*Garcinia livingstonei*) – which remind me of a bomb exploding, as all the stems grow out straight from the top – jackalberry (*Diospyros mespiliformis*), sausage tree (*Kigelia africana*), leadwood (*Combretum imberbe*) and knobthorn (*Senegalia nigrescens*).

As you move further south in the reserve, around Lebala Camp, you're getting into the northern side of the Magweqgana or Selinda Spillway, and here the riverine forest opens out, becoming a mosaic of open areas covered in low bushes and grasses. These open areas are often dominated by wild sage (*Pechuel-loeschea leubnitziae*) and interspersed with patches of woodland, which become smaller and more island-like as you move further south.

These forest patches and islands contain many of the same riverine tree species, though in increasingly fewer numbers, and you'll also find marula trees (*Sclerocarya birrea*), occasional baobabs (*Adansonia digitata*) and increasing numbers of real fan palms (*Hyphaene petersiana*), plus many camelthorns (*Vachellia erioloba*) and the invasive candle-pod acacia (*Vachellia hebeclada*).

Further south still, the land becomes even more open as you approach the reserve's southern boundary and the Selinda Reserve.

Fauna Like the Linyanti and Selinda, Kwando's resident game is augmented in about June by migrant game which arrives here from the drier areas south and west, attracted by the permanent waters of the Kwando River.

Common species found here include impala, red lechwe, kudu, giraffe, steenbok, warthog, baboon and vervet monkeys. Roan, sable, tsessebe and common duiker also occur, but not frequently. Lion, leopard and spotted hyena are common, while cheetah traverse between Kwando and Selinda. Hippo and crocodiles frequent the river, along with the playful spotted-necked otters.

Herds of wildebeest and zebra are resident from about May to December. Elephants and buffalo follow a similar pattern with individuals around all year, and larger breeding herds arriving around June–July and staying until December. These large herds are particularly common near the river during the dry season, and with 20 years having passed since hunting took place on the concession boundary, the herds' behaviour is now notably more relaxed.

Kwando is also a good reserve for seeing wild dog, especially in the dry season, helped by Kwando Safaris' policy of actively 'tracking' animals across the bush, and having both a tracker and a driver/guide on each of its vehicles. In 2023, wild dog were regularly seen denning near both Lagoon and Lebala camps.

Highlights of the night drives here include Selous's mongoose, genets and aardwolf – along with more usual sightings of scrub hares, spring hares, bushbabies, genets, civets, honey badgers and porcupines.

Birdlife The birdlife here is almost identical to that of the Linyanti Reserve (page 288), with plenty of variety. I particularly remember a huge colony of carmine bee-eaters that we seemed to have discovered by accident when stopping for a sundowner drink.

Sacred and hadada ibis are particularly common in the waterways, while rarer residents include slaty and black egrets, and rufous-bellied herons.

WHEN TO VISIT Game viewing revolves around the reserve's riverfront on the Kwando River and its adjacent riverine forest, so note the comments made on page 109, and also the specific comments made for the Chobe riverfront area, on page 114. The Kwando's riverfront has broadly similar game movements to the Chobe or Linyanti riverfronts. In short: game concentrates around here when it needs the water, and spreads away again when it can easily drink elsewhere.

This means that the game viewing improves as the land dries out. Then buffalo and elephants move into this area from the west and south and zebra and wildebeest move in from the great plains of the Chobe. Later, when it rains, so the animals will move away – although birdwatchers will find more of interest in the wet season when there's a greater variety of bird species, many in breeding plumage.

GETTING THERE AND AWAY Like most of Botswana's private concessions, Kwando is reached by a short flight from Maun, Kasane or one of Botswana's other camps. There are two main airstrips in the concession: one near Lagoon (Kwando airstrip), and the other near Lebala. Both the camps here work out their logistics well in advance. Trips are always pre-arranged, and they don't welcome drop-in visitors, nor ever really get any.

Thus virtually nobody would consider self-driving into these camps, even by prior arrangement. However, if you did then you'd pre-arrange your visit with the camps and take the transit route north through Selinda. It's about 14km in a straight line from Selinda to Lebala, and a further 30km by road from there to Lagoon.

WHERE TO STAY *Map, page 284*

Both the camps here are owned and run by **Kwando Safaris** (page 215), who are based in Maun.

Lagoon (8 tents) ✈ LAGOON 18°12.980'S, 24°24.790'E. Overlooking a bend in the Kwando River, Lagoon is the more northerly of Kwando's 2 camps in the riparian forest belt. It stands amid tall, mature forest that includes some fine marula & jackalberry trees.

Large chalets, set on stilts along the river, are designed to maximise the views from both the veranda & each area of the interior. The front walls are made entirely of gauze, & this, together with a ceiling fan over the bed, ensures that everything is cool & breezy. In the split-level interiors, there's a comfortable seating area at the front, a dbl or twin beds set higher up, & an en-suite bathroom with a claw-foot bath & outdoor shower.

The food at Lagoon is good, served buffet-style in a thatched dining room facing the river. The bar is largely self-service, & an extensive curio shop has local handicrafts & some useful books. The lounge area has comfortable armchairs, a small library & various local board games. Wildlife frequently wanders into camp & on our last visit an elephant had broken the main deck overnight to uproot a small tree.

Lagoon Camp has a plunge pool for the hotter months, but its main activities are 4x4 game drives & boating excursions, usually 1 early in the morning, & the 2nd in late afternoon, which usually turns into a night drive as the light fades. With a tracker accompanying every drive, & a max of 6 people per vehicle, there's a willingness to drive cross-country & actively track coveted game, such as big cats & wild dogs. The guides are enthusiastic about their big game, & sometimes positively zealous in their tracking of it. For gentle sundowner cruises (subject to water levels) there is a 2-storey floating pontoon-type boat on the river, & if you're keen on fishing, you can try your hand at spinning for tigerfish & bream. Lagoon's atmosphere is laid-back, friendly & not at all regimented – mealtimes are usually adjusted around game-viewing times, rather than vice versa. A slight minus is that the tents are quite close together (although all have canvas blinds that can be closed). *From US$950–1,320 pp Nov–Jun (US$150 Xmas surcharge) to US$1,750 pp Jul–Oct, FBA inc conservation fee.* ⊕ *All year.* 🛏🛏🛏🛏–🛏🛏🛏🛏🛏

❋ **Lebala** (8 tents) ✈ LEBALA 18°24.760'S, 23°32.540'E. Lebala is in a very different setting to Lagoon; the name means 'open space', which is appropriate as the camp overlooks the surrounding plains. It's just 14km from Selinda & yet 26km (measured in a straight line) from Lagoon – so it's no surprise that its environment is close in character to that of Selinda.

11

The camp's substantial & custom-designed tents are on raised decking made of polished Zimbabwe teak. Sliding doors lead to a large bedroom, with 2 ¾-size beds & simple teak furniture. Screened 'shade cloth' walls mean that wildlife can be watched from your room, with curtains & blinds to control the level of light. Outside is a private veranda for sitting out, with 2 chairs & a coffee table. Canvas room-divisions separate the bedroom from the 'entrance hall', where there is a spot to put suitcases, a hat-&-coat stand, a large wardrobe & a writing desk. The large bathroom has a standalone claw-foot bath, his & hers washbasins & a separate toilet, while outside is a dbl shower. (Hot water comes very efficiently from individual gas geysers.)

In a thatched dining area behind the tents, good meals are served communally with guides & managers, & often under the gaze of the resident bushbuck, Norman. Adjacent is a thatched, open-fronted lounge with a well-stocked, self-service bar, a good reference library of nature books & a souvenir shop. Overlooking the plains, it's a cool spot to while away siesta time & see what wanders by. There's a central campfire for the cooler months, & a 'naturally solar-heated' plunge pool for the warmer ones.

Activities concentrate on 4x4 game drives & walking. As at Lagoon, the guides always drive with a tracker & will actively seek the game. *From US$950–1,320 pp Nov–Jun (US$150 Xmas surcharge) to US$1,750 pp Jul–Oct, FBA inc conservation fee.* ⊕ *All year.* ♨♨♨♨–♨♨♨♨

12

The Okavango Delta – Moremi Game Reserve

Much of what is covered in this section – especially concerning flora and fauna, and when to visit – is applicable to the Okavango as a whole. Therefore I've covered this information here in detail, and made reference to it elsewhere where appropriate. The map of the Delta in the first colour section relates to the whole area.

Remember that Moremi and its surrounding reserves are separated only by lines on a map; their ecosystems blend together seamlessly. Birds and animals move without hindrance across almost the whole of the Okavango, Linyanti and Chobe regions. Thus all the country covered in *Chapters 12–16* is really one continuous area dedicated to environmental and wildlife conservation. The enormous size of this, and the diversity of ecosystems that it contains, are two of the main reasons why the wildlife of northern Botswana is so spectacular.

BACKGROUND INFORMATION

HISTORY In his *Missionary Travels and Researches in South Africa* (page 544), David Livingstone recounts what he was told by the local people near Lake Ngami in 1849 about the origin of a river there:

> While ascending in this way the beautifully wooded river, we came to a large stream flowing into it. This was the Tamunak'le. I enquired whence it came. 'Oh, from a country full of rivers – so many no-one can tell their number – and full of large trees.'

However, within 100 years of Europeans finding this 'country full of rivers', its environment and wildlife were under threat. In an exceedingly far-sighted move, the Batawana people proclaimed Moremi as a game reserve in 1962, in order to combat the rapid depletion of the area's game and the problems of cattle encroachment.

Initially, Moremi consisted mainly of the Mopane Tongue area; then in the 1970s the royal hunting grounds of Chief Moremi, known as Chief's Island, were added. In 1992, the reserve was augmented by the addition of a strip of land in the northwest corner of the reserve, between the Jao and Nqoga rivers. This was done to make sure that it represented all the major Okavango habitats, including the northern Delta's papyrus swamps and permanent wetlands which had not previously been covered.

As an aside, this is often cited as the first reserve in Africa that was created by indigenous Africans. This is true, and recognises that the indigenous inhabitants

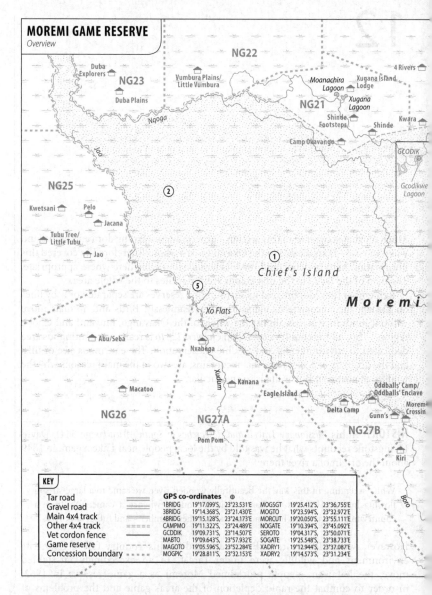

MOREMI GAME RESERVE
Overview

NG22

Duba Explorers
NG23
Duba Plains

Vumbura Plains/
Little Vumbura

4 Rivers

Moanachira Lagoon
Xugana Island Lodge

NG21
Xugana Lagoon

Nqoga

Shinde Footsteps
Shinde

Camp Okavango

Kwara

GCODIK

Gcodikwe Lagoon

NG25

②

Kwetsani
Pelo
Jacana

Tubu Tree/
Little Tubu
Jao

①
Chief's Island

⑤

M o r e m i

Xo Flats

Abu/Seba

Nxabega

Xudum

Kanana

Oddballs' Camp/
Oddballs' Enclave

Macatoo
Eagle Island

Morem Crossin

NG26
NG27A

Delta Camp
Gunn's

NG27B

Pom Pom

Kiri

Boro

KEY

Tar road	═══
Gravel road	═══
Main 4x4 track	━━━
Other 4x4 track	=====
Vet cordon fence	────
Game reserve	─ ─ ─
Concession boundary	· ─ · ─

GPS co-ordinates ⊕

1BRIDG	19°17.099'S,	23°23.531'E	MOGSGT	19°25.412'S,	23°36.755'E
3BRIDG	19°14.368'S,	23°21.430'E	MOGTO	19°23.594'S,	23°32.972'E
4BRIDG	19°15.128'S,	23°24.173'E	MORCUT	19°20.050'S,	23°55.111'E
CAMPMO	19°11.322'S,	23°24.489'E	NOGATE	19°10.394'S,	23°45.092'E
GCDDIK	19°09.731'S,	23°14.507'E	SEROTO	19°04.317'S,	23°50.071'E
MABTO	19°09.643'S,	23°57.932'E	SOGATE	19°25.548'S,	23°38.733'E
MAGOTO	19°05.596'S,	23°52.284'E	XADRY1	19°12.944'S,	23°37.087'E
MOGPIC	19°28.811'S,	23°32.153'E	XADRY2	19°14.573'S,	23°31.234'E

were the prime movers here, rather than the colonial authorities. However, beware of ignoring the fact that Africa's original inhabitants seemed to coexist with the wildlife all over the continent without needing any 'reserves', until Europeans started arriving.

GEOGRAPHY Moremi Game Reserve protects the central and eastern areas of the Okavango Delta. It forms a protected nucleus for the many wildlife reserves/ concessions in the region. Physically Moremi is very flat, encompassing extensive floodplains, some seasonal, others permanent, numerous waterways and two main land masses: the Mopane Tongue and Chief's Island.

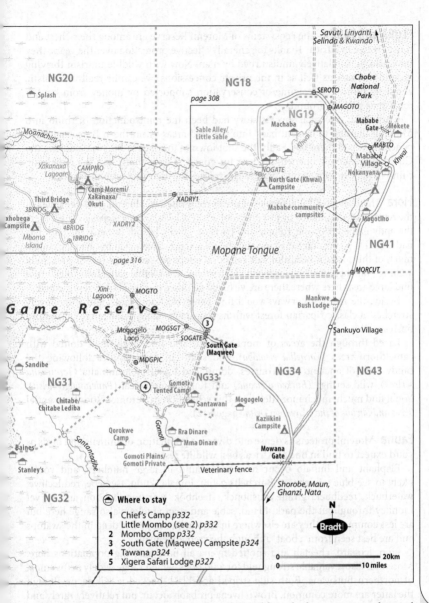

page 308

NG20

🏕 Splash

Moanachira

Xakanaxa
Lagoon   CAMPMO

Camp Moremi/
Xakanaxa/
Okuti

Third Bridge
3BRIDG

xhobega
Campsite
4BRIDG   1BRIDG
Mboma   XADRY2
Island

page 316

NG18

page 308

SEROTO

MAGOTO

Sable Alley/
Little Sable

NG19

Machaba

Khwai

NOGATE

North Gate (Khwai)
Campsite

Mababe
Gate   Mekete

MABTO

Mababe
Village
Nokanyana

Mababe community
campsites

Magotlho

**Chobe
National
Park**

NG41

MORCUT

XADRY1

Mopane Tongue

Game   Reserve

Xini
Lagoon   MOGTO

Mogogelo
Loop   MOGSGT

SOGATEX

South Gate
(Maqwee)

MOGPIC

NG31

Sandibe

Chitabe/
Chitabe Lediba

Gomoti
Tented Camp

Santawani

NG33

NG34

Mogogelo

Kaziikini
Campsite

Mankwe
Bush Lodge

Sankuyo Village

NG43

Qorokwe
Camp

Rra Dinare

Mma Dinare

Baines

Stanley's

Santantadibe

Gomoti

Gomoti Plains/
Gomoti Private

Mowana
Gate

Veterinary fence

NG32

🏠 **Where to stay**
1 Chief's Camp *p332*
   Little Mombo (see 2) *p332*
2 Mombo Camp *p332*
3 South Gate (Maqwee) Campsite *p324*
4 Tawana *p324*
5 Xigera Safari Lodge *p327*

*Shorobe, Maun,
Ghanzi, Nata*

Bradt

N

0 ————————— 20km
0 ————————— 10 miles

Savuti, Linyanti,
Selinda & Kwando

Its area is defined in some places by rivers, although their names and actual courses are anything but easy to follow on the ground. Its northern boundary roughly follows the Nqoga–Khwai river system, while its southern boundary is defined in sequence by the Jao, Boro and Gomoti rivers.

It's worth noting that since the middle of the last century it seems that the western side of the Delta (specifically the Thaoge River system) has gradually been drying up. As this has happened, an increasing amount of water is entering the Moanachira–Khwai river system, on the eastern side of Chief's Island – helping to raise water levels around the Khwai River area, and increase the incidence of flooding on the roads there.

FLORA AND FAUNA The ecosystems of Moremi Reserve are among the richest and most diverse in Africa. Thanks to generally effective protection over the years, they have also been relatively undisturbed by man. Now with wildlife tourism thriving around the park as well as in the private concessions, we can be really optimistic about its future. The regime of conservation supported by money from benign tourism is gaining ground.

Until 2021, one such success story had been the reintroduction of rhino into Moremi: the first to be sent back into the wild areas of northern Botswana since poaching wiped them out. Sadly, the shutdown of tourism in Botswana during the Covid-19 pandemic opened the door for poachers once more, and the remaining rhino have been moved into private sanctuaries for their protection (page 330).

Flora There are over 1,000 species of plants recognised in Moremi, yet large tracts of the reserve are dominated by just one: mopane (*Colophospermum mopane*). This covers the aptly named Mopane Tongue and parts of Chief's Island. Because the park has had effective protection for years, and the soils are relatively rich but badly drained, much of this forest is beautiful, tall 'cathedral' mopane – so called for the gracefully arching branches which resemble the high arches of a Gothic cathedral. You'll often find large areas here where there are virtually no other species of trees represented.

Beside the many waterways you'll find extensive floodplains, and some lovely stretches of classic riparian forest with its characteristically wide range of tree and bush species.

Laced through the areas of mopane you'll also find open areas dotted with camelthorn trees (*Vachellia erioloba*), and sandveld communities following the sandy beds of ancient watercourses, dominated by silver terminalia (*Terminalia sericea*), wild seringa (*Burkea africana*) and Kalahari appleleaf (*Philenoptera nelsii*). You'll find much, much more detail on this vegetation in Veronica Roodt's essential *Trees and Shrubs of the Okavango Delta* (page 542).

Fauna Moremi protects as dense and diverse a population of animals and birds as you'd expect to find in one of Africa's best wildlife reserves.

Elephant and buffalo occur here year-round in large numbers, and you're likely to see blue wildebeest, Burchell's zebra, impala, kudu, tsessebe, red lechwe, waterbuck, reedbuck, giraffe, bushbuck, steenbok, warthog, baboon and vervet monkey throughout the park. Eland, sable and roan antelope also range here but are less common, as they are elsewhere in Africa. Sitatunga live deep in the swamps and are best seen from a boat, although they remain elusive.

Lion, leopard, cheetah and spotted hyena all have thriving populations here. Moremi is also a valuable stronghold for wild dogs, which range widely across most of northern Botswana. Both side-striped and black-backed jackal occur, though the latter are more common. Brown hyena probably occur, but relatively rarely and only in the drier areas, with lower densities than the other large predators. Similarly, bat-eared fox are found, though in much smaller numbers than in Botswana's drier areas. There is a wide variety of mongooses, including the banded, dwarf, slender, large grey, water and Selous's mongoose. Meanwhile in the water, African (Cape) clawless and spotted-necked otters are often glimpsed though seldom seen clearly.

Serval, caracal, aardwolf and aardvark are found all over the park, though are seldom seen due to their nocturnal habits. Pangolin are also found here, and seem slightly less rare than in other areas of their range.

Although night drives aren't allowed within the reserve itself, some of the camps near North Gate will finish their afternoon drives outside the park, and hence do short night drives back to camp. Then you have a chance to see scrub hares, spring hares, lesser bushbabies, porcupines, genets (small-spotted and large-spotted), civets, African wildcats and honey badgers. Black-and-white-striped polecats are also nocturnal, though very seldom seen.

Birdlife Moremi boasts over 400 bird species, a great variety, which are often patchily distributed in association with particular habitats; though visiting any area, the sheer number of different species represented will strike you as amazing.

Although there are no birds that are truly endemic to Botswana, the Okavango is a hugely important wetland for many species, among which are a number of rarities worth noting. Top of the Okavango's list of 'specialities' is the slaty egret. Expect to find this in shallow, reedy backwaters and pans. Besides the Okavango, this rare egret is only resident in the quieter corners of the Chobe and Linyanti rivers, and the Bangweulu Wetlands in Zambia. To identify it look for its overall slate-grey colouring, except for its lower legs and feet which are yellow, as are its eyes and some of its face, while the front of its neck is a rufous red. (The more common black heron – formerly the black egret – lacks the yellow on the legs and face, or the rufous neck.)

Much easier to spot are magnificent wattled cranes which can be seen in the Delta fairly readily, usually in pairs or small groups wandering about wet grasslands or shallow floodplains in search of fish and small amphibians and reptiles.

For keen birdwatchers, other specials here include brown firefinch, lesser jacana, coppery-tailed coucal, Bradfield's hornbill, rosy-throated longclaw and the inconspicuous chirping cisticola.

PRACTICAL INFORMATION

WHEN TO VISIT See page 109 for more general comments on the whole of northern Botswana, and note that the best times to visit are dependent upon how you intend to visit, exactly which camps you are visiting, and why.

Flora and fauna The flora and the birdlife are definitely more spectacular during the rains. Then the vegetation goes wild, migrant birds arrive, and many of the residents appear in their full breeding plumage. So this is a great time for birders and those interested in the plants and flowers.

The story with the animals is more complex. In most of Moremi there is water throughout the year. Higher water levels here simply means less land area available for animals that aren't amphibious. However, around the edges of the Delta, animal densities are hugely affected by the migration towards the water from the dry central areas of the country.

Thus game viewing generally gets better the later in the dry season that you go… although this trend is probably less pronounced in the centre of the Delta than it is at the edges.

Activities The water levels will affect the activities that you can do while here. In some areas mokoro trips are possible only for a few months every year, when water levels are high enough. Similarly, the game drives from a few of the camps are generally possible only when water levels are low enough.

Costs The cost of some camps in the Okavango varies with the season. This depends very much on the company owning/marketing the camps, but in general you can expect July–October to be the period of highest cost, December–March to be the time of lowest cost, and November, April, May and June to be pitched somewhere in the middle.

GETTING THERE AND AWAY

Flying in If you're flying into a camp in Moremi or the Delta then the season won't make much difference to the access. The Okavango's camps used to close down during January and February, but now most stay open throughout the year, despite being much quieter during the green season (December to March).

In terms of vehicle access to the various game-viewing areas from your camp, the rains are typically less of a concern than the flood, the peak of which usually lags behind the rains by several months (depending on how far up the Delta you are). However, generally there will be the most dry land from about August to January.

Driving in If you're driving yourself into Moremi, it's important to understand that only a restricted area of the reserve will be accessible to you, and the wet season will make this access even more difficult. As the rains continue, their cumulative effect is to make many of the roads on the Mopane Tongue much more difficult to pass, while it simply submerges others. Thus only the experienced and well equipped need even think about driving anywhere through Moremi between about January and April.

Most visitors who drive themselves come to Moremi in the dry season, between around May and October. Then the tracks become increasingly less difficult to navigate, although even then there are always watercourses to cross. As with all national parks, the speed limit in the park is 40km/h, with no vehicles allowed on the roads between sunset and sunrise.

ORIENTATION Moremi Game Reserve covers a large tract of the centre of the Okavango Delta, and a wide corridor stretching east to link that with Chobe National Park.

At the heart of Moremi is a long, permanent island, Chief's Island, oriented from southeast to northwest. At about 60km long and around 10km wide this is the largest island in the Delta, and it's usually cut off from the mainland by waterways and floodplains. Within the eastern side of Moremi is a triangular peninsula of dry land covered (mostly) in mopane trees, known as the Mopane Tongue.

Between and around Chief's Island and the Mopane Tongue, Moremi is a mosaic of rivers, lagoons, floodplains and small islands which slowly and gradually change with the passage of time.

Maps Once again, the Tracks4Africa maps (page 142) and Veronica Roodt's definitive map of Moremi Game Reserve can't be recommended too highly for visitors to Moremi, and are essential for anyone planning a self-drive trip there. Tinkers' Moremi Game Reserve map (w tinkers.co.za) is also available from Tracks4Africa and includes GPS points and distance markers within the reserve.

GETTING ORGANISED

Booking and park fees If you're flying into an organised camp, then park fees will probably already be included in the price that you've paid. If you're driving in you'll need to have booked all your campsites and paid all your park fees in advance; see page 127 for details of how to go about this, and a scale of the fees. On arrival at the park gate, you'll need to present your confirmation documents confirming that you have pre-booked your campsites, and paid your park fees, before you are allowed to proceed.

Opening hours (⏰ Apr–Sep 06.00–18.30 daily, Oct–Mar 05.30–19.00 daily) As with other national parks, Moremi's opening hours vary with the season, roughly corresponding to 'dusk til dawn'. You're not allowed to drive in the park outside of these hours.

THE MOPANE TONGUE

Within eastern Moremi, the dry triangle of the Mopane Tongue juts into the Delta from the east, between the Khwai and Mogogelo rivers. Each side of this is about 40km long, and roughly marking the corners are the campsites of South Gate (Maqwee), North Gate (Khwai) and Xakanaxa – a reminder that this is the only area of Moremi that is accessible for visitors driving themselves.

Aside from the riverine forest which lines its edges, most of the interior of this peninsula is covered in forests of mopane, including many stretches of very mature and beautiful forests.

KHWAI RIVER AND NORTH GATE (KHWAI) – NG19 Near the northeastern edge of Moremi, the waterways of the Okavango gradually narrow to form the Khwai River, which – along with various channels – is spanned by several wooden pole bridges. The tracks beside the river and around the floodplains are often stunning in their beauty, and prolific in their wildlife. It's a spectacular area, and especially so if approached from the dusty heartlands of Chobe during the dry season.

While this stretch of the Khwai River is within the community-run NG19 Concession, it falls naturally on the route between Chobe and Moremi, and thus – especially for self-drivers – it feels more logical to include it here. Most of the lodges in this area conduct their activities along the river, although some do occasionally go into Moremi. The downside of that is that it can get quite busy around key sightings.

Flora and fauna
Flora All along the edge of the Khwai's floodplain you'll find some of the region's most beautiful, mature riverine forest. Stunning trees, tall and old, abound, including a large number of camelthorn (*Vachellia erioloba*) and some almost pure stands of leadwood (*Combretum imberbe*). There are also patches of acacia woodlands, usually standing on sandy patches of ground between the river valley and the mopane woodlands of the Tongue's interior.

Fauna The Khwai area seldom fails to deliver some very impressive wildlife spectacles when visited in the dry season. This is perhaps to be expected, as it marks the boundary of the Okavango's waters that flow east and north – and so is the closest drinking water for large numbers of thirsty animals in southern Chobe during the late dry season.

We've had some particularly good leopard sightings here, seeing the cats lounging around in shady trees during the day, usually on the edge of the riverine forest. Mixed areas of broken woodlands and open areas is classic leopard territory, and because it's been protected for so long, many of the residents are very relaxed in the presence of game-viewing vehicles. Well suited to this environment, too, are wild dogs, which are known to den close to the river and are regularly seen with their pups, and spotted hyena.

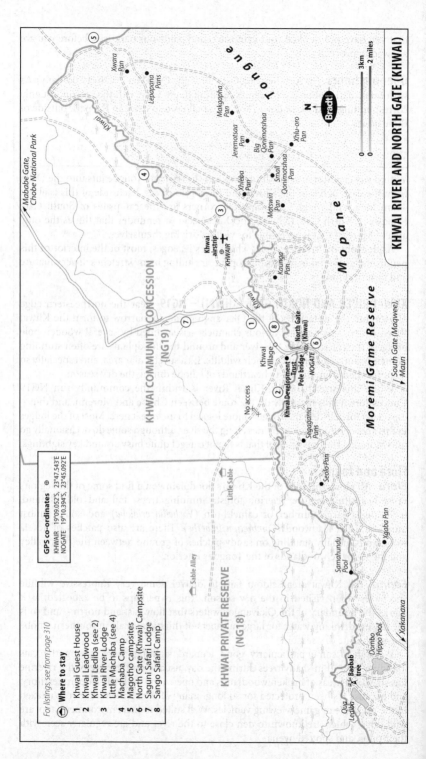

KHWAI RIVER AND NORTH GATE (KHWAI)

For listings, see from page 310

Where to stay
1 Khwai Guest House
2 Khwai Leadwood
3 Khwai Lediba (see 2)
4 Khwai River Lodge
  Little Machaba (see 4)
  Machaba Camp
5 Magotho campsites
6 North Gate (Khwai) Campsite
7 Saguni Safari Lodge
8 Sango Safari Camp

GPS co-ordinates ⊕
KHWAIR 19º09.052'S, 23º47.543'E
NOGATE 19º10.394'S, 23º45.092'E

KHWAI COMMUNITY CONCESSION (NG19)

KHWAI PRIVATE RESERVE (NG18)

Moremi Game Reserve

Mababe Gate, Chobe National Park

South Gate (Maqwee), Maun

As well as the almost ubiquitous impala, you're likely to spot kudu and waterbuck in this environment, and you probably have a better chance than in most places of seeing the normally elusive roan antelope, which regularly come down to the river to drink.

Birdlife Khwai's birdlife is varied, like the habitats found here, though with only a narrow channel of water in the dry season, you'll usually have to search elsewhere for large numbers of the more aquatic species. That said, even in the dry season you will find storks (saddle-billed and marabou) and wattled cranes pacing around the open areas in search of fish, frogs and reptiles to eat.

Khwai does have a reputation, especially towards the end of the dry season, for having a very high density of raptors – with which I can concur. I've been closer to a martial eagle here than anywhere else, and had a lovely sighting of a marsh harrier hunting, and both bateleur eagles and giant eagle owls seem particularly common. So as you drive along, keep glancing into the sky and checking the tops of trees for the distinctive outline of a perched raptor.

Getting there and away
By air Most visitors to the lodges arrive at the airstrip (⊕ KHWAIR 19°09.052'S, 23°47.543'E), which is close to Khwai River Lodge. This is a short hop from Kasane, Maun or any of the other airstrips in the region. There are no facilities at the airstrip; it's just a flattish section of low grass with a windsock next to it. As in all areas of the Okavango these days, helicopter transfers to individual camps are also possible.

By car If you're driving into the Khwai area from Savuti, Xakanaxa, South Gate or Maun, see the directions given on page 321, and simply follow them in reverse – or check out the individual 'getting away' sections for these places.

Orientation It's relatively easy to orient yourself here, although since the opening of the mostly good gravel transit road, most self-drivers simply pass through this area, glimpsing the Khwai River only from the bridge. The Okavango's waters approach from the west down the Khwai River. To the west they're flanked by floodplains, loops, meanders and lagoons, but gradually travelling east this valley narrows and concentrates the river water into a small channel.

Central to the whole area is the bridge at North Gate (now more commonly called Khwai), which spans the channel. South of this is Moremi Game Reserve, and north are the small settlement of Khwai Village (home to around 400 people), the community-controlled concessions of NG18 and NG19 (page 341), and the area's airstrip. Access to the area along the river is from the village of Khwai.

Getting organised There are a few small shops in Khwai Village, a welcome sight if you've been driving for several days and supplies are running low. Most sell just a few cans and soft drinks, but ask around and you might find potatoes and other fresh vegetables, and even fresh bread. There are also baskets for sale. There is a small outdoor café, **Afro Ville** (m 7305 2699; ⊕ 08.00–20.00 daily), where owner Mike has a bougainvillea-covered canvas café serving cold drinks and snacks, alongside a small general store that may be able to supply you with firewood, water and ice.

On the edge of the village, near the bridge across to North Gate, is the office of the **Khwai Development Trust**. The small NG19 Concession, which stretches north of the Khwai River bordering Moremi, and east to Chobe National Park, is owned and managed by the community of Khwai Village. Here the people have formed the trust, originally funded at least in part by auctioning off their hunting quota to various organisations (though hunting is no longer allowed in Botswana). Unusually for the private concessions, self-drivers are allowed to explore this area, on payment of a concession fee of P350 per person per day (this is included if you are camping at one of their campsites), but it is not permitted to drive beyond the concession boundaries into NG18 and towards the Linyanti and Selinda reserves.

The trust's office (680 1211, 683 0272; e khwai@btcmail.co.bw; w khwaitrust. co.bw; ⊕ 08.00–16.00 Mon–Fri, 08.00–12.30 Sat) is where you pay your concession fees, but note that their self-drive campsites (Magotho 1 and 2) must be pre-booked through their Maun office (page 217). While there is no requirement to have a guide, you can pick up a community 'escort guide' here, or organise one in Maun. Their role is simply to show you the routes, which is valuable in an area where it's surprisingly easy to get lost, but they are not trained wildlife guides. There is no charge for their services, as they are paid by the trust – though a tip is normally expected – but if you'd like the guide to stay with you at one of the trust's campsites (page 313), you will need to provide all his/her food and drink.

You can also book cultural tours from Khwai (P2,000/group), which will include the opportunity to visit Khwai Village, talk to the villagers about the culture of the Khwai Bushmen, and watch a performance of dancing and singing.

🏠 Where to stay *Map, page 308*

Accommodation in this area has burgeoned. All the lodges and self-drive campsites are sited on the north side of the river, between Chobe National Park and North Gate, and all must be pre-booked; you are likely to be turned away if you simply roll up.

Camps and lodges

Khwai Guest House (6 chalets) Contact Bush Ways Safaris (page 216); w khwaiguesthouse.com; ⊕ KHWAIG 19°09.505'S, 23°45.662'E. On the edge of Khwai Village as you're coming in from Mababe, Khwai Guest House is under the same ownership as Sango Safari Camp (page 312). It's a welcoming but very low-key spot, popular with self-drivers & plugging a big gap in the market: affordable, attractive & convenient accommodation. The cool, thatched elephant-grey chalets have comfortable beds, thoughtful, neat interiors, fans & en-suite bathrooms with semi-open-air shower & separate toilet. They are light, bright & welcoming retreats.

The circular mess tent is a convivial place for meals or to while away the siesta hours. Curved concrete benches are covered in cushions, meals are taken family-style & a firepit surrounded by directors' chairs glows of an evening. Options here are flexible, from a fully inclusive package to B&B or dinner, B&B with additional meals (US$17/25 lunch/dinner) on request, & game drives from US$60 pp. *From US$310 pp Jan–Mar & Dec to US$370 pp Jul–Oct, FBA. Self-drive*

rates available from US$155–215 pp dinner, B&B only. Children all ages; 6+ for activities. ⊕ All year. 🛏🛏🛏–🛏🛏🛏🛏

Khwai Leadwood (6 tented chalets, 1 family suite) Contact African Bush Camps (page 214); ⊕ KHWAIL 19°16.631'S, 23°73.448'E. Opened in 2021, Khwai Leadwood is an attractive, contemporary camp overlooking a picturesque bend in the Khwai River. It's a well-priced, family-friendly base from which to explore the Khwai area & Moremi.

Set back among sycamore & leadwood trees within the Khwai River floodplain, the camp has 4 standard & 2 family chalets, all with solid walls, thatched roofs & private verandas. Inside, stone floors make the chalets feel cool & there are twin or dbl beds with bedside tables & lamps, a writing table & some comfy chairs. One chalet has a low mezzanine bedroom & lounge below with a warming fireplace for the winter months. En-suite bathrooms have basins, a shower & a flush toilet. The family chalets are similar but larger, with 2 bedrooms & 2 bathrooms. Unlike the linear set-up of many riverside camps, the 7 tents at

SAFARI DRIVE

— Since 1993 —

The ultimate way to explore Botswana

Safari Drive has been organising tailor-made, self-drive safaris in Botswana since 1993.

With expert knowledge of the roads, driving conditions and routes, Safari Drive gives you the freedom and security to embark on the adventure of a lifetime. Self-drive safaris offer versatile, independent travel with the freedom to explore at your own pace.

Personal itineraries are tailored to your time frame, level of 4x4 driving experience and budget.

Choose from a range of accommodation, from luxury lodges to camping. Additional activities can be booked such as sleep-outs on the salt pans, riding safaris and scenic flights.

Safari Drive trips include:

- Expedition-equipped 4x4s for up to five people
- In-country briefing & backup
- Satellite phone
- Handbook
- Roof tent
- Water tanks
- Satellite navigation with Tracks 4 Africa
- All camping equipment

 +44 (0)1488 71140 | info@safaridrive.com ABTOT

www.safaridrive.com

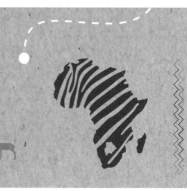

Khwai Leadwood form a semi-circle from the main area, making everything very easily accessible, albeit a little closer together. Each chalet does still have a river view from their private veranda day bed though.

The main tented area has a wide veranda leading out from the inviting lounge, complete with log burner & dining areas, with a low-level firepit under the trees with views along the river. Sharing those views is a lovely infinity pool. Activities here include 4x4 game drives (day & night), walking safaris, mokoro trips when the water is high enough & visits to Khwai Village. *From US$675 pp Jan–Mar & Dec to US$1,340 pp Jun–Oct, FBA inc conservation fee. Children all ages.* ⊕ *All year.* 🏺🏺🏺🏺–🏺🏺🏺🏺🏺

Khwai Lediba (6 tented chalets, 1 family suite) Contact African Bush Camps (page 214); ⊕ KHWAIT 19°15.178'S, 23°77.110'E. Formerly the well-known Khwai Tented Camp, the camp relocated 30mins west of the village to beside Khwai Leadwood in 2023 & reopened as the beautiful Khwai Lediba.

Small & intimate, it combines the simplicity of an old-style safari camp with modern creature comforts & really beautiful, contemporary styling. Its simple canvas-&-timber rooms are raised on wooden decking, with elegant interiors & comfortable furniture. There are twin or dbl beds with leather headboards, huge picture windows taking in the view, open shelving storage, & an en-suite bathroom complete with an indoor corner shower, pole-screened outdoor shower, bath & a toilet cubicle behind a privacy curtain.

The tented communal area is open-fronted & tiered. The homely lounge is filled with eclectic curiosities, quirky swinging chairs & African patterns & textures. Adjacent is a deep corner sofa, plenty of decking, & an open kitchen (complete with wood-fired pizza oven) overlooking the family-style dining table, where convivial meals are shared together. There's also a circular firepit, front & centre of the camp, & a swimming pool for cooling off.

Activities are fairly flexible, from walking safaris & 4x4 game drives (day & night) to mokoro trips when the water is high enough. Most visitors arrive by air; self-drivers are welcome on the same basis – which includes doing all activities with the camp's staff. *From US$675 pp Jan–Mar & Dec to US$1,340 pp Jun–Oct,*

FBA inc conservation fee. Children 12+. ⊕ *All year.* 🏺🏺🏺🏺–🏺🏺🏺🏺

Khwai River Lodge (15 chalets) Contact Khwai Development Trust (page 217); ⊕ KHWAIL 19°08.860'S, 23°48.019'E. Among the leadwood trees on the edge of the floodplain, Khwai River Lodge is one of the Okavango's oldest lodges. Once a cluster of understated bungalows, it transformed into an opulent lodge under Belmond Safaris, who operated Khwai River for decades before the lease was reallocated to the Khwai Development Trust in December 2023. While the camp structures remain in place, at the time of writing in mid-2024, an investment partner was still being sought to operate the lodge and it remained closed for now.

With high game densities here, particularly during the latter parts of the dry season, when the camp does reopen, guests can expect to see an abundance of wildlife, & the lodge's location within a community concession means that visitors can enjoy day & night drives as well as guided walks.

☀ **Little Machaba** (4 tents) Contact Machaba Safaris (page 215). Little Machaba is hidden a few hundred metres south of Machaba Camp (page 312), overlooking a wide bend in the Khwai River. The team didn't change their successful formula, & so the feel, layout & facilities of the tents is very similar to those of Machaba, albeit perhaps slightly smarter & more contemporary in their choice of colours.

It's smaller than Machaba, with just 4 tents, 2 of which are family units, but they are exceptionally well-thought-out in design. From the natural light pouring through the large mesh sides to the use of pale canvas & the practical ergonomics of lighting & mirrors, alongside extremely comfortable beds & chairs, the tents are a joy to stay in. Built on low, timber decks with boardwalks meandering to the main area, each tent has a lounge area, en-suite bathroom (3 have outdoor showers & all have a bath) & a veranda. In-room massage, charged separately, is available from the resident therapist.

The main area at Little Machaba is a welcoming, tented lounge, bar & dining area, with beautiful views across the river into Moremi Game Reserve. Furnished with plump cushions on big armchairs, assorted books & a self-service bar, it's the perfect spot to relax any time of day. There is also a small, circular swimming pool & sunloungers overlooking the floodplains. B/fast & brunch are served at individual tables, with communal dining at one long, social table in the evening, usually served by candlelight under the stars.

Most activities here are game drives, but walking safaris are an option, as are mokoro trips when the water is high enough; the boat station is 30mins' drive from camp. *From US$660 pp mid-Jan–Mar to US$1,190 pp Jun–Oct, FBA. Children 12+, unless exclusive use.* ☉ *All year.* 👣👣👣👣–👣👣👣👣👣

Machaba Camp (10 tents) Contact Machaba Safaris (page 215). ⊕ MACHAB 19°07.371'S, 23°48.820'E. Delightfully positioned on a wide, shallow stretch of the river frequented by elephants & hippos, Machaba is a welcoming, hospitable camp that strikes a good balance: comfortable & attractive while still at one with the environment.

At the heart of Machaba, 2 open-fronted tented wings spread from the entrance. One is furnished with armchairs & sofas, its tables dotted with books, magazines & sweets, its walls adorned with maps. In the other, tables set with white linen are backed by a buffet. & in front, directors' chairs surround a warming firepit by the river. It's the kind of place that invites conversation. The attention to detail runs through to the spacious tents, reached along sandy paths beneath shady trees, & accessible by those with limited mobility. Spacious & uncluttered, these are a twist on the traditional safari camp, their floors dotted with rugs, their metal basins in pairs beneath hanging mirrors, & their en-suite 'bucket' showers boasting hot running water. In 2 family tents, a central lounge separates 2 bedrooms which share a bathroom & outside shower. In-room massage is offered at extra cost by the resident therapist.

At the far end of the site is a secluded circular pool, a real draw during the heat of the day; no doubt elephants would be attracted too, should the river ever dry out! Even the curio tent (including baskets made by the staff) is appealing rather than simply functional. Game drives are the backbone of activities here, but walking safaris are an option, & mokoro trips (some distance away) when the water is high enough. The guiding is both good & personable, & if you'd like to see behind the scenes, just ask. *From US$680 pp mid-Jan–Mar to US$1,220 Jun–Oct pp, FBA inc conservation fee. Children all ages.* ☉ *All year.* 👣👣👣👣–👣👣👣👣👣

Saguni Safari Lodge (17 tents) m 7338 7715; f sagunilodge. Located on an island surrounded by mature trees, Saguni is a large, affordable camp overlooking Mbudi lagoon to the north of Khwai Village. The simple, comfortably furnished accommodation is divided between 9 forest tents & 8 river tents, which overlook the Sable River. Each tent has either twin or dbl beds on polished timber floors, with plenty of mesh windows, en-suite bathrooms & small private decks with directors' chairs. There's a dining tent where buffet meals are eaten communally, a pole-shaded deck with simple seating, a basic bar facing the river & a plunge pool. Activities include game drives (day & night), mokoro excursions, subject to water levels, guided walks & village trips. *US$485 pp Nov–Apr, US$671 pp May–Oct, FBA. Children 6+.* ☉ *All year* 👣👣👣–👣👣👣👣

Sango Safari Camp (6 tents) Contact Bush Ways Safaris (page 216); w sangosafaricamp. com; ⊕ SANGO 19°09.826'S, 23°45.771'E. Sango is that rare find: an old-fashioned camp that focuses on safaris rather than frills. It's set back from a shallow section of the river, just a short drive from Khwai Village. Self-drivers (who must pre-book all meals & activities), should turn off the road just metres north of Khwai Guesthouse (⊕ 19°09.578'S, 23°45.594'E), from where a track leads to the camp.

Squashy cushions bring comfort to the airy mess tent, which is open to the view, & dinner is often taken under the stars. Guests stay in traditional en-suite Meru tents, set along sandy paths on low varnished wooden decks with small verandas. Each is well thought out, with proper twin or dbl beds flanked by bedside tables & lights & surrounded by mosquito netting. A fan is welcome in the heat of summer, as are the outside shower & the small plunge pool, complete with shaded loungers.

Game drives are at the heart of Sango's activities, with full-day options, afternoon drives continuing after sunset on the way back to camp, & night drives on request. Even at camp you can take in the action on the river, perhaps from the camp's tall observation hide. There are also nature walks with an armed guide, mokoro trips on a tributary of the Khwai, & village tours – which may include the opportunity to watch basket weavers at work. *From US$400 pp Jan–Mar & Dec to US$710 pp Jul–Oct, FBA. Self-drive rates available from*

US$295–560, exc activities & park fees. ⏱ All year. 🛖🛖🛖–🛖🛖🛖🛖

Camping

Magotho campsites (15 pitches) Contact Khwai Development Trust (page 217). Reached from a turning south off the main transit road between Mababe & North Gate (◈ MAGOTO 19°05.596'S, 23°52.284'E), these 2 campsites – Magotho 1 (8 pitches) & 2 (7 pitches) – are set in tall grass under mature camelthorn trees. Each 'pitch' has a firepit & access to simple shared ablution blocks (theoretically each has a solar-powered shower & toilet, though water supplies can be sporadic). You will need to bring everything you need with you, including all water, & be sure to take everything out, including waste. Campsites must be pre-booked. *P350 pp.* ⏱ *All year.*

North Gate (Khwai) Campsite (10 pitches) ☎ 686 5365; Contact SKL (page 213); ◈ NOGATE 19°10.394'S, 23°45.092'E. Khwai is situated on a lovely site to the south of the Khwai River, immediately on your left as you enter Moremi Game Reserve at North Gate. Its pitches are dotted amid tall woodlands, some along the river, where fireflies put on a mesmerising display as night falls, & the grunts of hippos form the bass notes to the general cacophony from baboons & spurfowl. There are good, clean ablution facilities, & each site has a braai stand, firepit & waste bin. Do be aware that monkeys & baboons here can be a real menace. Like many campers, we have had them openly steal from our vehicle as we stood close by, & others have reported tents being opened as they search for anything sweet-smelling: food, toiletries & medicines. If you do stay, look out for especially impressive specimens of sickle-leaved albizia. Their fine leaves & flattened seedpods might look like acacias, but trees of the albizia family don't have thorns. You'll also find a few huge sycamore figs, easily spotted because of their yellow-orange bark & a tendency for parts of their wide trunks to form buttresses. Old Africa hands will avoid camping directly under a fig tree, though, as their fruits are sought after by everything from baboons & bats to elephants – any of which can make for a messy tent in the morning, & a very disturbed night's sleep. *US$50 pp, exc bed levy & park fees.* ⏱ *All year.*

What to see and do Wherever you stay, however you travel, your activities during the day will largely focus on game drives, as walking and night drives are forbidden by park rules, and the Khwai is too shallow and narrow for safe boating. Mokoro trips, however, are possible on several nearby channels – and offer a tranquil opportunity to explore the river up close.

Game-viewing roads and loops spread out on both sides of North Gate, to the west and east. Most stick close to the Khwai River, either exploring the river's floodplain or the adjacent band of riverine forest. You'll need Veronica Roodt's map of Moremi to get the best from these, as they're not shown on the main map of Botswana, or the Tracks4Africa app.

One particularly attractive loop within the game reserve, almost 14km west of North Gate and signposted 'Hippo Pool', leads to a large, shallow lake where hippos wallow in the permanent water. At one end of the pool is a tall bird hide, with a toilet at the base, so you can leave your vehicle and spend time in the heat of the day observing waterbirds such as Egyptian and spur-winged geese, knob-billed and white-faced ducks and woolly-necked storks.

GETTING AWAY FROM NORTH GATE

Driving from North Gate (Khwai) to Savuti, Chobe National Park This route used to be very confusing, but the gravel road running parallel to the old sand tracks near the Khwai River has simplified navigation considerably. On the downside, the route no longer takes you along the stunningly beautiful Khwai River, which is now largely the preserve of the lodges dotted along its banks (page 310).

From the park entrance at North Gate (◈ NOGATE 19°10.394'S, 23°45.092'E), cross the pole bridge over the Khwai River, and follow the road through Khwai Village, then over (or around) another small river to a steel bridge (◈ STEELB

19°07.564'S, 23°45.840'E). A little over 2km from here, the road turns sharply to the right, then continues uninterrupted all the way to Mababe Village. For the Mababe Gate into Chobe National Park, turn left about 35.5km from North Gate (⊕ MABTO 19°09.643'S, 23°57.932'E), then follow that road for about 7.5km. At the gate, stop and sign in before continuing roughly north towards Savuti.

About 20km north of the Mababe Gate, the road splits. Both forks lead to Savuti. The right fork is the **marsh road**, which is more scenic, but can be very rutted and bumpy during the dry season, with great views of the marsh. It is certainly going to be the worse of the two during the rainy season, when you'd be wise to take the left fork, the more direct if less interesting, **sand-ridge road**. This stays closer to the Magwikhwe Sand Ridge, climbing on to it at one point.

After about 37km on the sand-ridge road, or 44km on the marsh road, these routes converge (⊕ MARSAN 18°36.078'S, 24°03.678'E) beside Leopard Hill Rock, which is about 5km south of the heart of Savuti.

Driving from North Gate (Khwai) to Xakanaxa This route is really very straightforward – although the introduction of a 'dry' route to avoid the oft-flooded sections on the old road has changed things a little. Start from the park's entrance at North Gate and follow the road southwest towards South Gate for about 1.2km. Here you'll find a substantial right turn signposted to Xakanaxa, heading in a more westerly direction. Follow this for almost 20km until you come to another junction

NEGOTIATING THE ROADS AROUND XAKANAXA

While the road has done much to alleviate the problems of getting from North Gate to Xakanaxa, tracks along the old route, and indeed off-road, can get pretty waterlogged. When I drove this route in 1999, most of the loops were fine. A few – often those marked as 'seasonal roads' on Veronica Roodt's map of Moremi – were tricky and required one to cross quite deep water in the vehicle. The scenery on the road around Qua Lediba (*lediba* is the local word for 'lagoon'), particularly looking out west towards the Xuku floodplain, was very beautiful as we meandered between the dappled light of the forest and open lagoons.

However, west of Qua Lediba, the road became progressively more difficult, with deeper and deeper stretches of water to cross. Several times we forded water across the road, until one large pool stopped us. Forest to the left and lagoon to the right. There was no easy way around. The track was flat sand; solid not slippery. Vehicle tracks had been this way recently – a good sign.

As we considered our next move, two large trucks, run by a mobile-safari operator, approached and drove across, showing us the depth; we crossed safely. We avoided the next pool, but in a third the vehicle lurched alarmingly to the right – my passenger falling across me as I drove. The Land Rover didn't blink though and pulled us through. Nerve-racking when alone, such puddles are more fun with a party of two vehicles, as then one can pull the other out of difficulty if necessary.

Back on the main road, heading west we found a drift, where the road had been washed away. Various alternatives circled off left, finding shallower, but more slippery, places to cross. The water at the main road was deeper, but the substrate was more solid. On the whole, a safer bet.

(at ✿ XADRY1 19°12.944'S, 23°37.087'E). Turning right here would lead you after a further 24km straight to Xakanaxa, mainly through old, established mopane woodlands. This route, however, has been frequently closed and at best very wet since the unusually high floods of 2009, so if you're planning to take it, do ask advice from the staff at the gate before you set off.

Turning left, however, leads on to a more circuitous but considerably more predictable 'dry route' that heads southwest for 12km before joining up with the main route from South Gate (✿ XADRY2 19°14.573'S, 23°31.234'E). From here, it's a further 11km or so northwest to the Xakanaxa Gate (✿ XAKGT 19°11.865'S, 23°25.865'E).

The real joy of this journey comes from the numerous side-loops that detour to the right of the road. If you feel lost, remember that heading west and south will generally keep you going in the right direction. Heading north will go deeper into the detours and usually bring you back to the Khwai River. While the 'dry route' itself is less rewarding, you will pass several of these loops during the first 20km stretch from North Gate, so you won't be missing out.

Drivers with reservations at the campsite or one of the lodges should sign in at the gate before proceeding, but if you're camping at Third Bridge, their paperwork is handled at the campsite.

Driving from North Gate to South Gate and Maun

This is a very straightforward route, on a very straight road. From North Gate's campsite you simply follow a substantial track for about 30km, which heads southwest, directly towards South Gate (✿ SOGATE 19°25.548'S, 23°38.733'E).

To continue to Maun, see page 325. Alternatively, and thus avoiding park fees, you could follow the first part of the driving instructions on page 313. Instead of turning off for the Mababe Gate, continue on the gravel road as far as Mababe Village, where you turn south on to the road to Sankuyo, Shorobe and ultimately to Maun.

TIP OF THE TONGUE: XAKANAXA AND BEYOND

One corner of the Mopane Tongue's triangular peninsula juts towards the centre of Moremi, and at the end of the tip is Xakanaxa Lagoon. Beyond it, on three sides, is the Delta's maze of channels, floodplains, lagoons and islands. A few of the larger, closer islands, such as Goaxhlo and the large Mboma Island, are accessible via simple pole bridges. Beyond this, Moremi becomes inaccessible without a boat: that's the realm of the small, fly-in safari camps.

The patchwork of environments found here is typical of the inner reaches of the Delta. It's also phenomenally beautiful, and one of the most reliably good areas for wildlife on the subcontinent. Expect extraordinary densities of game and birdlife and, as it's been protected for years, the wildlife is generally very relaxed.

For the self-driving visitor, the game and scenery here are as good as they get in Botswana – don't miss this area.

Flora and fauna

Picking out the wildlife highlights for an area like this, and trying to point out what's special, is virtually impossible. There's usually something extraordinary around every corner. It's not that you'll see different things here than you will elsewhere in Moremi, or even Botswana; it's just that you'll see them all in a very small area.

Getting there and away

Virtually all lodge visitors arrive and leave **by air**, via Xakanaxa airstrip, which is easily linked with any of the other airstrips in the region. For details on how to **drive** there, see opposite and page 324.

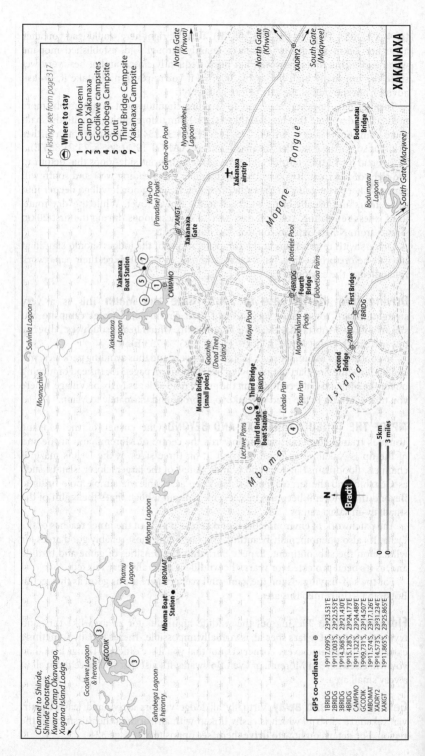

XAKANAXA

For listings, see from page 317

Where to stay
1 Camp Moremi
2 Camp Xakanaxa
3 Gcodikwe campsites
4 Gxhobega Campsite
5 Okuti
6 Third Bridge Campsite
7 Xakanaxa Campsite

GPS co-ordinates ⊕

1BRIDG	19°17.099'S,	23°23.531'E
2BRIDG	19°17.003'S,	23°22.553'E
3BRIDG	19°14.368'S,	23°21.430'E
4BRIDG	19°15.128'S,	23°24.173'E
CAMPMO	19°11.322'S,	23°24.489'E
GCODIK	19°09.731'S,	23°14.507'E
MBOMAT	19°11.574'S,	23°17.126'E
XADRY2	19°14.573'S,	23°31.234'E
XAKGT	19°11.865'S,	23°25.865'E

Orientation

The main route from North Gate to Xakanaxa roughly follows the northern edge of the Mopane Tongue. Similarly, the main road from South Gate to Third Bridge roughly follows the southern edge of the Tongue. This section covers the area around and between Xakanaxa and Third Bridge.

In Veronica Roodt's map of Moremi there are some detailed insets of the road layouts around this area, so make sure that you buy a copy of this before you get here. You'll also find plenty of useful references and background information on the reverse of the map.

Where to stay *Map, opposite*

Three long-established camps and one campsite cluster on the edge of Xakanaxa Lagoon, a vast waterbody fed by the Moanachira River. Access upstream to Camp Okavango, Shinde, and Xugana is prohibited. There's a second campsite at Third Bridge near Mboma Island, and camping is also possible on the islands northwest of here. Pre-booking is mandatory for all accommodations.

While lodges at Xakanaxa are discreetly fenced to deter elephants, other wildlife may still roam freely. Conversely, campsites are entirely open, inviting frequent visits from lions, hyenas, leopards, buffalos, wild dogs, and elephants. Hence, caution is advised, especially after dark.

Camps and lodges

Camp Moremi (12 tents) Contact Desert & Delta Safaris (page 214); ⊕ CAMPMO 19°11.322'S, 23°24.489'E. The furthest southwest of the camps here, Camp Moremi is set under huge old trees where natural papyrus & ferns nod over lawns cropped short by hippos. A lot of other animals venture into camp, too, though elephants are kept at bay by discreet strands of electrified wire around the perimeter.

At the heart of the camp is a series of decks raised up in a marvellous old jackalberry tree; although being set back from the lagoon, the views here are not as expansive as from the neighbouring camps. Accessed along a gradually ascending boardwalk, these decks are home to a dining area, housing long communal dining tables & a b/fast area; a bar; & 2 large lounge areas with plenty of comfortable seating. Behind these sits the reception area & a small curio shop. Back at ground level, heading towards the lagoon, a path winds through manicured lawns, past the camp's firepit to a boma area & on to the pool. The pool & surrounding sunloungers are right on the edge of the lagoon & have perhaps the best views in the camp.

The 12 tented rooms, with high thatched roofs, are built on low decks of their own. Inside each, a large open-plan space features a bedroom at one end, an en-suite bathroom at the other & a lounge area in the middle. Bi-folding glass doors open on to a private deck with sunloungers shaded by the surrounding mature trees. Unusually – & in contrast to the other camps in this area – the rooms at Camp Moremi are set back from the lagoon. Forfeiting a view of the lagoon, the rooms are instead surrounded by pristine bush, protected from elephant damage by the surrounding electric fence; mature trees provide shade, while the understory screens the rooms from each other, providing additional privacy.

Activities concentrate on morning & afternoon game drives, & motorboat trips around the lagoons & waterways. As Camp Moremi & Camp Xakanaxa are owned by the same company as Camp Okavango (page 348) & Xugana (page 349) in the Delta, it's a good idea to combine several nights in each of the 2 locations, sticking to game drives here, & switching to motorboat & mokoro trips there. *From US$645 pp Jan–Mar & Dec to US$1,160/1,566 pp/sgl Jul–Oct, FBA.* ☺ *Closed mid-Feb–end Feb.* 🏵🏵🏵–🏵🏵🏵🏵

Camp Xakanaxa (12 tents) Contact Desert & Delta Safaris (page 214); ⊕ XAKANA 19°10.973'S, 23°24.567'E. Less than 1km northeast of Camp Moremi, Xakanaxa (ka-ka-na-ka) is the oldest of Moremi's camps, established in the 1960s. From its hunting & fishing origins, it became a photographic camp in 1988, & although modernised in 2020, its intrinsic laid-back character remains intact.

The camp is in a truly beautiful location overlooking the lagoon from the banks of the

Khwai River, with plenty of natural shade from mature kigelia & leadwood trees, & a reputation for good game both inside camp & around it. Its raised, thatched dining area is memorable for an 18-seater table, made from reclaimed railway sleepers. There's a separate, open-fronted lounge/bar, a circular area built out over the water with armchairs around a fire, & an infinity plunge pool. A second, much larger & more secluded pool is tucked behind the curio shop.

The solid wood furnishings run through to the comfortable Meru-style tents, which stand on wooden decks beneath canvas shade cloths, their verandas facing the lagoon. Woven rugs, simple timber furniture & comfortable beds are standard, & spacious interiors allow for a child's bed to be added to 2 of the tents if required. At the back, screened by poles & reeds, are a hot shower, handbasin & flush toilet. Activities include 4x4 game drives & boat trips offered morning & evening. *From US$690 pp Jan–Mar to US$1,240 pp Jun–Oct, FBA. Children 6+.* ⊕ *Closed 1–13 Feb.* 👑👑👑–👑👑👑👑

Okuti (7 rooms) Contact Ker & Downey Botswana (page 214). Sandwiched between Camp Xakanaxa & the boat station, Okuti occupies quite a tight spot among shady trees overlooking the lagoon. Opened in the early 1980s, but completely rebuilt over the years, Okuti remains a very comfortable place to stay, albeit perhaps in need of a little refurbishment, which may well be on the cards soon. The current camp is an ingenious triumph of design over space – all barrel-vaulted ceilings & soft curves, with sand-coloured walls, an extensive circular deck that is partially open to the lagoon, & a pool enclosed by rough wooden stakes in the style of a rural kraal. The domed entrance, with shelves of books, opens on to the dining area & a separate lounge, where there's a help-yourself bar. From here, long wooden walkways are punctuated by huge, tunnel-like masasa rooms – a traditional house of reeds. Inside, twin or dbl beds & simple, practical furnishings sit beneath elegantly curved reed ceilings, & mesh sliding doors reveal a veranda over the lagoon. Every room has indoor & exceptionally private outdoor showers, which in the 2 family chalets are shared by 2 bedrooms, while the honeymoon suite boasts an outdoor bath. They are all calm, laid-back spaces.

Activities concentrate on well-guided 4x4 game drives with no more than 4 on a vehicle (except on request), & motorboat trips on the lagoon from their own jetty. With a curio shop that offers locally made baskets, it all adds up to a well-run & friendly camp in a good location. *From US$645/871 pp/sgl early Jan to US$1,160/1,566 pp/sgl Jun–Oct, FBA.* ⊕ *Mar–early Jan.* 👑👑👑–👑👑👑👑👑

Camping

Gcodikwe & Gxhobega campsites Contact Xomae Group (page 213). Wild camping on Gcodikwe (or Gcadikwe) & Gxhobega islands, just northwest of Mboma Island, must – like Third Bridge Campsite – be organised in advance. You'll find 3 sites across these islands, in the area of the Gcodikwe Lagoon, unimaginatively known as Gcodikwe 1 & Gcodikwe 2, & Gxhobega. Access to the islands is only by pre-arranged boat, which takes about 3hrs from Third Bridge boat station, though if water levels are low you'll go from Mboma. You'll need to bring in all your own equipment, food & water – & bring out all your rubbish – as there are no facilities whatsoever on the island (& that includes toilets). It's possible, though, that fully catered trips may be available on request. *Self-catered US$100 pp per night, plus P5,500 (US$397) for the boat & driver/guide per night.*

Third Bridge Campsite (9 pitches, 5 en-suite tents) Contact Xomae Group (page 213); ⊕ 3BRIDG 19°14.368'S, 23°21.430'E. Third Bridge is about 8km in a straight line from Xakanaxa Campsite, although by road it's about 18km, depending on the route used. Despite their relative proximity, if you're camping in the area for 4–5 nights, then ideally try to split your time between the 2 sites. Third Bridge is well located for visiting Mboma Island, & is a more open site, with plenty of tree shade. It used to be my favourite site in Moremi but with privatisation its inherent character as a wilderness destination has been compromised. Now – with an ostentatious DWNP gate to greet you on the 'dry' route from Xakanaxa, a clutch of staff houses & 2 large (clean) ablution blocks – it's lost its old allure.

Crossing the bridge, you'll see that the water's crystal-clear as it passes over the sandy bottom of the narrow waterway. People used to bathe here often, but despite the apparently impenetrable stands of papyrus, there have been regular attacks by crocodiles; hence the plethora of notices warning you against swimming. It is also worth checking in advance if the pole bridges are operational, as periodic detours are in place if these break during the rains. That said, a new bridge opened at Third Bridge in late 2022, making all crossings passable at the time of writing this edition.

The site itself is sprawling, with pitches spread out across 2 almost distinct areas. It's notable for some attractive large feverberry trees (*Croton megalobotrys*) & a particularly fine sausage tree (*Kigelia africana*). Third Bridge is also known for a troop of very cheeky baboons, who have developed stealing food into a form of sport. So what's good practice anywhere is vital here: lock everything away when you're not using it, & make sure any rubbish is securely fastened in the cage provided. When we last stayed, there wasn't a baboon in sight, but don't bank on it. There was, though, a bearded lioness that strolled through the camp.

There is Wi-Fi in the office, a credit-card machine, & a small shop selling a motley selection of goods from cold beer, baskets & even beef to tinned foods, charcoal & firewood, though don't rely on them; it's still best to arrive fully equipped. There are also motorboat trips (P900/hr up to 9 people) from the camp's own boat station (page 320). *Camping US$42 pp, self-catering tent US$100 pp, exc park fees.* ☺ *All year.*

Xakanaxa Campsite (8 pitches) Contact Kwalate Safaris (page 213); ⊕ XAKCMP 19°11.026'S, 23°24.986'E. To the east of Okuti, Xakanaxa Campsite stretches along this tip of the Mopane Tongue, almost adjacent to Xakanaxa Boat Station. On arrival, campers should sign in at the smart DWNP Xakanaxa Gate (⊕ XAKGT 19°11.865'S, 23°25.865'E) which is 3km southeast of the campsite. The site's roughly marked pitches, some only just off the dirt road (though there's no traffic to speak of), blend into one long camping area lining the river. Along with 2 ablution blocks that are generally well maintained, water taps are dotted around the site, with a motley selection of tables, benches & braai stands of varying quality.

I've always loved these sites, & on one September visit the purple hanging flowers of the Kalahari appleleaf were in full force, reminding me of small jacaranda trees. As with Third Bridge, this is an area of particularly dense game, so do keep your eyes open for animals at all times as you move about the campsite: lions, hippos & elephants are known to wander through camp. *US$20 pp, exc park fees & bed levy.* ☺ *All year.*

What to see and do Until relatively recently, self-drive visitors here conducted their own game drives, or perhaps took a boat trip for a few hours from one of the lodges. Now, more organised water activities are available for independent visitors too. But there's still lots of self-driving exploring to do in this area, which is veined with game-viewing loops and tracks. So take your time – and be aware that after heavy flooding some previously navigable tracks might be impassable. Drive around slowly, and stop frequently. There are a number of specific areas that you might aim for, or just end up at.

Floodplain roads The network of tracks to the west of the main track between Xakanaxa and Third Bridge is probably the most rewarding in Moremi for game. Many are also very beautiful, lined with glassy pools that attract considerable numbers of both game and birdlife.

Goaxhlo Island and Pan Also known as Dead Tree Island, you'll recognise it by the number of skeletal trees that surround the pan of open water. Like those at Savuti, these were killed by drowning – when the channels changed and inundated the area. Most are mopane trees, and because of their resistance to termites, and semi-submerged state, they're decomposing very, very slowly indeed. This is quite an eerie sight, and photographers will find plenty to inspire them, especially if there are any animals present. Keep a particular look-out for the graceful pink spoonbills that breed here.

Dobetsaa Pans Take a left in a southerly direction, perhaps 1km after crossing Fourth Bridge on the way to Third Bridge, and you'll find a short loop leading down past a few very scenic pans. Veronica Roodt comments that this is 'one of the few places in Moremi where the African skimmer can be seen'. But even without the skimmers it's a good birdwatching spot with some very open pans.

Mboma Island West of Third Bridge is a large, long island, circled by a loop road which stretches for about 50km around it. There's a spur to this at the north end, and a short cut back to Third Bridge halfway round. It's worth spending a day here, as Mboma's environments are varied and beautiful, though different from the floodplain loops nearer to Xakanaxa. I've had great sightings of cheetah on the northern side of the island, and the south is said to be a popular haunt of buffalo herds.

Boat trips We'd recommend that you take at least one trip by boat or mokoro on to the lagoons and waterways of Moremi. It's usually worth the cost, unless you're due to be going on to a camp with water-based activities. But remember that boat fuel is costly to buy and transport, and that you're in a very remote location, so these trips aren't cheap.

All the drivers are qualified guides, in as much as they can name the various birds and plants that you'll see, but their understanding of what you want may not tie up with yours. For this reason, do explain your objectives clearly before you set out, even to the lodge guides, or you may find yourself being driven at breakneck speed from one side of the lagoon to the other, watching a hastily named bird rise up in fright at the approaching roar of the engine, or veering away from the occasional pod of hippo. And do ask questions – your boat driver may well know the answers.

Aside from the lodges at Xakanaxa, three boat stations hold the exclusive rights to take boats on to the lagoons, although effectively there are four operators involved. This exclusivity is in part to help prevent the spread of *Salvinia molesta*, or Kariba weed, an invasive plant that is posing a serious threat to Botswana's waterways (page 17). You'll need a hat, suncream and drinks, but little else except, of course, binoculars and a camera. It is reasonably safe to leave a vehicle parked at either place.

There's little or no shade on most of the boats, so the best times to venture out are early morning, or in late afternoon, culminating in sunset over the lake. A couple of hours is really the ideal; less than that and it'll seem rushed so you'll miss out on the gentle beauty of the place. In theory there's no need to book, but the number of boats is limited so it makes sense to give them advance warning.

Mboma Boat Station m 7372 7929; e boatstation@mboma-island.com; w mbomaboatstation.com. The most established of Moremi's boat stations is at the far northwest tip of Mboma Island, about 1–2hrs drive (15km) from Third Bridge along deep sand, or 3hrs (63km) from South Gate. The turn-off from the main loop road is at ⊕ MBOMAT 19°01.574'S, 23°17.126'E, with the station about 1.5km west of there. Both 6- & 9-seater motorboats with a driver-guide can be hired by the hour (P1,475/hr, min 2hrs). For a more leisurely trip, you can go out on a mokoro with an experienced poler (P440 pp/hr for up to 2 people; min age 12), & even arrange an overnight island camping experience in small dome tents (P3,500 pp/night, min 4 people). The clear website includes online booking & pricing information.

Third Bridge Boat Station 📞 686 2221; e xomaesites@btcmail.co.bw. Based at Third Bridge Campsite (page 318) & also run by Xomae Group (page 213), there are 3 9-seater boats costing P900/hr per boat with driver. Typically you'll go out for 2–3hrs morning or afternoon, taking a slow cruise from the campsite & exploring 3 lagoons.

Xakanaxa Boat Station (Okavango Boating); 📞 686 0364; m 7349 7609; e okavangoboating@gmail.com; ⊕ dawn–dusk; ⊕ XAKABT

19°13.098'S, 23°22.247'E. Literally adjacent to the campsite at Xakanaxa (page 319), this enterprise – signposted as Okavango Boating – offers trips on the lagoon with several boats, including a double decker (P1,700/hr or 8,000/day for up to 16 people), a 12-seater (P1,400/hr or 7,200/day) & an 8-seater (P1,100/hr or 6,100/day). It is also possible to arrange for overnight trips. If you ask around at the campsite, you may well find others to share a boat with, thus cutting costs. Trips departing here have the advantage of starting on the large Xakanaxa Lagoon.

Gcodikwe Lagoon and heronry Gcodikwe (or Gcadikwe, Gcudikwa) Lagoon (◈ GCODIK 19°09.731'S, 23°14.507'E) is one of the Okavango's largest and most famous lagoons. A huge, almost circular oxbow lagoon encompassing several large tree-islands, it is reachable only by boat: a trip of about 90 minutes from Xakanaxa. It is perhaps best visited from one of the lodges just outside the park, the best being Kwara (6km northeast), Shinde (11km northwest) or Camp Okavango (15km west) – though you can double all these 'straight-line' distances to allow for meandering through the waterways.

The 'islands' are made up mainly of water-fig trees and a little papyrus growing in shallow water. Over the millennia these have accumulated a mass of bird guano and detritus under them to raise their levels and grow. Now they're large, but still isolated from any predators that are not aquatic. Hence they have become a vital breeding ground for the Okavango's waterbirds. Some years, including 2023, the heronry was much smaller than it used to be, in which case a further 5 minutes on the boat to a second heronry at Gxhobega will enchant even the most casual birdwatcher.

Thousands of birds come to these heronries to breed, including herons, egrets, storks, ibises, cormorants and many others. Most of the nest-building activity starts around August, and breeding seems to be timed so that the chicks hatch around October and November, when water levels are low and fish are easier to catch. Certainly when we've visited in late February, there have only been a few birds around.

Watch carefully and you'll see that the larger, more robust species like marabou and yellow-billed storks tend to nest in the canopy of the trees, while the smaller, more vulnerable species can be found within the trees. Also keep an eye out for water snakes and leguaans, which come here in search of chicks.

GETTING AWAY FROM THE MOPANE TONGUE
Driving from Xakanaxa to North Gate (Khwai) It's about 44km to drive directly from Xakanaxa to North Gate; just head east from the Xakanaxa Gate (◈ XAKGT 19°11.865'S, 23°25.865'E). However, ask advice from the camp's office before you set off as if this road is blocked by high water levels, you will need to take the 'dry' route to the south. For details, see below.

Driving from Xakanaxa to South Gate (Maqwee) Many would travel from Xakanaxa to South Gate via Third Bridge, using the route described in the next section, as the scenery's more varied and, in the dry season, I'd expect the game to be better – especially around the Mboma Island area.

However, the most direct route is along a track that heads southeast from near the western end of Xakanaxa's airstrip, taking about 42km to reach South Gate. The route is generally good, even when it's wet, apart from a number of clay pans which can be sticky.

Driving from Third Bridge to South Gate (Maqwee) The tracks around Mboma Island can be confusing, but to reach South Gate you set off west on to

Mboma Island from Third Bridge. Keep bearing left when the road forks and after 3–4km you'll be travelling south. The road then bends east, south and even west until you reach another pole bridge which is known, rather unimaginatively, as Second Bridge (✪ 2BRIDG 19°17.003'S, 23°22.553'E).

Crossing this, you'll then head southeast towards another pole bridge referred to as (surprise!) First Bridge (✪ 1BRIDG 19°17.099'S, 23°23.531'E). From here it's an uncomplicated drive southeast to South Gate, with most of the trip through mopane woodlands – which in turn conceal any number of elephants.

If time is on your side, consider a detour off the main track. There's a short, easy loop off to the south of the road, about 12km before the gate; it's clearly marked on Veronica Roodt's map of Moremi. Characterised by flat, open plains, dotted with anthills and small pans, this is a great place to look out for storks, with large numbers of marabou in particular when we visited at the end of the dry season. Don't worry if you miss the connection with the main road at the picturesque Xini Lagoon, which isn't at all clear on the ground when it's dry; the track links up almost seamlessly with the main road to South Gate, and the woodland landscape, just a couple of kilometres further on.

Very close to here, at ✪ MOGTO 19°23.594'S, 23°32.972'E, is a turning towards a series of tracks, signposted to Mogogelo Hippo Pool and Black Pools. The loops here are clearly marked, running around and across floodplains, shallow pans and areas of woodland. An added and unexpected bonus in the heat of the day is a picnic site (✪ MOGPIC 19°28.811'S, 23°32.155'E), with benches and tables set out in a beautiful shady grove of trees looking out on to a floodplain. If exploring at the end of the dry season, when most of the pools had dried up, was somewhat disappointing, Veronica Roodt claims that the area supports 'vast numbers of game'. Certainly all the signs were there, imprinted in the mud across numerous shallow depressions – and at the neighbouring Xini Lagoon, the scene was like something out of a picture book of African wildlife. If you follow the loops in an easterly direction, you can rejoin the main track about 4km west of South Gate at ✪ MOGSGT 19°25.412'S, 23°36.755'E.

SOUTH GATE (MAQWEE) South Gate (✪ SOGATE 19°25.548'S, 23°38.733'E), also known as Maqwee Gate, is usually treated as a transit stop by most visitors as it's in the midst of fairly unexciting mopane forest, with a small campsite sheltered among the trees.

Having described it as unexciting, this may just be my failure to really get to know the area well. We've only stayed a handful of individual nights, during different trips (always at the start or the end of a trip across Chobe and Moremi). However, on one of those occasions, just as we were getting up, about half-a-dozen wild dogs gently jogged through the camp and into the forest. I don't think our roof tent has ever been packed away so rapidly – but try as we might, tracking them was a waste of time, with park rules forbidding off-road driving in Moremi!

On another trip we found a whole pack of wild dogs lounging on the road a few kilometres south of South Gate, in the NG33/34 Concession area. They posed for photographs just a few metres from our vehicle for 20 minutes or so – totally unconcerned with our presence. So perhaps, especially in the earlier months of the year, South Gate warrants a closer look and more than just an overnight stop.

Flora and fauna

Flora Around South Gate the trees are almost all mopane (*Colophospermum mopane*), with their distinctive butterfly-shaped leaves. Tall, undamaged specimens can reach 18m in height, when they're known as 'cathedral' mopane for their gracefully arching branches. In neighbouring areas, where the nutrients are not as plentiful or the trees have been damaged by elephants, this same species grows much lower – and is known as 'stunted mopane'. In both you'll find their leaves hanging down and tending to fold together during the heat of the day, leaving little shade underneath.

This tremendously successful tree is one of the commonest species in the hot, dry areas of the subcontinent. It's notable for its tolerance of poorly drained, alkaline soils – and often occurs in areas where there's a lot of clay. Driving in mopane country during the rainy season usually involves negotiating lots of sticky, clay-filled mud-holes.

For the camper, the mopane wood is a dark-reddish colour, hard, heavy and termite-resistant. Thus even long-dead pieces won't have been completely eaten by termites. It burns exceedingly well, smelling sweetly and producing lots of heat. You're no longer allowed to collect firewood in Moremi, but it's worth seeking out outside the park. (Turn each piece over, looking under it carefully for snakes and scorpions, before picking it up.)

Fauna With relatively dense forests this area can seem devoid of wildlife. But don't be mistaken; it isn't. Because the soil in mopane forest areas is often very poorly drained, it's dotted with small pans – temporary shallow ponds – during and shortly after the rains. This allows most of the big-game species to leave the over-populated areas beside the watercourses and disappear into these huge areas of forests.

Elephant, zebra, impala, kudu, tsessebe, common duiker, bushbuck, steenbok, eland, roan warthog, baboon and vervet monkey can all be found here, as can lion, leopard, cheetah, spotted hyena, wild dog and many of the smaller mammals. But you will have to look much harder here for them than on the open floodplains and beside the watercourses where they congregate during the dry season.

What you are guaranteed to see at any time of year are lots of bush squirrels (*Paraxerus cepapi*), which are so common in mopane woodlands that they're often known as 'mopane squirrels'. See page 14 for more details.

Birdlife The high density of small rodents in mopane woodlands, especially bush squirrels, means that it's a good place for small raptors which hunt from perches (rather than the air). These include barn owls, smaller hawks and kestrels, and even martial eagles.

Meanwhile two species here are very common. The small, black-and-white Arnot's chat appears in pairs or small groups, often hopping about the ground or lower branches in search of small insects – memorably described by a friend on first sight as 'little flying zebras'. There's also the red-billed hornbill, which seems to be everywhere with its heavy flap-flap-flap...glide...flap-flap-flap... glide...style of flight. Remember Rowan Atkinson's performance as the hornbill 'Zazu' in Walt Disney's *The Lion King* and you'll never be able to watch one again without smiling.

Getting there and away For directions to South Gate, see pages 218 and 321.

Orientation Navigating around South Gate is very straightforward, with just five clear roads: one to Maun via the veterinary checkpoint; another to North Gate; one to Third Bridge, which stays close to the southern side of the Mopane Tongue; and a fourth to Xakanaxa which cuts through the heart of the Tongue. The fifth, now closed to self-drivers, leads to Santawani Lodge (page 398). There are now several game-drive loops quite close to the gate in Moremi; for details, see below.

 ## Where to stay   *Map, page 302*

In June 2024, Tawana became the first lodge to open in this southeastern area of Moremi. For self-drivers, there's a long-established campsite immediately next to the park gate.

Tawana (8 suites) Contact Natural Selection (page 215). Located on the banks of the perennial Gomoti River, Tawana is a collaboration between the local Batawana tribe & Natural Selection, & named after the Paramount Chief Tawana Moremi. Nestled beneath the shade of ancient ebony trees, the luxury lodge sits in the southeastern part of the reserve, offering panoramic vistas across the floodplains – a popular hang-out for grazing herbivores. 2 of the spacious suites are tailored for families & all embrace a contemporary aesthetic. Each sits under a trio of thatched roofs, with an interconnected bedroom, lounge & large en-suite bathroom with a bath & 2 showers – one outdoors. The curved deck along the front of the suites includes a circular plunge pool & a shaded outdoor sala, ensuring ample space & seclusion for guests. All suites have ceiling fans, AC & thoughtful amenities, from a stocked minibar to a Nespresso machine. Powered entirely by solar energy, Tawana has 24hr electricity & Wi-Fi throughout.

The lodge's central area encompasses a spacious lounge, dining area, & a library stocked with reference books. Dining options range from indoor settings to alfresco meals in an open-air kgotla, complete with a wood-fired pizza oven. A well-stocked wine cellar & an outdoor lounge with a firepit make for great sundowner drinks. Activities focus on Moremi game drives, while back at camp there's an on-site gym, 16m swimming pool & spa treatments. *From US$1,695 pp mid-Jan–Mar to US$3,495 pp Jul–Aug, FBA inc airstrip transfers & conservation fee. Children 6+.* ⊕ *All year.* 🦏🦏🦏🦏🦏

South Gate (Maqwee) Campsite (10 pitches) Contact Kwalate Safaris (page 213). Immediately next to the park gate, this well-managed campsite has 10 basic sand pitches & good privacy. There are 2 clean, shared ablution blocks with solar-heated water & standpipes (though elephants have been known to rip the taps off in search of fresh water). Pitches nearer the ablutions offer considerably more shade thanks to the tall mopane trees, but be warned these are popular hang-outs for baboons & monkeys. Each pitch has its own raised braai, rubbish bin (watch out for honey badgers at night) & a firepit, & some have concrete picnic tables too. No electricity or drinking water available, but firewood for sale. Book a pitch in advance. *US$40 pp, exc park fees & bed levy.* ⊕ *All year.*

GETTING AWAY FROM SOUTH GATE
Driving from South Gate (Maqwee) to Third Bridge
Take the most westerly exit from the campsite and the route is very easy. After about 24km you'll pass a right turn, marked by an old green cement block. One side of this notes that Mboma and Third Bridge are off to the left. There are no indications where the right turn goes, though it actually leads around the east side of the Bodumatau Lagoon.

Keeping on the main road (to the left), you'll then pass, in order, First Bridge (⊕ 1BRIDG 19°17.099'S, 23°23.531'E) and Second Bridge (⊕ 2BRIDG 19°17.003'S, 23°22.553'E), before finally reaching the campsite at Third Bridge (⊕ 3BRIDG 19°14.368'S, 23°21.430'E). At the time of writing, all of these bridges were passable, though they have been known to collapse after heavy rains, so always check conditions locally before embarking on this journey.

Driving from South Gate (Maqwee) to Xakanaxa
The more scenic route is to follow the directions to Third Bridge (see above), then continue southwest to Fourth Bridge (⊕ 4BRIDG 19°15.128'S, 23°24.173'E) and thence to Xakanaxa.

The 'new' bridge is already in poor repair, but the old one is still passable, and in the dry season it's possible to drive to the side. From there proceed broadly northeast to the Xakanaxa Gate (⊕ XAKGT 19°11.865'S, 23°25.865'E), where you turn west for the campsite and lodges. You can navigate through this labyrinth of game-viewing loops using Veronica Roodt's map, or by sticking to the main track, setting your GPS for Xakanaxa, and then keeping slightly east of the direct-line direction.

However, if it's late in the dry season and you've plenty of time, then you may want to take a detour around the Bodumatau Lagoon, which avoids Third Bridge completely. (This track is marked as 'seasonal' on most maps, and is much less reliable than the main track, especially when wet.) In that case, take the right turn at the green concrete block that is about 24km from South Gate. It's 16km to the Bodumatau Bridge from here, then a further 13km to Fourth Bridge. One local operator refers to the first part of this road after the green concrete block as 'Elephant Alley', for its winding road through dense mopane is often frequented by elephants. Drive carefully.

Alternatively, there's a shorter, alternative route marked on the Shell map. Head towards North Gate from South Gate for about 300m, then turn left for 10km to the Kudu Flats, where you bear left again and follow the road all the way to Xakanaxa. The final part of this ties up with the 'dry' route from North Gate to Xakanaxa.

Driving from South Gate to North Gate (Khwai)
A very direct, straight road leads about 30km north-northeast from South Gate to North Gate (⊕ NOGATE 19°10.394'S, 23°45.092'E). There are no game-viewing loops off this road as it's largely dense bush, used primarily as a transit route.

Driving from South Gate to Maun
Leaving the park from South Gate, after a few hundred metres there's a well-signposted fork. For Maun, take the main fork to the left, along a wide but badly rutted gravel road that is painfully slow going. The right fork leads into NG33 and the wild-dog research station near Chitabe (page 383), but this road is now closed to self-drivers.

Heading towards Maun, to the right lies the NG33 Concession, while to the left is an area managed by the community, NG34. Both are good wildlife areas, but because the land and the wildlife are managed, technically the road you are on is a 'transit route', and you are not allowed to stop and camp. The nearest place to camp is the community-run Kaziikini site (page 398).

After a further 17km you'll reach the sizeable village of **Shorobe**. Roadside vendors sell cold drinks, and there's a craft studio on the east side of the road, but little else to tempt the passing traveller. From here the road to Maun is tarred, passing the University of Botswana. The total journey from South Gate to the Engen garage, which is the first fuel station in Maun, is about 90km.

THE PRIVATE AREAS WITHIN MOREMI (NG28)

Aside from the Mopane Tongue, the only way to access any of the rest of Moremi is from one of the small private safari camps within the reserve. In 1992, the boundaries of Moremi Game Reserve were revised and extended to the north and east, resulting in the previously private concession of NG28 being incorporated into the reserve area. As a result, three upmarket safari camps now stand within Moremi itself: Mombo and Chief's Camp at the north end of Chief's Island, and Xigera right on the western edge.

These two areas are very different, and so we've sub-divided this former concession into two sections: one covering Xigera's area, and the other concentrating on Mombo and Chief's Camp.

It's also worth noting that there are a number of safari camps that border the edge of the park and conduct some of their activities within the park. These include those in NG19 near North Gate (page 341), camps in NG21 (page 346) and camps along the south end of the Boro River in NG27B (page 371).

XIGERA If you had to stick a pin on the map in the centre of the Delta, you'd probably put it near to here. The Xigera (pronounced 'kee-jera') area is near Moremi's western border. It can be visited any time of the year, but be aware that boating activities are seasonal.

Only pre-booked guests may visit this area, flying in to Xigera's own **airstrip** (✪ XIGAIR 19°23.155'S, 22°44.618'E). Note that there's no practical dry-land access from here to Mombo, Chief's Camp or the nearby Nxabega, and that driving in isn't an option.

Concession history Look at an old map of the Delta and you'll realise that the western boundary of Moremi used to be further east than it is now. Then the Xigera and Mombo areas were part of the NG28 Concession and outside the park. Xigera was originally built in 1986 by Hennie and Angela Rawlinson, two well-known Maun residents, at a place that Hennie called 'Paradise Island'.

Then, in 1992, Moremi was expanded westwards and northwards. This was done in order to bring under its protection all the major Okavango habitats, as until then none of the northern Delta's papyrus swamps or permanent wetlands had been included. This expansion swallowed up NG28, including the Xigera and Mombo areas. Thus these camps now occupy prime sites within Moremi Game Reserve.

In 1998, the Rawlinsons renewed the lease for another 15 years and shortly after, the camp was completely demolished, and rebuilt from scratch a short distance away. The lease then passed to Wilderness Safaris and now sits with the Tollman family and their Red Carnation Hotel group. Under this latest ownership, Xigera has its most opulent safari lodge.

Flora and fauna You're very close to the Jao River, which feeds the Boro and is one of the Okavango's major waterways. In the recent past, the area around Xigera was one of the Delta's few truly deep-water experiences, surrounded by apparently endless papyrus swamps, with only the odd island. But the situation is radically different now. The papyrus-lined channels have been completely replaced with grassy floodplains, the Xigera Lagoon hasn't flooded in the last five years and although the Seronga Channel remains deep, it is extremely narrow. While safari days spent predominantly on the water are over – at least for the moment – the flip-side is that the possibilities for game drives in the area have increased significantly. As the water has dried up, so the access by land has expanded and the visibility of predators has increased.

As far as **flora** is concerned, in the shallower sections of water you'll find large areas of common reeds (*Phragmites australis*) and the tall miscanthus grass (*Miscanthus junceus*). There are also a few lovely stands of pure water fern (*Thelypteris interrupta*) on the edges of some of the channels and lagoons. On the islands you'll find the normal trees of the Delta, including a good number of confetti trees (*Gymnosporia senegalensis*). The English name for these comes from the small, scented white flowers that come out around May–June, and then fall underneath the tree in large enough quantities to be scooped up. Fan palms are visible throughout the area.

On Xigera island itself, the lodge has taken preventative measures to protect the vegetation from elephant damage and rejuvenate the area. A high electric fence has been installed, preventing elephants from accessing the island's trees but allowing all other wildlife to pass freely through. With new baobabs and strangler figs planted, and time for the existing vegetation to grow unabated, the island itself is increasingly lush.

For **fauna**, elephants can be found in substantial herds of up to 50, and their impact on some of the large hardwood trees is evident. There are good sightings of big cats. Leopards have long been successful in the area and in 2024, eight were resident with as many as 16 known transient individuals. Additionally, four prides of lion operate here, with a total of 22 animals, their numbers indicative of the prey availability. Spotted hyenas cross the bridge to the island almost religiously every night, lion regularly and leopard occasionally too.

You've a good chance of spotting impala, lechwe, tsessebe, zebra and warthogs in the area, many of whom can also be spotted grazing on the floodplain beyond the camp's veranda. Buffalo herds are in evidence, as are spotted hyena, who have even been known to catch catfish here.

If you are visiting during boating season or head out on a mokoro, you can expect to see assorted **birdlife**, such as kingfishers, herons, egrets, saddlebill storks and other waterbirds. Included in this list, if you're lucky, will be purple (but not lesser) gallinules, lesser jacanas, moorhens, lesser moorhens and green-backed herons. Other unusual birds that enthusiastic ornithologists should look out for include chirping cisticolas, tawny-flanked prinias and palm swifts, all of which are regularly sighted here. Territorial wattled cranes are a lovely sight in the ponds around camp, with talk of a National Geographic researcher conducting a study of them in the area. Raptors, too, notably bateleur and fish eagles, are easily spotted.

Where to stay   *Map, page 302*

✳ **Xigera Safari Lodge**   (11 suites, 1 family suite) ☏ +27 87 743 2388; w xigera.com. Sited on the evocatively named Paradise Island, Xigera (kee-jera) was entirely reimagined & reopened in palatial style in 2020. If you've never been to the Delta, then simply conjure up an image of a beautifully luxurious safari camp in the heart of the swamps, enveloped by a lush, tropical abundance & you've probably come close to visualising Xigera.

Considerable grandeur & comfort are now its hallmarks, & Xigera caters unashamedly for those who would like room service, AC, flat-screen sat TV & vintage wines as part of their experience, as well as travellers with a keen eye for the pan-African art collection on display throughout the lodge.

Xigera's suites, each constructed from Japanese cedarwood topped by a sensuously curving canvas roof, take in endless views of the surrounding floodplains. From bespoke cabinetry to hand-thrown ceramics, custom-print textiles & bronze-cast lilies (the lodge's ever-present icon), every room is grand & individually styled, including the classic, dark-wood neutrality of the Mangosteen

Suite & the bold, ruby-red patterned style of the Sausage Tree Suite. The 11 2-person suites feature a separate lounge, bedroom & dressing room area – as well as an extensive outside deck, complete with gazebos & king-size day beds. All are raised high enough to have wildlife wander underneath, & each is named & themed after a local tree. There is also a larger Xigera Family Suite with 2 en-suite bedrooms sharing a very lovely lounge that opens out on to a wide deck: an ideal spot for families or travelling friends.

For something special, a 3-storey, 10m-high steel baobab-inspired structure is available for treehouse sleepouts 1km from camp. Complete with its own bedroom, bathroom & lounging deck, guests can choose to stay here for a night during their stay.

The opulence & space extend into the main areas of the lodge, where the lounge & dining room overlook a perennial channel. There's also a cocktail bar, wine cellar, library with AC, stylish boma & an outdoor firepit, swimming pool, gym & spa, as well as a serious boutique showcasing choice pieces from acclaimed African artisans.

Activities on land & water are available, with game drives (daytime only), guided walking (sensibly within the Nxabega Concession to allow for an armed guide), fishing (exc Jan–Feb), double-decker motorboat cruises (seasonal) & mokoro trips all offered with flexible departure times.

Photographers with long lenses will appreciate the adjustable armrests on vehicles & experience of the guides. *From US$2,597 pp 6 Jan–Apr to US$4,846 pp Jun–Oct, FBA exc transfers. Baobab Treehouse sleepout US$250 pp supplement. Children 6+.* ☺ *All year.* ♛♛♛♛–♛♛♛♛♛

MOMBO AND CHIEF'S CAMP

Mombo and Chief's share a concession within Moremi, but they are about 25km apart – which is a long way in the Okavango. Hence, unless they want to cross paths, you'll never normally see vehicles from one camp in the other camp.

Concession history From the mid-1980s, the rights to run Mombo were owned by the now defunct Jao Safaris, who sub-leased the area to many safari companies including Ker & Downey, Bonadventure (who were one of the main tour agencies when I first visited Maun in 1987) and Wilderness Safaris. During this time, and especially in the latter years, it gained a first-class reputation for game.

When Jao Safaris' lease expired in 1998, stiff competition was anticipated for such a prime area, resulting in the government's Land Board allowing two sites to be put up for tender, at opposite ends of the concession. There was indeed tremendous competition: 29 companies entered the bidding war. Eventually two bids were accepted, one from Wilderness Safaris (page 216) and another from Abercrombie and Kent (whose Botswana operation is now called Sanctuary Retreats; page 215). Each company had to promise the government the highest possible revenue, as well as the most sustainable and productive management plan.

To achieve this, both companies arrived at the obvious solution: each built one of the country's most upmarket camps, and attached an appropriately high price tag to it. It was the only proposition to make financial sense given the high concession fees. Thus, the new, luxurious Mombo came into being, near the old Mombo site, and Chief's Camp was created south of that, on the northwestern side of Chief's Island. The tender process had maximised the government's revenues, and pushed part of the area's tourism a step further upmarket.

Flora and fauna

Flora The environments found here aren't unique in the Delta, but they are old, established, and have long been protected – and so are basically pristine and undisturbed.

Perhaps the most interesting, and certainly the most photogenic, habitats here are the shallow floodplains which surround the northern end of Chief's Island. It's such a distinctive landscape that an image of it has remained deeply ingrained in my mind since my first visit here, in the mid-1990s.

Looking at the whole Delta, you'll realise that this area is very close to the permanent swamps at the base of the Panhandle. Because of this, the floods here are more regular and predictable than they are lower down the Delta. This regular seasonal flooding has created a very photogenic environment of short-grass plains, among which are a number of tiny islands fringed by dense, feathery stands of wild date palms (*Phoenix reclinata*). For me, this is the quintessential Delta landscape – and it's sufficiently open to be excellent for game viewing.

Away from the Okavango Delta, the only place that I've seen which is similar to this in southern Africa is the Busanga Plains of northern Kafue, in Zambia. Again, these are consistently flooded every year, and have very little disturbance.

Go back on to the dry land of Chief's Island and you'll find a range of more familiar landscapes and floral communities. Across southern areas of the island (albeit not visited on game drives) are some areas of impressive, tall 'cathedral' mopane (*Colophospermum mopane*), often a popular retreat for game during wetter months.

Running through this you'll find lines of Kalahari sandveld, reflecting the locations of old, long-dry watercourses. Here you will see sand-loving species like the silver cluster-leaf (*Terminalia sericea*), the Kalahari appleleaf (*Philenoptera nelsii*), perhaps some camelthorn (*Vachellia erioloba*) and umbrella thorns (*Vachellia tortilis*), and the odd leadwood tree (*Combretum imberbe*).

Where the land meets the water, there are bands of classic riverine forest including fine specimens of raintree (*Philenoptera violacea*), sausage tree (*Kigelia africana*), jackalberry (*Diospyros mespiliformis*), African mangosteen (*Garcinia livingstonei*), figs (mostly *Ficus sycomorus*) and some wild date palms (*Phoenix reclinata*). Throughout the area's forests you'll occasionally find huge old baobab trees (*Adansonia digitata*) – which probably have lived long enough to see the environment change around them!

Fauna The game in this area is at least as dense as anywhere else in the Okavango, and probably more so as a result of historical peat fires on the north of Chief's Island releasing nutrients en masse into the ecosystem. Because the area's a private one, the game viewing is just about the best you'll find in southern Africa. It's dense, varied, and good sightings of predators are virtually guaranteed.

See *Flora and fauna* at the start of this chapter for more extensive comments on Moremi as a whole; in this particular area impala, tsessebe, zebra and giraffe are usually the most numerous of the larger herbivores – although warthogs are remarkably common. (So numerous that they have become a major prey species for both lion and leopard.) Elephant and buffalo are resident here in good numbers, with more individual animals seen during the rains, and generally larger herds recorded as the dry season progresses. Rhino have had an especially rough ride, as in much of Africa (page 330).

Zebra populations are far denser than elsewhere in the Delta. Herds of red lechwe are common in the flooded areas when the water's high, but they rarely venture into the drier parts of the reserve. Kudu and wildebeest also occur, as do the occasional reedbuck and steenbok; sable and roan are usually never seen here.

Though the majority of the Delta's usual line-up of nocturnal animals do occur, without taking night drives most are difficult to spot. The exception seems to be honey badgers, porcupines, civets and spring hares, which are sometimes seen around the camps at night.

The area has a justified, first-class reputation for excellent predator sightings. Spotted hyena are probably the most successful large carnivore in the area, though lion are also common – as they are in many areas of the Delta. And cheetah, very much at home among the sprinkling of slightly raised date palm islands and termite hills that make ideal look-out posts, have become widespread.

There are good numbers of leopard around – although their appearances during the day are relatively limited. Originally Mombo, and this area, built its reputation on some of Africa's best sightings of wild dog – largely because of a very large and successful pack of about 40 dogs that denned here for several years in the mid-1990s. With this pack in residence, visitors were virtually guaranteed amazing sightings, and the area's dry open floodplains proved marvellous for following the animals as they hunted. Then that pack broke up, as is the usual process when the alpha female dies, but two other packs now operate in the area, so sightings remain pretty good.

Until the middle of the 20th century, white rhino were common across northern Botswana, while the less populous black rhino held its own in the area around the Kwando and Chobe rivers. However, protection was inadequate, and illegal hunting was spurred on by the value of rhinoceros horns on the world market. By 1992, the area's population of black rhino had been wiped out, declared 'locally extinct', and white rhino numbers were down to a critical 19. As a result, the remaining white rhinos were removed to wildlife sanctuaries for their protection.

Gradually, a more effective anti-poaching operation was formed by the Department of Wildlife and National Parks (DWNP), backed by the Botswana Defence Force (BDF). By 2001, the Botswana Rhino Reintroduction Project was born, a collaborative venture between the DWNP and Wilderness Safaris (page 216). Under its auspices, four white rhinos were initially reintroduced on to Chief's Island: two females and two males. Two years later, four black rhinos were released to roam in the Delta. These small initial populations thrived and gave confidence that further reintroductions could build the population to sustainable levels.

The cause of conservation had always enjoyed enthusiasm from stakeholders in the tourism industry, and during this period, it had real support in the government, from President Khama down. The DWNP's Anti-Poaching Unit, backed by the BDF, took a zero-tolerance approach to poaching – so the Delta's embryonic new rhino population remained relatively unscathed.

Meanwhile, poaching in some areas of Africa was reaching epidemic proportions. In South Africa, more than 6,000 rhinos had been killed for their horns in just a decade. To counter the real threat of extinction, Rhinos Without Borders (w rhinoswithoutborders.com) was launched, spearheaded by two

Birdlife At the heart of the Delta, and with a large and diverse area of dry land and floodplains, this area of Moremi gets periodic visits from virtually all of the birds in the Delta, so singling out a few to mention here is inevitably a flawed process.

However, top of the list for a special mention are the vultures, attracted by the game densities and predator activity. Most numerous are the white-backed, hooded and lappet-faced vultures – though you'll also find a surprising number of white-headed vultures. Palm-nut vultures occur, too (usually frequenting the real fan palms), though they're not common.

Also attracted by the game are both kinds of oxpecker – though yellow-billed (which feed on the backs of hippos) seem more common than the red-billed variety.

As happens everywhere in the Delta, when the waters recede, isolated pools of fish are left behind. As these gradually dry up the fish become more and more concentrated, attracting the most amazing numbers of predatory birds. Pick the right day (usually one between about May and October) and the right pool, and you'll be entertained for hours by large concentrations of pelicans, saddle-billed storks, marabou storks, black egrets, grey and Goliath herons to name but a few. It's an amazing sight. In other receding pools you'll find congregations of pelicans or, in those which aren't so frantic, painted snipes can be seen if you look hard (or have a good guide!).

The short-grass floodplains here suit wattled cranes, which are often found in numbers, and on the drier plains watch for secretary birds and kori bustards. The latter occasionally have carmine bee-eaters using their backs as perches. In plains with longer grass you may be able to spot an African crake, while ostriches are very rarely seen (perhaps because there are too many large predators).

concerned tour operators, Great Plains Conservation and &Beyond (page 214). They aimed to raise enough funds to move 100 rhinos out of South Africa into the relative safety of Botswana. At a cost of US$45,000 per rhino, it was an expensive mission, but by the end of 2015, 25 animals had been moved, and by about 2018, this number had grown to 87. After release, they were closely monitored, and the project proved successful: Rhinos Without Borders noted that 'every sexually mature female that they translocated had had a calf'. They were also spreading out more widely, with reports of individuals roaming as far as the Makgadikgadi Pans. At the end of 2017, a CITES report estimated Botswana's rhino population at a much healthier 502 rhinos (50 black and 452 white); only six rhinos had been poached since 2006.

However, in April 2018, when Mokgweetsi Masisi became president, the climate for conservation seemed to change. Poaching began to increase; a report by the Environmental Investigation Agency noted: 'At least 92 rhinos were killed between January 2019 and July 2020, according to the government, though the true poaching figures may be significantly greater.'

Then came the disruption of the Covid-19 pandemic in 2020. Travel restrictions and reduced tourism revenue was coupled with lower surveillance during lockdowns, which almost certainly compounded this rise by giving poachers freer rein.

Since then, the remaining rhinos in most areas of northern Botswana have been relocated to 'safe areas', with few remaining truly in the wild. Sadly, for the visitor, this means that, aside from one or two specific concessions, you're unlikely to see rhinos in northern Botswana.

On the water look for pygmy geese and dwarf jacanas in the quieter areas, along with many species of more common waterbirds. There's often a good number of the relatively rare slaty egrets about too.

When to visit Given that the focus here is firmly on game viewing, the dry season is the obvious time to visit. That's when the game is at its most visible and most dense. That said, from July to October the camps (especially Mombo) have substantial 'high-season supplements', which can make the costs at other times of the year seem very attractive.

If you decide to come at a less popular, and cheaper, time then remember that Chief's Island is a large, permanent island with its own large, permanent population of game. Thus you'll still see some first-rate game even if the game viewing isn't quite as good as it would have been during October, though do be aware that no off-road driving within Moremi will impact on guides' abilities to follow or track predators.

Getting there and away Only pre-booked guests flying in visit this area, as there is no practical dry-land access to Chief's Island. Driving here isn't an option. Each camp has its own airstrip on Chief's Island; Mombo's airstrip is at ⊕ MOMBOA 19°12.680'S, 22°47.510'E.

Where to stay *Map, page 302*
Both Mombo and Chief's are top-of-the-range camps in one of southern Africa's very best game areas – though Mombo is a notch above Chief's and the game

12

viewing arguably slightly better in the Mombo area. Both come at a high cost – though Chief's hasn't been around long enough to build up quite the same reputation that Mombo has. However, note that some safari purists contend that elements of the clientele who visit this camp are attracted more by the image of the camp rather than the reality of the game viewing, which can be to the detriment of the atmosphere at times.

Chief's Camp (10 suites, 1 family villa) Contact Sanctuary Retreats (page 215). About 25km from Mombo (see right), just off the western side of Chief's Island, this is the pride of Sanctuary Retreats' operations in Botswana. A stunning camp, the main area is raised on decking where its high thatched roof covers a large, open-plan area. This encompasses a reception desk, lounge & a well-stocked bar, with wooden coffee tables & both leather & cloth sofas, & a dining room with a number of tables. Here guests tend to dine with their own guide, who is generally allotted to you when you arrive (you usually stick with the same guide & take all your drives with him/her). Chief's food is generally outstanding, & accompanied with an impressive selection of wine. Outside this dining/lounge area, an expanse of wooden decking acts as a veranda, where you can sit in the shade of large jackalberry & marula trees. An 8m-long swimming pool is surrounded by cushioned loungers facing the water & a small sala. Those with a passion for shopping might seek out the efficient shop stocked with books, clothing & some stylish curios.

Chief's secluded 'pavilion' tents are set on each side of the main area, & reached from a simple sand path that is lit at night by electric hurricane lamps. All are slightly raised off the ground on decking, & have private verandas overlooking the plains (which usually flood around Jun–Aug, when the water may come all the way up to the lodge). Each tent has a wooden door & polished wood floor, with very stylish, calm, modern décor. Beside the twin or dbl beds, adjustable coil lamps attached to a wooden headboard flank the twin or dbl beds. There's an open wardrobe, a couple of chairs & tables, a stone-decorated chandelier & a ceiling fan, powered by 24hr electricity. The bathroom, adjacent to the main body of the tent, is bright & open, with proper partition walls, twin washbasins beneath a large mirror. Doors lead out to a massive open-air shower, separated by the sliding glass doors of a large indoor shower. The toilet is behind a wooden door – completing the impression that this is the bathroom of a plush hotel rather than a safari camp. For families or groups of up to 6, the Geoffrey Kent Suite has 2 en-suite bedrooms & its own kitchen, lounge, dining & plunge pool area.

Set at the far end of the tents is Chief's dedicated spa. Small but well equipped, it offers treatments including massages, facials, manicures, body scrubs & wraps – all of which can be experienced from a deck overlooking the floodplain. *From US$2,400 pp Jan–Mar & Nov–Dec to US$4,350 pp Jun–Sep & festive season, FBA. Children 6+. Geoffrey Kent suite from US$11,520 Jan–Mar & Nov–Dec to US$20,880 Jun–Sep & festive season, FBA. Children 6+.* ⊕ *All year.* 🐘🐘🐘🐘🐘

Little Mombo (3 tents) Along a meandering walkway, past the shared gym, spa & lap pool, is Little Mombo, the tiny sister camp to Mombo (see below). Although adjacent to the main camp, Little Mombo operates as a separate entity. Its trio of tents have the same design & its central area is similarly furnished, albeit smaller, but it's a more intimate place, perfect for a small group travelling together or those seeking highly personalised service. *Rates as Mombo Camp (see below).* 🐘🐘🐘🐘🐘

Mombo Camp (9 suites) Contact Wilderness Safaris (page 216). This is the flagship Wilderness Safaris camp in Botswana & one of the most expensive photographic camps in Botswana. Raised on wooden decking beneath tall shady trees, the camp was completely rebuilt in 2018, & while many of the original features, such as the iconic wooden front doors into the tents, have been retained, others have been recycled – so old floors now do service as wood panelling & even b/fast counters. Further additions have been made, from plunge pools to solar power. The large main area has beautifully furnished seating areas & a library with a good selection of reference & fiction. At one end is a well-stocked bar (⊕ all day). The deck in front of this main area is the venue for alfresco dining, complete with pizza oven. A second, covered dining area lies off to one side with a long polished wooden table for candlelit dinners. Dividing the bar & main indoor dining areas, there is a tall, double-sided fireplace for cool winter evenings. There's an elevated infinity lap pool, with self-service bar, reached via the walkway that links Mombo Camp to its smaller, sister camp, Little Mombo (see opposite). There's also a well-equipped gym with great views across the floodplain.

The 9 timber-framed, tented suites are large & luxurious, with sliding mesh doors on to pole-shaded decks, affording panoramic views across the floodplains from circular plunge pools & day beds. Interiors are in natural tones & evoke the Mombo of old: vintage leathers, oak & antique brass finishings. Each suite is furnished with an extremely comfortable, king-size bed, large writing desk with plenty of USB charging points, & a lounge for lazing on the sofa & enjoying the tasty snacks. The open-plan bathroom has his & hers showers (as well as another outside), twin basins, a shiny brass bath & a separate toilet cubicle. *From US$2,805 pp 6 Jan–Mar to US$4,846 pp Jun–Oct, FBA.* ⊕ *All year.* 🥘🥘🥘🥘🥘

What to see and do Game drives are the main activity at Mombo and Chief's camps, though both are constricted to some extent by the park's rules. Night drives and fishing are not currently allowed.

Chief's Camp also offers mokoro trips, subject to water levels. When the floods arrive, up to 70% of Chief's Camp's network of roads becomes covered in water, and mokoro trips can start off right at the lodge.

13

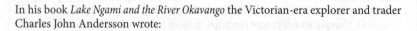

The Okavango Delta – Private Reserves Around Moremi

In his book *Lake Ngami and the River Okavango* the Victorian-era explorer and trader Charles John Andersson wrote:

> On every side as far as the eye could see, lay stretched a sea of fresh water, in many places concealed from sight by a covering of reeds and rushes of every shade and hue; while numerous islands, spread over its whole surface, and adorned with rich vegetation, gave to the whole an indescribably beautiful appearance.

For modern visitors the Okavango Delta has lost none of its beauty – something that was internationally recognised in 2014, when it was designated the 1,000th UNESCO World Heritage Site. However, finding reliable information on the various areas from brochures can be as challenging as Andersson's expedition. This chapter aims to demystify these areas, and to identify some of the strengths and weaknesses of the areas and their camps.

Here I will cover all of the private reserves around the Okavango and the main camps within these. But before you read any of my comments, here are a few general observations on the chapter:

- I've covered the reserves in the order of their concession numbers, from NG12 to NG43.
- There are virtually no fences between these areas, so the game flows freely between them, and won't always be where I suggest it is.
- Remember that differences in environment and game can be as great within a reserve as they are between one reserve and its neighbour. Despite this, some trends are evident, which I've tried to draw out.
- The marketing leaflets of the reserves usually claim that every animal/bird is found in their particular areas – particularly the 'sexy' ones like wild dogs and Pel's fishing owls! There is some truth in this, in that virtually all the animals/birds do occur in all the reserves. However, I've tried to get behind the spin with a realistic assessment of what you're most likely to see, and where you're most likely to see it. I've tried to make my comments reflect realistic probabilities, but they can't be definitive.
- I've made comments largely from my own first-hand experience, informed when in these areas by guides and experts. Occasionally, I have used reliable local sources. That said, I have not spent a year in each reserve, so my observations have been snapshots from the times that I've visited, augmented

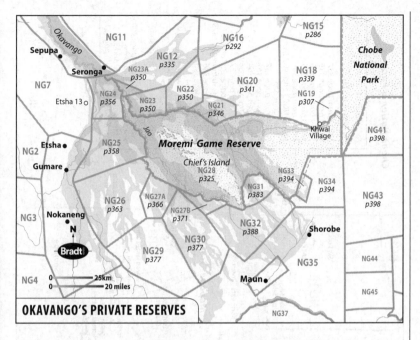

by comments from my team of Botswana experts and the travellers who visit with my travel company. They don't pretend to be comprehensive, systematic surveys, but I do believe that they're broadly representative.

- Under each reserve I've tried to cover the basics of the wildlife and the practicalities. This has necessitated some repetition, but it's a reflection of the fact that there are more similarities between the various reserves in the Delta than there are differences.

MAPULA AND KADIZORA (NG12)

Outside the buffalo fence, north of Vumbura and Duba Plains, the Magweqgana or Selinda Spillway starts in an environment similar to southeast Vumbura – though generally NG12's islands are bigger and its vegetation more established. In the south are good game viewing and extensive mopane woodlands, and cheetah have been known to hunt here.

Several villages stand on this concession's northern boundary, including Seronga, Beetsha (Betsaa), Eretsha (Eretsa), Gunotsoga (Ganitsuga) and Gudigwa. There are two established lodges – Mapula Lodge and Kadizora Camp – and a recent flurry of exciting new openings (page 337), all backed by seriously knowledgeable Botswana enthusiasts, which makes this concession a new standout area for high-quality, original Delta experiences.

Visitors to all lodges in NG12 arrive by **air**. The trip takes 40 minutes from Maun, and costs around US$226 per person each way in a fixed-wing plane or US$734 by helicopter.

FLORA AND FAUNA The NG12 Concession is bisected by the Okavango's main buffalo fence, though it has been burned many times and is badly damaged these days, allowing almost a free flow of game from one side to the other. Both

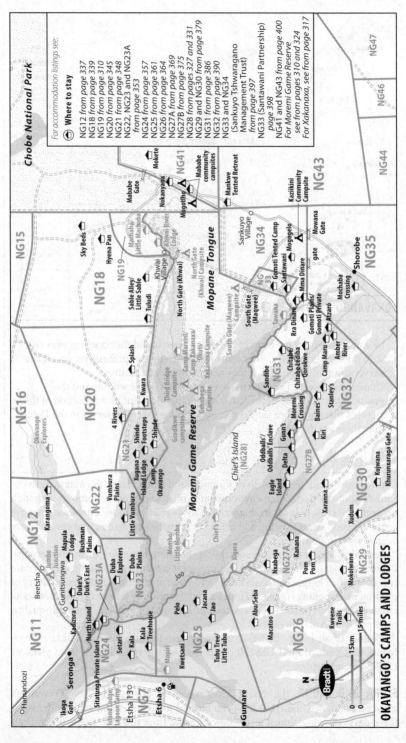

OKAVANGO'S CAMPS AND LODGES

Chobe National Park

For accommodation listings see:

(i) Where to stay

NG12 from page 337
NG18 from page 339
NG19 from page 310
NG20 from page 345
NG21 from page 348
NG22, NG23 and NG23A from page 353
NG24 from page 357
NG25 from page 361
NG26 from page 364
NG27A from page 369
NG27B from page 375
NG28 from pages 327 and 331
NG29 and NG30 from page 379
NG31 from page 386
NG32 from page 390
NG33 and NG34 (Sankuyo Tshwaragano Management Trust) from page 397
NG33 (Santawani Partnership) page 398
NG41 and NG43 from page 400
For Moremi Game Reserve see from pages 310 and 324
For Xakanaxa, see from page 317

NG47

NG46

NG44

NG43

NG41

Mokete

Mababe community campsites

Nokanyana

Mababe Gate

Magottho

Mankwe Tented Retreat

Kaziikini Community Campsite

Mowana Gate

NG15

Sky Beds

Hyena Pan

Machaba/ Little Machaba

Khwai River Lodge

NG19

Sable Alley/ Little Sable

Tuludi

Khwai Village

North Gate (Khwai)

North Gate (Khwai) Campsite

Mopane Tongue

Sankuyo Village

NG34

Gomoti Tented Camp

Santawani

Mogogelo

gate

Mma Dinare

Mochaba Crossing

Shorobe

NG35

NG18

NG16

Splash

NG20

4 Rivers

Third Bridge Campsite

Camp Moremi Camp Xakanaxa/ Xhuti/ Xakanaxa Campsite

South Gate (Maqwee)

South Gate (Maqwee)

Tawana

Rra Dinare

Gomoti Plains Gomoti Private

Atzaró

Okavango Explorers

Kwara

Goodkwe campsites

Gcobega Campsite

NG33

NG31

Sandibe

Chitabe Chitabe Lediba

Qorokwe

Camp Maru

Amber River

NG32

NG21

Shinde Footsteps

Shinde

Xugana Island Lodge

Camp Okavango

Moremi Game Reserve

Moremi Crossing

Baines'

Stanley's

Kiri

NG22

Vumbura Plains

Little Vumbura

Chief's Island (NG28)

Oddballs'/ Oddballs' Enclave

Eagle Island

Delta

Gunn's

NG27B

NG12

Karangoma

Mapula Lodge

Bushman Plains

Duke's/ Duke's East

Duba Explorers

Duba Plains

NG23A

Mombo/ Little Mombo

Chief's

Xaranna

NG30

Kujwana

Khurunkaraga Gate

Beetsha

Gunitsungwa

Jumbo Junction

NG11

Kadizora

North Island

Setari

Kala Treehouse

NG24

Xigera

Jao

Jacana

Pelo

Abu/Seba

Macatoo

NG26

Nxabega

NG27A

Kanana

Pom Pom

Xudum

Mokolwane

NG29

Seronga

Hamandozi

Ikoga Gate

Sitatunga Private Island

Island Lodge Lagoon Camp

Etsha 13

NG7

Etsha 6

Mopiri

Kwetsani

NG25

Tubu Tree/ Little Tubu

Kweene Trails

Pom

Gumare

0   15km
0   15 miles

N

Bradt

Mapula and Kadizora are just north of the buffalo fence line, but operate on both sides.

Wildlife here reflects the variety of habitat in this area, though it is more prolific to the south. Zebra and giraffe are common, as are a range of antelope, from red lechwe and waterbuck to impala, wildebeest and kudu. These in turn attract the predators, including leopard and lion, but also wild dog, which den here regularly. Buffalo and elephant are permanent residents. The birdlife, too, is exceptionally varied. This is a good place to spot the endangered wattled crane, as well as carmine bee-eaters, and the African paradise flycatcher.

WHERE TO STAY *Map, opposite*

Bushman Plains Camp (4 tents)
✛ 18°55.336'S, 22°46.428'E; e info@ bushmanplains.com; w bushmanplains.com. Bushman Plains proudly states that it is the only safari camp in Botswana primarily owned by Bushmen. Operated by 3 Bushmen – Olatotse, Ditshebo & Tshosa – & veteran safari guide Peter Comley (author of *The Field Guide to Botswana Mammals*), the camp blends experiences of the nomadic hunter-gathering Bukakhwe Bushmen clan with the classic Delta wildlife safari. All of the owners have significant past experience with some of the Delta's top safari operators, giving this camp terrific potential to offer a high-quality, alternative Okavango experience.

Set on the edge of a pretty palm island, the camp itself is currently a very simple affair: 4 large Meru tents with a neat dbl bed, solar lighting & en-suite bathrooms (flush toilets & hot-water bucket showers on request). The main 'mess tent' is a no-frills timber dining table & a small bar, where guest gather to socialise & eat together. Expect simple meals using local ingredients, with traditional dishes available, & a nightly campfire.

Activities centre on game drives (day & night), mokoro trips, boating (seasonal), bush walking & cultural visits from the Gudigwa Village community. Opportunities to learn about the lifestyle & survival skills of the Bushmen here are authentic & fascinating. The area around camp offers good predator sightings. With 2 packs in the area, large wild dog sightings are promising. The 2 lion prides here are known for their impressively large kills of buffalo & hippo. Significant herds of buffalo & elephant are spotted year-round, while rarely seen wildlife is a treat on activities here, notably the sable antelope – of which we saw 30 around camp during research – endangered wattled cranes & Pel's fishing owl.

At the time of research, we understood that this camp was due to be taken over, rebuilt & run by a well-known operator, but this had yet to be finalised. If it goes ahead, the Bushmen owners will remain & we'd expect high standards of guiding, comfort & service in line with the operator's other properties. *From US$525 pp Jan– Mar & Dec to US$950 pp Jul–Oct, FBA. Children 6+.* ⏱ *All year.* 😋😋😋–😋😋😋😋

Duke's Camp (8 tents) Contact Natural Selection (page 215). Opened in 2022, Duke's Camp is a lavish, remote camp situated on Kgao Island at the foot of the Panhandle. Impeccable attention to detail defines the experience, evident in the perfectly appointed tented chalets & the main area's unique style. Whether you're out on safari or sharing a meal under the soft glow of lanterns sparkling off polished crystal glasses & silverware, every moment is thoughtfully curated.

The creation of Ralph Bousfield, the visionary guide behind Jack's Camp in Makgadikgadi Pans (page 471), there is a similarity in the chintzy, richly patterned interior design & vintage campaign furniture. The tents are indulgent: a leather-upholstered chaise-longue on the deck, Persian carpets, brass-trimmed mahogany chests, & sumptuous fabrics around a high, four-poster bed. There's a spacious en-suite bathroom to the rear (& an additional outdoor shower in the family suite), while the front of the tent opens on to a private deck overlooking a permanent lagoon. In spite of being relatively new, there were plans to refurbish Duke's Camp in 2024 when the tents would be supersized to mimic those at Duke's East (page 338).

The main area is equally opulent. Reminiscent of a Bedouin tea tent, oversized cushions & plush pouffes surround low tables, & leather directors' chairs overlook the floodplains. Communal meals are served banquet-style under giant ebony &

13

leadwood trees, there are cabinets of African curiosities to investigate & a firepit. Duke's Camp is not just about luxury though; it's about idyllic Delta surroundings & high-quality guiding, both of which it delivers. Game drives & mokoro trips are available, as is catch-&-release fishing (exc Jan–Feb) & overnight 'fly-camping' sleepouts on a secluded private island. *From US$1,100 pp Jan– Mar to US$1,890 pp Jul–Aug, FBA inc conservation fee. Children 6+.* ☺ *All year.* 🐘🐘🐘🐘🐘

Duke's East (4 tents) Contact Natural Selection (page 215). The smaller sister camp to Duke's Camp (page 337), Duke's East offers the same style & activities, in a more intimate setting. With just 4 enormous tents – inc a family unit with a plunge pool – it's perfect for exclusive-use groups of families & friends. While the patterned, vintage décor is identical to Duke's Camp, the tents here are almost double the size, with an additional lounge area of plush velvet-covered seating. Raised wooden decks overlook the Delta, & there's a separate swimming pool pavilion & central mess tent, complete with scallop-edged canvas roofs & old-world curiosities. *From US$1,100 pp Jan–Mar to US$1,890 pp Jul–Aug, FBA inc transfers & conservation fee. Children 6+.* ☺ *All year.* 🐘🐘🐘🐘🐘

Kadizora Camp (9 tents, 1 family unit) m 7338 7715, 7264 7810; e book@kadizoracamp.com; w kadizoracamp.com. Kadizora lies some 15km northwest of Duba Plains in the remote north of the Okavango Delta. The camp has 9 generously sized, tented rooms, each with large mesh windows opening on to a wrap-around deck, which is thoughtfully positioned to ensure privacy. Inside, there are dbl or twin beds on large rugs, comfortable armchairs, & a spacious en-suite bathroom with twin basins, a claw-foot bath with a view & an outdoor shower. There is also a separate family unit, catering for up to 4 people in 2 bedrooms.

In the main area, a trio of open-fronted tents surround a central firepit. These house the lounge, a raised bar & the dining areas, although, weather permitting, meals are often taken outside on the deck. There is also a small pool surrounded by sunloungers & umbrellas. Activities include mokoro trips through intricate waterways, boat trips (seasonal; usually Aug–Sep), catch-&-release fishing (exc Jan–Feb), community visits to Gunotsuga Village, game drives (day & night) &

nature walks. *From US$769 pp Jan–Apr to US$1,324 pp Aug–Oct, FBA. Children 6+.* ☺ *All year.* 🐘🐘🐘

Karangoma (6 tents) e wea.res@wild-expeditions.africa; w wild-expeditions.africa. The newest camp in NG12 – opened May 2024 – Karangoma is a small, classic safari camp tucked among ancient leadwood & sausage trees on a forested peninsula extending into the Okavango's floodplains. Each of its 6 spacious tented suites – including one for families – are raised on low wooden decks (for high flood years). Modern interiors inspired by local Hambukushu basketry patterns are stylish & understated, with comfortable beds & small lounges; large mesh windows afford all-round views & a welcome breeze, & en-suite bathrooms feature indoor & outdoor showers. Winding paths lead to the central tent, where guests can meet for drinks, shared meals & campfire stories of an evening.

As at Bushman Plains (page 337), Karangoma has been set up in partnership with the Bukakhwe Bushman community in Gudigwa (30km), allowing guests here to spend time with the Bushmen, learning about their lifestyle & involvement in the area's conservation. For safari activities, the camp's location between woodlands to the north & the Delta's floodplains allows for both land- & water-based activities, including 4x4 drives (day & night), guided walks & boat or mokoro trips (seasonal) along the Magweqgana Channel. The wild dogs were out in force for the opening of this camp & you can expect to see a good range of herbivores, with particularly high densities of elephant & zebra. Buffalo, wildebeest & lechwe occur in good numbers, with good sable, roan & lion sightings. *From US$650 pp Dec–Mar to US$1,050 pp Jul–Sep, FBA inc conservation fee. Children 8+.* ☺ *All year.* 🐘🐘🐘–🐘🐘🐘🐘

Mapula Lodge (9 chalets) Contact Natural Selection (page 215). Occupying a stunning position on the edge of seasonal floodplains, Mapula Lodge overlooks a permanent lagoon complete with a large contingent of resident hippos. It has a relaxed, homely atmosphere, with boho-chic décor, and many of its staff come from nearby villages. Its comfortable, open-sided lounge & dining area under thatch extends to a large deck in the shade of an ancient African ebony, & beyond to a sunlounger placed enticingly at the end of a long jetty. More loungers around a small pool are an inviting spot to relax in the afternoon, while the bush bar comes into its own as the sun dips below the horizon. Solidly built chalets are raised up on private decks fronting the lagoon, with views from the four-poster canopy bed, rattan armchairs, & en-suite bathroom with (very good) outside shower. Activities focus on day & night game drives on both sides of the buffalo fence (the range covered depending on flood levels, but drives can be quite long), as well as boat trips (when water levels permit), mokoro excursions & guided walks.

Resident herds of elephant & buffalo, frequent lion sightings & good numbers of plains game make for productive game drives, with vehicles often using a guide & tracker. Mapula has undergone several management changes in recent years, but its most recent partnership with the excellent team at Natural Selection will hopefully bring the stability & expertise that will allow this camp to really shine. Closed for further refurbishment in late 2024, it's one to watch. ⊕ *All year.*

KHWAI PRIVATE RESERVE (NG18)

From its southern border with Moremi Game Reserve, the private NG18 Khwai Concession stretches north to the Linyanti Concession (NG15), west towards Kwara (NG20) and east to Chobe National Park, covering an enormous 2,000km².

For many years, it was a hunting concession, only turning its attention completely to photographic safaris in 2014 as the economic benefits of Botswana's high-end, conservation-tourism model spread. Working with Natural Selection (page 215), the community here have created a significant extension in the protected area between Chobe, Moremi and the Linyanti private concessions. As time has passed since the hunting stopped, the wildlife here is noticeably more relaxed, and the game viewing in the area is beginning to benefit from increasing wildlife movements between the long-established protected areas on its boundaries, as well as the magnetic draw of the water along the pretty Khwai riverfront.

Most guests at lodges in the reserve arrive by **air**. From the airstrip it's just a 10-minute drive to Sable Alley, an hour's drive to Hyena Pan and a further 30 minutes on to Sky Beds.

FLORA AND FAUNA Khwai Private Reserve incorporates some of the most diverse habitats in northern Botswana and the Okavango Delta. Riverine woodland and open floodplains flank the Khwai River to the south and attract herds of plains game, along with the predators that hunt them. Away from the river, the papyrus-lined channels and picturesque, lily-covered Delta lagoons, the environment changes to somewhat monotonous mopane woodland in the centre and north of the concession, although these areas are dotted with open grasslands which, together with the abundance of water, draw herds of elephant (best in the dry season from around July to October), and buffalo.

The presence of water attracts a wide array of species, naturally including hippos, crocodiles and a variety of bird species, from pelicans to kingfishers.

The wildlife here has relaxed considerably in the last decade, gradually becoming more habituated to game-drive vehicles. Wild dogs pass through the area frequently, and have been known to den close to Sable Alley (page 340), as have hyena, and there are good numbers of leopard and lion in the area. Large populations of zebra, alongside red lechwe, sable, kudu and waterbuck, occur. Night drives provide opportunities to see African wildcats, civets and spring hares.

WHERE TO STAY *Map, page 336*
The camps here are all operated by **Natural Selection** (page 215), who are responsible for the shift from hunting to photographic trips in this concession, and a considerable amount of community and conservation work.

Hyena Pan (8 tents) This camp is set deep in mopane woodland overlooking Hyena Pan itself: one of the few permanent water sources in the area &, at the end of the dry season (Sep–Oct), a magnet for a variety of game, including elephant, buffalo, wild dog, lion & leopard. In years of exceptional rains, the water has been known to come right up to camp.

The main area sits about a metre off the ground under a high thatched roof, sharing the view of the pan with the firepit below. The dining area, dominated by a long communal table, leads on to a lounge area with comfortable sofas & armchairs, with more seating under canvas by a small infinity-style plunge pool. The small, quirky bar is made out of an old log, & the whole area is adorned with local artefacts, old suitcases & fun ornaments. Scatter cushions & an eclectic mix of furniture add splashes of vibrant, ethnic colour.

The large Meru-style tents have twin or dbl beds. Vibrantly coloured wooden headboards screen the en-suite facilities behind, which include a large mirror, flushing toilet & shower screened by polished timber poles. The tents are not overly luxurious but are comfortable & attractively furnished, with pops of colour & quirky light fittings.

The combination of thick mopane in this area & relatively unexplored terrain means that game drives are often also conducted in the Khwai Community Concession (NG19). Photographers will enjoy visiting the underground waterhole hide. For combinations with Sky Beds, see page 341. *From US$795 pp Apr–May & Nov–19 Dec to US$1,040 pp Jul–Aug, FBA inc conservation fee & transfers.* ⊕ *Apr–9 Jan.* 🏕🏕🏕🏕–🏕🏕🏕🏕🏕

Little Sable (8 tents) Originally a small photographic camp known as Pangolin Khwai Camp, & then Jackal & Hide, in 2021 Little Sable was reinvented as the 'free-spirited little sister to Sable Alley' (see right). In spite of it sharing many design elements, there is a somewhat more down-to-earth atmosphere here, not to mention a lower price tag.

Little Sable is situated away from the riverfront, yet it enjoys a picturesque vantage point nonetheless. A thatched lounge/dining area is surrounded by expansive decking & a sizeable firepit that welcomes guests for drinks at sunrise & sunset. Positioned to overlook the favoured grazing spots of passing elephants & plains game,

it's a good spot for socialising before communal meals & middle-of-the-day relaxation.

Tucked into the bush are 8 traditional Meru tents. They are simple, stylish retreats with inviting king-size beds under timber headboards & ceiling fans. There's a writing desk, spacious en-suite bathroom (with an additional outdoor shower) & a private veranda overlooking the grassy plains & passing antelope. Tents are bright & airy thanks to large mesh windows all around, with the view taking centre stage. If you fancy a night completely at one with nature, though, combine a stay here with a stay at Sky Beds (page 341).

Guides are knowledgeable & activities include game drives (day & night), mokoro & boating trips (May–Oct) & fishing (exc Jan–Feb). There is also a sunken photographic hide (90min by road or short helicopter trip) for capturing eye-to-eye images of thirsty elephants & bathing birds. *From US$680 pp 10 Jan–Mar to US$1,400 pp Jun–Oct, FBA inc conservation fee. Children 6+.* ⊕ *All year.* 🏕🏕🏕🏕–🏕🏕🏕🏕

Sable Alley (12 tents) Overlooking a deep, lily-filled lagoon connected to the Khwai River, Sable Alley is a friendly, professionally run lodge, in an area where the wildlife is increasingly relaxed.

At the heart of this contemporary camp is a lofty, thatch-covered main area set on stilts overlooking the water towards Moremi Game Reserve, where hippos & elephants are frequently seen drinking, eating & cooling off. It's a vast space, so even when camp is full you can be as social or as reclusive as you wish. There are separate seating areas, with tasteful furniture & objets d'art all complementing the pale green & brown colour palette, making for plenty of places to chill out with a book, a board game or your binoculars. Steps lead down to the firepit – a popular spot for pre-dinner drinks & warming b/fasts during winter; the plunge pool, equipped with comfortable loungers & changing facilities; & relaxing hanging chairs on the sunken deck. Towards the back of the camp, a curio shop serves as the hub for 'bush Wi-Fi'. Meals are generally eaten communally in the dining room, & the bar impresses with probably the widest selection of gins in a Botswana camp.

There are 12 spacious, tented chalets, including 1 honeymoon tent (with a bath) & 2 family tents consisting of 2 interconnected standard tents. All are elevated on stilts & have a veranda, from which sliding doors open to reveal a bright room with twin or dbl beds. A tall wooden screen separates the bedroom from a wardrobe, his & hers basins, a large shower that opens on to an outdoor shower with views over the lagoon, & a toilet in a separate cubicle.

Consider requesting a back-of-house tour to gain insights into the camp's functioning & learn about initiatives promoting sustainable & renewable energy usage at this new breed of safari camp. There's a range of activities, including both day & night game drives, seasonal mokoro excursions & guided walks for the more adventurous, & the option to spend a night at Sky Beds (see below). Sable Alley combines well with many camps & makes a great private reserve alternative to the Khwai area. *From US$1,100 pp Jan–Mar to US$1,890 pp Jul–Aug, FBA inc conservation fee & transfers.* ⏲ *All year.* 🏅🏅🏅🏅🏅

Sky Beds (3 platforms) Acting as a fly-camp, Sky Beds can be booked as an excursion from either Sable Alley, Little Sable or Hyena Pan; it cannot be booked independently. The camp is made up of 3-tier raised platforms, each set about 70m from the edge of a permanent waterhole & roughly 50m apart. At the top is an open bedroom where you sleep under the stars, with a mosquito net depending on the season. The area below, with an enclosed shower & flushing toilet, also provides a private changing area. Hot water is pumped up from a little generator when needed. An additional platform serves as the bar, affording great 'sundowner'

views over the pan, & simple but convivial meals are taken near the fire around a long camp table. It's a rustic camp that offers something totally different so would be a great choice for the more adventurous. Game, such as elephant, buffalo, roan, kudu, wild dog & lion visits the waterhole (at its best Aug–Oct). *Rates as at Hyena Pan (see opposite). Min 2 people. Children 16+.* ⏲ *Apr–Oct.* 🏅🏅🏅🏅–🏅🏅🏅🏅🏅

Tuludi (7 suites) Tuludi is in a superb setting, overlooking a permanent waterhole surrounded by vast seasonal floodplains & backed by towering riverine forest. Its 7 expansive treehouse-style suites are shaded by giant leadwood trees. Under a high, pale canvas roof, the interiors of each are a tasteful blend of contemporary design & fairly traditional styling: black-&-white prints, maps, soft rugs & a modern room divider. Each suite includes a distinct dressing & sleeping area, an en-suite bathroom with both indoor & outdoor showers, a bath, an outdoor sunken seating area, & a private plunge pool.

The main area offers numerous serene corners, including a spacious lounge, an indoor dining room leading to an expansive deck, a creatively designed bar, a swimming pool, & a high treehouse library, complete with a slide! Activities include game drives, walking safaris & water-based game viewing in mekoro if water levels allow. *From US$1,395 pp 10 Jan–Mar to US$3,195 pp Jun–Oct, FBA inc conservation fee. Children 6+.* ⏲ *All year.* 🏅🏅🏅🏅–🏅🏅🏅🏅🏅

KHWAI COMMUNITY CONCESSION (NG19)

On the southern edge of the small NG19 Concession you'll find a collection of lodges benefiting from the beautiful frontage along the Khwai River. These are managed by the community-run Khwai Development Trust, and fall naturally on many travellers' itineraries between Chobe and Moremi. So, given its proximity to Moremi's North Gate entrance and for the sake of logical continuity, this concession and its safari options are covered in *Chapter 12* (page 301).

KWARA (NG20)

The Kwara Concession covers a huge 1,750km², in the middle of the Delta's northern edge. It's bounded to the north by Selinda (NG16), to the west by Vumbura (NG22) and to the east by Khwai Private Reserve (NG18). On the south side, the reserve is adjacent to Moremi Game Reserve and the small enclave of NG21 (which includes Camp Okavango, Xugana and Shinde). This location means that the reserve spans the transition from deep-water areas on the extreme north of the Delta, through very large areas of open floodplains, many of which are dry for much of the year, to the substantial dry areas of its northern section.

This geography means Kwara Concession has a wider range of activities available through the year than many camps in the Delta. Game drives and night drives are the norm, and the camps never have more than six guests on a vehicle (four at Kwara), plus a guide and tracker. Together with the impressive knowledge of the guides, this makes the game-viewing experience here among the best in the Delta, and certainly better in the green season than most dry-land camps. Much of this is due to their commitment to actively tracking the wildlife, heading off-road and into the bush at the slightest sign of something interesting. It is an engaging, and often exhilarating, experience, which reliably delivers good predator sightings.

On the water, motorboat and mokoro trips are possible all year, and Splash Camp and Kwara Camp also have a double-decker pontoon boat. Sitting on top of this as it moves through the papyrus-lined channels is magical, and will give you a completely different view of the waterscape.

As with most areas in the Delta, it is also possible to arrange scenic helicopter flights (from US$345 pp for 30mins) and day trips from all of these camps.

CONCESSION HISTORY Kwara has been an established safari camp since the mid-1990s. It was initially privately owned and run, before being operated first by Bird Safaris, then by Ker & Downey, with the marketing taken on by Wilderness Safaris. In 1999, the camp was taken over by the Kwando Safaris team, who bought the rights to the concession around 2008.

For many years, only two camps existed here – Kwara and Little Kwara – but in 2018 Kwando Safaris received permission to build more camps in this concession and Splash Camp duly opened in June of that year. The original camps were demolished, with Kwara rising again in a more luxurious form in 2019 and including a satellite 'Enclave' camp, and subsequently a new camp, 4 Rivers, completed the concession's camp trio in 2023. This is a large concession, leased by one operator, so the camps here can avoid overlapping their activities.

FLORA AND FAUNA Kwara is a vast reserve comprising a diverse mix of habitats, from deep-water lagoons and thick papyrus swamps to dry-country scrub and mopane woodland, creating a unique and varied ecosystem. Therefore, trying to describe here any dominant species of plants or animals is at best inconclusive, and at worst completely misleading.

These are a few general notes on what you're likely to find here, plus observations of what we have found most interesting on our visits over the years.

Flora South of the camp lie the permanent swamps: a true deep-water environment. You'll find large stands of both papyrus and phragmites reeds, often with waterberry and water-fig trees dotted among them. Look down in some of the deeper main channels and you'll find the water opaque, heavy with sediment.

However, in most of the lagoons and the slower channels you'll be able to see right to the Kalahari sand at the bottom, and any water creatures or plants there. Among the mass of weeds, ask your guide to point out the delicate web of stems belonging to one of the Okavango's many species of bladderwort (*Utricularia* species). These usually form a submerged tangle of green, hair-like stems with tiny, thin leaves. Dotted among these are numerous small 'bladders' which, when touched by a small invertebrate like a mosquito larva, can suck the animal in and capture it. The bladder then digests the animal, and in the process gets valuable

The two main species of waterlily in the Okavango are the day-lilies (*Nymphaea nouchali caerulea*) and the night-lilies (*Nymphaea lotus*), which are sometimes called lotus lilies. The day-lilies are more common, and the species are fairly easy to tell apart.

The large floating leaves of day-lilies have smooth edges. As you might expect, the flowers open in mid/early morning, and close in the afternoon; they start off as a delicate shade of violet-purple (earning them the name of 'blue lily'), with only the centre having a yellowish tinge. These last for about five days, gradually turning whiter as they age, before the stem twists and drags the pollinated seed-head underwater. There it matures until the seeds are eventually released, complete with air-filled bladders to help them float and disperse better.

Night-lilies are similar but have much darker green leaves, sharply serrated at the edge. The flowers have creamy white petals, edged with yellow, and a strongly yellow centre; these flowers often lie very flat on the surface, facing directly upwards. They open in the late afternoon and close in the early morning, relying for their pollination on night-flying insects.

nitrogen, which is in very short supply in the mineral-impoverished waters of the Okavango.

Much easier to locate, floating on the surface of the lagoons, you'll find the fan-shaped, serrated leaves of the water chestnut (*Trapa natans*). This is often found on the edges of the lagoons, and is interesting not so much for its white flowers, but for the horned seedpod which it forms. The barbs on this will latch on to the fur or skin of animals, as an aid to dispersing its seed. Their large size suggests that the area's numerous hippo are involved.

Move away from the water, north of camp, and you'll start entering the drier parts of the Kwara Reserve. You'll see that between the dry and wet, there's a transition zone where the bush is a mixture of ancient tree-islands surrounded by plains that were once flooded. The tree-islands were once more distinct, and surrounded by true floodplains, but as this area has dried out, the vegetation on the plains has grown and blurred the distinction between plains and tree-islands. Similarly, the salt deposits that are often found at the heart of the tree-islands have dissipated.

Like many areas on the edges of the Delta, this is in the extremely slow process of change. This zone was once wet, and now its landscapes and vegetation are very, very gradually reverting to landforms and vegetation of the drier areas – a process that will take millennia to complete. Here you'll find most of the Delta's usual species of trees, from African mangosteens to jackalberries, and both real fan and wild date palms. Plus a few species more often seen in the drier areas of Chobe, like Kalahari appleleaf (*Philenoptera nelsii*) and silver cluster-leaf (*Terminalia sericea*).

Fauna In the drier areas, Kwara's dominant herbivores appear to be tsessebe and impala, with very healthy populations of reedbuck, kudu and giraffe. You'll also find wildebeest, zebra, waterbuck, warthog and steenbok, plus a liberal sprinkling of elephant and the odd herd of buffalo. On the floodplains around camp, lechwe are also common, while deep in the papyrus there are sitatunga, though these are not often seen.

The Okavango Delta – Private Reserves Around Moremi   KWARA (NG20)

13

When I first visited this area in 1996, most of the reserve was still in the grip of hunting, with dismal game viewing and a bleak outlook. The few game drives I went on yielded remarkably little. Antelope would flee at 500m, and we had almost no sightings of big game. Since then, the wildlife situation has changed immeasurably and photographic camps have been run successfully in the area by Kwando Safaris for some years. This is an interesting reflection of what's been happening in northern Botswana in the past 20 years, as areas that had been used for hunting have been supplanted by photographic camps.

Large areas of this concession are open and dry for most of the year and Kwando Safaris' approach is to track the big predators actively wherever possible. So now all the big cats – lion, leopard and cheetah – are around and regularly seen, and it's a particularly good area for seeing wild dog. I made one visit here a long time ago in February, which is usually a very difficult time for spotting predators. But despite the thick, green vegetation the guide and spotter managed to locate a pack of wild dogs and track them for several kilometres across the bush until we caught up with them as they killed an impala. The effectiveness of excellent trackers being paired with safaris guides on every drive here does make a real difference to predator sightings.

Birdlife As with the range of animals, the birdlife is inevitably varied. About 6.5km southwest of Kwara is Gcodikwe Lagoon. This is within Moremi Game Reserve, but Kwara is the nearest camp to it, so makes a good base for visits here. (See the more comprehensive comments on page 321 about Gcodikwe, but note that within a boat ride you'll find one of the region's most important breeding colonies of storks, egrets, herons and spoonbills.) It is at its busiest between September and November, but there are always a few birds there.

Elsewhere in Kwara you'll find a good range of the usual species found in and around the Delta. The more common residents include reed cormorants, darters, African and lesser jacanas, malachite and pied kingfishers, pygmy geese, fish eagles and marsh harriers. Meanwhile the coucals are particularly well represented, with Senegal, coppery-tailed and (in summer) even black coucals all seen. More unusual sightings include African crake, swamp boubous, black and slaty egrets, black-crowned and white-backed night herons, and the occasional migrant osprey.

In the drier areas north of the permanent waterways, some of the more common residents include blacksmith lapwings, red-billed spurfowl, double-banded sandgrouse, lilac-breasted rollers, red-billed and Bradfield's hornbills, Meyer's parrots, fiery-necked nightjars, palm swifts, Hartlaub's babblers, red-eyed and Cape turtle doves, black-crowned tchagras, white-browed robin-chats, ground hornbills, saddle-billed storks and black-breasted snake eagles. More unusual sightings might include western banded snake eagles, Dickinson's kestrels (often perching on dead palm trees), red-necked falcons, bat hawks, swallow-tailed bee-eaters, red-billed helmet shrikes, brown-throated weavers and wattled cranes.

WHEN TO VISIT As with much of the Delta, the big game here is invariably more prolific during the dry season; and although many of the birds breed between December and March, Gcodikwe is generally at its most spectacular between September and November. That said, visiting in February still allowed me some first-class game viewing, including wild dog, as noted above. So don't write off the green season as a universally lousy time for game: it just takes a bit more tracking down.

GETTING THERE AND AWAY Kwara can be reached by **boat** from the Xakanaxa area, but in practice virtually all visitors arrive by **air** to one of the small airstrips close to the camps. Kwara airstrip is about 15 minutes from its namesake camp, and plans are afoot to construct another close to 4 Rivers.

🏠 **WHERE TO STAY** *Map, page 336*
This concession is owned by Kwando Safaris (page 215) who run all the camps here. Like most camps in the Okavango, you can't just drop in, and even if you could, the camp wouldn't welcome you. It's essential to pre-book your visit.

4 Rivers (8 tents, 1 family unit) Nestled within ancient woodlands & overlooking a clear permanent channel towards Maboa Island, 4 Rivers opened in mid-2023 in the western area of the Kwara Concession, where no people had been present for some considerable time. As such, the area is still being explored & new game-drive roads opened. Given the beautiful, wildlife-rich landscapes, we'd expect this to rapidly become a firm favourite: think herds of 400 zebra, frequent lion sightings & an array of general wildlife.

Surrounded by a mosaic of waterways, expansive plains & forested islands, it's an intimate camp with a distinct wilderness feel. The 9 spacious, light tents are surrounded by huge mesh-covered picture windows & furnished in a relaxed, contemporary style. A great family unit with 2 bedrooms & 2 bathrooms is also available. In every tent, sink into the comfortable armchairs for a perfect vantage point of the lagoon & its birdlife, & enjoy indoor & outdoor showers.

The thatched, split-level main lounge/dining area includes deckchairs by a small pool & a circular firepit on the edge of the water. Venturing in search of wildlife, you'll be accompanied by both a guide & tracker, whether you're exploring the reserve on a game drive (day or night) to the vast floodplains or tall leadwood forests, or stepping out on foot (seasonal) through the forested Maboa Island – look out for sable & roan antelope! On the water, you can navigate the intricate channels by mokoro (May–Oct). The dedicated tracking on vehicles often produces some superb sightings, perfect for wildlife enthusiasts, but the sometimes single-minded pursuit of predators may not be to everyone's taste, so do talk to your guide to tailor your experience. *From US$620 pp 15 Nov–31 Mar to US$1,470 pp Jul–Oct, FBA inc conservation fee. Children 6+.* ⊕ *All year.* 🛏🛏🛏–🛏🛏🛏🛏🛏
Kwara Camp (9 tents) Kwara stands on a small, forested island, overlooking a seasonal

lagoon amid the floodplains. Rebuilt in 2019, its traditional tents have been replaced with smart suites & an adult-only policy has been instated, though it remains a good-value Delta camp. Slightly raised on decking beneath a large jackalberry tree, Kwara's thatched bar-lounge, small library & dining area are cosy & comfortable. The open sides of these communal spaces offer panoramic views of the shallow lagoon, which often attracts good numbers of wildlife. It's a friendly place & a relaxed spot for engaging in a traditional game of morabaraba with the team, or simply enjoying the vista. Down some steps towards the water, a firepit is a good spot for an early-morning bite or evening drink. There are also 2 small swimming pools at opposite ends of the camp, offering a refreshing escape from the summer heat.

The generous tented chalets all overlook the lagoon. Crafted from timber & stretched-canvas walls, each room is divided into 3 distinct sections: an inviting lounge with a plush sofa, 2 armchairs & a writing desk complete with wildlife magazines; the slightly elevated bedroom (twin or dbl) cooled by a ceiling fan; & an en-suite bathroom, separated from the main room by a linen curtain. There are indoor & outdoor showers, a bath & separate toilet. Interiors are classically furnished in polished wood & neutral tones.

Kwara shares a fairly informal approach with its sister camps, Lagoon & Lebala, which are all designed slightly differently. While each aims to provide a very comfortable camp, the accent is firmly on the activities & guiding rather than creature comforts. Game drives with both a guide & tracker are enthusiastic, fast-paced & often focused on tracking predators – which they do extremely successfully. Boat & mokoro trips on the camp's lagoon, guided walks & fishing (exc Jan–Feb) are also available. *US$1,135 pp 15 Nov–31*

13

Mar to US$2,120 pp Jul–Oct, FBA inc conservation fee. 18+ only. ⊕ *All year.* 🛏🛏🛏🛏🛏

❋ **Splash Camp** (10 tents, 2 family units) Negotiating the sizeable water crossings necessary to reach this camp, the origin of the name 'Splash' becomes clear. Situated in the heart of the Delta, Splash is in a prime game-viewing area with the same distinct focus as Kwando's other camps: delivering fantastic game-viewing & great value for money. Our own wildlife sightings here would certainly endorse this, from successfully tracking wild dogs that had passed through camp to locating an incredibly relaxed aardwolf.

In camp, Splash's clear focal point is a prominent waterhole, visible from nearly every vantage point: the rooms, lounge, plunge pool & firepit. It's easy to understand why: as the dry season progresses, this waterhole is a magnet for a variety of wildlife. Under shady trees, the central, open-sided hub has a contemporary lounge with inviting sofas, black-&-white artwork & a small reference library, a bar & a large dining table for shared meals under ceiling fans. There's a firepit immediately in front of camp, as well as a curio shop. A short walk from the main area is a small pool set within a teak deck dotted with sunloungers & a pergola to provide some welcome shade.

Well-spaced rooms, constructed primarily from wood with canvas walls, are smartly appointed, flooded with light & benefit from sweeping panoramas from both the veranda & comfortable bed. Naked wood, canvas, cow skin rugs & tasteful photographic wall hangings give a contemporary, Scandinavian feel to the interiors, which overlook a small, sapphire-blue plunge pool in the decking.

At one end of the camp is a second smaller main area with its own bar, dining area, lounge & plunge pool. Combined with 3–6 rooms (min 6 adults), this makes up the exclusive use of Splash Enclave, effectively a private camp within a camp. Here, travellers will enjoy their own private dining & activities, & the min age requirement is waived, making this a great option for families & groups of friends.

Splash places a premium on wildlife experiences. Safaris here involve 4x4 vehicles, with an experienced guide as well as an impressive tracker on every vehicle – they really specialise in predator tracking, though the general game is good here. Seasonal activities include gentle mokoro rides along shallow waterways or motorboat excursions to nearby heronries, particularly appealing to birdwatchers & photographers. *US$950 pp 15 Nov–31 Mar to US$1,770 pp Jul–Oct, FBA inc conservation fee. Children 6+; all ages at Splash Enclave.* ⊕ *All year.* 🛏🛏🛏🛏–🛏🛏🛏🛏🛏

Tsum Tsum [not mapped] At the time of writing, a new camp was planned for the Kwara Concession. Located on the site of a long-defunct hunting camp, Tsum Tsum would sit on the northern side of the concession between 4 Rivers & Kwara. The plans for the new camp were still being finalised, though activities would follow the same pattern as those at 4 Rivers (page 345).

XUGANA, CAMP OKAVANGO AND SHINDE (NG21)

This concession is relatively small by Botswana's standards, but shares a long southern boundary with Moremi Game Reserve, and was devoted to photographic safaris long before many other areas. To the north, NG21 adjoins the Kwara and Vumbura concessions.

Within the reserve, the activities are primarily water-based. Xugana, Camp Okavango and Shinde all operate motorboat excursions to explore the lagoons, plus mokoro trips to visit the areas of shallower water nearby. Often the mokoro trips are combined with walking on the islands, though some camps offer these walks without an armed guide, so read my comments on walking (page 178) first. Note that if you're keen to visit Gcodikwe Lagoon then Camp Okavango or Shinde are much nearer to it than Xugana. All water activities are primarily for birdwatching and scenery rather than game viewing, though it's also possible to go fishing (bream and tigerfish) from the motorboats.

In addition, Shinde, Shinde Footsteps and Xugana offer 4x4 game drives day and night, with both Shinde camps conducting walks accompanied by an armed guide and tracker. Those more serious about walking can also book specialist walking guides for US$550 per night. As with most camps in the Delta, it is also possible to arrange scenic helicopter flights.

FLORA AND FAUNA NG21 is adjacent, and in many ways very similar, to the southern parts of the neighbouring Kwara Reserve, NG20. Thus read our comments on the flora and fauna there (page 342) for a complete picture. That said, a greater proportion of NG21 Reserve is permanent swamp, as it has several large, permanent rivers flowing through it. The Moanachira passes through, heading east to feed the Gcodikwe Lagoon, before flowing into the Xakanaxa Lagoon. This in turn forms the source of the Khwai River that eventually reaches to the far eastern corner of the Delta.

A less clear channel, the Mborogha, flows southeast almost to Chief's Island where it ultimately feeds into the Gomoti and Santandibe rivers, both important watercourses of the lower Delta (though in the last few decades there seems to have been a change of flow between these two major rivers, from the Mborogha to the Moanachira).

In *Okavango: Jewel of the Kalahari* (page 541), Karen Ross notes that the eastern rivers, the Moanachira and Mborogha, carry far more water today than they did 100 years ago. So with all these waters concentrated into NG21 it's perhaps not surprising that it's an area where you'll find plenty of deep-water lagoons and channels.

Most of NG21 Reserve has too much water to be one of the Delta's prime game-viewing areas, but in the dry area around Shinde you'll still find good densities of game, including impala, red lechwe, tsessebe and giraffe. Lone bull elephants are around for most of the year, while the breeding herds migrate here from the dry interior towards the end of the dry season.

Kudu, sable and buffalo are infrequently seen. Sitatunga, while common in the areas of thick papyrus, are rarely sighted. NG21 is also a good place to look for water-based mammals like the very common hippo and the more elusive Cape clawless otters.

The dominant predators are lion and hyena, with leopard and wild dog also found here. In recent years, a pack of wild dogs has regularly used the area around Shinde Footsteps as a den site, often moving between here and Kwara.

WHEN TO VISIT While game viewing under the clouds of the green season can be quite rewarding, most people need at least dryness and preferably a blue sky and tropical sun to appreciate the magic of boating through the Okavango.

During one visit in the green season, the weather one morning was glorious. This prompted the enthusiastic manager to ask me why Expert Africa sends relatively few visitors to the Okavango between January and March. 'It's almost empty of visitors and often the weather's superb,' he beamed. Later that day the clouds drew in and it rained on and off for 36 hours, foiling any ideas I had about photography for the rest of my stay. Hence I'd still advise that water-based camps like Xugana and Camp Okavango are best visited during the dry season.

GETTING THERE AND AWAY All guests pre-arrange their trips here, and fly in to the camps' own airstrips, which are all nearby. Camp Okavango's (⊕ CAMPOA 19°07.720'S, 23°05.930'E) is a short walk behind the camp, and from the air you'll realise that it takes up most of the very small island on which the camp is situated!

Shinde's airstrip (⊕ SHINDA 19°07.070'S, 23°09.180'E) is a 5-minute drive northeast of the camp. Xugana's (⊕ XUGAIR 19°02.200'S, 23°05.710'E), too, is very close and northwest of the camp.

Guests heading for Footsteps arrive at Shinde by plane, then have a leisurely 1½-hour transfer. This varies but will sometimes involve a game drive, followed by a short river crossing by mokoro, and a final drive to camp. A 3-minute helicopter transfer is also an option from Shinde Airstrip at an additional cost.

🏠 **WHERE TO STAY** *Map, page 336*

Camp Okavango (11 suites, 1 family suite) Contact Desert & Delta Safaris (page 214). On the south side of this concession, Camp Okavango overlooks floodplains & channels. It's a measure of the meandering geography of the Delta's waterways that although its sister camp, Camp Moremi, is only about 33km away as the egret flies, the most direct route by boat (coincidentally via the Gcodikwe Lagoon) is slightly over 60km.

'Camp O', as it's usually known, was started by an American woman, Jessie Niel, in the early 1980s, & was swiftly followed by Camp Moremi. She ran & marketed them as a pair under the banner of Desert & Delta Safaris until, in the mid-1990s, the operation was taken over by a group called Chobe Holdings, associated with Chobe Game Lodge & AfroVentures – though the name was kept.

Despite being quite large by Okavango standards, the whole camp is built on raised platforms with the suites & main area linked by wooden walkways. For seclusion during the day, there's a raised viewing hide that is built into a sausage tree & 3 knobthorn trees near the end of the jetty. It's a nice spot to relax with comfy chairs & the view over the papyrus & reeds might interest patient birdwatchers. However, the infinity pool (which overlooks the same floodplain) & the sundeck probably make better places to relax.

Wooden walkways lead to the spacious suites, each with twin or dbl beds, crisp linen, tea & coffee station, lounge area & deck complete with sunloungers. The en-suite bathrooms come with hot his & hers showers, his & hers washbasins & a flush toilet. For guests staying 3 nights, there's also the option to sleep out on the 'star bed' platform.

Although the camp focuses on boat & mokoro trips, bush walks on the islands are possible, though see our comments on walking trips in Botswana (page 178) before you set off. Camps like this which concentrate on water activities tend to have a slower pace than those which also offer game drives; you'll have more time just to relax. *From US$645 pp Jan–Mar & Dec to US$1,160 pp Jun–Oct, FBA. Children 6+. ⊕ Closed mid-Feb– 1 Mar.* 🏠🏠🏠–🏠🏠🏠🏠

Shinde (8 tents) Contact Ker & Downey Botswana (page 214). Long established, Shinde stands in an intrinsically beautiful, tree-shaded spot in the heart of NG21, about 6km east of Camp Okavango, 12km west of Kwara & 8km southeast of Xugana. It's a well-run camp, with a long-serving team of staff & a very flexible approach. The camp is set on a picturesque channel that feeds the Moanachira River, so with land-based as well as water activities, there's plenty of choice; if you have the energy to do 3 activities in a day, then that can be accommodated.

Under a thick canopy of ebony, mangosteen & water-fig trees, Shinde's heart has a wonderful treehouse feel, with the lovely lounge & dining areas built on a series of polished teak platforms, rising towards an unusual bowed canvas roof that's a little like an old wagon. Below, guests can help themselves to drinks from the bar, peruse the collection of baskets made by the staff, or browse the books in the excellent reference section, before gathering round the extensive, water-level firepit deck for a drink & an alfresco dinner. Behind a pole screen is a small, sheltered pool with sunloungers & views across the water.

Sharing the view are 8 large tents – 3 of them forming the distinct **Shinde Enclave**. The tents are built on low wooden platforms protected by large shade cloths that also shelter a porch with a couple of comfy chairs. Inside are twin beds (or a king-size dbl), their crisp white linen offset by neutral canvas & dark-wood furniture & traditional wall hangings. Persian rugs dot the wooden floors, mesh windows allow the air to flow freely, & a separate room behind the bed houses an en-suite shower, basin & flush toilet. They are spacious & comfortable retreats.

Families or groups of up to 8 seeking a more exclusive set-up can book the Shinde Enclave, a 'camp within a camp' that comes with a dedicated waiter & guide, & has its own bar, firepit, dining area & lounge, & a small deck overlooking an expanse of papyrus & reeds dotted with palm islands.

Activities at Shinde include game drives (day & night) – where we've had excellent dry-season sightings – guided walks, birdwatching, catch-&-release fishing (exc Jan–Feb) & motorboat or mokoro trips (usually available year-round). *From US$650 pp Jan–Feb to US$1,490 pp Jun–Oct, FBA. Add US$550 per night for Shinde Enclave. Children 7+.* ⏱ *Year-round.* ♔♔♔♔–♔♔♔♔♔

❋ **Shinde Footsteps** (4 tents) In operation since 1998 but completely rebuilt & reopened in May 2023, Footsteps is a lovely, personal camp & the standard of guiding is excellent. As with any camp historically renowned for good walking safaris, the guest numbers are small (max 8 guests or a family group of up to 10). Though the newly rebuilt camp now offers game drives, boat & mokoro trips, as well as walking, it's retained that down-to-earth intimacy.

The main area, overlooking a permanent hippo pool, features 2 small, open-fronted tents: 1 with a smart, family-style dining table surrounded by large wildlife images, & the other a curved lounge area with soft, sunset-coloured seating. Between them, a simple firepit marks the heart of camp, & the morning & evening social meeting point. There's also a great photo-editing suite, with desks, charging ports & storage cabinets to ensure the safekeeping of camera kit, & large screen monitors to view your images.

The khaki tented chalets are simple yet comfortable, with twin, dbl, or a 2-bedroom family configuration available. Sitting on low decks with cushioned day beds & a curved walkway to the open-air shower, the rooms are immediately along the water's edge. Interiors feature soft rugs, comfortable beds & open shelving with roll-down canvas covers. All rooms are en suite, with indoor & outdoor showers.

Despite the camp's remote location, the standard of food is excellent, with plenty of fresh fruit & vegetables, newly baked bread each day & a well-stocked bar. If you'd like to take a look 'backstage', they're usually very happy to show guests around. Meals are often eaten alfresco & wildlife regularly roams through camp. Footsteps offers a mix of water- & land-based activities: game drives (day & night), mokoro excursions, boat cruises &, of course, walking safaris. For those focused on walking, timings & distances are flexible. It is also one of the bases for Ker & Downey's Young Explorers safari (page 113), for which the camp

is always booked exclusively. *From US$650 pp Jan–Feb to US$995 pp Jun–Oct, FBA. Children 7+.* ⏱ *Year-round.* ♔♔♔♔–♔♔♔♔

Xugana Island Lodge (8 chalets) Contact Desert & Delta Safaris (page 214). Xugana is one of the Delta's older camps; it is said to have been started as a hunting camp as early as the 1960s & was then a private family retreat, before later opening as a safari camp. It enjoys a spectacular location on the banks of a forested island beside a large, deep lagoon, about 7.5km north of Camp Okavango (yet the most direct route by boat covers about 16.8km of waterways). For many years Xugana used the lagoon itself as a swimming pool, suspending a crocodile-proof wire cage in the lagoon for bathers to cool off in. While environmentally admirable, some of the camp's less enlightened guests found this pool's occasional murkiness off-putting, so a swimming pool was built among the landscaped lawns at the centre of camp. These are dotted with natural vegetation, with everything protected from hungry elephants by an electric fence. (The old pool was renovated & converted into a floating deck, used for special occasions, the odd alfresco dinner & sundowners.)

The camp's open-sided lounge, bar & dining areas under thatch are set back slightly from the jetty, facing the water. In good weather, most meals are taken on the spacious deck overlooking the lagoon, shaded by fig & leadwood trees, & with a fireplace perched above the water. A good small curio shop sports a fair selection of local books & wildlife guides, plus T-shirts, handicrafts & postcards.

Xugana's chalets are built of reed & thatch, raised up on wooden decking, with twin beds or a dbl under a large, walk-in mosquito net. Rooms are traditionally styled with polished timber furniture & each has a ceiling fan under its high roof, operated by the camp's generator during the day. There's a 12V lighting system in the rooms for use at night. The bathrooms are en suite with a walk-in hot shower, flush toilet & washbasin, & outside, facing the lagoon, is a private wooden deck with a pair of canvas safari chairs. Water is heated by solar power.

Activities are largely water-based, with mekoro & motorboats available, catch-&-release fishing & guided nature walks on the surrounding islands. *From US$645 pp Jan–Mar & Dec to US$1,160 pp Jun–Oct, FBA. Children 6+.* ⏱ *Closed mid-Feb–1 Mar.* ♔♔♔♔–♔♔♔♔

VUMBURA AND DUBA PLAINS (NG22, NG23 AND NG23A)

Immediately north of Moremi's Mombo Concession, the Vumbura and Duba Plains reserves (NG22 and NG23) share many similarities of game and landscape with Mombo. NG23A is a wedge shape just north of the Duba Concession, with idyllic surroundings. There has been some controversy over the lease of this concession, but this will matter little to visitors, who will simply enjoy beautiful landscapes and great wildlife. This northern area of the Delta is one of our favourites, but because of the similarity between Vumbura and Duba, if you are planning a trip to this area then it's best to include only one of them in your itinerary.

THE ANATOMY OF A COMMUNITY PARTNERSHIP

Though 'community-based natural resource management' is recognised as one of the main strategies for achieving sustainable development in the rural areas of Botswana, really good examples of it are few and far between. Wilderness Safaris have a strong track record with successful community projects in other countries, like Damaraland Camp in Namibia, and here in Botswana their flagship community project is the Vumbura and Duba concessions. The camps in these private reserves or concessions started in 1997 when the safari company and their partners made an agreement with the community to which the government had given management of concession areas NG22 and NG23. Great Plains continues to liaise and work with the local communities in much the same way that Wilderness still do.

The community, in this case, consists of five villages to the north of the Okavango Delta: Seronga, Eretsha, Beetsha, Gudigwa and Gunitsungwa. The villagers had to set up a trust, with a fully constituted board to represent all the villages and people of the area in their dealings with the government, the Land Board and the safari companies. The ten-person board is made up of two elected people from each of the five villages. Wilderness Safaris/ Great Plains Conservation pay a six-figure US-dollar lease fee each year to the board (this is a lot of money in rural Botswana). The board decides how to use that money for the benefit of the community. Further, as part of the deal, the two safari companies have to employ at least 118 people from the villages (though they actually ended up giving jobs to around 150), and to deliver on a number of community projects. These projects have resulted in the setting up and supporting of a number of secondary cottage industries in the villages, like basket weaving and vegetable gardens; in addition they have sponsored an inter-village football tournament; helped with transport problems; and set up village shops, mortuaries, etc.

Perhaps the most difficult issue about this kind of agreement for any safari company is the short duration of the leases; the community can swap their safari company after the first year if it wishes to, then again after the second year, the fifth year and the tenth year. Given the huge investment in infrastructure and the long-term nature of the marketing, this is difficult for most safari companies to contemplate. Two decades into the project, the safari companies are slowly starting to reap the benefits of a stable, long-term relationship with the community as their partner. Equally, guests to these camps know that their safari is actively benefiting both the communities in the area, and thus, in turn, the local wildlife.

Vumbura is a varied reserve, and the areas through which you drive are often very pretty. Much of its landscape consists of wide-open plains with tiny islands – almost a cliché of the Okavango. Vumbura's game is notably diverse, so most visitors will see a wide range of antelope and have a good chance to spot the less common predators. With year-round access to deep permanent water, boat trips are possible from Vumbura and the island at any time, with opportunities to fish and take a mokoro trip if you wish.

Duba Plains, to the west of Vumbura, is visually similar but with larger open plains, long water crossings and vast floodplains. Its volume and diversity of game is the stuff that wildlife documentaries are made of. Historically, the big attraction here was the long-standing battles between large herds of buffalo and sizeable prides of lion. Thus, it has often provided a very impressive spectacle of big game, particularly during the drier months of April to November. In the wet season (December to March), when the buffalo are fitter from eating the lush grass, the lions focus more on the large numbers of lechwe and warthog.

Boating at Duba Plains, however, is dependent on water levels, and there are no mekoro here. All the camps also have 4x4 game drives day and night (though night drives are sometimes restricted when flood levels are very high, between May and August). Short walks are offered by these camps, though I would generally go to a specialist walking camp if that is of particular interest.

CONCESSION HISTORY Until around 1997 when Wilderness Safaris opened the Vumbura, Little Vumbura and Duba Plains camps, this was a hunting area. And indeed, for several years afterwards there were two small, seasonal hunting camps running in the northeast of the Vumbura Concession. Both have been closed since 2001 and these areas are now used solely for photographic safaris.

In 2012, Duba Plains split from Wilderness Safaris and is now owned and managed by Great Plains Conservation, along with its sister camps in the Selinda Reserve (page 292) and Sitatunga Private Island Camp (page 355) in NG23A. Dereck and Beverly Joubert, the wildlife film-makers, are closely involved with this venture, while Vumbura and Little Vumbura are still very much a part of Wilderness Safaris.

As is increasingly the case with reserves in Botswana, both Duba and Vumbura have an element of local community involvement. Five local villages – Seronga, Eretsha, Beetsha, Gudigwa and Gunitsungwa – have some control over the concession, and derive considerable benefit from its success. Most of the staff for the camps come from these villages too, so there's a flow of revenue from these camps back to the communities by way of wages (see opposite and also page 335).

FLORA AND FAUNA Both these reserves are broadly similar in character, although Duba Plains (as you might expect) has more extensive open plains, whereas the plains at Vumbura are often partially flooded and are broken up by more islands.

Flora Much of these concessions consist of very beautiful, open floodplains dotted with islands, many of which are tiny. The vegetation of the larger islands is dominated by many of the Okavango's usual tree species, including the apple leaf (*Philenoptera violacea*), leadwood (*Combretum imberbe*), African mangosteen (*Garcinia livingstonei*), jackalberry (*Diospyros mespiliformis*), sausage tree (*Kigelia africana*) and sycamore fig (*Ficus sycomorus*).

You'll also find knobthorn trees (*Senegalia nigrescens*), although relatively few of them, and some particularly large, wonderful specimens of feverberry trees (*Croton*

13

megalobotrys), named after the anti-malarial properties of the seeds and the bark. (These properties had been known to local African residents for centuries, but were brought to the attention of a wider audience by an article in the medical journal, *The Lancet*, in 1899. Apparently there has still not been any detailed research on these medicinal properties.)

Among the main bushes that you'll find here are the Kalahari star apple (*Diospyros lycioides lycioides*), which is often also called the blue bush, for its overall bluish tinge, or the 'toothbrush bush', as its roots can be peeled and used as a toothbrush. (Veronica Roodt reports that on using it 'at first my mouth burned and I became extremely worried when my whole mouth turned yellow. The result, however, was remarkable – white teeth and fresh breath.') Another very common bush in this area is the evergreen magic gwarri bush (*Euclea divinorum*), also sometimes known as the 'toothbrush bush' for the use of its branches. Both these bushes produce dyes that are used in Botswana to colour palm leaves for weaving baskets.

In the northeast of Vumbura there are some fine acacia woodlands, while as you travel west from Vumbura into Duba you'll find more and larger open floodplains, slightly less thick wooded islands, and more clusters of the wild date palm (*Phoenix reclinata*).

As well as the drier areas, there are many small channels near the Vumbura camps, and some open, lightly reeded lagoons. The channels are lined intermittently with a mixture of papyrus and common reeds, and periodically open out on to floodplain areas. Scenically the areas near these camps don't quite match up to the sheer beauty of the Jao Flats, as there are very few feathery real fan palms or lily-covered lagoons.

Fauna When I last visited, I was very impressed by the varied line-up of antelope that I saw in the Vumbura Reserve. Unlike many of the areas further from the heart of the Delta, there wasn't just a high density of one or two species, to the virtual exclusion of the rest.

Species that you can expect to see here include tsessebe, impala, lechwe, kudu, zebra, wildebeest, giraffe, warthog and steenbok. Sable are seen fairly often, especially near the airstrip. Waterbuck are common; Vumbura is one of the few places within northern Botswana where you'll find good numbers of them. Duiker, reedbuck and bushbuck are seen infrequently, while roan antelope are rare, though have been seen occasionally in the late dry season. I know of just one (February) sighting of sitatunga in Vumbura.

Wild dogs regularly den here, and one year I was lucky enough to be able to watch a beautiful pack with pups at its den, situated in the mopane woodlands on the east side of the Vumbura. However, in this thick band of mopane woodland it wasn't possible to follow them when they moved off.

Cheetah are occasionally seen, though like the rest of the smaller game they will move through the buffalo fence and out into the huge NG12, to the north. In the dry season, when many of the open floodplains are dry, the open environment is perfect for cheetah, rather like Mombo and parts of Selinda, so it's a better time of year to seek them.

Leopard are occasionally seen on night drives, including on the small islands. Lion and spotted hyena are both relatively common. Both black-backed and side-striped jackals occur here, though the black-backed are seen much more regularly.

Moving westwards, Duba Plains is noted not only for its huge open plains, but has long had a reputation for high concentrations of buffalo, and particularly for lion–buffalo interactions. Larger herds of buffalo usually congregate in the Delta during the dry season, though they have been seen in Duba less, and spend more of their time to the north and towards Vumbura. When present, these usually attract the attention of the larger lion prides which have more experienced hunters, and lion have always been very much the dominant predator in the Duba Plains area. The converse of this is that in the past, Duba hasn't had quite the same balance of species, or the diversity, that you often find in Vumbura. Wild dog, cheetah and impala have been largely absent, while very good populations of lechwe have diverted the lions' attention, along with reedbuck, bushbuck, waterbuck and kudu. And the area is curiously popular with warthogs! Spotted hyena are flourishing, despite the sizeable prides of lions, and side-striped jackals are seen fairly frequently, but black-backed are largely absent.

In recent years, we've seen a reduction in the number and size of the buffalo herds, and far fewer lion–buffalo interactions, but a rise in the number of other species, including cheetah.

Birdlife The birdlife here is as varied as you'll find in any area of the Delta with a good mix of dry and wet environments. Certainly in one afternoon of very casual bird spotting on the river you can expect to find a range of kingfishers (malachite, pied and giant), jacanas, several species of egrets (including black and slaty), black-winged stilts, open-billed storks and reed cormorants. In addition, the open floodplains with short grass seem to attract very good numbers of various waders plus saddle-billed storks, glossy and sacred ibises, spoonbills and – relatively unusually – pelicans. Over several previous trips the quality of birdlife has been particularly impressive. As well as large numbers of common species, we spotted comparative rarities such as the pink- (or rosy-) throated longclaw, wattled crane and Stanley's bustard. Pel's fishing owls can also be found in the area, and in unusually high water years, the waterlogged plains of the Duba Concession have been known to play host to a very unusual sight in the Delta: flamingos.

WHEN TO VISIT As elsewhere in the Delta the big game is more diverse and prolific during the dry season, although the birdlife is generally better between December and March. Driving around the reserve can be more difficult then, as there's usually a lot of water around and many roads are submerged. To deal with this problem, vehicles at Duba Plains have been modified to be higher off the ground.

GETTING THERE AND AWAY All the camps here only accept pre-booked guests who fly in. Driving isn't possible without permission – and permission is never given. Camps use the nearest airstrip within the concession, notably Vumbura (VUMAIR) at ✪ 18°57.504'S, 22°49.063'E, and Duba (OMDOP) at ✪ 19°01.039'S, 22°41.059'E.

🔖 **WHERE TO STAY** *Map, page 336*

Duba Explorers Camp (5 tented rooms) Contact Great Plains (page 214). Situated on a tree-studded island in the secluded northern expanse of the Duba Concession, this intimate camp is surrounded by floodplains & woodland in an area celebrated for its wildlife encounters & exceptional birdwatching (400 species). Under a peaked canvas roof at the centre of camp is a cosy lounge & dining space, furnished with traditional leather sofas, inventive woven lampshades & a communal dining table.

There's a self-service bar, a shady deck overlooking the floodplains & marsh that teem with wildlife, a plunge pool, social firepit area & a small curio shop.

Its 5 expansive, expedition-style tents each enjoy captivating views from their veranda sofas & spacious beds. Elegant lamps, Persian-style rugs on wooden floors, polished storage trunks & a writing desk lend a sophisticated air to the interiors.

Land-based activities include game drives (day & night) & guided walks &, water levels permitting,

13

there are also mokoro & motorboat trips. *From US$1,220 pp 11 Jan–Mar to US$2,260 pp 15 Jun–Oct & festive season, FBA exc transfers. Children 8+.* ⏱ *All year.* 🛏🛏🛏🛏🛏

✷ **Duba Plains** (5 tents, 1 2-bed suite) Contact Great Plains (page 214). Duba Plains is strategically positioned on an island surrounded by expansive floodplains, affording breathtaking views of the surrounding landscape. These days it's a very smart camp modelled on 1920s safari-chic, & it's retained an authentic atmosphere. Thanks to a great team & consistently exciting wildlife interactions, it makes for a super safari spot.

Under majestic ebony & jackalberry trees, the hub of Duba Plains is an elevated central dining area with a peaked canvas roof. There's a comfortable lounge, a library, an excellent open kitchen, a wine cellar & a photography centre for reviewing those prize-winning shots.

Well-appointed accommodation blends seamlessly with the environment from atop upcycled railway sleeper decks. Each tent offers high levels of comfort, with luxurious furnishings, en-suite bathrooms & private verandas with pools to soak in the views.

Game drives explore the diverse ecosystems & prolific wildlife: the camp has historically been renowned for its unique interactions between lions & buffalo, providing extraordinary sightings for wildlife enthusiasts & photographers alike. In more recent times, the lions have shifted their prey preferences to lechwe. Like all Great Plains camps, camera mounts, beanbags & guides familiar with positioning their vehicles for photography are standard. Guiding is excellent, with individual guides knowledgeable about the dragonflies & butterflies. With Duba's location near the Panhandle, it's one of the first camps in the main Delta to be flooded, so from about May to Aug, the shallow-water plains around camp usually have enough water for mokoro trips. Boat safaris & walking safaris are also available. *Tent: from US$1,753 pp 11 Jan–Mar to US$4,201 pp 15 Jun–Oct, FBA. Suite (4 people): from US$9,290 11 Jan–Mar to US$17,590 15 Jun–Oct, FBA. Children 6+.* ⏱ *All year.* 🛏🛏🛏🛏🛏

✷ **Little Vumbura** (5 dbl tents, 1 2-bed family tent) Contact Wilderness Safaris (page 216). Although less than 2km from its larger sister camp (see opposite), Little Vumbura (⊕ LVUMBU 19°00.070′S, 22°51.710′E) feels quite separate,

perhaps because it's on a small island (& soon to be relocated to another nearby island) & is always approached by boat.

The main areas feature circular tented roofs that contribute to a cool & spacious ambience. The lounge, adorned in vibrant blue tones, offers a refreshing departure from the traditional safari khaki. Comfortable sofas, armchairs & coffee tables are orientated to maximise views over the water. For a more secluded experience, there's a small library resembling a treehouse built around a vacant termite mound, with reference books, magazines & information on wildlife research conducted in the area. There's a dining area, a well-stocked help-yourself bar, a star deck & a firepit. Set back is a secluded plunge pool, surrounded by a decked area furnished with sunloungers & a large shaded sunbed.

Elevated wooden walkways, designed to accommodate fluctuations in Delta water levels, connect the central area to the tented chalets. All interiors are spacious, sophisticated & extremely comfortable. Pale timber floorboards, floor-to-ceiling mesh windows & canvas, circus-like tented roofs make for a light, bright space, & every room has dbl or twin beds, comfortable chairs both indoors & on the deck, an en-suite shower room & a separate toilet. A honeymoon tent has an outdoor bathtub on the private deck too.

Activities are varied, with both water & dry land excursions. Game drives are rewarding, although there are no night drives given the island location. Deep-water channels allow for motorboat trips, while shallow channels enable excursions by mokoro. *From US$1,480 pp Jan–Mar to US$2,940 pp Jun–Oct, FBA exc transfers. Children 6+.* ⏱ *All year.* 🛏🛏🛏🛏🛏

North Island (4 tents) Contact Natural Selection (page 215). In quintessential Delta territory, where floodplains & savannah grasslands are criss-crossed by channels & calm lagoons are dotted with tree islands, North Island Okavango opened in Jun 2023. Set on a private island, lush with mature ebony, mangosteen & wild fig trees, it's an intimate camp with beautiful interiors & superb surroundings.

Its 4 secluded suites are set in gorgeous tents, raised on wooden decking complete with private plunge pools & panoramic lagoon views. Sophisticated, contemporary interiors, with African influences & a refined natural palette, make for an exquisite retreat. A floating bed overlooks the lagoon & a beautiful bath takes in the same views from the en-suite. There's an alfresco shower, inviting lounge with a minibar & a Nespresso machine, & myriad little touches to enhance a stay. In-room spa treatments are available too.

The air of refined exclusivity extends beyond the suites, permeating every facet of the camp. Under towering trees, there's a camp library, a well-equipped outdoor gym & a lovely central bar-dining area, from which decks lead out into super spots over the lagoon, one offering a perfect firepit boma where evenings can be spent sipping cocktails in the sunken seats, listening to hippos & a chorus of frogs. Food, by executive chef Lugile Mbangi, is a delight.

Excellent guides offer game drives & more serene journeys along the waterways by boat or mokoro. For an alternative perspective, helicopter or hot-air balloon trips can be arranged, or take a trip to the nearby village to learn about the importance of wildlife conservation & community development in the area. *From US$1,445 pp 10 Jan–Mar to US$3,245 pp Jul–Aug, FBA inc conservation fee. Children 6+.* ⊕ *All year.* ☀☀☀☀☀

Sitatunga Private Island Camp (2 dbl suites, 1 2-bed family suite) Contact Great Plains (page 214). Opened in Jul 2023 as the latest in the impressive Great Plains portfolio, this is a secluded, exclusive retreat. Situated just north of Duba Plains Camp, it is in a serene setting surrounded by the watery, natural beauty that draws many to travel to the Okavango. This camp is exclusively water-based & so access is by a scenic helicopter transfer from the Duba Plains airstrip (10mins), or by motorboat (2hrs).

Surrounded by this stunning wetland landscape, the camp's design draws inspiration from local fishing artefacts, using solid wood poles & oversized baskets to mimic the funnel-like reed traps used by local fishermen. The rich tones of the timber interiors are speckled with deep blue details, mirroring the surroundings. Persian carpets, beaded chandeliers, delicate silk & linen fabrics & soft leather sofas exude style, but it is unfussy & without pretence. It is simply a beautiful, carefully curated camp. The open-sided lounge is comfortable & in the evenings the firepit provides a cosy gathering spot, & the camp's wine cellar shines during delicious dinners, which are typically enjoyed in

the main area, though private veranda dining is also available.

With only 2 tented suites & 1 exclusive-use family suite (2 bedrooms, a lounge, firepit, pool & boat), an intimate & highly personalised experience is guaranteed, & the team are known to deliver consistently high standards. Each suite has an elevated veranda & a private plunge pool, a large lounge area & en-suite bathroom; they are designed with comfort in mind & make a luxurious space for relaxation. Beds are sumptuous & the bathroom boasts a bathtub, indoor shower, twin basins & – unusually on safari – a hairdryer. Mosquito netting incorporated into the canvas sides of the tent allows for a gentle breeze, & there's solar-powered AC & fans above the beds. There's a yoga mat, light weights & an exercise bike for fitness enthusiasts, & in-room massage for those seeking indulgence.

Activities are primarily water-based, including wildlife viewing from flat-bottomed motorboats, with swivel chairs for photography, peaceful mokoro excursions, birdwatching & catch-&-release fishing (exc Jan–Mar). As with all the Great Plains camps, photography is a central theme & each suite comes equipped with high-quality binoculars & a professional Canon camera, with lenses available for guest use. The photos can be downloaded on to a USB flash drive at the end of the stay. Enthusiastic guided walks are available on request, but there are no game drives due to the island location. Guiding standards are very high & when researching this edition we learned that one guide was so passionate about the environment that he was teaching the entire staff about the birdlife to allow everyone to contribute to the guest's wilderness experience. *Dbl: from US$1,550 pp 11 Jan–Mar to US$2,935 pp 15 Jun–Oct & festive season, FBA. Family suite (4 people): from US$7,440 11 Jan–Mar to US$14,090 15 Jun–Oct & festive season, FBA. Children 6+.* ⊕ *All year.* ☀☀☀☀☀

Vumbura Plains (8 rooms North, 6 rooms South) Contact Wilderness Safaris (page 216). Vumbura Plains was a 'contemporary lodge in the bush' trailblazer. To be precise, Vumbura Plains is in fact 2 near-identical, adjacent safari lodges run semi-independently to give the discerning visitor a top-of-the-range experience without large numbers of guests: Vumbura Plains North, which incorporates 2 family rooms & perhaps enjoys a

13

nicer setting, & Vumbura Plains South. They are linked by a walkway, but have separate central areas & management, so feel more intimate, softening what could otherwise be a slightly corporate effect.

Modern in design, each of the large, square rooms (emphatically not tents) features light-coloured wood & its own sizeable private deck with plunge pool & a small sala, lit by soft spotlights. In the spacious bedroom area, voluminous white net curtains slide on ceiling rails, acting as room dividers, & wardrobes are cleverly concealed along one side. One quarter of the room houses a square sunken lounge with low seating & soft, pastel cushions; another part features a free-standing shower on a concrete slab with a view through the large windows (or shower curtains for privacy) – & there's another completely outdoor shower too. It's all quite unexpected & very different from a traditional safari camp.

For families, Vumbura Plains has a big plus: 2 private family suites, each having a completely separate en-suite room for children (age 6+). Linking the 2 rooms is a private deck with 3 enclosed sides, which means that – unusually – children can be slightly independent of their parents.

At the heart of each camp, set beneath indigenous trees overlooking the plains, is a wooden platform sheltered by a roof supported by poles. When it's raining or blowing a gale, wooden slatted blinds protect guests from the worst of the elements, but during the dry season, this makes for dining or relaxing almost alfresco, with a cool through breeze. As elsewhere, the décor is contemporary & quite fun: plenty of soft comfortable sofas & modern objets d'art. The stylish mode of the camp extends to meals, which are served to a table set with sparkling cutlery & crystal glasses. A cappuccino maker is on hand throughout the day, & the bar is particularly well stocked.

The service is friendly & staff try very hard to meet the high standards set by the camp. Activities include the usual 4x4 safaris, walking & boats/mokoro trips. There's also a well-stocked curio shop between the camps – & shared by guests at both.

Over the years, we have found that camps like Vumbura, Mombo & Chitabe attract some of Wilderness's more ambitious & keen guides, who certainly rank among the best in the company. *From US$1,848 pp Jan–Mar to US$3,830 pp Jun–Oct, FBA exc transfers. Children 6+.* ☉ *All year.* 😋😋😋😋

JEDIBE COMMUNITY AREA (NG24)

Located at the base of the Panhandle, where the Okavango River fans out into the Delta, Jedibe is a maze of deep-water, papyrus-edged channels, spectacular floodplains, lagoons laced with lilies and lush islands of tall palms, giant leadwoods and shady jackalberries: a stunning and exotic water wonderland.

Jedibe is not a place to choose for animals and adrenalin encounters. Although there are animals on the islands, you should treat any big-game sightings as a bonus. Instead, come for the super bird- and water-life, spending gentle days paddling the waters (or sitting back with a drink and binoculars on a motorboat) to seek out delicate painted reed frogs, nesting skimmers and Pel's fishing owl.

Once the location for one of Wilderness Safaris' earliest photographic camps in the Delta – Jedibe Camp – the concession was without a safari operation for close to 20 years after its closure in 1999 when lease negotiations between the government, the community (the Okavango Jakotsha Community Trust) and potential operators failed. A combination of the business costs associated with operating so far from Maun and its supplies, and the burgeoning success of other parts of the Delta, notably places where land and water safari activities were both possible, left Jedibe looking less commercially viable, at a time when the local community was expecting to get more for the concession.

Since 2018, however, Jedibe has enjoyed a revival. The opening of a trio of comfortable camps (see opposite) is once again making these beautiful water areas accessible, with motorboats, mekoro and island walks enticing birdwatchers, wilderness enthusiasts and fishermen (the phenomenal barbel run is between August and October).

FLORA AND FAUNA Jedibe is a classic deep-Delta environment, veined by a network of fast-flowing channels, peaceful waterways, lagoons and seasonal floodplains. The channels are lined with thick banks of **papyrus**, phragmites reeds and swamp grass, which occasionally break away, drifting down the channels to alter the watercourse and the Delta's ever-changing pattern. In the slower channels and mirror-like lagoons, **water-lilies** flourish, opening by day to reveal their white and pink blooms.

Dotted around the water are beautiful **tree islands**, like those where the three safari camps are located. Rich in riverine hardwood species – sausage trees (*Kigelia africana*), jackalberries (*Diospyros mespiliformis*), leadwood (*Combretum imberbe*) and waterberry (*Syzygium cordatum*) – as well as wonderful wild date palms (*Phoenix reclinata*), which sadly appear to be disappearing from many other Delta areas, these islands are dense and verdant, attracting myriad bird species.

As for **wildlife**, water-based activities dominating, there are good opportunities to see pods of hippos, sunbathing crocodiles and water monitor lizards, all of which appear in good numbers. Antelopes, such as reedbuck and the illusive sitatunga, can be spotted coming to drink, as well as elephants and buffalos, who appear as the floodwater recedes and the grass floodplains are revealed. Hyena, leopard and occasional lions may be sighted, with troops of baboons known to hang around the tree islands.

The Jedibe Concession is a haven for **birdwatchers**, boasting a diverse range of habitats – waterways, floodplains, and woodlands – which entice an array of both resident and migratory birds. Along the water's edge and in the shallow wetlands, spot the iridescent colours of an African swamphen, African jacana or the impressive Goliath heron. With raptors such as African fish eagles and African hawk-eagles plying the skies above, and kingfishers, including the vibrant malachite kingfisher and pied kingfisher, skimming the water's surface, there are avian delights all around.

Wading birds like white-necked storks and sacred ibises are a common sight, as are waterfowl such as herons, egrets, Egyptian geese and knob-billed ducks. There is a seasonal heronry – a breeding colony featuring both herons and egrets – allowing close-up views, and good photographic opportunities of the birds nesting and raising their young.

Come nightfall, owls and nightjars are a treat, with especially reliable sightings of the usually shy Pel's fishing owl.

 WHERE TO STAY *Map, page 336*
After a long absence of lodges in this area, a trio of camps has opened here in recent years. Operated by the competent team at Setari, each lodge has a different feel and environment, but all are well run and comfortable.

Kala Camp (6 tents) Contact Setari Camp (page 215). Launched in May 2022, Kala Camp nestles in permanent wetlands at the base of the Panhandle, just 12km from sister camp Setari & only 6km from Jedibe airstrip. Kala's allure lies in its intimacy: just 6 comfortable tents, perched on wooden platforms, overlooking a seasonal river & lush palm forest island. All enjoy relaxing interiors in natural tones, en-suite bathrooms & a timber decked veranda to take in the scenery.

The camp's main areas are elevated too, & feature a simple but inviting open-fronted 'mess tent', with a leather sofa, communal dining table, delightful little swimming pool with loungers under umbrellas, & an open-air boma for evenings round the firepit.

13

While Kala may not be known for big-game sightings, it embraces its classic Okavango landscapes, showcasing its rich flora & fauna. Characterised by a network of deep-water channels, lagoons & small islands, this region of the Okavango is a good spot for water safaris regardless of the season. Guests here can explore papyrus-lined water channels by boat (seasonal), try their hand at fishing, or glide across floodplains in traditional mekoro. Guided walking safaris on the palm islands offer excellent birdwatching opportunities too, but no 4x4 game drives are on offer here. *From US$480 pp 10 Jan–Mar to US$949 pp Jul–Sep, FBA. Children 12+.* ⊕ *All year.* 🐘🐘🐘🐘–🐘🐘🐘🐘🐘

Kala Treehouse (3 suites) Contact Setari Camp (page 215). The latest addition to the Setari trio of camps, Treehouse is only available on an exclusive-use basis. Elevated amid the trees, as its name suggests, though without the rustic buildings one imagines, Treehouse accommodates only 6 guests in 3 spacious, en-suite canvas suites. Each has extra-length beds, a neat desk & a fan-cooled lounge. At the front, overlooking the floodplains, a spacious veranda, complete with loungers, makes a super sundowner spot.

Much like Kala, Treehouse is fundamentally a water camp May–Oct, enabling guests to go in a boat or mokoro right from the camp's jetty. After Oct, as floodwaters recede, the surrounding grassy floodplains are revealed, inviting herds of buffalo & elephant to graze, with opportunist lions hot on their heels. Walking can be arranged & birdwatching is always productive here, though especially so in Nov–Mar. Exclusive use *US$7,000, FBA inc helicopter transfer from Jedibe. Min 2 nights. Children 12+.* ⊕ *All year.* 🐘🐘🐘🐘🐘

Setari Camp (8 tents, 1 family suite) ☏ +44 7724 138637 (UK); e reservations@setaricamp.com; w setaricamp.com. Close to the base of the Okavango's 'Panhandle', where the Okavango River starts to fan out & the Delta 'proper' starts, Setari Camp occupies a pretty, palm-dotted island, known as Little Duba & spanning just 1.2km by 700m. Encircled by permanent channels, expansive green reedbeds interspersed with clusters of papyrus, & tranquil lily-covered lagoons, this area boasts deeper waters than most other camps in the Delta, making it a super choice for year-round water activities & magical birdwatching.

The double-tented suites are perched high in the giant riverine trees to provide panoramic views of the surrounding floodplain from wide sundecks. Spacious interiors are classically furnished, with comfortable beds, woven rugs & a sofa facing the mesh picture window. The en-suite bathrooms include a freestanding bath, twin sinks & a separate indoor & outdoor shower with a picturesque view. The family suite accommodates up to 4 guests, with 2 separate but adjoining tents, both equipped with en-suite bathrooms & conveniently located close to the main area & pool.

Envisioned as a complex of treehouses, Setari's rooms are linked by high, winding boardwalks through the lush canopy, alive with birdsong. There's a central thatched area, where communal meals take place on the deck & leather sofas encourage relaxation. There's a pleasant pool, with shaded loungers & views of the floodplains framed by palm fronds, a gym, small curio shop & firepit.

Unlike the traditional game-focused safaris, Setari's emphasis lies on walking & boating, giving an alternative perspective to this watery ecosystem. 2-storey pontoon boats are super for spotting wildlife & birds, with the extra height a real asset for photographers too. Traditional mokoro excursions are also on offer, as well as catch-&-release fishing (tigerfish & bream) & gentle bush walks (max 6 guests) on the neighbouring islands. A full-day mokoro excursion, including a picnic lunch & island walk, is also on offer. As a camp constructed in partnership with the community, Setari also offers visits to nearby Jao Village, where you can meet the community & the resident basket-weavers. *From US$480 pp 10 Jan–Mar to US$949 pp Jul–Sep, FBA. Children 6+.* ⊕ *All year.* 🐘🐘🐘🐘–🐘🐘🐘🐘🐘

JAO, KWETSANI, JACANA, TUBU AND PELO (NG25)

Close to the Panhandle, west of Moremi, NG25 is a particularly beautiful concession covering about 600km² of the upper Okavango Delta. Most of this is a fairly wet environment, with extensive floodplains, especially around the Jao Flats, though there is a substantial drier section, where Tubu Tree Camp is situated, to the west of the reserve. The annual flood generally reaches this reserve around April or May, instantly expanding the area of the floodplains, although water levels are proving increasingly difficult to anticipate. As with most camps, flying in here is the only option, and is always booked in advance. Driving in is totally impractical.

Visit Jao, Kwetsani and Jacana primarily for their water activities – trips by boat and mokoro – which are generally offered all year (though motorboats at Kwetsani may be restricted by water levels around October–January). That said, Kwetsani offers slightly better game viewing. Both camps offer day and night game drives (and sometimes short walks on the islands) nearby, which are a real bonus. Game drives, offered by all three camps, are often taken on Hunda Island, which is reached by a short boat ride. As the largest swathe of dry land in the area, it's a wildlife hotspot for giraffe, kudu, wildebeest and zebra, alongside the predators who hunt them.

The other camps in the concession are extremes. Pelo is all about the water – in fact, because of concession limits it has no vehicle of its own – while Tubu Tree is a dry-land camp focused on game drives, though mokoro trips can be organised when the flood levels are high. A couple of nights at Jacana or Pelo, and a few at Tubu Tree, make a good combination for variety.

The game drives in this reserve tend to be in vehicles with three rows of three seats, of which the centre seats are often left empty. When I last went walking, the guide was a capable, experienced walking guide who gave an appropriate pre-departure safety briefing and clearly knew how to use the rifle that he carried. He also escorted the mokoro trip, which I was pleased to see eschewed the easier hippo trails in favour of a more difficult, but much safer, route through a shallow floodplain. Though he's now left this reserve, I hope that the standards of safe practice which he set will remain.

FLORA AND FAUNA The area around Jao and Jacana feels very much like most people's image of the Okavango: watery and terribly picturesque. It's a lovely environment, one that is mirrored at Kwetsani when the flood arrives. While the game diversity in the area might not quite match some of the areas further east, lechwe and lion are generally common and those alone will keep most people entertained. That said, visiting on one occasion in April, we didn't see a single lion; and conversely, on another occasion we spotted an unusually large number of sitatunga.

The birding is also good, with enough diversity of habitat to mean that you'll find most Delta species here if you look hard enough. I've had great luck in the past here with gallinules and pink-throated longclaws.

Hunda Island, the area around Tubu Tree Camp on the western side of the concession, is much drier and totally different from the eastern part of the reserve where the three older camps are situated. Historically this area had a reputation as a good place to see leopard, but since the arrival of small prides of lion, leopard sightings have been less frequent.

Flora The reserve's most memorable area must be the beautiful Jao Flats, a series of huge open floodplains, dotted with tiny islands that are often only a few metres across. These vast floodplains are covered in a mix of very sparse vegetation, much of which is the aptly named hippo grass (*Vossia cuspidata*), which has round, slender leaves, pointing periodically out of the water by up to a metre. Often these have a tiny flower spike on top, reminiscent of a minute papyrus head.

Much taller and denser are the stands of tall common reeds (*Miscanthus junceus*), and even areas of the attractive bulrush (*Typha capensis*). The latter have distinctive

13

velvety seedheads and edible roots (which taste a little like chewing gum or sugarcane!). As you'd expect in such a watery area, the deeper parts have thick stands of papyrus.

There's usually plenty of open, shallow water around, and in the slow-flowing channels look out for water lettuce plants (*Ottelia ulvifolia*) underwater, with their wavy leaves, long trailing stems and delicate, trumpet-shaped flower held above the surface by a single air bladder.

The many small islands in the area are often little more than bases for the emergence of a ring of bushy wild date palms (*Phoenix reclinata*), and perhaps the odd real fan palm (*Hyphaene petersiana*), springing up through the centre of the low canopy, perhaps around a termite mound.

Also look out for the wild dagga plant (*Leonotis nepetifolia*), with its bright-red flowers, like baubles from a Christmas tree. These will remain standing long after they turn brown and die. There are also thickets of the uncommon magic gwarri bush (*Euclea divinorum*), which is believed by some local people to have wood with supernatural powers. Above these you'll find raintrees (*Philenoptera violacea*), woodland waterberry trees (*Syzygium guineense*) and the occasional bird plum or motsentsela (*Berchemia discolor*).

Some of the bushes on the larger islands are more typical of drier areas, including the Kalahari appleleaf (*Philenoptera nelsii*) and the Kalahari star apple (*Diospyros lycioides lycioides*), with its blueish tinge which sometimes gives it the name of 'blue bush'. Ask your guide and s/he may show you how its twigs can be used as a toothbrush!

Similarly these larger islands have bands of acacias, including the umbrella thorn (*Vachellia tortilis*). These become more prevalent as you move further east in the reserve, where you find larger islands, with thicker belts of acacia bush and areas of mopane also.

Fauna Most of the reserve around the Jao Flats is a good area for lion and superb for lechwe. The lechwe occur in large herds and will frequently startle; listen to them splash as they run across the flooded grasslands. Lion are certainly the dominant predator.

Other game is usually present in lower densities, but in the eastern section you can expect to spot blue wildebeest, zebra, small groups of tsessebe and elephants. Kwetsani, in particular, is noted for the increasingly relaxed bushbuck which seem to frequent its island. Sable and roan are virtually never seen here, but the large areas of papyrus are home to sitatunga, though as ever these take a lot of effort to see.

Lone male buffalo will pass through, especially from June onwards, and later in the dry season larger breeding herds move across the reserve. Elephants have a broadly similar pattern, and their herds get larger as the dry season progresses.

Cheetah aren't usually seen on the eastern side of the reserve until the waters have receded a long way, which means around October. Then they'll move west again as the waters rise in February. Hyena and leopard are seen occasionally but infrequently throughout the reserve and the year. Although sightings of wild dog are unusual, your best chance has recently been in the area near to Tubu Tree.

The western area of the reserve, accessed from Tubu Tree and Little Tubu, is a much drier habitat where you can expect giraffe, kudu, tsessebe and impala in the mixed acacia woodlands.

Like most of the reserves around the Okavango, Jao Reserve was previously used for hunting, which may not have been at all ethical. It is alleged that leopard were baited and snared in numbers, and hyena shot. This would have enabled the lion prides to grow with little competition, thus satisfying the demand for lion trophies – and explaining the once very high numbers of lion and relative scarcity of other predators.

Fortunately all commercial hunting was stopped here well over a decade ago, and the animal populations are returning to a more natural balance.

Birdlife This is a good reserve for birdwatching, particularly for some of the less common water-based species. During a few gentle boat rides on the eastern side of the reserve, I had good sightings of many of the commoner waterbirds, plus lesser jacanas, lesser moorhens, purple and green-backed herons, slaty egrets, white-faced whistling ducks, and both African swamphens and Allen's gallinules. The number of waterbirds peaks during September and October, notably in the channels between Jacana and Jao, while between October and November, wattled cranes are here in good numbers, too. Very occasionally, visitors are treated to the sight of African skimmers, of which there is a breeding colony near to Pelo.

Meanwhile driving in the drier areas we came across a similarly good range, and noted several flocks of Meyer's parrots, Dickinson's kestrels nesting at the top of an old palm tree, a very unusual melanistic Gabar goshawk, wattled starlings and a tree full of open-billed storks. Then, again near Kwetsani, we found some very uncommon pink (rosy)-throated longclaws (a big tick!) in a wide marshy plain where they seem to be resident.

Though not too unusual, African snipes can be found here. Listen carefully around dusk, as the sun sets and darkness falls. Then, during the breeding season, the birds fly high and zoom back to the ground. Their fanned-out tail feathers make a noise like a percussion instrument – called 'drumming'.

The western side of this reserve, around Tubu Tree, should have a wider range of raptors than the east (Jao, Kwetsani and Jacana), simply because it's drier.

WHEN TO VISIT For the water activities, any time is fine as long as it doesn't rain. Hence from April to November would be my choice of time to visit. However, if you're on a serious game-viewing trip then it's better to come towards the end of the dry season when this area's diversity of species does pick up, with dry-country species like cheetah being seen here periodically.

WHERE TO STAY *Map, page 336*
All six camps in the Jao Reserve are marketed by Wilderness Safaris (page 216). They range from the opulence of Jao to the relative simplicity of Pelo. All cater exclusively for fly-in visitors.

Jacana Camp (5 tents) Although less than 4km north of Jao, Jacana is a 35min boat ride away. It stands on an island in the very beautiful Jao Flats area, & as at Jao, the density of date palms lends the feeling of a tropical island hideaway. In years where the flood levels in the Delta are high, the area around Jacana is completely flooded. Consequently, the camp is known for mokoro excursions, while game drives entail a 20min boat ride to reach their vehicles.

Jacana started life as a base for mokoro excursions for small escorted-group itineraries across Chobe & Moremi, before being upgraded to one of Wilderness Safaris' 'classic' camps, & then rebuilt in 2019.

The main double-storey central area sits under an overlapping tent structure, featuring a first-floor dining room that opens on to a balcony, with views stretching far across the floodplains. There's a mezzanine-level bar & an open-plan lounge on the ground floor which extends to the main deck, connecting to the adjacent pool, jetty & 'floating' firepit boma.

The spacious canvas & timber tented rooms each have a small veranda, with wicker chairs & a coffee table. Inside is a comfortable dbl or twin bed

13

beneath a ceiling fan, a writing desk, good storage & largely open-plan bathroom, including both indoor & outdoor showers & a separate alfresco claw-foot bath.

The camp is a good option at any time of the year for those wanting water-based activities, & is pretty good value for a couple of nights, especially towards the end of the dry season. *From US$900 pp 6 Jan–Mar to US$1,475 pp Jun–Oct, FBA.* ⊕ *All year.* 🐾🐾🐾🐾–🐾🐾🐾🐾🐾

Jao Camp (5 dbl rooms, 2 villas for 4 people) Standing on the southeast side of the Jao Reserve, Jao has always been one of Wilderness Safaris' flagship 'premier' camps.

Approaching Jao by boat, you navigate through gentle waterways surrounded by reeds before the camp is revealed. Jao was always a strikingly beautiful lodge, but its 2019 rebuild has created an ultra-luxurious Delta retreat.

The main area, seamlessly integrated into the tree canopy as in the original lodge design, encompasses beautiful indoor & outdoor lounges, dining spaces, a satellite kitchen, private dining areas & a beautiful, cushioned fire deck. Its 2-storey 'Centre of Knowledge', at the heart of the main area & centred around a towering giraffe skeleton, is a museum-style space that showcases maps, local curiosities & botanical pressings by E E Galpin, a renowned botanist & the great-grandfather of Cathy Kays, who co-owns the Jao Reserve. There's also a small library, seating area, lecture space for talks by visiting researchers, a well-stocked wine cellar (including French & Italian vintages) & a curio shop. A secluded spa has 2 treatment rooms surrounded by water to create a serene ambience. Even the gym on the island's edge offers idyllic views across lush waterways. The stunning main pool sits at the end of a boardwalk extended into the floodplain, providing a panoramic vista of the Delta from under its distinctive, nest-like lattice canopy.

The huge tented suites offer refined, natural interiors: exposed rafters, soft linens, muted colours & ceiling-to-floor glass panels making the most of their raised positions. Each has an infinity plunge pool & sunken firepit on the veranda, an indoor lounge & private dining area, & a contemporary bathroom complete with indoor & outdoor showers. The 2 exclusive-use villas include a private vehicle, guide, chef & butler.

The camp is both visually impressive & exceedingly comfortable, an obvious choice for honeymoon couples. It's worth noting that guests here tend to like their privacy rather than mix socially, so it doesn't have quite the sociable feel of some of the smaller camps. Activities by boat and mokoro are highlights here, for fishing trips, birdwatching or scenery. Game drives day & night, or a boat & 4x4 excursion to Hunda Island. *Suite: from US$1,848 pp 6 Jan–Mar to US$3,830 pp Jun–Oct, FBA. Villa: from US$8,272 6 Jan–Mar to US$15,319 Jun–Oct, FBA.* ⊕ *All year.* 🐾🐾🐾🐾🐾

Kwetsani (5 tents) Kwetsani faces east, towards the rising sun, from a long, narrow, palm-studded island about 10km northwest of Jao, its larger, more opulent neighbour. (This can take 40mins if the roads are dry, or 1hr by boat.)

The main lounge/dining room area at Kwetsani is slightly raised & stands under a high thatched roof, with one open side overlooking the plain. There's a dining table under part of this, as well as a lounge area with comfy chairs, a leather sofa & a small bookshelf. Nearby is a well-stocked bar, complete with a jackalberry tree (*Diospyros mespiliformis*) growing up through it.

The wooden decking floor extends from under the thatch on to a wide veranda, which has been built around a huge sycamore fig, a marula & a sausage tree. There's usually a spotting scope standing on the deck. Nearby is a guest washroom/toilet, which not only has a tree growing up through it, but also has half of its wall cut away, affording a great view. Down a sloping walkway, almost on the level of the surrounding plains, a few sunloungers, umbrellas & chairs surround a small splash-pool, & from here, more steps lead down to a firepit at ground level, which is perfect for pre-dinner drinks.

Modern, open-plan tents with 2 ceiling fans incorporate a lounge area with a comfortable L-shaped sofa, & a desk with a couple of chairs. Further back, twin beds or a dbl are surrounded by a large mosquito net; & at the end is the bathroom – partly open plan, but with the toilet in a separate cubicle. There are both indoor & outdoor showers. At the front of the tent, large glass doors can be almost fully folded back, allowing easy access to the spacious deck.

Kwetsani is a lovely camp, which is smarter & more modern than many other camps in the concession. However, activities, particularly game drives, may feel limiting here, as a boat transfer is needed to reach Hunda Island & you must return on the boat before dark. *From US$1,300 pp 6 Jan–Mar to US$2,230 pp Jun–Oct, FBA. Children 6+.* 🕐 *All year.* 🐘🐘🐘🐘🐘

Little Tubu (3 tents) Adjacent to Tubu Tree (see right), & with the same 'treehouse' feel, the much smaller Little Tubu affords a more intimate & exclusive option. Shaded beneath a riverine canopy & overlooking the floodplain, the elevated dining area & bar, & a raised pool, are well placed to watch the abundant wildlife. Sharing the views are Little Tubu's spacious en-suite tents, which are almost identical in design to those at Tubu Tree. There is also a honeymoon tent here, which is further away from the main area than the other chalets, offering greater privacy, & it also has a sala day bed raised among the trees. *From US$1,480 pp 6 Jan–Mar to US$2,229 pp Jun–Oct, FBA.* 🕐 *All year.* 🐘🐘🐘🐘🐘

Pelo Camp (5 tents) Set in the centre of the concession, Pelo is the simplest camp in the reserve: a seasonal camp focusing on mokoro excursions, boating & fishing. The canvas structure incorporates a dining & lounge area set beneath jackalberry, wild date palms & mahogany trees, alongside an outdoor 'boma' area & a viewing platform on an old anthill. Modest tented rooms have twin or dbl beds, a writing desk & sofa chairs, with a basin at the back & 2 screens providing privacy for the flush toilet & shower. In front of the tent is a covered porch with safari chairs, & an outdoor bucket shower with views over the floodplain.

Pelo is not a place for those in search of dry-land activities: it opens when the flood arrives & closes when the waters recede. It's also important to realise that as Pelo is situated on an island, all activities must finish before dark; no boats are permitted on the water after sunset. On the other hand, the camp takes advantage of its westerly facing firepit & has sundowner drinks ready for your return to camp. *From US$658 pp 6 Jan–Mar to US$1,148 pp Jun–Oct, FBA. Children 13+.* 🕐 *Seasonally (variable).* 🐘🐘🐘🐘🐘

Tubu Tree Camp (8 tents) West of the other camps in the concession, & another of Wilderness Safaris' 'classic' camps, Tubu Tree has a treehouse feel, with elevated buildings & high wooden walkways through the canopy that link the tents to the main area.

Under a marula tree, the central area has great views over the surrounding seasonal floodplains. Inside, there's a large, simply furnished dining area & a relaxing, open-sided lounge with sofas & some interesting reference books. A spotting scope enables guests to focus on the comings & goings of wildlife on the floodplains. From a quirky bar, built around the trees & with a top carved from a sausage tree, a walkway leads down to a small pool & sundeck with loungers. Beyond, a firepit is the venue for evening get-togethers.

Tubu's large, bright tents – 2 of them designed for families – stand on wooden decks, each with a veranda & a couple of directors' chairs affording super vistas over the floodplains. Open-plan interiors are elegant & unpretentious, with plenty of thoughtful touches. Dbl or twin beds, a writing desk & a couple of soft chairs furnish the bedroom, while a divider behind the bed separates this from the en-suite shower, toilet & washbasin, plus a separate outside shower. The baboons here have been known to be quite bold & were periodically breaking into empty rooms to eat soap, play with shiny things & generally be a nuisance, so guests should keep medication, valuables & scented items locked in the safe.

Tubu has access to large areas of dry mopane & acacia woodlands. From around Apr–Sep, & perhaps later, mokoro trips & fishing ought to be possible, but for the rest of the year activities are generally limited to game drives & walks on Hunda Island. That said, at drier times they will often use different launch points for the mekoro to extend their seasonal use. There are also 2 hides for photographic opportunities, one of which is a raised platform on which 'star-bed' sleepouts can take place on request. *From US$1,480 pp 6 Jan–Mar to US$2,940 pp Jun–Oct, FBA.* 🕐 *All year.* 🐘🐘🐘🐘🐘

13

ABU, SEBA AND MACATOO (NG26)

In this large concession, west of Moremi Game Reserve, the focus was traditionally on specific activities rather than the environment, from elephant-back safaris (now discontinued) at the well-known Abu Camp to specialist horseriding safaris at Macatoo. And while the riding safaris here continue to thrive, the shift to more conventional wildlife safaris is in evidence elsewhere.

In February 2024, Wilderness Safaris' long-standing contract to manage and market Abu and Seba camps ended, and the camps ceased operating. It is widely understood that the camps have been purchased by Danish billionaire Anders Holch Povlsen, and that the management will ultimately be taken over by upmarket ecotourism operator Singita (page 215), who had begun recruiting in Maun in early 2024.

However, bureaucratic challenges, perhaps most notably pressure from Botswana's Competition and Consumer Authority to have Povlsen cede 30% of his shares to local operators, have significantly slowed the process. Negotiations have already been underway for a few years. Hopefully, within the lifetime of this guide, contracts will finally be agreed to allow for safaris to resume here. We would envisage that if this deal does complete, the resulting camps will be beautifully styled and deliver the high level of service for which Singita is known elsewhere.

Unusually for the Delta's private concessions, Beagle Expeditions (page 216) also run mobile safari operations here.

Given that the focus of a trip here is either the experience of horseriding or the elephants and predator interactions, travel is fine any time, as long as you avoid the **rains**. So visit anytime from April to November.

The only option for reaching this area is to make advanced bookings and **fly** in. There's an airstrip near Abu Camp and a second close to Macatoo. Driving here is not possible.

FLORA AND FAUNA Most of the Delta's usual big game, including elephant, buffalo, giraffe, blue wildebeest, kudu, tsessebe, red lechwe, impala, zebra, reedbuck, steenbok, warthog, baboons and vervet monkeys, are in evidence in this concession. Lion and spotted hyena are the dominant predators, with occasional appearances by leopards and wild dogs.

That said, like NG25 to the north, and NG29 and NG30 to the south, the variation and density of game are not quite up to the levels of, say, central Moremi or some of the areas on the north side of the Delta. There is little doubt that, at present, the changing watercourses of the Delta are resulting in less floodwater in these western areas, and with that comes shifting wildlife patterns. However, rest assured that you'll still see plenty of game when visiting here.

It's perhaps also worth noting that for those on the dedicated horseback safaris, the finer details of the wildlife in this concession tend to be eclipsed by the thrilling adventure of being on horseback and in close proximity to animals in the wilderness.

WHERE TO STAY *Map, page 336*

Safari camps Although closed at the time of writing this guide, we understand that Singita (page 215) are in the process of taking on the lease for Abu Concession, and with it the operation of two long-standing luxury safari camps: Abu Camp and Seba Camp. As a result, we anticipate that the camps' names and aesthetic will likely change over the lifetime of this guide.

For now, Macatoo Camp (page 366), the base for African Horseback Safaris (see opposite), is the only camp still operational.

Mobile safaris

Beagle Expeditions: The Kweene Trails m 7645 6198, 7178 3077; e res@ beagle-expeditions.com; w beagle-expeditions. com. Towards the south of this huge private reserve, just west of the Sandveld Tongue, Beagle Expeditions operate superb mobile safaris (4–10 guests) between 2 locations, known as the Kweene Trails. Impeccably hosted & guided by husband-&-wife team Marleen & Simon Byron, these remote mobile camps may be simple in structure, but they're big on experience. This is a high-quality operation with excellent guiding & service.

Although all trips are tailor-made, everyone arrives here by helicopter – the only option to this corner of the Delta. Time is then divided between Kweene River Camp, in the arid floodplains surrounding the southern part of the Kweene River, & travelling north to the perennial swamp at Magwegwe Camp, & its surrounding forest 'islands'. On 'moving day', guests travel by foot, mokoro or game drive through the reserve, whatever their preference & possibilities given the water levels.

The camp itself consists of a central 'mess tent' for shared meals, a firepit complete with bar, & up to 5 en-suite Meru tents. With enormous mesh picture windows (with zipped, roll-down sides for overnight) the views are immersive. There are comfortable camp beds with luxury linen, a table, wardrobe, & a bathroom at the back, complete with a neat composting toilet & hot-water bucket shower. The atmosphere in camp is laid-back & convivial, with the depth of experience of this team evident in everything, from guiding knowledge to the delicious meals prepared on the fire by the bush chefs, & the impressive team who pack up & relocate the whole camp in time for sundowners on 'moving day'.

Activities focus on exploring the diversity of the area's varied ecosystems predominantly on foot, but also by boat, mokoro or 4x4. Each trip is tailored to the group's individual interests & requirements, & the seasonal options. Beagle Expeditions donates US$30 pp/night to Wild Entrust, an organisation at the forefront of predator conservation in Botswana & behind some great community initiatives in the villages of the nearby Habu Conservancy. *US$1,385 pp, FBA. Min 4 nights. Children all ages.* 🐘🐘🐘🐘🐘

Horseriding safaris Contact African Horseback Safaris (page 218). These riding safaris were established by British rider Sarah-Jane Gullick, who set up the operation in 1995, originally with Ker & Downey Safaris (based out of a camp called Macateer Camp). Today, the operation is run by John Sobey, who was the camp's first head guide and has experience of guiding riding trips in both East and southern Africa.

The general comments on Okavango Horse Safaris (page 218) about the fascinating experience of riding through the Okavango apply equally well to this operation. Suffice to say that once you step into the saddle, most of the Okavango's resident game will treat you and your horse as a single, composite four-legged herbivore. So antelope will relax around you, and predators will give you pause for thought!

Below is some basic information for these trips. Contact African Horseback Safaris for more precise details.

The horses The horses (there are over 50) are a variety of thoroughbreds, Namibian Hanovarians, Arabs and Kalahari–Arab crossbreeds ranging from 14 to 18 hands (140–180cm) high.

Tack and clothes Good-quality English- and Western-style trail saddles are supplied, each with its own water bottle. Guests may borrow half chaps; long leather boots are impractical.

African Horseback Safaris does not supply hard hats or safety helmets; you must bring your own and it's essential that properly fitted, recognised riding helmets are worn for most insurance companies to offer cover. It's suggested that riders wear their riding clothes and shoes/boots on the plane, and bring their hat and wash bag as hand luggage, in case luggage gets delayed. A recommended packing list is detailed on the African Horseback website.

Information about you These safaris are for **experienced** riders aged 12 years and over. Riders over 60 need to be 'riding fit' and strong. Trips usually involve about 4 to 6 hours in the saddle each day, and riders need to feel competent about keeping up with the group, and capable of riding at all paces, and in variable temperatures. They may also be required to gallop out of trouble, so these trips do not take beginners. For safety reasons, if they think that your riding is not up to standard, you won't be allowed to ride here.

There's a **weight limit** of 15 stone (210lb or 95kg) per person, above which they can sometimes make special arrangements for advanced riders. Guests over 100kg can only participate in non-riding activities.

About the trips African Horseback Safaris offers a range of safaris from three to ten nights, giving plenty of scope. Following arrival in camp, each trip starts with an introductory talk on the safari, and a safety briefing. While safaris were once timed to start and finish on Tuesdays and Fridays, guests are now welcome to choose the dates that best suit their itinerary.

The riding groups have a maximum of six to eight guests. Trips normally incorporate not only riding but also the occasional game drive, walk and night drive, while the more adventurous may opt to spend a night in the 'treehouse', sleeping high up in the tree canopy under the African night sky. Boating, canoeing and fishing are also possible sometimes, depending on water levels.

Two guides accompany each riding safari, carrying a first-aid kit, rifle, radio and GPS.

The riding camp Macatoo Camp [map, page 336] (8 tents; Contact African Horseback Safaris, page 218; 🐾🐾🐾–🐾🐾🐾🐾) is modest but comfortable and, as with most camps, the service is very friendly and of a good standard. Its six standard tents are large and simply furnished, with comfortable twin beds and an en-suite shower and toilet. There is also a honeymoon suite, with a bath on a raised platform and a large private deck, and a 'friends and family suite' with two tents linked by a walkway and viewing deck. Meals are social, with dinner usually a stylish, three-course affair served by candlelight, with high-quality food freshly prepared. There is a furnished mess tent and a small splash pool for afternoon relaxation – equally popular with the local baboon families.

The costs From January to March, and December, rates are £585 per person per night, including all meals, drinks and activities. This rises to £765 from April to mid-June and mid-October to November, while in the peak season (July to the end of October) the cost is £940 per person. Note that in common with all riding safaris here, prices are quoted in pounds sterling, rather than the more usual US dollars. Air transfers to/from Maun are £280 per person one-way, or £390 from Kasane. Those coming from Kasane will not be able to ride on the day of arrival due to flight timings.

POM POM, KANANA AND NXABEGA (NG27A)

This large, strictly photographic concession is effectively split between three safari companies: Ker & Downey Botswana (who run Kanana), &Beyond (who run Nxabega) and Kwando Safaris (who run Pom Pom).

CONCESSION HISTORY By the early 1970s there were a number of camps throughout the Delta, most of which accepted either hunting or photographic guests. One of the bigger companies involved here was Safari South, who ran many camps including Khwai River Lodge, 4 Rivers Camp, Queenie, Splash, Jedibe, Machaba, Mombo, Pom Pom and Shinde.

Around 1985, Ker & Downey was split from Safari South, as a wholly owned subsidiary, to differentiate the photographic camps from those used for hunting. Ker & Downey then had four photographic camps in the Delta: Shinde, Mombo, Jedibe and Machaba.

A company called Jao Safaris owned Mombo at that time. Various contracts changed, which resulted in Ker & Downey leaving Mombo and Jedibe. (These were eventually taken up by Wilderness Safaris, in 1989.) Meanwhile, the government had designated NG27 for photographic use only, and Ker & Downey took over the running of Pom Pom, which had been another old hunting camp run by Safari South.

From 1985 Pom Pom was the only major camp here, but in 1990 they started a 'partnership' with Randall Jay Moore. Moore brought trained African elephants over from the USA to start Elephant Back Safaris, and Ker & Downey built Abu Camp (page 363) from which to run these, on the site that Nxabega now occupies in the north of the reserve. In 1993, I was very excited to visit Pom Pom – and to get here I took my first flight over the Delta! It was then one of Botswana's most upmarket camps, and the rest of the clientele during my stay were all from America. The combination of Pom Pom and then Abu Camp was a winning one; business was good for them. (Note that throughout this time there were also a few simple bush camps in the area, used by various operators.) However, the following year Randall Moore tendered for, and obtained, his own concession next door: NG26. This upset the apple cart, as he then built the camp that is today known as Abu Camp – thus taking away a highly profitable chunk of business from Ker & Downey.

The NG27 Concession has always been subdivided. First AfroVentures (who subsequently merged with CC Africa, now &Beyond) built Nxabega Camp on the site of the old Abu Camp, in the north. Then, in 2000, Ker & Downey opened their own camp, Kanana.

In 2001, Wilderness Safaris took over the marketing and management of Pom Pom, building a completely new small camp here, but keeping the name and location of the 'old' Pom Pom. Since then, it has changed hands again, and is now operated by Kwando Safaris.

FLORA AND FAUNA Travelling from south to north, the landscapes, flora and fauna change very slowly, but there are slight differences between the various parts of the reserve. Bear in mind while reading this that the similarities between the different areas are much greater than their contrasts.

Flora The NG27 Concession is in the heart of the Delta and contains most of the typical Delta environments: thickets and stands of riverine forest; more open areas of invasive bushes; and occasional floodplains.

The area around Pom Pom is very open and pretty, notable for many tiny islands amid wide open floodplains, which are often submerged between May and September. These distinct islands, surrounded by large marshy floodplains, are home to quite a few baobabs, with fairly sparse forest patches in the area.

Moving northeast to the area of Kanana, there are fewer flat, open plains and more areas colonised by expanses of wild sage. Around these are larger islands and woodland patches with plenty of the Delta's usual riverine tree species: sausage trees (*Kigelia africana*), jackalberries (*Diospyros mespiliformis*), knobthorns (*Senegalia*

13

nigrescens), the occasional marula (*Sclerocarya birrea caffra*) and the odd raintree (*Philenoptera violacea*). (The raintree, also sometimes called the appleleaf, gets its name from the droplets which are secreted by froghopper insects as they suck the sap from the leaves. This keeps the soil beneath the tree moist, and in exceptional cases can even form pools.)

Further northwest, around Nxabega, the forests become more in evidence with large, dense lines of broadleaf forests and patches of acacia. Mixed with these are a few open plains, fringed by significant numbers of real fan palms (*Hyphaene petersiana*) and stands of riverine trees. It really is incredibly scenic. In the midst of the larger floodplains you'll see occasional islands crowned with an African mangosteen (*Garcinia livingstonei*), or perhaps a large sycamore fig (*Ficus sycomorus*), growing out of an old termite mound perhaps surrounded by a few russet bush-willow bushes (*Combretum hereroense*). Some of the Nxabega's floodplains have thick coverings of hippo grass (*Vossia cuspidata*) that turn a lovely shade of orange-red around September.

Fauna The variety of game in NG27 certainly seems wider to me than that found in areas further south and west – though I feel that it's not as wide as some of the reserves on the northeast side of the Delta. Tsessebe, impala, wildebeest, lechwe, steenbok, baboon and zebra are all common and seen very regularly. Giraffe do particularly well here, they're very relaxed among the many acacia thickets, and there is a good number of resident elephants.

Lion and spotted hyena are the commonest large predators, though the mixed woodland is a perfect habitat for leopard, which are numerous and spotted with increasing regularity. Cheetah are seen only rarely, when the reserve is at its driest (October to March); they're not at all common. Wild dog pass through periodically (as they do through most areas of northern Botswana) though not frequently. Both black-backed and side-striped jackal are common.

As with most of the Delta there's always plenty of smaller animals, too widespread to be worthy of particular comment…though I recall a great sighting of an entertaining troop of dwarf mongooses here once!

THE LIZARD

There's a tale of a slightly fussy, older woman coming to stay on her own in a tented safari camp. Over lunch she complained about a lizard in her room, but was told this was nothing to worry about – and it'd probably vanish of its own accord soon.

That afternoon after lunch, while most of the camp was having a siesta, she wandered out in search of one of the staff. 'That lizard is still in my room,' she proclaimed, with agitation, to one of the managers that she found in the dining room. He then explained that this was really nothing to worry about, as lizards often came in and out of the rooms. In fact, he elaborated, 'it's very good as they're a natural way of keeping the mosquito population down.' So, she could go back and sleep, relaxed in the knowledge that it wouldn't do her any harm at all.

Off she went, but 20 minutes later she was back again. She couldn't sleep, claiming that the lizard was making too much noise. Unimpressed, but determined to satisfy the guest, the manager took her back to the room – only to be completely embarrassed to find a huge monitor lizard thrashing about, trying to find a way out of the tent.

Birdlife The birding is good and very varied in this concession. Kanana has immediate access to the deep Xudum River that is lined with a mixture of water figs, huge floating mats of graceful papyrus and anchored sections of miscanthus grass (*Miscanthus junceus*). Among the birdlife, there's a notable profusion of squacco herons. However, what is really interesting is the Kanana heronry (⊕ KANHER 19°30.02'S, 22°51.10'E), discovered only in 2001. Like the heronry at Gcodikwe, the shallow floodplain is dotted with tree-islands, primarily of water-fig trees interspersed with waterberry. Protected in some measure from predators, these in turn attract countless waterbirds during the breeding season, which starts in July and reaches its peak between September and December.

When found, many birds were breeding here, including yellow-billed, marabou and open-billed storks, darters, cormorants, herons and egrets, while a survey by BirdLife Botswana confirmed the presence of vulnerable pink-backed pelicans from mid-July. How such a large heronry went 'unnoticed' for so long is a complete puzzle, but the survey concludes that it is 'the most dynamic and vibrant heronry that we have ever visited in Botswana'. However fascinating, visitors must remember the problems that disturbances can cause to the birds; don't encourage your guide to approach too close to the heronry.

Nxabega doesn't have the heronry, though one September over 500 open-billed storks and about 1,000 squacco herons were seen gathering to roost just a little west of Nxabega. It does, however, have a couple of very old pole bridges across small waterways in its reserve. These prove particularly attractive perching places for waterbirds that can then be seen while driving. (This is an advantage if, like me, you prefer a stationary base from which to use a camera and tripod, rather than a rocking boat.) There are lots of kingfishers, hamerkops, small herons, egrets (including a good number of slaty), black crakes and bee-eaters.

Read the marketing literature for almost any camp in the Delta and you'll realise that claims for sightings of 'the elusive Pel's fishing owl' are a tedious marketing cliché. Every camp simultaneously trumpets their rarity, and yet claims you'll see one while staying there. That said, when I last visited Nxabega, one such owl was making predictable, regular appearances on one of the old bridges, and the guides advised that three pairs were regularly seen in different locations in the area.

Having said all that about the resident birds that associate with water, you'll find an equally good variety of drier-country birds in this reserve. On my last visit, among the eagles, I spotted tawny, bateleur, Wahlberg's and, most remarkably, a martial eagle battling with a large monitor lizard on the ground beside our vehicle, near Pom Pom. (We found both locked in combat, but at a stalemate. Eventually they disentangled themselves and the great lizard made a hasty retreat under a bush.)

WHEN TO VISIT The area is lightly less seasonal than those further south and west, though there's still a big difference between the game densities through the seasons: they're a lot better when it's drier. As usual, the birding is as good as it gets during the wetter time of the year (December to around March).

GETTING THERE AND AWAY All of these camps work only with guests flying in, usually having made their bookings months before they travel. Driving here is not possible without permission, and is anyway totally impractical.

➤ **WHERE TO STAY** *Map, page 336*
The camps are totally different from one another, perhaps because they're run in different ways by different companies.

Kanana (9 tents) Contact Ker & Downey Botswana (page 214). Opened in 2000 & refurbished in 2019, Kanana stands roughly in the centre of NG27, overlooking the reedbeds of the Xudum River. This gives the camp access to a permanent, deep-water channel, allowing close to year-round boating opportunities. Occasionally, when the waters are very low (Nov–Feb) these may be stopped.

The rooms are expansive, tent-like structures spread out along wooden walkways & elephant-dung paths (more pleasant than it sounds!). All offer views of the channel or seasonal floodplains in front of the camp. The interiors are light & airy, with twin or dbl beds, a circular sisal rug, leather benches & a tree trunk coffee table. On a writing/vanity table there's information about the camp & surrounding area, while the wardrobe includes a small safe. Considerate touches, such as a tin of homemade biscuits & the evening appearance of a whisky decanter, are particularly welcome. The spacious en-suite bathroom, accessed through a wooden door at the back of each chalet, features a modern glass-fronted walk-in shower, his & hers washbasins, & a selection of organic & environmentally friendly complimentary toiletries.

Outside on the shaded veranda, to the front & side of the tents, there's a table & smart wicker chairs, & all the tents face the river from under a cover of riverine trees – jackalberries, knobthorns & sausage trees. These, & the plunge pool, are all linked by sandy paths, illuminated at night by lanterns. There is a fence surrounding the camp to restrict elephant movement, but which allows free movement of other game.

Kanana's main area is a U-shaped wooden building with a large tree in the centre & an alfresco dining deck, several small lounge areas (one with a small library), a bar &, down nearer the water, a 'sandpit' for fires.

Though the comfortable game-drive vehicles have been carefully thought out, with storage for binoculars & lots of space, the camp's strongest suit is its mokoro trips, often including short island walks. It's particularly convenient that when water levels are good, these can be launched directly from the side of the lodge's main area, & into the reedbeds which surround the Xudum River. There are also boat trips, including fishing for bream or catfish (Mar–Dec). A real highlight, especially around Sep–Dec when many species of birds are breeding, is a boat trip to the heronry. As with most camps, Kanana works on the basis of one long safari activity after b/fast, then siesta time after lunch, & another activity following afternoon tea, before dinner. Late-night drives after dinner are also possible. *From US$650 pp Jan–Feb to US$1,355 pp Jun–Oct, FBA exc transfers. Children 7+.* ☉ *All year.* 👑👑👑👑–👑👑👑👑👑

Nxabega Okavango Tented Camp (9 tents) Contact &Beyond (page 214). Nxabega is the most northerly of the camps in NG27, occupying an area of 70km². It's about an hour's drive north of Kanana (though only around 12km as the birds fly) & 11km south-southeast of Xigera, which is in Moremi.

Nxabega's main building is constructed on a grand scale around a huge jackalberry tree, from local timber & reeds, with a high shaggy thatched roof. Inside, it is swish but understated, with clean lines & teak-panelled walls. Lounge seating is warmed by a log-burner in the evenings, the large dining area has an open kitchen & the bar is exceedingly well stocked with obscure liqueurs, imported spirits & good wines. (Unlimited house wine, beers & soft drinks are normally included in the rate, but if you want to drink their cellar of vintage wines dry, they'll charge extra.) There's a lovely large swimming pool, with deep-cushioned loungers, where you'll find staff have ensured your favourite drinks sit in a cooler box, as well as an impressive curio shop & a massage sala.

The large, high-quality tents are raised on wooden platforms about a metre above the ground, with verandas overlooking the floodplain. All are well spread out, with a discreet 30–40m between them. Inside, on sisal mats laid on a smooth wooden floor, twin or dbl beds are draped with embroidered cotton linen, down duvets & assorted pillows. Each tent is thoughtfully furnished with chairs, a dressing table, luggage rack, wardrobe & bedside lamps (powered by a solar-powered battery system). At the back of each tent is an en-suite bathroom with a flush toilet, twin sinks & shower, plus an outdoor rain shower. For families, 2 of the tents have an enclosed connecting walkway.

Activities include 4x4 game drives, mokoro excursions & seasonal boat trips, with good catch-&-release fishing possible on the Boro River. Nxabega has been constructed with great care & generally seems to be run with a higher complement of staff than most lodges, which lends it an air of quality. The food is particularly good, but what is often appreciated most is the flexibility that visitors have over everything: from the timings of meals to the scheduling of activities. These are seldom regimented, & the staff make real efforts to organise activities to suit you. *From US$1,270 pp 11 Jan–Mar to US$3,100 Jun–Oct, FBA. Children all ages.* ☺ *All year.* 😋😋😋😋😋

Pom Pom Camp (8 dbl tents, 1 2-bed family unit) Contact Kwando Safaris (page 215). One of the original upmarket camps in the Delta, Pom Pom is barely 5km southwest of Kanana, yet a game drive between the 2 camps would take 45mins. The camp's classic Meru-style tents incorporate a private lounge area, secluded veranda & a spacious interior, all overlooking a small permanent lagoon. The design is an eclectic mixture of solid wood & African furniture, including twin or dbl beds. Each also has an en-suite bathroom, behind a wall & partially open to the stars.

A central area under thatch brings together the dining area, bar & a curio shop; there's also a small pool. Well-guided activities include day & night drives, mokoro trips from the front of camp, & short walks. There is the opportunity to fish, or watch game & birdlife, from a boat at all times, but only when water levels are very high can you take a boating excursion. (The main flood hits here around May, often filling the dry lagoon in a day. The area's highest water levels usually occur around Jun–Aug.) *From US$600 pp 15 Nov–Mar to US$1,450 pp Jul–Oct, FBA. Children 6+.* ☺ *All year.* 😋😋😋–😋😋😋😋😋

DELTA, ODDBALLS', GUNN'S AND EAGLE ISLAND (NG27B)

Between NG30, NG32 and Moremi Game Reserve, stands a fairly small photographic reserve, just off the southwest side of Chief's Island. This was the first area of the Okavango where tourism really took off in volume, and it's been very interesting to see it transition to smaller numbers of visitors, and more upmarket camps.

Though the camps here differ slightly in their activities, most offer guided mokoro trips along the Boro River and walking on the islands. Bush-wise local guides, whose local knowledge can be excellent (even if their English is more variable), run both excursions. They will almost never be carrying firearms for protection (that's not allowed inside the Moremi Game Reserve), so see *Walking in the bush* (page 177) for a discussion of the safety issues. The exception here is Eagle Island, who will on request walk with rifles on their concession outside the reserve.

CONCESSION HISTORY A short history of the Delta and Oddballs' camps is an interesting illustration of the transition between different types of tourism mentioned previously. It started shortly after Lodges of Botswana bought Delta Camp in 1983. During their first year they not only catered to upmarket visitors, but also used the camp as a base for the mokoro trips of more budget-conscious travellers.

This mix didn't work in one camp, and so in 1984 they built a separate lower-budget camp at the other end of their island. The nickname of their first manager was 'Oddball', and so this became – tongue in cheek – Oddball's Palm Island Luxury Lodge. Oddball's marketing was astute and well targeted, portraying a relaxed, hippie hang-out where spaced-out campers could find paradise on their own island in the Delta. This became a buzzing base for budget mokoro trips in the heart of the Delta – *the* backpacker's place in the Delta, known in hostels from Nairobi to Cape Town, and beyond.

It was very successful. At first they just had showers, toilets and a (fridge-less) bar; campers brought all their own food and kit. It grew fast, eventually encompassing a shop for campers and food, as well as chilled drinks from a fully fledged bar.

When business peaked during the late 1980s and early 1990s, they had up to 120 visitors *per day* flying in, some camping for a night in the camp and others heading out on mokoro trips. Then there were no limits on how many visitors the camp

13

could accept. The camp had a rule that every visitor had to stay at Oddball's for at least one night.

Then two things happened which changed this business. First, in July 1989, the government began raising its national park fees significantly: first from P10 per person per week to P30 per person per day, then to P70, and up to today's P270 per person per day. Mokoro trips from Oddball's had always been to Moremi, but this move increased their prices dramatically.

Second, there had long been a process of tendering for camps, whereby safari operators bid for leases to operate safari camps. In 1996, the government introduced new leases to camps in many of the Delta's reserves, insisting that safari companies not only produce large cheques for rental and royalties (per visitor), but also a 'management plan' for the reserves. These became effective in January 1997.

In drawing up these detailed management plans, the safari companies were forced to look not only at their game and environmental policies, and the sustainability of them, but also how they trained their staff, and what they were doing to help the wider community in the area. This process raised the issues of sustainability, responsible tourism and community development – and placed them in the centre of the government's decision-making process. Thus, it made them important to the safari operators.

Oddball's had started a programme of training their polers as early as 1988. Like all camps, it now insists that all of its polers have a qualification as a professional mokoro guide. The government requires that standards like these are now applied across the board for all the camps in the region.

By 1997, Oddball's alone had about 35 mokoro guides working for them. They were able to renew their leases on Oddball's and its smaller, upmarket sister camp, Delta Camp. However, the government had made a hard bargain: they had to reduce the number of visitors to a maximum combined total of 60 people at any one time. That was 40 guests at Oddball's and 20 at Delta Camp, a fraction of past numbers.

Immediately prices had to be increased in order to cover their costs from a much smaller base of visitors. In December 1999, both camps were extensively renovated; economics dictated that they had to move more upmarket, charging more, to stay in business. The camp on the Oddball's site was rebuilt in much greater style, as a fully fledged upmarket camp that could command high prices. Then the names of the two camps were switched. This newly built camp on the site of Oddball's old site is now known as Delta Camp, while the older camp which was once known as Delta Camp became Oddballs' (with the apostrophe moved to reflect a change of emphasis).

Thus the 1980s camp has become an upmarket camp for the next century, while the original budget camp has been totally rebuilt and refurbished as a new luxurious camp, to standards which are now much higher than they were.

This is a textbook example of what has happened right across Botswana. Pressure from the government, using park fees and the concessions as tools of implementation, has led to lower numbers of visitors to Botswana's wild areas, and hence to more costly safaris and more upmarket lodges. For their money visitors now get a much more exclusive experience, with mokoro guides who have more training and better skills than before – and are paid better as a result.

In summary: the environment benefits, the local people benefit, Botswana's finances benefit, and even the visitors get a better experience – that is, of course, those who can still afford to visit!

GEOGRAPHY As with the whole Delta, the floods in this area are variable and unpredictable, in both duration and timing. The flood usually arrives between

March and May, and remains for an average of four months. However, hydrologists note that since the late 1980s, there was a measured decrease in the amount of water flowing down the Boro River. In the 1994–95 period of water inflow, it was estimated that the lower Boro River received little over half of its long-term average. That water flow then gradually decreased, until – due to heavy rainfall in Angola – water levels rose again, and by 2009 were back to those of the 1980s. The flood levels continued to be very impressive through 2010 and 2011, before starting to return to more normal levels from 2012 to 2017, and declining in the last few years, with the effect of El Niño perhaps having an additional effect in the last year.

Changes in water levels could also be explained by postulating that the western side of the Delta is gradually rising relative to the eastern side. Hence the Thaoge is gradually flooding less, and the Khwai is flooding more. The Boro is fairly central to the Delta, and derives its flow from the Nqoga River (the source of the Khwai River). However, it breaks from this at a very sharp, acute angle, and hence some experts suggest that it should be considered as being influenced the same way as the rivers on the western side of the Delta.

Having said all this, some say that changes in water flows could be caused simply by a hippo changing its regular path in the higher reaches of the Delta or shifting agricultural practices in Angola diverting increasing amounts of water to paddy fields. Whatever the cause, this reduced flow isn't necessarily good or bad for the visitor; but it is a help in understanding some of the gradual changes which are happening to the area's vegetation.

FLORA AND FAUNA The Boro River and its associated floodplains dominate this reserve. A land survey in 1996 estimated that only about 4% of the whole reserve was permanent swampland, but 75% was classed as seasonally inundated swamp and grasslands. The remainder is dry land: riverine forests and grasslands on the islands. So this is a very seasonal environment, which changes annually with the floods.

Flora As just noted, there is relatively little permanent swamp here. Small patches of papyrus are found though, usually in photogenic little clumps beside the main Boro River. Look carefully and you'll also find areas of common reeds (*Phragmites australis*), Miscanthus grass (*Miscanthus junceus*), bulrushes (*Typha capensis*) and a number of floating-leafed, emergent and submerged species.

Perhaps the major feature of the area is some splendid, mature patches of riverine forests that line sections of the Boro River. Here you'll find lots of real fan palms (*Hyphaene petersiana*), often in beautiful dense stands. There's also a scattering of all the 'usual suspects' that you'd expect in riverine forest in the region, including leadwoods (*Combretum imberbe*), jackalberries (*Diospyros mespiliformis*), knobthorns (*Senegalia nigrescens*), sausage trees (*Kigelia africana*), large fever-berries (*Croton megalobotrys*), woodland waterberries (*Syzygium guineense*) and occasional baobab trees (*Adansonia digitata*). However, perhaps the area's most unusual flora are the huge strangler figs (*Ficus* species, probably *thonningii*, *natalensis* or *fischeri*). There are several specimens here enveloping large leadwood trees – an amazing sight.

On the larger island, and particularly on Chief's Island (in Moremi, but visited from these camps), you'll find permanently dry forest areas. These vary from mopane woodlands in areas of clay soil, to areas of acacias where there's more sand.

In the deepest areas of sand you'll find *Terminalia sericea*, the source of the best wood from which to craft traditional mokoro poles.

Adjacent to the river are large areas of very shallow floodplains. A wide variety of grasses, sedges and herbs are found in these areas with various species of *Eragrostis*,

13

Imperata, Panicum, Aristida and *Cymbopogon* being common. More than 200 plant species have been recorded here, though the floodplains are very often dotted with a sparse covering of *Imperata cylindrica,* sometimes known as 'silver spike', with long, rigid leaf spikes growing from a rhizome, some with a small 'spikelet' at the end.

Fauna Of the camps in this reserve, only Eagle Island Lodge (see opposite) conducts game drives, and then only when it is dry enough to do so. As such, a visit here is usually much more about the ambience of the Delta than about spotting game. Come for the experience, let any game sightings be a bonus, and you'll have a good trip.

That said, there are good game densities in the area, and especially on the adjacent Chief's Island. Even from a mokoro you're likely to see hippopotami and crocodiles in the water. Elephants are frequently seen in the drier months, from May to October, wandering through the floodplains; from December to April they are around in smaller numbers.

When out walking on the islands there is a chance of much more game. The area's dominant antelope is the red lechwe, but you will also find tsessebe, impala, zebra, kudu, reedbuck, giraffe, warthog and buffalo. As the area becomes drier with time, blue wildebeest are being seen more often. Roan, sable and waterbuck remain absent from this area. When the flood is at its height, sitatunga are occasionally seen.

The most common predators are lion, spotted hyena and side-striped and black-backed jackals. Leopard are rarely seen, but they will be relatively common as the riverine forest suits them perfectly. Wild dogs and cheetah also occur, but are rare sightings – though we were once lucky enough to see a pack of some 15 dogs from Eagle Island Lodge.

Birdlife Birding is an important feature of all the trips here; you'll probably spend much of your time exploring the area from a mokoro. As mentioned on page 372, the water levels can vary hugely – in October 2002, they dropped by 15cm in just three weeks. So expect the channels and the birdlife to vary greatly through the seasons.

When water levels are lowest, around November to February, you may find skimmers on some exposed sandbanks. Meanwhile knob-billed ducks, long-toed and blacksmith lapwings, and saddle-billed storks are among a whole host of permanent residents. As levels rise, red-winged pratincoles gather in large flocks, and there is always a good variety of kingfishers, from giant and pied to the tiny pygmy and malachite. Woodland kingfishers – insectivorous birds which are usually seen hunting for insects in the riverine forest – appear for the summer around the end of October. They arrive with a variety of migrants, including carmine bee-eaters, aerobatic yellow-billed kites, and paradise flycatchers, the males of which have the most spectacular tails. I have also had a reliable report of black coucals in front of Delta Camp, but haven't seen them there myself.

Much of the Boro channel sees the annual catfish run (page 406), and this area is no exception. If you're lucky enough to catch this then you can spot 30 species or more in a 100m stretch of waterway. Pelicans, skimmers and a wide variety of herons, egrets, storks, stilts, snipes and cormorants all appear in quantity then, to take advantage of the abundant food.

WHEN TO VISIT Though open all year, these camps rely primarily on mokoro trips and so are certainly at their best when the sun is shining and the sky blue, ie: between April and November. If you're camping out then it makes for a better trip if it's not too cold at night, so my favourite months for visiting here would be around

May–early June (though those months can be cold, too) and September–October time. However, these activities heavily depend on water levels – mainly to ensure that guests and guides avoid the hippo population.

GETTING THERE AND AWAY It is possible to embark on a boat transfer to this area from Maun, heading up the Boro River, but this tends to be more costly and take much longer than flying, which is the usual means of transport into this concession. There are several airstrips, including Delta airstrip (✈ DELAIR 19°31.840'S, 23°05.430'E), which is closest to both Oddballs' and Delta Camp, and, about 4km southwest from there, Xaxaba airstrip (✈ XAXAIR 19°33.220'S, 23°03.510'E).

🏠 **WHERE TO STAY** *Map, page 336*

Delta Camp (7 chalets) Contact Lodges of Botswana (page 215). This charming camp overlooks the Boro River from its site next to Moremi Game Reserve. Its 7 rustic, open-fronted reed-&-thatch chalets are consciously incorporated into the landscape, with occasional tree trunks poking through floorboards & leaves hanging down from the thatch. It's a very low-key, immersive, back-to-nature experience. Shaded verandas enjoy views northeast into Moremi, simple timber furniture & pretty basketry is handmade by the local communities, & solar power feeds the lighting & hot-water system. All have an en-suite bathroom, including a shower, toilet & washbasin. There is also a marvellous treehouse in the fork of a jackalberry tree, reached up some steep steps, with a small balcony & a hammock from which to look out over the channel & the wildlife beneath.

Activities centre around walking in Moremi Game Reserve & mokoro trips, with your local guide poling the mokoro & leading walks on the islands. With a little advance notice, it's possible to go on day trips with picnic lunches. *From US$505 pp Dec–Mar to US$900 pp Jul–Oct, FBA. Children all ages. ⏲ All year.* 🛏🛏🛏–🛏🛏🛏🛏

Eagle Island Lodge (12 tented rooms) Contact Belmond (page 214). One of the Delta's first photographic camps, Xaxaba Camp was built here at Xaxaba Island (usually pronounced 'Ka-kaa-ba', unless you're fluent in Khoisan 'click' languages). Changing hands many times over the years, a small bush camp is now on the same spot, known as Baboon Camp & used by wildlife researchers, but close by is this reserve's plushest & most imposing safari lodge: Eagle Island.

Built to a similar design & specification to its sister camp, Savute Elephant Lodge (page 277), guests here can expect hotel-like amenities & high standards of luxury. Each large, opulent tented room, set beneath a thatched roof, has a wide veranda at the front & an outside lounge with an infinity plunge pool. They're well spread-out & linked by well-lit pathways. Inside, each tent is grand: fully furnished with polished wooden floors, rugs & luxurious furniture. The wider-than-usual twin beds, which can be made up as a king-size dbl, have high-quality cotton bedding, bedside tables & twin lamps, all surrounded by a mosquito net. The rooms come with many of the accoutrements of a top city hotel, such as a minibar, safe & AC. At the back, as well as a walk-in dressing room, are his & hers basins, indoor & outdoor showers, a polished black bath & a separate toilet.

The expansive main area includes an open-fronted dining area, where meals are usually served individually, an open kitchen with pizza oven, a comfortable lounge area arranged around a large fireplace, & a swimming pool. There is also a curio shop, a TV room & – down a long grassy spit towards the boat station – the romantic Fish Eagle sundowner bar.

Eagle Island is primarily a camp for water-based activities – mainly mokoro trips & guided walks on the islands, plus motorboat trips during high-water periods (usually Jun–Sep). For most of the year there's also a large 14-seater 'sundowner cruiser' which can slowly coast along the main channels. Helicopter safaris – a great way to see the scenery & animals from a different perspective – are also on offer. When it becomes so dry here that there's not enough water for good mokoro & motorboat trips, game drives are also on offer. *From US$825 pp Jan–Mar & 15 Nov–23 Dec to US$2,862 pp Jun–Sep & festive period, FBA. Children 6+. ⏲ All year.* 🛏🛏🛏🛏🛏

13

Gunn's Camp (6 tents) Contact Kwando Safaris (page 215). Situated on the Boro River, overlooking Moremi Game Reserve, in the 1980s Gunn's ran week-long 'fitness in the wilderness courses'. Now part of Kwando Safaris' Delta collection, things have definitely changed.

Though still a small, classic tented camp, it's more upmarket these days. Twin-bedded Meru tents feature neutral colour tones, teak furniture & en-suite bathrooms with flush toilets, standalone bathtubs & outdoor showers. At the front of each tent is a small, enclosed lounge area with 2 large armchairs, footstools, a desk & electric lighting. Each room also has a wide deck with outdoor seating. The central dining/bar area is set across 3 levels & constructed of canvas & thatch; the upper seating area is noteworthy for excellent views across the river & floodplains. There is also a small swimming pool & a campfire.

Activities are organised in the morning & evening &, like all the camps in this area, usually involve mokoro trips & perhaps a walk on one of the islands. If water levels in the Boro are high enough, boating & fishing are possible. With prior notice, overnight mokoro trips can be arranged, camping on an island with dinner around a campfire & a walk the following morning. At times when the water levels here drop significantly, making water activities impossible, game drives are available. *From US$580 pp Nov–Mar to US$870 pp Jul–Oct, FBA inc conservation fee. Children 12+.* ☉ *All year.* ♛♛♛–♛♛♛♛

Moremi Crossing (16 tents) Contact Kwando Safaris (page 215). The former bush camp of Gunn's Camp (see above), Moremi Crossing has been completely refurbished & renamed, drawing a definitive line under the lower-budget camping options of times gone by. One of the Delta's largest camps, its 16 en-suite Meru-style tents, which include 2 family tents, are all shaded by African ebony, sycamore fig & palm trees. Interiors are simple but comfortable, with dark, polished wood floors, electric lanterns, neat beds & an alfresco shower.

Meals are served in a large thatched central area, which also houses a bar, lounge & curio shop. Most appealing is its crescent-shaped deck that overlooks the permanent Boro River & Chief's Island. Tucked behind is a swimming pool & sundeck with a few sunloungers. The camp aims to be 100% ecofriendly, with solar power & modern waste disposal technology, though it does have a back-up generator.

Activities combine mokoro trips with walks on the islands, as well as motorboat cruises & wilderness camping in dome tents on nearby islands – though this option must be requested in advance. As an alternative to the flight into camp, it's possible to take a boat transfer from Maun as an optional extra (US$120 pp each way, min 2 people). *US$580 pp 15 Nov–31 Mar to US$870 pp Jul–Oct, FBA inc conservation fee. Children 6+.* ☉ *All year.* ♛♛♛–♛♛♛♛

Oddballs' Camp (15 dome tents) Contact Lodges of Botswana (page 215). Southeast of Delta Camp, but also beside the Boro River, Oddballs' (named after its first manager!) was one of the original Okavango camps, welcoming backpackers for budget mokoro trips into the heart of the Delta. It was a buzzing hang-out, listed on noticeboards in hostels from the Cape to Cairo. Today, its clientele will certainly need bigger budgets, & will likely be on shorter trips, but Oddballs' is still full of character & considered a good spot in the Okavango for budget-conscious travellers.

For your money, you now have your own Meru tent, which features a low platform bed with crisp white linen, an alfresco en-suite shower & toilet, & a veranda with a small table & stools looking out over the Delta. There's also a central lounge area with a separate bar, a hammock-strewn chill-out area, a reed-walled massage area & a social firepit.

Unlike the backpackers' camp of old, a stay here now includes all meals & activities. On arrival, guests are allocated a guide for the duration of their stay & activities focus on mokoro trips (they are one of the last camps in the Delta still to use traditional wooden mekoro), & walks on nearby Chief's Island. It is also possible to do a longer mokoro trail that usually includes a 1st & last night at Oddballs' itself, with the intervening nights camping out on islands. Most of your camping kit & food is provided on the mokoro trail, but you must bring your own sleeping bag & drinks, & you generally all muck in & cook together over an open fire. It's essential this is booked in advance, though. There are no motorised activities at Oddballs' – it's a place to enjoy the peace & soak up the Delta atmosphere. *From US$325 pp Jan–Mar to US$530 pp Jul–Oct,*

FBA exc P200 pp wilderness camping fee for mokoro trail. Children all ages. ⏰ All year. 🛏️🛏️🛏️

✳️ **Oddballs' Enclave** (5 tents) Contact Lodges of Botswana (page 215). This slightly more upmarket offshoot of Oddballs' was built in 2009 on the other side of the same island. Depending on water levels, guests will either be transferred by mokoro to camp or take a short walk from the airstrip. The enclave's 'mini-Meru' tents are comfortable but fairly basic & all come with twin or king-size beds, solar lighting & open-air en-suite bathrooms at the rear. The main area, although quite compact, is smartly decorated with a bar & lounge, a large communal dining table &, among other seating options, a fun swing chair made from an old mokoro. The staff here are an established, friendly bunch. The activities are the same as at Oddballs' (see opposite). *From US$440 pp Dec–Mar to US$660 pp Jul–Oct, FBA. Children all ages.* ⏰ *All year.* 🛏️🛏️🛏️–🛏️🛏️🛏️🛏️

XIGERA, MOMBO AND CHIEF'S CAMP (NG28)

Although technically in the NG28 Concession, on the north and west side of Chief's Island, Xigera, Mombo and Chief's Camp were effectively swallowed up by Moremi Game Reserve in 1992. Thus these three private camps and their satellites are covered from page 325.

XUDUM, XARANNA AND OHS (NG29 AND NG30)

Together these equally large concessions cover a total of about 2,500km² on the southern edge of the Delta, sandwiched between southern Moremi and the Sandvelt Tongue. There are two operations here: Xudum and Xaranna run by &Beyond, and a specialist horseriding operation run by Okavango Horse Safaris. The reserves are so large that horse riders and safari campers are most unlikely to come across one another. Travellers should realise that these areas don't have the best game densities, but they are perfect for keen birdwatchers, and there are relatively frequent sightings of lion.

GEOGRAPHY Be aware that the western side of the Delta (from the Thaoge into Lake Ngami) has been drying up since the middle of the last century. As a result of this (or vice versa) an increasing amount of Okavango's water is finding its way into the Muanachira–Khwai system, on the eastern side of Chief's Island.

Thus the floodplains of the west are gradually drying out and being invaded by flora used to drier conditions, while the drier areas of the Khwai River, and areas like Sandibe, are gradually becoming wetter.

FLORA AND FAUNA Visiting one September, I concentrated my time in the far northern corner of the concession, close to Moremi Game Reserve – and probably its most productive area for wildlife. There the land was relatively dry, with only a few areas of floodplain, which is probably fairly typical of these areas towards the southwest edge of the Delta. Because of this location, the annual flood hits these areas relatively late – typically around the end of May or June. Then good water levels last until around the end of October or November.

Further south, around Xudum, there have been extensive changes in water levels over the last decade, which has impacted significantly on the wildlife in this area. We have found February to offer the best birding here.

Flora Across the reserve there are lots of large, open plains covered in tall grass and interspersed with dry established thorny thickets and expanses of turpentine grass (*Cymbopogon* spp). Tall and with sharp barbs, it is widely used for thatching. Among these are dense stands of leadwood trees (*Combretum imberbe*) and knobthorns (*Senegalia nigrescens*). The latter are so numerous that their beautiful, creamy flowers combine to form a powerful perfume.

Perhaps as the result of fires in the past, there are large areas of chest-high wild sage, amid occasional 'islands', typical of the Delta, where termite mounds are dotted among African mangosteens, raintrees, marulas, sausage trees and jackalberrys. Among the larger stands of trees are umbrella thorns (*Vachellia tortilis*) and real fan palms (*Hyphaene petersiana*). But these islands of forest are relatively infrequent and quite poorly defined.

In the far north, the concession has a short boundary with Moremi: the Boro River, which is one of the Delta's best-known channels and is lined in parts by mature riverine forest.

Overall the mixed environment contains a wide variation of tree and plant species, though it doesn't have the beauty of some of the more mature, established forests or floodplain areas.

Fauna There's a good range of species here, typical of the Delta, though game densities are probably not as high as further north. They are certainly highly seasonal with animals proving scarce during the rains, and then numbers improving as the land dries out in the dry season. In the deeper waters around the Boro River, there's no shortage of hippos or crocodiles.

In the north, the dominant antelope is probably tsessebe (in one study of the Delta these made up 70% of all lion kills), though impala are also fairly common, occurring frequently in small groups. Family groups of giraffe and small numbers of zebra and wildebeest are also seen in the drier areas, along with kudu and steenbok, but rising water levels around the Xudum River over the past decade have impacted on the wildlife in this area. Populations of red lechwe and reedbuck have swollen, while those of the plains game such as zebra and wildebeest have declined. Roan, eland and gemsbok are seen very rarely, and generally only in the drier areas on the south side of the NG29 Concession.

Between about December and June elephants occur in small family groups (this is typical of their behaviour in the whole region when food is plentiful). Then they tend to be most frequently found in the mopane scrub areas in the south of the concession. Later in the year, as the land dries up, they gradually coalesce into larger herds, hundreds strong, which move north and east, nearer to the heart of the Delta. Buffalo tend to occur in large herds that move through the concession in the dry season; smaller groups are seldom seen.

Of the predators, lion are by far the most common in these concessions, although numbers have reduced as the plains game moved away. Leopard are also permanent residents and, though generally shy, are increasingly seen around the camps. I didn't see any spotted hyena on my last visit, though they're almost certainly around. Cheetah are very scarce, and generally only seen in the driest of months, around October to December. Then the grass is shorter, and there's more dry land, and so less pressure from lion. At other times of the year the cheetah tend to move away from the water, south and west out of the concession.

Birdlife The varied habitat leads to good birdwatching, and explorations both of the Boro River area and further south can be excellent. Along the river, very large flocks of red-winged pratincoles congregate on the exposed sandbanks, where the grass is cropped short thanks to the grazing lechwe. May witnesses the biggest pratincole colonies, which first appear as the Boro River begins to rise. Before that, while the sandbanks are exposed, you'll sometimes find African skimmers around. Old favourites include saddle-billed storks, knob-billed ducks, night herons, long-toed lapwings and spurwing geese. Look out, too, for the relatively uncommon lesser jacana among the more common African jacanas, and the rufous-bellied heron. With luck, you might even spot the rare grey-tit flycatcher.

In the area's drier grasslands black-bellied korhaans are highly visible, with their eye-catching courtship displays. The wild sage areas here are often burned and, immediately after this, wattled cranes arrive in numbers to dig up snails and other creatures that are exposed by fires.

Raptors which are frequently seen include various vultures, bateleur, fish and tawny eagles, both the black-chested and brown snake eagles, and the occasional martial eagle. The opportunist yellow-billed kites and steppe eagles usually start arriving for the summer in late August, and while the smaller raptors are more scarce, black-shouldered kites are often spotted (and easily recognised because they hover in mid-flight). Trees on the islands also shelter both eagle owls and the occasional Pel's fishing owl, its tawny plumage unmistakable against the dark foliage.

WHEN TO VISIT These areas on the edge of the Delta have more seasonal variation than areas further north, so the game really is significantly better later in the dry season than earlier. As with anywhere in the Delta, the wetter times of the year are better for birdwatching.

GETTING THERE AND AWAY Access is by light aircraft into Xaranna Airstrip; from here it is a 20-minute drive to Xaranna. Road transfers from the airstrip to the riding camps is possible only between about June and September; the alternatives are a helicopter transfer, or a 4-hour road/boat trip from Maun. Guests must have a prior reservation. No self-driving visitors are allowed into these areas, though in case of emergency, it's sometimes possible to access the camps by road – a dusty, bumpy 6 hours from Maun.

WHERE TO STAY *Map, page 336*

Traditional safari camps There are two &Beyond safari camps in this concession – Xaranna and Xudum, both of which are located in the south of the concession. Sadly, fire destroyed Xudum in 2019 and the camp has yet to reopen, so at the time of writing only Xaranna is operational. Its high ratio of staff to guests allows considerably greater flexibility in choice of activities than is often the case, though it's a place for beautiful waterscapes and birdlife, rather than big game.

Xaranna Okavango Delta Camp (9 tented chalets) Contact &Beyond (page 214). Spread out among mature jackalberry & sycamore fig trees, Xaranna Camp faces east across a seasonal lagoon & occupies a super birding spot. It can offer mokoro trips from camp throughout the year, as well as fishing, bush walks & game drives, with trips by motorboat an added option in the winter months, usually Apr–Sep. There's considerable emphasis on flexibility, which is wonderful for guests.

The camp's pale timber construction, offset with olive green & lily-pink interiors, has the strong imprint of a designer at work. The wide, open-fronted central area, under canvas raised on heavy poles, is divided neatly into sections at different levels. At one end is a circular boma-style area & firepit, while at the other is a comfortable lounge, with comfortable chairs & sofas, all in the hallmark green & white; there's even a green-covered Scrabble set! A good library of brown-paper-wrapped books contrasts with other volumes bound in pink & green, & monochrome photos are used to dramatic effect both on walls or under glass as tables or counters.

13

In the centre is a round long table, while more comfortable chairs around the outside invite guests to relax with a drink. The theme continues on to the deck, & even on to the jetty where a family of white-painted hippos is in residence. A curio shop offers a range of items, from the lodge's own sarongs to beaded jewellery, baskets, candles & a few field guides, as well as clothing essentials & even binoculars. There's a guest computer & Wi-Fi in the main area.

To each side of the main building lie chic tented chalets, with gauze panels & coloured blinds. From the private bar at the entrance to the private plunge pool at the back, it's clear that these are far removed from the standard safari tent. In the middle is a good-size bedroom, its twin beds (or a king-size) under walk-in mosquito nets affording a view across the channel. To one side, sharing the view, the bathroom features twin basins, a separate toilet, a free-standing bath, & showers inside & out. A narrow deck runs around the front, linking a sheltered circular day bed to the pool. It's clear that plenty of thought has gone into kitting out these rooms. As well as AC, there are fans on each side of the bed, attached to the bedposts.

Camp-style hanging wardrobes contain everything from toiletries to a hairdryer & torch, & for those in need of activity, each room has its own 'gym in a basket', offering the potential for a workout after all those game drives. There's even a couch in the bathroom, with stylish sarongs as well as bathrobes & slippers, & it's possible to arrange in-room massages. An inverter system means that lights & fans operate at night, while a generator powers appliances (including AC) during the day.

For those who put style & service high on their agenda, this – & its sister camp, Xudum, when it reopens – should be serious contenders. It's a great spot for birdlife & gliding the truly idyllic waterways, though less strong for serious concentrations of big game.

As an amusing aside, rumour has it that the lodge's San-sounding name – 'Xaranna' – is in fact a nod to the concession's previous owner, professional hunter Jeff Rann, who insisted his name be used in that of any lodge here. As far as we know, this name bares no relation to any real word in any of the San languages. *From US$1,495 pp Jan–Mar to U$3,300 pp Jun–Oct, FBA. Children 6+.* ⊕ *All year.* 😮😮😮😮–😮😮😮😮😮

Riding safaris Contact Okavango Horse Safaris (OHS; page 218). Provided that you are a competent rider, seeing the Okavango from horseback can be totally magical. From the point of view of most of the wildlife in the Delta, once you step into the saddle you become part of a four-legged herbivore (albeit a strangely shaped one). Thus generally they relax around you, so you can ride with herds of antelope without disturbing them, and see the environment from a kudu's-eye view. The palm islands, grassy floodplains, mopane forests and clear streams all ensure that the ground beneath you is always changing. Your horse will wade from island to island, where the going is normally quite good and firm along the edges – allowing the rider to move on at a trot and canter.

Having said all this, just as the herbivores perceive you as an antelope, so will the predators. Hence the emphasis on safety that a horseriding operation must have in this environment: it's not unusual to have to gallop to safety from a pride of lion – usually with the guide at the rear, gun in hand.

Perhaps unlike most of the other camps in this book (except African Horseback Safaris, page 218), the precise details of Okavango Horse Safaris' camps are really much less important than the arrangements made for the riding activities. Thus here I'll cover briefly the basics of these safaris, before mentioning the camps and costs.

The horses The 60 horses owned by OHS are all full and part thoroughbred, Pure Arab, Anglo Arab, Friesian cross and Botswana Warm Blood (American Saddlebred cross African Boerperd) horses. All are between 14 and 17 hands high, well schooled and responsive, and have fairly even temperaments. The team will make every effort to match the horse and rider carefully.

Tack and clothes The tack used is English style as well as South African Trail saddles, and each saddle has a seat saver for comfort. Tack is of high quality and kept in good condition. An assortment of saddles is used, including well-known makes such as Albion, Ideals and Symonds. All horses go in snaffle bridles.

OHS produces specific 'clothes lists' for their trips, but they can do laundry in their camp. Like all operations, the air transfers dictate that you stick to a strict weight limit (excess can be left in Maun). Note that proper riding clothes, and clothes of bush colours, are important here. A limited assortment of half chaps and riding gloves is kept in the camp for guests' use, but it is strongly recommended that riders bring and wear their own hats.

Information about you To book a place on one of their trips, OHS will ask you for your age, weight, height and riding experience – as well as the more usual questions of your preference in drinks, specialised dietary requirements, allergies, etc. They'll also require you to fill out an indemnity form in camp before beginning your trip, a practice which is now widespread in camps throughout southern Africa.

Children must be over 12 years old and have a Pony Club certificate or qualified teacher recommendation to attest that they are strong, competent riders.

You must be able to **ride well**. This isn't a place to learn to ride, or to come if you feel at all nervous on a horse. This means being able to 'post to the trot' for 10 minutes at a time, being comfortable at all paces, and being able to gallop out of trouble. It is a great advantage if you are fit and a proficient rider as you'll be in the saddle for 4–6 hours a day, with breaks for meals and refreshments. A separate programme can be organised for non-riding partners, on request, focusing on game drives, walks and mokoro trips.

The maximum **weight** for any rider is 90kg (14½ stone or 200lb), and OHS insist that potential riders may be required to step on a pair of scales!

About the trips Having established that you can cope with the rigours of a riding safari, you have a choice between five-day, seven-day and ten-day safaris, which include rides between some or all of OHS's camps detailed on page 218. The longer trips are scheduled in advance on set dates throughout the year. While this does lack flexibility, it means that you are with a group of people and can get to know each other. Generally, the best time to go is in the latter half of the dry season, between August and October.

On all trips there's a demonstration and talk at the beginning of the safari on how to handle big-game situations, as well as a familiarisation session with the tack. After that, expect to spend between 4 and 6 hours in the saddle each day, broken by refreshment stops. Typically this means that you'll have some picnic breakfasts and lunches, and also 10-minute walks every couple of hours spent in the saddle. (This acts to rest the rider by giving him/her the chance to use different muscles, and it also helps to relieve the horse from the constant pressure of a rider's weight.)

Although the focus here is firmly on horseriding, alternative activities are often possible during afternoons which are not 'day rides'. These can include game drives, birdwatching walks, mokoro rides and night drives.

Riding in big-game country can be difficult, especially when a horse looks very much like an antelope to a hungry lion. Thus safety is a big issue; it's at the root of why this isn't a place for inexperienced riders. An extremely experienced guide accompanies every ride, and they do carry a .375 rifle in case of emergency.

These riding itineraries take a maximum of eight riders at once (again, for safety reasons). They will accept children (recommended 12+), though these must be strong, competent riders (a Pony Club or licensed teacher test pass is compulsory).

The riding camps These aim to be comfortable and simple, and all are staffed. Three meals a day are prepared, with vehicle-supported picnic lunches and bush breakfasts. As with most camps, they emphasise fairly healthy food with fresh vegetables and salads, and bake fresh bread each day. Dinner is often a three-course affair, usually served by candlelight at a dining table beside the campfire. Lighting and power for charging of cameras is supplied by a solar system and there is even Wi-Fi at the main Kujwana Camp.

The camps are spread out over a considerable distance, with Kujwana – the company's base, where the horses are stabled – in the centre and the other permanent camp, Mokolwane, almost 20km to the southeast. All of which goes to emphasise what a large amount of ground these horseriding safaris can cover.

Kujwana Camp (6 tents) Kujwana is Okavango Horse Safaris' base, & this is where the horses are stabled. It is situated on the Xudum River, on a hippo-shaped island of mature trees about 8.5km southeast of Xudum lodge.

At the heart of the camp, overlooking the river, is a raised open-sided 'treehouse' complete with a bar, relaxing day beds & a separate dining area. Adjacent is the central firepit, where b/fast & pre-dinner drinks focus daily.

Stretching out from one side of this main area are 4 Meru-style tents, each on a raised deck with a shaded veranda & twin or dbl beds, a flush toilet & hot-water shower en suite. There are also 2 more spacious, riverside suites for those craving a more decadent bolthole – The Hippo Cradle & The Rocking Horse – which command a modest supplement.

There's a decked area with pole-shaded seating & a refreshing little swimming pool, beside which meals can be taken together.

Laundry is done every day except when the camp is on the move. The camp has 220V solar power & also Wi-Fi, so it's possible to recharge camera batteries & keep in touch with the outside world! There's a serious tack room, training area & lunge ring for the young horses, & barn tours to see all the horses are popular of an evening. 🥄🥄🥄🥄–🥄🥄🥄🥄

Mokolwane Camp (7 tents) Contact Natural Selection (page 215). Mokolwane, known simply as 'Mok', is the most northern of the OHS camps, barely 5km southwest of Pom Pom in the adjoining

NG27A reserve. It is situated among mature trees on a small island, facing east across open plains & a tributary of the Matsebi River. In winter, when the river is full, access is by water only.

While the camp is in part a satellite of Kujwana, this is no longer its sole focus. As well as riding, guests can choose from mokoro trips, game drives & walking. Central to the camp is an open-sided green canvas-roofed dining area, built on 2m stilts beneath a mature African ebony overlooking the plain, & with drop-down sides to keep out the worst of the elements. A levelled-off termite mound under a neighbouring sycamore fig forms a convenient bar area. Sharing the view, & the height, are canvas 'treehouses', spaced out on either side along sand paths. They are simple but very spacious, with twin or dbl beds under mosquito nets, polished wooden floors & a large en-suite bathroom with a hot-water shower overlooking the plains. 🥄🥄🥄🥄–🥄🥄🥄🥄

Fly-camp [not mapped] (6 tents) To the more remote southeast side of the reserve the fly-camp's exact location varies depending on the location of the game. Accommodation is on single stretcher beds supplied with bedrolls, cotton sheets & duvets, & surrounded by mosquito nets. The bathroom facilities include a long-drop toilet, wash stand & a bucket shower (that's the type where the bucket is filled with hot water & raised on a pulley for you by the camp staff!). 🥄🥄🥄🥄–🥄🥄🥄🥄

The costs Unusually for Botswana, but in common with the other riding camps, prices here are quoted in pounds sterling rather than US dollars. Rates range from

£700 per person in January–March and December (no minimum stay) to £1,020 in June–September (set departures for five, seven or ten nights). All rates are full-board, including local drinks, riding, game drives, walks, boats and mokoro trips (water levels permitting). The cost for a child is the same as for an adult.

Between January and March and in December, only Kujwana is used for accommodation, with Mokolwane on request. Between March and November, both camps and fly-camping are used. Guests staying at Kujwana can upgrade to either Hippo Cradle or Rocking Horse riverside suites for £100 per night.

The flight between Maun and airstrip costs £240 per person, with a 1-hour drive to the camps, or £325 for a 25-minute scenic helicopter flight from Maun, which lands directly on the camp island.

CHITABE AND SANDIBE (NG31)

NG31 Reserve covers a relatively small 360km² of the eastern Okavango Delta. However, it's a superb location which looks on a map like a bite out of the southern side of Moremi Game Reserve – between Chief's Island and the Mopane Tongue. Sandibe and Chitabe share this reserve, though generally keep to their own sides. Sandibe has about 160km² on the northern side, and Chitabe (with the adjacent Chitabe Lediba) occupies the southern 200km². The two camps are relatively close, about 12km apart, and they share a central airstrip.

Recent decades have shown the geography of the reserve to be experiencing a period of change, largely attributed to tectonic movements altering the Delta's watercourses. The result is increased water flowing into the eastern portion of the Delta. The Gomoti River, which forms the northern and eastern border of this reserve, was dry from about 1984, but began to flow again in 1999, spilling on to the seasonal floodplains and dramatically increasing the amount of water in this area. Around Chitabe, however, it is much drier, with limited permanent water and only seasonal flooding.

The camps here differ little in their activities: all three are essentially dry-land camps, which concentrate on day and evening game drives, plus guided walks during the dry season, when the grass is low.

FLORA AND FAUNA NG31 is a varied reserve: there are quite marked differences between the northern sides (east and west) and also between these two and Chitabe's area further south, even if the list of species which occur in both are broadly the same. There is a complex mix of environments in this reserve; what follows here is very much a simplification.

The most striking difference is that the northwest of the reserve is a wetter environment than the rest. Just north of this reserve, in Moremi, the Mboroga River flows south between the dry-land areas of Chief's Island and the Mopane Tongue. Forming a number of large lagoons, it splits into two channels. One branch, the Gomoti River, then forms part of this reserve's northern boundary, and all of its eastern side. The other branch, the Santantadibe River, is a deep, wide channel that leads to lots of lagoons and runs down this reserve's southwestern side.

Flora Sandibe overlooks the permanent Santantadibe River from within this watery northwestern corner. Around it there are plenty of open-water areas and floodplains, fringed by belts of riverine vegetation with a high proportion of real fan palms (*Hyphaene petersiana*). The islands here can be large, with the occasional baobab trees growing – an indication that they've been dry islands for a long time.

13

The northeastern side of the reserve, around the location of the airstrip, is a spit of dry land where the habitats seem to occur in belts. There are belts of thick mopane forest interspersed with belts of dry 'acacia thornveld', where you'll find mixed stands of camelthorn trees (*Vachellia erioloba*), umbrella thorns (*Vachellia tortilis*) and the very similar, but thornless, sickle bush (*Dichrostachys cinerea africana*); also buffalo thorn (*Ziziphus mucronata*), with its two types of thorn, which snag on any passing animal (and on clothing) and have earned it the Afrikaans name *wag-'n-bietjie*, meaning 'wait-a-bit'.

There are also bands of lower, more 'scrubby' vegetation, including classic species of deep Kalahari sand like the silver cluster-leaf (*Terminalia sericea*), and some very striking areas forested with large numbers of dead leadwood trees (*Combretum imberbe*). These trees, with their hard, termite-resistant, wood were killed when the water levels in the area changed – some believe the cause is flooding, while others point to the years of drought, which have caused the water table to fall and the trees to absorb increasing levels of salt. Sadly, the result, either way, is the loss of high numbers of hardwoods. They will likely stand for many years, looking from the air like a river of dead trees.

Moving to the south side of the reserve, nearer to where Chitabe stands, you will find a lot of mixed forest areas with classic riverine species of trees like the large feverberry (*Croton megalobotrys*), sausage tree (*Kigelia africana*) and jackalberry (*Diospyros mespiliformis*).

Around here there are some smaller islands surrounded by shallow floodplains covered with hippo grass (*Vossia cuspidata*). The deeper channels are mostly lined by phragmites reeds (*Phragmites australis*) and miscanthus grass (*Miscanthus junceus*). These are permanent channels which don't dry up, and seem to have relatively little seasonal variation; they simply spread out on to wider floodplains when the flood finally arrives, which is increasingly later in the year (around July–August). The waters then begin to recede in September.

At the southern end of the reserve is a belt of soil with a high clay content, providing the perfect substrate for large stands of mopane trees (*Colophospermum mopane*), which sometimes seem so uniform that it almost appears to be a monoculture.

Increasing elephant numbers in the area are having an impact on the vegetation, with the loss of baobabs (*Adansonia digitata*) around Sandibe, marula trees (*Sclerocarya birrea*) and the removal of young leadwoods.

Fauna This reserve has a wide range of game species, dominated by impala, tsessebe, kudu and, on the floodplains, red lechwe. Zebra are fairly numerous, blue wildebeest less so, and giraffe are very common in the bands of acacia thornveld. Reedbuck, duiker and steenbok are often seen, with tsessebe, lechwe and impala present. Eland and roan are found only very rarely (usually towards the south of the reserve), while sable seem to be totally absent.

The sightings of buffalo and increasing numbers of elephants here seem to follow the same broad patterns. Throughout the year there are small resident herds of both around, plus odd old bulls and small bachelor groups numbering around 200. However, from around June to October large breeding herds pass through. Then buffalo herds can number well over a thousand, and herds of a hundred elephants are not unknown.

The key to understanding this is to realise that when there has been rainfall, usually starting around November–December, the big herds move into the large swathes of mopane forest between the Okavango and the Kwando–Linyanti river system; that is, into the interior forests of Kwando (NG14), Linyanti (NG15), Selinda (NG16), Khwai Community (NG18) and Kwara (NG20). While there, their water needs are sustained by the seasonal clay pans which hold water. However, when these pans start to dry up, around May or June, they move back to the areas of permanent water, including this reserve.

The reserve has plenty of lion and recently they seem to have specialised in taking down giraffe. There are two male lions whose territory centres on Chitabe Camp, making sightings – and evening calling – a regular occurrence.

Leopard are common here, with the mixed woodlands and floodplains being an ideal habitat for them. We've had one of our best leopard sightings in Botswana near Chitabe, spotting an astonishing seven leopards including three cubs in 12 hours during a stay at Sandibe, and to reinforce our view that this is one of the country's best concessions for leopard, we saw a male casually reclined in a tree for a photoshoot right outside Chitabe Lediba as we researched this latest edition.

Cheetah stay here throughout the year, and are most frequently seen in the centre of the concession in the area around the airstrip.

The reserve seems to have made a name for itself for wild dog. This may partially be due to the involvement in the reserve's management of Dave Hamman, who took many of the photographs for the book *Running Wild* (page 541), about the 'Mombo' pack of wild dogs in Moremi.

There certainly is a healthy population of dogs here, with the concession once home to a 30-strong pack reputed to be the biggest in the Delta at the time. While this pack is no longer present, the 'Chaos' pack are currently moving between five dens in the concession, successfully hunting and raising a healthy litter of puppies in 2023. They seem to like the marginal floodplains, and will flush the antelopes through plains and islands to catch them. We tracked them hunting impala while researching this guide and watched their emotional return home to the puppies and 'babysitter' dogs. Their interactions are unquestionably some of the most endearing and interesting.

An increasing population of spotted hyena patrol the concession, with vocal clan members often spotted in the vicinity of wild dog kills.

Aardvarks are also sometimes seen here at night, and good sightings of aardwolf occur around Chitabe. Equally, there are excellent porcupine sightings, and both caracal and serval sightings have increased over the last few years. Perhaps this is really a reflection of the camps' enthusiasm for (or at least willingness to organise) serious late-night game drives, rather than a higher density of these animals in this area per se, but either way opportunities exist for the observation of some more elusive creatures here.

Birdlife An avian survey counted 386 species in this immediate area. In general, Sandibe is the better location for waterbirds, although this is by no means exclusive. Along with many more common species, Okavango 'specials' like the Pel's fishing owl, wattled crane, slaty egret (thought to be the world's rarest heron), black coucal and black egret have been recorded. There is excellent birdlife along the Gomoti River by the northeastern boundary of the concession, where malachite kingfishers are particularly keen on perching to fish from the pole bridges.

Chitabe has a wider variation of dry-country birds, with its most common raptor being the bateleur eagle, though there are also good numbers of many other eagles including martial, brown snake, black snake, tawny and western banded snake eagles. Marsh harriers are found in the wetter areas, along with the inevitable fish eagles and even the uncommon migrant European marsh harriers. There are often good sightings of African harrier hawks around Chitabe Camp, while hooded vultures nest in the trees around Chitabe Lediba. Look out for bat hawks in the late evening. Less spectacular, though almost equally uncommon, brown firefinches can certainly be found here.

WHEN TO VISIT As with the rest of the Okavango, the big game here is more diverse and prolific during the dry season, although the birdlife is generally better between December and March. That said, NG31 is in the heart of the Okavango where the water is for the most part permanent, and so these differences aren't as great here as you'll find in some of the more outlying, western areas of the Delta.

GETTING THERE AND AWAY All visitors to these camps pre-book their time and fly to the camps. NG31's main airstrip (⊕ CHITAA 19°27.952'S, 23°22.443'E) is about 7km north of Chitabe and 8km east of Sandibe. This is barely 60km from Maun, making it one of the closest of the Delta's airstrips for camps. However, this doesn't usually affect the price of a trip. Wilderness Safaris, for example, usually charge a set rate for a package including time at its camps and flights to/from them. This price doesn't vary with the position of the camp within the Delta.

🏠 **WHERE TO STAY** Map, page 336
There are three choices, all very good, if very different. Chitabe and Chitabe Lediba are run by Wilderness Safaris (page 216), as part of a joint venture with Flamingo Investments, which has resulted in a very loyal staff: many have been at these two camps for ten years or more. Sandibe is run by &Beyond (page 214).

Unusually for the Delta, both Sandibe and Chitabe Lediba welcome children. At Sandibe they're even given a workbook to keep them busy while teaching them about the area, and the camp staff are adept at ensuring that they don't disrupt the activities or ambience for the other guests. At Chitabe Lediba there are two family tents consisting of two twin-bedded en-suite rooms; in one of these the rooms are linked by an internal hallway, making it well suited for families with younger children. That said, Chitabe Lediba limits children to those aged six or over, unless the whole camp is taken over, and those travelling with under 12s must book a private vehicle.

Chitabe Camp (8 tents) Contact Wilderness Safaris (page 216). Chitabe is set facing southwest across a channel on an old, established tree-island. It first opened in 1997, but since then has been considerably revamped, taking the camp more upmarket. In accordance with Wilderness's current policy, the entire site has step-free access throughout.

Accessed along a sweeping sloped walkway, the whole camp is raised up on wooden decking under typical tall, shard trees of riverine forests, including jackalberries, knobthorns & sausage trees. High, sinuous walkways lead between the tents, the lounge & the dining areas that form the centre of the camp. Here you'll find a large central area with a bar on one side, under thatch, & a separate dining area. Scattered around the open areas of decking are tables &

chairs, & a walkway leads from here down to a lovely lap pool (8m x 3m) alongside a small spa & gym, making it a great spot for siesta relaxation.

The thatched main area is stylish, housing comfortable sofas & a bar creatively crafted from a marula tree trunk. A staircase leads to the firepit, where guests gather for afternoon tea or evening drinks, & there's a lovely library with tree-inspired seating, & a separate dining room with a Japanese feel, with sliding timber-&-gauze doors opening to reveal a beautiful banqueting table, open kitchen & serving counters made of beautifully polished old tree trunks.

The 8 raised tented rooms are spacious, with contemporary interiors, comfortable beds & private verandas. All rooms are en-suite, with an additional outdoor shower.

The camp offers 4x4 game drives (day & night) in covered open-sided vehicles, & its guides have a good reputation for both knowledge & friendliness. *From US$1,480 pp Jan–Mar to US$2,940 pp Jun–Oct, FBA. Children 6+.* ⊕ *All year.* ♛♛♛♛♛

✳ **Chitabe Lediba** (5 tents) Just a few hundred metres from Chitabe Camp (see opposite), on the other side of the same tree island. While sharing the same kitchen & guiding team, & offering the same level of care & service, Chitabe Lediba has a more laid-back, intimate vibe.

Accommodation is very similar, but here there are just 5 tented rooms (2 of which are for families) situated on low wooden decks. Each room has a veranda at its front, complete with cushioned chairs & a table, providing an ideal spot to observe passing wildlife heading to the small 'lediba' (waterhole lagoon). Through sliding glass doors, there's a very pleasant, classic bedroom: smart but unfussy. In the room's centre is a comfortable dbl or twin bed, with a large mosquito net conveniently enveloping the bed & side tables. Additional furnishings include a writing desk & a leather chair with a footstool, & terrific wildlife photographs taken by the camp's owner, Dave Hamman, an acclaimed photo-journalist, hang on the walls.

A super-size polished wooden headboard separates the bedroom from the en-suite bathroom, which has twin basins & a separate shower & toilet cubicle. The outdoor shower is more appealing under the trees. Practical amenities abound, including ample shelving, hanging space & a safe.

The 2 family units (4 guests each), feature 2 en-suite bedrooms (one with an outdoor shower) & sharing a common veranda. One of these chalets features an internal hallway, making it an excellent choice for families.

The camp's open-sided, thatched main area is orientated to give wide views of the floodplains. There's a small bar at one end, deep-cushioned leather sofas in the central lounge, & a long banqueting table at the other end for buffet-style meals. There's a walkway to a small wooden deck on the floodplain edge, perfect for solitary game viewing in the middle of the day or hanging out around the firepit in the evenings. An inviting swimming pool is tucked behind pole fencing, complete with sunloungers & shaded seating. Behind the central area, steps descend to a

boma, where traditional meals & barbecues are occasionally served. There is a playroom for younger children, with 'Bush Buddies' available to look after & entertain children in camp.

The true heart of this camp, however, is its deeply loyal, friendly staff, 8 of whom have been here over 2 decades. It's a testament to the positive relations with owners Dave & Helene & initiatives such as the staff profit-share scheme & the annual 'Educate a Child' payment. Everyone is cheerful & ready to engage in conversations about the camp & the surrounding wildlife. The guiding services are typically excellent, with guides mindful of vehicle positions & lighting to capture great photographs. If you're keen to be out game viewing early, ask for the Monkey Run 'grab & go' b/fast or take a picnic lunch for full days out.

This is one of our favourite camps in the Delta; we often prefer the smaller, more intimate camps & the experience that we had here on our last visit was magical. *Rates as Chitabe Camp (see opposite).* ⊕ *All year.* ♛♛♛♛–♛♛♛♛♛

Sandibe Okavango Safari Lodge (12 suites) Contact &Beyond (page 214). Set in a band of thick riverine vegetation facing the Santantadibe River, Sandibe's architecture draws its inspiration from nature, & its unique wooden structures, all on elevated decks, & its excellent service make for a luxurious, sustainable camp. The main lodge mimics the curvature of a pangolin in shape & houses a beautifully styled indoor & outdoor dining area, as well as the lounge & bar. The décor here is cool minimalist, with plenty of whitewashed wood & a muted sandy pallet enlivened by stylish highlights, notably a suspended copper mokoro. From the bar, a raised deck extends out toward the river, offering a serene spot for a sundowner. As at its sister camp, Nxabega (page 370), Sandibe has a well-stocked wine cellar, which is also used as a venue for private dinners. (Although good-quality house wine is included as part of your stay, the vintage wines & more esoteric, imported spirits cost extra.) There is also a small but interesting curio shop. There's an open kitchen, complete with a pizza oven, & food is a real highlight.

Sandy paths connect the central area with the large suites, which are set on sizeable wooden decks raised up on stilts. Each is clad in the same wooden tiles as the main building to create a modern, almost spherical cabin amid the trees, with the aim of replicating the nest of a golden

13

weaver bird. Inside, timber dominates the design of the open-plan room, with slatted shutters, a cosy lounge & fireplace for the winter months. Past the dbl or twin beds, enclosed in a large mosquito net & cooled by AC, are the bathroom & a walk-in dressing room, divided by an island with suspended oval mirrors & copper basins. A rare use of concrete at Sandibe creates a tube with a skylight at the top, forming an indoor shower, & there is also a spacious outdoor shower. Outside, a private deck, hugged by a low woven fence, is split over 2 levels: the upper with a large sofa & the lower with a circular plunge pool & day bed. There is also a family suite where 2 rooms are linked by a covered walkway.

Regular suite: from US$1,850 pp 11 Jan–Mar to US$4,100 pp Jun–Oct & festive season, FBA. Family suite: from US$6,475 11 Jan–Mar to US$14,350 Jun–Oct & festive season, FBA. Children all ages. ⊕ *All year.* 🐗🐗🐗🐗🐗

STANLEY'S, BAINES', GOMOTI PLAINS, QOROKWE AND BUDGET MOKORO TRIPS (NG32)

This 'multi-purpose area', covering over 1,500km², in the extreme southeast of the Delta is controlled by the local communities through the Okavango Kopano Mokoro Community Trust, which represents the interests of six villages. They have divided the concession into several areas and grant the operational leases to safari companies – perhaps because of this, operations continue to change and evolve here more than they do in most of the Okavango's private areas.

There are currently five separate safari companies with camps in the concession, each with distinct areas in which they operate. An entirely separate area is also used for budget mokoro trips by operators from Maun, who journey along the Boro River. Given that these are so distinct from the safari camps in the area, they're described separately.

FLORA AND FAUNA
Flora NG32 is the concession on the northern side of the buffalo fence that separates it from the more populated areas around Maun. It's at the southern end of the Delta, relying on the Boro and Santantadibe rivers for flooding – and last in line to receive the water. In a dry year, the floods can be very low and patchy.

This means that there are relatively few short-grass plains that are regularly flooded, but significant patches of floodplains that are only intermittently wet. These provide an ideal base for a profusion of the invasive wild sage (*Pechuel-loeschea leubnitziae*), which covers large open areas with its aromatic grey-green foliage. Where they've had slightly longer to become established, you'll find the distinctive rounded outlines of candle pod acacia bushes (*Vachellia hebeclada*) starting to appear in these areas – as one of the first shrubs to move in it usually indicates that an area has been dry for many years. In some of these open areas where the recent floods haven't reached, you'll find a profusion of termite mounds.

Aside from this, driving around NG32 near Stanley's the vegetation seems to occur in strips, including linear expanses of riverine forest where the major tree species are leadwoods (*Combretum imberbe*), jackalberries (*Diospyros mespiliformis*), marula (*Sclerocarya birrea*) and sausage trees (*Kigelia africana*). There are relatively few areas of deep, deep sand here and not that many acacia glades, but there are some quite dense – and very attractive – concentrations of real fan palms (*Hyphaene petersiana*).

When visiting with a mokoro poler, you'll see a very different side to the area. Unless the flood has been very high, you'll probably be poling within the vicinity of the Boro or the Santantadibe. This is at the very shallowest end of the Delta, so expect large areas of miscanthus grass (*Miscanthus junceus*) and common reeds

(*Phragmites australis*), plus the occasional floodplains of hippo grass (*Vossia cuspidata*). In the east of the concession, around Qorokwe and Gomoti Plains, poling is on the tributaries of the more open Gomoti and Santantadibe rivers, where vegetation is far more varied.

If you do pole up the Boro, then you'll find the environment generally gets more interesting as you continue. After a few days, you'll leave behind some of the more boring stretches of reeds, and start finding wider floodplains around you, and more lagoons. Wherever you pole, the islands on which you stop will often be classic little palm islands fringed with palms and the riverine forest.

Fauna   The game densities generally get better as you head further northeast in the area, around Qorokwe and Gomoti Plains, both of which are close to the Gomoti River. Certainly, the game around Stanley's and Baines' is generally quite sparse, with the exception of elephant.

Impala are probably the commonest antelope, with tsessebe a close second and red lechwe certainly dominating any areas which are flooded. Kudu, giraffe, zebra, reedbuck, warthog and occasionally wildebeest are all found here; sable, roan and waterbuck are not. Elephant and buffalo occur singly during the wetter parts of the year, and pass through in larger herds as the dry season reaches its end.

When the flood is at its height, there may be the occasional sitatunga around, but apart from a few places on the rivers, there aren't enough papyrus reedbeds to support them.

Lion are around in good numbers, and while leopard occur, they're not frequently spotted. Wild dog pass though, and sightings of them seem to increase between about October and December. However, the open wide plains where you could follow them are limited in the concession.

Cheetah are certainly around and often seen in the drier areas – on one drive here during a fairly brief visit one of this book's contributors spent a magical 25 minutes with a male cheetah as he strolled from termite mound to termite mound searching for the perfect vantage point.

In 2017, both black and white rhino were relocated into this vast concession from South Africa. However, due to increased poaching concerns (page 330), these rhino have been relocated to the Khama Rhino Sanctuary (page 486).

Birdlife   NG32 is a classic edge-of-the-Delta reserve that has a good mix of dry-country and shallow-water bird species. The most common species include red-eyed, mourning and Cape turtle doves, which all greet the morning with a variety of gentle coos. Identify the last by their lyrical exhortations to 'work harder, work harder'.

Other birds frequently seen here include long-tailed shrikes, red-billed quelea, buffalo weavers, lilac-breasted rollers, blacksmith lapwings and long-tailed and glossy starlings. Crimson-breasted shrikes provide startling flashes of red; Meyer's parrots can often be seen as a flash of colour flying at speed.

In more open areas you'll find red-billed and Swainson's spurfowl, flocks of helmeted guinea fowl, kori bustards and occasional ostriches. Sandgrouse are common in acacia groves, as are yellow-billed hornbills, while their red-billed cousins prefer the reserve's mopane woodlands.

The floodplains support a varied cast of waders and waterbirds, including the occasional wattled cranes. This is a good reserve for raptors: bateleur (short-tailed) eagles, black-breasted and brown snake eagles are especially common, and Gabar goshawks are frequently seen.

WHEN TO VISIT Like most of the areas on the edge of the Delta, the game densities are better during the dry season than during the rains. So while from June to October is the best time to visit for game, the birdwatching is usually more interesting during the rains, from around December to March.

GETTING THERE AND AWAY For those staying at Stanley's and Baines' camps, access is by air to the nearby airstrip; you're not allowed to drive yourself.

WHERE TO STAY *Map, page 336*

There are five very different safari operators in the concession. The western side is home to Sanctuary Safaris' long-established, classic camps: Stanley's Camp and Baines' Camp. Further east, Wilderness Safaris' Qorokwe stands close to the Santantadibe River. Machaba Safaris operate two camps: Gomoti Plains and their latest addition, Kiri Camp which opened in 2022 in the far west of the concession. Okavango Hidden Gems have two camps – island-based Amber River Camp and Camp Maru which opened May 2024. Also opened in 2024, African Bush Camps' latest boutique-style property, Atzaró Okavango, is the furthest south of the camps.

Amber River Camp (6 tents) Contact Okavango Hidden Gems (page 215). A 30min mokoro ride downstream from its sister camp Camp Maru (see opposite), Amber River Camp offers the same classic tented style & activity options from its island location. It's a lovely spot with 6 spacious tented suites on low decks – 3 on each side of the island – with elegant canvas shades extending over the tents & veranda areas. Unpretentious but thoughtfully furnished, each tent has an outdoor bath & shower as well as a standard en-suite & comfortable bedroom with separate sitting area. Decked footpaths lead to the central area campfire & lounge/dining tents, where friendly staff are always on hand.

Mokoro rides, walking & game drives are on offer year-round, & there's a swimming pool with sundeck for relaxation between game viewing. *From US$600 pp mid-Jan–Mar to US$1,250 pp Jun–Oct, FBA exc transfer from Maun (from US$100/200 by road/helicopter each way). Children 12+.* ☺ *All year.* 🐗🐗🐗-🐗🐗🐗🐗

Atzaró Okavango Camp (8 tents, 2 villas) Contact African Bush Camps (page 214). Opened in Mar 2024, Atzaró is the latest luxury offering from this long-established operator. There is nothing 'bush camp' about Atzaró though. It is very much styled on a 'boutique hotel in the bush' model, with bar staff donning flat caps to serve cocktails from the jade-green marble bar, & decadent, super-size interiors. There's a 2-storey, circular central lounge for relaxing, with views across the palm-fringed lagoon, dining on the deck under ivory umbrellas & a lower-level firepit with a sweeping, cushion-covered semi-circular bench.

Atzaró has 8 indulgent suites with AC & 2 tented villas for families. These enormous rooms feature soaring ceilings, plush interiors, en-suite bathrooms with inside & outside showers, private plunge pools & minibars. Chesterfield sofas, deep-pile rugs, sash curtains & oversized lampshades all give distinctly traditional grandeur.

There's a range of facilities such as a 20m freshwater lap pool overlooking the lagoon, a spa & wellness centre, a well-equipped gym, & Wi-Fi in the rooms. Away from camp, activities include walking safaris, catch-&-release fishing, mokoro excursions (depending on water levels) & game drives (day & night) with off-roading capability. *From US$775 pp Jan–Mar & Dec to US$1,575 pp Jun–Oct, FBA inc conservation fee. Children all ages.* ☺ *All year.* 🐗🐗🐗🐗🐗

Baines' Camp (6 rooms) Contact Sanctuary Retreats (page 215). Built in 2005, Baines Camp was then a trail-blazing camp in Botswana's creation of luxury, fly-in safaris. Named after the Victorian explorer & artist Sir Thomas Baines, its 2019 refurbishment has given this intimate camp a more funky edge. Vibrant bursts of colour in the soft furnishings & objets d'art are a refreshing departure from the neutral tones typically found in safari camps, & its innovative construction using recycled drinks cans & elephant dung-infused plaster is impressive. Plus, even by Botswana's high standards, the view from Baines' Camp is breathtaking.

With just 6 suites, it's an exclusive experience. The thatched suites, all raised on high wooden decks overlooking the surrounding bush & tall papyrus beds that flank the Boro River, are lovely. Their stylish décor includes a four-poster bed, private deck & an en-suite bathroom with a unique outdoor 'star bath'. A highlight here are the private 'star beds', which are set four-poster style under mosquito nets, & can be rolled out on to the decking under the stars.

The main area of the camp has a lovely lounge, waterfront dining area where sitatunga have been known to graze as you eat, & a spacious self-service bar with a pizza oven. There is also a pretty infinity pool & sundeck with shaded day beds.

Activities include 4x4 game drives (which in low water can include the southern section of Chief's Island in Moremi Game Reserve), boat excursions & mokoro trips (depending on water levels), & walking safaris on request. *From US$1,271 pp 3 Jan–Mar & Nov–20 Dec to US$2,400 pp Jun–Sep & 21 Dec–2 Jan, FBA inc airstrip transfers. Children 16+.* ⊕ *All year.* 🛡🛡🛡🛡–🛡🛡🛡🛡🛡

Camp Maru (6 tents) Contact Okavango Hidden Gems (page 215). Reopened in May 2024, Camp Maru is inspired by the classic safari camps of the early 20th century: simple but comfortable & stylish. Within a grove of giant leadwood trees, there's a central tent that boasts a well-stocked library, small lounge & communal dining area. There's also a swimming pool surrounded by loungers & a firepit for evenings beneath the stars.

Inside each of the 6 spacious tents, king-size or twin beds are made with crisp white bedding, & soft blankets are folded & tied with tan leather straps. Neat timber furniture, flasks of cold water & diamond-patterned matting are all smart, functional & low-key. The en-suite bathrooms share the same unpretentious elegance, with a lovely timber vanity, silver sink & hot-water shower. Solar power is used throughout the camp.

The location, at the far southern reaches of the Delta's annual floods, means water arrives here last & leaves first. However, Maru does benefit from being sited beside an expansive permanent lagoon, & its water is therefore a draw for a plethora of animals & birds, from resident hippo bloats to elephants & buffalo quenching their thirst.

Year-round water & land activities are on offer: game drives, mokoro trips & walking safaris. There are also opportunities to see some of the camp's projects, like beekeeping. Camp access is either by a 2½hr road transfer from Maun or a 25min helicopter trip. *From US$600 pp mid-Jan–Mar to US$1,000 pp Jun–Oct, FBA exc transfer from Maun (US$100/200 by road/helicopter each way). Children 12+.* ⊕ *All year.* 🛡🛡🛡🛡–🛡🛡🛡🛡

Gomoti Plains Camp (10 tented rooms) Contact Machaba Safaris (page 215). Under the same ownership as Machaba Camp (page 312) in the Khwai area & Kiri Camp (page 392) to the western side of this concession, Gomoti Plains is a masterclass in understated safari chic. Overlooking a seasonal side channel of the Gomoti River & its fan palm-fringed floodplains, it's a smart, relaxed tented camp with a supremely professional management team. It's designed with solar power, low-energy appliances & sophisticated waste-disposal systems to minimise its impact on the environment.

The linear central tent is the hub of camp activity & a delightful place to hang out. The lounge is tastefully furnished with generous sofas & high-backed wicker chairs. Planet-like woven lampshades hang from the canvas ceilings, sizeable bookcases house a wide range of books on local wildlife, plants, geography & history, & there's even a felt-topped games table for afternoon dominoes or cards.

A small self-service bar ensures you're always able to get a drink – hot or cold – & a tasty treat. The adjacent dining area has tables set up individually for b/fast & lunch, which is served from the new open kitchen area, but in the evenings, these are usually combined – & often moved under the stars – to create a more sociable atmosphere. The friendly team here are flexible & happy to accommodate guests' preferences though.

The central tent opens on to a narrow decking area with additional seating, leading to a tidy sandy space where early morning coffee or tea & pre-dinner drinks are served around a campfire. At night, glowing paraffin lamps hanging from shepherds' crooks create a nostalgic safari ambience. Between activities, there's a really lovely curio tent for souvenir shopping: safari clothes, stylish hats, books & locally made crafts. A short distance away, a large swimming pool overlooks

13

the river, with carefully sloping sides into the water should an elephant end up inside. The pool area features a pole-shaded deck with sunloungers & umbrellas, providing a tranquil spot to unwind after a game drive.

The 10 smart tents are fronted by a timber deck where you'll find a day bed & a couple of directors' chairs, & most overlook the channel. A zipped door opens into a dbl or twin bedroom with its own sofa, good lighting, plenty of hanging space, & a neat en-suite bathroom with inside & outside showers & a separate toilet. For families or friends travelling together, there are 2 specially designed units – Hippo & Elephant – where 2-bedroom tents share a bathroom & small lounge. Alternatively, small groups (4–6 people) should consider the adjacent private camp – Gomoti Private (see below).

Gomoti Plains benefits from proximity to a 3km stretch of Gomoti riverfront, making game viewing & birdwatching productive & the landscape attractive. There are herds of buffalo up to a 1,000 strong in the area, who flock to the water in Jun–Nov. Along with day & night game drives, there are motorboat & mokoro excursions (seasonal, usually Jun–Sep), guided walks & – back at camp – the option of a spa treatment (extra cost) by a qualified therapist in the privacy of your own room. It all adds up to a well-designed camp in an area of very good game. *From US$1,080 pp 11 Jan–Mar to US$1,930 pp Jun–Oct, FBA inc conservation fee. Children all ages; private vehicle US$500/ night – necessary if children are under 6. ⊕ All year.* 🐘🐘🐘🐘🐘

Gomoti Private   (2 tented suites, sleeps up to 6) Contact Machaba Safaris (page 215). Nestled at the far end of the Gomoti Plains camp, Gomoti Private mirrors the design of the main camp but on a smaller scale. Featuring just 2 tented rooms – one a spacious 2-bedroom family room & the other a charming tented suite with an outdoor bath – this exclusive-use mini-camp operates completely independently from the main camp, offering privacy & flexibility. With its own lovely tented lounge & dining area, infinity pool, excellent manager, private chef & guide, it's a wonderfully personalised service, making it a great option for small groups & families. Guests here are welcome to visit the souvenir shop & larger pool at Gomoti Plains too. Activity choices are the same as at the main camp (page 391). *US$2,230/1,530 adult/child*

up to 11 years (min 4 guests), FBA inc conservation fee. Children all ages. ⊕ All year. 🐘🐘🐘🐘🐘

Kiri Camp   (10 tented suites) Contact Machaba Safaris (page 215). Machaba Safaris' 2nd camp in this concession opened in Jun 2022, under a lush canopy of towering jackalberry & ebony trees. Set on an island with panoramic views across the seasonal Kiri Channel, the superb safari-chic aesthetic that Machaba Safaris do so well is very much in evidence here. It's managed by a supremely friendly & professional team, & maintains a strong commitment to minimising its environmental impact.

On a sprawling central deck, punctuated with living tree trunks & a large termite mound, a duo of open-fronted tents house the cosiest of lounges filled with deep cushioned sofas & beautiful objets d'art & a welcoming dining room. Sweeping, lantern-lit stairs lead to a lower-level firepit surrounded by leather directors' chairs, & a network of sandy pathways through the bush fan out to the tents & swimming pool.

The well-spaced 8 standard & 2 family tents are all elevated on decks that offer sweeping panoramas across the floodplains. Each tent is equipped with twin or dbl beds under cooling ceiling fans, shaded verandas with comfortable seating to spot wildlife between activities, & spacious en-suite bathrooms, thoughtfully designed to allow for open-air showers & a gorgeous bath. The family tents consist of 2 rooms, each with an en-suite bathroom, connected by a communal sitting area. The design in all the rooms is pared-back, casual elegance.

Kiri Camp offers both land- & water-based activities, with the latter contingent on water levels; typically these are limited during the drier months (Apr–Sep). Day & night drives, guided walking safaris on nearby islands, mokoro excursions navigating the shallow lagoons, boat trips & catch-&-release fishing on the Kiri River are all on offer. Relaxation between activities can be enhanced with in-room massage services. *From US$1,080 pp 11 Jan–Mar to US$1,930 pp Jun–Oct, FBA inc conservation fee. Children all ages; private vehicle US$500/night – necessary if children are under 6. ⊕ All year.* 🐘🐘🐘🐘🐘

Qorokwe Camp   (9 suites) Contact Wilderness Safaris (page 216). This feather in Wilderness Safaris' cap is a 'classic' camp, putting it in line with the likes of DumaTau (page 289), Chitabe Camp (page 386) & Little Vumbura Camp (page 354). Qorokwe is contemporary, with industrial-design overtones, making it quite distinct from traditional tented safaris. Its main area features a geometric wrought-iron & wood structure, open to views of the lagoon & woodland beyond, & a pleasant swimming pool & firepit. Telescopes on the deck provide closer observation of passing wildlife & birds near the permanent lagoon, & there's a small linear pond with a few papyrus plants. Inside, the main area mixes modern & traditional elements with cowhide patchwork rugs, woven stools, lovely baskets & terracotta pots. There's a central bar, plentiful seating, including a swinging sofa, & a large separate dining room.

Qorokwe's 9 suites, sharing the same flat-roofed, angular design as the main area, are perched on high black steel frames above the ground, to offer wide views of the lagoon & bush beyond. Inside, they exude modern elegance, with leaf-veined timber, burnished metal latticework, floor-to-ceiling windows, retractable curtain panels, large sliding doors on to the deck & beautifully curated soft furnishings. There's a spacious open-plan room with a lounge area, a bed surrounded by a mosquito net, ample storage, ceiling & standing fans (no AC), & even a yoga mat with dumbbells. The deep free-standing bath has a super view & the shower has a sliding wall for a semi-outdoor experience. One of these is a spacious family unit with 2 bedrooms either side of a shared lounge, & a bonus plunge pool on the veranda.

Qorokwe's staff consistently provide friendly service, & activities at the camp focus on game drives, but depending on water levels, guided walks, mokoro excursions & boat trips on the nearby Santantadibe River are also possible. Qorokwe has access to a 9km stretch of the Gomoti waterfront, which offers more productive game viewing in a pretty area, albeit at the far side of the concession & a reasonably long drive. If you plan on visiting this area with your guide, we recommend requesting a picnic lunch & making a day of it. Back in camp, the in-house beauty therapist offers in-room treatments & there's a shop selling various items including baskets made by the staff. *From US$1,480 pp 6 Jan–Mar to US$2,940 pp Jun–Oct, FBA. Children 6+.* ⊕ *All year.* 👑👑👑👑👑

Stanley's Camp (10 tents) Contact Sanctuary Retreats (page 215). Originally built by a maverick local character, Alistair Rankin (the subject of a number of local bush myths – some involving mokoro trips, buffalo & uncomfortable nights spent in trees!), Stanley's was completely rebuilt by Sanctuary Retreats at the turn of the millennium, & fully refurbished in 2017.

The open-plan dining-lounge area sits under a large canvas tent (think 'big top' circus), on slightly raised wooden decking. Wildlife photos printed on oversize canvases stand out from the cream walls, with the odd woven basket or wooden carving. The sitting area takes centre stage, with a couple of comfy sofas & a few leather chairs. The library is a slightly eccentric collection of novels, magazines & reference books, with an enormous vintage map of Africa of the wall. There's a separate bar constructed round a tree & a small curio shop that also showcases baskets made by the staff. A short wooden walkway leads to a small pool with sunloungers, a couple of umbrellas & unobstructed views of the floodplains, where elephants regularly congregate.

Dinner may be a social affair, with everybody eating together, but other meals are usually taken at individual lantern-lit tables. If you're staying for a few days you can request a picnic lunch, so that you can stay out in the bush all day. After dinner, there are often night drives, but otherwise guests usually retire for drinks & a chat to a small firepit.

The camp's tents are to one side of the main area. A covered deck extends from the front of each, with a day bed & a hammock for that all-important midday siesta. Inside, a contemporary twist on classic safari tents is evident: polished wooden floors, beautifully made beds, pale timber furniture, leather headboards, angle-poise bedside lights & pale linen curtains to cover panoramic ceiling-to-floor gauze windows. Each tent has its own Scandi-chic en-suite bathroom with a separate toilet & shower cubicle.

Activities include 4x4 game drives (which in low water can include the southern section of Chief's Island in Moremi Game Reserve), mokoro trips (Jun–Sep, depending on water levels), & walking safaris. Our own experience of wildlife in this area over the last decade has been highly variable, from visits when we've seen leopard & hyena cubs, lions, herds of over 2,000 buffalo & great general plains game, to trips when we've seen little bar small elephant herds. That said, the birdlife is invariably very good. *From US$1,050 pp 3 Jan–Mar & Nov–20 Dec to US$2,150 pp Jun–Sep & 21 Dec–2 Jan, FBA inc airstrip transfers. Children 6+ ⊕ All year.* 🌺🌺🌺🌺

BUDGET MOKORO TRIPS NG32 is the end destination for virtually all of the one- to four-day mokoro trips offered from Maun, through the Okavango Kopano Mokoro Community Trust (OKMCT). These must be booked through a private tour operator in Maun, who will organise a road transfer into the Delta; you cannot just turn up. For full details of how to choose a trip, and what to expect, see page 211.

These trips aren't really about game, although you may see some. Relax, take a bird book and a pair of binoculars, and enjoy the experience of being poled along the waterways, and seeing some of the birdlife, and water-life, close up. My first trip into the Delta was like this – and it was enchanting. Subsequently I've seen more interesting areas of the Delta, and infinitely better game, but it's still hard to beat the sheer joy that you'll get from floating around on a mokoro in such an amazing environment for the first time.

From my experience, mokoro trips are much more fun when the sun's shining and the sky is blue; grey skies and (even worse) rain do take the edge off it. Thus best avoid January and February if you have a choice – and ideally come between about April and the end of October.

See my comments on walking (page 178) before you set off on foot with your poler in search of big game – as none of these trips is likely to be led by someone that I'd describe as a professional walking guide, and none of the polers carries any guns.

SANKUYO TSHWARAGANO MANAGEMENT TRUST (NG33 AND NG34)

NG34 covers an area of about 900km², an area with good game that encompasses part of the road between Moremi's South Gate and Maun. Thus, and very unusually for the region, it's a private concession through which you can drive yourself, albeit only on the main gravel road leading into and out of the area. The concession is now divided into five zones, each run by a different operator.

NG34 is run for the benefit of the local community, through the Sankuyo Tshwaragano Management Trust – and it's a reserve that has seen more frequent changes than most. Until about 2001 it was the location for Gomoti Camp, which has since been rebuilt and renamed a number of times, before Kwando Safaris opened Rra Dinare here, and then its nearby partner camp, Mma Dinare, in 2018. In 2022, Motswana-owned tour operator Stars of Africa opened a camp towards the centre of the concession (Mogogelo).

Meanwhile there's long been an intermittent presence here of animal researchers, many of whom seem to have subsequently written books. Naturalist and lion researcher Peter Katz was based here for several years. His book, *Prides*, was published in 2000, and more recently the three children staying with him and his partner wrote *The Lion Children* (page 546).

Before that, John 'Tico' McNutt began a wild-dog research unit here in 1989, co-authoring *Running Wild: Dispelling the Myths of the African Wild Dog* (page 541). The project has broadened and developed since then, and now – as the Botswana Predator Conservation Trust (w bpctrust.org) – conducts research into leopard, lion, cheetah and spotted hyena, as well as wild dog.

FLORA AND FAUNA Ancient floodplain habitats dominate large tracts of land in the reserve, with mature acacia trees and fertile grasslands, while away from the floodplain, mopane woodland comes into its own. Most of the area around the Gomoti River, where Rra Dinare and Mma Dinare camps are based, is an attractive combination of big open floodplains with occasional islands.

Like much of the Delta around eastern Moremi, the flood patterns here do seem to have changed recently. When Tico McNutt first came in 1989, the Mogogelo River, near Santawani, still had water in it; since then this has dried up and hasn't flowed for many years. Similarly, while it still fills seasonally, in recent years the Gomoti River has not been flooding as much or for as long as it used to.

With something as complex as the changes in water flows and levels in the Delta, everyone has a slightly different opinion. Perhaps one of the most pertinent comments on this was, allegedly, from local wit Willy Philips, who commented that 'the only reliable water in the Okavango is the water in the toilets'.

Flora Although parts of NG34 feature quite thick, and relatively unproductive, mopane woodlands, the floodplains that spread out from the rivers, including the western side of the reserve adjoining the Gomoti River, are much more interesting.

Even driving on the main road south from South Gate to Maun you'll get a flavour of this, as you pass through some stretches of open acacia savanna – where you'll find very good populations of giraffe, if you're not travelling through too fast. The dominant species here is camelthorn (*Vachellia erioloba*), though you'll also find a few umbrella thorns (*Vachellia tortilis*) and some stately old leadwoods (*Combretum imberbe*) among them. In recent years, a rise in elephant ringbarking has caused the death of a number of the largest acacia and knobthorn trees, transforming some of these areas into acacia scrub, as young trees are effectively coppiced by the wildlife. This is classic mature Kalahari sandveld – and matches many people's image of Africa. These areas run like veins through the reserve, marking out the areas of deepest sand.

Around the Gomoti River, things are different. Here you'll find plenty of lovely areas of old riverine forest, containing all the usual species including sausage trees (*Kigelia africana*), marula trees (*Sclerocarya birrea*), jackalberries (*Diospyros mespiliformis*) and African mangosteens (*Garcinia livingstonei*). You'll also find knobthorns (*Senegalia nigrescens*), which are immediately obvious around September and October for their creamy-white flowers and almost sickly-sweet perfume. Occasionally you'll find small islands, or patches, of these standing together.

The floodplains here come in two broadly different varieties. Those plains that still regularly flood are usually covered with short grass – a photogenic environment that's easy for game viewing. The others, which have been dry for a number of years, have often been largely covered with wild sage (*Pechuel-loeschea leubnitziae*). This classic 'pioneer species' thrives in areas that have recently been disturbed and can quickly take a hold when a floodplain dries out. Other, slower-growing species of shrubs and trees will eventually germinate and take over these areas.

Amid all of these plains, you'll find islands, large and small. These have riverine trees and shrubs on them, including a scattering of real fan palms (*Hyphaene petersiana*) and a notably high density of knobthorn trees (*Senegalia nigrescens*). In recent years, the inner areas of some islands have become noticeably more Kalahari-esque with the loss of mature, hardwood trees and the increasingly exposed sand covered with little other than wild sage. Areas newly colonised by feverberry, Kalahari apple leaf, blue bush and shepherd trees are visibly stunted by elephants.

Fauna My first memory of this area was in May 1993, when I'd been driving myself through Chobe and Moremi. It had been a good trip, though we were disappointed not to have seen any wild dogs. By the time we left South Gate, in the heat of midday, we had given up trying to spot animals. We were in NG34, but didn't think of this as a wildlife reserve.

After about 14km along the main track, we slowed down to find our way blocked by a large pack of very lazy wild dogs wandering about the road, and lounging by the side of it, yet showing little interest in our vehicle. They posed for photographs, as harmless as lapdogs, for about 30 minutes until they finally wandered off – thus providing us with one of the best game sightings of our whole trip. Only now, knowing how long researchers spend following the dogs in this area, do I understand why these dogs were so totally relaxed with our vehicle.

The most common antelope here is probably the impala, a favourite prey of leopard and wild dog, but you'll also find good numbers of tsessebe and kudu, along with giraffe, zebra, wildebeest and warthog. Elephant and buffalo are seen year-round, with large herds often moving through the area in the dry season. Roan are also seen occasionally.

Of the predators, lion dominate, although the area certainly has a permanent presence of wild dog, and there's no shortage of spotted hyena. The landscape is a good habitat for leopard, too, and they have become less shy in recent years. Cheetah occur, but tend to hide in the mopane away from the floodplains so aren't seen often.

Birdlife The birdlife reflects the variety that you'll find anywhere in the Delta, and obviously depends heavily on the water levels. One checklist for NG34 and the small NG33 lists 208 species, but doesn't even pretend to be exhaustive.

However, the more common birds which are most frequently seen on the Gomoti floodplain around the lodges and campsite include the long-tailed and glossy starlings (from which the former Starling's Camp took its name), plus red-eyed, Cape turtle and mourning doves; blacksmith and crowned lapwings; long-tailed and crimson-breasted shrikes; red-billed queleas; buffalo weavers; lilac-breasted rollers; and white-backed and hooded vultures. Pelicans, several species of egret, ibises and yellow-billed storks jostle for position in the pools, and wattled cranes and paradise flycatchers or whydahs are also spotted periodically.

Meanwhile in the acacia woodlands, along with the ever-present doves, you're likely to find kori bustards; large flocks of helmeted guinea fowl; red-billed and Swainson's spurfowl; southern ground and grey-, red- and yellow-billed hornbills; Meyer's parrots; double-banded, Burchell's, Namaqua and yellow-throated sandgrouse; plus the occasional Gabar goshawk, bateleur and ostrich.

WHEN TO VISIT Big-game animals are more prolific here during the dry season, as with the rest of the Okavango – although the birdlife is generally better between December and March. Because NG34 is on the southwest side of the Delta, the flood reaches it last. Also note that NG34 contains some of the closest dry-season watering points for the game that spreads out towards Nxai and Makgadikgadi during the rains. Around this, there is a much higher density of game in the dry season than the wet. That said, quite a lot of the reserve is mopane woodlands, a favourite location for animals during the rains and early dry season – so expect it to have some game around all year.

GETTING THERE AND AWAY Most visitors arrive by air into the Santawani airstrip (✥ STWAIR 19°30.621'S, 23°37.372'E) in NG33, which is about 10km from the lodges. If you're driving yourself, you can follow the main route through NG34 between Maun and Moremi Game Reserve or Chobe National Park, but driving off this route is no longer permitted without an escort. The campsite is along the road towards Moremi's South Gate. For details of these routes, see page 218.

🏠 WHERE TO STAY *Map, page 336*

With the introduction of Rra Dinare and Mma Dinare, accommodation in this reserve is looking up. As in almost all the concessions, all lodges must be pre-booked, but if you find yourself travelling between South Gate and Maun and need a space for the night, your best option is Kaziikini Campsite, which lies right on this road (opposite the cultural village of Shandereka). Alternatively, you could divert about 30km towards Mankwe Tented Retreat in NG43 (page 398). From west to east, you'll find:

Rra Dinare (9 tents) Contact Kwando Safaris (page 215). Rra Dinare faces the Gomoti River across the floodplains towards NG32. This stands under a huge marula tree (*Sclerocarya birrea*), around which a few smaller knobthorns (*Senegalia nigrescens*) are clustered. From its classic wood-&-thatch main area to very well-spaced tents, the camp is designed to maximise the views; thus you can watch wildlife from almost anywhere, whether that's the lounge, your tent, the open pool deck, the chairs around the firepit, or even the loo with a view. Connecting it all are lengths of high walkways – broken by the occasional wildlife 'corridor' to allow larger game such as elephant & buffalo to pass through without damaging the structure.

Big airy tents house a small lounge area, & twin or king-size beds beneath a mosquito net & ceiling fan. To the back of the tent is an en-suite toilet & ceramic basins plus an outside shower. A family tent consists of 2 standard tents joined by a short corridor, & share a bathroom, so may not work for a group of friends. To make you feel at home in the main area, there's a help-yourself bar, a tea & coffee station, & a constant supply of filtered water. Power comes entirely from solar panels, albeit with a generator as back-up.

Game viewing led by a guide & tracker team in 4x4 vehicles explores both riverine & dry areas day & night. The guiding team here can also communicate with the guides from Mma Dinare (see right), maximising the potential for sightings, although in busy times, this might congest sightings despite a max vehicle policy on the concession. You can also drift down the Gomoti River in a mokoro, or take a nature walk – albeit well away from the area's buffalo, after which Rra Dinare ('Sir Buffalo') is aptly named! Both walking & mokoro trips are seasonal. *US$620*

pp 15 Nov–31 Mar to US$1,470 pp Jul–Oct, FBA inc conservation fee. Children 6+. ⊕ *All year.* 🛁🛁🛁–🛁🛁🛁🛁

Mma Dinare (10 tents) Contact Kwando Safaris (page 215). Just 3.5km south as the crow flies of Rra Dinare, Mma Dinare opened in mid-2018 beneath mature trees on the edge of the Gomoti River, with beautiful views across the floodplains & good wildlife in the dry Santawani area. It shares a similar design & ambience, although the 2 camps operate independently.

The 10 safari tents feature a spacious private deck, ideal for relaxation. Inside, there's a lounge area, king-size or twin beds, & an en-suite bathroom with twin basins & an outdoor shower. The 2-bed 2-bath family tent accommodates up to 4 guests. Tents connect to the main area via raised walkways, where there's a dining space, a lounge/viewing deck, & a curio shop. On another level is a pool on a wooden deck & a social campfire.

Activities include game drives, mokoro excursions & walking safaris. As in Kwando's other camps, both a guide & tracker are on every game drive, ensuring active predator tracking. Mokoro trips are offered throughout the year, but their duration may vary based on water levels, which are lowest in Nov–Dec. *US$620 pp 15 Nov–31 Mar to US$1,470 pp Jul–Oct, FBA inc conservation fee. Children 6+.* ⊕ *All year.* 🛁🛁🛁–🛁🛁🛁🛁

Mogogelo Camp (10 tents) Contact Stars of Africa (page 215). Opened in 2022, Mogogelo Camp is a classic, tented camp with traditional Meru-style canvas tents elevated on wooden decks. Simple but functional interiors feature an en-suite bathroom, comfortable bed, free-standing fan & storage, while outside a small deck overlooks the camp's waterhole.

13

At the heart of camp is a thatched, open-sided dining area with a bar, a small seating area & swimming pool, & to the front, a traditional firepit. Local guides take game drives (day & night) in this area of private concession, & offer bush walks. *From US$425 pp Dec–Mar to US$650 pp Jul–Oct, FBA. Children 6+.* ⊕ *All year.* 🛖🛖🛖–🛖🛖🛖🛖

Kaziikini Community Campsite (2 tents, 10 camping pitches) 📞 680 0664; m 7770 7081; e kaziikinistmt@btcmail.co.bw; w kaziikinisafaris. com; ✪ KAZIIK 19°35.425'S, 23°48.190'E. Some 28km from South Gate, Kaziikini is run by the Sankuyo Community & occupies a lovely wooded setting just off the road. Its camping pitches, all named after trees, are large, shady & well kept, each with its own water tap, braai (firewood for sale), solar light & rubbish bin. These share 3 ablution blocks, with reliable hot-water showers from the solar geyser & toilets, with 2 en-suite, twin-bedded tents.

There's a thatched bar & simple restaurant (snacks available; meals must be ordered in advance) overlooking a small artificial waterhole, & a sizeable craft shop selling locally made basketry.

Kaziikini is a pleasant spot to regroup & watch some of Botswana's more common birds, but probably isn't a place to linger. At a push you could use Kaziikini as a base for driving into Moremi or Chobe, but within the reserve itself, self-drive game drives can be conducted in your vehicle with a community escort (not a professional guide). Alternatively, you can take a full-day's guided game drive in their vehicle, with lunch. Campers here have reported elephants, hyena & even honey badgers around the sites. *Camping US$40 pp, tent US$100 pp.* ⊕ *All year.*

SANTAWANI PARTNERSHIP (NG33)

The small Santawani Reserve, covering just 60km², is really an enclave that has been cut out of NG34. It borders Moremi, and in character is very similar to the area around South Gate and parts of NG34.

In the past, this hasn't proved an easy area in which to run a standalone camp. Santawani Safari Lodge – one of the Delta's older photographic camps – has periodically fallen into disuse and has undergone several changes of management in the last two decades alone. Taken over by Wilderness Safaris in 2016, Sanatawani, like Gomoti Tented Camp, is currently used for private group-travel bookings only.

GETTING THERE AND AWAY At present, access to the lodges is exclusively by air into Santawani airstrip (✪ STWAIR 19°30.621'S, 23°37.372'E).

 WHERE TO STAY *Map, page 336*

The two camps in the reserve are not currently open to independent travellers, but are booked on an exclusive-use basis only for group trips from the US. **Gomoti Tented Camp** (5 tents; w nathab.com; ⊕ all year), not to be confused with Machaba's Gomoti Plains Camp (page 391), is a small camp largely used by US operator Natural Habitat, set beneath shady acacia trees, with classic safari-style tents and a thatched central area. **Santawani Lodge** (6 tented chalets; w oattravel. com; ⊕ all year) is operated by Wilderness Safaris offshoot OAT, with Meru-style tented structures looking out over the floodplain, and a small waterhole in front of the lodge that attracts good numbers of game.

MABABE AND MANKWE (NG41 AND NG43)

These two concessions lie to the east of the Delta. NG41 is leased to the proactive Mababe Zokotsama Community Development Trust and shares its northern and western boundaries with Chobe National Park. On its southern border is NG43, which is essentially a huge (3,460km²) patch of the Kalahari.

Until 2024, this vast area was solely the base for two small bush lodges under the same ownership, which could prove convenient stops between Maun and either Moremi or Chobe. Over time, as the areas under wildlife protection have effectively expanded, the Mababe reserve is beginning to be viewed as a game-viewing destination in its own right. The arrival of Wilderness Safaris into the concession, with the opening of Mokete in 2024, is certainly sure to increase the area's visibility to overseas travellers.

Should you wish to explore NG41, note that there is a P60 concession fee payable, and that you must have a community escort guide with you in your vehicle to show you the various game-drive routes (and make sure you don't go off-road). There is no charge for this – the escorts are not qualified guides – but they will in all likelihood expect a tip.

It is worth noting that both NG41 and NG43 are mixed-use concessions, with both hunting and photographic safaris in operation. After the five-year nationwide suspension of hunting was overturned in 2019, citizen and trophy hunting licences once again became available at annual auction. In 2023, both NG41 and NG43 were issued with licences to hunt 11 elephants, alongside other wildlife. Traditionally, the argument has been made that hunting takes place in only marginal areas where photographic safaris are not viable. With the arrival of long-established photographic safari operators like Wilderness Safaris to the concession, this argument becomes harder to make here. Some conservationists have expressed concern that allowing hunting to resume in NG41, which forms a migration route between Chobe National Park and the Okavango Delta, undermines other protection efforts and potentially stores up behavioural issues in young males if older bulls are targeted (as is common practice in trophy hunting). Most people with any significant knowledge of wildlife in Africa are aware that animals, especially those with long memories like elephants, will be extremely skittish in areas where hunting takes place, and indeed for some time afterwards. For this reason, we would expect game viewing here to be less reliable than in areas where photographic safaris have long been established.

Sandwiched between NG41 and the Khwai Community Concession (NG19) is a wedge of land that forms part of Chobe National Park (CH3). The Mababe local community have long campaigned for this area to be allocated for their use, specifically to create a campsite; however, in mid-2023, their requests were again declined.

FLORA AND FAUNA In spite of its classification as an Okavango Private Reserve, NG41 is not the lush, watery wilderness that perhaps implies. For much of the year the Mababe Depression is largely a **dry landscape**, characterised by mixed Kalahari bushveld, open savannah plains scattered with large camelthorn (*Vachellia erioloba*) trees, and – especially thanks to Wilderness Safaris' new camp – a sprinkling of small waterholes. However, in years when the Okavango's annual floodwaters reach right down as far south as the Khwai River, it will sometimes get as far as the Mababe, creating marshy areas here too, making red lechwe sightings possible.

As for **wildlife**, there are large populations of elephant in NG41, with 2018 aerial surveys estimating over 2,800, predominantly in breeding herds. A few impressive old bull elephants are around, though largely to the north of the concession. Seasonally, during the summer rains, the area is known to have sizeable herds of zebra (December and March) and buffalo several thousand strong, who migrate through the area in search of water and fresh grass brought on by the rains. Good numbers of hyena and lion will invariably be on their trail, and can generally be

13

spotted year-round. Wild dogs and cheetah do range here but are less commonly spotted. General plains game commonly found in the area include giraffe, blue wildebeest, impala and tsessebe, with more elusive species of antelope like roan and sable rarely seen.

Over 100 species of **bird** have been recorded in Mababe. The fertile soils of the Mababe Depression support a host of nutritious grasses, whose seeds attract a diverse range of colourful finches, waxbills and whydahs, notably the violet-eared and black-cheeked waxbill, and the impressively long-tailed paradise whydah. In woodland areas, bee-eaters, weavers, warblers and scarlet-chested sunbirds can be spotted.

Northern black korhaans, southern ground hornbills and stalking secretary birds can be seen hunting snakes and rodents in the grasslands, while the area's raptors – myriad eagles from tawny to martial, steppe and Wahlberg's – can be spotted, alongside raptors such as the red-necked, Amur and Lanner falcon, little sparrowhawk, and pairs of gabar goshawks and shikra.

GETTING THERE AND AWAY Virtually all visitors travelling directly between Maun and Chobe will pass through sections of both NG43 and NG41, even if they aren't aware of it.

To reach Mankwe from Maun, head towards Chobe's Mababe Gate (that is, follow the directions to Sankuyo on page 219). The turning to the lodge is clearly marked, 7km north of Sankuyo Village. Mogotlho Safari Lodge (⊕ MOGOT 19°13.109'S, 23°57.365'E), in NG41, is about 20km north of Mankwe Tented Retreat – or some 10km before Mababe Village. Visitors to Mokete park and leave their vehicles at Mababe village for a transfer on to camp.

 WHERE TO STAY *Map, page 336*

NG41

Mababe community campsites Run by the Mababe Zokotsama Community Development Trust; m 7466 5349; e mztfund@gmail.com; f Mababe Zokotsama Community Development-Trust. 12km from the Mababe Gate into Chobe, Xanakgaei (aka Tshaa) & Dizhana campsites are situated on the Khwai River. There are large pitches with firepits & shared ablutions. Water standpipes (prone to elephant destruction), bins & firewood (additional cost) are available on site. *P350/150 adult/child.* ⊕ *All year.*

Mogotlho Safari Lodge (13 tents) +27 21 671 7729; e info@hideawaysafrica.com; w mogotlholodge.com; ⊕ MOGOTL 19°13.840'S, 23°58.696'E. Opened as a hunting camp in 2000, Mogotlho switched allegiances to photographic safaris back in 2008, & more recently undertook a complete aesthetic renovation. It lies 2.5km east of the road, in NG41, its large central deck with a firepit occupying a lovely spot above the Khwai River, shaded by camelthorn (*mogotlho*) trees, after which the camp is named. The large, thatched camp hub has a lounge, curved bar, communal dining area & a pleasant pool deck.

Also overlooking the river, simple but spacious en-suite tents are set on low decks, with polished floors, cow-hide rugs, comfortable beds, open shelves & storage chests. Large en suites have twin sinks & an enclosed glass shower. There are 2 large tents designed for families, with internal canvas flaps separating the dbl and twin-bed sections.

Day & night game drives, mokoro trips & bush walks are centred on the area around the Khwai River, although full-day trips into Moremi can be arranged. Through their partner company, Kalahari Tours (page 238), they can also organise activities in Chobe for those heading north. Village trips to Mababe community are possible. *US$595–695 pp, FBA. Children all ages.* ⊕ *All year.* 🛇🛇🛇–🛇🛇🛇🛇

Mokete Camp (9 tents) Contact Wilderness Safaris (page 216). Opened in Apr 2024, Mokete Camp is a 'Limited Edition' camp, essentially meaning that the camp in its current form is only temporary, & will be replaced with a more permanent lodge by 2026. This is largely a new area for photographic safari operators, so it's likely this period will be a time of learning while Wilderness is finalising its long-term plans here.

In this initial period, rates are relatively low by Botswana standards.

Mokete, however, is already a smart, modern tented affair, with private tents raised on low decking, comfortable interiors & a highly original, retractable canvas roof that slides down to allow for bedtime stargazing. Shaded verandas & outdoor showers take in the surrounding savannah views.

The main area of the camp is a V-shaped duo of open-sided, elegant tents, with a lounge, dining area, small plunge pool & a central firepit.

Game drives (day, night or all day long), guided walks, community village visits & hot-air ballooning (Apr–Sep) are on offer, or guests can make use of the sunken photographic hide to simply wait & see what wanders by. Birdwatchers especially will appreciate the range of species found around the Mababe marsh. It is possible to self-drive from Maun, Moremi or Chobe & leave your vehicle in secure parking at Mababe Village to stay in the camp, or fly in to the new Mababe airstrip. *From US$1,145 pp Jan–Mar to US$1,418 pp Jun–Oct. Children 16+.* ⊕ *All year.* 👑👑👑👑👑

Nokanyana Lodge (7 dbl & 3 family tents) m 7747 9188; e res@rootsandjourneys. com; w rootsandjourneys.com. Situated at the confluence of the Khwai & Mababe rivers, Nokanyana, meaning 'little river', has spacious, comfortable tented rooms overlooking an expansive floodplain from the riverbank. Filled with natural light, tasteful interiors & smart, contemporary furnishings, the rooms are restful retreats. Each offers a king-size bed, modern en-suite bathroom (indoor & outdoor showers available) & shaded private deck. The family tents (4–5 people) are set a little further away from the main area.

Winding timber walkways lead from each room to the central hub of camp, where a high-thatched, open-sided lounge/dining-bar area awaits. Communal meals are often served on the deck & there's a sandy boma centred on the fire, & a lovely separate swimming pool. It's a low-key, laid-back place.

Activities include game drives within the Chobe section of the concession or towards the Mababe Depression & village visits to Mababe. Excursions towards the Khwai riverfront are usually undertaken as part of a leisurely airstrip transfer, & all-day activities with picnics are available. *From US$370 pp Jan–Mar & Dec to US$690 pp Jul–Oct. Children 6+.* ⊕ *All year.* 👑👑👑–👑👑👑👑

NG43

Mankwe Tented Retreat (10 tents, camping) ☎ 686 5787/8, reservations +27 21 203 5173; e reservations@sundestinations.co.za; w mankwe-bush-lodge.com; ✪ MANKWE 19°21.769'S, 23°53.775'E. In the northwest corner of NG43, about 7km north of Sankuyo village, Mankwe is set among mopane trees to the west of the road (2hrs from Maun). The camp has pared-back, natural African–Scandi styling, with a central, open-sided dining & lounge area raised on low decking overlooking the campfire, & 2 plunge pools surrounded by sunloungers. Overlooking the surrounding bush, fairly large Meru-style tents on wooden decks are simple but pleasantly furnished, with twin beds, battery-powered lights & an en-suite flush toilet, basin & gas-fired shower.

About 1.5km from the lodge, beneath camelthorn & mopane trees, are 6 private campsites, each with its own flush toilet, bucket shower & washbasin. Firewood is available, but otherwise you'll need to be fully equipped, with all your own drinking water, as well as food & fuel. That said, with a couple of hrs' notice, campers may eat at the lodge (3-course dinner P265).

You can use Mankwe as a base for self-drive day trips into Moremi Game Reserve, or take part in their organised activities. These include 3–4hr afternoon drives with a sundowner in the NG43 Concession (P525 pp based on 4 people), & full-day drives (P1,400 pp), usually into the Khwai River area. Guided bush walks & night drives are further options, along with 4x4 trails across NG43, accompanied by a local guide. *US$370 pp Dec–Mar, US$485 pp Apr–Jun & Nov, US$690 pp Jul–Oct, FBA exc park fees & Maun transfer (US$280/vehicle). Children 2+.* ⊕ *All year.* 👑👑👑–👑👑👑👑

13

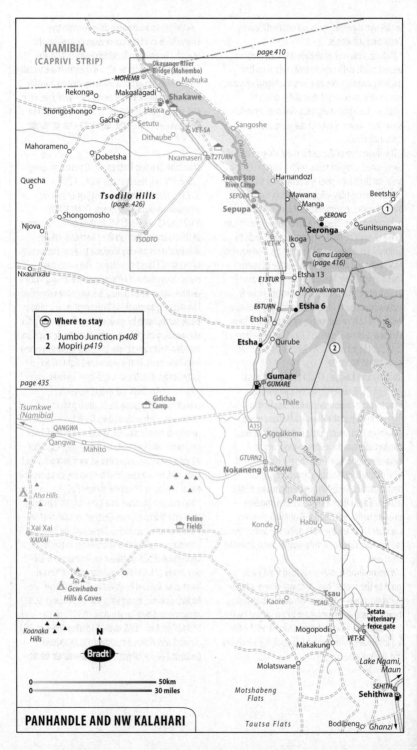

NAMIBIA
(CAPRIVI STRIP)

page 410

Okavango River
Bridge (Mohembo)
MOHEMB
Muhuka

Rekonga
Makgalagadi
Shakawe

Shongoshongo
Gacha
Hauxa
Setutu
Sangoshe

Mahorameno
Dithaube
VET-SA
Okavango

Dobetsha
Nxamaseri
T2TURN

Quecha
Swamp Stop
River Camp

Tsodilo Hills
(page 426)
Hamandozi

Mawana
Manga
Beetsha

Njova
Shongomosho
SEPUPA
Sepupa

SERONG

TSODTO
VET-IK
Ikoga
Seronga
Gunitsungwa

Nxaunxau
Guma Lagoon
(page 416)

E13TUR
Etsha 13

Mokwakwana

⊕ **Where to stay**
1 Jumbo Junction *p408*
2 Mopiri *p419*

E6TURN
Etsha 6

Etsha 1

Etsha
Qurube

page 435

Gumare
GUMARE

Gidichaa
Camp
Thale

Tsumkwe
(Namibia)
QANGWA
A35
Kgosikoma

Qangwa
Mahito
Thaoge

GTURN2
Nokaneng NOKANE

▲
Aha Hills
Ramotsaudi

Xai Xai
XAIXAI
Feline
Fields
Konde
Habu

Gcwihaba
Hills & Caves

Kaore
Tsau
TSAU

Koanaka
Hills

N
Mogopodi
Setata
veterinary
fence gate
VET-SE

Bradt!
Makakung
*Lake Ngami,
Maun*

0 ——— 50km
0 ——— 30 miles
Molatswane
SEHITH
Sehithwa

PANHANDLE AND NW KALAHARI
*Motshabeng
Flats*

Tautsa Flats
Bodibeng *Ghanzi*

14

The Okavango
Panhandle and
Northwest Kalahari

If much of the Okavango Delta is the preserve of the privileged few who can afford to fly in to exclusive safari camps, then the Panhandle presents a few more egalitarian options. Here you'll find the raw edge of Botswana's safari industry, camps and houseboats on the edge of the Delta run by idiosyncratic owners or local communities. This is the Okavango's safari scene as it was 25 years ago!

Go west, into the Kalahari, and it's wilder still. Here there's almost nothing organised, yet the amazing Tsodilo Hills were declared Botswana's first UNESCO World Heritage Site in 2001. Adventurers may want to soak up the region here and explore the caverns of the Gcwihaba Hills or the remote Aha range.

THE PANHANDLE

Look at a map of the Okavango Delta and you'll see that it's shaped like a frying pan, with the main river flowing down the centre of the handle, from the northwest. Hence this area is known as the Panhandle.

GEOGRAPHY All of this area is in the Kalahari, though here it's dominated by the influence of the Okavango River. This flows south into Botswana from the Angolan Highlands, having crossed Namibia's Zambezi Region (Caprivi Strip). Entering Botswana, the river's gradient is very low. However, it is constrained from spreading out by steep riverbanks on either side. Underneath the sand lies a more fundamental constraint: parallel faultlines in the earth's crust that run southeast, about 10–15km apart. Thus the river meanders gradually southeast, between them,

GPS CO-ORDINATES FOR MAP (OPPOSITE)			
E6TURN	19°06.706'S, 22°16.152'E	SERONG	18°48.771'S, 22°24.988'E
E13TUR	19°00.793'S, 22°17.356'E	T2TURN	18°35.834'S, 21°59.986'E
GUMARE	19°22.242'S, 22°09.242'E	TSAU	20°10.294'S, 22°27.265'E
MOHEMB	18°15.700'S, 21°45.768'E	TSODTO	18°47.378'S, 21°44.981'E
NOKANE	19°39.694'S, 22°11.184'E	VET-IK	18°50.327'S, 22°13.756'E
QANGWA	19°31.868'S, 21°10.281'E	VET-SA	18°29.256'S, 21°55.142'E
SEHITH	20°28.259'S, 22°42.372'E	VET-SE	20°15.775'S, 22°33.926'E
SEPUPA	18°44.150'S, 22°10.625'E	XAIXAI	19°52.867'S, 21°04.934'E

forming a series of wide, sweeping curves and the odd oxbow lagoon – but always remaining within the constraints of the banks.

Where the river's meanders kiss the banks at the edge of the floodplain, villages have sprung up: Shakawe, Sepupa and Seronga. The southern extent of the faultlines lies around Seronga, so south of here the river begins to spread wider to form the main body of the Delta.

FLORA AND FAUNA The Panhandle isn't a prime area for game viewing, so don't come here expecting masses of big game or you'll be disappointed. That said, you may catch glimpses of the occasional sitatunga or small herds of lechwe, and you're almost bound to see numerous hippo and crocodile. However, there are some first-class areas for birding, and plenty of areas with deep-water channels and lagoons.

Flora Looking from the Panhandle's banks, often all you can see is a gently swaying mass of feathery papyrus heads. Here, more than anywhere else in the Delta, the environment is polarised: there are deep-water channels, and there are the papyrus beds that surround them.

Occasionally you'll find sections of phragmites reeds and, when the waters are low, open stretches of sandbanks. Sometimes the odd day-lily (*Nymphaea nouchali caerulea*) will take hold in a quiet inlet on the edge of the channel, but mainly the vegetation here is huge expanses of floating papyrus.

Birdlife The birdlife here is as varied as anywhere in the Delta, though getting to actually see the birds that inhabit the papyrus can be tricky. Some of the more sought-after sightings would be painted snipes, rufous-bellied herons, lesser jacanas, chirping cisticolas, brown-throated weavers and coppery-tailed and white-browed coucals. Greater swamp warblers and swamp boubous can often be heard calling from the papyrus, but are less easy to spot.

The Panhandle is a particularly good area for the white-backed night heron. Look out, too, for white-backed ducks (sometimes in large numbers) perching on the sandbanks, as well as long-toed lapwings, red-winged pratincoles and, of course, the Panhandle's most acrobatic birding attraction: the African skimmer. These distinctive, black-and-white birds fly south to the Delta between about September and December. They mainly come to breed on the sandbanks of the Panhandle, which are exposed while the water is low. Gathering in small flocks, each pair excavates a shallow depression in the sand where they'll lay their eggs and raise their young.

One of the Delta's most amazing sights is to watch these birds feed. With long, graceful wings they fly fast and low, holding their elongated lower mandible just low enough to cut the water's surface. This is hollow and has sharp edges, shaped to minimise its drag in the water. When this touches a small fish near the surface, it is quickly raised against the upper mandible, trapping the fish firmly. I always marvel at their flying skill, moving their body in all directions while their bill traces a constant, steady path through the water.

Note that because African skimmers nest very near the waterline, on low sandbanks, their nests and young are very vulnerable to both predators and to damage from the wash caused by fast-moving motorboats. So boats operating in these areas should never be driven too fast.

Another spectacular migrant, better seen in the Panhandle than anywhere else in the Delta, is the carmine bee-eater. These come to southern Africa to breed, and stay from about October to March. They nest in large colonies, building their

The graceful, feathery papyrus is a giant sedge that dominates large areas of the Okavango. It grows in areas of permanent swamp in thick floating mats, unmistakable for its feather-duster heads that sway in the breeze.

The secret lies in remarkable adaptations. Firstly, papyrus has adapted well to the nutrient-poor Kalahari sands beneath the water: it has nitrogenous bacteria between its scale-leaves which 'fix' nitrogen from the air into a form that the plant can use; it also photosynthesises using a special 'carbon-4' pathway, making more efficient use of the sun's energy than most plants.

With these adaptations, plus water and sunshine, papyri are among the fastest-growing plants in the world. Plus, despite having thick and strong stems, they are very light, so the plant commits relatively little energy or materials to growing a tall, strong stem.

In fact, papyri store most of their energy in long, thick rhizomes which form part of the tangled floating mat. From this base, their shoots can rise up to about 2.5m high, and yet typically have a life cycle of only three months. Within this they grow swiftly to maturity, flower and die – leaving a tangle of brown, dead stems near water level. The nutrients from these old stems are withdrawn back into the rhizome, ready to power the birth of another shoot. This rapid recycling of nutrients is another key to the plant's lush, vigorous growth.

But papyrus swamps are in many ways a difficult habitat. Below the waterline, little light penetrates the floating mat of dead stems. The constant decomposition means much organic debris and water that is acidic and low in oxygen. With no light, there's no chance for algae or any other higher plant life.

Above the waterline the stems form a dense, tangled mass. The stems themselves are fibrous, difficult to digest and very nutrient-poor. Combined with a floating base that can't support any weight, this makes life here almost impossible for most larger animals. Only the specially adapted sitatunga antelope is at home here.

For animals as small as rats and mice, the situation isn't so bad. They don't generally stay in the papyrus beds, but they are light enough to make forays there. Greater cane rats are the largest of these, growing up to about 80cm on a diet of papyrus shoots, reeds and other vegetation. Although they swim well, they normally live in small family groups in burrows on permanent dry land, leaving these at night to forage in the reedbeds and papyrus.

A few birds also use the papyrus for shelter and nesting, including several species of weavers, the red-shouldered widow and red bishop bird – which will tear the feathery umbels of the papyrus as material to weave their intricate nests. Many more will come into papyrus areas to hunt for fish or insects, and there will be very few trips here when you won't see at least a few malachite and pied kingfishers.

nests underground at the end of tunnels which they excavate into the side of sandy riverbanks. You won't forget the sight of hundreds of these bright carmine-pink birds twittering around a riverbank that's holed with nests like a piece of Swiss cheese.

Above the water you'll regularly spot African fish eagles; marsh harriers and even the occasional migrant osprey are also sometimes seen. On the banks beside the

The Okavango Panhandle and Northwest Kalahari THE PANHANDLE

14

The amazing phenomenon of the catfish run is unique to the Okavango Delta. It happens every year, between early August and the end of November, though its timing is difficult to predict precisely.

As the water level starts to drop in the northern part of the Panhandle, it is still rising in the southern part of the Delta. The catfish runs start in the north of the Panhandle, where the lowering water levels concentrate the Delta's smaller fish – especially the relatively small churchill (*Petrocephalus catostoma*) and bulldog (*Marcusenius macrolepidotus*) – in the channels and papyrus banks.

The main predatory species involved include the sharp-toothed catfish (*Clarias gariepinus*), a hardy, omnivorous species which grows up to 1.4m in length and 59kg in weight, and the much smaller blunt-toothed catfish (*Clarias ngamensis*). These catfish hunt in packs and a 'run' starts with the catfish swimming upstream inside the papyrus banks. Here they slap their powerful tails on the surface of the water, making a noise like a gunshot, and against the papyrus, to stun the smaller fish, their prey.

Hundreds and sometimes thousands of catfish will work their way upstream like this, making the water 'boil' with their frenzy of activity. All this noise and commotion attracts an eager audience of herons, storks, egrets, fish eagles and other fish-eating birds on the banks, while crocodiles, snakes and tigerfish lurk beyond the papyrus in the deeper channels waiting to snap up anything that escapes into open water.

Although in each run the catfish swim upstream, when it's finished they pause and drift back down, subsequently rejoining other catfish and starting new runs. So as the water levels drop further down in the Delta, the location of the runs moves south also.

These runs occur in many different sizes. There will be several per day in different areas of the Delta, each covering a distance of a few kilometres before fizzling out. A couple may be longer than this, perhaps continuing for as long as two weeks and covering a lot of distance, but these are the exception rather than the rule.

Eventually, signalled by the onset of the rising waters, the catfish will themselves move out on to the floodplains and spawn.

waters and papyrus there's a narrow band of thick riverine forest, before the bush becomes that of the dry Kalahari. Here there's a wide variety of different birdlife – typical of any of the riverine areas in this region. Notable sightings would include the tiny brown firefinch, Bradfield's hornbill, the western banded snake eagle and Pel's fishing owl.

ORIENTATION The Panhandle's western side is very easy to access with a 2WD, as the road between Sehithwa and Shakawe is tar. Once you leave the main road and the larger settlements, however, a high-clearance 4x4 is essential to cope with the often deep sand in the area.

In 2022, after six years of construction, the new Okavango River Bridge at Mohembo (aka the Mohembo Bridge) finally opened, connecting the communities either side of the water, who had previously depended on an unreliable pontoon or mekoro to cross. The 1.2km pedestrian and vehicle bridge is cable-stayed, with

a distinctive crossed tusks design in honour of the region's elephant population. Approximately 3km of tar road access extends either side of the bridge, and though the track that follows the river on the eastern side is used much less, it's not intrinsically difficult, and the advent of the bridge may well open up this hitherto less-visited side of the Panhandle.

GETTING THERE AND AROUND

By air There are small airstrips dotted around, so if you charter a plane you can get to most places here: Shakawe, Nxamaseri, Nokaneng, Tsau and Guma Lagoon. Tsodilo Hills also has an airstrip, but you really need a vehicle while you're there to get the most out of it. This is also true for the Gcwihaba or Aha Hills, which can alternatively be accessed via the airstrip at Xai Xai.

By car The main tar road on the west side of the Panhandle offers relatively straightforward driving in a 2WD. That said, the stretch between Gumare and Shakawe was riddled with pot-holes in early 2024, although there does seem to be a concerted if slow effort to repair the surface.

For anywhere else in this area, you really need your own fully equipped 4x4, with gravel or sand roads the norm – they're often impassable in the rains. Fuel supplies in Shakawe, Gumare and Sehithwa are relatively reliable but it's wise to come prepared and fill up whenever you can – carrying plenty of spare fuel with you.

By bus Basic buses ply the road between Maun and Shakawe several times a day, starting at around 08.30, with the last departure of the day at 16.30 in each direction. The whole trip takes about 5–7 hours and costs a total of P125. Buses stop at the main villages on the way, turning off to the larger centres such as Gumare and Etsha 6, but near the smaller villages they just pick up and drop off passengers on the main road.

THE EASTERN PANHANDLE Although visitors relatively rarely see the side of the Okavango's Panhandle to the east of the river, those who do usually come for the mokoro trips. These have long been run by the Okavango Polers' Trust (☏ 687 6861; e mbiroba@gmail.com) – a community-based organisation dedicated to preserving the traditional culture and skills of the local community, particularly the art of poling mekoro – though other companies have now stepped into the market. For travellers who are constrained by a relatively tight budget, this is one of the few options left to see any of the Okavango.

A single deep-sand road runs down the eastern side of the river from Mohembo to Seronga, making a high-clearance 4x4 essential. Between the two you'll find numerous smaller villages which survive mainly on fishing and, away from the river, a number of tiny 'cattlepost' settlements used by people tending their cattle in the interior of NG11 – which is fairly continuous cattle-ranching country.

Getting there and away

By air Seronga has an airstrip (✦ SERAIR 18°49.180'S, 22°25.020'E) that is by far the easiest and most convenient way for most travellers to access the village. Check in Maun for details of the options.

By car The only practical way to access the eastern side of the Panhandle with a (4x4) vehicle is to cross the Okavango River at the new bridge at Mohembo, in the far north.

There appears on many maps to be another route, which seems to go around the eastern side of the Delta and link into Seronga from the Linyanti area, via the village of Beetsha. However, the tracks on this side have very few users and no signposts. They cross a number of different private concessions, none of which would welcome your visit: straying off designated transit routes will get you into trouble. Meanwhile, when the tracks meet villages they split and vanish. But perhaps the greatest danger is of water blocking the route. It's easy to get dangerously lost in this region and then to run out of fuel, water or supplies. There's no mobile signal or help at hand, so we'd strongly advise against trying to use any of these tracks.

By bus/boat Both Shakawe and Sepupa are fairly easy to access on one of the local buses that run up and down the road to the west of the river, between Shakawe and Sehithwa. There are bus stops either side of the new bridge at Mohembo, though currently few buses on the eastern side, making travel by public transport here a challenge.

The once-regular motorboat ferry between Sepupa and Seronga Boat Station (⊕ SERBOA 18°49.316'S, 22°24.855'E) remains out of service, but the team at Swamp Stop River Camp (page 415), Okavango Houseboats (page 414) or one of the lodges at Guma Lagoon (page 417) may be able to assist with crossing if you're staying; arrange this in advance.

Seronga Seronga (⊕ SERONG 18°48.771'S, 22°24.988'E) is a sizeable village at the eastern base of the Panhandle. It's the regional centre for a number of small settlements to the east of it, along the northern edge of the Delta, as well as a focus for the people who still live in the northern areas of the Delta. It has essential services – accommodation, basic shops and local restaurants – if you're passing through the area.

 Where to stay Mbiroba Camp, run for years by the Okavango Polers' Trust, seems to have disappeared off the radar. The only viable option in this area at present offers several options. **Jumbo Junction** [map, page 402] (2 chalets, 7 tented rooms; m 7310 6501, 7276 0245; e reservations@jumbojunction.com; w jumbojunction.com; ⊕ JUMBO 18°49.31'S, 22°36.19'E; US$530–650 pp, FBA; ♨♨♨) is situated some 28km east of Seronga on the northern bank of the lower Selinda Spillway and has a couple of spacious, well-furnished en-suite chalets, seven twin-bed, luxury tented rooms under pole-shaded arches and an island bush camp that includes some permanent tented accommodation. Central to the camp is a large, semi-circular, thatched bar and restaurant, a campfire overlooking a permanent lagoon, and a swimming pool. Activities, all dependent on water levels, focus on boating, mokoro trips, island walks, fishing and game drives. Flights from Maun to Seronga can be arranged, as can boat transfers from Sepupu to Seronga for self-drivers.

THE WESTERN PANHANDLE
Mohembo border Mohembo – almost 16km north of Shakawe – marks the road border at the top of the Panhandle between Botswana and Namibia's Zambezi Region (Caprivi Strip). Here you'll find a neat customs and immigration area (⊕ MOHEMB 18°15.700'S, 21°45.768'E; \ 687 5505; ⊕ 06.00–17.00 daily) where the formalities are normally handled promptly and efficiently. Possibly as a result of unreliable banking services in the Panhandle and Zambezi Region, the authorities on the Botswana side of the border now accept card payments for cross-border fees.

Shakawe This sprawling town stands east of the main road on the northern banks of the Panhandle of the Delta, some 16km south of the Mohembo border post, and 281km north of Sehithwa. Driving into the old village used to feel like entering a maze of reed walls, each surrounding a small kraal, as the track split countless ways between the houses. The odd trap of deep sand was enough to stop you for an hour, and thus serve up excellent entertainment to numerous amused locals.

Today, Shakawe is a bustling little town, founded on fishing but catering to the needs of locals and long-distance travellers, albeit still something of a backwater. Just a stone's throw from the tar road you'll find a significant base for the Botswana Defence Force, as you'd expect in one of the country's more sensitive border areas, and a major police station.

Of particular importance to drivers are the two fuel stations (one of which advertises 24-hour service, perhaps for the trucks passing through) and ZAIB Motors (✆ 687 5101; e janizeb@yahoo.com), who can assist with minor mechanical and tyre repairs. There's a Barclays Bank (with an ATM) and a branch of Choppies supermarket with a good range of produce, while other, smaller shops and a post office are largely concentrated within the small shopping centre around the bus stop.

If you fancy a break before driving on, you could try a guided tour of **Krokovango Crocodile Farm** (⊕ KROKO 18°25.817'S, 21°53.682'E; m 7230 6200; ⊕ 08.00–17.00 Mon–Sat; P25/15 adult/child), about 10km south of Shakawe. The farm is in an attractive woodland setting, with 8,000 crocs at all stages of growth from hatchling to enormous 5m-long adults. They're at their most active at feeding time, usually at 11.00 on Tuesday and Friday – though the adults are not fed at all between May and July, so the first feed in August could be quite a spectacle! There's also a museum on the history of crocodile farming and a shop for croc-skin products.

Getting there and away There are good daily bus services to Maun via the rest of the western Panhandle from the centre of town. Of these, the fastest service is the Golden Bridge Express (m 7140 5528; ■), which departs at set times throughout the day, taking about 5 hours to reach Maun, while Gibfly (m 7468 8155) operate an overnight bus departing Maun at 23.00 and arriving at 06.00. Minibuses are cheaper but very cramped and take at least an hour longer; they also only depart when full.

Self-drivers will need to allow around 4 hours to reach Shakawe from Maun. And for fly-in guests, there's the option of charter flights taking about 45 minutes. The airstrip is to the west of the main road, just 400m off the tarmac.

Where to stay *Map, page 410*
In Shakawe itself, the options are many, though the better places are outside of town. About 10km south of the centre, there are a number of camps on the river catering mainly for fishing and birdwatching. Houseboats have added further variety, moored on the river near Shakawe and offering the opportunity to explore the western fringes of the Delta while based on the river itself. It's an entirely different approach, and may well appeal to those seeking a more relaxing trip with less of an emphasis on fishing (although fishing is still an option!). For a general overview, contact Okavango Houseboats (e houseboat@okavangohouseboats. com; w okavangohouseboats.com), who offer exclusive-use, crewed boats (with or without catering), from P12,085 for the boat per day, plus P848 per person for three daily meals. Alternatively, consider one of those listed from page 412.

With the increase in the number of travellers along the Zambezi Region, trade here has picked up over recent years, so you will often need to book.

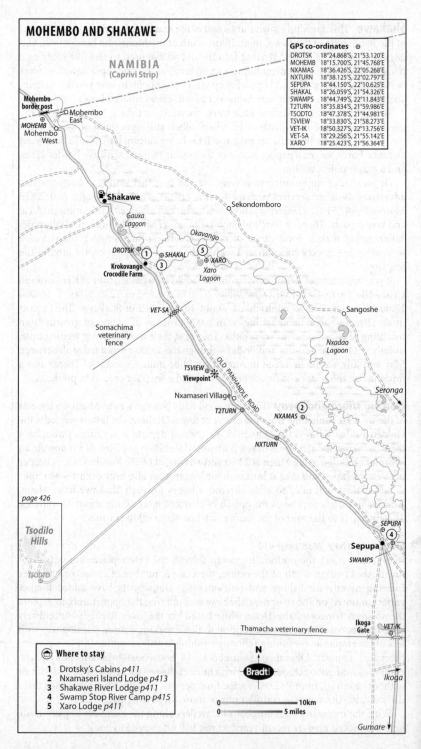

MOHEMBO AND SHAKAWE

NAMIBIA
(Caprivi Strip)

Mohembo border post
MOHEMB
Mohembo West
Mohembo East

Shakawe

Gauxa Lagoon

Sekondomboro

Okavango

DROTSK ⊕   ⊕ SHAKAL   ⊕ 5
①
③
Krokovango Crocodile Farm
⊕ XARO
Xaro Lagoon

VET-SA ✕

Sangoshe

Somachima veterinary fence

Nxadao Lagoon

OLD PANHANDLE ROAD

TSVIEW ✳
Viewpoint

Nxamaseri Village

Seronga

T2TURN ⊕
②
NXAMAS ⊕

NXTURN ⊕

page 426

Tsodilo Hills

TSODTO ⊕

SEPUPA
④
Sepupa
SWAMPS

Ikoga Gate
VET-IK ✕

Thamacha veterinary fence

Ikoga

N
Bradt

Gumare ▼

0   10km
0   5 miles

⊖ Where to stay
1 Drotsky's Cabins p411
2 Nxamaseri Island Lodge p413
3 Shakawe River Lodge p411
4 Swamp Stop River Camp p415
5 Xaro Lodge p411

Lodges

Drotsky's Cabins (10 chalets, camping)
\ 683 0226; m 7496 8638; e info@drotskys.
com; w drotskys.com; ✆ DROTSK 18°24.868'S,
21°53.120'E. Almost 8km south of Shakawe you'll
find a left turn off the tar road on to a sandy
track. This leads east, crossing the old road up
the Panhandle for about 3km to reach the lush,
manicured lawns of Drotsky's Cabins. You should
be able to drive this track in a normal 2WD car,
though the sand can be very thick, so some driving
skill is needed.

This once-small fishing camp is still run by
owners Jan & Eileen Drotsky & their family, who
have seen Shakawe change from a remote outpost
to a thriving little town over their 30 years here. The
central area is designed like a vast log cabin on high
stilts, under a thatched roof, & is approached by an
almost palatial series of steps & walkways. Adorned
with wrought-iron chandeliers & wood carvings,
& with a separate bar under whirling fans, it may
sound rather grand, but the effect is homely rather
than ostentatious. The log-cabin theme continues
in the large, twin-bedded, en-suite chalets, each
of which is also raised up on stilts, overlooking the
trees & Okavango River. AC, fans & flat-screen TVs
are standard, while high-backed armchairs & ornate
ceramic basins add a touch of traditional comfort.
Outside, beautifully tended gardens sweep around
a pool to the river beyond. The main area is entirely
wheelchair-accessible, as is one of the chalets.
Activities focus on the river with boat cruises &
fishing trips. It is also possible for self-drivers to
use this as a base for the Tsodilo Hills, 65km away,
although this is a long round trip.

Campers enjoy a shaded but sandy campsite
with 20 pitches, each with lights, electric points
& a firepit – but watch out for the local monkey
population. There are sparklingly clean ablution
blocks here, a communal boma campfire, shared
lounge area & meals can be arranged at the main
camp with advance notice.

Drotsky's is an authentic, traditional camp, where
hospitality hasn't been learned from a manual.
It can be a super lodge & offer you fascinating
insights into the area, its history & its ecosystems,
& there's superb birdwatching to be done without
leaving the grounds. *Camping P250 pp; chalet rate
is exc b/fast.* **$$$**

Shakawe River Lodge (10 chalets, camping)
m 7211 9400; e shakawe@scadvlodges.com;

w scadvlodges.com; ✆ SHAKAL 18°26.059'S,
21°54.326'E. Known for decades as Shakawe
Fishing Camp, this lodge has risen from humble
surroundings. Gone is the simple fishing camp of
yore, its expansive river frontage now hosting a
more modern, albeit low-key, open-fronted lodge
that's all neutral colours beneath a topping of
smart thatch. From the entrance, you're greeted
by a riverside vista of palm trees & papyrus,
where basket chairs hang enticingly in the breeze.
Sunloungers on a raised pool deck catch the river
view across the well-tended lawn, too, as do the
restaurant & lounge. Most of the twin & king-size
dbl en-suite chalets with sliding glass doors are
lined up along a rather reedy section of the river,
their contemporary décor enhanced by AC, TV & a
bar fridge.

Downstream, the shady old riverside campsite
has had a makeover, but remains relaxed &
unpretentious, with 10 clearly demarcated pitches
(sites 1–7 boast the best river views if you're
booking in advance), its own bar, & spotless if
well-worn showers & toilets. Campers are welcome
to dine at the lodge, where an à la carte menu
features a good selection of pizzas. Beside the
slipway, look out for the hulk of an old houseboat,
a relic of the Angolan war from the late 1970s.
Apparently it was used by 32 Battalion of the
South African forces, who were stationed in the
Zambezi Region (Caprivi Strip), but it broke loose
& drifted south, & has been gently rusting in
Botswana ever since!

The lodge is clearly signposted some 2.5km
east of the main road, about 5.5km north of
the Somachima veterinary fence (✆ VET-SA
18°29.256'S, 21°55.142'E), or 11km south of
Shakawe, & is accessible by 2WD. Guests have
always come here to fish, especially during the
peak season of Jun–Aug, & certainly fishing is
still a focus; boats can be hired by the hour or day
(from P250 pp/hr, P1,400 pp/day, exc fuel), but
birdwatching, as well as day trips to the Tsodilo
Hills & Mahango Game Reserve add another
dimension. *Lodge P2,690/dbl; camping P2,565/135
adult/child.* **$$$$**

Xaro Lodge (9 Meru tents, 1 Suite) Contact
Stars of Africa (page 215); m 7280 7476;
e reservations@xaro-lodge.com; w xaro-lodge.
com; ✆ XARO 18°25.423'S, 21°56.364'E. Xaro
is about 10mins by boat from its boat reception
in Samochima Village – self-drivers can leave

vehicles at Xaro's secure parking here. The lodge itself is set in 30ha on an outcrop from the mainland, in an established grove of knobthorn, mangosteen & jackalberry trees, while in the garden you'll find a host of succulents & cacti, banana trees & even a small baobab. Originally built in the mid-1980s by Hartley's Safaris, & run by the Drotsky family for many years, Xaro passed through several hands until it was most recently acquired by Christo Vorster. The origins of a beautiful, old-style Okavango camp remain though in the thatched, stone dining area, where the polished wood banqueting table overlooks the lawns towards the river. There's a comfortable lounge area & a bar with an amazing sunset view & myriad outdoor spots for dinner. Raised on timber decks, the large Meru tents all have en-suite facilities, solid timber furniture & plenty of thoughtful home comforts, from snacks to fresh flowers. Sliding glass doors lead on to verandas on the edge of the Okavango River & make a lovely spot for afternoon relaxation. 2 of the tents can be accessed with a wheelchair.

The birdwatching & photography is superb here, with sightings of Pel's fishing owls all but guaranteed, while the lily-strewn Ngarange Channel supports kingfishers & jacanas, & guided walks are on offer to look for woodland species. Guided day trips to Tsodilo Hills can also be organised & souvenirs purchased from the small curio shop featuring staff-crafted products. *US$580/room, FBA inc boat cruise & island walk, exc drinks; US$665/room, FBA inc boat cruise, island walk & Tsodilo Hills trip, exc drinks (min 3 nights); US$40 pp Shakawe return boat transfer.* 🛏🛏🛏–🛏🛏🛏🛏

Houseboats [not mapped]
Kabbo (8 cabins) Contact Wilderness Dawning Safaris (page 217). This 2-storey 'floating lodge' is designed to make the most of its location.

On the lower deck, each of the 8 en-suite cabins has sliding glass doors just above water level, for super river views, while the upper deck – 3m above the water – offers panoramas from the dining area, bar & sundecks. Boating & fishing trips (catch & release) from the 2 tenders are available or – if you tire of the water – there are visits to the Tsodilo Hills by road or plane. *US$1,920/night (min 8 people), FBA inc 1 water-based activity/ day, exc transfers. Tsodilo Hills (by road) day trip US$80 pp.* ☺ *Apr–Oct.* 🛏🛏
Kubu Queen (2 cabins, sleeps 6) ☏ +27 76 585 5052; m 7230 6821; e oldafricasafaris@ngami. net; w kubuqueen.com. From its base just north of Shakawe, the *Kubu Queen* is moored at a different spot each night, with tender boats to enable guests to explore the river & its channels & go fishing (exc Jan–Feb). Nature walks on some of the larger islands are also a lovely option. Inside, there's a lounge, bar & dining area. Each of the 2 cabins has a dbl bed, while a further 2 guests can sleep under the stars on the upper deck, where simple twin beds are set up under mosquito nets. The shower & toilet are shared, but groups are not mixed, so you won't be sharing with strangers. Another option is to camp in en-suite dome tents on one of the islands (max 12 guests).

The boat is owned by Greg & Kate Thompson, who have worked in the safari industry in the Okavango for almost 25 years; Greg is an enthusiastic professional guide on hand to share river stories, predict fishing hotspots & enthral with knowledge of the area's flora & fauna. In years of very high floodwater (in Jul–Aug), *Kubu Queen* offers a 7-night Trans-Okavango trip from Shakawe to Maun, camping on remote islands along the way. *US$590 pp/night (min 4), FBA inc drinks, guide, fishing & permits, fuel for houseboat & tender boats & airstrip transfers.* ☺ *All year.* 🛏🛏

Nxamaseri

Though the small village of Nxamaseri is not a stop for most visitors, I've included this section because the surrounding area is a very interesting one, offering an insight into the attractions of the Delta that are on a par with most of the reserves further east.

The Nxamaseri Channel is a side-channel of the main Okavango River. When water levels are high, there are plenty of open marshy floodplains covered with an apparently unblemished carpet of grass, and dotted with tiny palm islands. It's very like the Jao Flats, and is one of the Okavango's most beautiful corners.

Like Guma Lagoon, further south, it's fairly easily accessible due to the presence of a lodge. If you want a real Delta experience in the Panhandle, then this should be high on your list of places to visit – though getting here requires either your own vehicle or a flight.

Flora and fauna The Nxamaseri Channel is north of the point where the main Okavango River divides at the base of the Panhandle, and is a stretch of open, clear water up to about 30m wide in places. Beside the edges you'll find stands of papyrus and common reeds, while its quieter edges are lined by patches of waterlilies, including many night-lilies (also known as lotus lilies; *Nymphaea lotus*) as well as the more common day-lilies (*Nymphaea nouchali caerulea*). Look out also for the heart-shaped floating leaves, and star-shaped white or yellow flowers of the water gentian (*Nymphoides indica*).

As with the rest of the Panhandle, this isn't a prime area for game viewing. You may catch glimpses of the odd lechwe or the shy sitatunga, and you're almost bound to see hippo and crocodile, but big game is scarce. However, the channel is a super waterway for birdwatching, home to a tremendous variety of waterbirds. Without trying too hard, my sightings included many pygmy geese, greater and lesser jacanas, lesser gallinules, colonies of reed cormorants, darters, several species of bee-eater and kingfisher, green-backed herons, a relaxed black crake, numerous red-shouldered widows and even (on a cloudy morning in February) a pair of Pel's fishing owls. Beside the channel are pockets of tall riverine trees and various real fan and wild date palms, whose overhanging branches house colonies of weavers (masked, spotted-backed and brown-throated). Upstream of the lodge, on the main Okavango River, there's a colony of carmine bee-eaters at a location known locally as 'the red cliffs'. This is occupied from around early September to the end of December, but is probably at its best in late September or early October (the best time for most migrant species here). While watching for birds, keep an eye out for the elusive spotted-necked otter (*Lutra maculicollis*), which also frequents these waters.

Getting there and away Nxamaseri (also spelt Nxamasere) Village lies about 37km south of Shakawe, or 19km north of Sepupa. From the north, follow the tar road to the Somachima veterinary fence (⊕ VET-SA 18°29.256'S, 21°55.142'E), then after 10km you'll pass a slight rise marked by a sign as 'Tsodilo View' (⊕ TSVIEW 18°33.830'S, 21°58.273'E). From here, on a clear day, you should be able to see the Tsodilo Hills to the southwest, but thick vegetation has obscured the view, and sand sprinkled with broken glass makes it a far from attractive place for a break. Less than 3km south of this viewpoint you'll pass a sign to Nxamaseri, which leads to the village of the same name. The turning to Nxamaseri Island Lodge (⊕ NXTURN 18°38.125'S, 22°02.797'E) is clearly signposted almost 9km south of the village turn-off. Advanced reservations are essential; this is not a place to try and drop into unannounced. Most visitors are transferred to the lodge (⊕ NXAMAS 18°36.426'S, 22°05.268'E) from the airstrip, but self-drivers leave their vehicle in the guarded parking spot by the turning, and are transferred by 4x4 vehicle and boat for the final few kilometres.

Where to stay *Map, page 410*

✴ **Nxamaseri Island Lodge** (9 chalets)
m 7132 6619; e info@nxamaseri.com;
w nxamaseri.com; run by Desert & Delta Safaris

(page 214). One of the Okavango's oldest lodges, Nxamaseri started as a fishing camp in about 1980, & though sensitive refurbishments over the years have ensured higher standards of accommodation & food are on offer, it has retained a strong sense of place & remains a wonderful, friendly lodge that justifies a stay of at least 2 days.

Built on an island surrounded by deep-water channels, Nxamaseri sits within a thick, tropical patch of riverine vegetation. All around are knobthorn, waterberry, sycamore fig, mangosteen, jackalberries, sausage trees & some of the most wonderfully contorting python vines that you'll see anywhere.

Its wide, thatched lounge/dining area is built around a pair of lofty old jackalberry trees, with an open frontage to the river: it's comfortable, cosy & well thought-out, but not ornate. From here, a jetty extends for boats, & wooden walkways lead to 9 thatched chalets tucked within the lush vegetation. Spacious, simple bedrooms feature twin or dbl beds, crisp white linen & down duvets, & make a serene retreat. Each chalet has an en-suite bathroom, complete with a large shower & separate toilet, large mesh windows & folding doors leading to a private wooden deck with river views. There's a light, airy ambience & a seamless connection to the surrounding bush. For extra seclusion, the Tsodilo Suite, slightly larger than the others, caters to honeymooners & those celebrating special occasions.

It is claimed that fly-fishing in the Delta was pioneered at Nxamaseri, & certainly it remains an attraction for people who fish seriously, but to this have now been added 1st-class boat trips for birdwatching, visits to a local village to watch basket making, & day trips to the Tsodilo Hills. There tends to be less emphasis on mokoro excursions, but these are also possible (& magical) when the water levels are high & there are suitable areas of shallow water nearby. Fly-fishing & lure/spinning fishing with top-quality equipment under expert guidance are possible throughout the year. That said, the very best tiger fishing months are Aug–Nov, while the best times for bream are Mar–Jun. During the first 3 months of the year the rain & new floodwaters are said to disturb the fish, which move out to the floodplains, so fishing in the channels can be more difficult. Nxamaseri's record tiger fish catch is about 10kg, though in a normal season they'd expect to have 10–15 catches over the 6kg mark. Like most Okavango lodges, Nxamaseri operates a 'catch-&-release' system, except for the occasional bream that has been damaged. They have a large, flat, barge-like boat which provides a particularly stable platform for several people fishing, & is also ideal for photography, plus a fleet of aluminium-hulled craft. *US$895 pp Apr–May & Nov, US$1,160 pp Jun–Oct, US$645 pp Dec–5 Jan. Sgl supplement US$406, peak season only. All rates FBA inc fishing tackle & transfers from airstrip/road. Children age 6+.* ⊕ *1 Apr–5 Jan.* 🏆🏆🏆–🏆🏆🏆🏆

Sepupa (⊕ SEPUPA 18°44.150'S, 22°10.625'E)

Sepupa, sometimes spelled Sepopa, is 1.7km east of the main road, about 223km north of Sehithwa and perhaps 58km south of Shakawe. Here you'll find a few shops including a bottle stall and a general dealer.

Most visitors, however, are looking for Swamp Stop (see opposite). The lodge is clearly signposted from the main road; just follow the access road to Sepupa Village for 1km until the pot-holed tar runs out, then turn right and continue for a further 2.5km; the track is fine for a 2WD car.

 Where to stay *Map, page 410*

On dry land, long-established Swamp Stop is the place to stay here, but as at Shakawe, there are a few **houseboats** moored on the river here, affording an entirely different perspective on life in the Delta. Three of these – the *Inkwazi*, *Inyankuni* and *Madikubu* – are operated by Okavango Houseboats (e houseboat@ okavangohouseboats.com; w okavangohouseboats.com), who offer exclusive-use, crewed boats and cruise between Sepupa and Seronga. If you're prepared to bring all your own food and drinks, you can hire one of these boats and the tender boats outright for P12,085 per boat per day, excluding fuel and transfers, but with a crew available to prepare your meals. Alternatively, you can organise to stay on a full-board basis (boat rental plus P848 pp for 3 meals/day). The boats are accessible by road, but transfers from Sepupa to Seronga can be arranged at P1,025 per person return, while airstrip transfers are P195.

Swamp Stop River Camp (12 chalets, 5 tents, camping) m 7261 0071; e swampstop@ gmail.com; w swampstop.co.bw; ✪ SWAMPS 18°44.749'S, 22°11.843'E. This established backpackers' & overland stop has undergone exciting transformations. The original riverside campsite, shaded by magnificent trees, still stands, offering open pitches adorned with power points & lighting. An ablution block ensures your comfort, while a 2nd site at the back features 8 neatly swept pitches enclosed with reed fences. Each pitch boasts its own barbecue & cooking area, a firepit, & the convenience of power & light. Quirky metal doors in a reed enclosure lead you to the showers & toilets, with handbasins artfully set within upturned mekoro, & a separate washing-up area. Occasionally, overlander groups, who have their own dedicated camping space, share access to the same amenities. For those without their own camping kit, twin-bedded Meru tents, raised on wooden decks, make up the 'Mokoro Beach Camp' and are equipped with electric lights, simply furnished but neat bedrooms & open-air en-suite bathrooms. There are also semi-detached chalets,

for couples & families, offering river or garden views, which are a haven of privacy, complete with AC, minibar, en-suite bath & shower, & a private deck.

Adjacent to twin oval pools, the Swamp Stop's riverside bar & restaurant has an upstairs deck with views over the papyrus to the main channel of the Okavango. Down below, meals from b/fast selections to main courses of burgers, curry & steaks are on offer. For many, a refreshing beer at the bar is the perfect opportunity to soak up the views.

Swamp Stop has garnered a reputation as a budget-friendly gateway to the Delta & a springboard for getting to Seronga. Guests have the opportunity to explore the river by motorboat, with hourly rentals starting from P612. Angling enthusiasts are welcome to bring their own fishing tackle & adventurers can take a mokoro journey (P1,860 pp) along the Delta's serpentine channels. Day trips to the Tsodilo Hills are also possible. *River chalet P1,814/dbl; garden chalet P1,544/ dbl; tent P1,155/dbl; camping P230 pp.* ⊙ *All year.* **$$–$$$**

THE DELTA'S WESTERN AND SOUTHERN FRINGES

Ordered from north to south, here's a brief listing of the main landmarks and villages on the road between Sepupa and Sehithwa. If it gets a little repetitive, then take that as a fair reflection of the road, which is long and well surfaced with tarmac. Most of this area has a low, wide verge of groundcover which is often cut – helping to ensure that big game can be seen before it is standing in front of you. But for all this visibility, the scenery is uninteresting.

Although you're travelling at times very close to the western edge of the Okavango Delta, the road passes through apparently undistinguished areas of bush. You may see the occasional animal, but with man and cattle as the dominant species in this area, only birdwatchers are likely to find much of interest on the drive.

SEPUPA TO ETSHA 13 North of Etsha, the road condition improves, with pot-holes present but fairly consistently being repaired. The greater danger to self-drivers here are wandering cattle in the road, so take care.

About 12km south of the Sepupa turn-off, or 211km north of Sehithwa, you may have to stop at the **Ikoga Gate** (✪ VET-IK 18°50.327'S, 22°13.756'E), which is a checkpoint on the Thamacha veterinary fence. About 206km north of Sehithwa, there's another turning east, this time to **Ikoga**. Some 32km south of the Sepupa turn-off, or 191km north of Sehithwa, is a turning (✪ E13TUR 19°00.793'S, 22°17.356'E), which leads slightly over 3km east to **Etsha 13**. This small village has a few basic shops, but little more. More important for visitors, it marks the access road to Guma Lagoon and Guma Lagoon Camp.

GUMA LAGOON
On the western side of the Delta, at the very base of the Panhandle, Guma is a large, papyrus-lined lagoon. It is linked to the Thaoge River, the main eastern finger of the Okavango River system, by a short channel (40 minutes by boat from the camp or the lodge). Both Guma Lagoon and the main Thaoge River are excellent spots for fishing and birdwatching – a combination that, with relatively easy 4x4 access from around Etsha 13, has encouraged two very different camps to set up here. Note that during heavy rains or high water, alternative access routes to the camps may be put in place. These are often extremely sandy with some water crossings, and can be difficult to navigate, so a high-clearance 4x4 is essential.

Flora and fauna
Guma isn't a place for big game; it's a deep-water environment that offers good birdwatching and fishing.

The vegetation around the lagoon is mainly papyrus, though you'll also find large stands of phragmites reeds. You'll also find the odd waterberry (*Syzygium cordatum*) and water fig (*Ficus verruculosa*), especially in the smaller channels and backwaters.

On the banks, the riverine vegetation is thick and lush. It includes plenty of wild date palms (*Phoenix reclinata*), river beans (*Sesbania sesban*) and potato bushes (*Phyllanthus reticulatus*), which are members of the euphorbia family and are not related to potatoes at all – but smell the air on a warm evening and you'll realise where their name comes from.

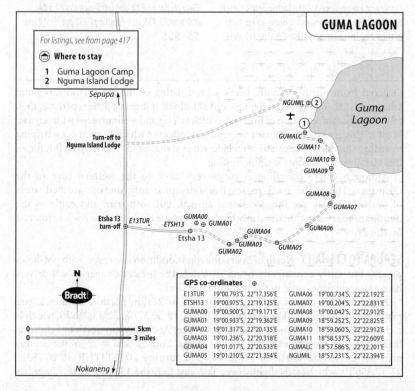

GUMA LAGOON

For listings, see from page 417

⊙ **Where to stay**
1. Guma Lagoon Camp
2. Nguma Island Lodge

Sepupa ↑

Turn-off to
Nguma Island Lodge

Etsha 13
turn-off ⊕   E13TUR   ETSH13 ⊕ ⊕ GUMA01
                       GUMA00
            Etsha 13   ⊕ GUMA03
              GUMA02   GUMA04
                       GUMA05

NGUMIL ⊕ 2
✚
①
GUMALC
GUMA11
GUMA10 ⊕
GUMA09 ⊕
GUMA08 ⊕
GUMA07
GUMA06

Guma Lagoon

N
Bradt

0 —————— 5km
0 —————— 3 miles

Nokaneng ↓

GPS co-ordinates ⊕

E13TUR	19°00.793'S, 22°17.356'E	GUMA06	19°00.734'S, 22°22.192'E
ETSH13	19°00.975'S, 22°19.125'E	GUMA07	19°00.204'S, 22°22.831'E
GUMA00	19°00.900'S, 22°19.171'E	GUMA08	19°00.042'S, 22°22.912'E
GUMA01	19°00.933'S, 22°19.362'E	GUMA09	18°59.252'S, 22°22.825'E
GUMA02	19°01.317'S, 22°20.135'E	GUMA10	18°59.060'S, 22°22.912'E
GUMA03	19°01.236'S, 22°20.318'E	GUMA11	18°58.537'S, 22°22.609'E
GUMA04	19°01.017'S, 22°20.533'E	GUMALC	18°57.586'S, 22°22.201'E
GUMA05	19°01.210'S, 22°21.354'E	NGUMIL	18°57.231'S, 22°22.394'E

Also keep an eye out for large sour plum (*Ximenia caffra*), water pear (*Syzygium guineense*), jackalberry trees (*Diospyros mespiliformis*) and the occasional sausage tree (*Kigelia africana*) – one of which greets you as you enter Guma Lagoon Camp. Further from the water, you'll often find acacias: camelthorn (*Vachellia erioloba*), knobthorn (*Senegalia nigrescens*) and umbrella thorn (*Vachellia tortilis*) are the main species here. There are a few baobabs (*Adansonia digitata*) in the area, but they're not common.

The more common birds include fish eagles, many species of herons, egrets, warblers, bee-eaters and kingfishers, pygmy geese and greater and lesser jacanas. Look for red-shouldered widows in the papyrus, and reed cormorants and darters sunning themselves on perches over the water.

In the riverine forest areas you can find white-browed robin-chat (formerly known as Heuglin's robin), crested and black-collared barbets, green pigeons, various sunbirds and, in summer, the spectacular paradise flycatchers in breeding plumage.

Getting there and away Despite their proximity, the two lodges at Guma Lagoon are normally accessed from two separate points along the main road: Guma Lagoon Camp (and the lagoon itself) via Etsha 13, and Nguma Island Lodge from a well-signposted turning about 3km further north. You'll need a 4x4; if you're driving a 2WD then with prior notice the lodges can arrange to collect you at a pre-agreed location, leaving your car somewhere safe while you're at the camp.

The actual routes depend on the conditions. Signboards to Nguma Island Lodge make their access drive of 12km or so relatively straightforward. Although it changes according to the prevailing conditions, it is usually well marked. Alternatively, Nguma Island Lodge has an airstrip (about 5 minutes from the lodge), or you can fly in to the small airstrip at Gumare and be collected from there. It may also be possible to fly in to Seronga, and be transferred to the lodge by boat from there.

However, the track to Guma Lagoon Camp, although marked with arrows, is very sandy and considerably more circuitous; it's easy to get lost. The first hurdle is finding the right track out of the small village of Etsha 13 (⊕ ETSH13 19°00.975'S, 22°19.125'E). In theory there's a sign saying 'camp' on a telephone pole, but it's none too clear. This will take you through the village on a track going east-southeast. Gradually this turns east, then northeast, and finally north – and the scenery gets prettier, with fewer domestic animals and settlements, and more small date palm islands and open floodplains. The distance varies between 10km and 13km, and you'll need to allow around 45 minutes. As a guide, GPS waypoints for just one possible route are shown on the map on page 416. There are certainly more direct routes than this, as the whole area is criss-crossed with confusing bush tracks. However, many will be seasonal and depend on the water levels, so beware of getting lost and stuck!

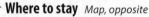 **Where to stay** *Map, opposite*
There are only two choices at this lagoon. Though both have campsites as well as tented rooms, they are each quite different and don't generally work closely together.

Guma Lagoon Camp (16 cabins, camping)
m 7757 0658; e info@guma-lagoon.com;
w guma-lagoon.com; ⊕ GUMALC 18°57.586'S,
22°22.201'E. Relaxed, friendly & popular
with anglers, Guma Lagoon Camp occupies a
picturesque spot with open views across the

lagoon. It focuses mainly on self-drive, self-catering visitors, although meals can be provided with advance notice.

Nestling among the trees at the water's edge are en-suite 'cabins', constructed of wood & canvas on raised decks to catch the breeze. With twin/dbl beds, wooden floors, electric lights & a veranda over the lagoon, they're comfortable, but not luxurious. At the campsite, each of the 6 pitches has its own toilet, hot shower & braai pit. Guests prepare meals in the self-catering kitchen, where fridge/freezing facilities are available, before congregating in the shaded dining/bar area with a deck extending over the lagoon. A small pool is a welcome place to cool off, perhaps after a game of volleyball.

In addition to boating & fishing (boat hire from P381/hr exc fuel), there is the option of a full-day mokoro trip (P1,530 for 2 people), or staying overnight on one of the islands (P1,915 pp plus P480 for a luggage mokoro); note that children under 12 may not take part in mokoro excursions. Camping equipment can be hired, & food/drinks organised by the camp with advance notice. *Cabin P1,542; camping P188 pp. Rates exc transfers (P138 pp from Etsha 13) & concession fees (P120 pp).* **$$$**

Nguma Island Lodge (20 Meru tents, 6 self-catering tents, camping) ✆ 683 0159; m 7356 0120; e info@ngumalodge.com; w ngumalodge.com; ✪ NGUMIL 18°57.231'S, 22°22.394'E. Situated on the northwestern edge of the lagoon, this lodge was opened in 2000, & is owned & run by Nookie Randall, who has lived in the area for over 20 years. Her late husband, Geoff, played an important part in pioneering the fiberglass mekoro in the area – & thus is partially responsible for saving an enormous number of the Delta's old trees!

It's a linear site, neatly divided into 2. At one end, where the lodge is based, tents are spread out among the trees along fairly high wooden walkways & raised up on high wooden decking. Inside you'll find comfortable twin beds with percale linen & colourful cushions, chairs, a bedside table & a wrought-iron hanging unit. At the back of each tent is an en-suite shower, toilet & washbasin. Power comes from a generator, with a system of back-up batteries for the lights at night; batteries can be charged in the main area.

Walkways continue to the raised main area, so everything is above water if levels rise to a high flood. Normally the ground beneath is dry, with cool lawns dotted with date palms. A comfortable lounge, dining room & well-stocked bar are housed in a large log cabin. There's a better collection of local baskets & craftwork than in most curio shops, & some are for sale in the small shop.

At the other end of the site, but under the same cool canopy of trees, is the Delta Dawn campsite. As well as camping pitches, there are pre-erected twin tents with linen & towels provided. Ablutions are simple, with wooden-clad showers & toilets. There are also braai stands & facilities for washing up, as well as a bar & restaurant (P125 b/fast, P270 2-course dinner). Fishermen should note that there is no freezer space at the camp but cables can be provided to plug in vehicle freezers.

Activities include ½-day, full-day & overnight trips by mokoro, as well as boat trips by the hour (for up to 6 people). Fishing tackle is available for hire, & lures, etc, for sale. Other options include island walks & birding excursions. *Lodge P2,495 pp, camping P256.50 pp, dome tent with bedding P593 pp. P3,230 boat hire/day exc fuel; P1,550 pp full-day mokoro trip inc lunch; transfers from parking P314 pp.* ⊕ *All year.* **$$$**

What to see and do Precise activities depend on where you're staying, though boat trips are really the main draw. On the whole, the water's deep enough to limit the scope of mekoro for most of the year, and so motorboats are the vehicle of choice. If you're not a devout angler or birdwatcher, then just take a few rods and a pair of binoculars and do a little of both – it's very relaxing.

ETSHA 6 TO SEHITHWA Although the A35 along the western side of the Delta is tarred, it merits careful driving. Significant sections are riddled with often large pot-holes and the edge of the road is quite literally crumbling.

Etsha 6 About 45km south of the Sepupa turn-off (178km north of Sehithwa) there's a signposted turning (✪ E6TURN 19°06.706'S, 22°16.152'E) to Etsha 6, which is less than 3km east of the road. For the traveller, it's a reasonable halfway point between the turn-offs to the Gcwihaba Caves and the Tsodilo Hills.

THE ETSHA VILLAGES

In 1969, the war in Angola (which, in many ways, was an extension of the Cold War using African proxies) displaced a large number of mostly Hambukushu people from the Caprivi area into Botswana. There they were accepted as refugees. Initially they were received at Shakawe, but eventually the plan was to move them to a new village to the south, called Etsha (pronounced 'Etsa').

However, while the refugees were at Shakawe it's said that they naturally split into 13 separate groups. So when they were moved, they naturally split into 13 villages, which spread out along the western edge of the Delta, 1km apart. They were called, somewhat unimaginatively, Etsha 1, Etsha 2, Etsha 3 and so on up to the most northerly, Etsha 13.

Now the old track that links them and runs close to the Delta has been largely superseded by the new tar highway, which takes a more direct route on the east of the old road. However, you'll still find tracks linking the two, one of which is close to Etsha 13, and another close to Etsha 6.

There is a defunct fuel station, opposite which is a Co-op that stocks tinned food, soft drinks and basic staples like rice and maize in quantity, though there's very little fresh produce.

Turning right on to the old Panhandle road at the T-junction near here will bring you to the post office, and a further kilometre or so along the road, there's a craft shop run by the Botswana Council of Churches (BCC) that sells very nice baskets woven on the premises, though opening hours seem erratic.

Where to stay Map, page 402

Mopiri (10 tents) 680 0021; m 7747 9188; e res@rootsandjourneys.com; w rootsandjourneys. com; ◈ 19.42.000'S, 22.906.108E. 14km from Etsha 6, Mopiri Lodge sits on the western bank of the Weboro Lagoon. With 7 luxury tents & 3 family units, the spacious accommodation offers relaxing, comfortable spaces to unwind. The interiors of all the tents are open & contemporary, decorated with quality furnishings & amenities in neutral, earthy tones. They have comfortable beds dressed in high-quality linens, smooth polished floors & rain showers. Ceiling fans keep rooms cool & private verandas provide an excellent location to take in the panoramic views of the lagoon & surrounding vegetation.

There's a comfortable, multi-level lounge & dining area, a campfire, an inviting pool surrounded by loungers under sail-cloth shade, & an inviting Delta pool. Activities include nature walks, boating safaris, mokoro trips & fishing expeditions. Self-drivers can leave their vehicles at Mopiri's secure parking in Etsha 6 & transfer to the lodge with their guide. *US$370 pp Jan–Mar & Dec, US$485 pp Apr–Jun & Nov, US$690 pp Jul–Oct. FBA. Children all ages.* ⊕ *All year.* **$$$–$$$$**

Gumare An ostentatious 'bus rank' on the main road signals the turn-off to the east for Gumare (aka Gomare), which lies about 146km north of Sehithwa, 37km from Nokaneng, and 77km south of Sepupa. There are both Shell and Engen fuel stations here, making Gumare one of the more reliable places to fill up along this side of the Delta.

The town itself (◈ GUMARE 19°22.242'S, 22°09.242'E) is one of the main towns of the Panhandle area, with over 8,500 residents, and it has clearly seen considerable growth and investment in recent years. The roads into town are tarred, there are two fuel stations, an Auto Repair shop (limited range) and a tyre repair service. As if vying for attention with the bus station, there's a smart branch of Barclays

Bank with a (usually working) ATM, a post office, hospital, a branch of Choppies with an attached off-licence and a large Shoprite supermarket, which is great for stocking up on supplies.

If you've time to spare, it's worth seeking out the small craft shop, **Ngwao Boswa Basket Shop** (⎆ 686 4431; m 7437 9830; w crafthood-unite.com; ⊕ 08.00–16.00 Mon–Fri), beside the bus rank. It was founded by a group of 40 weavers in 1986 under the co-operative name Ngwao Boswa, meaning 'Culture is heritage' in Setswana. Aiming to empower vulnerable women in the community, the shop sells a variety of handcrafted baskets made from palm leaves and grass, skilfully woven by 65 local artisans and sold at reasonable prices.

Where to stay While there are several guesthouses in Gumare, most are extremely overpriced for what they offer. If you're heading towards Namibia, or indeed coming from the Dobe border post, and are looking for creature comforts in the bush, consider stopping at Gidichaa Camp (see below) instead.

Ramorwa Guest House (10 rooms) ⎆ 687 4556; m 7169 4999; e ramorwag@btcmail. co.bw; 🅕 ramorwaguesthouse; ⊕ RAMORW 19°21.770'S, 22°09.973'E. About 1.3km from the centre of Gumare, & well signposted, Ramorwa is tucked away down a quiet residential street. Small but comfortable rooms lead off a tree-shaded courtyard, a pleasant place to make use of free Wi-Fi access. With AC, TV & fridge, & a dbl bed under mosquito nets, they're well equipped but not fancy. If you can't face the walk into town, you can get traditional or international-style meals here, too. *P350/room, exc b/fast.* **$**

Sexhebe Guesthouse (10 rooms) ⎆ 687 4340; m 7176 0038; e bookings@sexhebe.co.bw; w sexhebe.co.bw. This russet-coloured guesthouse lies on the main road, just north of the turn-off to the town, & has simple en-suite rooms, all with AC, TV & an en-suite shower. The more expensive category of room boasts carpet, a mirror & huge wardrobe. Meals are available on request, & there's Wi-Fi & guarded parking. *P500–800/room.* **$–$$**

Where to eat and drink There's a franchise of **Zebro's** at Rail Park Shopping Centre, serving barbecue chicken and chips, and similar fare is offered at The Grill (m 7575 9336; e kukafood@outlook.com), where it's served on simple outdoor tables under cover. If all you're after is food for a picnic, there's also a good bakery in town, and a couple of grocery stores: Shoprite and Choppies.

Nokaneng The village of Nokaneng (⊕ NOKANE 19°39.694'S, 22°11.184'E), about 114km south of Sepupa, 109km north of Sehithwa, is marked by a radio mast amid a group of houses. There's little to detain the visitor here except a small grocery shop and a bar.

More significantly for travellers, shortly north of the radio mast is a road heading west signposted '120 to Qangwa' (⊕ GTURN2 19°39.577'S, 22°11.010'E). This leads eventually to the Namibian border (Dobe border post), near Tsumkwe, where you'll need Namibian dollars or South African rand to pay the necessary fees to cross. Before the border, the village of Qangwa marks the point where you can turn south and access both the Aha Hills area and, eventually, the Gcwihaba Hills and Caves. See page 434 for more on these areas. If you're heading this way in a 4x4, consider a stop at Gidichaa Camp, a new, family-run camp offering high levels of service and complete solitude.

Where to stay Map, page 435
Gidichaa Camp (3 tents) m 7789 5191; e info.gidichaacamp@gmail.com; w gidichaacamp.com; ⊕ 19°27.264'S, 21°46.271'E. Once an old hunting camp, the

refurbishment of Gidichaa Camp has been a labour of love for owners Ian & Cici. Having operated luxury yacht charters around the world for 30 years, they are no strangers to hospitality & have brought their commitment to highly personal service to this corner of the Kalahari (the NG3 Concession area). Opened in 2020, Gidichaa has just 3 tents & operates on an exclusive-use basis, even if only 1 tent is occupied, to ensure the feeling of wilderness serenity.

Situated in a natural depression with several natural pans, the camp attracts a diverse array of birds & wildlife, even during the dry season when they're drawn to the area's only water: a pan filled with pumped water. Thirsty elephants, wild dogs, kudu & wildebeest stop by, Meyer's parrots congregate in the birdbaths, there's the occasional honey badger, & check out the rafters for passing owls & squirrels.

Set on russet timber decking overlooking the waterhole, the main area is open-sided & homely, with areas for deep-cushioned leather sofas, a stuffed bookcase, communal dining table for tasty home-cooked meals & an adjacent, pole-shaded pool & bar. There's also a campfire boma & a separate 2-tier shaded viewing platform for in-camp game viewing.

Accessed along sandy paths, the tented accommodation is classic safari style: simple but comfortable with solid timber furniture, crisp bedding, a small deck with chairs & an en-suite bathroom.

Game drives are available, along with guided walks to learn about the flora & fauna, cultural experiences with local communities, & birdwatching at the nearby pans. There is no mobile phone signal & limited internet access.

Self-driving from Sehithwa, the signposted turn-off to camp is 20km north of Nokaneng on the A35 tar road. It's then 37km along a cutline west towards the Dobe border post, before another signposted turn north for the final 10km to camp. The road varies from hard pan to soft sand, which is firm & easy to drive up until the end of Apr. *P2,950 (US$740) pp, FBA inc concession fees, exc alcohol.* 👑👑👑👑

Tsau About 180km south of Sepupa or 43km north of Sehithwa, you'll come across a turning to the village of Tsau (often written 'Tsao'), just to the east of the main road (⊕ TSAU 20°10.294'S, 22°27.265'E). Its prominent radio mast is quite a landmark, too. Here you'll find lots of small houses, though relatively little tree or vegetation cover, and a few small, general shops. Back on the main road, there's a small stall announcing 'tyre fix' – handy in an area where punctures are all too frequent.

Some 10km north of Tsau is a large banner on the side of the road (⊕ GTURN1 20°07.047'S, 22°22.291'E), marking a more southerly turn-off to the Gcwihaba Hills and Caves.

Setata veterinary fence gate About 27.5km north of Sehithwa you'll have to stop and pass through the Setata Gate (⊕ VET-SE 20°15.775'S, 22°33.926'E) in the veterinary fence. Here, as at other veterinary checkpoints, self-drivers and campers may have their vehicles searched for red meat, which you are not permitted to take across the vet fence.

Sehithwa Coming from the Panhandle, you'll reach a T-junction, where you meet the tarred A3. Turning left will bring you to the turn-off for Sehithwa, and on to Toteng and Maun, while right leads to Ghanzi, some 195km away.

The village of Sehithwa (⊕ SEHITH 20°28.259'S, 22°42.372'E) itself lies just south of the main road, about 93km from Maun. There's a Puma fuel station close to the turning, and it remains sensible to fill up wherever you can. If you're camping, it's also worth picking up your braai charcoal (P30/4kg bag) from the Lake Ngami Conservation Trust in town (📞 687 2090; e lngamitrust@gmail.com).

Sehithwa is a more substantial settlement than Toteng, with a couple of small, basic guesthouses, of which one – Ditoro Guest Lodge – is 1km or so from the main

14

road. You'll also find a few general shops and liquor stores, and a not-inconsiderable police station. Sehithwa and Toteng have a significant Herero population, and you will often pass women in the typical Victorian-style full-skirted dress and striking headdress.

LAKE NGAMI The existence of a great lake within the Kalahari was known to Europeans from early reports of Bakwena and Batawana people, though it wasn't reached by them until the mid 19th century. David Livingstone arrived on 1 August 1849, with Cotton, Oswell and Murray, narrowly beating Charles Andersson, who set out specifically to reach it from present-day Namibia.

In his book, *Lake Ngami and the River Okavango* (page 543), Andersson was hugely disappointed with what he first took to be Lake Ngami.

He wrote:

> At last a blue line of great extent appeared in the distance, and I made sure it was the long-sought object; but I was still doomed in my disappointment. It turned out to be merely a large hollow in the rainy season filled with water, but now dry and covered with saline encrustations.

However, he hadn't reached the lake at this stage, and after getting beyond some pans and reedbeds, and over a series of sand ridges, he finally glimpsed the water, and described the moment:

> There, indeed, at no very great distance, lay spread before me an immense sheet of water bounded only by the horizon – the object of my ambition for years, and for which I have abandoned home and friends, and risked my life.

Visiting the lake is certainly easier now than it was for those first explorers, though signposting is poor, and at times it can still be very disappointing. Even after the exceptional rains of 2008–09, much of the lakeshore was lined by shoulder-high thistles, so while the lake had plenty of water, it was still far from being an attraction in its own right.

Note that although the lake is very large when full, a high rate of evaporation and a very shallow profile means that the area covered by water can vary enormously.

When to visit The pithy answer to this question is 'whenever it's full of water!' And therein lies the rub; it's only worth going if there's water in the lake, but few people will have been there and be able to tell you. Your best chance of getting up-to-date information is probably from operators in Maun, and especially the pilots, because if the lake is just a wide expanse of clay, it's better to save yourself a trip.

The state of this mystical lake varies greatly, depending upon whether the Delta's flood, which has historically been Lake Ngami's main source of water, has been high enough to overflow into the Kunyere River which feeds the lake. The lake was an empty dustbowl for the late 1980s and 1990s, but then filled to a shallow depth during 2000 and 2001. After the exceptional rains of 2009, Ngami held a serious amount of water until 2016. However, from 2018 to 2021 the water receded dramatically, with periods of serious drought (there was no water at all in 2019–20). So ask around to find out what the latest situation is before making the journey.

If and when it really floods, Lake Ngami comes alive with birdlife, and has been identified as one of Botswana's 'important bird areas' (IBAs). From October, the ducks, geese, waders and other northern migrants arrive, lining the muddy shores until the weather cools towards the end of April. The flamingos, both greater and lesser, don't choose their times so carefully – being found here in their thousands whenever the conditions are right for the algae on which they feed. They appear from the shore as a pink haze settled on the water's surface.

Getting there and away The lake's bed is surrounded by a triangle of good roads, so approaching it is in theory a matter of turning off one of these and following your nose (or, perhaps better, your compass or GPS). However, it's one of those areas where all roads seem to lead back to where you first started – often enough to Sehithwa – so while you can strike out on your own, there's a simpler way.

About 3.5km north of Sehithwa, on the main road towards Toteng and Maun, there is a clear sign to the lake pointing to the south of the road (✛ LKNGTO 20°27.021'S, 22°44.427'E). Turn down that track and after continuing straight for about 2km you should get to the lake (✛ LNGAMI 20°27.812'S, 24°45.247'E).

🏠 **Where to stay** There's nowhere official to stay near the lake, but the land is open enough to camp rough – provided that you ask permission first from the nearest local villagers. On my last visit the villagers suggested that I go a few kilometres away from the lake to avoid the mosquitoes. This was a very wise move. You'll need to be self-sufficient, of course; and don't count on finding any drinkable water.

What to see and do This is purely a birding destination, though because visitors here are really very rare there are no tracks or pathways (for 4x4s or walkers) designed for birdwatchers. All the tracks have been made to serve the villagers and their many, many cattle. All this makes getting around time-consuming and at times difficult – but if there's water here then it might be worth it.

Lake Ngami is part of the Okavango Delta management plan, which has long proposed developing tourist facilities along the Panhandle and creating a scenic route along this western side as far as the lake. If birdwatching tours start up here, perhaps with the opportunity to take a canoe out on the lake, it could be quite a draw – when the lake is full of water! If you're interested in birdwatching in the area, the team at Letaka Safaris in Maun (page 217) include a stop here in their 16-night Livingstone Birding Trail through Botswana and Zambia.

TOTENG TO MAUN Though a significant dot on the map, Toteng (✛ TOTENG 20°21.407'S, 22°57.204'E) is little more than a road junction at the centre of a sprinkling of small cattle-farming homesteads. Once it marked the turning southwest to Ghanzi, but now that the tarred A3 goes via Sehithwa, it's easy not to notice the place at all. If you're looking for the old road to Ghanzi, you'll find it at ✛ GH2OLD 20°21.407'S, 22°57.204'E, on the west side of the main road.

Despite its apparent insignificance, Toteng has historical importance as a centre for the Batawana; in his *The Guide to Botswana*, Alec Campbell (page 546) comments that: 'When they arrived in Ngamiland in 1795 they settled at Kgwebe and later moved to Toteng.' This was also one of the areas that received an influx of Herero people after their defeat at the Battle of Waterberg.

Beyond Toteng, the tar road leads in around 64km to Maun. If you're planning to stop en route, there's a delightful small camp, Tshima Bush Camp, about equidistant between Toteng and Maun, though you do need to have a reservation; for details, see page 202.

This area is Botswana at its most enigmatic. Here you'll find huge tracts of the Kalahari, punctuated only by isolated Bushman settlements. It's an area where you need to have a good 4x4 (or two), and for the most part you must be totally self-sufficient – travelling with all your own food, water, fuel and equipment.

It's not somewhere which will attract visitors for its game viewing or birdwatching, though you will find both game and birds. In fact, it's not an area that attracts many visitors at all. But old Africa hands are drawn here for its isolated ranges of hills. One displays a breathtaking cultural heritage of paintings, another hides a labyrinthine cave system, and a third – well…the Aha Hills are just there. On the map. In the middle of the Kalahari. Waiting to be visited.

For more information on the science and explorations of this area, interested readers are directed to numerous articles in *Botswana Notes and Records*, some of which are noted on page 545.

 ## WHERE TO STAY *Map, page 435*

You can camp at the Tsodilo Hills, the Gcwihaba Caves and the Aha Hills (see the relevant sections later in this chapter for details), but if you're looking for something that's arguably even more isolated, there is a lodge a couple of hours' drive west of Tsau that might fit the bill.

Feline Fields Lodge (6 suites, 1 villa)

🖊 686 5756; m 7222 2302; e info@felinefields. com; w felinefields.com; ⊕ FELIN 19°58.560'S, 21°48.800'E. This ambitious property is set in the northern reaches of the Kalahari, about halfway between the main Sehithwa–Shakawe road & Gcwihaba Caves: a 3hr drive from Maun or a 50min helicopter ride. The brainchild of Marjan Blom & Raphaël del Sarte, it was designed & built to be 'the perfect safari lodge', focused on empowering local people & connecting visitors with their surroundings. It's fair to say that they have gone a long way to achieving their goal.

The main area is a large thatched wooden building that houses an open-fronted kitchen, where you can watch the chefs as they prepare varied & delicious meals for you to eat in the communal dining area. To one side is a library with a Mac for guests to use, free Wi-Fi & seating that includes an inviting sofa swing; to the other side is a well-stocked bar. Activity is key, here, with a 25m lap pool surrounded by sunloungers & giant beanbags, a small but well-equipped 'bush' gym, an outdoor hard tennis court & a golf driving range.

The well-spaced suites come in 2 styles – thatched 2-storey pool suites & smaller tented bush suites – their décor combining modern styling with safari classics & personal touches. Each of the 3 pool suites, which include free Wi-Fi & a polaroid camera

for guests to use, has a raised super-king-size bed, separate day bed, writing desk & chair, fans, a mini-fridge & an enormous en-suite bathroom with a shower, bath, his & hers sinks & a separate toilet. Upstairs, a day bed makes the most of the Kalahari views, while at the front, a private 4m x 6m swimming pool is set into a large teak deck. The 3 tented suites come with twin beds or a dbl & have the bonus of an outdoor 'star bath'. There is also a lovely 2-bedroom family villa, complete with its own private pool deck. Distances between the accommodation & the main area are such that fat bikes are parked outside for guests to get around easily on the sand. Not surprisingly, mountain biking is included in the activities here, along with golf, tennis, early-morning horseriding, spa treatments & nature drives. The lodge's proximity to the Aha Hills, Xai Xai & the Gcwihaba Caves allows superb access to San cultural experiences, & a San guide from Xai Xai can be arranged on request to show you the caves or perform a trance dance in the Aha Hills; it is also possible to visit a San village.

Feline Fields is not a safari destination but a few days here will allow guests to indulge in relaxation & great food, & to experience a taste of San culture. *Bush suite US$1,000–1,300 pp, pool suite & family villa US$1,200–1,800 pp, FBA inc road transfers, exc specialised San activities & air transfers.* ⊕ *All year.* 🏕🏕🏕–🏕🏕🏕🏕

TSODILO HILLS (📞 687 8025; ⏰ 07.30–17.30; admission P50 plus P120 for a guide; camping P130 pp/night) Rising above the bush-covered undulations of the western Kalahari, the Tsodilo Hills consist of four hills, roughly in a line, with names from San folklore: the Male Hill, the Female Hill, the Child Hill and a smaller unnamed kopje. Highest is the Male Hill, reaching 410m above the surrounding bush, and – at over 1,400m in total – often considered to be the highest point in Botswana. The San believe that the most sacred place in the hills is near the top. Their tradition is that the first spirit knelt on this hill to pray after creating the world, and that you can still see the impression of his knees in the rock there.

The Female Hill, which covers almost three times the area of the Male, is a little to its north, but reaches only about 300m above the plain. This is where most of the main rock art sites can be seen. Then there's the Child Hill, 2km further north again, and smaller still at only about 40m high. And another 2.2km northwest of the Child is a yet-smaller kopje that is said by the San to be the first wife of the Male Hill, who was then left when he met the Female Hill.

Archaeologists say that the hills have been sporadically inhabited for about 60,000 years – making this one of the world's oldest historical sites. For only about the last millennium has this included Bantu people; for thousands of years prior to that, the San lived here, hunting, using springs in the hills for water, and painting animals (over 2,000 of them) on the rocks.

For both San and Bantu, the Tsodilo Hills were a mystical place, a 'home of very old and very great spirits' who demanded respect from visitors. As told in *The Lost World of the Kalahari* (essential reading before any visit here; page 540), these spirits created much trouble for some of the first Europeans to visit – and were still doing so as recently as the 1950s. Long ago it must have been, in van der Post's words, 'a great fortress of living Bushman culture, a Louvre of the desert filled with treasure.'

The Tsodilo Hills remain a remarkable place, an important national monument which, in 2001, was declared a UNESCO World Heritage Site. While this should help to safeguard the hills for future generations, I can't visit without wondering what it was like when the San were here. What we regard now as the high art of an ancient people is remarkable, but it's very sad that our understanding of it is now devoid of the meaning and spirituality with which it was once imbued.

Visitors are no longer permitted to explore the Tsodilo Hills alone, but it's still worth spending several days searching out the paintings along the marked trails with a guide. However, after several visits over the years, I am left remembering the captivating feeling of spirituality in the hills far more than simply the images of the paintings, however remarkable. I've known this to disturb some visitors profoundly; they were uneasy to the point of wanting to flee the hills, and couldn't wait to get away, while others find the hills entrancing and completely magical.

So if you come here, then do so with respect and take your time – don't just come to tick it off your itinerary and leave.

A word of warning: in *The Lost World of the Kalahari* (page 540), you can read Laurens van der Post's story of his first visit to the hills: of how his party ignored the advice of their guide, and disturbed the spirits of the hills by hunting warthog and steenbok on their way. Once at the hills, his companion's camera magazines inexplicably kept jamming, his tape recorders stopped working, and bees repeatedly attacked his group – and the problems only ceased when they made a written apology to the spirits.

So perhaps the spirits here are one more reason why you ought to treat the Tsodilo Hills with the very greatest of respect when you visit them.

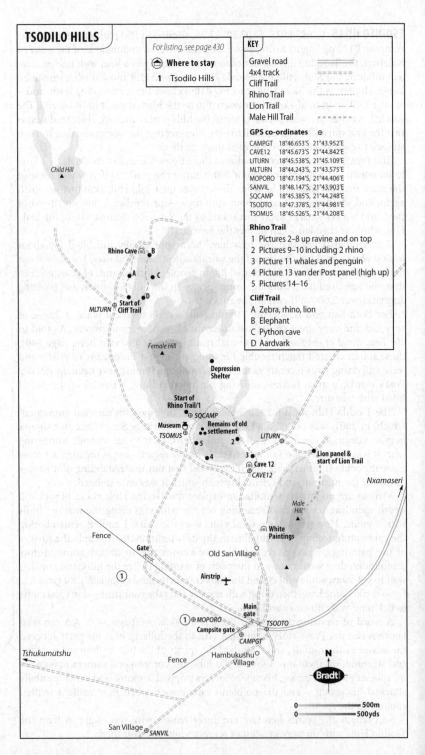

TSODILO HILLS

For listing, see page 430

⌂ **Where to stay**
1 Tsodilo Hills

KEY

Gravel road	
4x4 track	
Cliff Trail	
Rhino Trail	
Lion Trail	
Male Hill Trail	

GPS co-ordinates ⊕

CAMPGT	18°46.653'S, 21°43.952'E
CAVE12	18°45.673'S, 21°44.842'E
LITURN	18°45.538'S, 21°45.109'E
MLTURN	18°44.243'S, 21°43.575'E
MOPORO	18°47.194'S, 21°44.406'E
SANVIL	18°48.147'S, 21°43.903'E
SQCAMP	18°45.385'S, 21°44.248'E
TSODTO	18°47.378'S, 21°44.981'E
TSOMUS	18°45.526'S, 21°44.208'E

Rhino Trail

1 Pictures 2–8 up ravine and on top
2 Pictures 9–10 including 2 rhino
3 Picture 11 whales and penguin
4 Picture 13 van der Post panel (high up)
5 Pictures 14–16

Cliff Trail

A Zebra, rhino, lion
B Elephant
C Python cave
D Aardvark

Child Hill ▲

Rhino Cave ⌂ B
A   C
D
Start of Cliff Trail
MLTURN

Female Hill ▲

Depression Shelter

Start of Rhino Trail/1
⊕ SQCAMP

Museum ⌂
TSOMUS ⊕

Remains of old settlement

5   2   LITURN

4   3   ⊕ Cave 12
CAVE12

Lion panel & start of Lion Trail

Nxamaseri →

Male Hill ▲

White Paintings ⌂

Old San Village ○

Fence

Gate

①

Airstrip ✈

① ⊕ MOPORO
Campsite gate
CAMPGT ⊕

Main gate
TSODTO

Fence

Hambukushu ○ Village

Tshukumutshu
═══

N
↑

Bradt!

0 ─────── 500m
0 ─────── 500yds

San Village ⊕ SANVIL

Background information The Tsodilo Hills hold a special spiritual significance for the people of the region, and are of immense archaeological value to the wider world for what can be learned about some of our earliest ancestors.

Folklore The San believe the hills contain the spirits of the dead, and that their powerful gods live in caves within the Female Hill, from where they rule the world. They believe that these gods will cause misfortune to anyone who hunts or causes death near the hills.

They have many beliefs, all specific to places within the hills. For example, there's a cave on the western side of the Female Hill that contains a permanent source of water and, the San believe, a giant serpent with spiralling horns, like a kudu. If a San guide takes you around the hills, then ask them about legends and stories associated with the places that you visit on the hills.

Meanwhile the Hambukushu people, who also live in the area, believe that God lowered man to earth at the site of the hills, and he landed on the Female Hill. For proof they point to footprints engraved into the rock, high up on the hill. However, modern sceptics claim these are simply natural marks in the rock, or suggest that they might even be the footprints of dinosaurs!

Archaeology Archaeologists think that people (*Homo sapiens* as opposed to *Homo erectus*) have occupied the area for at least 60,000 years. Estimating the age of rock paintings is very difficult, and is usually done by linking a style of painting with nearby artefacts which can be scientifically dated with precision (eg: by carbon-14 dating techniques).

However, the Tsodilo Hills have been the subject of more archaeological research than most of southern Africa's sites – so we do have an idea about the people who lived here. So far, most of the evidence unearthed dates from the Middle Stone Age period. There have been several major excavations, including ones at the Depression Shelter, the Rhino Cave and White Paintings. (See page 544 for articles in *Botswana Notes and Records* with more details. There's also a more personal view of a visit to one of these excavations in Mike Main's *Kalahari: Life's Variety in Dune and Delta*.)

Excavations at White Paintings, a site at the base of the Male Hill, indicate habitation going back at least 40,000–50,000 years. For this the archaeological team excavated as deep as 7m below ground level, finding a variety of stone blades and scrapers. It's estimated that over 55% of the raw materials for these tools don't occur in the hills, and must have been brought in from outside. This at least indicates a movement of people, and perhaps early bartering or trading networks.

Excavations at the Depression Shelter certainly indicate that people were using coloured pigments here, probably for painting, more than 19,000 years ago. However, despite what you'll often read, nobody really knows exactly how the artists made their paints. Many things have been suggested, but animal fats and derivatives of plants seem the likely binding agents, probably mixed with pigments obtained largely from ash, various minerals and plant dyes. Iron oxide, in the form of ochre, seems a particularly likely mineral to have been used.

Meanwhile much more recently, about AD800–1000, specularite was being mined here intensively. This mineral was historically used for cosmetic purposes by groups within southern Africa, further emphasising the likelihood of a long-standing trade network that included the people of the Tsodilo.

The paintings The paintings at the Tsodilo Hills chart thousands of years of human habitation, and include some of the world's most important and impressive rock art. Its special nature is augmented by the realisation that these hills are 250km from the nearest other known rock art. They are totally removed from all of southern Africa's other rock paintings. Even within the hills, some of the paintings are located on high, inaccessible cliffs, with commanding views over the landscape. This was surely a deliberate part of the paintings for the people who created them – although soil erosion has probably also played its part.

Campbell and Coulson, in their excellent book *African Rock Art* (page 546), assert that the Tsodilo Hills 'contain some 4,000 red finger paintings composed of about 50% animals, 37% geometrics, and 13% highly stylised human figures'.

The paintings belong to several different styles and if you take the time to look closely at them will often amaze you with their detail. Although most of the animals painted are wild, Campbell and Coulson noted that there is a much higher incidence of paintings of domestic stock than at any other similar sites in southern Africa.

The human figures include many schematic men painted with erect penises. It's thought that these could be associated with the trance dance – a traditional dance of the San in which rhythmic breathing often produces an altered state of consciousness.

Geology The Tsodilo Hills are formed from metamorphic rocks that are technically known as micaceous quartzite schists. These started out as shales, probably deposited as mud on the surface of an ancient sea. Great heat and pressure in the earth changed them, and you can see the small crystals of minerals formed during this process if you look carefully.

Tsodilo's schists have particularly high mica and quartz contents, and a coarse-grained surface. Conveniently, this texture means that rocks give a good grip to rubber-soled shoes, so they're relatively easy to clamber around. In many places there are piles of boulders, and you'll often need to hop between these if you want to explore the hills.

There are a few permanent springs of water in the hills, but these are very difficult to find without a local guide. They were certainly important to the early inhabitants of the area though, as they would have been the only water sources for kilometres around.

Flora and fauna Unlike most destinations for visitors in Botswana, a visit to the Tsodilo Hills really isn't about looking for animals, birds or plants. The focus is much more cultural and historical. That said, don't forget that you are in a very sparsely populated area of the northern Kalahari and there is wildlife around.

On the roads that approach the hills I've been very aware of fresh elephant dung, and fleeting glimpses of occasional fleeing small buck. There are certainly kudu, steenbok and duiker here permanently, as well as leopard and probably spotted hyena.

In his 1934 book *The Mammals of South West Africa* (page 544), G C Shortridge records that klipspringer were found here at the hills, although I've not come across any reports of them more recently, so it seems unlikely that there is any population of them left now.

Everywhere around the hills you'll find quite a wide variety of birdlife, including the ubiquitous grey hornbills – easily heard as well as seen with their descending call of 'phe, phephee, pheephee, pheeoo, phew, pheeoo-pheeoo' (with thanks to Kenneth Newman for expressing this song so well on paper; page 542).

Look out also for the Tsodilo gecko (*Pachydactylus tsodiloensis*), a small, nocturnal gecko with yellow and brown stripes which is endemic to these hills.

Looking at the vegetation, keep your eyes open for stands of mongongo trees (*Ricinodendron rautanenii*), which occur on the hills and sometimes in pure stands on the Kalahari's sand. These can reach 15–20m in height, and are characterised by smooth, often peeling bark on grey to light-brown stems and compound leaflets a little like the chestnut trees of Europe. After sprays of yellow flowers around October–November, they produce egg-shaped grey-green fruits from February onwards. These can be up to 3.5cm x 2.5cm in size, covered with smooth hairs. Inside these are mongongo nuts, which can be cracked open to reveal an edible kernel – one of the most important, and celebrated, foods for the San across the Kalahari. Coates Palgrave (page 541) comments that this is a protected tree in South Africa, and that its light, strong wood is sometimes used as a substitute for imported balsa wood.

Although large animals aren't prolific in this area, there is big game in the bush around the hills, including elephants, so drive carefully when you are in the area.

Getting there and away

By air There's a bush airstrip at the hills, so it's quite possible (albeit at significant cost) to charter a plane to get you here from Maun or elsewhere in the region. However, once on the ground you'll need a 4x4 to get to the base of the hills, and to the start of the various walking trails, which would need to be organised in advance – perhaps with one of the lodges along the Panhandle if you're staying with them. The other option is to take a helicopter day trip from Maun or one of the Delta lodges, where you'll be met by a 4x4 vehicle from the helipad and enjoy the guided walks and a picnic before your return flight.

Approaching from the air you'll appreciate the hills' uniqueness within the surrounding flat desert landscape, though perhaps miss the excitement as they're first sighted over the treetops.

By car Access to the Tsodilo Hills was improved immeasurably around 2004 with the construction of a new route from the main Shakawe–Sehithwa road. With a relatively smooth gravel surface, it has cut down driving time during the dry season to about 40 minutes, and in so doing has completely changed the nature of a visit here. After heavy rains, however, the gravel road can become very muddy, so in those conditions you'll need to allow nearer to 2 hours for the journey. This road is normally accessible by 2WD, but when you arrive at the hills, a high-clearance vehicle may be advisable.

In the past, there were two access routes: both difficult, sandy, 4x4-only routes, taking about 2½–3 bone-shaking hours (mostly in low-range gear) to complete. Both boasted an unusual type of corrugation which made the whole vehicle bounce up and down. Drive faster than about 10km/h and you found your head hitting the ceiling. It was painful, and ensured that getting to the hills was always a long and tedious drive.

Now, however, the bush is gradually reclaiming these old routes, and only the one road in – and out – remains, starting from close to the village of Nxamaseri. The turning off the main road (✪ T2TURN 18°35.834'S, 21°59.986'E) is indicated by a large green signboard that is surprisingly easy to miss, so do keep your eyes open. It's almost 15km south of the Somachima veterinary fence (✪ VET-SA 18°29.256'S, 21°55.142'E), or 25km north of the turning to Sepupa. From there the track heads southwest until after 34.4km it reaches a right turning clearly signposted 'Tsodilo 5km' at ✪ TSODTO 18°47.378', 21°44.981'E. This leads after just 0.4km to the main entrance gate to the hills (✪ TSGATE 18°47.275'S, 21°44.856'E), kitted out in the smart green livery of the hills.

Getting organised Access to the hills is now firmly controlled, with all visitors passing through the entrance gate, where you'll pay your entrance fees. The site is managed by the local community, and fee increases over the years have been significant – but at least it is now the local people who benefit from the extraordinary heritage that is on their doorstep.

Whereas once the hills were a place to explore for yourself, preferably with a local guide, nowadays you must hire a **guide** – either at the entrance gate or by the parking area, where picnic benches are laid out in the shade. The cost varies depending on the trail (P120–175/group), so do give yourself plenty of time to investigate each of the paintings as you go; 2 hours is probably about average, but you may wish to take longer. Some of the guides are truly excellent, while others are less well qualified, so if you're genuinely interested in understanding more about the hills, it may be well to ask a few salient questions before you agree on a guide.

Next to the parking area you'll find a small **museum** (✪ TSOMUS 18°45.526'S, 21°44.208'E) – more a series of contemplative thoughts about the hills than an exhibition of artefacts, but interesting nonetheless. This is where you'll pay for your guide, and can sometimes buy cold drinks, and a small selection of handmade jewellery. A large ablution block contains not just toilets, but showers, too – useful for sluicing off the inevitable dirt that will have accumulated if you've tackled one of the more arduous trails (though there are no towels). For the trails themselves, do wear good, strong shoes or boots, and take a hat, suncream and plenty of water. A walking pole might be a useful extra.

Most visitors spend their time on Female Hill, and may visit the Male. Without a special permit, visitors are not allowed to the Child Hill or the kopje beyond, to which there are no vehicle tracks. Ideally, plan your day to start walking as early as possible – which given that the park gates don't open until 07.30, will not be much before 08.00. Campers, though, can gain a good half an hour on this, which is well worthwhile to avoid walking in the heat of the day.

 Where to stay *Map, page 426*
There has long been talk of a new tented camp opening at the hills, but for now, your options are limited to camping.

Tsodilo Hills campsites (6 pitches) Camping in this area, under the control of the Tsodilo Community Trust, is now limited to one very large open area, with a rather over-the-top entrance gate (🕒 07.00–16.30), exclusively for campers. You'll find this gate, clearly proclaiming 'Tsodilo Community Trust Campsite', at right angles to the main gate to the hills. If you're camping, you can pay both your camping (P130 pp/night) & entry fees (P50 pp/day) here.

Although you'll be told more or less where to pitch your tent, the pitches are only roughly demarcated, & quite far apart, so unless it's busy it's really a question of finding one that you like. 4 of them – the Mopororo (✪ MOPORO 18°47.194'S, 21°44.406'E), Dimbo, Dimbo da diwe & Aininai sites – are only about 1km from the gate, sharing a small modern ablution block that would be fine

if the goats would stay out & the local baboons weren't so intent on turning on the taps. The pitches themselves have a standpipe for water, & a firepit, so it's all fairly civilised. Wherever you camp, do be aware that you might find domestic animals around.

Having paid their entry fees along with the camping fee, campers have their own entrance to the hills – a gate in the fence (✪ CAMPGT 18°46.653'S, 21°43.952'E) that separates the 2 parts of the site. From the ablution block to the gate it's about 2km, then a further 2.4km from the gate to the parking area. Thus as a camper, you can be at the museum & ready to start on one of the trails slightly earlier than those driving in. There's no great advantage in this except when it's very hot – when the earlier you start, the more pleasant it will be exploring the trails.

Some years back, before there were any organised guides to the hills, I drove to the San village of Hambukushu – which had been moved from its old location between the hills to a new location (⊕ SANVIL 18°48.147'S, 21°43.903'E) about 3.8km south-southwest of there, well away from the hills. With sign gestures and improvisation, I tried to ask for a guide. The man of the family that I was speaking to eventually sent me off with two of the children, a boy called Xashee, aged 10, and a girl called Tsetsana, aged 16.

At first I thought that I'd been fobbed off with the children, who were silent in the presence of their family. However, as soon as we got into our car to drive back to the hills, it transpired that Tsetsana was on holiday from school, and spoke excellent English. Her brother spoke much less to us, but seemed to know more of the sites with rock art. They bounded up the hills with bare feet, faster than we could in walking boots. They knew their way about very well and although we only followed on the 'standard' trails, we would have missed many of the paintings without their help.

Perhaps these children, or their friends, are among the guides who show people around the hills today.

What to see and do Visitors have the option of four trails on the hills: the Rhino Trail, the Cliff Trail, the Lion Trail and the Male Hill Trail. References to other trails, however enticing, are irrelevant: you are no longer permitted to explore beyond these guided routes. The old Divuyu Trail, for example, can be visited only by archaeologists engaged in scientific research.

In theory, guides will tailor your walk as required, taking into account both what you want to see and the level of exertion required. In practice, however, visitors are usually encouraged to take the Rhino Trail, at the north end of the Female Hill, which is the most accessible trail, and features the most well-known paintings. The best guidebook to the area is *Guide to the Tsodilo Hills World Heritage Site*, which is available from Ngami Data Services in Maun (page 192).

The notes that follow are from my own and readers' observations. I'm aware they may contain errors as well as omissions, but I hope that they'll spur other readers to explore – and perhaps send me any corrections or additional comments.

Rhino Trail (P120/guide; approx 2½hrs) In theory this trail is marked with sequentially numbered posts, though despite walking the trail on several occasions, some of them have proved elusive, especially in the lush vegetation early in the year.

The trail starts from close to the old Squirrel Valley Campsite (⊕ SQCAMP 18°45.385'S, 21°44.248'E), a short walk from the museum and car park. The numbered posts are clearer at the end of the dry season, and the GPS references here should be a help to make sure you're in roughly the right place, but if your guide doesn't know the trail well, you may still have to search a bit to find the paintings. Note that some of the numbered posts indicate features of archaeological interest, rather than paintings, such as an old waterhole or a place where hunters would have sharpened their spears – though steps are being added in some places to improve access.

The first marker, **No 1**, sets the scene with a granite rock whose deep grooves suggest that it served for sharpening spears.

Picture 2 (⊕ PICT2 18°45.331'S, 21°44.225'E) is deeper into the ravine and higher up, at an altitude of 1,063m. There's quite a lot of steep rock-hopping to climb up this ravine at the beginning of the trail. It won't be suitable for anyone who is uncomfortable clambering around rocky slopes.

Less than 100m north-northwest of No 2, but higher up again, is **Picture 3** (⊕ PICT3 18°45.291'S, 21°44.239'E), a beautiful silhouette of a rhino that's perhaps 100cm across, with gemsbok below.

By the time you reach **Picture 5**, which includes an impressive giraffe, the trail starts to open out, and you're heading towards the centre of the Female Hill. Here **No 7** marks another spear-sharpening rock on the site of an old San settlement. It's a large, relatively flat and secluded area, where the head of the tribe and his family would have been well protected. Another grooved rock here indicates where tools were sharpened, and the geometric designs painted on the rocks suggest the presence of shaman.

Found under an overhang, **Picture 8** (⊕ PICT8 18°45.150'S, 21°44.576'E) – known as 'the dancing penises' – depicts several men in what is considered to be an initiation ceremony. It lies at an altitude of 1,102m, from where you can see the Male Hill.

Continuing downhill, you'll come to the site of a lower settlement, whose inhabitants' role was to protect the upper settlement from invasion. Here, the white domestic animals of **Picture 9** (⊕ PICT9 18°45.437'S, 21°44.723'E) were created more recently than most of the paintings – around 1,000 years ago. Their chalk-based pigments have survived the elements as they're sheltered beneath a cave overhang. Almost adjacent, the main figures of **Picture 10** consist of two rather beautifully painted rhino, for which the Rhino Trail is named. These are the most famous of Tsodilo's paintings, as they now form the logo of The Botswana Society.

Shortly, this trail joins the main track which leads west between the Female and Male hills. Detour to the right of this, and you'll find **Picture 11** (⊕ PICT11 18°45.635'S, 21°44.862'E), which appears to include a penguin and at least one whale. Arguably this is one of the pieces of evidence that indicates that the Bushmen travelled far more widely than is commonly believed, adding weight to Robert Gordon's contention in his *Bushman Myth: The Making of a Namibian Underclass* (page 544), that our view of the Bushman is often misguided.

This trail then leads around to **No 12** (⊕ CAVE12 18°45.673'S, 21°44.842'E), a large cave at the base of the Female Hill, facing the Male Hill. Known locally as the Makena Cave, it is said to be where a woman who went missing for several months was found, over a thousand years ago. From here there's a short tunnel back to the path, where – if you look up – you'll see an extraordinary rock formation that resembles a three-dimensional map of Africa.

Following the main track north along the west side of Female Hill brings you to **Picture 13** (⊕ PICT13 18°45.627'S, 21°44.436'E). Move closer to the hill here, then look up and slightly back at the hills; there, high up, you'll see what is now known as the '**van der Post panel**'. In his inimitable style, Laurens described first seeing this:

> Over the scorched leaves of the tops of the bush conforming to a contour nearby, and about a hundred feet up, was a ledge of honey-coloured stone grafted into the blue iron rock. Above the ledge rose a smooth surface of the same warm, soft stone curved like a sea shell as if rising into the blue to form a perfect dome. I had no doubt that I was looking at the wall and part of the ceiling of what had once been a great cave…

But what held my attention still with the shock of discovery was the painting that looked down at us from the centre of what was left of the wall and dome of the cave. Heavy as were the shadows, and seeing it only darkly against the sharp morning light, it was yet so distinct and filled with fire of its own colour that every detail stood out with a burning clarity. In the focus of the painting, scarlet against the gold of the stone, was an enormous eland bull standing sideways, his massive body charged with masculine power and his noble head looking as if he had only that moment been disturbed in his grazing. He was painted, as only a Bushman, who had a deep identification with an eland, could have painted him.

This footpath, which follows the west side of Female Hill, heads roughly north. Very close to the path, **Picture 14** depicts rhino, warthog and several antelope. Next, less than 400m from the start of the trail, **Picture 15** (⊕ PICT15 18°45.556'S, 21°44.361'E) includes lots of very clearly painted giraffe, rhino, gemsbok and other antelope on a wonderfully colourful outcrop of rock.

Finally, just before arriving back at the old Squirrel Valley Campsite, **Picture 16** includes a curious circular design – almost geometrical – that is reminiscent of a shield, the shell of a tortoise or even a wheel; this, like similar earlier paintings, is considered to be a shaman symbol.

Cliff Trail (P175/guide; approx 3hrs) This is at the north end of Female Hill, starting near the old Malatso Campsite, which is found by forking right at ⊕ MLTURN 18°44.243'S, 21°43.575'E. You'll reach the steep base of the cliffs, about 50m away, where there's a turning circle for vehicles.

The trail circles broadly clockwise around the northern part of Female Hill, before taking a short cut back to near its start over a col.

Reader Jon Williamson walked the Cliff Trail in 2011, and sent us the following report:

The Cliff Trail is fairly similar in appearance to the Rhino Trail, but the path was not as cleared. Some points along the trail were partly obstructed by tree damage caused by elephants. The cliff paintings were as frequent as those found along the Rhino Trail, but not as grandiose: we saw impressions of lion, rhino, zebra, aardvark, elephant and scorpion, as well as some geometric shapes:

zebra	⊕ 18°43.917'S, 21°43.734'E
rhino	⊕ 18°43.908'S, 21°43.735'E
lion	⊕ 18°43.899'S, 21°43.741'E
zebra	⊕ 18 43.659'S, 21°43.810'E
elephant	⊕ 18°43.669'S, 21°43.880'E
scorpion	⊕ 18°43.712'S, 21°43.896'E
aardvark	⊕ 18°44.196'S, 21°43.732'E

The most exciting part of the Cliff Trail was actually just off the trail: a cave (⊕ PYTHCV 18°43.863'S, 21°43.870'E) containing a rock formation shaped like a large snake. Before our trip, we had read that the earliest evidence of practised human rituals was found in a cave in Botswana, so we persuaded our guide to show it to us.

Lion Trail (P175/guide; approx 2hrs) This trail stays at ground level, and doesn't include any climbing. It overlaps with some of the Rhino Trail's paintings at the base of the south end of Female Hill, as well as visiting sites on the north side of

Male Hill. It starts at the base of the Male Hill, reached by turning off the track between the Male and Female hills at ⊕ LITURN 18°45.538'S, 21°45.109'E.

Male Hill Trail (P175/guide; approx 2hrs) Also known as the Summit Trail, this starts from the same place as the Lion Trail, though it eventually goes to the top of Male Hill, then back down the same route. The route has some strenuous scrambles, so good footwear and relatively good fitness are essential, but the views from the summit are well worth the effort.

Around the hills Just south of the entrance gate to the hills is a small settlement, **Hambukushu**, with some corrals for animals. Further away, on the way from the main gate to the San Village, a track heads off right, on a northwest bearing of about 305°. I've followed this for 7–8km, and it remains a good track, which I believe heads for a place called **Tshukumutshu**. I'd welcome more information on it if readers have gone further.

AHA AND GCWIHABA (Admission P100 pp; camping P450 pp/night) Over 150km southwest of the Tsodilo Hills lies an even more remote area, populated by scattered San villages and dotted with a number of hills. This is one of the most remote areas of the Kalahari, and it attracts the most experienced bush travellers simply 'because it's there'. This is expedition territory, best reserved for those who are well equipped and bush-wise. Most go to visit the Aha Hills, straddling the border with Namibia, and the nearby Gcwihaba Hills, which contain the fascinating Gcwihaba (or Drotsky's) Caves. These are easily located and not commercialised.

In reality, though the Gcwihaba Caves are the only cave system here that's practical for most visitors to see, there are a number of others in the area which have been unearthed by local scientists in the last few decades. The locations of these are usually kept secret to avoid visitors damaging them or having a serious accident (which would be all too easy).

History Though people have occupied the area for at least 12,500 years, it doesn't seem as if the caves were used extensively. Excavations in Gcwihaba Caves (in 1969 by Yellen et al; page 545) did find evidence of charcoal, ostrich eggshell and bone fragments, thought to be the remnants of human occupation, but the finds were limited and there is no rock art here at all.

These caves were first brought to the attention of the outside world in June 1932 when the local !Kung people showed the cave to a farmer from Ghanzi, Martinus Drotsky. Hence for many years this was known as Drotsky's Cave. (As an aside, Martinus was the grandfather of Jan Drotsky, who runs Drotsky's Cabins, near Shakawe.)

GPS CO-ORDINATES FOR MAP (OPPOSITE)					
DOBEVI	19°34.830'S, 21°04.428'E		QANGWA	19°31.868'S, 21°10.281'E	
GCWIHA	20°01.250'S, 21°21.230'E		TSAU	20°10.294'S, 22°27.265'E	
GTURN1	20°07.047'S, 22°22.291'E		WAXHUN	19°43.532'S, 21°03.489'E	
GTURN2	19°39.577'S, 22°11.010'E		WAXHUS	19°46.643'S, 21°02.518'E	
GTURN3	19°54.286'S, 21°09.418'E		XAIXAI	19°52.867'S, 21°04.934'E	
GTURN4	19°57.556'S, 21°44.541'E				

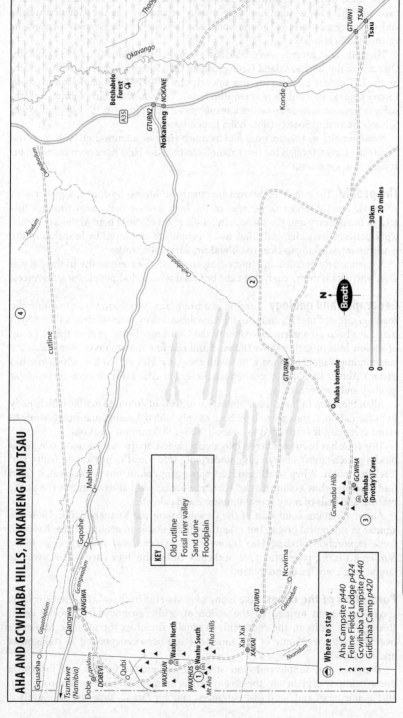

AHA AND GCWIHABA HILLS, NOKANENG AND TSAU

Bradt

N

30km
0
20 miles
0

KEY

Old cutline
Fossil river valley
Sand dune
Floodplain

Where to stay

1 Aha Campsite p440
2 Feline Fields Lodge p424
3 Gcwihaba Campsite p440
4 Gidichaa Camp p420

The local !Kung refer to these hills as '/twihaba' – hence the hills, and main cave and this cave system, are now usually referred to as the Gcwihaba Hills and Caves respectively (although you'll see this spelled in a variety of ways in various publications).

The hills and caverns were declared a national monument in 1934 and the Director of the Bechuanaland Geological Survey visited the caverns with Drotsky in 1943. The first cave survey was undertaken in 1970 by a school group from Falcon College in Zimbabwe (then Rhodesia). Various scientific explorations and surveys have been done since then, including an expedition in 1991 by the British Schools Exploring Society (now BSES Expeditions).

Nowhere else in this area has had as much time or attention given to it as the Gcwihaba Caves, though the two sinkholes in the Aha Hills have been surveyed on at least two occasions.

The people The people of the area are mostly Ju/'hoansi Bushmen, together with a few Herero (Mbanderu). Because of the lung disease that swept through this area of the country and the subsequent eradication of cattle here in the late 1990s, work patterns have changed. Thus many people are employed by branches of the government, working to clear roads and similar public works.

A particularly detailed and interesting article on the community in the Xai Xai area, with details from a study there, can be found at w kalaharipeoples.org/resources.

Geography and geology Turning east from Tsau, you'll soon start to notice the road's gentle decline. It's entering the Gcwihaba Valley, a fossil river valley which may have been an ancient extension of the Okavango Delta. Within this, a group of six low hills protrude above the sand and rise to a maximum of 30m above the surrounding valley. (Compare this with the Male Hill at Tsodilo, which reaches 410m.) About 40–50km northwest of these, the Aha Hills share a very similar geology and appearance.

All of these low hills are made almost exclusively of dolomite marble which, early in its formation, is thought to have been steeply folded, causing many of its strata to stand vertically. It's estimated to be about 800–1,000 million years old.

This rock has been weathered into a very jagged, sharp surface and many loose blocks which aren't always easy underfoot. Underneath, numerous faults and fractures split it. When weathered it appears a grey colour, but if you break it you'll find a pearly-white colour inside. There are occasional bands of muscovite in the marble, and beds of more recent limestone and calcrete.

About 15–20km southwest of the Gcwihaba are the Koanaka Hills. These are similar in geological origin, but essentially inaccessible to visitors. There has been some exploration of these (see *Discovery and Exploration of Two New Caves in the Northwest District*, page 545). One of them – called the 'blue cave' – is Botswana's largest cave complex found to date.

Formation of the caves Like many cave systems in the world, the Gcwihaba Caves have been formed by the action of acidic groundwater flowing down through the faults in the rock. This gradually dissolves the alkaline limestone over the centuries. Some of this limestone has been redeposited as stalagmites and stalactites.

That said, this simple and quite standard explanation for the cave formation doesn't entirely explain why the cave system is more or less horizontal throughout. (It has northeast and southeast entrances, and appears to have had two levels at different times.) Because of this, Cooke and Baillieul note (page 544) that from the size of the caves and passages, it seems likely that very large volumes of groundwater must have moved within the rock here – perhaps an underground course of the old Gcwihaba River. This would explain the sheer size of some of the caves.

For that to have been the case, the area's water table must have been much higher for at least one period historically, and probably two. After these levels had subsided, and the caves emptied of water, then stalagmites and stalactites would have been formed gradually by a trickle-through of more moderate volumes of water (eg: rainfall) through faultlines.

Flora and fauna
Though visits to this part of the Kalahari are usually for caves and culture, there is some wildlife around. As with most places in the Kalahari, this area is at its most beautiful and the flora and fauna are at their most vibrant during and shortly after the summer rains (January to about April).

Flora This classic Kalahari environment is dominated by the silver terminalia (*Terminalia sericea*), identified by the silvery sheen on its blue-grey leaves, and the Kalahari appleleaf (*Philenoptera nelsii*). You'll also find some bushwillows (*Combretum collinum*) and wild seringa bushes (*Burkea africana*).

Raisin bushes (*Grewia flava*) are here accompanied by sandpaper raisin bushes (*Grewia flavescens*) and the false sandpaper raisin bushes (*Grewia retinervis*). Rub a leaf of either of the latter between your fingers and you'll soon realise how they got their common names.

One tree worth noting here is the Namaqua fig (*Ficus cordata*). This is well known throughout the central highlands of Namibia and down to the Cape – but otherwise unrecorded in Botswana. Here you'll find it growing all over the hills, its roots often flattened against the rocks. Several strong specimens grow around the entrances to the Gcwihaba Caves, green and thriving even during the dry season, perhaps due to the cooler, moister microclimate in the air of the caves.

Similarly, the mopane aloe (*Aloe littoralis*) is found here and throughout Namibia, but nowhere else in northern or central Botswana. It's a striking plant with a single, vertical stem, succulent leaves with serrated edges and a flower head that branches into pointed spikes of red flowers.

All around the region you'll certainly find the Devil's claw creeper (*Harpagophytum procumbens procumbens*). Recognise it by its pinky-mauve flowers with a hint of yellow in the centre in January to March, and after that its small but wicked oval fruit that has hooks on all sides – like some tiny medieval jousting ball with grappling hooks. (This could be confused with the large Devil's thorn, *Dicerocaryum eriocarpum*, which has a brighter pink flower but a much less elaborate fruit.)

The Devil's claw is found all over the Kalahari. It's in demand from overseas for its medicinal properties, with herbal extracts variously claimed to aid in the treatment of intestinal complaints, arthritis and many other ailments. Hence anywhere near a centre of population is likely to be largely devoid of these plants, but in the more remote areas of the Kalahari you'll often find it beside the sandy track.

Fauna Big game is present throughout this area, but it's relatively scarce especially near to settlements where you're more likely to come into contact with dogs and domestic stock. That said, gemsbok, springbok, eland, steenbok, duiker and kudu all occur in the area. Veronica Roodt reports seeing six very relaxed wild dog near the entrance to Gcwihaba Caves, and there are also occasional lion, leopard, cheetah and spotted hyena around. Hence there must be a reasonable population of their antelope prey – even if these seem elusive due to the relatively thick vegetation, and lack of waterholes at which they might gather and be more easily spotted.

Given the huge distances that elephant can cover, and the spoor that I've seen near the Tsodilo Hills, I wouldn't be surprised to find lone bulls wandering around during the wet season. Drivers, be warned.

If approaching this area then, while looking for big game, don't forget the smaller stuff. Small seasonal pans will fill with a noisy mélange of bullfrogs which have spent the dry season underground, attracted by the water and the number of grasshoppers and crickets around.

There's no better time to see plenty of small reptiles, from the Kalahari serrated tortoise, with its bold, geometric patterns, to the flap-necked chameleon. Around sunset, and for the first few hours after that, listen out for the *click-click* of the barking gecko, sometimes described as like rattling a box of matches. The onomatopoeic name 'Aha' is said to come from the sound made by these often-unseen residents.

Inside the Gcwihaba Caves is a different story. Some of the earlier scientists to visit the cave noted that leopard inhabited it, and found fresh spoor. Meanwhile, its name derives from the !Kung word for 'hyena's hole'. While I don't know of any more recent visitors who have come across large predators in here, you can't help but notice the bats! These can be noisy and smelly, but are otherwise harmless.

The most common species here is probably the insectivorous Commerson's leaf-nosed bat (*Hipposideros commersoni*). These are the largest insectivorous bats in southern Africa which, although they only grow to a weight of about 120g, can have a wingspan as large as 60cm. These have short, pale fawn-coloured hair all over, and black feet. Males have distinctive tufts of white fur on their shoulders. These are the bats that leave the caves in large numbers at dusk.

Also found in numbers are the tiny Dent's horseshoe bat (*Rhinolophus denti*), which weigh a mere 6g and measure about 7cm long, with a wingspan of 20cm, when fully grown. Horseshoe bats like this are identified because of complex 'nose-leaf' structures on their face between their mouths and their foreheads (used to locate their insect prey using the animal equivalent of radar).

A third common bat here is the Egyptian (also called 'common') slit-faced bat (*Nycteris thebaica*), which is easily identified by its long, rounded ears and the 'split' running down the centre of its face. They fly efficiently but relatively slowly, eat insects, and grow to about 10cm long with a wingspan of about 24cm.

Given the presence of these bats, it's quite likely that they support a small ecosystem of invertebrates in the caves. In similar caves in Namibia, several hundred kilometres to the west of here, scientists have also discovered small but highly poisonous spiders. So tread carefully…

Birdlife As with anywhere in the Kalahari, the birds here can either survive without drinking water, or will routinely fly long distances to find it every day. Guineafowl and red-billed spurfowl are very common, though coqui and crested francolin also occur. Sandgrouse are common, particularly the namaqua and double-banded species, though you'll also find Burchell's and, occasionally, the yellow-throated varieties. Doves are here too, with Cape turtle, laughing and namaqua species always around.

The area's LBJs ('little brown jobbies', as keen birdwatchers refer to the plethora of smaller, brown birds whose similarities tax their identification skills) include chestnut-backed finchlarks, sabota larks and penduline tits.

Larger and more visible birds, which are easier to spot and identify, include double-banded coursers, and black-bellied and red-crested korhaans. Both of these korhaans show interesting displays during the mating season. You may also come across the world's heaviest flying bird, the kori bustard, and ostriches are not unknown, though they are very uncommon.

Of the raptors, by far the commonest is the pale chanting goshawk, which is usually seen perching atop a bush, small tree or post, surveying the area. When disturbed it'll usually swoop off, flying low, to a similar perch not far away. The very similar, but slightly larger, dark chanting goshawk may also be found here, on the edge of its range. (These are distinguishable in flight, from above, as the pale variety has a white rump, whereas the dark chanting goshawk has a darker colouring and a darker, barred rump.)

Getting there and away

Two roads head west from the main Shakawe–Sehithwa road, the A35, and then loop around and join up with each other around the Aha Hills. Both are very long. The southern route is very sandy and very hard-going, while the northern route is longer, but better as far as Xai Xai. Either way, navigation is reasonably straightforward, and a 4x4 remains essential.

The northern route About 300m north of the centre of Nokaneng there's a track heading west (✢ GTURN2 19°39.577'S, 22°11.010'E). This is the longer of the two routes, but the surface is now gravel, so although it can still be heavy going, it's usually the easier option. From here to Xai Xai, you can expect the drive to take about 3–4 hours.

From Nokaneng, the road twists and turns quite a lot but after a little over 120km, or around 3 hours, you'll reach the tiny village of **Qangwa** (✢ QANGWA 19°31.868'S, 21°10.281'E), sometimes spelled 'Xangwa', or even 'Gcangwa', which supports a small shop.

From Qangwa the gravel road continues west towards Namibia, ultimately to Tsumkwe (✢ TSUMKW 19°35.507'S, 20°30.184'E). For the hills, take the track that leads southwest for over 10km to another small village, Dobe (✢ DOBEVI 19°34.830'S, 21°04.428'E). From there the track picks its way through the Aha Hills, heading due south. It passes west of the small group of hills which contain Waxhu North Cave, or sinkhole (✢ WAXHUN 19°43.532'S, 21°03.489'E), and east of the main range of hills, within which is found the Waxhu South Cave, or sinkhole (✢ WAXHUS 19°46.643'S, 21°02.518'E). That said, the relatively thick bush found in the area makes these caves difficult to find, even with the aid of a GPS. Finally, after about 37km, the road reaches the village of **Xai Xai** (✢ XAIXAI 19°52.867'S, 21°04.934'E).

In some literature you'll find this designated as Nxainxai, CaeCae or, more recently, /Xai/Xai. However you want to spell it, this is one of the largest villages in the area, with a population of about 300–400 Ju/'hoansi San people, and perhaps 50 Herero (Mbanderu) people, who are mostly cattle farmers. The village has a borehole, a small primary school, a basic health post and a few shops, as well as an airstrip.

From Xai Xai the route turns east, becoming the southern route described below, which ultimately ends on the main road near Tsau. About 10km east of Xai Xai you pass a clear right turn (✢ GTURN3 19°54.286'S, 21°09.418'E) to the Gcwihaba Hills and Cave (✢ GCWIHA 20°01.250'S, 21°21.230'E), a distance of almost 30km.

The southern route A large banner on the side of the road some 10km north of Tsau (✢ GTURN1 20°07.047'S, 22°22.291'E) clearly marks the correct path to follow for the southern route. This is the shortest route to the hills and caves (the

14

latter being relatively well signposted), but it can become a quagmire if there has been rain in the area.

During the dry season, the first few hours from Tsau are generally fairly easy driving, as the hard, compacted track gently descends into the fossil river valley. However, during the rains a number of wide, shallow pans hold water here, turning it into a series of connected mud-holes and a challenging route even for experienced drivers. After that, the country becomes rolling duneland with thick sand, which is slow going but not as treacherous as the mud.

About 90km from Tsau there's a left turning (⊕ GTURN4 19°57.556'S, 21°44.541'E). This passes the Xhaba borehole, a satellite cattle post of Xai Xai Village, after about 26km, and then reaches the hills another 26km later. It's the quickest way to the hills. If you miss this turn-off then continue on to the main turning (⊕ GTURN3 19°54.286'S, 21°09.418'E) used by the northern route, and take a left there. This is over 150km from Tsau.

Getting organised To get the best out of such an experience, you're probably wisest to come here with an experienced mobile-safari operator who – and this is vital – knows the village and villagers well. They'll also know what's possible, while the community benefits in just the same way. This will be more costly than trying to do something yourself, but probably much more satisfactory.

Alternatively you might drive yourself, with at least one fully equipped 4x4, and with all your fuel, food and water. Although water is usually available at Xai Xai Village, and basic supplies may be found both there and at Qangwa, it's better to bring with you everything that you might need.

As with any tracks in the Kalahari, and especially those that are rarely used, a major danger is fire caused by grass seeds and stems blocking up your vehicle's radiator, or collecting near its exhaust system. If you're driving here, especially during the first few months of the year, you must take steps to prevent this (page 172).

A third option would be to fly in, using the airstrip at Xai Xai, although with the exception of Feline Fields Lodge (page 424) there is a lack of accommodation in the area for fly-in guests.

To explore the caves you'll need several good torches, plus extra batteries and bulbs (a fail-safe emergency back-up is essential, as there's no-one here to help you), and perhaps a lighter or matches. A large ball of string would also be handy to prevent you getting lost.

⌂ Where to stay *Map, page 435*

Managed by the Xaixai Tlhabobologo Development Trust, there is a rudimentary campsite at the Aha Hills and Gcwihaba. Since these are not signposted, it's best to contact the Concession Manager, Eric Keharara (m 7375 6518; e ekeharara@yahoo.com) in advance. He can then direct you to the exact location – and collect your fees for camping (P450 pp), the concession (P100 pp), vehicle entry (P50) and entry to the site (P100 pp).

Aha Campsite Located close to Waxhu South Sinkhole, there is no water at this campsite (the nearest is at Xai Xai), nor any other facilities, including toilets, so it's vital that you bring everything that you need with you, & take away all your rubbish (or at least everything that cannot be burned & reduced to ash). Take a spade, so you can bury your waste deeply, & always burn your toilet paper. *P450 pp.*

Gcwihaba Campsite Located about 3km from the caves themselves, the 5 pitches at the campsite have largely been abandoned.

However, the ablution block showers & toilets were still functional in 2023. So while you may be able to get water here in an emergency, we would recommend that you take everything you might need – & remove all your rubbish. *P450 pp.*

What to see and do

Aha Hills   About 40–50km northwest of the Gcwihaba Hills, and visible from them, is a range of low, rounded hills: the Aha Hills. These straddle the Botswana–Namibia border, and are among the most remote and little-visited destinations in Botswana.

Like the Gcwihaba Hills, this range is made of dolomite marble that has been split by weathering into numerous faults and fractures. This presents a very jagged surface, with many loose blocks underfoot, and isn't easy to walk on.

The range covers about 245km², most of which is in Botswana, and very little of which has been properly mapped or documented. With the access road to Xai Xai, visitors can now reach the hills from both Botswana and Namibia with relative ease.

In some ways the hills are attractive simply because they're so remote. Even though there are now designated campsites, this is a place that few visitors ever get to.

Clambering around isn't as much fun here as in the Tsodilo Hills, simply because the rock surface is totally different. Instead of large boulders with an even surface and an easy grip, the Aha Hills are made of endless jagged little blocks. So if you do come here, stout walking shoes with strong soles make clambering around a lot easier.

Two sites on the Botswana side have attracted some interest, and both are sinkholes – large holes in the ground. The local people apparently know both simply as 'Waxhu', which means 'house of god'. Both can only be visited using specialist climbing/caving equipment, so don't be tempted to try and climb down. There are no mountain-rescue teams in Botswana!

Waxhu North Cave (✪ WAXHUN 19°43.532'S, 21°03.498'E) was first described in 1974 and is about 70m deep.

Waxhu South Cave (✪ WAXHUS 19°46.632'S, 21°02.518'E) is also known by some of its recent visitors as 'Independence Cave', because they first visited it on the fifth anniversary of Botswana's independence. This cave is about 50m deep.

Botswana Notes and Records (page 544) records many more details on these sinkholes, including rough maps of them and information about the various expeditions that have explored them recently.

Gcwihaba Hills and Caves   The low, rounded hills here are not the attraction, but beneath them is a labyrinth of passages and caves, some with enchanting rock formations of stalagmites, stalactites and spectacular 'flowstones' which seem like waterfalls of rock.

Some of these chambers reach up to 10m in height, while other passages are so narrow that you'll need to clamber and squeeze through. All were formed by the dissolving and depositing action of acidic water on the limestone of the rocks around, though now the caves are totally dry.

There had been plans under Ian Khama's tenure as president to develop the caves for better tourist access, with professional cave guides and motion-sensitive lighting illuminating the geological features. With the change of president, these plans are currently on hold. For now, at the time of writing a team of French researchers were working with Botswana National Museum archaeologists to explore human evolution in Gcwihaba. Should they succeed in identifying hominid

14

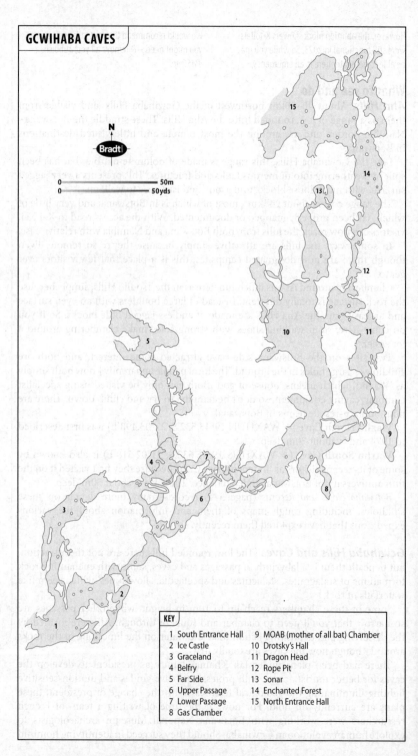

GCWIHABA CAVES

N

Bradt

0   50m
0   50yds

KEY

1 South Entrance Hall	9 MOAB (mother of all bat) Chamber
2 Ice Castle	10 Drotsky's Hall
3 Graceland	11 Dragon Head
4 Belfry	12 Rope Pit
5 Far Side	13 Sonar
6 Upper Passage	14 Enchanted Forest
7 Lower Passage	15 North Entrance Hall
8 Gas Chamber	

fossils, Botswana would join the countries in the 'Cradle of Humankind' and seek to secure UNESCO World Heritage Site status for the Aha Hills, Gcwihaba Hills and Koanaka Hills.

The string that used to mark the route through the total darkness of the caves has been removed due to disrepair and the chance of tourists getting lost, making it more important than ever that you attempt this route only with a local guide.

There are two main entrances to the caves, about 250m apart, each marked with a monument. Although there is a route between them, it's not straightforward or obvious, so getting through may tax your map-reading skills. (You won't be able to rely on your GPS either, as they're useless under the rock ceilings of the caves!) There are lots of dead ends, closed-off passages and caverns to penetrate. If your curiosity flags, then remind yourself of the legend of Hendrik Matthys van Zyl, the wealthy founder of Ghanzi, who is said to have stashed a portion of his fortune here in the late 1800s.

Most of the caves are on one level, though there is a section, slightly nearer to the south entrance than the north, where several of the corridors split into two different levels, one raised several metres above the other. You can expect a considerable amount of bat guano underfoot, but at least the complete lack of natural light means that you shouldn't need to worry about snakes.

Start exploring the caves from the main (north) entrance. Here, on one of the large boulders towards the right of the main entrance hall, you'll find the inscription 'Discovered 1 June 1932, M Drotsky'.

The route starts at the lower entrance, and proceeds down an increasingly steep and narrow passageway. There's a short vertical climb down into what's been christened the 'rope pit', before you emerge up the other side on to a shelf. Then it's a bit of a squeeze before you find yourself in a large chamber.

From here the route basically climbs, though there are lots of side-passages to distract you, and part way through is where there are two different levels to the passages. You'll also come across the chambers with bats in them, deep within the cave complex, before finally emerging from the southern entrance (where there's a ledge that is now used as a roost by a resident barn owl).

15

The Kalahari's Great Salt Pans

The great salt pans lie in the heart of the northern Kalahari, forming an area of empty horizons into which the blinding white expanse of the pans disappears in a shimmering heat-haze. In winter, dust devils whirl across the open plains; in summer many become undulating seas of grasses beneath the turbulence of the stormy skies. It is a harsh, spare landscape, not to everybody's taste, but it offers an isolation as complete as anywhere in southern Africa, and a wealth of hidden treasures for those prepared to make the effort – including Stone Age ruins and prehistoric beaches.

The wildlife is rich, but highly seasonal and nomadic. At times you'll find great concentrations of plains game, with all their attendant predators, and, in good years, spectacular breeding colonies of flamingos crowd the shallow waters of Sua Pan. At other times the stage seems empty. But even then, there is always a cast of smaller Kalahari residents behind the scenes – from coursers and korhaans to mongooses and mole-rats.

BACKGROUND INFORMATION

GEOGRAPHY AND GEOLOGY The Magkadikgadi Pans consist of an immense expanse of largely flat and featureless terrain in the north of the Kalahari. The pans themselves are located roughly between the diamond town of Orapa in the south, the village of Nata in the northeast and the Boteti rivercourse in the west. This falls away northwards towards the Mababe Depression and the Chobe–Zambezi river catchment system. At its centre lie two huge adjacent salt pans – Sua (to the east) and Ntwetwe (to the west) – which cover an estimated combined area of roughly 12,000km². Around them are a number of smaller pans, including Nxai Pan to the north and Lake Xau to the south.

To grasp the complex geology of this area, you really need a broader understanding of the way in which the whole Kalahari was formed (page 4). In brief, the pans are the desiccated vestiges of the huge superlake which, several million years ago, covered most of central Botswana and moulded the landscape of the entire region. Subsequent climate change, seismic upheavals and the diversion of rivers (the details of which divide geologists) starved this lake of its water supply, shrinking it to today's flat, caustic depressions of grey clay, and withering its surrounding wetlands into arid savannah.

Today the pans generally receive no more than 400–500mm of rain annually and have no permanent standing water. After good rains, however, they briefly become shallow saline lakes again, fed by the seasonal Boteti River from the west – bringing the overspill from the Okavango – and the Nata River from the northeast.

FLORA AND FAUNA The plant and animal life of the region reflects its harsh climate. The plants are hardy and resilient species; the animals comprise either nomadic species that follow the rains in large seasonal movements, or specialised sedentary species adapted to arid Kalahari conditions. Populations fluctuate wildly according to rainfall. Consequently wildlife viewing is a hit-and-miss affair, depending entirely on the time of year and local conditions. However, in the right place at the right time, it can be spectacular, and the wide, open spaces make for excellent visibility.

Flora The flora of the Makgadikgadi Pans region can be graded into a loose series of zones, each determined by the soil in which it grows. At the centre lie the pans themselves: barren, windswept and devoid of any plant life. These sterile, salty dustbowls are surrounded by extensive grasslands which flourish on Kalahari sands, comprising a mixture of salt-tolerant species around the pans, coarse 'finger' grasses across the sandy plains, and nutritious 'sweet grasses' on the margins. The grasslands are punctuated with scattered trees and thickets, consisting primarily of acacia species.

Further from the pans, where the soil has a richer sand and clay mix, this acacia savannah becomes a denser bush, interspersed with other woodland trees, including various combretum and terminalia species. To the north and east, the acacias are replaced by a belt of mopane trees (*Colophospermum mopane*), which flourish on the more heavily clay soils.

To the west, the alluvial soils and hidden water table of the Boteti riverfront support a strip of dense riverine woodland. Here typical Kalahari species, such as camelthorn (*Vachellia erioloba*) and blackthorn (*Senegalia mellifera*), grow alongside riverine giants such as sycamore figs (*Ficus sycomorus*), sausage trees (*Kigelia africana*) and many of the other riverine species that are usually associated with wetter areas.

Across the region, towering real fan palms (*Hyphaene petersiana*) cluster in elegant, waving stands above the grasslands, forming extensive groves of palm woodland to the west of Ntwetwe Pan. Equally conspicuous are the scattered baobabs, which sprout incongruously around the pans and on isolated rock outcrops, each with centuries of history recorded in its swollen limbs.

Fauna
Mammals Fossil evidence unearthed on the pans shows that in wetter, prehistoric times, the region supported the whole spectrum of African big game – including abundant elephant, buffalo and rhino. Today, the selection of large mammals is more limited than in the game-rich areas of Moremi and Chobe to the north and west. Rhino have disappeared altogether, while elephant and buffalo occur only occasionally, in small numbers on the fringes.

However, the grasslands draw huge herds of grazers, which can, despite recent declines, still rival anything outside Tanzania's Serengeti for sheer numbers. Zebra and wildebeest gather in tens of thousands, supported by smaller numbers of gemsbok, eland and red hartebeest. Movements are unpredictable, but in general the highest concentrations occur in the western Boteti region during the late dry season (August–November) and further north in the Nxai Pan area during the rainy season (December–March).

Hardy springbok are impervious to drought and remain scattered across the grasslands throughout the year. In the Nxai Pans area, the mopane woodland shelters browsers, including impala (which supplant springbok where the bush thickens), kudu, sable and tsessebe. Here, giraffe are common and a few breeding elephant frequent the fringes of the northern pans.

Another pocket of diversity occurs along the Boteti River, where the thicker bush provides cover for grey duiker, bushbuck and waterbuck. Giraffe and elephant also

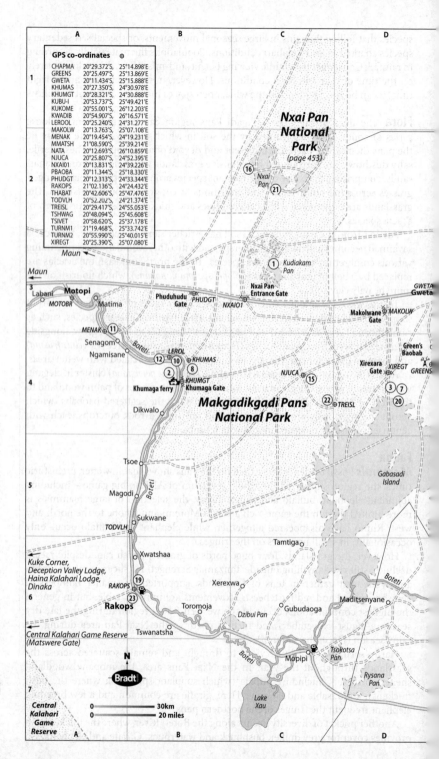

Nxai Pan National Park (page 453)

Makgadikgadi Pans National Park

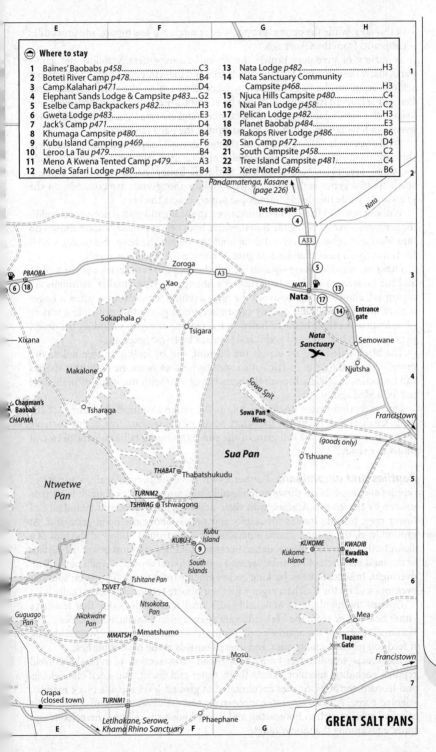

⊙ **Where to stay**

1	Baines' Baobabs p458	C3
2	Boteti River Camp p478	B4
3	Camp Kalahari p471	D4
4	Elephant Sands Lodge & Campsite p483	G2
5	Eselbe Camp Backpackers p482	H3
6	Gweta Lodge p483	E3
7	Jack's Camp p471	D4
8	Khumaga Campsite p480	B4
9	Kubu Island Camping p469	F6
10	Leroo La Tau p479	B4
11	Meno A Kwena Tented Camp p479	A3
12	Moela Safari Lodge p480	B4
13	Nata Lodge p482	H3
14	Nata Sanctuary Community Campsite p468	H3
15	Njuca Hills Campsite p480	C4
16	Nxai Pan Lodge p458	C2
17	Pelican Lodge p482	H3
18	Planet Baobab p484	E3
19	Rakops River Lodge p486	B6
20	San Camp p472	D4
21	South Campsite p458	C2
22	Tree Island Campsite p481	C4
23	Xere Motel p486	B6

Pandamatenga, Kasane (page 226) ↓

GREAT SALT PANS

visit this area, while the permanent pools even support a few hippos and crocodiles – emigrants from the Okavango.

A variety of predators prowls the region. Lions generally follow the game, particularly the zebra herds in the Boteti area and the winter springbok in Nxai, but seldom occur on the pans themselves. Cheetah are most often seen around Nxai Pan, while leopard frequent the denser bush of the Boteti waterfront. Spotted hyena keep to the woodland fringes in small numbers and are rarely seen, while the brown hyena – a Kalahari specialist – is found around the pans themselves.

Wild dogs are highly nomadic and, though unusual, can turn up anywhere. Here they are most often seen in the vicinity of Nxai Pan. Smaller predators include bat-eared fox, black-backed jackal, aardwolf, honey badger, African wildcat, small-spotted genet and striped polecat. Yellow mongooses are common on the grasslands, while the slender mongoose prefers acacia thickets.

Without much in the way of fruiting trees, the Makgadikgadi is not a good region for primates – except along the Boteti, where both vervet monkeys and baboons do find food and cover. However, throughout the region the lesser bushbaby, which feeds mostly on insects and acacia gum, thrives in the acacia savannah.

Other mammals of the grasslands include the ubiquitous aardvark and porcupine, and the bizarre spring hare is particularly abundant. Most smaller mammals are nocturnal, allowing them to avoid the high daytime temperatures, when a larger surface area to body ratio quickly causes overheating. On this principle a variety of rodents make their home in burrows and emerge at night, including the desert pygmy mouse, hairy-footed gerbil and Damara mole-rat (page 492).

The black-tailed tree rat avoids the burning sun by hiding in tree holes, and protects the entrance to its lair with a scruffy 'nest' of twigs. At night this species can be seen scampering through the branches of a camelthorn, using its prehensile tail for added agility.

One exception to the nocturnal rule is the ground squirrel, an animal of the deep Kalahari that occurs in the sandy south of the region. This highly sociable rodent can forage in the full glare of the sun by using its tail as a parasol to cast protective shade.

Reptiles and amphibians Further down the evolutionary scale, a variety of reptiles and amphibians thrive in Makgadikgadi's arid expanses, though most pass unseen by the visitor. Acacias, with their deeply fissured bark and abundance of insect prey, provide havens for skinks and geckos above the open grassland. At ground level, the ground agama ambushes termites from a hollow at the foot of a shady bush, while the legless Kalahari burrowing skink swims just below the surface of the sand in search of beetle larvae, and is often found drowned when pans fill up overnight. In sandier areas, barking geckos emerge from their burrows on summer evenings and fill the Kalahari night with their bizarre territorial clicking calls.

Perhaps the highlight of Makgadikgadi's smaller animals is one that few have either heard of or seen: the Makgadikgadi spiny agama (*Agama makarikarica*). This is a small species of the agama family – a lizard – that's endemic to Makgadikgadi. It feeds on termites and beetles, and lives in tunnels at the base of bushes.

The acacia woodland is home to a broad cross-section of typical bushveld reptiles, including monitor lizards (both water and rock), flap-neck chameleons and leopard tortoises. Snakes encountered at ground level include black mamba, snouted cobra, African egg-eater, mole snake and the ubiquitous puff adder, while arboreal species such as boomslang and spotted bush snake hunt chameleons and birds' eggs among the thorny tangle.

To survive this harsh habitat, many frogs aestivate below ground during the dry season. Giant bullfrogs emerge from their mud cocoons after seasonal rains to take over temporary pans in a frenzy of breeding. These frogs are so aggressive that they have even been observed snapping at lions. The much smaller rain-frogs of the *Breviceps* genus, like the bushveld rain-frog (*Breviceps adspersus*), have toughened feet, evolved for digging their burrows. They also appear with the rains, and gather at the surface during termite emergences, cramming in as many of the hapless insects as time will allow.

Invertebrates The Kalahari teems with invertebrate life. Good years bring swarms of locusts and mass migrations of butterflies to the grasslands, while countless termites demolish and carry away the dead vegetable matter that carpets the ground. Termites are fundamental to the ecology of the region. Not only do they recycle and enrich the soil, but they are also a vital prey species for everything from eagles and aardvarks to skinks and spiders.

There are 14 genera of termites, each of which has a different mode of foraging: harvester termites (*Hodotermitidae*) nest in underground burrows, while

HIGH-RISE LIVING

The towers of mud built by termites, known as termitaria, are often the only points of elevation for kilometres across the Makgadikgadi grasslands. Not all termites build mounds – harvester termites (*Hodotermitidae*), which are common on Kalahari sands, leave little evidence of their underground tunnels above the surface – but those that do, the *Macrotermitinae* species, are responsible for one of the true wonders of nature.

Communicating entirely through pheromones, millions of blind worker termites can raise several tonnes of soil – particle by particle – into an enormous structure over 3m high. Below the mound lies the nest, where separate chambers house brood galleries, food stores, fungus combs (where termites cultivate a fungus that can break down plant cellulose) and the queen's royal cell. The queen produces up to 30,000 eggs a day, which means – since she lives for many years – that the millions of inhabitants of the colony are all brothers and sisters.

The whole structure is prevented from overheating by a miraculous air-conditioning system. Warm air rises from the nest chambers, up a central chimney, into thin-walled ventilation flues near the surface (you can feel the warmth by placing your hand just inside one of the upper vents). Here it is cooled and replenished with oxygen, before circulating back down through separate passages into cavities below the nest chambers. Finally, before returning to the nest, it passes through specially constructed cooling veins, kept damp by the termites. In this way, termites maintain the 100% humidity and constant temperature of 29–31°C required for successful production of eggs and young. (These conditions are exploited by monitor lizards, who seal their eggs inside termitaria for safe incubation.)

After the rains, when conditions are right, the queen produces a reproductive caste of winged males and females – known as imagos – who leave the colonies in huge swarms to mate, disperse and establish new nests. Mass termite 'emergences' are one of the bonanzas of the bush, offering a seasonal feast to everything from frogs and spiders to kites, falcons and tawny eagles.

15

Odontotermes termites of the *Macrotermitinae* family construct the enormous raised mounds that can be seen for kilometres across the grasslands – each one a miracle of air conditioning (page 449).

Among a multitude of other insects are the wingless tenebrionid beetles, which scuttle rapidly across open ground on long legs and squirt a noxious fluid at attackers. More visible are the chunkier dung beetles, which swarm on strong wings to fresh animal dung, then roll it away and bury it as 'brood balls' in which their eggs are laid and their larvae mature.

On hot summer days, thickets throb with the stridulating calls of cicadas, the adults having only two weeks of life in which to mate and deposit their eggs, after up to 17 years' underground larval development.

Termites and other insects feed a host of invertebrate predators. Sand divers (*Ammoxenidae*) are small, fast-moving spiders that paralyse termites with their venom and bury themselves if disturbed. Golden orbweb spiders (*Nephilidae*) string their super-strong webs between thorn bushes to ensnare flying insects.

Contrary to popular belief, sun-spiders, or solifuges (*Solifugae*), are not venomous, but pursue insects at high speed across the ground and despatch them audibly with powerful mandibles. You'll often see these large arachnids running across the ground at night near campfires. Though frightening at first, they're totally harmless and don't bite people!

Not so harmless are the resident scorpions, which detect the vibrations of prey through their body hairs. As a rough rule of thumb for the nervous, species with larger pincers and slimmer tails have less powerful venom than those with smaller pincers and larger tails.

Red velvet mites are parasites on larger invertebrates and often gather in sandy areas in the early morning after rain showers, looking like tiny scarlet cushions. Another tiny parasite, the voracious tampan tick, lurks in the sand beneath camelthorn trees and, chemically alerted by an exhalation of its victim's CO_2, emerges to drain the blood from any unsuspecting mammal that fancies a nap in the shade.

Birdlife The great salt pans region offers several distinct habitats for birds. The open grasslands support typical ground-nesting, arid country species such as coursers, korhaans, sandgrouse, chats, larks and pipits. Both the world's largest bird – the ostrich – and the world's largest flying bird, the kori bustard, strike conspicuous figures in this featureless terrain, while greater kestrels, pale-chanting goshawks, marsh owls and the statuesque secretary bird are among the more common resident predators.

Any isolated stands of trees are beacons for birds: red-necked falcons breed in fan palms, while baobabs provide roosts for owls and breeding sites for hornbills and rollers. Elsewhere, typical arid woodland residents dominate the thicker scrub, including red-billed spurfowl, grey lourie, fork-tailed drongo, pied babbler, glossy starling, white-browed sparrow weaver and a wide variety of shrikes, barbets, flycatchers, robins, sunbirds, warblers, waxbills and whydahs.

Eagles, including martial and bateleur (or short-tailed eagle), roam the skies. Smaller predators such as Gabar goshawk and pearl-spotted owl hunt the thorn scrub, and vultures follow the herds across the region, hoping for casualties.

In summer the resident bird population is swelled by a huge influx of migrants drawn to the seasonal bonanza of seeds and insects. Some are non-breeding visitors that come from as far afield as Europe and central Africa. White storks (from Europe) and Abdim's storks (from East Africa) arrive wheeling on thermals to stalk the savannah; carmine and European bee-eaters hawk their insect prey just above the grass; shrikes, including red-backed and lesser grey, claim prominent territories on thorn bushes from where they ambush hapless lizards and grasshoppers.

Other more local breeding visitors include seed-eaters such as wattled starlings, doves, finchlarks, canaries – and the prolific red-billed quelea, whose flocks reach swarm proportions. Migrant raptors are lured by the brief abundance of prey, with many different species – including western red-footed falcons, steppe buzzards, yellow-billed kites and tawny eagles – congregating at mass termite emergences (page 449).

After good rains, when Ntwetwe and Sua Pans turn briefly into glassy lakes, waterbirds arrive in their thousands. The shallow, saline conditions are ideal for both greater and lesser flamingos, which construct their clay nests under the blazing Kalahari sun and filter-feed on algae and brine shrimps. Meanwhile pelicans, darters, cormorants and ducks flock to the brackish waters of the Nata River delta, in the northeast of Sua Pan. Here, waders such as stilts, sandpipers and avocets forage along the shoreline, while jacanas, pied kingfishers, weavers and bishops frequent the reedbeds.

PRACTICAL INFORMATION

ORIENTATION The tarred Nata–Maun road bisects this barren region. In May 2017, the road was badly flooded and partially destroyed by an unusually wet rainy season, and while some repairs have been undertaken along this major route since, pot-holes are considerable. The best stretch of road is from Maun to Motopi, after which the road degenerates, with the section from Gweta to Nata devoid of its original tarmac in parts and taking on an almost lunar quality. The government has committed the budget to repairing this road over the next few years though, so hopefully there will be a material change to the journey.

To the south of the road lies Makgadikgadi Pans National Park and the vast, dry depressions of Sua Pan and Ntwetwe Pan, with their scattered 'islands' of granite and fossilised dunes, fringed by grassland and acacia savannah. To its north is the Nxai Pan National Park, including Nxai and Kgama-Kgama pans, now grassed over, and Kudiakam Pan, overlooked by the famous Baines' Baobabs.

Much of the region is unfenced ranching country, where wildlife has largely been supplanted by cattle. However, the fauna and flora are protected in a number of reserves. Makgadikgadi Pans National Park extends south of the Nata–Maun road, between the western shore of Ntwetwe Pan and the Boteti River. Nxai Pan National Park adjoins this to the north of the Nata–Maun road, and includes the Nxai Pans complex and Baines' Baobabs. The much smaller Nata Sanctuary, established to protect the seasonal breeding waterbirds of the Nata River delta, is situated in the northeast corner of Sua Pan. Each of these areas has its own distinct attractions and seasonal peculiarities.

Maps Veronica Roodt's *Shell Tourist Map of Botswana* covers this area well, with a variety of useful GPS points, as does the Tracks4Africa map and app (page 142).

If you plan on exploring a lot of the pans, then you should also get hold of a copy of the excellent *African Adventurer's Guide to Botswana*, by Mike Main (page 546). This has a number of carefully described routes through the area, as well as much interesting general information. However, do be aware that tracks can change, so always be vigilant.

GETTING ORGANISED Once you leave one of the few main roads in this area, you generally need to be in a self-sufficient 4x4 vehicle. Bringing along all your food and water is always a good idea, as while you will find water in some places, there is very little in the way of shops. A few towns around the pans (page 481) can be good sources of fuel, but generally supplies are limited and/or intermittent.

If you're venturing off across Makgadikgadi, then you really should take at least two vehicles and have a GPS, a compass and a map; an environment of flat salt without any landmarks at all can be very disorienting, especially during a windstorm. In such a situation, breaking through the pan's crust and getting stuck can create a life-threatening situation.

If you want to stay in either of the national parks then you must book ahead for a campsite. See page 127 for details and fees for these national parks. Similarly Jack's Camp, San Camp and Camp Kalahari should be booked in advance, and it is also advisable to reserve the campsite at Nata Sanctuary if you plan to stay. That said, most of Sua and Ntwetwe pans fall outside the control of the authorities, so independent travellers can camp anywhere that appeals – though do first read the notes on safety on page 465.

NXAI PAN NATIONAL PARK

Nxai Pan National Park lies to the north of the Nata–Maun road at the northern fringe of the ancient Lake Makgadikgadi basin. It is contiguous with Makgadikgadi Pans National Park, to the south of this same road. Nxai is probably the easiest area of the pans to drive yourself into, and from December to around July will also have the best game. Add in the spectacular sight of Baines' Baobabs to make a super destination for a three- to four-day self-drive trip.

Note that Nxai is usually pronounced to rhyme with 'high', unless you're familiar with the clicks of the Khoisan languages, in which case the correct pronunciation of the 'x' is actually a palatal click (ie: press tongue against the roof of your mouth, and then move down).

GEOGRAPHY The park covers an area of 2,658km², comprising Nxai Pan itself, Kgama-Kgama Pan complex to the northeast, and the Kudiakam Pan complex (including Baines' Baobabs) to the south. The baobabs were added to the original park in 1992.

The pans themselves are ancient salt lakes, ringed to the south and west with thick fossil dunes of wind-blown Kalahari sand. Today they are completely grassed over, but scattered across their surfaces are smaller pans or waterholes that fill up during the rainy season. Two of these are artificially maintained by the park authorities to provide surface water throughout the year, but the watercourses that once fed the area from the northeast have long since dried up.

The park's general topography is flat and featureless, with the famous baobabs being the most striking landmarks, and one of the higher points of elevation. To the north and east the soils become increasingly clayey, supporting the encroachment of mopane woodland and integrating with the dense mopane woodlands of the Chobe–Zambezi river catchment system.

FLORA AND FAUNA

Flora The open grassland that covers the pans consists of many palatable 'sweet' grasses (eg: *Themeda* spp), which sustain the large herd of grazers that invade the area in summer. These grasslands are studded with 'islands' of acacias, consisting

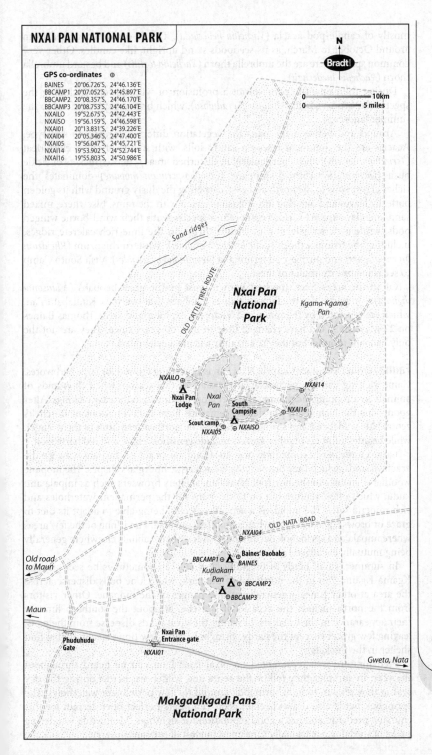

NXAI PAN NATIONAL PARK

GPS co-ordinates	⊕
BAINES	20°06.726'S, 24°46.136'E
BBCAMP1	20°07.052'S, 24°45.897'E
BBCAMP2	20°08.357'S, 24°46.170'E
BBCAMP3	20°08.753'S, 24°46.104'E
NXAILO	19°52.675'S, 24°42.443'E
NXAISO	19°56.159'S, 24°46.598'E
NXAI01	20°13.831'S, 24°39.226'E
NXAI04	20°05.346'S, 24°47.400'E
NXAI05	19°56.047'S, 24°45.721'E
NXAI14	19°53.902'S, 24°52.744'E
NXAI16	19°55.803'S, 24°50.986'E

N

Bradt!

0 ———— 10km
0 ———— 5 miles

Sand ridges

OLD CATTLE TREK ROUTE

Nxai Pan National Park

Kgama-Kgama Pan

NXAILO ⊕
▲ Nxai Pan Lodge

Nxai Pan

South Campsite ▲

NXAI14 ⊕

⊕ NXAI16

Scout camp ⊕
▲ NXAISO
NXAI05

OLD NATA ROAD

⊕ NXAI04

BBCAMP1 ⊕ ▲ **Baines' Baobabs**
⊕ BAINES
Kudiakam Pan
▲ ⊕ BBCAMP2

⊕ BBCAMP3

Old road to Maun

Maun

✕ **Phuduhudu Gate**

✕ **Nxai Pan Entrance gate**
NXAI01

Gweta, Nata

Makgadikgadi Pans National Park

mostly of candle-pod acacia (*Vachellia hebeclada*). This is easily recognised from around October to March, as its seedpods stand upright, like candles. Other very common species here are the umbrella thorn (*Vachellia tortilis*) and bastard umbrella thorn (*Vachellia luederitzii*).

During the rains, the pans sprout a profusion of wild flowers, including the spectacular brunsvigia lily (*Brunsvigia radulosa*), which brings a splash of red to the summer landscape.

Around and between the pans the vegetation differs according to soil type. Acacias are the dominant trees on sandy soils, with stands of silver clusterleaf (*Terminalia sericea*), and – particularly in disturbed areas – dense thickets of sickle bush (*Dichrostachys cinerea*). Mopane (*Colophospermum mopane*) dominates the richer clayey soils to the north and east, carpeting the dusty ground with its golden butterfly leaves and bursting into a flush of green with the rains. Elsewhere, mixed sand and clay support various combretum species, with their wind-borne winged pods, while a richer selection of shrubs thrive on the lime-rich calcrete ridges, including the trumpet thorn (*Catophractes alexandri*), Western rhigozum (*Rhigozum brevispinosum*) and purple-pod terminalia (*Terminalia prunioides*). Visit South Camp to see some fine examples of these.

Of all the area's trees, the best known must be the great baobabs (*Adansonia digitata*) – in particular the famous Baines' Baobabs that overlook Kudiakam Pan, which were painted by the renowned Victorian explorer and artist Thomas Baines on 22 May 1862, and have changed little in the 160 years since. They are not the only baobabs around, but they're certainly the most celebrated.

Fauna   From December to April, Nxai Pan is a breeding ground for large herbivores. Game viewing can be spectacular at the start of this season, when thousands of animals are dropping their young and predators are drawn to the easy pickings. After good rains the lush green grasslands teem with huge concentrations of Burchell's zebra, blue wildebeest and springbok (here at the northeastern limit of their range), while healthy numbers of other grazers include gemsbok, eland and red hartebeest.

Large giraffe herds, sometimes over 40 strong, move across the pans between the acacia 'islands', which they prune into characteristic hourglass shapes. The mopane woodland, mainly to the north of Nxai Pan, shelters browsers such as impala and kudu, which often venture out on to the pans for the permanent waterholes and rich mineral salts. The impala is a versatile species, being able to adapt its diet to graze or browse, according to what is on offer, and Nxai Pan is one of the few areas where impala and springbok occur side by side – their habitats elsewhere generally being mutually exclusive.

In summer, small herds of breeding elephant can sometimes be seen around Kgama-Kgama Pan in the northeast of the park, while lone bulls disperse across the area at other times – generally on the fringes of the mopane. Other visitors from the north include the occasional tsessebe, at about the southern limit of their appearance in the Kalahari. In winter the great herds disperse from the pans, leaving few grazers except the hardy springbok, and a few timid steenbok that find shelter in the thickets.

Predators are well represented on Nxai Pan. Lion can be heard throughout the year: in summer they follow the zebra and wildebeest herds; during the dry season they remain to hunt springbok around the few permanent waterholes. The springbok herds also draw cheetah: Nxai Pan offers perfect open terrain for this coursing predator, and has a good reputation for sightings. Meanwhile wandering packs of wild dog occasionally turn up in pursuit of the same quarry.

During Botswana's annual zebra migration, tens of thousands of zebra embark on a remarkable journey. Travelling in two distinct groups, one from the Okavango Delta to Makgadikgadi Pans National Park and the other from the floodplains of Chobe National Park to Nxai Pan National Park, this migration is now recognised as the longest terrestrial wildlife migration in Africa.

Confirmed by tracking collars, the migration sees the movement of over 20,000 zebras, walking a round-trip distance of around 500km – a longer journey that that undertaken by the Serengeti's famed wildebeest. As in Tanzania, the zebras' migratory pattern is influenced by the availability of grazing resources in different areas.

The zebras here take advantage of the floodwaters of the Okavango Delta during the dry season (June to November), and as the dry season progresses, the zebras move towards areas where there is better access to water and fresh grass. Taking two to three weeks, this movement is crucial for their survival and is driven by their instinct to seek out optimal feeding grounds.

Witnessing the zebra migration is a truly awe-inspiring experience. The sight of thousands of zebras travelling in unison, their black and white stripes fanning out across the landscape, is spectacular.

Spotted hyena can sometimes be heard at night, especially when there are large concentrations of game around, while the more elusive brown hyena hunts and scavenges for smaller prey items around the pans. Black-backed jackal and honey badger are both versatile smaller predators that occur throughout the area, the latter sometimes foraging in association with the pale-chanting goshawk.

Aardwolf and bat-eared fox snap up harvester termites on the open grasslands. The former is strictly nocturnal and seldom seen; the latter is diurnal in winter and nocturnal in the hotter summer months, foraging in loose family groups with ears cocked to the ground for termite rustlings.

African wildcat and small-spotted genet hunt the acacia bush after dark for small rodents and roosting birds, while by day yellow mongoose comb open sandy areas for scorpions, slender mongoose hunt the acacia scrub, alone or in pairs, and banded mongoose rummage through the woodland in large, sociable colonies.

Other smaller mammals found here include lesser bushbaby, aardvark and porcupine, with spring hare on the grassland and scrub hare in the woodland. By day, tree squirrels are common and noisy inhabitants of the mopane.

Birdlife Nxai Pan's rich avifauna comprises a mixture of grassland, acacia scrub and mopane woodland birds, with a total of 217 species recorded in Hugh Chittenden's *Top Birding Spots of Southern Africa* (page 546).

Grassland birds include ant-eating chat, white-browed sparrow weaver, capped wheatear and pale-chanting goshawk. White-browed robin, pied babbler and chinspot batis are found in the acacia scrub. Red-billed hornbill, red-billed spurfowl and barred owl prefer the mopane.

The distinction between adjacent habitats is reflected in the parallel distributions of similar species. For example, double-banded coursers and northern black korhaans – both Kalahari specialists – occur only on the open grasslands, while bronze-winged coursers and red-crested korhaans, their close relatives, stick to the surrounding woodlands.

15

Cuckoos are not the only cheats of the bird world. Whydahs (*Viduidae*) are also brood parasites that lay their eggs in other birds' nests. Like cuckoos, each species of whydah exploits a specific host, and all of them choose waxbills or estrildid finches (*Estrildidae*). However, unlike cuckoos, whydahs do not evict the eggs or nestlings of their host, so young whydahs grow up alongside their step-siblings, not instead of them.

To enhance the deception, a whydah's eggs – and there are usually two of them – perfectly mimic the colour of their host's clutch, and, once hatched, the whydah nestlings have exactly the right arrangements of gape spots inside their bills to dupe their step-parents into feeding them. A male whydah can even mimic the song of its host to distract it from the nest while the female goes about her devious business undisturbed. Breeding male whydahs are lively, conspicuous birds, who flaunt extravagant tail plumes in dancing display flights – though outside the breeding season they are indistinguishable from the drab females.

Three species of whydah occur in the pans region, of which the most typical is the shaft-tailed whydah (*Vidua regia*), easily recognised by the long, thin tail-plumes of a breeding male, each tipped with a pennant. This species frequents sandy clearings in acacia thickets, often in association with its host, the violet-eared waxbill, and apparently without any animosity between them. The other two species are the pin-tailed whydah (*Vidua macroura*), which parasitises the common waxbill and prefers well-watered areas, and the paradise whydah (*Vidua paradisaea*), which parasitises the melba finch and is a common bird of acacia savannah.

Resident raptors, such as bateleur (or short-tailed eagle), martial eagle, tawny eagle and brown snake eagle, are joined in summer by an influx of migrants, including steppe buzzard, western red-footed kestrel and yellow-billed kite. Raptor watching can be superb at this time, with more unusual species such as lesser-spotted eagle and hobby sometimes joining the throng at termite emergences.

Kori bustards, secretary birds and (in summer) white storks hunt the grasslands, and after good rains wattled cranes sometimes appear on the flashes. In spring the air resounds to the breeding displays of larks, including sabota, rufous-naped, red-capped, fawn-coloured, dusky and clapper. During summer the game herds are a focus of bird activity, with carmine and blue-cheeked bee-eaters hawking insects around the feet of springbok and zebra; red-billed and yellow-billed oxpeckers hitching rides on giraffes; and white-backed and lappet-faced vultures dropping from the sky on to carcasses.

Away from the pans, the campsites are a good place to search out the smaller passerines: violet-eared, black-cheeked and blue waxbills occur in the sandy acacia scrub together with melba and scaly feathered finches, while shaft-tailed and paradise whydahs – brood parasites on other birds (see above) – dash about in extravagant breeding finery. Baobabs are always worth checking, since they often provide roosting or nesting sites for rollers, hornbills and various owls.

WHEN TO VISIT The game at Nxai is fairly erratic – it can be excellent, though sometimes it will disappoint. If there have been good rains, then between December and April you have a very good chance of witnessing large herds of springbok, gemsbok, giraffe and migrating zebra, plus a scattering of other species. However, note that this is also the time when the pans are at their most treacherous, and driving at its most muddy.

During a year of good rains, we've seen good general game in February, with large numbers of zebra, although in two days we didn't see a single large carnivore. Conversely, a visitor in April was rewarded with sightings of both cheetah and lion during a one-night stay. Reliable reports suggest that game densities remain more or less constant until around August, when – as the dry season progresses and the waterholes dry up – the game becomes sparser and less dependable. Nxai can be a hot and unrewarding park at the height of October's heat.

GETTING THERE AND AWAY Unless you are staying at the lodge, in which case you will normally arrive by air, you really need a vehicle to visit Nxai Pan National Park. Whether you have your own or are driven by one of the mobile-safari operators from Maun, you should come with all your fuel, water and food – there are no shops or fuel pumps here.

The route is very easy to find. The gate on the main road (⊕ NXAI01 20°13.831'S, 24°39.226'E), 0.5km to the east of the old cutline, heralded a new entrance in 2009. This is about 135km from Maun and 157km from Nata, and is very well signposted so you're unlikely to miss it. This is where you need to sign and present your entry permit.

There's one track north here, paralleling the old cutline (which until 2009 was the only access road to the park), and leading after some 36km to the scout post. After driving on sand for around 18km, you'll reach a junction, where a right turn leads to Kudiakam Pan and Baines' Baobabs (see page 459 for directions). Continue straight, bearing north-northeast for a further 18km and you'll reach the scout camp (⊕ NXAI05 19°56.047'S, 24°45.721'E), which is at the south end of the main pan, near the waterhole. Nowadays this is fundamentally a base for the staff looking after the campsites but you can also get information here about the state of the roads and ask the guides about game movements within the park.

If you're driving yourself, follow the track round the pan from the scout camp to a junction. Here, turn west towards the Old Cattle Trek Route, pass the sign for the HATAB campsite, and continue for a further kilometre.

WHERE TO STAY Nxai Pan accommodation options are limited but offer something for all safari styles and budgets: a long-established campsite close to the park entrance, a smart lodge (Nxai Pan Lodge) to the west, and the mobile camping experience offered by Migration Expeditions. There are also campsites close to the famous Baines' Baobabs.

Migration Expeditions [not mapped] (4 tents) Contact African Bush Camps (page 214). Opened for its first season in 2019, this camp is only the second in the park (although it's seasonal, not permanent) & is run by the same team as Linyanti Expeditions (page 292). The main focus is to catch the great Zebra Migration, the longest in Africa (page 455). In keeping with park rules, Migration Expeditions is packed up & moved every 6 days, so by necessity the camp provides a pared-back safari experience. The simple main area consists of a mess tent split in two with a dining area & bar to one side & a lounge area on the other.

A shaded porch with two directors' chairs leads through a zippered door into the Meru-style tents. Inside, twin beds, a small writing desk & a tea & coffee station provide everything you need to be comfortable, but no frills. Through another canvas door is an en-suite bathroom with a chemical toilet, copper basin, mirror & small hanging rack. A final zip door leads out the back of the tent to a bucket shower screened by canvas for privacy.

Battery-operated fans & lights are solar-charged during the day & provide just enough light/cooling for most days, although both can be a little feeble at times. Guests can charge electrical equipment in the main area, where batteries are predominantly charged by solar power, with a small generator to supplement the system.

Activities here focus on morning & afternoon game drives, with the times governed by park rules. Full day trips to see Baines' Baobabs are also offered & are well worth considering. *US$540 pp, FBA inc conservation fee.* ⏰ *Dec–Mar.* 🦏🦏🦏

Nxai Pan Lodge {446 C2} (9 chalets) Contact Kwando Safaris (page 458); ⊕ NXAILO 19°52.675'S, 24°42.443'E. Opened in Feb 2009, & still the only permanent camp inside the national park, Nxai Pan is located on an area of flat, open grassland, 47km from the newer park gate, or 8.3km from the old one. The lodge forms a shallow crescent facing west over a distant waterhole that attracts a phenomenal number of elephants in the dry season (Jun–Oct). A particularly welcoming local team affords a homely atmosphere that is quite a highlight.

At the heart of camp is a substantial if narrow thatched building, entirely open on one side, but with roll-down canvas blinds with plastic 'windows' to keep out the worst excesses of the weather. Inside, light wooden furniture lends a somewhat Scandinavian air to the bar, lounge & dining area, which flow almost seamlessly from one end to the other. These look over an extensive wooden deck with a small pool near the bar, & a firepit in front. A telescope/spotting scope situated on the main deck is the perfect opportunity to explore the night sky, with the help of a guide, while a curio shop at the back offers a range of gifts & merchandise.

Flanking the main building, & mirroring it in style, are individual chalets, linked by raised wooden walkways that snake behind the complex. A door at the back of each leads into a long & open room, with twin beds – or a dbl – in the centre, & sliding doors with mesh panels opening on to

a wooden deck. At one end, there are inside & outside showers, twin washbasins & a separate toilet, while at the other are a desk, low table & chairs. A family room has a 2nd small twin room attached to the lounge. As of 2023, the camp is also surrounded by an unobtrusive electric fence to keep the park's larger & more dangerous residents out.

Morning or afternoon game drives within the immediate area can be extended to full-day trips to Kudiakam Pan & Baines' Baobabs, with late-evening drives also an option, & overnight trips on the pans planned too. Short informative nature walks are possible, too, since although the lodge is inside the national park, it sits within its own 5ha concession. These are conducted by a Bushman tracker, & are a great opportunity to share in their knowledge, sense of humour & passion for the land. *US$800 pp (US$150 festive supp't 20 Dec–4 Jan), FBA.* ⏰ *All year.* 🦏🦏🦏

Baines' Baobabs [446 C3] (3 sites) Contact Xomae Group (page 213). There are 3 separate campsites around Baines' Baobabs. The closest one to the famous baobabs themselves, at ⊕ BBCAMP1 20°07.052'S, 24°45.897'E, is on an island, separated from the baobabs by a salt pan. The other 2 sites (⊕ BBCAMP2 20°08.357'S, 24°46.170'E & ⊕ BBCAMP3 20°08.753'S, 24°46.104'E) lie further south along the eastern edge of the pan. Each of the sites is equipped with a long-drop loo & bucket shower, but there is no water, so make sure you bring everything you need for the duration of your stay. *US$42 pp, exc park fees.* ⏰ *All year.*

South Campsite [446 C2] (10 pitches) Contact Xomae Group (page 213); ⊕ NXAISO 19°56.159'S, 24°46.598'E. The closest campsite to the entrance, South Camp is probably the busier site – but it benefits from a lovely location. It's situated in a grove of purple-pod terminalia trees, which cast a good shade, making it relatively cool. There are separate ablution blocks for men & women, each with showers & flush toilets. *US$32 pp, exc park fees.* ⏰ *All year.*

WHAT TO SEE AND DO Nxai's a great park for watching the herds of plains game, and is certainly somewhere that you need to be patient. Don't rush around in search of predators; instead take your time and you'll see much more. The waterholes are very open and exposed here, so park a good distance away and you won't disturb the animals drinking.

Finally, note that the night sky here is often phenomenally clear – as it is across the centre of the Kalahari. So if you can bring a star chart as well as your route maps, you'll enjoy it all the more. First on your list should be to identify the Southern Cross, and use it to find due south. When gazing up, try using your binoculars and you'll be amazed how many more stars you can see.

Nxai and Kgama-Kgama pans These are the main pans of the complex. They're covered with grasses and dotted with clumps of acacias – and have always provided me with the best game viewing in this park.

In the dry season you'll find most of the roads in the area of the pan are good and hard, a pleasant contrast to the thick sand that you ploughed through to reach here. When the rains come you'll have to be much more careful as many roads on the pan itself turn very muddy. Then the sand road in will be the easiest section, and the park itself will provide the problems. Make sure your self-sufficient vehicle includes a spade, and always carry some wood with you, both for campfires and for sticking under the wheels when you get stuck.

The road that leads off east towards Kgama-Kgama Pan runs through dense bush, affording little visibility either side. To reach the pan, head east from the scout post for about 10km, passing South Camp on your right. This should bring you to a junction of the tracks (⊕ NXAI16 19°55.803'S, 24°50.986'E). From here one track (clearly marked on most maps) leads off to loop around to the southeast and then turn north.

However, another track leads off heading north of east, before turning northeast, and after almost 5km reaches another junction (⊕ NXAI14 19°53.902'S, 24°52.744'E). The alternative, which leads roughly west, across the north end of the small pan to the east of Nxai, heads through an interesting area of mostly mopane woodland, mixed with some denser groves of terminalia, and even in May, some of the pans here retained water. This eventually leads west to Nxai Pan.

Kudiakam Pan and Baines' Baobabs Sandwiched between Nxai Pan and the main road, Kudiakam is the largest of an interesting complex of pans lying in sparse bush east of the track to Nxai. The game here doesn't usually match Nxai's, but the main attraction is an extraordinarily beautiful group of trees known as Baines' Baobabs, which stand at a spectacular site on the eastern edge of the pan. They were immortalised in a painting by Thomas Baines who came here in May 1862 with James Chapman and wrote:

A lone circuit brought me, with empty pouch, to the clump of baobabs we had seen yesterday from the wagon; five full-sized trees, and two or three younger ones were standing, so that when in leaf their foliage must form one magnificent shade. One gigantic trunk had fallen and lay prostrate but still, losing none of its vitality, bent forth branches and young leaves like the rest…The general colour of the immense stems was grey and rough: but where the old bark had peeled and curled off, the new (of that peculiar metallic coppery-looking red and yellow which Dr Livingstone was wont so strenuously to object in my pictures) shone through over large portions, giving them, according to light or shade, a red or yellow, grey or a deep purple tone.

The baobabs themselves have changed very little since Baines painted them, and the one lying prostrate is still thriving, having lost none of its vitality.

Having thought of the baobabs with reference to a fairly recent Victorian painter, it's perhaps worth reminding ourselves that Baines was far from the

15

first person here. Lawrence Robbins (page 545) and others have conducted archaeological surveys of this area and discovered extensive remains dating from the Middle Stone Age period, 'especially on the eastern side within a 4km radius of the Baines baobab grove', according to Robbins. Many stone tools were found, plus ostrich eggshell remains, a zebra's tooth and the fossilised bone of a hippopotamus.

This site has been dated to about 105,000–128,000 years old, around which time this was probably a beach location on the edge of the great superlake. This Middle Stone Age period has a special resonance, as this is the period during which we think the first *Homo sapiens* appeared.

Getting there and away   The easiest way is to follow the directions to Nxai Pan by turning off the main Maun–Nata road at the new gate (⊕ NXAI01 20°13.831'S, 24°39.226'E) into the national park, which is well signposted. After heading north for 18km, you'll find a track off to the east. This track splits very soon, after about 0.9km, and both roads lead to the baobabs.

In the **dry season**, take the right fork, which heads almost directly for Baines' Baobabs (⊕ BAINES 20°06.726'S, 24°46.136'E). It is the more direct route, but it crosses the surface of the pans, so do not try this unless you know what you're doing and are sure they will be dry. (It should be fine after about August, though don't take this as a guarantee!) Even the guides at the main gate mentioned that they always try to take the more northerly wet-season route where possible.

In the **wet season**, or if you're unsure of conditions, taking the left fork is more reliable, as it bends around slightly to the north, taking about 14.4km to reach a crossroads at ⊕ NXAI04 20°05.346'S, 24°47.400'E. Here you meet the old road between Maun and Nata; this is about 3.6km from the trees themselves. There's a network of small tracks around here, so head straight and then look for tracks off to the right, or turn right and find a track to your left – you can't miss them (⊕ BAINES 20°06.726'S, 24°46.136'E).

MAKGADIKGADI PANS

The Sua and Ntwetwe pans that comprise Makgadikgadi cover 12,000km² to the south of the Nata–Maun road. The western side is protected within a national park, while the east is either wilderness or cattle-ranching land. These are among the largest salt pans in the world and have few landmarks. So you're left to use the flat, distant horizon as your only line of reference – and even that dissolves into a haze of shimmering mirages in the heat of the afternoon sun. During the rains this desolate area comes to life, with huge migrating herds of zebra, wildebeest, and occasionally (if the pans fill with water) pelicans and many thousands of flamingos. A couple of odd outcrops of isolated rock in and around the pans add to their sense of mystery, as well as providing excellent vantage points from which to view the endless expanse of silver, grey and blue.

Makgadikgadi Pans National Park lies on the west of the pans, incorporating the western end of Ntwetwe Pan and a larger adjacent area of grassland and acacia woodland. The flora and fauna there are sufficiently different, especially around the Boteti River, to warrant a separate section, towards the end of this chapter, entitled *Makgadikgadi Pans National Park* (page 473).

This section concentrates on the main salt pans, Sua and Ntwetwe, and the areas of grassland immediately around them which encompass many scattered smaller pans.

GEOGRAPHY AND GEOLOGY   As discussed on page 466, Sua and Ntwetwe lie at the centre of the great prehistoric lake basin that circumscribes the whole region. On top of this is an ancient mantle of wind-blown Kalahari sands – deposited during the Tertiary period, as the subcontinent was levelled by erosion. Exposed rock is a rarity on the surface of this scrubbed and scoured landscape. However, beneath the sand lie ancient Karoo deposits 300 million years old, comprising basalt larva, sandstone and shales and containing such valuable minerals as gold, silver, copper and nickel.

During the Cretaceous period, 80 million years ago, rifts and buckles in the earth's crust allowed 'pipes' of molten material – known as kimberlite – to punch their way up from below. Diamonds formed under conditions of massive heat and pressure in these kimberlite pipes. Today they are mined at Orapa, just south of Ntwetwe Pan.

A few isolated outcrops of igneous rock extrude from the surface of the pans, notably Kubu Island and Kukome Island on Sua Pan. Apart from these, and some fossilised barchan (crescent-shaped) dunes to the west, the pans themselves are flat and featureless expanses of dry, sterile salt. However, after good summer rains they are transformed into shimmering lakes, giving a glimpse of what the great superlake must once have been like. The rainwater that pours down on them is augmented in really wet years by seasonal flows from the east: the Nata, Tutume, Semowane and Mosetse rivers. Also, again only in exceptional years, an overspill from the Okavango makes its way to the west side of Ntwetwe, via the Boteti River.

FLORA AND FAUNA   The saline conditions of the pans themselves have a strong local influence on their surrounding vegetation. Broadly speaking this becomes richer and more diverse the further you travel from the pan edges, creating a loose concentric series of 'succession' zones, each of which supports a distinctive fauna. These zones effectively chart the gradual demise of the ancient superlake.

Flora   There is no plant life on the surface of the pans, since nothing can tolerate the excessively high concentration of mineral salts, and wind erosion scours the exposed dusty surface, quickly denuding it of any vegetation that tries to take hold. The immediate fringes are carpeted with more or less uninterrupted grassland, consisting primarily of *Digitaria* species, which can survive despite the irregular herd movements. Between the pans can also be found patches of prickly salt grass (*Odyssea paucinervis*), a yellowish, spiky species that tolerates high salinity (salt crystals can sometimes be seen on the leaves).

Summer rains bring lush growth to the grasses, which flower in a wind-rippled sea of green. Then you'll also see a scattering of short-lived wild flowers bloom among the grasses, including crimson lilies, acanthus and wild hibiscus (*Hibiscus calyphyllus*). In areas of thicker sand ridges, the runners of the tsamma melon (*Citrullus lanatus*) sprawl across the sand, its swollen fruit providing life-sustaining moisture for a myriad animals, from gerbils to gemsbok. In winter, cropped and shrivelled, the grasses are reduced to a sparse golden mantle over the dusty plains, scattering their seeds to the wind.

Here and there, small hollows in the rolling grassland trap wind-blown detritus, creating pockets of richer soil that support scattered trees and shrubs. The most common trees are various acacia species, such as the umbrella thorn (*Vachellia tortilis*), which, with their fine leaves for minimising water loss and wicked thorns to deter browsers, are ideally suited to survive this arid environment. The hardy camelthorn (*Vachellia erioloba*) thrives in areas of deeper sand, often in an almost

There are at least eight species of the pumpkin family in Botswana, of which the tsamma melon (*Citrullus lanatus*) is the most distinctive and frequently seen. It is found throughout the region, and is particularly common after a good rainy season. Then, even after most of the rest of the vegetation is brown and shrivelled, you'll find tempting round melons beside the sandiest of roads – often apparently on their own.

During the dry season these become important sources of moisture for many animals, especially the gemsbok, and are also used by the local people. To get drinking water from one of these, you first cut off the top, like a boiled egg. The centre can then be cut out and eaten. Then take a stick and mash the rest of the pulp while it's in the melon, and this can be eaten. Take care not to eat the pips. These are best roasted and pounded, when they make an edible meal that can be cooked with water. Sometimes you'll come across a bitter fruit, which you should not eat as it may cause poisoning.

Another fairly common species is the gemsbok melon (*Citrullus naudinianus*), which has similar sprawling tendrils and an oval fruit, covered in blunt fleshy spines. Unlike the tsamma melon, this is a perennial plant with a long underground tuber. Inside the fruit is a jelly-like, translucent green which can be eaten raw (again, discarding the pips usually), though it doesn't taste very good. It's slightly more palatable when roasted beside the fire overnight – but I wouldn't recommend that you throw away your muesli or yoghurt before tasting it!

lifeless state of disintegration, by tapping deep reserves of groundwater with its long roots.

The shepherd's tree (*Boscia albitrunca*) with its distinct white trunk and dense, invaluable shade, is another versatile pioneer of sandy Kalahari soils. The grasslands are studded with stands of fan palms (*Hyphaene petersiana*), with their hard, cricket-ball-size fruit known as vegetable ivory. Thick groves of this elegant tree occur beyond the northwest shores of Ntwetwe Pan and along the Maun–Nata road.

In the far northeast of Sua Pan, the seasonal Nata River spreads out into a small delta formation which is quite different from the rest of the region. Here there's a band of tall dry riverine forest along the banks of the Nata, and a thickening of the ground cover lining the braided channels. Phragmites reeds thrive in the brackish conditions here, and when this delta is in flood the area can seem quite lush.

Further from the pans, the grassland gives way to a denser bush. To the east, a mixed sand and clay soil supports a greater variety of woodland trees, including tamboti (*Spirostachys africana*), marula (*Sclerocarya birrea*) and monkey thorn (*Senegalia galpinii*), while a belt of mopane woodland (*Colophospermum mopane*) also grows in the more heavily clayey soil around Nata and along the eastern boundary of Sua Pan.

The mighty baobabs (*Adansonia digitata*) are perhaps the region's best-known and most easily identified trees. These iconic, drought-resistant giants occur scattered around the pans and on isolated rock outcrops such as Kubu Island, where they have stood as landmarks for millennia. The swollen trunks of many are engraved with the signatures of generations of thirsty travellers. Among the baobabs on Kubu some other more unusual species take advantage of this rocky, island niche, including the African star-chestnut (*Sterculia africana*) and common corkwood (*Commiphora pyracanthoides*).

Fauna Large mammals are scarce around the pans. This is partly because of the hostile nature of the terrain, partly because this is cattle-ranching country, where wild animals have been marginalised by the activities of people, and partly because of the destructive effect that veterinary control fences have had on animal migration patterns.

There is no doubt that cattle fences to the south have had a significant impact on the populations of herbivores, and especially the blue wildebeest. Now blue wildebeest are seldom seen around Sua Pan and certainly not in the vast herds that built up during the 1950s, when populations are estimated to have peaked at about 250,000. Further west, though, in the area where Ntwetwe Pan borders the national park, great numbers of zebra and wildebeest arrive with the rains between November and December, feeding on the nutritious new grasses. Many move on in February and March, but others stay, attracted by regularly pumped waterholes in the area.

A permanent scattering of springbok inhabits the grasslands around the pans, too. These hardy and versatile antelope manage without water for long periods, and withstand the harshest daytime temperatures by orientating their white rumps towards the sun to deflect the worst of its ultraviolet rays.

Other large mammals are thin on the ground, being more abundant towards the west of Ntwetwe and the adjacent grazing grounds of Makgadikgadi Pans National Park (page 473). However, a scrutiny of the pan surface can reveal the tracks of a surprising range of visitors, including rare wandering elephants or giraffe. Zebra and gemsbok are sometimes seen trekking wearily through the heat haze as they cross the pans between grazing areas, while red hartebeest are frequent visitors to the grasslands, where they can subsist on poorer grasses than many species.

The encrusted tracks of lion or cheetah sometimes appear on the pan surface, particularly towards the west, but the comparative lack of large herbivores means that larger predators are scarce, and a wandering lion is apt to be shot by cattle ranchers. More common are the smaller nocturnal carnivores that can survive the harsh conditions and thrive on smaller pickings.

Brown hyena inhabit the area, and occasionally these elusive predators may be observed at close quarters from Jack's Camp, San Camp and Camp Kalahari on the western shores of Ntwetwe, where they have been studied by zoologists. Their catholic diet includes tsamma melons and ostrich eggs, as well as spring hares, young springbok, smaller mammals and carrion.

Black-backed jackal, bat-eared fox and African wildcat are widespread, while yellow mongoose is common in sandy areas, where it is an accomplished killer of

SPRING HARES

The spring hare is actually a true rodent, and not a hare at all. Weighing about 3kg, this bizarre animal looks like a cross between a rabbit and a kangaroo, with its long ears and thick black-tipped tail. It progresses in ambling hops on long hind legs, with forelegs clasped in front and tail balanced behind.

Spring hares live in burrows by day, in which they doze off upright, having plugged the hole with dirt. By night they graze on grass and crops, and dig for roots, corms and tubers. This animal is a prized delicacy for many nocturnal predators, including owls, honey badgers and caracals. It also figures prominently on the local human menu. It has been estimated that over 2.5 million spring hares are hunted annually in Botswana – hooked out of their holes during the day – providing the protein equivalent of 20,000 cows.

scorpions. At night, a legion of smaller mammals moves out across the grasslands. Spring hares thrive on damaged grassland and are common around villages, where up to 60 may occur per hectare. Their eyes shine brightly in torchlight, and casting a beam around your campsite will usually reveal at least one foraging nearby.

Aardvarks are found (though seldom seen) in open areas with plenty of termites, scrub hares hide up in acacia thickets, and porcupines occur anywhere. Acacias provide shelter for lesser bushbabies, which feed on their gum during winter when insects are less abundant. This diminutive, nocturnal primate performs astonishing leaps from tree to tree and seldom comes to the ground, progressing on its hind legs in huge hops when it does. Common rodents include typical Kalahari species such as ground squirrel, Damara mole rat, hairy-footed gerbil and black-tailed tree rat.

Birdlife The Makgadikgadi Pans are perhaps best known for their birdlife, specifically the great concentration of waterbirds in the Nata River delta after good rains (December–March). In good years, tens of thousands of flamingos, both lesser and greater, arrive to breed, visible from the air as a pink shimmer across the surface of the lake. They are sustained by a rich soup of algae – and brine shrimps, whose eggs lie dormant in the baked clay of the pan surface throughout the dry season.

This gathering represents the largest breeding flamingo population in southern Africa, and can peak at over 100,000 birds. However, it is a very unpredictable phenomenon. Even after good rains the flamingos have a life-and-death race against time to breed before the waters dry up, and they may not return again for years. In 1976, over 5,000 young flamingos, still unable to fly, were observed from the air trekking en masse across the barren pans in search of new water when their breeding shallows evaporated. What became of them is not recorded.

The flamingos can best be seen in the Nata Sanctuary (page 467). Here, when the flood is full, you will also find pelicans (both white and pink-backed), herons and egrets, cormorants and darters, waders (including avocet, black-winged stilt, blacksmith lapwing, wood sandpiper and ruff), black-necked grebe, red-knobbed coot, and ducks (including red-billed teal and white-faced duck). Other species more typical of the Okavango floodplains also occur at this time, including fish eagles, saddle-billed storks and, occasionally, wattled cranes. The reedbeds themselves provide a breeding habitat for weavers, bishops and reed warblers.

The open grasslands surrounding the pans are home to many typical Kalahari ground-nesting birds, including ostriches, which are sometimes seen far out on the pans themselves, kori bustards and secretary birds. Some smaller species, including capped wheatear and ant-eating chat, take this a stage further by nesting, like rodents, in underground burrows. All four of southern Africa's sandgrouse (Namaqua, Burchell's, double-banded and yellow-throated) occur around the pans. These delicately plumaged birds are most often seen in the evening, flying rapidly towards a waterhole with rippling calls. Males will waddle in to immerse their absorbent belly feathers and carry water back many kilometres to their young on the nest.

More conspicuous by day is the boldly marked male northern black korhaan (renamed the white-quilled bustard, though the new name is not in common usage yet), who calls with a noisy 'karak karak karak' as he takes off and circles slowly in territorial display, before fluttering to the ground with yellow legs dangling. Like all korhaans, the brooding female relies on her cryptic camouflage to remain hidden. Another common species, the double-banded courser, is superbly adapted to withstand the harsh conditions of the pans. It does not need any drinking water, and can survive extreme overheating while protecting its single egg from the fierce Makgadikgadi sun.

In this largely featureless habitat, any point of elevation can prove a good spot for birds. The baobabs on Kubu Island provide roosting and nesting sites for barn owls and rollers (both lilac-breasted and purple). Many tall stands of date palms harbour breeding palm swifts, and the occasional pair of red-necked falcons. Isolated thorn trees support the massive untidy nests of secretary birds or vultures (both white-backed and lappet-faced).

The acacia woodland holds a wide selection of birds typical of this habitat across the region (page 450). Red-billed spurfowl, white-browed robin and violet-eared waxbill forage low down in the thickets, while lilac-breasted roller and long-tailed shrike perch more conspicuously in the taller acacias. Bateleurs (or short-tailed eagles) and martial eagles patrol the skies, and a host of bulbuls, babblers, hornbills, barbets, sunbirds, flycatchers and others occupy the niches in between.

The area around Nata Lodge is particularly rich in woodland species. In summer, migrant raptors such as steppe buzzard, western red-footed kestrel and yellow-billed kite join resident predators such as greater kestrel, pale chanting goshawk and marsh owl, and after good rains, Montagu's and pallid harriers may be seen quartering the grasslands in drifting, elegant flight.

Other common summer migrants include white stork, red-backed and lesser grey shrikes and European and carmine bee-eaters, while seed-eaters such as red-billed quelea and black-eared finchlark arrive to breed in large numbers, taking advantage of the seasonally abundant grass seeds.

GETTING AROUND With a large number of tracks in the area, I have not even tried to describe them all in detail here. However, if you're driving around by yourself, rather than with a local guide who knows the area well, then navigation issues should preoccupy you. Outside the national park, visiting the pans is all about exploring for yourself. If you want set routes to follow, perhaps it's not for you.

If you're ready for a small expedition, then take note of the highlights and landmarks mentioned here, with GPS co-ordinates, and use the Shell map (mentioned on page 141) to keep some realistic idea of where you are. That said, because of the size of the pans and their very remote situation, you must follow some basic safety rules:

- Take at least one reliable GPS with you – and many more batteries than you think you'll need.
- Carry much more fuel than you expect to use.
- Carry enough water and food for your whole time in the pans area, plus a few days' safety margin.
- Travel with a minimum of two fully equipped 4x4s, and preferably also a satellite phone.
- Arrange a rendezvous for when you leave the pans, and someone to raise the alarm if you don't arrive. Leave a rough route plan with them.

It's difficult for me to emphasise enough just how dangerous the pans can be. There are periodic deaths of people who visit the area without the proper back-up and preparation, and then get into difficulties. It's different from many areas in Botswana because:

- The sun is merciless on the pans' surface; there's absolutely no shade.
- If you break through the crust of the pans to the wet silt beneath, then getting out is very difficult, even with a second vehicle. Remember: there will be no wood around; no branches to put under the wheels.

- There are so many different tracks on the pans (each diverging vehicle makes a new one), that often there simply isn't a 'right' track which most vehicles take. Thus, it may be weeks or months before someone takes the same route that you do, and passes you.

SUA PAN Sua Pan is the eastern of the twin pans, and extends roughly southwards from the town of Nata (page 481) in its northeast corner. On its southern shore is the village of Mosu; to its north lies the Maun–Nata road; to its west it is divided from Ntwetwe Pan by a thin strip of grassland.

Sua (sometimes spelled 'Sowa') is the Setswana word for 'salt', and it is this mineral residue from the vanished superlake that dominates the geology and ecology of the pan. Once, salt was laboriously collected from the pan surface by the San and carried away on donkeys. Today, it is mined by Botswana Ash (Botash), a joint enterprise in which the Botswana government is the major shareholder, and taken out by road and rail. The company supplies sodium carbonate on an industrial scale for use in the manufacture of paper, glass and steel. Their mine is

FLAMINGOS

Of the world's half-dozen or so species of flamingo, two are found within southern Africa: the greater (*Phoenicopterus ruber*) and the lesser (*Phoenicopterus minor*). Both species have wide distributions, from southern Africa north into East Africa and the Red Sea, and are highly nomadic in their habits.

Flamingos are usually found wading in large areas of shallow saline water where they filter feed by holding their specially adapted beaks upside down in the water. The lesser flamingo will walk or swim while swinging its head from side to side, mainly taking blue-green algae from the surface of the water. The larger greater flamingo will hold its head submerged while filtering out small organisms (detritus and algae), even stirring the mud with its feet to help the process. Both species are very gregarious and flocks can have millions of birds, though a few hundred is more common.

Only occasionally do flamingos breed in southern Africa, choosing the Makgadikgadi Pans, Namibia's Etosha Pan or even Lake Ngami. When the conditions are right (usually March to June, following the rains), both species build low mud cones in the water and lay one or (rarely) two eggs in a small hollow on the top. These are then incubated by both parents for about a month, until they hatch. After a further week the young birds flock together and start to forage with their parents. Some ten weeks later the young can fly and fend for themselves.

During this time the young are very susceptible to the shallow water in the pans drying out. In 1969, a rescue operation was mounted in Namibia when the main Etosha Pan dried out, necessitating the moving of thousands of chicks to nearby Fischer's Pan, which was still covered in water.

The best way to tell the two species apart is by their beaks: that of the greater flamingo is almost white with a black tip, while the lesser flamingo has a uniformly dark beak. If you are further away then the body of the greater will appear white, while that of the lesser looks smaller and more pink. The best place to see them in Botswana is certainly Sua Pan – although even there they will only appear if the rains have filled some of the pan.

situated along the Sua Spit, a tongue of grassland that extends halfway across the pan from its eastern shore.

The Nata River feeds Sua Pan from the northeast (bringing the rains from Zimbabwe) and, in good years, it floods from December to March with shallow, warm water. Where the fresh water of the river meets the saline pan, a brackish delta of silted reedbeds has formed. In summer, this corner of the pan attracts great concentrations of breeding waterbirds, notably flamingos (see opposite). This delta – an area of 230km² – is now protected within the community-run Nata Bird Sanctuary (see below). The flamingos can usually be viewed from the bird hide on the eastern shore, but after heavy rain, access may not be possible.

Evidence of the former lake exists in the form of fossil pebble beaches along the shores of Kubu Island and other granite outcrops around the pan, and fossil diatoms and molluscs on the pan surfaces. These reveal that there was a prolonged wet period about 14,000–17,000 years ago and, more recently, a flood only 1,500 years ago. Near the village of Mosu in the south, an escarpment rises some 40m above the edge of the pan, showing the erosive force of the great lake that once washed against these cliffs. Here there is also one of several subterranean springs that emerge around the fringes of the pans.

The pan is a remarkable area, with the occasional spot like Kubu Island that has a magic all of its own. That said, there's a lot more than just Nata Sanctuary and Kubu here – but it does need time to explore it. Read my warning on page 465; then get a copy of Mike Main's book (page 547) and a few good maps, and enjoy it!

Most visitors to this area spend the night at one of the variety of options in Nata (page 481). An alternative would be to camp at Nata Sanctuary (see below). There has been sporadic talk of a new lodge to be built at Sowa for some time now, but this has yet to be substantiated.

Nata Sanctuary [447 H4] (⊕ all year 07.00–19.00 daily; P100 pp, plus P50/vehicle, camping P80 pp) A conservation area was originally established in the northeast corner of Sua Pan with the help of the Kalahari Conservation Society in the 1980s, to protect the important seasonal wetland areas around the Nata Delta. However, although the villagers at Nata were consulted about the plans, the wider community in the area didn't benefit from it.

This area encompassed cattle-grazing land owned by four communities: Nata, Sepako, Maposa and Mmaxotae. In the early 1990s, it was realised that without the support of these communities, conservation in the area couldn't be effective. Eventually, as part of a ground-breaking community project, the communities moved about 3,000 head of cattle out of the area, and fencing began. In 1993, Nata Sanctuary was opened to the public, and in the same year it won the prestigious Tourism for Tomorrow award for the southern hemisphere.

Now Nata Sanctuary conserves an ecologically sensitive and important natural environment, and also effectively returns money to the communities for doing so. That said, the fences have become less effective over the years, so you'll probably see the odd cow as you drive around. Consider this an illustration of the increasing difficulties facing wildlife conservation areas in marginal regions of Africa. But don't be put off – this is still an excellent area for birding and it is well worth exploring.

Nata Sanctuary generally makes a very easy place to visit for a day or two, either based in Nata or camping at the sanctuary itself. That said, while the birding is at its best during the rainy season, this is also the time when the roads are likely to be impassable, so if you're intent on spending some time in the sanctuary, then it's wise to check the situation before you set off. Arguably the best time to visit is around April, at the end of the rainy season.

See page 461 for notes on the general **flora and fauna** of the pan, but note that a number of mammals have been enclosed (or reintroduced) within the fenced boundaries of the Nata Sanctuary, including gemsbok, springbok, hartebeest, kudu, eland, zebra, reedbuck, jackal, fox, monkey, steenbok, squirrel and spring hare.

The colourfully decorated entrance to Nata Sanctuary is about 17km southeast of Nata, next to the main road to Francistown. It's very well signposted in both directions.

Where to stay Many visitors to the sanctuary stay at one of the lodges in nearby Nata (page 481), but the sanctuary does have its own campsite, the **Nata Sanctuary Community Campsite** [447 H3] (P80 pp). Sadly, it is fairly run-down these days, with little investment or maintenance in its facilities and staff. It's quite close to the main road so expect traffic noise, but equally it's only 300m from the sanctuary entrance and a straightforward drive to the viewing platform across Sua Pan. There are a few large, relatively shady pitches, each with concrete braai stand and picnic table. Single-sex ablution blocks have toilets and showers – although there's no guarantee that either are working. There have been some reports of theft at this campsite.

Kubu Island [447 F6] In the southwest of Sua Pan lies an isolated granite outcrop some 10m high and 1km long, known as Kubu Island or Lekhubu. It forms the shape of a crescent, and its slopes are terraced with fossil beaches of wave-rounded pebbles, providing startling evidence of the prehistoric lake's former water levels. Crowned with an array of ancient, gnarled baobabs and surrounded on three sides by a vast grey emptiness, Kubu has a unique atmospheric beauty.

At night, with the wind moaning through the baobabs, it is easy to imagine the waves of a great inland sea lapping at its pebble beaches. Many of the island's rocks are white, covered in ancient, fossilised guano from the waterbirds that used to perch here when it was surrounded by the lake. The moonlight reflecting off the pan's white surface gives the place an almost supernatural atmosphere, which is heightened by the mystery of Kubu's former inhabitants. The shoreline is littered with Stone Age tools and arrowheads, while concentric drystone walls on the islands survive from a much more recent village, perhaps around AD1400–1600, and outside this are a number of stone cairns.

Archaeologists have linked these walls and cairns with the dynasty of Great Zimbabwe, and think that they were probably at the southwesternmost tip of that state. In *The Riddle of the Stone Walls* (page 544), Alec Campbell suggests that they could have been remote 'circumcision camps', to which the boys of the tribe were taken for circumcision and ceremonies leading to adulthood. It is suggested that perhaps ceremonies took place within the walls, and every class that 'graduated' then built a separate cairn.

Campbell also noted that the people of the nearest village, Tshwagong, hold Kubu and the nearby Thithaba Islands as sacred, and men over 16 years of age visit the islands to make contact with God, singing a particular song for rain and leaving offerings on the ground.

Kubu is a national monument, under the management of the proactive, efficient Gaing-O Community Trust (w kubuisland.com), and there is a team stationed here to ensure that visitors to the campsite and island are both assisted and educated about the geological and cultural significance of the area. Guided walks are available, though visitors are also welcome to explore independently – albeit while respecting the sanctity of the location for the local community, admiring the historical stone walls and leaving archaeological and geological discoveries in place.

Getting there and away One of the few operators to run trips to this area Uncharted Africa (contact via Natural Selection, page 215), which offers quad-bike excursions here from all their camps. In addition, their Kubu Island Adventure safari includes time at Kubu Island, travelling by quad bike and sleeping under the stars. Alternatively, you can drive yourself.

It is not possible to reach Kubu Island in the rainy season, so if in any doubt, contact the island custodians at the Gaing-O Community Trust, who will provide up-to-date information on the road conditions.

From the north there are endless possible routes to Kubu Island (⊕ KUBU-I 20°53.737'S, 25°49.421'E), and you can expect it to take about 4 hours from the main Maun–Nata road along sandy tracks, sometimes clear and swift and at other times overgrown.

Easiest is probably to take one of the many tracks that leave the main road between about 30km and 15km west of Nata. Follow your nose (or, more practically, your GPS) towards Thabatshukudu Village (⊕ THABAT 20°42.606'S, 25°47.476'E), which is about 70–75km south, depending on the track that you take.

From there it's about 10km southwest to the Tshwagong Veterinary Gate, through which any north–south traffic between Sua and Ntwetwe pans passes – so tracks will lead you there. This is about 3km north of the small village of Tshwagong [447 F5] (⊕ TSHWAG 20°48.094'S, 25°45.608'E), from where it's about 14km in a straight line southeast to Kubu Island. (There are several tracks here, so just head southeast and follow your GPS.)

Note that the track that leaves Gweta in a south then southeasterly direction, ending at the Tshwagong Veterinary Gate, passes over several long stretches of Ntwetwe Pan, and so is dangerously muddy during the wetter months of the year. Do not ever be tempted to cross the pans if wet: you will get stuck and there is no phone signal and few villages in the vicinity. Driving and navigating across the pans can be notoriously challenging: the disorientating nature of endless vistas, glue-like mud hidden beneath the surface crust, and the curved horizons all make getting stranded or lost distinct possibilities, so take no chances.

From the south it's best to start by heading for the village of Mmatshumo (⊕ MMATSH 21°08.590'S, 25°39.214'E). You'll find a number of tracks from the Orapa–Francistown road which will lead you here; the shortest leaves the main road around ⊕ TURNM1 21°19.468'S, 25°33.742'E [447 F7]. From there it's about 23km to Mmatshumo. Heading north from there, there's a good view of the pan to your right after about 5km, before the track bends west and back north to cross the small Tsitane Pan, crossing the veterinary fence at ⊕ TSIVET 20°58.620'S, 25°37.178'E [447 F6]. Then a straight track heading north-northeast brings you to Tshwagong (⊕ TSHWAG 20°48.094'S, 25°45.608'E) after about 20km.

Note that during the dry season you can take a short cut about 7km north of the vet fence, at around ⊕ TURNM2 20°55.990'S, 25°40.015'E [447 F5], which heads east-northeast across the pan to Kubu; but don't even think of attempting this when the pans are wet!

Where to stay

Kubu Island Camping [447 F6] (13 pitches, tents) m 7549 4669, 7310 9996; e kubu. island@btcmail.co.bw; w kubuisland.com. Known as a striking granite outcrop with panoramic views of Makgadikgadi, Kubu Island is a remote camping experience operated by the Gaing-O

Community Trust. Pitches under ancient baobabs with braai facilities, firepits (firewood P20/ bundle) & basic long-drop toilets are available, & there are also tents with 2 mattresses & solar lighting. Guided walks are on offer & are a good way to explore while gaining an understanding of the island's archaeological & cultural significance. It is possible to explore independently; be sure to arrive in time to take in the idyllic sunsets. *Kubu Island entrance P50 pp/day; camping P160 pp inc government levy; equipped tent P250/night; guided walk P60 pp.*

Other landmarks around Sua Pan

Places detailed here run south from Nata and Nata Sanctuary, then west and north to Kubu Island and beyond. Note that you should never attempt to drive across the pan from the east side to the west, or vice versa, even during the dry season.

Sowa Pan Mine [447 G4] (soda-ash factory) This modern industrial complex seems strangely out of place here, especially as it is easily reached, 40km along a tarred road. The turn-off is about 48km south of Nata on the road to Francistown.

Kukome Island [447 G6] On the eastern shore of Sua Pan, roughly opposite Kubu, Kukome (also spelled 'Kukonje') Island (✥ KUKOME 20°55.001'S, 26°12.203'E) has similar fossil beaches and ancient remains. To reach here, first head for the Kwadiba Veterinary Gate (✥ KWADIB 20°54.907'S, 26°16.571'E) on the east side of Sua Pan, from where a track leads west for about 7km to Kukome Island.

Mmatshumo [447 F7] Mmatshumo (✥ MMATSH 21°08.590'S, 25°39.214'E) is a small village on the south side of the pans, between Sua and Ntwetwe pans, as well as an important waypoint when you're navigating yourself around.

South Islands [447 F6] About 7km south of Kubu, far out on the pan, are two other small islands. They too have baobab trees and the larger one, on the east, has a series of rock cairns along its spine.

Thabatshukudu [447 F5] Thabatshukudu (✥ THABAT 20°42.606'S, 25°47. 476'E) is another village – notable for the landmark of its colourfully painted general dealer's store – and another useful waypoint when navigating yourself around.

NTWETWE PAN

Ntwetwe Pan is the western twin of Sua, and is of a similar size and general topography, though aligned more east–west. It lies due south of the Nata–Maun road, between Gweta in the north and Orapa and Mopipi in the south. One finger extends to the north of the road, while to the southwest the pan breaks up into several smaller pans, including Lake Xau, just south of Mopipi. The old north–south trading route between Gweta and Mopipi crosses the centre of the pan, and the two famous isolated baobabs (Green's Baobab and Chapman's Baobab) that marked this route for early European explorers – including Livingstone, who left his initials here – still serve as landmarks for today's travellers.

Ntwetwe lacks the famous granite outcrops of Sua; its main points of elevation are fossilised barchan dunes that once crept across the surface of the lake during a dry period and were left stranded when waters rose again. Gabasadi Island is the largest of these. The profiles of the dune islands show steps and lines of vegetation which, like Sua Pan's pebble beaches, are evidence of former higher lake levels.

Stone Age sites are scattered among the smaller pans that form the western shore of Ntwetwe. At Gutsha Pan, near Chapman's Baobab, there is a perennial spring.

Here the San once dug pit traps lined with poisoned stakes to trap the plentiful game that came to drink. The remains of these traps, and the calcrete blinds behind which the hunters hid, are still visible today.

Where to stay
There are three well-known camps on the northwest side of the pan: Jack's Camp, San Camp and Camp Kalahari, in that order of luxury. Though these are the only camps on the pans themselves, you could also visit this area on a day or overnight excursion with Planet Baobab or Gweta Lodge (page 483). Both offer a cheaper option, aimed at backpackers and people driving along the Nata–Maun road.

All three camps are usually reached by light aircraft or helicopter from Maun; a private airstrip (⊕ SANAIR 20°29.504'S, 25°11.054'E) is 20 minutes' drive from camp and a flight transfer is US$396 per person (one-way). That said, they do accept self-drive vehicles in the dry season, although all self-drive vehicles must be escorted to the camps from Planet Baobab (page 484). Road transfers to/from Planet Baobab are US$455 per person return, or escorted self-drive transfers are US$135 per vehicle return.

Camp Kalahari [446 D4] (12 tents) Contact Natural Selection (page 215). Standing among real fan palms & acacias, the former Makgadikgadi Camp is just 5mins from the edge of Ntwetwe Pan, south of Gweta. The low-key little sister to Jack's & San Camp, Camp Kalahari is a family-friendly spot with activities galore. Central to the camp is a small, open-sided V-shaped structure under a thatched roof, with a decked pool area & social firepit. One 'wing' houses a long teak dining table, the other a cosy lounge. The style has a distinctly tribal feel, with furniture from Ethiopia & Sudan, whereas the tented rooms hark back to the 1940s, complete with twin or dbl metal-framed beds & campaign safari furniture, offset by rich Indian & Moroccan textiles. 21st-century creature comforts come in the form of an en-suite bathroom & separate toilet, shower, solar-powered lights & a solar hot-water system. There are 2 dedicated family tents with interconnecting rooms. In the front, safari furniture sits on a wooden veranda. Batteries can be charged both in the tents & the main building. As an aside, there is a discreet electric fence around the camp, largely to protect the trees, but it doesn't entirely deter elephant or lion.

In addition to the activities detailed on page 472, Camp Kalahari also offers horseriding safaris, including 2hr activities (US$175 pp), 3-night set-departure safaris based in camp with riding every day, & more bespoke options including fly camping on request. The open pans & sparse vegetation combined with relatively low levels of dangerous game in the area make this ideal riding country.

The style might be more laid-back than Jack's & San, but the activities (& effectively the location) are the same, making this a winning combination at a fraction of the price. *From US$775 pp 10 Jan–Mar to US$1,205 pp Jul–Aug, FBA inc drinks, laundry, conservation fees. Children all ages.* ⊕ *All year.* 🛏🛏🛏🛏🛏

Jack's Camp [446 D4] (9 tents) Contact Natural Selection (page 215). Jack's Camp was the original camp on the pans. When all the other safari operators in Botswana focused on wildlife & the Delta, Jack's dared to offer something totally different – & succeeded in style, becoming one of the country's best-known camps.

A bush camp was originally started in this area in the 1960s, by the late Jack Bousfield. After his tragic death in an aircraft accident, his son, Ralph, built a camp for visitors here which first opened in 1993. It's set in a grove of mokolwane fan palms, on grasslands on the edge of Ntwetwe Pan, overlooking Makgadikgadi Pans National Park.

Although entirely rebuilt in 2021, Jack's remains classically furnished in a bold East African 1940s campaign safari style. It's very comfortable, with first-class attention to detail & a distinctive aesthetic. The 9 enormous, khaki tents are built on decks & set under rustling palm fronds. Inside, the interiors are a striking vision of colour, texture & pattern, with canopied four-poster beds made up with down pillows & duvets, Persian rugs on polished floors, vases of ostrich feathers &

mahogany furniture, from travelling trunks to brass-handled chests of drawers: a glamorous step back in time. Each tent now has a comfortable lounge area complete with its own curiosities cabinet, an en-suite bathroom with indoor & outdoor showers, & a veranda with velvet chairs & a plunge pool. At night, lighting is by solar lanterns & there's an over-bed air-cooling system in place.

Jack's central 'mess tent' is a grand, canvas pavilion. The interior is lined with coral printed cotton, the lampshades are fringed with tassels, & everything is patterned or embellished. There is a museum air to the eclectic selection of (mostly local) items filling glass cabinets & tabletops around the area: stone tools, fossils of extinct mega-fauna (like giant zebra), prints, maps, historical etchings, & a fair-sized collection of Bushman beadwork. Communal dining is around the 1820s officers' mess table, & there's a well-stocked drinks' cabinet, library area & an antique pool table. There's a separate open-sided pavilion over a pool, & a Bedouin-esque tea tent, its floor scattered with a mass of Persian rugs & cushions, the venue for tea & delicious cakes before afternoon activities.

For guests seeking an exclusive-use escape, Jack's Private Camp opened as a 2-bedroom private retreat in 2024 for families or travelling couples. Set apart from the main camp, & with a private guide, vehicle, pool & a satellite kitchen, it offers both space & seclusion.

Jack's Camp from US$1,215 pp 10 Jan–Mar to US$3,445 pp Jul–Aug, FBA. Private Camp from US$6,950 10 Jan–Mar to US$11,445 Jul–Aug, FBA. ⏲ *All year.* 🛏🛏🛏🛏🛏

❋ **San Camp** [446 D4] (7 tents) Contact Natural Selection (page 215). This smaller, but no less exclusive, satellite of Jack's Camp lies 20mins' drive away, right on Ntwetwe Pan, & is open only during the dry season (usually Apr–mid Dec). Run by the same team as Jack's, it works in the same way, with similar activities & approach. Like Jack's, it's rustic but traditionally stylish & comfortable, with classic Meru tents in white to reflect the stark surrounding landscape – lending San Camp something of an *Arabian Nights* feel. 3 llnked billowing pavilions, incorporating a central dining area flanked by a library to one side, & a tea tent & 'relaxation area' to the other, are lined in a subtle pinstripe, with brass-trimmed mahogany furniture offset by Persian rugs. In addition, a yoga & meditation pavilion is situated right on the edge of the pan. In the individual tents, a veranda with a day bed leads through to a sitting area, then on to the bedroom (2 with four-poster dbl beds; the rest with twins), dressing room, & bathroom with flush toilet & hot water at the back.

Both Jack's & San camps are excellent, something totally different from virtually all of the rest of Botswana's camps. San is slightly cheaper than Jack's (though both are expensive), while activities are the same. Personally, we actually prefer the atmosphere & environment at San, though either makes a great 3-night stop, best placed at the very end of a fly-in trip to Botswana.

From US$1,895 pp Apr–May & Nov–19 Dec to US$2,380 pp Jul–Aug, FBA inc drinks, laundry & conservation fees. ⏲ *Closed 10 Jan–31 Mar.* 🛏🛏🛏🛏🛏

Activities At these camps, activities vary with the season. When it's dry, around April–November, there's likely to be very little game around. That's fine, as it's not the focus of a trip here. Instead you'll explore the pans in **4x4s**, on individual **quad bikes** and on **foot**, often with a Bushman tracker. These trips concentrate on the area's smaller wildlife, and also touch on its history and archaeology. At a nearby pan, old Stone Age flint axe-heads and arrowheads can be found on the surface, though (quite rightly) the guides insist that they should be left there.

During the wet season, around December–March, the pans can become quagmires. It's often impossible to use the quad bikes, and the 4x4 drives tend to stick to the grasslands on the edges of the pans. However, then there is a much greater density of wildlife around, with many migrant birds – including flamingo – and if you're lucky, large herds of plains game, including zebra and wildebeest. Throughout the year you may see brown hyena, and you can have the fascinating experience of interacting with a gang of habituated meerkats. As the camps are outside the national park, night drives are possible – when there's often more wildlife around than during the day.

Horseriding activities to explore the Makgadikgadi Pans are run by the experienced team from Ride Botswana (w ridebotswana.com) (page 218), and are available from all three camps. Riders can traverse the ancient lakebed, grasslands and sand dunes in the company of experienced guides. Various horseriding safaris are on offer, ranging from shorter rides of around 2 hours (all abilities) to multi-day adventures (experienced riders only).

What to see and do

Like Sua Pan, Ntwetwe is an area for experienced Africa hands to explore in their own vehicles – though bear in mind our comments on safety on page 465. Alternatively, and much safer (albeit very expensive), fly in from Maun to one of the camps for three or four days and explore the pans and surrounding area with expert guides: on foot, by 4x4 or on quad bikes.

Ntwetwe Pan doesn't have anything quite so spectacular as Kubu Island, though it does have a few marvellous old baobabs and an island of its own.

Chapman's Baobab [447 E4] This famous landmark (⊕ CHAPMA 20°29.372'S, 25°14.898'E), the only one for hundreds of kilometres, was named after South African big-game hunter and explorer James Chapman, who passed through this area with Thomas Baines in 1861. One of the largest trees in Africa (David Livingstone recorded its circumference as 25.9m!), and designated a national monument, it used to be visible from some distance away, guiding early explorers across the narrowest stretch of the pans. It was seemingly also used as a historical 'post office', with passing travellers leaving notes in cavities in its six-stemmed trunk and even carving into it.

Sadly, in January 2016, quite unexpectedly, it split into three and fell prostrate. No conclusive reason has been given for its demise, though late rains, high temperatures and simply old age have all been sited.

Parts of the tree are most definitely dead and decaying, though some roots are very much alive and small shoots and leaves continue to appear along some of the limbs, so it remains to be seen if some of these might serve to continue the tree's long line.

Note that there are endless tracks to the west of here, many made by nearby private safari camps, and so navigation can be especially difficult, rendering a GPS essential.

Green's Baobab [446 D4] Less well known than Chapman's Baobab, but still very much alive, this tree (⊕ GREENS 20°25.497'S, 25°13.869'E) is close to the only permanent spring in the area, Gutsha Pan, and still bears the inscription 'Green's Expedition 1858–1859' carved into its bark by the Green brothers, Fred and Charles, an intrepid duo who paused their wagons here en route to Matabeleland in Zimbabwe.

Gabasadi Island [446 D5] In the middle of Ntwetwe, to the west of the usual north–south route across the pans, Gabasadi Island is a low mound protruding from the surface of the pan. It's actually a fossilised, crescent-shaped barchan dune, which you'll realise if you climb it.

MAKGADIKGADI PANS NATIONAL PARK

Makgadikgadi Pans National Park covers about 3,900km² in a roughly square-shaped block to the west of the pans. It extends from the western edge of Ntwetwe Pan – one corner of which is incorporated within the park, fragmented into a myriad smaller pans – westwards to the Boteti River, which marks the park's western boundary. To the north it meets the southern boundary of Nxai Pan National Park, from which it is separated only by the main Maun–Nata road. While for administrative purposes the two parks are often lumped together as Makgadikgadi and Nxai Pan National Park, here they are treated individually, as a reflection of their very different attractions.

GEOGRAPHY AND GEOLOGY About one-fifth of the national park consists of salt pan. The rest is rolling grasslands on Kalahari sands, rising here and there into fossilised dunes and low hills of thicker sand which mark prehistoric limits of the great Makgadikgadi superlake. The great breadth of the sandy Boteti watercourse and the riverine woodland that lines its steep banks are evidence of a major river that once carved a channel across central Botswana, carrying the waters of the Okavango into the Makgadikgadi basin.

Until 2008, the Boteti hadn't flooded properly for 16 years, but in early 2009 the water returned and began to advance south again. Today it flows right through to Lake Xau and stays throughout the dry season. That said, in 2013, many locals were predicting that after a couple of years of lower rainfall and floods, the river may gradually revert back to its previous dry-season state in the coming years. Time will tell but for now the transformation is quite something.

FLORA AND FAUNA Makgadikgadi Pans National Park really contains a spectrum of environments, flora and fauna. Its east side, especially the southeast, is dominated by salt pans and grasslands – very much the same as the rest of Sua and Ntwetwe further east. Its western border, the Boteti River, is lined by thick riverine forest; here the wildlife has more in common with that found beside the Chobe or the Linyanti, or in the Okavango Delta. Between these two very different environments lies the body of the park.

Flora The vegetation on the east side of the park is very similar in pattern to that of the Makgadikgadi Pans (page 461). Its diversity increases westwards as the saline influence of the pan is left behind; from the bare surface of the pan itself, through rolling grassland and the vegetated dunes of Njuca Hills, into thicker acacia scrub, and eventually to the dense riverine woodland along the banks of the Boteti River. Along the eastern border there are areas of palm-tree woodland, where groves of vegetable ivory palms (*Hyphaene petersiana*) grow among the tracts of tall grassland.

On raised ground between the salt pans, yellowish patches of prickly salt grass (*Odyssea paucinervis*) flourish, contrasting with clumps of the dark succulent Chenopodiaceae species. Along the pan edges you may also find a cactus-like succulent, *Hoodia lugardii*, which periodically produces striking maroon flowers. The open grasslands are studded with islands of trees and denser vegetation, with such species as the trumpet thorn (*Catophractes alexandri*) and western rhigozum (*Rhigozum brevispinosum*) flowering among the acacia scrub.

Beside the deep sand that normally characterises the Boteti River, camelthorns (*Vachellia erioloba*), blackthorns (*Senegalia mellifera*) and silver clusterleaf (*Terminalia sericea*) dominate the riverine forest, interspersed with a few other riverine giants such as sycamore figs (*Ficus sycomorus*) and sausage trees (*Kigelia africana*). From the early 1990s until 2009, most of the 'riverbed' itself consisted of a sandy channel carpeted in grasses and punctuated by occasional muddy pools of water. Then, following the spectacular rains of 2009, the Boteti enjoyed a period of sustained flow. Today, the river appears to have reverted to a more seasonal pattern.

Typically, the river flows for a period of 20–40 years, followed by a similar period of seasonal flow only. The water remains higher than it was in the 90s but no longer flows year-round.

Fauna

Mammals In the wet season, Makgadikgadi Pans National Park boasts good concentrations of grazers that rival those of Nxai Pan to the north, and an aerial view shows the area to be latticed with a dense network of game trails. From about June onwards, herds of Burchell's zebra and blue wildebeest start a westward movement towards the lush grazing around the Boteti River, accompanied by smaller numbers of gemsbok, eland and red hartebeest. (The latter tend to come slightly later, in years when the rains have been exceptionally good.) These herds gradually congregate along the waterfront until, by November, this area becomes jam-packed with game. In attendance are leopard and lion, attracted by the high concentration of prey.

In the ecozone between grassland and woodland, browsers such as kudu, bushbuck and grey duiker find a permanent home, while troops of baboons and vervet monkeys forage beneath the trees, and small numbers of giraffe and elephant often occur. The area also supports a small waterbuck population, resident pairs of bushbuck (locals say the same subspecies as the Chobe bushbuck) and – when the Boteti flows – the occasional hippo. There are also some huge crocodiles, many of which survived for years in the caves along the banks of the riverbed & reap the rewards of their patience when the river flows.

In peak season, from September to November, the area around the Boteti can offer truly outstanding wildlife watching, and the air is filled with the braying calls

THE LIONS OF MAKGADIKGADI

Makgadikgadi is an erratic and uncertain place for lions. With the first rains, huge herds of zebra and wildebeest move out on to the plains to graze on the succulent grasses and drop their young. In the dry months this pulse of life ebbs back to the Boteti River, 50km to the west, leaving the plains largely deserted by large ungulates. The lions have had to adapt to these huge fluctuations and the unpredictability.

For some the solution is simply tracking the herds back to the Boteti for the dry months, where they must dodge the human residents on the west side of the river. Others stay behind amid the parched grasses, swirling dust devils and spring hares. This is not the place for huge ungainly prides; rather lionesses pair up and wander over large areas, often in excess of 1,000km^2, in order to find sufficient food. Males typically spread their time between two or more of these small, efficient prides. They can maintain territories of almost double that, walking up to 50km a night to patrol their vast swathes of baked wasteland.

Water is unavailable for up to seven months a year for these lions, so they must gain all their moisture from their prey. Immediately after killing large prey such as gemsbok they snick open the belly and stomach, slurping up the juices before they soak away into the sand. However, large prey is hard to find during the dry season, so they will hunt aardvarks and porcupines, and they increasingly look outside the eastern and western boundaries of the park for sustenance from herds of dopey, slow-moving livestock.

The brown hyena (*Hyaena brunnea*) is one of the three hyena species in southern Africa, the other two being the spotted hyena, a successful hunter and scavenger, and the insectivorous aardwolf. The rarest of the three, the brown hyena is officially classed as 'near threatened', with a global population estimated to be between 4,000 and 10,000. Of these, around 150 adults live within Makgadikgadi Pans National Park.

The brown hyena occurs at low densities throughout southern Africa. This shy, nocturnal animal has evolved to live in desert systems: it is a solitary forager that can survive independently of permanent surface water. Brown hyenas will eat virtually anything, apart from grass or herbage – and here their diet ranges from old carcasses or ostrich eggs to melons and even scorpions.

For over a decade, the Makgadikgadi Brown Hyena Project operated near Jack's Camp in a bid to improve the management and conservation of this elusive carnivore. Researchers investigated foraging strategies, scent-marking behaviour, space and resources requirements, and the impact of the Makgadikgadi game fence on the populations of brown hyenas living on both sides of the fence, through changes in food availability and loss of access to the cattle areas.

It was observed that individuals frequently covered over 65km in a night when foraging in the Makgadikgadi, with lion kills forming an important food source. Over the wet season, these are often zebra and wildebeest, while over the dry season, when food is scarcer, they can frequently be cattle.

Brown hyenas are not truly solitary animals; they live in clans of between two and ten members. While clans' territories cover 200–1,000km², clan members are rarely seen together since they forage alone, only interacting either by a chance meeting while scavenging, or at a cool, communal den site underground. Some brown hyenas, the males in particular, are not part of a clan but are nomadic. Clan members will often be tolerant of an intruder of the opposite sex, but will chase away same-sex intruders.

Brown hyenas are usually almost silent. Long-distance communication is by a unique double scent mark deposited on grass stalks. These marks can be made as often as every 150m of foraging, and as well as communicating with other clan members, the scent mark is also a marker for the clan's territory. Defecations are also used as territorial markers and can be found in concentrations in 'latrine sites' along territorial boundaries. The presence of brown hyenas is more often indicated by their spoor or scent marks, as sightings of the animal in the wild are very uncommon.

of the milling zebra herds. However, with the arrival of the rains in December–January, the herds disperse. Some head north towards Nxai Pan; others gather in the grazing grounds of the southeast, where their migration route beyond the park to the Central Kalahari is partially blocked by a veterinary fence, although there are several gaps in the fence these days. At this time, zebra and gemsbok may often be seen out on the pans in search of the mineral salts that are lacking on the Kalahari grasslands.

A healthy population of large predators, protected in the park from persecution by ranchers, includes lion, cheetah, leopard, spotted and brown hyena. Lion can be common during peak migration, with prides knocking down more zebra than they can consume and (be warned) sometimes wandering inquisitively through the campsites. Cheetah are less common, but may turn up anywhere where there are springbok, while leopard are permanent residents of the denser bush along the Boteti. Spotted hyena, like lion, follow the dry-season herds, while brown hyenas find life more productive (and less competitive) along the park's eastern side.

In the east of the park the campsite at Njuca Hills offers a panoramic base from which to explore the wildlife of the pans and grasslands. Herds of springbok, well adapted to survive the arid and exposed conditions, are common around the pans, while steenbok – usually found in pairs – are also widespread. Nocturnal predators of the pan fringes include brown hyena, aardwolf, bat-eared fox and striped polecat, while black-backed jackal, African wildcat, honey badger and small spotted genet can occur anywhere in the park. Other small mammals include porcupine, aardvark, spring hare and scrub hare, as well as a host of smaller rodents and insectivores (see the general section on pans fauna, page 461).

In sandy areas, ground squirrels (here at the northern limit of their Kalahari range) forage by day in small colonies, holding up their tails as parasols against the fierce sun and dashing for their burrows at any hint of danger. These sociable rodents associate amicably with yellow mongooses, who share their burrow systems and help keep a look-out for predators.

Reptiles Perhaps the most bizarre report from this park is of some of the Boteti's larger crocodiles which, when the river drops drastically during the dry season, or dries up completely, retreat into holes in the riverbank that they have dug for themselves. One such lair that I saw was a good 4–5m above the level of the water even in May, and would have been completely high and dry by October.

Birdlife The birdlife of Makgadikgadi Pans National Park is largely the same as that elsewhere in the greater Makgadikgadi region (page 450), with a grading of species according to habitat, and a large summer influx of migrants.

The denser woodland along the Boteti also harbours more cover-loving species such as Meyer's parrot, woodland kingfisher, Burchell's coucal and White-browed robin-chat (formerly known as Heuglin's robin), while higher water levels have attracted waterbirds such as black-winged stilts, pelicans, cranes and African fish eagles. Many raptors cruise the skies over the park, with Gabar goshawks hunting the thickets, secretary birds stalking the savannah, and vultures following the game herds in search of carcasses. In summer, storks, bee-eaters, kites, shrikes and other migrants move in and fan out across the grasslands.

OSTRICH BREEDING

Ostriches are particularly common in the eastern grasslands, and can often be seen from the main Nata–Maun road. These huge birds breed before the rains, with several females laying in a single scrape that may hold over 30 eggs. Incubation tends to rotate between the male at night (when his dark plumage is no longer vulnerable to overheating), and the female by day (when her drab plumage provides more effective camouflage). Youngsters from several broods gather together in large crèches, presided over by one adult pair, and can sometimes be seen gathering in the shadow of an adult for shade.

15

GETTING AROUND If you're self-driving, ensure you have the Tracks4Africa paper map and GPS (page 142), the Tinkers map (page 142) or the Shell map of Botswana (page 192), with its wealth of GPS co-ordinates. Then take to heart my caveats on page 465, and you're ready to explore.

In most cases you can sign in and pay park fees at one of the three main gates: Makolwane [446 D3] (✪ MAKOLW 20°13.763'S, 25°07.108'E), Phuduhudu [446 B3] (✪ PHUDGT 20°12.313'S, 24°33.344'E) on the Maun–Nata road, and Khumaga [446 B4] (✪ KHUMGT 20°28.321'S, 24°30.888'E). The gates are all open 06.00–18.30 (winter) and 05.30–19.00 (summer).

When the Boteti River is full, the Khumaga Gate is reached by a small but adequate ferry (P150/vehicle). When the river is lower the crossing becomes a ford or even completely dry and driveable. Please note that the ferry operating times are the same as the park opening hours; however, if no-one is around when you arrive at the ferry, it's worth calling Boteti River Camp (see below).

There is a further, little-used gate, the Xirexara Gate [446 D4] (✪ XIREGT 20°25.390'S, 25°07.080'E), on the eastern side of the park, but it is not currently possible to pay park fees here, so entry permits must be arranged in advance if you plan on accessing the park from this direction.

Note that if you enter the park at any other point – and there are several – go straight to one of the gates to sign in. Meandering through the park without having signed in first is against the rules. If you have not paid park fees on entry you will need to ensure you leave the park through one of the gates where you can.

Driving around, you'll find a basic network of sandy tracks that are clearly defined even in the rainy season, when the grass is very high. Moving away from these, though, the tracks are increasingly overgrown and difficult to follow. The more southerly roads, crossing the pans, are particularly hard to locate; arguably they are simply non-existent, washed away with each year's rains. Equally, those around the centre of the eastern side of the park are so numerous that they're totally confusing, complicated by a whole network of tracks used by the camps in the area.

Many visitors enter the park on one side and leave from another – which can make perfect sense. However, with the Boteti River periodically flowing all the way to Lake Xau, it's important to check that you can cross the river by ferry or ford before committing yourself to entering or leaving the park through the Khumaga Gate.

Just to emphasise the safety issues raised about travelling in any of the pans, visitors Richard and Vikki Threlfall once wrote to us to say: 'We broke down at Njuca Hills Campsite and were not found until the third morning after discovering the problem! And then it was only pure chance.' This cautionary tale happened at one of only three official campsites in the park, and realise that it would have taken a full-scale air search to find them if they'd been off the main routes. Do take heed of the safety issues detailed on page 465, before you drive anywhere in the pans area.

 WHERE TO STAY The trio of upmarket lodges north of Khumaga have spectacular, elevated settings on the western bank of the Boteti River, overlooking the park. There are three campsites within the national park: Khumaga, Njuca Hills and Tree Island. As with all national parks' sites, these must be booked in advance (page 212). In Khumaga Village itself, near to the ferry and the park entrance, Boteti River Camp is a small, budget option for campers and non-campers alike.

Camps and lodges

Boteti River Camp [446 B4] (8 chalets, tents, camping) ☎ 686 3763; e reservations3@ bushways.com; w botetirivercamp.com; ✪ TIAAN 20°28.165'S, 24°30.875'E. Formerly Tiaan's Camp, this spot on the edge of Khumaga Village is now part of the Bush Ways collection (page 216) & offers affordable accommodation & camping with easy access to the national park: the camp is right next door to the park gate & ferry across the river (you can drive over in the dry season).

Its 8 flat pitches have shade, a water standpipe, firepit, braai & electricity, as well as access to clean ablution blocks with hot-water showers & flush toilets. There are also pre-erected mini Meru tents & 8 en-suite chalets, 2 of which cater for families, with twin beds & bunkbeds in spacious, connecting rooms. They are light & airy with simple but comfortable décor & welcoming AC for summer.

Available to all guests is a small pool under blue shade cloth & an open-sided restaurant, festooned with hanging plants & overlooking the Boteti River. Given its proximity to the village, the sound of music & dogs can sometimes be heard. *Chalet from US$110 pp Jan–Mar to US$165 pp Jul–Oct, dinner, B&B; camping US$20 pp; erected tent US$40–50 pp. Meals US$15–28; game drive (3–4hrs) US$80 pp inc park fees.* **$–$$$**

Leroo La Tau [446 B4] (12 chalets) Contact Desert & Delta Safaris (page 214); ✪ LEROOL 20°25.240'S, 24°31.277'E (turn-off from road ✪ LEROTO 20°26.231'S, 24°27.935'E). This long-established lodge, perched 15m above the Boteti River, lies in an area that can provide remarkable game spectacles.

The star draw of the lodge is its extensive hide overlooking the Boteti River &, when it's not flowing, a large waterhole in the riverbed. Elephants & other wildlife are in regular attendance here. Regardless of water levels & the changing game dynamic, the hide, & another above by the firepit, always look out on to some fantastic scenery, with animals often coming down to drink on the opposite bank of the river.

Up a few steps from the firepit is a small pool, surrounded by a lawn set with wooden loungers. The main lodge is set back again, one long wall fronted by a shady veranda. Inside, it's light & modern, with teak flooring, leather directors' chairs & a signature pop of turquoise colour. Most visitors dine together, but individual tables are always an option. Upstairs, above the bar, upholstered chairs & sofas are an enticing place to relax with a book, or to keep an eye on the river from the look-out window. Back at ground level, there's a shop, selling books & reasonably priced curios.

Guests stay in smart thatched chalets, well spaced along the treeline, overlooking the Boteti. Each has a large, timber veranda with smart loungers & a table, from which sliding doors lead into the bedroom. Furnished with contemporary beds, sisal rugs, simple furniture & a comfortable armchair, these are clutter-free, modern spaces. In the spacious, tiled en suite, there is a toilet, twin sinks & a huge shower, all with an impressive view.

Visitors explore beyond camp on morning & afternoon game drives in 6-seater vehicles, either in a stretch of land enclosed by a loop of the Boteti or into the national park. Either way, this represents lots of riverfront – which is where the game is usually concentrated. Despite being on a bend in the river within the park's perimeter fence, & surrounded by it on 3 sides, the lodge remains technically outside the park – so game drives can continue after dark. Guests staying 3 nights or more can opt for a full-day trip to Nxai Pan & Baines' Baobabs, but this must be pre-booked. *From US$645 pp Jan–Mar & Dec to US$1,160 pp Jun–Oct, FBA exc Maun air transfer (US$284 pp one-way). Children 6+.* ⏲ *All year.* 🛏🛏🛏–🛏🛏🛏

Meno A Kwena Tented Camp [446 A3] (10 tents) Contact Natural Selection (page 215); ✪ MENAK 20°19.454'S, 24°19.231'E (road turn-off ✪ MENATN 20°16.310'S, 24°15.577'E or, slightly further south, MENATS 20°20.538'S, 24°17.848'E). Set on top of a 40m-high bank overlooking a bend in the seasonal Boteti River, Meno A Kwena has a highly unusual location for a camp in a largely flat country like Botswana: here, the camp's elevation affords superb views down to the river below & national park beyond. A laid-back, good-value, family-friendly spot, Meno A Kwena is a gentle safari camp, with armchair game viewing possible from your veranda or the rock-hewn swimming pool.

Each of the classic, Meru-style tents is built inside its own kraal – an enclosure of narrow tree trunks – with views over the river. The tents themselves are spacious, with comfortable beds, down duvets, tribal rugs & simple, campaign-style furniture. Sliding doors open on to a shaded veranda complete with a pair of safari chairs & a wooden lounger from which to take in the panorama. En-suite bathrooms at the rear have a toilet, twin sinks & a pebble-floored shower.

15

Sand paths through the bush link the rooms to a central tent of traditional green canvas, complete with guy ropes. The space is split between a fairly large bar, a dining area whose huge dining table is inset with glazed panels displaying local artefacts, & a comfortable lounge area, complete with leather sofas & a log-burner for winter. To the front is a sandy courtyard area, while overlooking the river is a rock pool that does service as a plunge pool, flanked by 2 small canvas shelters, & out of sight below is a wildlife hide. The relaxed atmosphere is accentuated by hand-crafted wrought-iron furniture & an eclectic selection of books; it feels like the sort of place where someone might pick up a guitar & start strumming around the campfire.

While the normal 2 activities/day with a rest in between is on offer, there's considerable choice. From camp, activities focus on seasonal boat trips, & game drives to the Hippo Pools area of the park; normally this involves a boat into the park, then a game drive south, returning via the Khumaga ferry & a drive back to camp opposite the park. Seasonal day trips to Nxai Pan & Makgadikgadi Pans can be organised on request, as can mobile safaris to the salt pans & a meerkat colony or visits to the CKGR (both min 3 nights). For something slower-paced, there's a floating game-viewing hide in the river to simply sit back & watch the wildlife. Perhaps more than most camps, Meno A Kwena attracts a wide range of visitors, from expats escaping Maun to international safari-goers. *From US$645 pp 10 Jan–Mar to US$1,205 pp Jul–Aug, FBA inc conservation fee, exc Maun road transfer (US$145 pp return). Children all ages.* ⊕ *All year.* 🛏🛏🛏–🛏🛏🛏🛏

Moela Safari Lodge [446 B4] (8 rooms) m 7199 5522; e reservations@ thelandstravel.com; w thelandstravel.com. Opened by none other than President Masisi in Nov 2023, Moela Safari Lodge is the latest camp on the high banks overlooking the Boteti River. It's a stylish, contemporary lodge with curvaceous adobe walls, sculptural tree trunks supporting thatched roofs, & a low-key aesthetic punctuated with vibrant painted doors.

The 8 en-suite rooms are elegant, with whitewashed interiors, modern pared-back styling & elements of traditional African architecture, from the handmade brick construction to the artisan lampshades. Cool & open-plan, with private verandas overlooking the river & passing wildlife below, they are calm, spacious retreats.

At the centre of camp, the thatched lounge/ dining area has quirky alcoves stocked with books, a lantern-lit table for delicious, freshly prepared communal dinners, a bar & a pizza oven, all overlooking the sweeping swimming pool, complete with pole-shaded loungers set in sand. There are views down to the river & a great, shaded waterside deck, accessed by stairs down the bank, affording close-up views of the wildlife.

Activities include game drives within the national park & concession, a Bushman experience, walking safaris, & trips to the Makgadikgadi Pans & Nxai Pan. *From US$575 pp Jan–Mar to US$1,125 pp Jul–Oct & 15 Dec–10 Jan, FBA inc conservation fee. Children all ages.* ⊕ *All year.* 🛏🛏🛏–🛏🛏🛏🛏🛏

Camping

Khumaga Campsite [446 B4] (10 pitches) Contact SKL (page 213); ⊕ KHUMAS 20°27.350'S, 24°30.978'E. Khumaga, sometimes written 'Xhumaga', stands near the east bank of the (normally dry) Boteti River, close to one of the scout camps. It's a large, flat, sandy site, with extensive tree shade in a number of spots. Each pitch has a water tap (slightly sulphurous & definitely not potable), steel drum braai, concrete disk firepit & rubbish bin. There are 2 modern, clean, thatched ablution blocks, each divided for male & female campers, with flush toilets, washbasins & solar-heated showers, & a cold-water washing up area. As an unfenced campsite close to the river, wildlife is known to wander through camp on occasion, so do be aware.

Firewood is available to buy at the site, but nothing else, although basic supplies (meat & drinks) are available in the village 2km away. Be aware that there will likely be light noise from the village audible at the site, & vervet monkeys are adept thieves. The camping costs here are considered high by some travellers. *US$50 pp, exc park fees & bed levy.* ⊕ *All year.*

Njuca Hills Campsite [446 C4] (2 sites) Contact DWNP (page 213); ⊕ NJUCA 20°25.807'S, 24°52.395'E. This basic campsite in the heart of the park, about 38km east of Khumaga, is slightly elevated on one of a series of low, fossilised dunes (no more than about 20m, so

'Hills' seems somewhat hyperbolic), which makes for a moderately difficult drive. There's no water or firewood, but there are positives (aside from the seclusion): there's an outcrop of trees for shade & each site has a firepit, bucket shower & a long-drop toilet. Expect the main wildlife to be barking geckos & perhaps the odd curious yellow mongoose. *P200 pp, inc park fees.* ☺ *All year.*

Tree Island Campsite [446 C4] (3 sites) Contact DWNP (page 213); ✿ TREISL 20°29.417'S, 24°55.053'E. On the edge of a deep pan, about 8km southeast of Njuca Hills, this is one of the most remote & isolated campsites in northern Botswana, & considered more attractive than Njuca Hills (see opposite) by some. Opened a decade ago, it remains the newest camp in the area & certainly provides a remote, wilderness experience. There is no water available: just long-drop toilets & bucket showers. Access is along a bumpy, little-used track, frequently overgrown with vegetation, so it's advisable to use a radiator seed net on your vehicle. *P40 pp, exc park fees.* ☺ *All year.*

WHAT TO SEE AND DO Like the bulk of Sua Pan or the rest of Ntwetwe Pan, the Makgadikgadi Pans National Park is really an area for experienced Africa hands to explore in their own vehicles – though bear in mind my comments on safety on page 465. That said, in the late dry season you won't be quite so isolated if you stick to the road in the park which runs beside the Boteti River and stay at Khumaga Campsite, which will then have quite a few visitors. Alternatively, and much safer, stay at one of the lodges outside the park, exploring each area with their expert local guides: the pans on the eastern side with Jacks, San or Camp Kalahari, or the contrasting Boteti riverfront with Leroo La Tau, Moela or Meno A Kwena.

TOWNS AROUND THE PANS

The small towns around the pans, from Nata west to Motopi then south to Rakops, are rarely seen by those flying into the area's camps and tend to be used by self-drivers to refuel and replenish basic supplies. All the towns along this route have mobile-phone coverage, but don't expect any signal in the areas between them.

NATA [447 G3] Nata itself is a small place at the junction of the tar road to Maun, Kasane and Francistown. For many years it was little more than a filling stop for most people, where the vital garage relied on hand-cranked petrol pumps, and the well-stocked Sua Pan Bottle Store was always busy. Fuel is still the main reason for people to stop, though now the town boasts three modern fuel stations at the junction (✿ NATA 20°12.693'S, 26°10.859'E), each with either a shop or a fast-food outlet. With these, plus a branch of Barclays Bank with an ATM, a post office, a new Choppies superstore with a Liquorama bottle store next door (over the river on the Francistown road), and a handful of local shops, Nata is a reasonable place to get organised. And if you're in need of repairs to your vehicle, try contacting Nata Garage on the Kasane road (✆ 621 1450).

With some decent places to stay, Nata is also a good choice for an overnight stop. Those planning to linger might seek out the nearby Nata Sanctuary (page 467), on the northern edge of Sua Pan, or use it as a base for exploring the pan as a whole. As an aside, staff at Pelican Lodge talk with enthusiasm about the wildlife at Dzibanana Pan, about 5km north of town close to the Zimbabwean border, which is reported when filled with water (roughly between April and August) to attract buffalo and sable.

Where to stay and eat There are many accommodation options in and around Nata, from campsites and backpacker pads, to the more upmarket, long-running Nata Lodge to the west of town. For campsites and lodges north of Nata, see page 483.

15

Most visitors to Nata are either self-catering or eat at their lodge. For those just passing through, the restaurants at Nata and Pelican lodges are open to non-residents. Alternatively, there's fast food in the form of Barcelos Flame-Grilled Chicken at the Engen garage, or a Wimpy at Caltex.

In and around Nata

Nata Lodge [447 H3] (22 chalets, 10 Meru tents, camping) `247 1112; e reservations@natalodge.com; w natalodge.com; ⊕ 20°13.448'S, 26°16.052'E. Nata Lodge lies about 10km east of Nata towards Francistown, & is well signposted just off the main road. It stands in a patch of light woodland with real fan palms & marula trees.

Thatched wooden chalets raised on stilts have neat, comfortable interiors, with twin beds, AC & en-suite facilities incorporating a claw-foot bath & an outdoor shower. 2 of the rooms have extra bunk beds, for families, & a 3rd is designed for improved access for those with limited mobility. The en-suite safari 'glamping tents', also with twin beds & an outdoor shower, are tucked into the bush, with a shared braai stand if you want to self-cater.

Nearby is a large, shady campsite with space for 150 campers & separate male & female ablution blocks. The restaurant has seating indoors & out under the dappled light of the trees. At lunchtime there's a 'terrace menu', with evening meals either à la carte or, when it's busy, a braai dinner (P205). The swimming pool, with shaded pairs of loungers, is right in front of the bar area, & there's also a shop selling curios, as well as books, maps, cuddly toys & an array of hats.

Trips into Nata Sanctuary, village tours & sunset drives on to the pans can be arranged. *Chalet US$105 pp; tents US$90 pp; camping US$20 pp.* ⊕ *All year.* **$$$**

Pelican Lodge [447 H3] (66 rooms, camping) m 7364 4444; e reservations.pelican@thewildlodges.com; w thewildlodges.com. About 7km south of Nata, on the Francistown road, Pelican Lodge is more a stark hotel than a lodge, though it makes an adequate overnight stop. With a series of large concrete, thatched buildings linked by thatched walkways on concrete slabs, it dominates a vast site. An indiscreet 3m fence surrounds the whole property, which at least helps to keep out livestock.

There's an à la carte restaurant, 200-seat conference room & the 'Boma Bar' – a more informal restaurant where b/fast is served. At the front of all this is an inviting swimming pool which, in keeping with everything else, is large & spread out. Most of the en-suite chalet rooms are twin or dbl, but 3 are for families; all have AC. Furthest away from the road, a well-designed campsite has a central braai & washing-up area, as well as a large ablution block & a communal firepit. 3 sites sport their own private ablution blocks & braai stands. Activities include a tour of a local village, trips to Nata Sanctuary, game drives to Dzibanana Pan & bush walks. *Room rate is exc b/fast; camping P90 pp.* ⊕ *All year.* **$$–$$$**

Eselbe Camp Backpackers [447 H3] (1 chalet, tents, camping) m 7605 7089; e eselbecamp@outlook.com; w eselbecamp.com. Clearly signposted down a sandy track off the Kasane Road (2km north of the Shell fuel station), Eselbe Camp is a quirky place, offering a range of budget-friendly accommodation & camping. Built & run by Rupert Barstow, Eselbe is working hard on its eco credentials – solar power, a UV & reverse-osmosis water filtration system, & myriad upcycling schemes (check out the wine-bottle walls in the chalet) – & on providing a warm welcome for the travellers who stop here. It's working, too: guests here – from touring motorcyclists to digital nomads (US$24/day for a tent, place at the table & Wi-Fi) & families – all attest to the relaxed friendliness of the camp. There is a distinct backpacker vibe; it's an eclectic, laid-back, 'no worries' place.

Accommodation ranges from the simple en-suite Hippo Chalet & en-suite safari tent to dbl & dormitory tents, & self-drive camping facilities. Those in tents & campers share communal facilities: hot showers & toilets in eccentric pole-&-mosaic bathrooms, as well as a fully equipped kitchen. There's a firepit, braai & small lounge area complete with resident bushbabies, & home-cooked meals are available to order (cooked b/fast P115, dinner P150, or they can recommend a butcher in town).

Eselbe's activities are naturally low-key: borrow a canoe (free) for a trip on the Nata River, take a riverside walk, play mini-golf or board games, try your hand at volleyball, & relax in hammocks. Trips can be arranged to the Nata Bird Sanctuary.

Hippo Chalet P610/dbl; en-suite tent P510/dbl; tent with shared ablutions P400–470; dorm tent P370 for 4 people; camping P125 pp.

Further afield
Elephant Sands Lodge & Campsite [447 G2] (14 chalets, camping) 247 0013; **m** 7344 5162; **e** bookings@elephantsandsbotswana. com; **f** elephantsands; ❖ ELESAN 19°44.935'S, 26°04.265'E. Around 53km north of Nata, just 7km south of the vet fence, Elephant Sands is about 500m west of the tar road & is clearly signposted. It's a reasonably large camp, with a reputation for the elephants who give the camp its name.

Accommodation options range from simply adorned, en-suite Meru tents, built on stilts overlooking the waterhole, to en-suite rondavels with open-air, semi-circular bathrooms at the rear & thatched family chalets for 4. There are also sandy grounds, which are popular with both independent campers & overlanders, who pitch in together & share rustic but clean open-air ablutions. There is little shade & pitches are not marked, so exercise consideration when choosing your spot during busy times.

It's also important to keep in mind that elephants frequently pass through this unfenced campsite, so do stay alert when walking around. Elephant viewing around the pumped waterhole is this camp's *raison d'être*, though, & the reason most visitors overnight here. There can be dozens of elephants crowding around the water & visitors must stay within the confines of the camp – though that's no hardship with a large restaurant area (dinner P240 with advance booking), a separate bar, swimming pool & a sunken boma overlooking the wildlife action. *Room rate is exc b/fast; camping P185 pp.* ⊕ *All year.* **$$**

GWETA Gweta [447 E3] (❖ GWETA 20°11.434'S, 25°15.888'E) is a small, old village about 2km south of the road between Nata and Maun, about 205km from Maun and 100km from Nata. There is a Shell **fuel station**, though its opening hours and fuel supply are notoriously unreliable, so don't count on its availability. In the village, the small Saverite **supermarket** (⊕ 07.30–20.00 daily) sells basics, plus some fresh fruit and vegetables.

Getting there and away
Gweta is very clearly signposted from the main road, in an area of mostly stunted mopane woodlands with the odd small clay pan. Turning off the main Maun–Nata road you'll come to a fork after about 2km, with a couple of shops on your right, and a post office on your left, before reaching the lodge, the entrance to which is visible from the fork on the left.

There are very regular **bus** services between Maun and Francistown, with up to five a day to and from Nata. They usually turn into town and stop in the centre. If not, ask the driver to stop on the road beside the turn-off to Planet Baobab. From here, the trip to Maun is about 3 hours and costs around P70.

Where to stay
The choices here are starkly different: the traditional Gweta Lodge in the village itself, or the funky, rustic-trendy Planet Baobab about 4km to the east. Both can be used as a base to explore Ntwetwe Pan or the Makgadikgadi Pans National Park, although most self-drive visitors will probably opt to camp nearer the pans instead. That said, both also offer day and overnight trips on to the pans, including quad-bike excursions, so can be ideal for those without a vehicle. For accommodation right on the pans, see page 471. There are also campsites in the national park (page 480).

Gweta Lodge [447 E3] (15 rooms, camping) 621 2220; **e** gwetalodge@botsnet.bw; **w** gwetalodge.co.bw. This old camp has undergone something of a transformation over the years. At the centre is a thatched bar & lounge area, with a small but sparkling pool in front. Twin, dbl & family en-suite rooms have fans, mosquito nets & tiled floors. The smaller, rustic rondavels offer fans & modern en-suite facilities. Across the entrance track is a level, grassy campsite, with

When Graham Hemson worked as a guide at Jack's Camp, he was studying for a PhD on lion ecology and conservation in the Makgadikgadi area as part of Oxford University's Wildlife Conservation Research Unit. In 1999, he estimated that there were about 39 lions in the Makgadikgadi area, where he investigated their impact on people, and vice versa.

Every year lions kill hundreds of domestic animals in and around the Makgadikgadi Pans National Park, which brings them into conflict with the herders and owners. In retaliation people have, in the past, laid out traps and poison, and hunted lions outside the park with ruthless efficiency. As a result, between November 1999 and May 2000, at least 12 lions were killed.

However, contrary to common belief, Graham's research indicated that livestock predation does not happen mainly inside the kraal, but rather out in the grazing areas and sometimes inside the park. Although lions will tackle livestock in the villages, often they can simply pick off the many untended stragglers. An interesting ecological response to the predictability of livestock as prey is that lions that eat livestock have substantially smaller home ranges than those that are dependent on migratory prey, or scarce desert species.

Typically, this livestock predation is only a problem when wild prey is scarce. When zebra and wildebeest migrate out of their territories, lions are forced to change their preferences abruptly.

After surveying the local inhabitants, Graham found that many of the people in charge of the livestock were elderly women; often their husbands were living in town, running more lucrative family businesses. These women were physically unable to keep track of their cattle – resulting in a large number of stray animals which made a veritable manmade buffet for lions.

Following Graham's conclusions, Botswana's Department of Wildlife has lobbied its Veterinary Department to consider rerouting a proposed disease control fence around the Makgadikgadi, to help prevent the wildlife from straying into cattle country. Meanwhile strategies have been developed to help the local people minimise their losses, and to discourage them from killing more lions before the fence is built.

toilets & showers, some pre-erected tents, & 3 further twin rooms. Campers can use the bar, pool & lounge at the lodge. Meals are served in the homely if old-fashioned restaurant, which is entirely separate.

Activities include village tours (P170 pp), ½-day Bushman nature walks on to the pans (P1,200 pp), & full-day trips to Nxai Pan, the Makgadikgadi Pans, Ntwetwe Pan & the Central Kalahari (around P2,240 pp/day, min 2 people). *Standard room P850–1,650 exc b/fast; family room P1,640 exc b/fast; camping P80 pp.* ⊕ *All year.* **$$**

Planet Baobab [447 E3] (18 huts, camping) ⊕ PBAOBA 20°11.344'S, 25°18.330'E; ✆ 684 0931; e res@planetbaobab.travel; w planetbaobab. travel. From the giant aardvark at the entrance

to the subterranean feel of the reception 'tunnel', Planet Baobab (run by Natural Selection, page 215) does indeed seem to be on another planet. Set in a grove of giant baobabs, it is just south of the main Nata–Maun road, & combines a Makgadikgadi Pans experience for a clientele who can't afford the prices of the trio of camps on the pans with somewhere interesting to stop for those driving past.

A sense of fun is evident in the well-furnished lodge, with bold local designs used to exuberant effect on the extensive surfaces of polished concrete. The focus is a funky bar area, dominated by a large, curved bar & lit by chandeliers made from local beer bottles. Seating is on hide-covered chairs at small concrete-plinth tables & there's a fine collection of interesting artefacts on the walls. Service is friendly & food – served here or in the similarly styled restaurant – is from a pan-African menu. Outside, behind a wavy ochre wall, is a superb 18m-diameter circular pool, with a shallow area for children & thatched gazebos at the side.

Traditional thatched 'mud' huts – actually brick clad in cement – are arranged in village-like clusters & offer intriguing accommodation. Inside, there's moulded concrete furniture, whitewashed walls & cheery African print bedding & wall hangings. Although similar in design, the Baobab chalets are slightly more spacious than the standard Bakalanga huts. A sgl bed is built into each side of the room, under a mosquito net, & there's an en-suite washbasin, toilet & shower. 3 family huts have a dbl bed too, & a designated parking spot outside. All are thoughtfully designed, with glazed windows, wall mirrors & electric lanterns.

There is also a small campsite with 6 pitches & 3 overland trunk spaces, all sharing immaculate showers & toilets (separated for men & women) built into a large & stylish thatched rondavel – complete with lights set into the walls & clothes-hooks made from branches. Each site has a thatched shelter with power & washing-up facilities to hand.

A variety of trips can be organised out of Planet Baobab. These include a guided 2hr village & cattlepost tour (US$90 pp), which takes in a visit to the local primary school, Gweta's kgotla (traditional court), & a stop at the traditional healer, as well as a meal with a local family (typically of sorghum, mealie meal, *seswaa*, wild spinach, mopane worms in season, wild beans & perhaps creamy baobab fruit milkshake). There's always a chance to sample some of the local sorghum beer, too (it's an acquired taste!). A 2nd option is a 2hr baobab bushwalk & sundowner (US$40 pp), concentrating on the environment, the traditional uses of plants & animals, the history of the area & perhaps some local stories.

Further afield are ½-day, full-day & overnight trips to Ntwetwe Pan (from US$210 pp, inc quad bikes; Jun–Oct only), & a full-day game drive to follow the zebra & wildebeest migration inside the national park (US$350 pp Nov–May). All excursions are for a min of 2 people, & on Nxai Xini Pan can involve sleeping out on a bedroll under the stars. With minimal dangerous game around, this is all you need & is a great way to sleep. *Standard huts US$150–185 pp, dinner, B&B; family hut US$150–185 pp, dinner, B&B; camping US$18 pp. Children all ages.* ☺ *All year.* **$$$**

MOTOPI [446 A3] A few kilometres west of the Makgadikgadi Pans National Park, this large village is linked to the main Maun–Nata road by a bridge (⊕ MOTOBR 20°12.723'S, 24°07.600'E) over the Boteti River. Apart from a few small shops, including a SPAR, Choppies and a Hungry Lion fast-food outlet in the centre of town, there's nothing to delay visitors. (Though as an aside, the original gravel road, signposted to Moreomaoto, leads to the river, affording some lovely views and a nice picnic spot.)

From Motopi, a good tarred road runs parallel to the western bank of the river as far as Rakops (126km) and Mopipi, then around to Orapa. From here the road splits, with one fork heading east for Francistown, and the other southeast for Letlhakane, Serowe and Palapye; both are tarred and of good quality. Most of this area is flat, cattle-farming territory, much of it lush and green during the rains, though with the vegetation thinning out as you head south towards Rakops. If you don't fancy pulling off into the bush, several picnic spots along the side of the road offer the chance to stop.

KHUMAGA The village of Khumaga just east of the main road marks another gate (KHUMGT 20°28.321'S, 24°30.888'E) into the Makgadikgadi Pans National Park, leading directly to the scout post and Khumaga Campsite via a ferry across the Boteti River. Boteti River Camp (page 478) is on the left as you approach the ferry crossing from the main road.

RAKOPS [446 B6] Reachable entirely on tarmac from Maun, Rakops (✪ RAKOPS 21°02.136'S, 24°24.432'E) is notable as the last outpost passed on many trips into the Central Kalahari Game Reserve.

The village itself sprawls to the east of the road. A ragged remnant of tar runs down the centre of the road, flanked by widely spaced huts and bungalows, and a few general stores. There is a fuel station, but supplies are erratic, so either call ahead (m 7264 3490/7131 6170) or join the many people who opt to travel the extra 60km to Mopipi.

Where to stay While there is nowhere to stay in Rakops itself, there's a useful little lodge and campsite just 7km north of the turning off the main road, and a similar-size motel just south of the town.

Rakops River Lodge [446 B6] (16 chalets, villa, camping) ☎ 393 2711; m 7143 4129; e bookings@ rakopsriverlodge.com; w rakopsriverlodge.com; ✪ RKRLO 20°59.189'S, 24°21.748'E. Close to the eastern side of the road, this simple, clean & very friendly motel has 10 standard chalets, each with dbl or twin beds & tiled, en-suite bathrooms, & 6 have AC. There are also family rooms, a 5-bed self-catering villa, & even a presidential suite. Alternatively, there are 9 camping pitches for self-drivers, with water, phone-charging points, a unisex ablution block & a central boma for preparing meals. Tents with beds can be hired too (P260/dbl). There are braai facilities for use by all guests, a restaurant & a swimming pool surrounded by a checkboard sundeck. *Standard dbl chalet P700; family chalet P1,000–1,400; villa P4,000; camping P130/100 adult/child.* ⊕ *All year.* **$$**

Xere Motel [446 B6] (11 rooms) ☎ 297 5068; w xeremotelrakops.com; ✪ XERMOT 21°02.834'S, 24°24.008'E. 3km south of Rakops, Xere Motel has small but clean & comfortable rooms, with AC, sat TV, a fridge & en-suite bathroom. There's an à la carte restaurant, laundry service & game drives to the pans & Central Kalahari (P800 pp). *Room rate exc b/fast.* ⊕ *All year.* **$**

ORAPA AND LETLHAKANE Orapa [447 E7] is at the heart of Botswana's diamond-mining operations. It's the world's largest diamond mine by area and produces 10.8 million carats of diamonds annually. This makes it by far the most important town in the country to Botswana's economy, and hence security there is very tight. You're not allowed in, or out, without permission from the diamond company Debswana, which isn't given easily. Hence it's effectively off-limits to visitors and there's a road that detours around the south side of the mine.

There's also a major diamond mine at **Letlhakane** [447 E7], about 30km southeast of Orapa, on the Serowe road, and there's active prospecting continuing throughout the region for more diamond pipes. More usefully for visitors, Letlhakane is also one of the few places where you can buy entry **permits for the national parks**.

For the safari visitor, the road south from Orapa is notable in that it leads, after some 220km, to the **Khama Rhino Sanctuary** [447 E7] (w khamarhinosanctuary. org.bw). Described by one mobile safari operator as 'a really well laid-out and cared-for park with good wildlife and excellent facilities', it's a refuge for both white and black rhino. While its location falls outside the scope of this guide, it's a good stopover on the road between Maun and the south for self-drive tourists and thus is worthy of mention.

16

The Central Kalahari

Covering about 52,800km², the Central Kalahari Game Reserve (or the CKGR, as it's usually known) is one of the world's largest game reserves. It dominates the centre of Botswana, the wider region that I refer to in this chapter as simply the 'Central Kalahari'. This is Africa at its most remote and esoteric: a vast sandsheet punctuated by a few huge open plains, occasional salt pans and the fossil remains of ancient riverbeds.

The CKGR isn't for everybody. The game is often sparse and can seem limited, with only occasional elephant and no buffalo; the distances are huge, along bush tracks of variable quality; and until 2009, the facilities were limited to a handful of campsites. So without a fully equipped vehicle (preferably two) and lots of bush experience, it was probably not the place for you. The converse is that if you've already experienced enough of Africa to love the feeling of space and the sheer freedom of real wilderness areas, then this reserve is completely magical; it's the ultimate wilderness destination.

There are, however, two small lodges within the reserve (although one was temporarily closed at the time of writing), which does open up the area to those who don't have the experience, time or equipment to embark on an expedition here alone. As a middle ground, there are also a number of mobile safaris (page 216) operating in the area.

Owing to limitations of space, this is only a short introduction to the area. It's intended to give you a feel for the Central Kalahari and the CKGR (the area of it which most visitors will see) and tell you how to get there and what it's like. I've assumed that most visitors will only be visiting the northern section of the park – Piper Pans and north – as that's generally regarded as the most interesting area. It's also the obvious part of the reserve to link into a trip with the more popular northern regions of Chobe and the Okavango.

BACKGROUND INFORMATION

HISTORY The Central Kalahari Game Reserve was declared a game park in 1961, on the very eve of independence. At that time, there was increasing international publicity about the San. With the prevalent view of their 'idyllic' hunter-gatherer lifestyle came a growing concern that this was threatened, and that they might become 'extinct'. The British Protectorate of Bechuanaland was the focus for this, so the authorities decided to protect the heart of the Kalahari for the San.

At the time, there was no way to set aside one particular area for an ethnic group. Neither the British authorities nor the Tswana, who were being groomed for government, wanted any discrimination among its citizens based on race. This

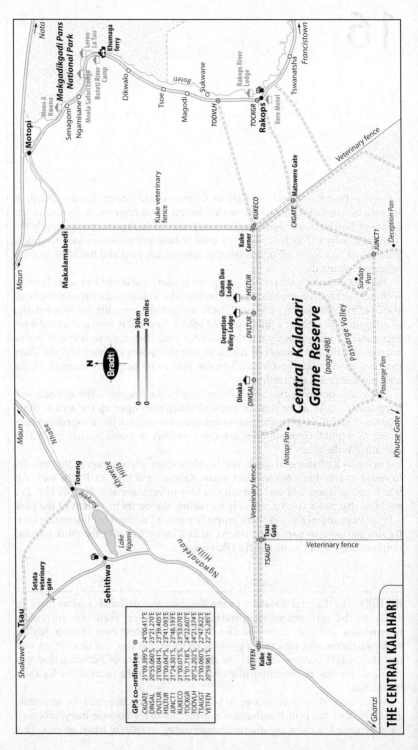

THE CENTRAL KALAHARI

GPS co-ordinates	⊕
CKGATE	21°09.399'S, 24°00.417'E
DINSAL	20°55.060'S, 23°21.270'E
DVLTUR	21°00.041'S, 23°39.405'E
HSLTUR	21°00.047'S, 23°41.093'E
JUNCT1	21°24.301'S, 23°48.193'E
KUKECO	21°00.075'S, 23°53.070'E
TOCKGR	21°01.718'S, 24°22.607'E
TODVLH	20°52.202'S, 24°21.374'E
TSAUGT	21°00.060'S, 22°47.822'E
VETFEN	20°59.961'S, 22°25.285'E

would have set a dangerous precedent, with echoes of the tribal 'bantustans' created by the apartheid regime in South Africa.

Back in the 1960s, legislation to proclaim a separate area for a separate ethnic group didn't exist. Nor was any wanted by a new country anxious to avoid ethnic divisions. Hence the heart of the Central Kalahari was protected from further development or agricultural encroachment as a 'game park' – even though it was intended as a place of sanctuary for the San. Thus the Central Kalahari Game Reserve was proclaimed. (Still to this day the Botswana government has a strict policy of not discriminating – positively or negatively – between any of the ethnic groups in the country. 'We're all Tswana' is their wise approach, designed to minimise any ethnic tensions. However, there lies the nub of a problem. If a group like the San are allowed to live and hunt in a 'game reserve', why shouldn't any other Tswana citizen? Many who are concerned for the San argue that they need positive discrimination, while others maintain that such moves would be racist.)

In keeping with its origins, the CKGR remained largely closed for around 30 years; visitors needed special approval and permits, which were not lightly granted. During this time its most famous visitors were probably Mark and Delia Owens, a couple of young and idealistic animal researchers from America who lived on a tree-island in Deception Valley for about seven years (1974–80), and subsequently wrote a best-selling book, *Cry of the Kalahari* (page 540), based on their experiences.

Then, in the late 1980s and early 1990s, the park started to open up more, first allowing in organised groups with tour operators and, only in recent years, individual travellers in their own vehicles. However, despite the opening of two small lodges within the reserve in 2009 (and especially with one temporarily closed), current visitor numbers remain largely limited by the number of campsites available, so it still feels very much a wilderness destination.

PEOPLE When the CKGR was declared a reserve, a population of around 5,000 San people lived within its boundaries. In the 1990s, a borehole had been installed at the small village of Xade, where some of the park's game scouts were based. Research in 1996 estimated that the population in the reserve had fallen below 1,500, a significant proportion of whom had moved to live in the vicinity of Xade, near this fairly reliable source of water.

In the 1980s, the government's stated policy was to encourage relocation of the people to New Xade, a village which was created outside the reserve. The resulting removals of the people, and the highly controversial court case that resulted, are discussed in detail on page 98. Note that this remains a very contentious and political topic.

GEOGRAPHY Despite its huge area, the Central Kalahari has relatively little scenic variation. Most of it is covered by an enormous, undulating sandsheet. Within the CKGR itself, the north of the park contains the most varied scenery; here you'll find a network of vegetated salt pans and a few fossilised riverbeds. There are a number of places within the reserve, including Motopi Pan, Passage Pan, Letiahau Pan and Piper Pans, where water is pumped by the park's authorities, creating permanent waterholes.

FLORA AND FAUNA If you're expecting to find stark differences between contrasting environments within this Kalahari reserve, you'll be disappointed. There are subtle changes between its different landscapes, but there isn't the variation here that you'll find around Chobe or the Okavango. Because of this, the animal species found here

16

vary little from area to area – and this is one reason why the Central Kalahari is an area for old Africa hands, and not first-time safari-goers.

Flora People on their first trip through the Kalahari are often struck by just how green and vegetated it is, in contrast to their mental image of a desert. In fact, most of the Kalahari is covered in a thin, mixed bush with a fairly low canopy height, dotted with occasional larger trees. Beneath this is a rather sparse ground-covering of smaller bushes, grasses and herbs.

To be a little more precise, the Central Kalahari's vegetation is dominated by *Terminalia sericea* sandveld (page 15), the silver cluster-leaf, a deciduous tree, growing up to 9m tall, which stands on deep sand. Other tree species you'll find include the Kalahari appleleaf (*Philenoptera nelsii*) and Kalahari sand acacias (*Vachellia luederitzii*), which occasionally form thickets. These vary from bushes to substantial trees, growing to a maximum height of around 10m. (Their flattened canopies are easily confused with the umbrella thorn (*Vachellia tortilis*), earning them the alternative name of bastard, or false, umbrella thorn.)

Other common trees include the distinctive purple-pod terminalia (*Terminalia prunioides*), which seem to grow best in areas where there is more clay in the soil; shepherd's trees (*Boscia albitrunca*), with their characteristic whitish bark; and feverberry trees (*Croton megalobotrys*). Bladethorns (*Senegalia fleckii*) and their close cousins the bluethorns (*Senegalia erubescens*), are common bushes with fine, feathery foliage but keen, curved barbs. Inevitably you'll spot plenty of old, gnarled camelthorn trees (*Vachellia erioloba*).

Beneath these you'll commonly find a variety of low bushes and shrubs including wild syringa bushes (*Burkea africana*) and bushwillows (*Combretum collinum*). Meanwhile on the ground one of the more common grasses is the lovely silky Bushman grass (*Stipagrostis uniplumis*).

Look carefully, perhaps helped by a good guide, and you'll find plenty to interest you here including, during the wetter months of the year, many flowers and herbs. The beautifully curving flowers of the cat's tail (*Hermbstaedtia odorata*) form spectacular pink patches in damper areas. More entertaining are the bright-red fruits of the balsam pear (*Momordica balsamina*) which, when ripe, fall to the ground and pop themselves open automatically if disturbed. In *Common Wild Flowers of the Okavango Delta* (page 542), Veronica Roodt reports that the young leaves of this plant are used as a vegetable, and while a few will use the fruits in cooking, many communities treat them as poisonous or use them in medicines.

Fauna Game viewing anywhere in the Central Kalahari area can be a stark contrast to the amazing densities of game that can often be seen in the Okavango–Linyanti–Chobe region. To get the best out of the CKGR, you'll require lots of time and patience, often just watching and waiting. The big game is here, but on average it occurs in very low densities – as you'd expect in such a harsh, arid environment. The only way to get around this is, as mentioned on page 493, to visit when it congregates on the open pans in the north.

Springbok are probably the most numerous of the **large herbivores** in the park today. That said, the game populations in the Central Kalahari seem to have been fluctuating fairly wildly, at least for the last century, and perhaps longer. In his book, *A Comment on Kalahari Wildlife and the Khukhe Fence* (page 544), Alec Campbell suggests that over this period human activities and interference have altered the balance of the wildlife populations in the Kalahari substantially, and led indirectly to population explosions and crashes.

Currently, springbok disperse in small herds across the park during the dry season, but congregate in very large numbers on the short grass plains found on pans and fossil riverbeds during and shortly after the rains. This is exactly the opposite of the usual situation for many mammals, including elephants and buffalo, which gather in larger herds as the dry season progresses, only to disperse during the rains.

These successful antelope are both browsers and grazers, which can derive all the moisture that they need from their food, provided that the plants they eat contain at least 10% water. They'll often rest by day and eat at night, thus maximising the moisture content of their fodder by including dew on it.

Springbok populations are very elastic: they are able to reproduce very speedily when conditions are favourable, allowing them to repopulate rapidly after a bad drought. With good conditions females can produce two calves in 13 months, while even six-month-old ewes will conceive, giving birth to their first lamb when they are barely a year old. To maximise the survival of their offspring, the females gather together in maternal herds and synchronise their births, thus presenting predators with a short-term surplus of easily caught young lambs.

The Central Kalahari's population of blue wildebeest has, at times within the last century, swelled to enormous proportions. In his work *A Comment on Kalahari Wildlife and the Khukhe Fence* (page 544), Campbell describes them as peaking in the 1960s when 'herds of 50 and 100 had so accumulated in the Matsheng and Okwa area that they stretched unbroken for many kilometres and numbered hundreds of thousands'. Thane Riney, an ecologist there at the time, was familiar with the vast herds of the Serengeti yet still referred to these as 'the largest herds of plains game left in Africa today'. Wildebeest populations were then estimated at up to 250,000 animals, but within a few years lack of water, grazing and the existence of veterinary cordon fences had conspired to wipe them out from much of the Central Kalahari. Today, you'll find small groups of wildebeest in the CKGR, but I've never seen them in large numbers.

Probably the area's most common large antelope are gemsbok (also known as oryx), which can be seen in congregations of hundreds on the short grass plains during the rains, but usually occur in smaller groupings during the rest of the year. These magnificent antelope are supremely adapted for desert living. They can survive fluctuations of their body temperature up to 45°C (when 42°C would kill most mammals) because of a series of blood vessels, known as the carotid rete, located immediately below their brain. These effectively cool the blood before it reaches the animal's brain – the organ most adversely affected by temperature variations.

Red hartebeest can also be found here in good numbers, as can eland and – an amazing sight – giraffe. Kudu occur, but generally in quite small numbers: either small bachelor groups or family groups consisting of an old male, several females and a number of youngsters. Common duiker are occasionally seen, too, but if you catch a glimpse of a small antelope bounding away from you, it's much more likely to be a steenbok.

The main **predators** here are lion, cheetah, leopard and spotted hyena, which generally occur in a low density, matching their prey species. The lion prides range over large territories and are bonded by loose associations; members spend most of their time apart from each other, living alone or in pairs, and meeting relatively infrequently. Individual lions will often hunt a variety of smaller prey, like bat-eared foxes and porcupines, as well as the larger antelope more commonly thought of as lion fodder.

Similarly, the Central Kalahari's leopard have a very catholic diet, ranging from mice and spring hares to ground squirrels and wildcats, plus steenbok, springbok and calves of the larger antelope.

The park's cheetah seem to be more nomadic than the lion or leopard. In other parks, where game densities are higher, cheetah often lose their kills to these larger cats. Thus the CKGR's relatively low density of predators makes it a good place for cheetah. Hence this is one of sub-Saharan Africa's better parks for spotting them – at least at times when the springbok concentrate on the pans and riverbeds.

Among the **scavengers and insectivores** found here are the brown hyena (the original object of study for Mark and Delia Owens; page 540), black-backed jackal, caracal, Cape fox, bat-eared fox, aardwolf, genet and wildcat. However, as there is no facility for night drives in the reserve, only black-backed jackal and bat-eared fox are commonly seen as they aren't strictly nocturnal.

TUNNEL VISION

Just below the surface of the Kalahari lies a labyrinth of tunnels excavated by the Damara mole-rat (*Cryptomys damarensis*), the only member of this endemic African family to occur in the Kalahari. Mole-rats are rodents, and unlike true moles, which are insectivores, they feed entirely on plant matter – specifically underground storage organs such as bulbs, corms, tubers and desert cucumbers.

They have plump, cylindrical bodies, short, sturdy limbs and formidable projecting incisors for chiselling out the tunnels in which they live their entire lives. Earth excavated by the teeth is shuffled backwards by the front feet, and when enough has accumulated the mole-rat reverses up a side tunnel, pushing it to the surface to form a 'molehill'. Digging is easiest when the soil is wet, so the rains prompt a flurry of activity: in one month, one colony of 16 Damara mole-rats was recorded digging 1km of tunnels and shifting 2.5 tonnes of soil to the surface. Not bad for an animal that weighs no more than 300g.

This Herculean effort uncovers enough food to last the colony through the dry season until the next rains. Meanwhile soil is shifted around and burrows modified to create a complex of chambers, passageways and latrines.

Damara mole-rats are the most sociable of their family. This is a necessary adaptation to the harsh Kalahari environment, where numbers bring more success to a team of blind foragers in search of an erratic, scattered food supply. Their complex societies are more like those of a social insect than a mammal. A colony averages around 15–25 members, occasionally up to 40, but only one pair – the dominant male and female – are reproductive. All others help forage, dig and rear the young, but suppress their fertility, being effectively like sterile worker-termites.

The dominant female breeds all year, producing a litter of between one and five pups after an 80-day gestation in a nest chamber 2m below ground. Hierarchies are reinforced aggressively, and each year about 10% of a colony's members leave to breed and found new colonies. Mole-rats communicate underground with snorts and squeals, and drum with their hind feet on tunnel walls to relay seismic messages to mates or rivals.

Though the casual visitor is unlikely ever to see a mole-rat, a range of canny predators, notably the mole snake (*Pseudaspis cana*), have learned to watch as a pile of fresh soil accumulates and will snatch the digger just as it approaches the surface.

Meanwhile the diurnal yellow mongoose is sometimes seen scampering around in search of insects, and families of meerkats (or suricats) are among the most entertaining and endearing of all the park's residents.

Birdlife The birdlife here is very varied, with Africa's largest bird, the ostrich, doing particularly well. I've never seen more free-roaming ostriches during May, when Deception Valley seemed to be dotted by large flocks of them.

Weighing 14–19kg, kori bustards are the world's heaviest flying birds and are also common, stepping around the plains in search of insects, small reptiles and mammals.

Closely related to the kori are the smaller korhaans; the northern black korhaan (or white-quilled korhaan, or white-winged) is one of the area's most obvious birds. The conspicuous black-and-white males have a harsh, raucous call and can be seen flying up and then falling back to the ground in endless display flights. Related red-crested korhaans are a little less obvious, and less common, though equally spectacular when displaying.

Doves are well represented with Cape turtle doves, laughing doves and, especially, Namaqua doves all being very common. All the species of sandgrouse found in southern Africa – double-banded, Burchell's, yellow-throated and Namaqua – live here. Watch in the mornings as flocks of Namaqua sandgrouse fly to waterholes. They drink and also wade into the water, where each male has specially adapted feathers on his breast, which act like a sponge to soak up water. He then flies up to 80km back to his nest, where the chicks drink from the feathers.

Large flocks of red-billed queleas resemble leaves blowing on a stiff autumn breeze as they swarm down from the trees in search of grass seeds or to drink from a muddy puddle. Even more colourful in the summer months are the male whydahs – pin-tailed, shaft-tailed and paradise – whose exuberant breeding plumage includes a disproportionately long tail. These are brood parasites – laying their eggs in the nest of other birds (page 456).

The Central Kalahari's most common raptor is the pale-chanting goshawk: a light-grey bird, with pink legs and black ends to its wings and tail. It's usually seen hunting from a conspicuous perch, perhaps a fence post beside a track or the top of a small thorn bush, or occasionally hopping about the ground foraging. If disturbed it'll usually fly off low, swooping to land on a similar perch – even if that's another fence post from which it'll shortly be disturbed again. Equally visible during the summer months is the yellow-billed kite.

Black-shouldered kites and rock kestrels, both of which often hunt by hovering in flight, are common here. Bateleurs (or short-tailed eagles), black-breasted and brown snake eagles, martial and tawny eagles, and lanner falcons are also around, with the last making something of a speciality of hunting birds as they come to drink at waterholes.

PRACTICAL INFORMATION

WHEN TO VISIT The Kalahari is really unlike any other game area in sub-Saharan Africa in that its game is probably at its most spectacular during and shortly after the rains – from around January to April. Then the animals gather where the best rain has been and the sweetest grazing is, which usually means on the pans. These can be a magnificent sight, with very large herds of springbok and gemsbok, accompanied by good numbers of giraffe and ostrich plus groups of blue wildebeest, hartebeest and eland. Inevitably these attract increased predator activity from lion, cheetah and the odd leopard.

Having said that, this is also the time when the weather, and in particular the driving conditions, can be at their least hospitable. If there has been much rain then the road from Rakops to the Matswere Gate and beyond becomes a series of mud-holes lined by black-cotton soil, which is rock-hard when dry, but feels like treacle when wet. Meanwhile areas of pans in the park become large, shallow lakes where both navigation and traction present a challenge to any vehicle. Any group coming at this time must be fully prepared for heavy rain, and should expect to have to dig out their vehicle from the mud a number of times.

As a compromise for those who are not fond of endless mud, a favourite time to visit is just after the rains, around March–May, depending on when the rains stop. Then most of the surface water has disappeared, and the black-cotton soil isn't nearly as treacherous as it would have been a few months earlier. The game concentrations will still be good, albeit perhaps not *quite* so spectacular, but your overall experience will probably be much more enjoyable. That is, unless you really enjoy digging your vehicle out of knee-deep mud…

GETTING THERE AND AWAY There are several entrances into the CKGR, but it's important to note that the reserve is not as developed as some other wildlife areas, and facilities can be limited. The most widely used entrance is the Matswere Gate (✪ CKGATE 21°09.399'S, 24°00.417'E), which is on the northeastern side of the reserve. It is accessible via a relatively good gravel road from the town of Rakops. From Matswere it's just 38km to the north end of Deception Valley and the nearest campsites.

The Tsau Gate (✪ TSAUGT 21°00.060'S, 22°47.822'E), in the northwest corner of the reserve, lies 39km east of the main Maun–Ghanzi road, along the southern side of the veterinary fence that defines the reserve's northern border. The closest campsites to the gate are at Motopi Pan.

The other entrances, Khutse Gate in the far south and Xade Gate to the west, some 80km from Piper Pans, are best suited to those exploring the more southerly areas of the reserve.

By car Driving yourself into the Central Kalahari is only a viable option for experienced and bush-wise adventurers with their own fully equipped 4x4s. Even they might consider travelling with two 4x4 vehicles and should have fail-safe plans for back-up assistance in the event of an emergency.

There are now four usual routes to the reserve, three to the Matswere Gate on the eastern side, and one to the Tsau Gate at the northwest corner.

From the Maun–Ghanzi road to the Matswere Gate About 119km from Ghanzi and 167km from Maun, on the tarred main A3 road between the towns, you'll have to stop and pass through the Kuke veterinary fence (✪ VETFEN 20°59.961'S, 22°25.285'E). Immediately north of this, you'll find a good, wide gravel road that heads off on a bearing fractionally south of east. After a few kilometres, this thoroughfare bends round to the left, and there's a small turning into the bush on the right. Take this, and you'll find a simple sand track with two clear ruts for your wheels (welcome to the Kalahari!). The veterinary fence will be literally inches from your right side.

Expect only the occasional 4x4 to pass you; this isn't a busy track. Beneath your wheels you'll sometimes find patches of hard ground with bands of calcrete rocks. Then there are mud-holes, where thick clay is a sticky hazard during the rains (when this route is perfectly possible, but time-consuming). However, most of the track is good, fairly hard sand on which a reasonably experienced bush driver should be able to average 50km/h.

At times now you'll find yourself travelling parallel to several fences, and sometimes with one on each side of you. Beware of startling antelope here; they'll run in front of the vehicle with no escape, and become exhausted easily if you drive too fast.

Around 128km after the tar you'll reach a left turning (⊕ DVLTUR 21°00.041'S, 23°39.405'E) which is clearly signposted to Deception Valley Lodge (page 500). The lodge is about 9km north from here along a winding track that crosses the lodge's own airstrip (⊕ DVLAIR 20°58.897'S, 23°39.515'E). Back on the main track, a further 3km brings you to the entrance to Gham Dhao Lodge (⊕ HSLTUR 21°00.047'S, 23°41.093'E).

Almost 23km after passing this, you'll reach Phefodiaka veterinary checkpoint, widely known as Kuke Corner (⊕ KUKECO 21°00.075'S, 23°53.070'E; ⏱ 06.00–22.00). Here a gate marks the junction of four veterinary fences. As at other vet-fence checkpoints, you will probably be asked if you're carrying any red meat, which cannot be taken east across the fence. To the left a straight cutline heads due north to Makalamabedi. Continuing straight on brings you after 52km to the main Maun–Rakops road, coming out north of Rakops (⊕ TODVLH 20°52.202'S, 24°21.374'E). To the right, a well-used track follows the line of the fence, roughly south-southeast (bearing about 143°). This can be quite rutted and tedious driving, but after about 21.5km leads to the Matswere Gate into the CKGR (⊕ CKGATE 21°09.399'S, 24°00.417'E).

From the Maun–Ghanzi road to the Tsau Gate The road east to the Tsau Gate is a turning off the Maun–Ghanzi road just south of the Kuke veterinary fence (⊕ VETFEN 20°59.961'S, 22°25.285'E). From here, it follows straight along the southern side of the fence for about 39km, to reach the Tsau Gate (⊕ TSAUGT 21°00.060'S, 22°47.822'E) into the reserve. After the gate, continue along the fence for a further 32km, before turning south (⊕ MOTCUT 21°00.194'S, 23°06.400'E) towards Motopi Pan. It's important to be aware that you cannot cross the vet fence into or out of the reserve at any point along its northern boundary.

From Rakops to the Matswere Gate Between Rakops (⊕ RAKOPS 21°02.136'S, 24°24.432'E; page 486) and the CKGR's Matswere Gate there is one main track, fringed by a few detours and side-tracks. The turning from the tar road (⊕ TOCKGR 21°01.718'S, 24°22.607'E) is clearly signposted to the west, just 200m north of the turning to Rakops.

The track is pretty clear on the ground, following a bearing of about 250° until after around 41km you reach the veterinary fence that doubles as the park's boundary. This is the location of the smart Matswere Gate (⊕ CKGATE 21°09.399'S, 24°00.417'E). When it's wet during the early months of the year, this is one of the muddiest, and hence trickiest, sections of track in the region, with patches of black-cotton soil that can trap even the most careful driver. I've heard tales of this section alone taking several days to pass, with frequent stops to dig out – so don't tackle it lightly. Later in the year, the track hardens to a roller-coaster ride where you bounce in and out of a succession of dry mud-holes; even then it's fairly slow going.

South along the cutline from Makalamabedi to the Matswere Gate We haven't driven the full length of this route, but we believe it's probably the most scenic route between Maun and the CKGR, though with the advent of the tar road

16

between Maun and Rakops it's probably no longer the quickest. You'll find the north end of this at the small village of Makalamabedi, southeast of Maun, and southwest of Motopi. If you're coming from Maun, turn south off the main Maun–Nata road just before the Makalamabedi control post (◈ MAKACP 20°11.219'S, 23°51.739'E), and take the tar road to Makalamabedi. From here, simply follow the cutline due south (driving on the eastern side of the veterinary fence) to Kuke Corner (◈ KUKECO 21°00.075'S, 23°53.070'E), then continue south for a further 21.5km to the main Matswere Gate (◈ CKGATE 21°09.399'S, 24°00.417'E).

Without your own vehicle If, like most visitors to Botswana, you don't have the knowledge, experience or equipment for this kind of a trip, there are now several options to visit the CKGR.

Fly-in trips Now that there are two exclusive lodges in the reserve (page 497), the option of incorporating a fly-in trip to the CKGR into a broader itinerary has become a reality.

Group trips A few of Botswana's larger safari companies have scheduled group trips, leaving on specific pre-planned dates, which include time camping within the CKGR; see the main listings on page 214. Check out what they have running and read between the lines to make sure you understand exactly how much of their time is within the CKGR: occasionally, quite long trips will spend far too short a time in the park. A few operators in Maun, like Letaka Safaris (page 217), offer set eight-night, guided mobile camping trips focusing on the CKGR, with prices at around US$6,500 (FBA inc transfers, park fees & professional guides), while Bush Ways Safaris (page 216) offers guided camping trips combining CKGR and Makgadikgadi, with six days costing around US$1,600 per person.

Private mobile trips If you have a fairly generous budget, then the same operators (and many of the smaller ones) will be delighted to organise a private trip for two or more people, for which you'll be able to specify the departure date and the timings. Expect the costs to be high though – in the region of US$300–500 per person per night. Larger groups and longer expeditions are generally less expensive than smaller groups and shorter trips.

GETTING ORGANISED A visit to the CKGR requires a lot of organisation before you even start to drive there. You must book a place to stay and make arrangements to bring all your water, food, equipment and supplies. Brackish water is sometimes available at the Matswere Gate, but it isn't safe to drink and cannot be relied upon. Note that all the land outside the park falls into private farms and concessions, and so camping 'outside the gate' is not a practical option.

GETTING AROUND The main entrance into the CKGR, and one of the few places where there's a break in the veterinary fence, is at the smart Matswere Gate (◈ CKGATE 21°09.399'S, 24°00.417'E). Here you can sign in, check on the state of the roads inside the park and use the toilet facilities. If you ask the scouts politely, it's sometimes possible to fill up with brackish water – which is fine for showers, but not suitable for drinking. (You should have arrived with all your own water, but if you didn't, then make the most of this. There are no waterpoints inside the reserve.) Remember that you must have prepaid your park entry fees at one of the designated points; see page 127.

The presence of a few signposts and distance markers within the reserve makes navigation a little easier than in the past, at least at first glance – but don't be fooled. Stray just a few metres from the main track and you could rapidly find yourself completely lost without a compass, a GPS, and a hefty degree of common sense.

Driving conditions In the dry season, the general quality of the tracks in the park is surprising. Many of them, particularly those which follow the valleys, are really very good. You might have expected to be constantly ploughing through deep sand, but it's not like that. Of course there are patches of deep and tricky sand, and also stretches of black-cotton soil (rock-hard when dry; virtually impassable if very wet), but many of the road surfaces are easy and hard when it's dry. During the rainy months it's important to seek advice from the wardens at the entrance gate, and from other visitors to the park. Some sections can be particularly treacherous, and you could save yourself hours – or even days – of digging.

WHERE TO STAY   *Map, page 498*

Visitors to CKGR can stay in one of the park's many demarcated campsites (page 500; booking essential), or in a lodge (one is temporarily closed, leaving Tau Pan the only option at the time of writing for those not keen to camp). While lodges open up the CKGR to a wider range of visitors, there are plenty of challenges, including a relatively limited road network. The companies operating here have a reputation for excellent guiding, though, so you should expect a real insight into the Kalahari's unique ecosystems, including the ways in which animals, birds and plants adapt to life in a region where lack of water is a serious problem.

It's also possible to stay at one of the three lodges outside the park boundary (page 500). Ideally these should be booked in advance, as if they're full it's a long way to the nearest alternative options. Note that they are at least 2 hours' drive from the Matswere Gate, and over 3 hours from Deception Valley, so they're not really close enough for day trips (though they remain useful either as destinations in their own right, or as comfortable stops at the start and end of trips into the park).

For those coming from the west, there are other accommodation options around Ghanzi, including Kalahari Arms Hotel (\ 659 6298; w kalahariarms.co.bw) and Grasslands Safari Lodge (m 087 057 4518; w grasslandsl.com), but these fall outside the scope of this book.

INSIDE THE PARK

Kalahari Plains Camp (10 tents) Contact Wilderness Safaris (page 216); ⊕ KALPLA 21°29.057'S, 24°00.470E. Located on an entirely secluded pan, 20km from Deception Valley, this camp was temporarily closed at the time of writing, but it's worth investigating if it has reopened by the time you're travelling.

Tau Pan Camp (9 chalets) Contact Kwando Safaris (page 215); ⊕ TAUPLO 21°27.033'S, 23°25.283'E. Built on top of a low ridge, dominating the surrounding bush & with commanding views west across Tau Pan itself, the lodge is named after the black-maned Kalahari lions (tau) who patrol the area &

lap at the permanent waterhole in front of camp.

The light design hand behind the camp at Nxai Pan has clearly been at work here, too: witness the long, narrow central building built in a slight curve, the pool to one side of the deck, & the curio shop at the back. Similar, too, is the open view across the plains, with roll-down blinds to keep the elements at bay. Here, though, the wood is darker than at its sister camp, & simple sand paths link the hub to each chalet. Sliding doors with mesh panels lead from a shaded deck into each spacious room, with roll-down blinds installed against the cold winter nights. Rooms are quite spacious, the centre is taken up by twin or dbl beds. To one side

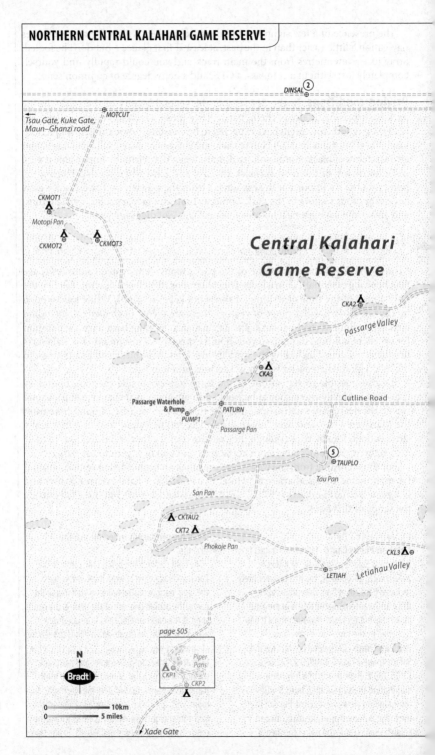

NORTHERN CENTRAL KALAHARI GAME RESERVE

DINSAL ②

MOTCUT

← Tsau Gate, Kuke Gate, Maun–Ghanzi road

CKMOT1

Motopi Pan

CKMOT2   CKMOT3

Central Kalahari Game Reserve

CKA2

Passarge Valley

CKA3

Cutline Road

Passarge Waterhole & Pump
PUMP1   PATURN

Passarge Pan

⑤ TAUPLO

Tau Pan

San Pan

CKTAU2

CKT2

Phokoje Pan

CKL3

LETIAH   Letiahau Valley

page 505

Piper Pans

CKP1

CKP2

N

Bradt

0 ————— 10km
0 ————— 5 miles

✓ Xade Gate

498

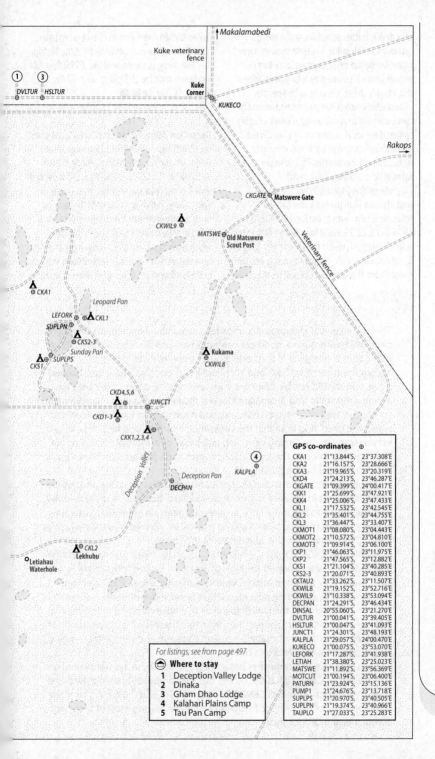

↑ *Makalamabedi*

Kuke veterinary
fence

Kuke Corner

① ③
⊕ ⊕
DVLTUR HSLTUR

⊕ *KUKECO*

→ *Rakops*

⊕ *CKGATE* ● Matswere Gate

▲ *CKWIL9* ⊕

MATSWE ⊕ Old Matswere
Scout Post

Veterinary fence

▲
⊕ *CKA1*

Leopard Pan

LEFORK ⊕ ▲ *CKL1*
SUPLPN ⊕
▲ ⊕ *CKS2-3*

Sunday Pan

▲ ⊕ *SUPLPS*
CKS1

▲ *Kukama*
CKWIL8

CKD4,5,6 ▲
⊕ *JUNCT1*

CKD1-3 ▲ ⊕

▲ ⊕
CKK1,2,3,4

④
⊕
KALPLA

Deception Valley

Deception Pan

⊕ *DECPAN*

▲ ⊕ *CKL2*
Lekhubu

○ *Letiahau
Waterhole*

For listings, see from page 497

⊖ Where to stay
1 Deception Valley Lodge
2 Dinaka
3 Gham Dhao Lodge
4 Kalahari Plains Camp
5 Tau Pan Camp

GPS co-ordinates	⊕	
CKA1	21°13.844'S,	23°37.308'E
CKA2	21°16.157'S,	23°28.666'E
CKA3	21°19.965'S,	23°20.319'E
CKD4	21°24.213'S,	23°46.287'E
CKGATE	21°09.399'S,	24°00.417'E
CKK1	21°25.699'S,	23°47.921'E
CKK4	21°25.006'S,	23°47.433'E
CKL1	21°17.532'S,	23°42.545'E
CKL2	21°35.401'S,	23°44.755'E
CKL3	21°36.447'S,	23°33.407'E
CKMOT1	21°08.080'S,	23°04.443'E
CKMOT2	21°10.572'S,	23°04.810'E
CKMOT3	21°09.914'S,	23°06.100'E
CKP1	21°46.063'S,	23°11.975'E
CKP2	21°47.565'S,	23°12.882'E
CKS1	21°21.104'S,	23°40.285'E
CKS2-3	21°20.071'S,	23°40.893'E
CKTAU2	21°33.262'S,	23°11.507'E
CKWIL8	21°19.152'S,	23°52.716'E
CKWIL9	21°10.338'S,	23°53.094'E
DECPAN	21°24.291'S,	23°46.434'E
DINSAL	20°55.060'S,	23°21.270'E
DVLTUR	21°00.041'S,	23°39.405'E
HSLTUR	21°00.047'S,	23°41.093'E
JUNCT1	21°24.301'S,	23°48.193'E
KALPLA	21°29.057'S,	24°00.470'E
KUKECO	21°00.075'S,	23°53.070'E
LEFORK	21°17.287'S,	23°41.938'E
LETIAH	21°38.380'S,	23°25.023'E
MATSWE	21°11.892'S,	23°56.369'E
MOTCUT	21°00.194'S,	23°06.400'E
PATURN	21°23.924'S,	23°15.136'E
PUMP1	21°24.676'S,	23°13.718'E
SUPLPS	21°20.970'S,	23°40.505'E
SUPLPN	21°19.374'S,	23°40.966'E
TAUPLO	21°27.033'S,	23°25.283'E

are a desk & leather armchairs; to the other, a bathroom – with inside & outside showers, twin basins & separate toilet. Lighting for ceiling & bedside lamps is powered by solar panels. There's also a family chalet, sleeping up to 4 people.

Game drives explore the remote area around the camp, with day trips to Deception Valley a further option. There are also nature walks, conducted by the lodge's Bushman trackers & some great birdwatching opportunities. Plus, with the huge Kalahari skies, stargazing is a must!

If you're driving yourself, follow the main westerly track from the Matswere Gate for 78km, then turn south to Tau Pan (⊕ TAUPTO 21°24.073'S, 23°25.656'E) for a further 6km to the lodge. The lodge is visible from kilometres around &, although its thatch is rapidly blending into the environment, the same can't be said for the metal-roofed kitchen, even with its coat of green paint. Most visitors, however, arrive by air at the airstrip, just 3km away, so see none of this. *US$560 pp, FBA inc conservation fee. US$150 pp suppt 20 Dec–4 Jan.* ⊕ *All year.* 🛏🛏🛏

OUTSIDE THE PARK

Deception Valley Lodge (8 chalets) ☎ 686 3685; m 7268 8208; e office@dvl.co.bw, lodge-res2@bushways.com; w deceptionvalleylodge.co.bw; ⊕ DVLOD 20°57.182'S, 23°38.988'E. Old-fashioned style & comfort are the watchwords at Deception Valley Lodge, which is set in one of the country's more remote locations. As with the wider Central Kalahari area, it has a relative lack of big game, which tends to suit old Africa hands more than first-time visitors. That said, lion numbers have increased in the last few years, sightings of brown hyena are

CAMPING

There are several designated campsites across the northern CKGR [map, page 498], with quite a good concentration around Deception Valley. Each of the sites is designed for just one group camping at any one time – with a maximum of three vehicles and six people – so once you have pre-booked a site, you should not be sharing it with anyone else. Most of the sites have a long-drop toilet and a separate bucket shower, enclosed by simple rush screens, as well as a firepit. That said, you must still bring all the food and water you need. And note that the vegetation around these facilities can get very overgrown, so digging your own toilet may be a more attractive option than fighting through the bush. (Don't forget a spade, and matches to burn any tissue paper before burying it.)

As with the rest of Botswana's parks, it's essential that you book and pay for these campsites in advance. Payment of park fees, however, is more flexible, with the option to pay in advance or at certain gates on entry. No matter how you pay, all fees must be settled before you will be allowed into the park. See page 127 for how to do this, and details of the costs.

Within the CKGR, six sites – Lekhubu, Letiahau, Piper, Sunday, Passarge and Motopi – are operated by Bigfoot Tours (w bigfoottours.co.bw; page 128), with rates for international visitors currently set at P357 per person (around US$26), excluding park fees. Other campsites within the reserve still fall within the remit of the DWNP (page 213), whose camping fees remain at P40 per person. It's worth noting, however, that there is a high expectation of park fees – and thus presumably attendant campsite and vehicle fees – being increased within the life of this book.

Each of the CKGR's campsites has a unique code. These are signposted on the ground as CKK1, CKK2, CKD1, etc, but for computer-booking purposes have been redesignated as CKKOR-01, CKKOR-02, CKDEC-01, etc. I've made notes on some of these in the following pages, identifying most of them with comments and GPS locations.

on the up & you may just spot elephant. For the most part, wildlife encounters here will more likely be with zebra, wildebeest, gemsbok & a host of antelope species, bat-eared foxes, jackals & genets.

Accommodation is traditionally styled. From a semi-circular veranda with simple chairs & a table, concertina doors lead into each thatched chalet. There's a bedroom, with campaign-style furniture & a comfortable bed under mosquito netting, a separate lounge area, where a leather sofa & beaten metal coffee table sit on a Moroccan rug, & a bathroom set between the 2 rooms, with a claw-foot bath & a door to the excellent outside shower.

The chalets are widely separated from each other, & linked by low wooden walkways to a good pool with sunloungers & the lodge's main reception. Here, the lounge & dining areas are furnished with careful attention to detail, including ostrich-eggshell lampshades, framed Bushman artefacts on the walls, & hand-crafted wrought-iron chairs. A curio shop sells a limited range of T-shirts, quilted jackets & souvenirs.

The veranda incorporates a large deck, where leather couches & low tables create an appealing outdoor seating area, while beyond is an outdoor dining area, a prime spot for watching the porcupine that roam through camp in the evening. About 75m in front is a productive waterhole, where on one visit, giraffe, oryx, zebra & wildebeest all turned up regularly.

Activities focus on day & night drives & walks on the lodge's 150km² concession, which shares its southern boundary with the CKGR. (Note that drives don't normally visit the game reserve, which – because of the location of the park gate – is too far for a comfortable day trip.) The landscape, flora & fauna are similar to that found on the fringes of the main reserve, although being much smaller & fenced, the concession doesn't get the large wet-season congregations that are a major attraction of the CKGR between Dec & May. In fact, the best season to visit Deception Valley Lodge is the more traditional game-viewing period of Jun–Sep. The reserve encompasses a number of waterholes & natural pans surrounded by larger trees, with a hide beside one that can be productive as game such as lion is not deterred by the fences. There's plenty to look at, & with good guiding – helped by San trackers – visitors should also spot many of the smaller attractions. 'Bushman' walks, accompanied by the lodge's San guides, incorporate genuine &

enjoyable demonstrations of their traditional skills. Children are welcome, but families must take a private game vehicle. The lodge has its own airstrip, but if you're driving yourself, see the directions on page 494. *Standard suite from US$500 pp Dec–Mar to US$750 pp Jul–Oct; family suite from US$585 pp Dec–Mar to US$835 pp Jul–Oct, FBA. Children all ages.* ⊕ *All year.* 🛏🛏🛏–🛏🛏🛏🛏

Dinaka (7 tents) Contact Ker & Downey (page 214); ⊕ DINSAL 20°55.060'S, 23°21.270'E. Set in its own 20,000ha private reserve on the northern edge of the CKGR, Dinaka is accessible by road, & also has its own airstrip. Taken over by established Botswana operator Ker & Downey in 2017, the lodge underwent substantial changes. The safari tents have modern, timber-panelled & khaki interiors, with both twin & dbl beds made up with crisp white linen. Each tent features a private en-suite bathroom with both indoor & outdoor showers. For families, there is a 2-bedroom tent with a generously sized shared en-suite bathroom. Dinaka's tents are thoughtfully positioned, elevated on wooden platforms, providing an ideal vantage point overlooking a year-round waterhole. The camp is designed for accessibility, with wooden walkways connecting all areas, making it suitable for wheelchairs.

Fronting the waterhole, Dinaka's main thatched area is in a rustic-chic style, with a comfortable lounge, bar & impressive banqueting table under white beaded chandeliers for social meals – although private dining can be organised too. A small pool is a boon during the hotter months, & a sleepout deck is lovely for a starlit night.

Activities encompass both morning & afternoon game drives conducted in open safari vehicles, with a max of 4 guests. Guided bush walks offer an opportunity to get up close to the environment, while on a San Bushman walk you can learn about the traditional lifestyle of the San. Bird enthusiasts will enjoy the prolific birdlife: over 200 distinct species, including a thriving population of Pale Chanting Goshawks. Dinaka also has strategically positioned hides & we're reliably informed that these offer productive game viewing in the dry season. Eland numbers are particularly good here, & lion & leopard have also been seen regularly. *From US$1,020 pp Mar–May & Nov to US$1,355 Jul–Oct pp, FBA.* ⊕ *Mar–Nov.* 🛏🛏🛏🛏🛏

Gham Dhao Lodge (11 rooms) ✆ 683 0238/9; ✉ res@evolveback.com, tessa.t@evolveback.com;

w evolveback.com/evolve-back-kalahari;
⊕ HAISAL 20°56.964'S, 23°40.689'E. Formerly the well-regarded Haina Kalahari Lodge, the lodge was renovated & reopened by the luxury Indian operator Evolve Back in 2019. On a 110km² private concession on the northern border of CKGR, & to the east of Deception Valley Lodge, Gham Dhao benefits from the same environment & wildlife, but with a more modern feel. It retains a reputation for the quintessential Kalahari experience with great service.

Central to the lodge is an open-sided timber & thatch hub, with views to the permanent, pumped waterhole in front of camp, & with roll-down canvas sides to guard against inclement weather. It houses the bar, elevated dining area, comfortable lounge, library complete with fireplace, & a curio shop for locally sourced souvenirs. To one side is a large boma for dining, with a firepit surrounded by chairs, & to the front is a pool surrounded by decking.

Accommodation is in tented rooms set amid the Kalahari bush, which are divided into 3 categories: Sky-Luxe, Classic & a family tent. The spacious timber-&-canvas Sky-Luxe tents are shaded under smooth thatch, with wide verandas & a raised sky-bed deck for starlit nights. Interiors are a contemporary take on classic safari style: polished wooden floors, four-poster beds taking in the gauze picture-window views, claw-foot baths

& a small lounge area for browsing books. The smaller Classic tents are shaded under neat pole arches & a dbl bed under mosquito netting, a tea/coffee station, & an en-suite bathroom featuring an indoor & outdoor shower. For families, there are 2 classic tents which share a communal deck & can accommodate up to 4 people. Some tents are a bit of a walk from the central area, offering an immersive wilderness experience, & vehicle collection from rooms is available for all guests. Power comes from solar panels, with a generator as back-up. Water is desalinated to make it drinkable & batteries can be charged at any time.

Activities at Gham Dhao focus on game drives (day & night) & walks with San guides. While big game is limited due to the arid environment, the fenced concession hosts plains game, jackals, bat-eared foxes, caracals & occasional large predators. Full-day drives into the CKGR are available (US$700/vehicle inc lunch & park fees). For self-drivers, the lodge is accessed from the same track as Deception Valley (⊕ HSLTUR 21°00.047'S, 23°41.093'E) & is clearly signposted. *Sky-Luxe tent US$1,200 pp Jul–Oct, US$800 pp Nov–Jun; classic tent US$800 pp Jul–Oct, US$550 pp Nov–Jun; family tent US$720 pp Jul–Oct, US$480 pp Nov–Jun; FBA exc CKGR trips & air transfer from Maun (US$320 pp). Children all ages.* ⊕ *All year.* 🏵️🏵️🏵️–🏵️🏵️🏵️🏵️🏵️

WHAT TO SEE AND DO

For most visitors, being in a pristine area that is as remote as the CKGR is an end in itself. Just being able to camp, move around and watch the wildlife at leisure in such a beautiful wilderness, with the certainty that you'll see very few other vehicles, is the real attraction here. So don't rush around looking for 'sights', as there really aren't any. Just take time to enjoy where you are!

That said, detailed here are some of the areas that you may visit, including a few notes on some of the various campsites, with their names, and both old on-the-ground codes and booking codes. Your permit for camping in the CKGR will specify the precise campsites booked for you on each night – and these can't be changed when you're here.

If you're entering and leaving via the Matswere Gate then a lovely week's circuit can be made by starting around Sunday and Leopard pans, then heading north and west along Passarge Valley, south via the western link to Piper Pans, and then returning northeast through Letiahau and Deception valleys. This is the order in which I've described these areas.

Should you want to stop closer to the Matswere Gate, there are two campsites along that route, the first, CKWIL-09, close to the old Matswere Scout Post (⊕ CKWIL9 21°10.338'S, 23°53.094'E), and the second, CKWIL-08, about 12km further into the reserve (⊕ CKWIL8 21°19.152'S, 23°52.716'E).

SUNDAY AND LEOPARD PANS Just north of Deception Valley are two fairly large pans: Sunday and Leopard. Both are surrounded by dunes and a waymarked 9km 'loop' – really more of a 5km semi-circular detour off the main track to Leopard Pan – allows you to drive around the edge of Sunday Pan rather than stick to the central track. The loop starts in the south at ⊕ SUPLPS 21°20.970'S, 23°40.505'E, continuing round to rejoin the original track at ⊕ SUPLPN 21°19.374'S, 23°40.966'E. Bat-eared foxes, springbok, gemsbok, kudu, black-backed jackal and honey-badgers seem to favour the area, with lions known to pass through on occasion too.

Any of the **campsites** around these pans make a good first stop if you enter the reserve via the Matswere Gate (66km) and plan on heading to the area around Passarge Valley. The four sites in this area were all renovated in 2019 and have long-drop toilets, bucket showers and firepits.

The more southerly Sunday Pan has three campsites. The first, set back from the pan under a grove of shady acacias, is CKS1, or CKSUN-02. It's slightly left of the track when you're driving north at ⊕ CKS1 21°21.104'S, 23°40.285'E. Further on, the turn-off to the second and third sites (CKS2 and CKS3, or CKSUN-04 and 03) is to the right, at ⊕ CKS2-3 21°20.071'S, 23°40.893'E. These two neighbouring sites are on a rise above the waterhole, making them especially popular, though all four are pleasantly sited on the edge of the bush close to the main open area of the pan.

Towards Leopard Pan about 5km further north, is a fourth campsite, CKL1, or CKSUN-01 (⊕ CKL1 21°17.532'S, 23°42.545'E).

PASSARGE VALLEY This is a long valley with many pans and several campsites. Approaching from the east, it's easily reached from Leopard Pan by finding the junction of tracks to the north of the pan (⊕ LEFORK 21°17.287'S, 23°41.938'E), and heading north from there.

Initially the landscape is quite a thick mixture of small trees and bushes: typical Kalahari sandveld. Then after about 13km you'll find an old green sign saying: 'Passarge Valley. Help keep this valley pristine by staying on the track'. Gradually – now heading southwest – you descend into a valley with a more open landscape and more grassland. About 9.5km further there's a turning south to **Manong Campsite**, coded CKA1/CKPAS-01 (⊕ CKA1 21°13.844'S, 23°37.308'E), a lovely campsite set very much on its own.

Continuing in the valley for another 18km you'll then find a track to the north signposted to Kgokong Campsite, CKA2/CKPAS-02 (⊕ CKA2 21°16.157'S, 23°28.666'E). Here the valley is really stunning: open grassland dotted with a few small tree-islands. The campsite is in the thickets just off to the side, slightly above the floor of the valley.

Further southwest (96km from Matswere Gate), the third of Passarge's campsites is Kukama Campsite, CKA3/CKPAS-03 (⊕ CKA3 21°19.965'S, 23°20.319'E), in a small group of trees. It's only 11km west of the waterhole, and its shady pitches offer long-reaching views and seclusion. There are no facilities here, bar a firepit, but giraffe, springbok, hyena and jackals are cited by campers here. This is about 12km northeast of the junction with the park's main east–west cutline track, at ⊕ PATURN 21°23.924'S, 23°15.136'E.

PASSARGE PAN AND MOTOPI PAN A little beyond the southwest end of the Passarge Valley track, Passarge Pan is on the south side of the track which leads to a water pump (⊕ PUMP1 21°24.676'S, 23°13.718'E).

North of here a track leads through some lovely country dotted with small pans to Motopi Pan, where three **campsites** have been established: CKMOT-01

(⊕ CKMOT1 21°08.080'S, 23°04.443'E), CKMOT-02 (⊕ CKMOT2 21°10.572'S, 23°04.810'E) and CKMOT-03 (⊕ CKMOT3 21°09.914'S, 23°06.100'E). This track leads ultimately to the double fence which is the northern boundary of the reserve (⊕ MOTCUT 21°00.194'S, 23°06.400'E). Note that there is no open gate here, and no direct way in or out of the reserve at this point. However, when you reach the fence you'll find a decent track that lies parallel to the fence. To the right, this runs east beside the fence, and then southeast from Kuke Corner (still confined within the park's boundary fence) to the main Matswere Gate. To the left a similar track runs west to the Tsau Gate (⊕ TSAUGT 21°00.060'S, 22°47.822'E), and from there to the Kuke Gate on the main Maun–Ghanzi road.

THE WESTERN LINK On the northeast side of Passarge Pan, the track south towards Phukwi, Tau, San and Phokoje pans starts at ⊕ PATURN 21°23.924'S, 23°15.136'E. This track is the start of the 'western link', which eventually heads south towards Piper Pans.

You'll see from the map that this track seems to zigzag, always heading either north–south or east–west; this is because the inter-dune valleys (with their string of pans) run east–west. These valleys usually make the best game-viewing areas. They are linked by tracks running north–south, across the top of the dunes.

Note that on this track, the first few kilometres south of the main cutline track (⊕ PATURN) are very boggy, so expect this to be exceedingly challenging during the rains.

For an alternative route south, you can enter the western link via Tau Pan. To do this, first turn east along the cutline towards the north end of Deception Valley. About 18km from ⊕ PATURN, there's a track which heads almost due south to Phukwi Pan with a campsite – CKTAU-02 (⊕ CKTAU2 21°33.262'S, 23°11.507'E) – on the route at San Pan. In addition, there is CKT2/CKTAU-03 (⊕ CKT2 21°35.278'S, 23°16.332'E), which is roughly halfway along the track that follows Phokoje Pan. Heading east along this, the track splits off southeast from Phokoje Pan about 18km before its junction (⊕ LETIAH 21°38.380'S, 23°25.023'E) with the main track from the Letiahau Valley to Piper Pans.

PIPER PANS Piper Pans are as far south as most people visit in the northern section of the park, and as far as I'll describe in this chapter. If you are wondering if it's worth the effort to get here, the answer is a resounding 'yes'. And that's despite a badly corrugated section of road just north of this area.

The complex of pans is only a few kilometres across, but it's a stunning stretch of perfectly flat grass. In the rains it's green, and often covered with springbok and gemsbok. By as early as May, it has usually turned a beautiful gold, like a field of ripe barley.

There are two **campsites** here. CKP1/CKPIP-01 (⊕ CKP1 21°46.063'S, 23°11.975'E), slightly further north, is in a grove of rather lovely trees on the west side of the track, but close to the edge of the pan.

The second site, CKP2/CKPIP-02 (⊕ CKP2 21°47.565'S, 23°12.882'E), is further south, up higher on a low fossilised dune. This is just beyond a prominent green water tank (⊕ WATANK 21°47.045'S, 23°12.755'E) which stands at the top of a fossilised dune, beside the track which leads, around 72km later, to Xade.

Around the outside edge of the pan itself there's a 7km circular track that is well worth exploring, although impassable during the rains. The eastern side of this (around ⊕ PIPERE 21°46.336'S, 23°15.039'E) is particularly treacherous black-cotton soil, while it often seems to disappear on the southern side. It's

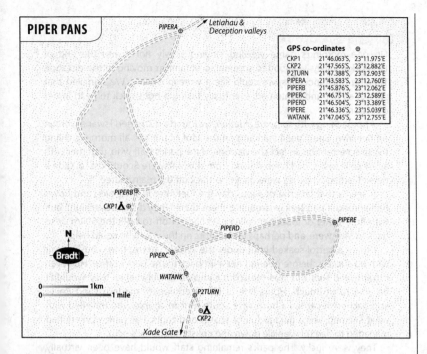

PIPER PANS

Letiahau & Deception valleys

PIPERA

GPS co-ordinates	⊕
CKP1	21°46.063'S, 23°11.975'E
CKP2	21°47.565'S, 23°12.882'E
P2TURN	21°47.388'S, 23°12.903'E
PIPERA	21°43.583'S, 23°12.760'E
PIPERB	21°45.876'S, 23°12.062'E
PIPERC	21°46.751'S, 23°12.589'E
PIPERD	21°46.504'S, 23°13.389'E
PIPERE	21°46.336'S, 23°15.039'E
WATANK	21°47.045'S, 23°12.755'E

PIPERB
CKP1
PIPERD
PIPERE
PIPERC
WATANK
P2TURN
CKP2
Xade Gate

N
Bradt

0 ____ 1km
0 ____ 1 mile

a lovely circuit, but very slow driving even when dry, as the hardened earth is very uneven.

LETIAHAU VALLEY Approaching from the south and Piper Pans, the road to Matswere leads first through Letiahau and then Deception Valley. About 12km northeast of the junction (⊕ LETIAH 21°38.380'S, 23°25.023'E), which is the turning north for the western link, the track enters the picturesque Letiahau Valley. A further 4km on there's a small turning south from the road which, after about 100m, leads to a group of trees in a bushy plain where the **Letiahau Campsite**, coded CKWIL-06 (⊕ CKL3 21°36.447'S, 23°33.407'E), is situated. Around 6km further east, a tiny loop takes a closer look at the permanent Letiahau waterhole.

About 20km east of the first campsite is a second one called Lekhubu, CKWIL-07 (⊕ CKL2 21°35.401'S, 23°44.755'E), off on the south side of the road. Continuing east from this, the track backs around to take a more northerly line as it approaches Deception Valley.

DECEPTION PAN Named for its striking mirage effect, Deception Pan (⊕ DECPAN 21°24.291'S, 23°46.434'E) is an open pan at the southern end of the valley, found by taking a short detour, about 1.5km from the main track. It fills with water during the rains and is home to large bullfrogs, whose loud nocturnal calls carry far and wide, but for the rest of the year it's just flat, cracked mud, tinged a vivid red colour by a small red water plant which flourishes when it's full. Springbok, giraffe, hartebeest and ostrich are regular visitors.

DECEPTION VALLEY This is a broad inter-dune valley running roughly north–south; it's thought to be the bed of a fossil river. During and after good rains this is carpeted in luscious green grass that attracts dense concentrations of game. It's the

On one morning's game viewing, driving slowly north into the end of Deception Valley, we spotted something unfamiliar moving in the distance. Training our binoculars, we could see a woman waving. We signalled that we'd seen her and continued, eventually taking a right track to head in her direction.

Approaching with some trepidation, we found a distressed Tswana woman on her own. She'd been standing on the roof of the 4x4 all morning, trying to attract attention. In fact she was one of the park's staff who, together with a few colleagues, had been driving from the Matswere Scout Post to Xade (I never learned why they were on a side-track off the main route!).

It seems that late the previous day the fuel filter in their old Land Rover had sprung a bad leak, marooning them there. They'd slept overnight but, with little water or food, her colleagues had set off to walk the 50km or so back to Matswere, and perhaps find visitors on the way who could help.

I spent a petrol-soaked hour under the vehicle, attempting a bush repair with no success, before offering her a lift back to the park's office. However, it transpired that this was the scout camp's only vehicle, so they wouldn't be able to do much. Hours later a better-equipped, modern Land Rover approached; it carried a bush-wise South African couple who travelled with what seemed like a garage full of spares and tools. The park workers had managed to flag this vehicle down and enlist the couple's help.

They were lucky. The park's remaining staff would have been virtually powerless to help, even if they'd known about the breakdown. Fortunately these visitors had the right tools and spare parts, so a repair was soon made. All set off again to Xade in their clapped-out Land Rover with few supplies. I hope they got there.

The morals of this story are simple:

- Don't expect any help from the park's staff: they probably won't have the vehicles or resources.
- Don't come to the CKGR without some basic spares, a simple tool kit and another vehicle to help you out.
- A satellite phone isn't totally necessary, but is a wise back-up, so bring one if possible.
- Ample food and water are absolutely essential: bring more than you expect to need.

park's most famous location, and where Mark and Delia Owens (page 540) lived. If you are visiting the northern section of the park for five to six days, then my advice is for you to save this as a highlight for your last couple of days.

As the park's most famous area, and relatively close (35km) to the Matswere Scout Post entrance, this is the place where you're most likely to see other visitors. It's also the area with the most campsites.

Towards the northern end of Deception Valley, on the west side, a track splits off to pass beside the four kori campsites (CKK1–CKK4, or CKKOR-01 to CKKOR-04), which are spread across a distance of almost 1km. The most southerly one is located at ⊕ CKK1 21°25.699'S, 23°47.921'E, and the most northerly at ⊕ CKK4 21°25.006'S, 23°47.433'E. They're in fairly sparse bush on the edge of the main pan, and generally very close to any animal action there – though with the exception of CKK4, views of the pan are usually obscured by vegetation. There's also limited privacy, as a track runs almost through some of the sites.

Deception Valley's other campsites are all set north of the pan, higher up in fairly thick woodlands with some of the best shade in the park. There are six of these (CKD1–CKD6, or CKDEC-01 to CKDEC-06), three on either side of the cutline road. CKD4 (✪ CKD4 21°24.213'S, 23°46.287'E) consists of a roughly circular area that has been cleared of trees and bushes. Each campsite is separated from its neighbours by a few hundred metres, making them feel very secluded and private.

When you leave the park, simply drive towards the north of Deception Valley. There you'll find several small junctions with signposts, as the tracks along the valley are intersected by the straight cutline road. Head east to ✪ JUNCT1 21°24.301'S, 23°48.193'E, and continue on to sign out at the Matswere Gate (✪ CKGATE 21°09.399'S, 24°00.417'E).

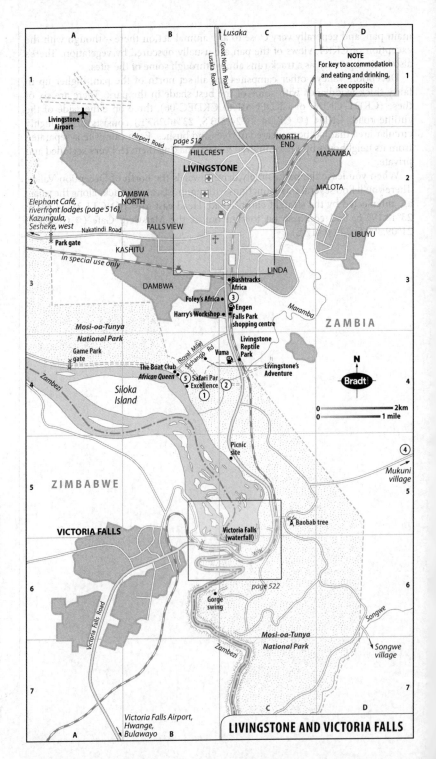

NOTE
For key to accommodation
and eating and drinking,
see opposite

↑ Lusaka

Livingstone Airport

Airport Road

page 512

HILLCREST

LIVINGSTONE

NORTH
END

MARAMBA

DAMBWA
NORTH

MALOTA

FALLS VIEW

Elephant Café,
riverfront lodges (page 516),
Kazungula,
Sesheke, west

Nakatindi Road

KASHITU

LIBUYU

Park gate

In special use only

LINDA

DAMBWA

●Bushtracks
Africa

Foley's Africa ● ③

ZAMBIA

Mosi-oa-Tunya
National Park

Harry's Workshop ●

Engen
Falls Park
shopping centre

Maramba

Game Park
gate

Livingstone
Reptile
Park

Zambezi

Royal Mile
Sichango Rd

Vuma

The Boat Club
African Queen

Safari Par
Excellence

⑤

①

②

Livingstone's
Adventure

N

Bradt

0   2km
0   1 mile

Siloka
Island

④

Mukuni
village

Picnic
site

ZIMBABWE

⑤

VICTORIA FALLS

Baobab tree

Victoria Falls
(waterfall)

Gorge
swing

page 522

Songwe

Mosi-oa-Tunya
National Park

Songwe
village

Victoria Falls Road

Zambezi

Victoria Falls Airport,
Hwange,
Bulawayo

LIVINGSTONE AND VICTORIA FALLS

508

17

Livingstone and Victoria Falls

Zambia telephone code +260

Many visitors on safari in Botswana will start or end their trips in Zambia, staying in Livingstone and visiting Victoria Falls. The Victoria Falls are certainly a magnificent sight, and, understandably, few can resist a couple of nights here.

The town of Livingstone itself is less well known than the small, nearby Zimbabwean border town that shares the name of the waterfall. However, Livingstone has developed rapidly since the early 2000s and there has been an impressive push to develop local infrastructure and improve the city, which continues today. Certainly, there are some excellent lodges along the Zambezi here and a wealth of knowledge and activities on offer from local tour operators. The Zambian and Zimbabwean sides offer different views of the Falls themselves, and if you have time it is worth seeing both to appreciate the whole waterfall.

This chapter aims to give you an overview of Livingstone and the Falls: what to do, where to stay and how to get organised. For comprehensive details on the area, and on Zambia as a whole, see the latest edition of our Bradt guide to Zambia (7th edition).

GETTING THERE AND AWAY

BY AIR Harry Mwaanga Nkumbula International Airport [508 A1] (code LVI) in Livingstone is just 5km northwest of the town centre on Airport Road. The glass entrance foyer has pleasant waiting rooms, airline offices, a bank (⊕ 08.00–16.00 Mon–Fri, 08.15–14.30 Sat) with an ATM, a post office and several car-hire kiosks. There's a simple snack bar (⊕ 08.00–18.00 daily) before passport control, a duty-free shop, and free Wi-Fi available throughout.

LIVINGSTONE AND VICTORIA FALLS
For listings, see from page 511

🛏 **Where to stay**

1 David Livingstone Safari
  Lodge & Spa...................................B4
2 Maramba River Lodge...................C4
3 Protea Hotel Livingstone............C3
4 Stanley Safari Lodge.....................D5
5 Victoria Falls Waterfront.............B4

✖ **Where to eat and drink**
  Victoria Falls Waterfront......(see 5)
  Off map
  Elephant Café...............................A3

Zambia Airways offers a direct, daily flight to Johannesburg (1hr 30mins). South African carrier **Airlink** also flies this route daily, as well as operating a daily flight to Kruger Mpumalanga Airport (1hr 40mins). **Kenyan Airways** flies twice weekly to both Cape Town (3hrs 10mins) and Nairobi (3hrs 15mins). Of the local **internal and charter airlines** that fly into Livingstone, Proflight (m 21 1 252452/476; m 977 335563; e reservations@proflight-zambia.com;

w flyzambia.com) and WildernessAir (✆ 0213 321578–80; m 0966 770485; e info@wilderness-air.com; w wildernessdestinations.com) have Livingstone-based aircraft.

BY BUS The modern intercity bus terminus is on Kafubu Road, although one of the town's most reliable companies is Mazhandu Family Bus Service, which is based on Mutelo Street [512 B2]. Buses gather in the early morning, most heading towards Lusaka (6hrs).

If you want to go west and cross the new bridge into Kasane, board the daily Mazhandu Family Bus that goes to Mongu. Expect the first buses to leave at around 06.00, with others to follow according to demand. The bus station can be chaotic, so it's wise to buy tickets the day before. It's also advisable to be at the bus station at least half an hour before departure, since buses may leave early if they're full, and overbooking is not unheard of.

DRIVING WEST Those heading west, into Namibia's Zambezi Region (Caprivi Strip), Botswana or western Zambia, should take the Nakatindi Road – signposted as the M10 – past the lodges by the river. After about 70km this comes to the Zambezi River at Kazungula – where Namibia, Botswana, Zimbabwe and Zambia all meet. Here you can continue northwest within Zambia to Sesheke, or take the fantastic new bridge across the Zambezi into Botswana, near Kasane.

GETTING AROUND

Livingstone town is fairly compact and surrounded by several small township suburbs, sprawling out from its centre. It's small enough to walk around, as is the Falls area.

The town has two main business areas concentrated along the all-important Mosi-oa-Tunya Road. Sections of this are lined with classic colonial buildings, some restored and others in a state of disrepair. The larger and busier central business district begins atop a small hill just past the museum, while in the lower part of town is a smaller but growing retail area known as '217'. Navigation is easy, even without a map, though signposts are often missing or may point to establishments no longer in existence.

Minibuses run to the Falls from the Town Centre Market [512 B2] in the centre of Livingstone throughout the day, departing when they are full. Expect to pay around K5 for the journey.

A **taxi** between town and either the Falls or the airport will cost around US$10 for up to four passengers. A taxi out to the riverside lodges will cost from around US$15, depending on the location; some are a considerable distance from town. Competition among taxi drivers can be fierce, so be sure to negotiate for the best deal and agree on the price in advance.

Driving yourself here is pretty straightforward, and most lodges, hotels and the larger restaurants have secure parking. There are several 24-hour fuel stations on the main Mosi-oa-Tunya Road. Cars can be hired with or without a driver (the former is often cheaper) or for a self-drive safari, you can rent a 4x4 with full kit; try **Hemingways** (m 977 866492, 870232; e info@hemingwayszambia. com; w hemingwayszambia.com) or **Voyagers** [513 D8] (163 Mosi-oa-Tunya Rd; ✆0212 627800; e rentals@voyagerszambia.com, livingstone@voyagerszambia.com; w voyagerszambia.com).

TOURIST INFORMATION

The **Zambia Tourism Board** [512 A2] (Mosi-oa-Tunya Rd; ☎ 0213 321404/87; e ztb@zambiatourism.org.zm; w zambiatourism.com; ⏰ 08.00–17.00 Mon–Fri, 09.00–noon Sat) is next to the Livingstone Museum, easily spotted for the two-seater plane outside. You can pick up brochures and get referrals, and details of what to see and do are also available at most places to stay, but **tour operators** are usually better geared to assist you with actual bookings:

Bushtracks Africa [508 C3] Mosi-oa-Tunya Rd; ☎ 0213 323232; e operations@bushtracksafrica.com; w bushtracksafrica.com

Livingstone's Adventure [508 B4] 4023 Sichango Rd; ☎ 0213 323589; m 0978 770175; e reservations@livingstonesadventure.com; w livingstonesadventure.com

Safari Par Excellence [508 B4] Zambezi Waterfront & Activity Centre, Sichango Rd; ☎ 0213 320606; m 0968 320606; e zaminfo@safpar.com; w safpar.com

Wild Side Tours & Safaris [513 D7] 131 Mosi-oa-Tunya Rd; ☎ 0213 323726; m 0978 323726; e karien.kermer@outlook.com

 WHERE TO STAY

Livingstone offers an enormous variety of places to stay for all types of travellers and budgets, and service, standards and amenities are consistently rising. Numerous bush lodges occupy lovely situations along the Zambezi River, some close enough to easily take advantage of the attractions and activities of the Falls; others further upstream are more remote. Closer to town, and to the Falls, an increasing number of upmarket hotels, some on the river and others in a more urban setting, offer creature comforts. At the cheaper end of the market, staying in a guesthouse or in-town lodge, where you may meet African travellers or volunteers from overseas, can add a multi-cultural dimension to your visit, while backpacker accommodation

ACCOMMODATION PRICE CODES

For urban establishments, and others offering B&B accommodation, rates are based on the cost of a double room with breakfast, unless otherwise specified. Single supplements average around 20%, but may be significantly higher. VAT may be charged extra.

$$$$$	US$250+	£165+	K1,875+
$$$$	US$150–250	£100–165	K1,125–1,875
$$$	US$80–150	£50–100	K600–1,125
$$	US$40–80	£25–50	K300–600
$	up to US$40	up to £25	up to K300

For all-inclusive places, such as safari lodges and camps, rates are per person and based on sharing a double room, including full board and activities (FBA).

♨♨♨♨♨	US$2,000+	£1,330+
♨♨♨♨	US$1,300–2,000	£865–1,330
♨♨♨	US$600–1,300	£400–865
♨♨	US$250–600	£165–400
♨	up to US$250	up to £165

Livingstone and Victoria Falls   WHERE TO STAY

17

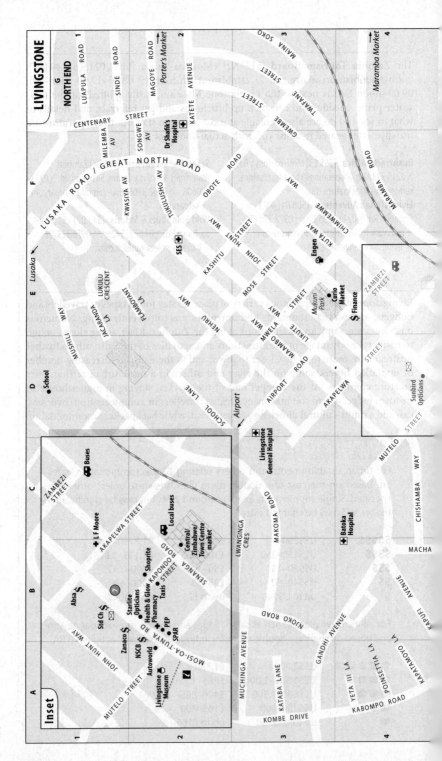

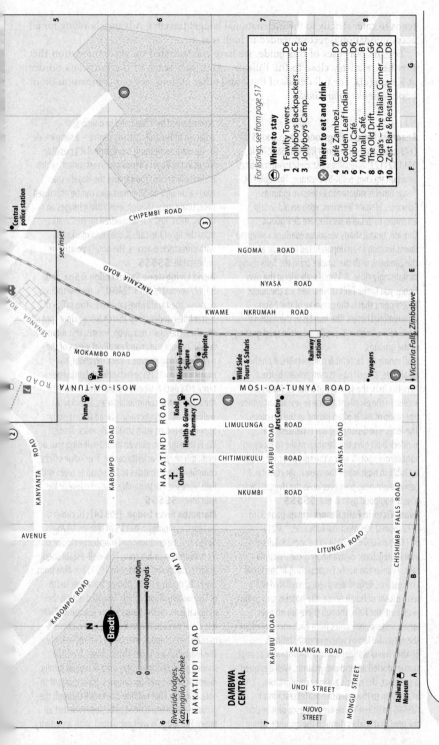

For listings, see from page 517

Where to stay
1 Fawlty Towers........................D6
2 Jollyboys Backpackers..........C5
3 Jollyboys Camp.....................E6

Where to eat and drink
4 Café Zambezi........................D7
5 Golden Leaf Indian...............D8
6 Kubu Café..............................D6
7 Munali Café...........................B1
8 The Old Drift.........................G6
9 Olga's – the Italian Corner....D6
10 Zest Bar & Restaurant..........D8

tends to cater strictly to the international budget traveller. Advance booking for all accommodation is recommended in high season.

For the purposes of this guide, we have concentrated on accommodation that is either relatively close to the Falls or within easy reach of the Botswana border at Kazungula. For full details of these and other options, see our companion Bradt book, *Zambia: Safari Guide*.

NATIONAL PARK AND VICTORIA FALLS

Anantara Royal Livingstone [map, page 516] (173 rooms) Mosi-oa-Tunya Rd; \ 0768 850446, 0213 321122; e royallivingstone@anantara.com; w anantara.com/royal-livingstone. This opulent 5-star hotel is situated in extensive grounds. Spacious, elegant interiors, with an old-world attention to detail & service, are de rigueur. Outside, broad, shady verandas overlook sweeping lawns leading to an unparalleled frontage along the Zambezi, with the 'smoke' from the Falls rising tantalisingly close. A 15min walk along the river brings you to the Falls themselves via the direct access point that is the preserve of the 2 Sun International hotels. The hotel is in the national park; zebra, impala & giraffe are often seen grazing in the grounds.

All rooms are tasteful & comfortable, if on the small side, & each has its own private balcony, & benefits from the services of a butler. Meals are served in the excellent à la carte restaurant where live piano music is often played in the evenings. The long, wood-panelled bar is relaxed, & a sundeck built over the Zambezi makes a pleasant sundowner spot, & when the spray from the Falls is visible in high water the view is spectacular. A grand swimming pool overlooks the river, & there's a well-equipped gym & spa. **$$$$$**

Avani Victoria Falls Resort [map, page 516] (212 rooms) 393 Mosi-oa-Tunya Rd; \ 0213 321122; m 0978 777044–7; e victoriafalls@ avanihotels.com; w avanihotels.com/victoria-falls. Avani is the lively 3-star sibling of the Royal Livingstone. Behind deep red, crenellated walls reminiscent of North Africa, the hotel is only 5mins' walk from the Falls, though there are no river views. Instead, balconies from each room overlook the extensive lawns where impala, zebra & giraffes freely wander among the ironwork animal statues dotted around the grounds. Well designed & compact, the rooms are very comfortable. In addition to the extensive buffet restaurant (US$40 pp), there's a relaxed alfresco grill beside the pool that snakes through the grounds, often

accompanied by a live band or dancers, or – adjacent to The Falls activity centre – a simple café. If you want something more formal it's possible to eat in the Royal Livingstone's restaurant, which is similarly priced. You can use the Royal's spa, too – although on-site massages can be organised here. Ultimately, though, everything hinges on the location. Just a few hundred metres' walk from the lip of the Falls & the curio market, & with unrestricted access, the hotel's position is unbeatable. **$$$$$**

David Livingstone Safari Lodge & Spa [508 B4] (77 rooms) \ 0213 324601; e res@anthology. co.za; w thedavidlivingstone.com. This efficient, 5-star hotel under steep thatch has a prime spot on the river. The main reception, rooms, restaurants & infinity pool command excellent views of the river & the lodge's own 3-deck riverboat, the *Lady Livingstone*. Huge basketwork lampshades, terracotta pots & wooden sculptures dominate the décor in the communal areas, & concrete walkways with rustic railings lead to tastefully appointed rooms with small balconies. There's Wi-Fi throughout, plus an award-winning spa, a gym, gift shop & activity centre. The lodge offers complimentary shuttles to Livingstone town & the Falls. *Rate inc 1 activity/day (sunset cruise or Vic Falls tour).* **$$$$$**

Maramba River Lodge [508 C4] (10 chalets, 26 tents, camping) \ 0213 324189; m 0976 587511; e reservations@marambariverlodge.com; w maramba-zambia.com. This well-established lodge & campsite, founded in 1991, lies 4km from the Falls, down a short, bumpy track just south of Livingstone Reptile Park. Situated within the national park on the banks of the Maramba River, it is a real oasis in the bush, with green lawns & mature trees, hippos, elephants & birds aplenty. The lodge has a relaxed atmosphere, & with a shaded pool, children's play area & several family rooms, it works well for families. It's important to note, though, that wildlife does walk through the grounds, so children need to be supervised at all times. The lodge is well appointed, with an activity booking office, craft shop, fully licensed riverside bar, simple restaurant, & free Wi-Fi available in the communal areas.

There are thatched en-suite chalets, spacious tents, small dome tents & a small, popular campsite. *Chalets US$145–169 pp; family chalets US$335/444 4/6 people; dome/large tents US$125–280; camping US$25/15 adult/ child. All B&B inc morning & afternoon tea.* **$$$**

Stanley Safari Lodge [508 D5] (4 suites, 6 cottages) Mukuni Rd; \ 0957 090441; e info@ robinpopesafaris.net; w robinpopesafaris.net. Set some distance back from the river & bordering the Mosi-oa-Tunya National Park, Stanley Safari Lodge is positioned at the top of a hill & enjoys sweeping views down towards the Zambezi. Spray from the Falls is often visible when the river is in full flow. It's best suited as a place to chill out, relax & unwind.

The main building is a beautifully designed thatched affair with an open-aspect lounge, bar & dining area, & a wine cellar for candlelit wine tastings. Large, formal gardens with a central infinity pool face west towards the Zambezi, as do the 6 stylish open 'cottages'. There's also a honeymoon suite with its own plunge pool, & 3 suites decorated in a colonial style with a lounge, fireplace, covered terrace & private plunge pool. Activities offered by the lodge include mountain biking, rhino tracking in the national park, & village & museum tours. *Cottage US$415–520 pp; open suite US$460–610 pp; closed suite US$520–680 pp. All FB inc local drinks, laundry & airport transfers.* **$$$$$**

Victoria Falls Waterfront [508 B4] (23 rooms, 20 tents, camping) off Sichango Rd; \ 0213 320606–08; m 0968 320606; e waterfront@ safpar.com; w safpar.com/lodges/victoria-falls-waterfront. This large, secure & affordable riverside complex, within the unfenced area of Mosi-oa-Tunya National Park, is only 4km upstream from the Falls. It's well equipped & positioned to take advantage of all Livingstone's activities. Its large teak deck, from which you can often see the spray from the Falls, is one of the best places to watch the sunset over the Zambezi. Outside, among palm trees, is a sunken pool overlooking the river. 8 large A-frame thatched chalets house individual rooms that are comfortable, light & airy, with ethnic touches. Beyond the main building is the Adventure Village, with a large natural-style

rock pool, another bar & a thatched auditorium where daily activity briefings are given & rafting videos are shown in the evening, accompanied by a barbecue. In the gardens, 20 permanent tents (US$30 pp, B&B) are perched on wooden platforms, each with 2 beds with bedding & linen (or bring your own). Further along, a separate grassed camping area takes about 75 campers (US$15 pp); it gets pretty noisy when it's busy with overland trucks. SafPar's activity centre is located upstairs in the main area, offering a full range of activities & excursions, many that they operate themselves; you will often begin & end your activities at the Waterfront, even if staying elsewhere in Livingstone. **$$$$**

BESIDE THE ZAMBEZI: UPRIVER [map, page 516] Lodges & camps are listed here in order of their proximity to the Falls.

Toka Leya (12 tented chalets) Contact Wilderness Safaris (page 216). Set within the national park, some 5km from Livingstone, Toka Leya's green canvas tents & timber decking blend into the riverine environment. Although each tented chalet faces the river, some lie well back, glimpsing the water through the trees rather than affording a panoramic view. Raised on wide wooden verandas, the rooms are airy & spacious, with 4-poster beds.

The understated style runs through to the main lounge & restaurant area, with linking walkways to a bar & a tree-shaded deck where steps lead down to a small sandy section of beach – a wonderful place to have dinner when the water is low. Nearby, sunloungers surround a small infinity pool, & by the river there's a simple spa for massages & manicures; for the more energetic, there's a riverside gym with AC. Dinner is often taken at a group table, though it can be served privately on your own deck, & there are individual tables during the day. Free Wi-Fi is available throughout the camp.

Boat trips, game drives & birding/nature walks are all possible, as are trips to the Falls, museum & market; most other activities can be booked. *US$750–950 pp, FBA exc spa treatments.* 🏵🏵🏵🏵

Sussi & Chuma (12 chalets, 2 houses) Contact Sanctuary Retreats (page 215). Named after the Zambian bearers who carried David Livingstone's

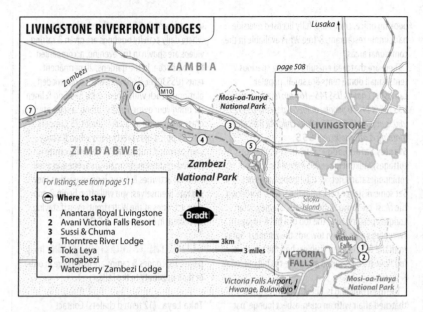

Lusaka ↑

ZAMBIA

Zambezi

M10

Mosi-oa-Tunya
National Park

page 508

LIVINGSTONE

ZIMBABWE

*Zambezi
National Park*

N

Bradt

Siloka
Island

Victoria
Falls

VICTORIA
FALLS

*Victoria Falls Airport,
Hwange, Bulawayo* ↓

*Mosi-oa-Tunya
National Park*

0 _____ 3km
0 _____ 3 miles

For listings, see from page 511

⌂ **Where to stay**
1 Anantara Royal Livingstone
2 Avani Victoria Falls Resort
3 Sussi & Chuma
4 Thorntree River Lodge
5 Toka Leya
6 Tongabezi
7 Waterberry Zambezi Lodge

body from Zambia to Dar es Salaam in Tanzania after his death, Sussi & Chuma lies within the national park, just 15mins' drive from Livingstone. Set among riverine ebony forest & constructed high up on wooden platforms, from the outside Sussi & Chuma's chalets are reminiscent of rustic treehouses. Inside, though, the rooms have a smart, modern feel to them, with large glass windows at the front where you can admire the views of the Zambezi. Alternatively, if privacy is preferred, the 2 separate Chuma houses each have 2 en-suite bedrooms, a private plunge pool, & a chef & butler.

The 2-storey thatched central area mirrors the circular design of the rooms, with an upstairs sitting room & lower dining area that extends on to a circular deck. The lodge has its own wine cellar, & a short walkway leads to a sheltered bend of the river, the location of a large infinity pool & a sundowner deck with firepits. Spa treatments are also available. There's Wi-Fi in all of the rooms, but not in the main areas.

Activities include game drives, walking safaris, boat cruises, fishing, a village tour & visits to the Falls. *US$755–1,150 pp (1–3 nights), FBA. Children under 6 in houses only.* ⊕ *All year.* 🏨🏨🏨🏨🏨

Thorntree River Lodge (10 suites) Contact African Bush Camps (page 214). The most luxurious lodge within the broader confines of Mosi-oa-Tunya National Park, Thorntree sits on private land 12km from the Falls & 10mins from town. Seriously

stylish, this beautiful lodge is a glamorous tented camp with every modern comfort & high levels of service.

The main area is a duo of stone-walled, peaked tents where a central fireplace makes for cosy evenings & a glazed folding wall leads on to an expansive deck overlooking the Zambezi. There are 4 seating areas filled with an array of beanbags, sofas & benches, all thoughtfully arranged under an eclectic arrangement of lights. The dining room, complete with a temperature-controlled wine cellar & open kitchen, serves delicious à la carte meals. There's also a circular, sandy boma complete with sculpted firepit. There's a lovely, 2-tier infinity pool overlooking the river, a small library, TV room &, in 2 traditional-style Lozi mud huts, a spa & gym. The suites themselves are characteristically elegant, with a glazed front wall opening on to the riverfront deck, complete with plunge pool. *US$603–974 pp, FBA inc airport transfers & community levy. Children all ages.* ⊕ *All year.* 🏨🏨🏨🏨

✷ **Tongabezi** (5 cottages, 7 houses) m 0979 312766; e reservations@greensafaris.com; w greensafaris.com/tongabezi. Set on a sweeping bend of the Zambezi, 15km west of the town centre, Tongabezi's lovely setting is matched by excellent service from a team of first-class local staff. Overlooking the water are 5 beautiful thatched cottages, full of character & furnished with contemporary Zambian fabrics & furniture, including deep cushioned sofas, large beds, linen curtains, en-suite bathrooms with river-view claw-foot bathtubs, & wide river-view decks. There are also 7 creatively designed, & amusingly named, houses; each is original in style & structure. For groups seeking exclusive-use, consider Tangala, the luxurious, 4-bedroom family home – complete with 2 resident dogs – with 250m of private riverfront, a large pool & oodles of homely, relaxing corners.

All Tongabezi's guests are welcome at the thatched, riverside boma, shaded by creeper-clad ebony trees & incorporating the bar, dining room & 2 intimate lounge areas, 1 with a fireplace. There's a large swimming pool, floating 'sampan' for romantic dinners (each course is hand-delivered by canoe) & in-room massage.

Tongabezi is well known for its long-running community initiatives, including a school, Tujatane, which provides free education for over 300 children – ask to visit. Otherwise, there's guided sunrise & sunset boat trips, canoeing, birdwatching, fishing, mountain biking, game drives (to Mosi-oa-Tunya National Park), island picnics, museum tours & gorge walks to enjoy. *Cottage from US$815 pp; house from US$1,023 pp; FBA exc park fees & museum entrance.* 👑👑👑👑–👑👑👑👑👑

✴ **Waterberry Zambezi Lodge** (7 chalets, 3 tents) 📞0213 327455, +44 1379 873474; e reservations@waterberrylodge.com; w waterberrylodge.com. Waterberry Lodge is set in a secluded position on the banks of the Zambezi, about 35mins' drive from Livingstone. It's a friendly, understated place, offering style, comfort & service at a modest price tag. Constructed of neat brick & thatch, Waterberry's rooms are dotted around lovely landscaped gardens, which include a lagoon & nature trail, making this a wonderful spot for birdlife.

The rooms are light, comfortable & clean. Polished concrete floors, splashes of vibrant colour, wrought-iron details & traditional thatched buildings all add to their character. All have en-suite bathrooms, AC, fans & mosquito nets. Most are grouped around the main building & swimming pool, but 2 larger rooms are set further back, with a private deck over the lagoon, & a secluded honeymoon suite sits at the river's edge. The 2-storey family room next to the main area is spacious & can sleep up to 6 people. For those seeking a secluded, peaceful hideaway, Waterberry

has opened 3 large, well-appointed tents – The Woodlands – in their own wilderness spot, dotted with waterholes popular with birds & bushbuck. Tucked away at the back of the gardens, this quiet little camp has its own butler & guard, with a shared open-sided lounge & campfire. Meals can be taken on your private terrace or guests are welcome to use all the facilities at Waterberry Lodge. The 2-storey central building at Waterberry has a dining area & ground-floor terrace, while upstairs the main bar & lounge are under deep thatch, with magnificent views over the lawns, river & Zambezi National Park beyond. Meals are tailored to fit around individual activities & there are island picnics & traditional bush dinners, too. Activities offered are very flexible, ranging from sunset & daytime cruises to birding, fishing, a tour of the Falls, & village & market visits. *Chalets US$546 pp; Woodlands US$441 pp; all FBA inc airport transfers & bed levy.* 👑👑👑

IN TOWN

Fawlty Towers [513 D6] (34 dorm beds, 33 rooms) 216 Mosi-oa-Tunya Rd; 📞0213 323432; m 0972 250154; e info@adventure-africa.com; w adventure-africa.com. This large, popular international backpackers' place – look for the blue, mural-covered building – feels spacious & a bit more upmarket than the other backpacker options in Livingstone. Light & clean dorm rooms, neat en-suite rooms & new garden twin rooms are all reasonably priced & have access to a self-catering kitchen, barbecue, lively bar, comfortable lounge, pool table & even a spa.

There's a tropical garden shaded by mango trees & coloured with bougainvillea around an inviting pool. Fawlty Towers is quiet, secure, well run & tremendously convenient for the centre of Livingstone. The atmosphere is informal & lively, & it's a great place to meet other travellers, but the bar closes early so you can still get a reasonable night's sleep. There is free Wi-Fi throughout the hostel & they offer free transport & transfers to Victoria Falls on select days (K20 pp). *Dorm bed US$12; en-suite room US$55; garden twin US$65; all rates exc b/fast.* **$–$$**

✴ **Jollyboys Backpackers** [513 C5] (14 en-suite rooms, 11 rooms/chalets with shared ablutions, 50 dorm beds, camping) 34 Kanyanta Rd; 📞0213 324229/322086; e res@ backpackzambia.com; w backpackzambia.com.

17

The ever-popular Jollyboys occupies a shaded site just behind the museum, a 2min walk from the town centre. Owner-operated, its reputation as the quintessential backpackers' lodge remains undimmed. The main facilities are set within a large, central thatched courtyard, with the dorms, reception area & ablutions around the perimeter. There are also 14 en-suite twin & dbl rooms with AC & mosquito nets. In the back garden are 2-bed A-frame thatched chalets & some lawned camping space, both sharing ablution facilities.

In the middle of the 'quad' is a wonderful sunken lounge – 'The Pillow Pit', with a firepit & colourful kitenge cushions – a perfect spot to chill out, read & meet fellow travellers. Above is a wooden deck from which you can see the spray from the Falls. A covered sitting area has comfy seating & table tennis, & looks out to an enticing rock swimming pool, lawns & gardens. Adjacent are the open-plan bar with sat TV, & a restaurant, where you can enjoy a home-cooked meal at reasonable prices. There's also a separate self-catering kitchen. Bikes can be hired (US$20/day), & there's a laundry service, book exchange (K2 per book, with proceeds to charity), Mon night movie, free weekly town walk, secure parking & short- & long-term baggage storage.

There's also a free airport pick-up service by arrangement & free lifts to the Falls at 10.00 daily. The atmosphere is relaxed & unpretentious, & even when busy, the bar shuts by 23.00 so noise isn't a major issue. *En-suite room US$68/80/90 sgl/dbl/ trpl; shared ablutions room/chalet US$48/63*

sgl/dbl; dorm bed US$20 pp; camping US$12 pp; all rates exc b/fast. **$–$$**

Jollyboys Camp [513 E6] (24 dorm beds, 9 en-suite rooms, 6 twin chalets, camping) 80 Chipembi Rd; `0213 324756`; e res@ backpackzambia. com; w backpackzambia.com. This offshoot of Jollyboys has all the hallmark offerings of its well-known parent, but with a greater focus on family accommodation. For campers, there are spaces both for tents & 4x4 vehicles with rooftop tents. All guests can use the bar, self-catering kitchen, braai facilities, Wi-Fi, baggage storage, secure off-street parking, swimming pool & free pick-up from the airport. Evenings around the firepit offer the chance to mull over the day's activities, & kids are catered for with their own jungle gym. *En-suite room US$68/80 sgl/dbl; shared ablutions room/chalet US$48/63 sgl/dbl; dorm bed US$20 pp; camping US$12 pp; all rates exc b/fast.* **$–$$**

Protea Hotel Livingstone [508 C3] (80 rooms) Mosi-oa-Tunya Rd; `0213 324630`; e reservations@phlivingstone.co.zm; w protea. marriott.com. Adjacent to Falls Park shopping centre, this is a surprisingly elegant hotel. From the entrance, flanked by giant pots overflowing with water, a wide tiled lobby, with a formal restaurant to one side, leads in turn through to a courtyard. Here, there's a rectangular swimming pool with its own bar & plenty of loungers. Dark-wood furniture & classic styling define the rooms, some of which face the courtyard. The hotel has its own activity centre & there's a secure car park. **$$$$**

 ## WHERE TO EAT AND DRINK

Meals are usually included in the rates of the upmarket, riverside lodges, and the food will be of a very high standard indeed. Many of the larger hotels' restaurants also serve international cuisine of a good quality. In recent years, several independent restaurants and cafés – hearty rather than haute cuisine – have opened up with

RESTAURANT PRICE CODES

Based on the average cost of a main course, which usually exclude VAT (currently 16%) and service of around 10%.

$$$$$	US$13+	£9+	K100+
$$$$	US$10.50–13	£7–9	K80–100
$$$	US$8–10.50	£5.50–7	K60–80
$$	US$5–8	£3.50–5.50	K40–60
$	up to US$5	up to £3.50	up to K40

cheaper prices. There are also several take-away chain restaurants in town; all are in the centre along Mosi-oa-Tunya Road, the Falls Park shopping centre and Mosi-oa-Tunya Square. We've listed the current pick of the bunch eateries here but it's always worth asking locally about the latest openings.

Café Zambezi [513 D7] Shop 214, 217 Area, Mosi-oa-Tunya Rd; m 0213 323189; e michelle. cafezambezi@gmail.com; f; ⊕ 08.00–21.00 Mon–Sat, 08.00–20.00 Sun. A popular local spot serving a well-regarded Jamaican goat curry, barbecue fare, burgers & Zambian beef stew. The best place to sit is under the mango tree in the outside courtyard. $

Elephant Café [508 A3] Nakatindi Rd, Mosi-oa-Tunya National Park; ☎ 0973 403270; w safpar. com; ⊕ 08.00–20.30 daily. Upstream of the Falls, inside the national park, the award-winning Elephant Café is far from a café: it's a sophisticated set-menu restaurant serving delicious, locally produced organic food, beautifully presented on a wooden deck over the Zambezi. Its name comes from the hand-reared rescue elephants who live here & with whom guests can interact. Road transfers are possible but it's pretty special to take the 30min Jetboat trip through the park. *Reservations essential. No children under 4; only children over 10 can interact with elephants. US$140–230 pp (price varies by time of day & road/ boat access)*. $$$$$

Golden Leaf Indian Restaurant [513 D8] 1174 Mosi-oa-Tunya Rd; ☎ 0213 321266; m 0974 321266; f; ⊕ 12.30–22.00 Tue–Sun. Serving homemade Indian delicacies here for over 20 years, this small, authentic restaurant has a good reputation, convivial atmosphere & loyal following. Consistently one of the better places to eat in town, the extensive menu includes fish masala, kadai chicken, spicy chilli naan & an extensive range of vegetarian dishes. You can order a take-away or eat in, although due to its popularity it's advisable to book in advance. $$–$$$

Kubu Café [513 D6] Kabompo Rd; m 977 653345; e kubucafe@zamnet.zm; ⊕ 08.00–23.00 Tue–Sat, 08.00–17.00 Sun–Mon. Next to Livingstone Fire Station, this consistently good café is a super spot for a full English b/fast, fresh salad, shwarma or simply a great cup of coffee & a slice of delicious carrot cake. There is ample seating both inside & outside, a children's play area, community noticeboard, book exchange & some great locally produced crafts & farm produce

to buy. The café serves milkshakes & coffees that go well with a slice of one of their homemade cakes. More substantial meals such as burgers, pizzas & steaks are also available, & there's a reasonably stocked bar. Wi-Fi is available to paying customers. $–$$$$

Munali Café [512 B1] Mosi-oa-Tunya Rd; ⊕ 08.00–21.00 Mon–Sat, 08.00–20.00 Sun. Another pleasant café in the centre of Livingstone, it serves pastries, samosas, sandwiches & basic hot food, & is a good place for a cheap & quick meal. The coffee is as good as any that you'll find in Livingstone. $

The Old Drift Restaurant [513 G6] The Royal Livingstone, Mosi-oa-Tunya Rd; ☎ 0213 321122; ⊕ 07.00–10.30, noon–15.00 & 18.30–22.00 daily. For old-world elegance & comfort, good service & fine dining, try the Royal Livingstone's à la carte restaurant: The Old Drift. It's formal & reasonably expensive. Enjoy a pre-dinner cocktail on the riverside Kubu deck, complete with views of rising mist from the Falls & resident grazing zebra. There is also a genteel afternoon tea option & a cosy piano bar complete with its own gin menu. Booking essential. $$$$$

✻ **Olga's – The Italian Corner** [513 D6] 20 Mokambo Rd; m 977 229083; e olgasproject2022@gmail.com; f; ⊕ 07.00–22.00 daily. Close to the Catholic church, this is *the* place for traditional stone-baked pizzas, as well as pasta dishes & salads. A thatched eating area incorporates crafts & furniture made by members of the Local Youth Community Training Centre & a school for disadvantaged & vulnerable youngsters, with profits from the restaurant fed directly back into the education centre. The restaurant has free Wi-Fi, & take-away is available. $$–$$$

Victoria Falls Waterfront [508 B4] Sichango Rd; ☎ 0213 320606–08; ⊕ 10.00–22.00 daily. The magnificent setting of SafPar's riverside watersports complex makes this a good place to dine after a day on the river (you can stay here too; page 515). Enjoy snacks, meals & sundowners on the banks of the Zambezi at affordable prices. The food is good & plentiful, with a variety of crowd-pleasing steaks, wraps, burgers & wood-fired pizzas served by friendly staff. There is also a full bar. While it is out of town, it's the kind of place you might go for a meal & stay for hours to savour the chilled riverside ambience. $$$–$$$$

Zest Bar & Restaurant [513 D8] 2616 Mosi-oa-Tunya Rd; m 0978 109392; f zestbarandrestaurant; ⊕ 08.00–midnight

daily. Opposite Zambian Railways, this casual spot is a local favourite serving popular *espetadas* (Brazilian hanging kebabs), pizzas & traditional Zambian fare – *vinkubala* (caterpillars) & *kapenta* (small fish) – as well as sharing platters. $$–$$$

SHOPPING

With the Falls Park shopping centre [508 C3] and Mosi-oa-Tunya Square [513 D6] (commonly referred to as the 'Shoprite Centre'), shopping in Livingstone has improved considerably in recent years.

Of the **supermarkets**, the newer Shoprite [513 D6] (Mosi-oa-Tunya Sq; ⊕ 08.00–20.00 daily) is the largest and has the best selection, and the new branch of SPAR on the corner of Mutelo Street [512 B2] (Mosi-oa-Tunya Rd; ⊕ 07.00–20.00 daily) is also useful and well stocked.

Several of the curio shops stock wildlife reference **books** and regional travel guides. Kubu Café (page 519) has a small secondhand bookshop selling books and slightly out-of-date magazines. Jollyboys (page 517) has a book-exchange system.

If you like bargaining and have lots of patience, then try one of the **craft markets** (page 527), either in town or next to the Falls. Alternatively, look out for the informal craft market in the car park at Falls Park shopping centre, where curio vendors lay out their goods on a more ad hoc basis.

If time isn't on your side, or you don't fancy the hassle of bargaining, then the hotel giftshops are generally good, or in town **Mosi-oa-Tunya Arts Centre** [513 D7] (123 Mosi-oa-Tunya Rd) and the **Museum Curio Shop & Art Gallery** [512 A2] (Livingstone Museum).

OTHER PRACTICALITIES

BANKS AND MONEY There are several major banks and various bureaux de change dotted throughout town. Most of the banks have ATMs, for which you'll generally need a Visa card rather than Mastercard.

The major **banks** are situated around the post office area, parallel to the main Mosi-oa-Tunya Road. Typically they open Monday to Friday 08.00–16.00, and sometimes on Saturday mornings, but get there early if you want to avoid long queues. The spacious air-conditioned interior and more private exchange facilities of Zanaco [512 B1] make it the preferred choice in town.

Many of these banks operate a **bureau de change** service and you can also exchange money at the post office [512 B1], though rates are likely to be lower at the private bureaux de change. More convenient still, but with the least favourable exchange rate, is to change money at a hotel or lodge. Avoid the freelance 'money-changers' who tend to congregate around the Capitol Theatre and at the border.

COMMUNICATIONS Driven by increasing expectations from international travellers, the majority of accommodation, and many restaurants, now offer free **Wi-Fi** access and/or computers with internet access. For those with a laptop, Kubu Café [513 D6] offers Wi-Fi to customers, so is a good place for a great cappuccino while you check your emails.

The prevalence of Wi-Fi and use of WhatsApp makes **phone** calls a great deal easier and cheaper than they once were. Any visitors spending any amount of time in Zambia, and especially those on self-drive trips, are advised to purchase a local **SIM card**. Those for Airtel, MTN and the state-owned Zamtel are easily obtainable from numerous outlets across town; look out for their signs at shopping malls and on Mosi-oa-Tunya Road. Expect to pay around US$4 for a week's unlimited data on a prepaid SIM card. After purchasing your SIM card (less than US$1), it must be registered at the main office of the supplier before it can be used. Airtel, MTN and Zamtel all have offices on Mosi-oa-Tunya Road and you will need to present your passport to complete the registration process.

POST You can't miss Livingstone's **post office** [512 B1] (912 Mosi-Oa-Tunya; 0213 322002; 08.00–18.00 Mon–Fri, 08.00–14.00 Sat) in the centre of town in a sprawling complex of banks and shops. If you splurge on a giant wooden giraffe or a heavy sculpture at the curio market, there are reliable international **couriers** (DHL and Fedex) who can assist.

CAR REPAIRS AND SPARES The two biggest workshops in town are **Foley's Africa** [508 C3] (639 Industrial Rd; 0213 320888; e info@foleysafrica.com, foleyscape@ foleysafrica.com; w foleysafrica.com; 08.00–17.00 Mon–Fri, 08.00–13.00 Sat), which caters for Land Rovers; and Bennet Quality Engineering, also known as **Harry's Workshop** [508 C3] (0213 322380; m 0978 308936; e hbennett@iconnect. zm), opposite Falls Park. Bennett services most of the tour operators' vehicles in town and is your best bet for more serious problems. For more basic repairs, punctures and tyre repairs, the main fuel stations will usually have someone who can assist. If it's parts or vehicle accessories that you need, the most central place is the large, well-signed **Autoworld** [512 A2] (Mosi-oa-Tunya Rd; 0213 320264; e autoworld@zamtel.zm).

HEALTH Medical facilities are limited in Livingstone, but in the event of an emergency you can contact the facilities listed here. For serious situations, SES (see below) are the country's premier emergency response unit, with a first-class service. Should you need an **optician**, head for Falls Park shopping centre [508 C3] or try Sunbird Opticians [512 D4] (3 Nongo Kalimba House, Mosi-oa-Tunya Rd) or Starlite Opticians [512 B2] (357 Mosi-oa-Tunya Rd). For toiletries or medicines, there are several good **pharmacies**. Each has a trained pharmacist, who can also offer advice on medications and fill prescriptions.

Dr Shafik's Hospital [512 G2] 1115 Katete Av; 0213 321130 (24hrs); m 955/966/977 863000; e shafikhosp@rocketmail.com. Dr Shafik is a surgeon & the hospital can also provide doctor consultations, nursing care & medication.

Health & Glow Pharmacy [512 B2] Mosi-oa-Tunya Rd; m 0967 319251, 0961 457104; w healthandglowpharmacy.com; 08.00–19.00 Mon–Sat, 09.00–13.00 Sun. With branches opposite Mosi-oa-Tunya Sq [513 C6] & next to Munali Café these well-stocked shops have helpful, knowledgeable staff.

L F Moore Chemists [512 B1] 133 Akapelwa St; 0213 321640; 08.00–17.00 Mon–Fri, 08.00–13.00 Sat. Established in 1936, L F Moore is a Livingstone institution. It remains one of the best-stocked chemists in town, with friendly staff who will go out of their way to help.

Speciality Emergency Services [512 E2] (SES) Emergency control centre; m 977 770302, 0962 740300, 977 740306/8; e livingstoneparamedics@ ses-zambia.com; w ses-zambia.com. Rapid emergency response teams with air ambulances can be deployed 24/7 from Lusaka & Kitwe, plus helicopters stationed in Livingstone.

The area around Victoria Falls has been a major crossroads for travellers for over a hundred years, from the early missionaries and traders to the backpackers, overland trucks and package tourists of the last few decades. Apart from simply marvelling at one of the world's greatest waterfalls, there are now lots of ways to occupy yourself for a few days.

VICTORIA FALLS The Falls are 1,688m wide and average just over 100m in height. Around 550 million litres (750 million during peak months) cascade over the lip every minute, making this one of the world's greatest waterfalls. Closer inspection shows that this immense curtain of water is interrupted by gaps, where small islands stand on the lip of the Falls. These effectively split the Falls into smaller waterfalls, which are known as (from west to east) the Devil's Cataract, the Main Falls, the Horseshoe Falls, the Rainbow Falls and the Eastern Cataract.

Around the Falls is a genuinely important and interesting rainforest, with plant species (especially ferns) rarely found elsewhere in Zimbabwe or Zambia. These are sustained by the clouds of spray that blanket the immediate vicinity of the Falls. You'll find various monkeys and baboons here, while the lush canopy shelters Livingstone's lourie, among other birds.

The flow, and hence the spray, is greatest just after the end of the rainy season – around March or April, depending upon the rains. It then decreases gradually until about December, when the rains in western Zambia will start to replenish the river. During low water, a light raincoat (available for rent on site) is very useful for wandering between the viewpoints on the Zimbabwean side, though it's not necessary in Zambia. However, in high water a raincoat is largely ineffective as the

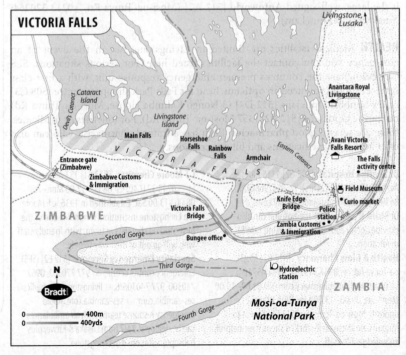

spray blows all around and soaks you in seconds. Anything that you want to keep dry must be wrapped in several layers of plastic or, even better, zip-lock plastic bags. The Falls never seem the same twice, so try to visit several times, under different light conditions. At sunrise, both Danger Point and Knife-edge Point are fascinating – position yourself carefully to see your shadow in the mists, with three concentric rainbows appearing as halos. (Photographers will find polarising filters invaluable in capturing the rainbows on film, as the light from the rainbows at any time of day is polarised.) Moonlight is another fascinating time, when the Falls take on an ethereal glow and the waters blend into one smooth mass that seems frozen over the rocks.

On the Zambian side (entry international visitors US$20/10/free adult/child/ under 6; vehicle US$5; gate ☉ 06.00–18.00 daily) Viewing the Falls here could not be easier, and every season brings a reason to visit. For photographers, the area is best explored in the early morning, when the sun is behind you and illuminates the Falls, or in the late afternoon when you may catch a stunning sunset. If you visit when the river is at its lowest, towards the end of the dry season, then the channels on the Zambian side may have dried up. Yet, while the Falls will be less spectacular then, their fascinating geology, normally obscured by spray, is revealed.

Viewing the Falls by moonlight (US$100 pp) is possible for four days at full moon, including two days before and one day after. Watch for a lunar rainbow at this time, too; it's an amazing sight. It's best not to go alone, as elephants occasionally wander about.

While you can easily explore on your own, most tour operators offer excellent guided tours of the Falls (both Zimbabwe & Zambia sides; around US$25–35 pp inc entrance fees) and the surrounding area, either stand alone or in combination with historical, cultural, game viewing and other sightseeing tours. These are highly informative, with professional guides offering detailed explanations of the formation of the Falls and gorges, the river, local history and flora and fauna.

From the Zimbabwean side (entry international visitors US$50/25/free adult/ child/under 6; lunar tour US$100; ☉ Sep–Apr 06.00–18.00 daily, May–Aug 06.30– 18.00 daily) Viewing the Falls is more regulated here, and may be easiest organised through a tour operator, who will also handle transport and visas to cross the border (US$55/70 sgl/dbl entry for UK, Irish & Canadian citizens; US$30/45 sgl/ dbl entry for citizens of USA, Australasia & much of Europe).

If you're planning to visit independently, allow at least half a day, and expect a fair delay at the border. Tickets are valid for the whole day, so you can return for no extra cost during the same day – though be prepared for the generally pleasant but very persistent vendors and 'guides' along the way.

LIVINGSTONE ISLAND (US$110 inc transfers, park fees, guide & gourmet meal; ☏ 0213 327450; m 0978 291886; e livingstoneisland@greensafaris.com; w livingstoneisland.com) Livingstone Island (also known as Namakabwa Island) lies in the middle of the great waterfall, and is the island from which Dr Livingstone first viewed the Falls. Trips are run exclusively by Green Safaris at Tongabezi (page 516) between July and March (subject to water levels), with guests transferred to the island from the Royal Livingstone launch site by boat. There you'll have the opportunity to take in the scene – gazing over the edge, perhaps chancing a thrilling dip in the Devil's Pool right on the Falls edge, and having a meal in an exclusive setting. Five trips are offered daily; choose either morning (called 'breezer'), with a full English breakfast, or go for lunch, or afternoon high tea with a full bar.

When the water's at its lowest (October–November), you can sometimes walk across the top of the Falls, climbing over rocks, exploring pot-holes and crossing small streams along the way – it's even possible to swim at the very edge of the Falls at the right time of year. These activities are only permitted if booked through Tongabezi.

RIVER CRUISES Floating on the Upper Zambezi with a glass in one hand, and a pair of binoculars in the other, is one of the region's highlights. Nowadays booze-cruise boats operate round the clock – and sometimes all congregate close together – but this is still a great way to take a gentle look around the Zambezi's islands, with national parks on both sides of the river. Most elegant of the river boats are the *African Queen* (sunset cruise US$75 pp; b/fast, mid-morning or lunch cruise US$65 pp; all inc open bar & a meal or canapés) and the *Lady Livingstone* (sunset cruise US$75 pp, inc drinks & snacks, exc US$10 park fees; b/fast cruise US$75 pp; lunch cruise US$80 pp), whose most popular excursions are the sunset cruises, which include a hotel pick-up. Smaller, less formal craft ply the same route at rather lower cost, with several leaving from Victoria Falls Waterfront Lodge (page 515).

FISHING EXCURSIONS (Angle Zambia; m 977 707829; e info@anglezam.co.zm; w zambezifishing.com; US$125/255 ½/full day inc lunch; multi-day trips on request) The Zambezi River is synonymous with great fishing for prized tiger fish and Zambezi bream. Angle Zambia, with their excellent local knowledge and friendly, personalised service, is highly recommended. Owner-operated by Vivienne Simpson, it runs half- and full-day fishing trips on the Upper Zambezi, about 30km from Livingstone, catering to both novice and experienced anglers, as well as fly-fishermen.

THRILLS AND SPILLS The Falls area is indisputably *the* adventure capital of southern Africa. There is an amazing and seemingly endless variety of ways to get your shot of adrenalin, though none comes cheaply. If you wish to do multiple activities, check out the many combination packages on offer as these can be slightly cheaper than booking individually. Whatever you plan, expect to sign an indemnity form before your activity starts.

Flight of Angels Named after Livingstone's famous comment, 'Flight of Angels' describes any sightseeing trip over the Falls by microlight or helicopter. This is a good way to get a feel for the geography of the area, and is surprisingly worthwhile. If you're arriving from Kasane, or leaving for there, consider combining a sightseeing flight and an air transfer.

Microlight Essentially sightseeing from a propeller-powered armchair 500m above the ground, this is the closest you'll get to soaring like a bird over the Falls. Microlights are affected by the slightest turbulence, so if you book in advance, it's best to specify early morning or late afternoon, when conditions are ideal.

Helicopter The most expensive way to see the Falls is tremendous fun. A 15-minute trip takes in the Falls and the national park, or for 30 minutes you will fly over the gorges below the Falls as well; at extra cost, you can stop in the gorge for a picnic, or – if you plan to raft or riverboard – you save yourself the walk up and take an exhilarating helicopter lift instead, gaining an aerial view of the Falls and Zambezi gorges.

Bungee jumping Organised by an offshoot of the original New Zealand bungee pioneers, you jump – solo or tandem – from the middle of the main bridge between Zambia and Zimbabwe. With the Zambezi 111m below you, it is among the highest commercial bungee jumps in the world, and not for the nervous.

Bridge walks There's no-one better positioned to show you the ins and outs (or the ups and downs!) of the Victoria Falls Bridge than the bungee folks, whose intimate bridge knowledge will not only fascinate you but have you clambering around and underneath the bridge like a monkey. With safety harness on and accompanied by a guide, you have the opportunity to explore the bridge's superstructure while hearing all about its construction and riveting history. While not as adrenalin-charged as bungee jumping, it's still bound to get your heart beating faster as you navigate your way high above the Zambezi.

Abseiling, high-wiring, gorge swing and slide A popular option on the adventure menu is the Zambezi swing, a cable swing set across the gorge which, together with a 90m-high cable slide (flying fox), abseiling (rappelling) and 'rap' jumps (rappelling forwards) down the side of the gorge, offers daring fun for all ages.

Swing participants are harnessed to ropes attached to the cable's sliding pulley and, after stepping off the cliff face, experience a heart-stopping 53m, three-second free-fall, followed by an exhilarating pendulum-like swing across the gorge, accelerating up to 140km/h (with a pull of roughly 2½ times that of gravity) for some 2 minutes before being lowered to the ground. It's definitely not for the faint-hearted, though participants of all ages are welcome. It's even possible to try it out in tandem.

Slightly tamer is the high wire or flying fox, set on another static cable stretched across the gorge. With harness and pulley, you leap off a platform and 'fly' (slide) across the gorge some 90m above the ground. It can be done in either a sitting or a flying position, and is suitable for children.

Canoeing on the Upper Zambezi Canoeing down the Upper Zambezi is a cool occupation on hot days, and the best way to explore the upper river, its islands and channels. Zimbabwe's Zambezi National Park stretches all along the western shore providing ample opportunity for game viewing, while lodges, farms, villages and bush dot the Zambian side as you head downstream. The silence of canoes makes them ideal for floating up to antelope, elephants or crocodiles. Birdlife is prolific – you may hear the cry of the African fish eagle or see pied kingfishers hover and dive. Hippos provide the excitement, and are treated with respect and given lots of space. All canoe trips are accompanied by a licensed river guide, and sometimes also a motorboat for additional safety. Canoes range from two-seater open-decked kayaks to inflatable 'crocodiles'.

No prior canoeing experience is necessary, and once you are used to the water, the better guides will encourage you to concentrate on the wildlife.

White-water rafting The Zambezi below the Falls is one of the world's most renowned stretches of white water. The rapids below the Falls are mostly graded IV and V – somewhere between 'very difficult' and 'for experts only' – but the majority of them don't need skill to manoeuvre the boat once it is within the rapids, so absolute beginners are usually allowed to take part. Nevertheless, although a trained river guide pilots every raft, you should think very carefully about committing yourself if you have no experience. Boats do flip over, and the consequences can be severe. It's also important to ensure that your chosen operator will give a thorough safety briefing before departure, explaining what to do in the event of a capsize.

Rafting is offered from both Zambia and Zimbabwe, but the entry points and length of trips vary according to the water levels. From July to January, when the water is low, and the river's waves and troughs (or 'drops') are more pronounced, there are full- or half-day trips, while in high-water months (February to July), only half-day trips are offered. If the water is too high, rafting is suspended until it recedes to a safer level.

River-boarding Thrilling for the fit who swim strongly, river-boarding is not for the faint of heart. After donning fins, lifejacket and helmet, you and your foam board (the size of a small surfboard) will be taught the basic skills before getting an opportunity to 'surf' the big waves of the Zambezi – accompanied by a safety raft. Experts can stand, but most will surf on their stomachs.

White-water kayaking Even those without experience can try tandem kayaking with a qualified guide, who manoeuvres the kayak through rapids while you assist with paddle power. All participants must be confident swimmers.

Jet-boating Undertaken in a 22-seater, 700-horsepower jet boat on the flatter sections of water (between rapids 23 and 27), the trip up and down the river reaches speeds of up to 90km/h, with 30 minutes of sharp turns and swift navigation of the small rapids ensuring that all occupants of the boat get suitably wet.

ROYAL LIVINGSTONE EXPRESS (Bushtracks, page 511; dinner train Nov–Apr 16.00 Wed & Sat, May–Oct 17.00 Wed & Sat; Sun lunch safari if enough demand; US$170 pp inc transfers, dinner & drinks; children welcome, recommended age 12+) The whistle of a steam loco rarely fails to stir a frisson of excitement, and Livingstone's foray into steam has proved a considerable success since its inaugural journey in late 2007. A joint venture between Bushtracks and Sun International, the train brings Zambia's railway history to life. It is pulled by one of two locomotives, the tenth-class *Princess of Mulobezi*, built in Glasgow in 1924 for Rhodesian Railways, or *Loco 204*, a 12th-class locomotive originally built in 1924. Both have been restored with meticulous attention and the locos and attendant wooden carriages are polished until they gleam. The train starts its 15km journey in a purpose-built station next to the Bushtracks office, getting up steam as it passes excited children and families gathering for the evening meal, heading to the Victoria Falls Bridge in time to witness the sun set behind the Falls. Wine, beer and soft drinks are served in air-conditioned comfort, with a cash bar on board for those who prefer spirits. Large windows, as well as an observation car, ensure good visibility for all, with game such as elephants and antelope often spotted en route to the bridge. After a 20-minute sundowner on the bridge itself, an unhurried five-course dinner is served as the train makes its way back towards Livingstone, prepared and served by staff from the Royal Livingstone Hotel, in an atmosphere enhanced by soft lighting and classical music.

CULTURAL ATTRACTIONS AND TOURS
Livingstone Museum [512 A2] (Mosi-oa-Tunya Rd; w livingstonemuseum. org; US$5/3 adult/child; ⏲ 09.00–16.30 daily) Livingstone's main museum more than justifies a visit. There's an excellent three-dimensional map showing how the

Zambezi River flows over Victoria Falls and downstream into the gorges, which puts everything into good perspective. There are several galleries focusing on the origins of humans in Zambia, the history of man in the country up to the modern age, the natural history of the area and an impressive gallery on traditional village life including a life-size village household. Watch out, too, for the David Livingstone gallery, with a unique collection of the famous explorer's personal possessions, including many of his letters: it's a must. The staff are friendly and knowledgeable and guided tours are included.

Railway Museum [~37d A8] (National Heritage Conservation Commission; Chishimba Falls Rd; US$15/7 adult child; ⊕ 08.30–16.30 daily) This collection of beautifully preserved old steam locomotives and memorabilia, and displays on railway history, originally belonged to the artist David Shepherd. It celebrates the iron horse's history in Livingstone since the 3ft 6in narrow-gauge railway was built by the British in 1905. Sadly a serious fire took its toll on the collections, but the engines themselves are in good condition, and will be of interest to railway buffs. There is also a small but informative Jewish museum on the site, a research centre and one of the oldest libraries in Zambia (⊕ 09.00–17.00 Mon–Fri).

Field Museum [map, page 522] Directly across from the entrance gate to Victoria Falls, this is signed as an information centre, but is more of a small interpretation centre. It's well worth a visit for an understanding of the geology, archaeology and history of the Falls.

Markets Livingstone has many colourful local markets. In addition to the large and fascinating Maramba Market [512 G4], there is also Porter's Market [512 G2] further north. For something smaller and closer to town, try Zimbabwe/Central/Town Centre Market [512 B2]. These markets offer everything from fresh produce to hand-crafted wood furniture and more. Bushtracks (page 511) runs 1½-hour **market tours** (US$54 pp).

Livingstone is one of the best places in Zambia to buy **crafts**. Just beside the entrance to the Falls is an outstanding curio market. The traders come from as far as the Democratic Republic of Congo and Malawi. In town, at **Mukuni Park Curio Market** [512 E3], craftsmen and traders sell their wares from stalls along the edge of the park. Both of these are excellent places to buy wooden handicrafts and are open during daylight hours throughout the week. The best buys are makenge baskets (these come exclusively from Zambia's Western Province), malachite and excellent-quality, heavy wood animal carvings. However, do consider the ethics of encouraging any further exploitation of hardwoods. Note, too, that some wooden items, especially wooden salad bowls and tall giraffes, are prone to cracking once you get them home due to changes in climate, and that very rarely are 'antiques' sold at craft markets anything other than fakes. Unless you have the expertise to tell the difference, it's better to buy such artefacts from a reputable shop in town.

Vendors will vie hard for your attention, and you can expect to bargain hard. When you start to pay, you will realise how sophisticated the traders are about their currency conversions, reminding you to double-check any exchange rates. Traders will accept most currencies and sometimes credit cards.

For something rather less demanding, there's an ad hoc craft and curio market in the car park at the Falls Park shopping centre [508 C3]. Buying items from street traders, however, is illegal, so stick to the designated markets.

Village visits (Mukuni Village: US$40 with Bushtracks, page 511; US$55 with SafPar, page 511) While some of the lodges organise independent visits to local villages, there are also several organised trips to different locations. Most popular among these is **Mukuni village,** east of the Falls. An organised tour here, lasting around 2½ hours, will give you a glimpse of how local people live and work in a traditional setting along with informative explanations. Further afield is **Songwe village**, about a 40-minute drive through the bush, and less commercial as it receives fewer tourists. The **Livingstone Quad Company** (contact Livingstone's Adventure, page 511) also offers guided quad-bike excursions to villages and the bush (US$140 pp; ⊕ 07.00–14.00 daily).

Historical and heritage tours Livingstone, the capital of Northern Rhodesia from 1907 to 1935, has a fascinating history marked by many old historical buildings and accented by colourful characters, intriguing tales and a once-vibrant social life. A guided historical tour (US$54 pp for 1½ hrs with Bushtracks, page 511; US$60 pp for 2½hrs with Wild Side, page 511) traces the town's history from frontier town to modern-day tourist capital.

Alternatively, the 'Mists of Time' tour (Bushtracks, page 511; ½ day US$137 pp, inc park fees & bottled water, min 4 people) takes in the Falls and one of the local villages. In the hands of Russell Gammon, whose family history in Africa dates back to the 19th century, the tour brings these sites to life through the stories of those who have left their mark on Livingstone over the years.

SPAS Many of Livingstone's hotels and lodges have small gyms, trained massage therapists and even tennis courts for their guests to use. Some of the better spas that welcome walk-in guests are **David Livingstone Safari Lodge & Spa** (page 514) and **Royal Livingstone Spa** (m 0978 7770447; w anatara.com).

WILDLIFE ENCOUNTERS
Mosi-oa-Tunya National Park (Park entry US$10; self-drive US$15 pp/day & vehicle US$15/day; guided game drive US$50 pp; game walk US$85 pp) Much of the Zambian area around the Falls is protected within the Mosi-oa-Tunya National Park. The park boasts tracts of riverine vegetation, dry mixed woodland and mopane trees. A few hours' driving could yield sightings of most of the common antelope and some fine giraffe, as well as buffalo, elephant and zebra. Although outside of the historical range of the white rhino, several attempts have been made to establish a population in the park. Today, only one white rhino remains. Always protected by armed rangers, it can sometimes be spotted from game drives, but a rhino walk with **Livingstone Rhino Walking Safaris** (US$105 pp; ☏ 0213 322267; w livingstonerhinosafaris.com) will give you a much better chance of a sighting, and a much closer experience. Wild dog are also present: a pack recently crossed the river from Zimbabwe. There are, however, no lion, leopard or other cats present.

Birdwatching Even the casual visitor with little interest will often see fish eagles, Egyptian geese, numerous kingfishers, bee-eaters, Hadeda and sacred ibis, and various other storks, egrets and herons. Meanwhile, avid birders will be seeking the more elusive birds like the rare Taita falcon, as Batoka Gorge (downstream from the Falls) is one of the best sites to look for them. Birdwatching excursions are an offered activity at many of the lodges along the river, often included in the nightly rate. Experienced guides can take you out either on foot or on the river. Alternatively, you can arrange to go out with a knowledgeable member of BirdWatch Zambia (w birdwatchzambia.org), who will be able to guide you to some great viewing spots and help with identification and general birding knowledge.

Horseriding Riding along the Zambezi and through the bush is a wonderful way to experience nature up close. Trips for all levels are offered from the fantastic stables at Chundukwa River Lodge (w chundukwariverlodge.com). The extremely experienced team here are skilled at pairing riders with suitable horses. All of the horses are well cared for and well behaved. Trips can last an hour to half a day and there are also champagne breakfast trips, or pony trails led by a guide on foot for younger children.

Livingstone Reptile Park [508 C4] (Gwembe Safaris; 🅕 livingstonecrocpark; w gwembesafrais.com; ⏱ 08.00–17.00 Thu–Tue; US$15/7.50 adult/child) Just to the south of Livingstone, the Reptile Park (still signposted 'Livingstone Crocodile Park') offers the opportunity to see some huge crocs at close quarters – from behind the safety of a chain-link fence or from covered walkways. Well-informed and friendly guides offer explanations about the behaviour and history of the animals, and feeding times (usually early afternoon) are posted at the entrance. The park also features some of Zambia's snakes, housed in glass cages. It, hopefully, will be your only chance to see Africa's most dangerous snakes – black mamba, cobra, puff adder – up close and personal; you can even hold the 'safe' snakes to get a feel for them.

Walking with lions and cheetah The opportunity to walk with lion cubs and cheetah is well advertised in Livingstone. The animals are bred specially for these programmes and for some visitors the activity is clearly very appealing and unusual. The authors' personal views are that this venture is unethical, and we would urge anyone considering taking part to read about the controversy surrounding this activity: it is well documented.

Appendix 1

TRACKS AND SIGNS

An extract from Southern African Wildlife: A Visitor's Guide *by Mike Unwin*

Animals seldom parade across the bush the way they do across a TV screen. In fact, the untamed wilderness, far from teeming with wall-to-wall wildlife, can sometimes seem a disappointingly empty place. But there is much more to see than simply the animals themselves, and the trained eye will find the land littered with evidence of their presence or passing: tracks and trails, pellets and droppings, diggings and rubbings, torn branches, flattened grass, feathers, nests and bones. These clues, often known by the Afrikaans word spoor, tell the story of what happened when nobody was looking.

Some awareness of tracks and signs will greatly enrich your own understanding of wildlife. Trackers, like forensic detectives, combine acute eyesight and vigilance with great patience, a photographic memory and the imagination to reconstruct a complete picture from a few scattered fragments. It is a humbling experience to watch an expert in action: a mere scratch in the soil can not only identify the animal responsible, but also reveal its age, sex, size, where it was heading, how it was moving, when it passed by and why.

MAKING TRACKS Every animal that touches the ground leaves tracks. Some are easily recognised; others are more puzzling. Most small creatures, such as lizards, can only be identified to a broad generic level, but many larger mammal species have unique signatures. No two individuals of any species are identical, and the tracks of many show marked differences of size and shape between forefeet and hindfeet or between male and female. Conditions underfoot are critical to tracking. The clearest tracks are laid on surfaces that hold an impression, such as firm mud or damp sand. Hard, baked soil is too resistant, while soft sand allows slippage that distorts the shape.

Weather is also important: wind and rain can help to date tracks, but may erode or completely obliterate them. Neither overcast weather nor a midday sun are very helpful to trackers. Early morning is the best time to look – partly because tracks are still fresh, but also because the low light and slanting shadows throw any imprint into sharper relief.

The heavy brigade The bigger the animal, the harder its footfall. Elephants leave huge, round tracks, up to half a metre across, with the hindfeet smaller and more oval than the forefeet. In soft mud they create knee-deep craters that become sunbaked into a treacherous pitted moonscape. On hard ground, the latticework of cracks on their soles leaves a distinct, mosaic-like impression, even though the circular track outline may be invisible. A small heap of soil in front of each print indicates the elephant's direction (the rear of each track shows a clean edge). Rhino tracks have a cloverleaf shape, with each foot showing three distinct toes. On hard ground only the curved outer rim of each toenail may be visible. White rhinos have larger tracks (up to 30cm long) than black rhinos (about 24cm), with relatively broader toe marks. Hippos leave tracks of a similar size, but spaced more closely together and showing four clear toes on each foot. Their regular trails to and from water leave two, deep, parallel ruts either side of a central ridge.

On the hoof
Most ungulates leave symmetrical cloven-hoofed tracks. Those of antelope differ in little other than size, though some, like an impala's, are pointed, while others, like a kudu's, are more rounded. Identification often depends upon other clues: for example, an impala's tracks are likely to be in a herd and unlikely to be on a hillside. A few antelope show more unusual tracks: a sitatunga's are very long (over 15cm in the male) and widely splayed for bounding over marshy terrain, while klipspringers drill neat round holes with their cylindrical tip-toed hooves. A giraffe's enormous hooves (up to 20cm long) leave imprints like a steam iron, spaced far apart by its great stride. A buffalo has tracks like a cow's – larger and rounder than any antelope's except an eland. A warthog's are also quite rounded, with the two halves clearly separated. Zebra, with only a single big hoof on each foot, leave horseshoe tracks, the size of a donkey's.

Pads, paws and claws
Most predator tracks show the typical pad and toes arrangement of domestic cats and dogs. The crucial things to look for are size, shape, number of toes and whether or not claws are visible. The male lion's are the biggest (up to 15cm long) and, like all cats, each shows four well-spaced, rounded toes and two small indentations in the back of the pad. Except for the cheetah, whose claws are permanently extended, cats do not leave claw marks. Conversely, all dog tracks show claws, and most have a longer, narrower shape than a cat's, with all four toes set in front of the pad. A hyena's tracks also show claws, but the curved toes are tucked closer together and the back of the pad slopes at a distinct diagonal. Spotted hyena tracks are about 10cm long, similar in size to a leopard's, and are commonly found around campsites. Mustelid tracks have five toes: an otter's show the hand-like spread of its dextrous fingers; a honey badger's show the furrows of its long claws, set well ahead of the toes. A genet's neat tracks resemble a tiny cat's – four-toed, clawless and rounded – but spaced close together by its short-legged gait. Most mongooses leave small, clawed tracks, some showing a fifth hind toe set back behind the four in front.

Mammal variations
An aardvark's tracks show only three toes on each foot, each one capped with a heavy claw mark, and its meandering trail is scattered with freshly excavated soil. Monkeys leave five-toed hand prints, with the opposable thumb or big toe clearly visible on each. A baboon's look particularly human, and are often confusingly overlaid where a whole troop has been active. A lesser bushbaby hops upright between trees, so leaves only the prints of its hindfeet. Squirrel tracks show longer hind feet than forefeet, and usually lead to and from a burrow or tree. A hare leaves tracks in sets of four, each of which shows the two front feet placed in line, one ahead of the other, and the overlapping back feet placed side-by-side in front. Rat and mice tracks are tiny and show four front toes, five hind toes and sometimes the drag mark of the tail.

Birds
Bird tracks can be roughly classified by the shape and arrangement of the toes. Most have three toes pointing forward and one back. In some, such as starlings or hornbills, the hind toe points straight back, while in others, such as doves, it is set at a slight angle. Korhaans and dikkops show no hind toe at all, while an ostrich shows only two toes in each of its enormous (20cm long) tracks and at least a metre's stride between them. The pattern of a bird's tracks reflects the way in which it moves: robins place both feet together in a series of well-spaced hops; doves follow a winding trail in which the feet move alternately in quick, short steps.

Scale trails
The undulating motion of a typical snake leaves a series of S-shaped ripples, where each curve has pushed against surface irregularities to propel the body forward. A

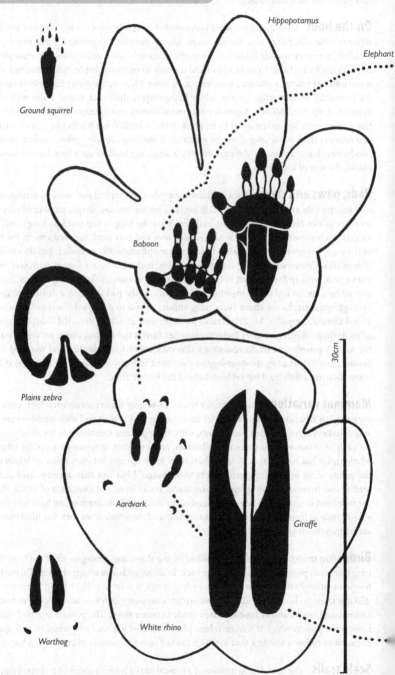

Hippopotamus

Elephant

Ground squirrel

Baboon

Plains zebra

30cm

Aardvark

Giraffe

White rhino

Warthog

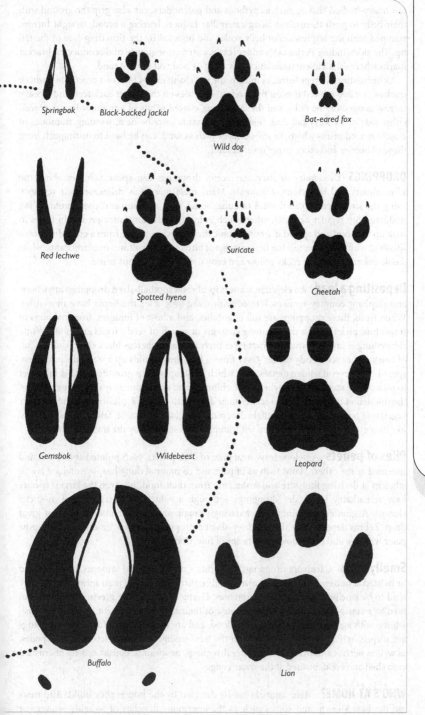

Springbok

Black-backed jackal

Wild dog

Bat-eared fox

Red lechwe

Suricate

Cheetah

Spotted hyena

Gemsbok

Wildebeest

Leopard

Buffalo

Lion

few heavy-bodied snakes, such as pythons and puff adders, can also grip the ground with their belly to push themselves along caterpillar-fashion, leaving a broad, straight furrow, stamped with the impression of belly scales and bisected by the thin drag-line of the tail tip. The sidewinding Peringuey's adder leaves a strange sequence of disconnected bracket marks where each violent undulation has flung its body off the hot sand.

Other distinctive reptile tracks include the riverbank mud-chute of a crocodile – whose tracks show five splayed toes on the forefeet, four toes on the longer back feet, and a heavy furrow gouged by the tail – and the large, long-clawed prints of a monitor lizard, spaced either side of its wavy tail drag line. Smaller lizards inscribe neat, winding tramlines of closely spaced prints which, in soft surfaces such as sand, can be hard to distinguish from those of beetles and other larger invertebrates.

DROPPINGS Unsavoury as they may seem, droppings can speak volumes about the whereabouts and behaviour of animals. Many male mammals delineate their territory using the strategically placed whiff of dung. Some, such as rhino and civet, build up big middens with regular deposits; others, such as hyena and many antelope, roll in theirs to soak up the scent and spread it around. Some droppings are visible from a great distance: a splash of white often reveals the nest or roost of birds such as vultures or cormorants, while dassie colonies stain the rocks yellow and brown with their viscous urine.

Depositing a load An elephant scatters its fibrous, football-sized droppings anywhere, and elephant country remains littered with dung long after the herds have moved on. When fresh, these droppings are full of goodies, and a host of foragers, from baboons to francolins, pick through the steaming contents in search of seeds, fruits and pods. White rhino dung is fine in texture, consisting entirely of grass, whereas black rhino dung is full of twigs and other woody matter. Over time, a bull rhino builds up a waist-deep midden, spread over several square metres, into which he scrapes deep grooves with his hind feet to pick up the scent. In areas where both rhino species occur, one may deposit its dung on the midden of the other. Hippo scatter their dung with their tail, plastering it messily over vegetation beside their trails. Buffalo droppings are black and loose, falling in folded 'pats' like domestic cattle's, and are often left trampled and smeared by the traffic of the herd.

Piles of pellets Antelope leave neat piles of dark pellets, each pointed at one end and indented at the other. Many, such as impala, use communal dung heaps. Antelope are so efficient at deriving moisture and sustenance from their food that even the largest species have remarkably small, dry droppings – though a wildebeest's may congeal in sticky clumps. A giraffe's droppings, also amazingly small, are widely scattered by their great drop. Zebras deposit their dark, kidney-shaped droppings in neat mounds, which grow paler with age and break down into heaps of fine, dry grass.

Smelly scats Carnivore droppings – or scats – are cylindrical sausages, often pointed or twisted at one end – as any dog-owner will confirm. Because of their meat content, they tend to be smellier than those of herbivores. Hyena droppings are green when fresh, but turn to a conspicuous chalky white because of their high bone content. A lion's may also whiten with age, but can be black with blood, and are usually full of fur. Civet droppings are surprisingly large, and often contain the hard undigested exoskeletons of millipedes, as well as berries and insect husks. Otter droppings, or spraints, consist mostly of crushed crab shell and are deposited at the water's edge.

WHO'S AT HOME? Many animals can be detected by the homes they build. Bird nests are the best known, and some, such as the enormous thatches of sociable weavers or hammerkops often provide shelter for a whole community of other animals. Tree holes offer a desirable residence to anything from hornbills and hoopoes to bushbabies and squirrels, and a promising-looking cavity is always worth watching during the breeding season. Burrows should be checked for signs of life: a complex of small holes may indicate a mongoose or ground squirrel colony, while a big burrow may house either the aardvark that dug it, or more recent tenants such as warthogs, wildcats or porcupines – so look out for signs of occupation, such as a snake skin or porcupine quill.

The state of an area's vegetation can also betray local residents with no permanent home. A flattened depression in long grass might be where a waterbuck bedded down for the night, while tattered bushes could be the work of a territorial bull sable, who thrashes them with his horns. Deep parallel gashes gouged into a tree trunk are the calling card of the local leopard, and a shiny tree stump beside a mud wallow is a 'rubbing post', polished to a smooth finish by generations of itchy rhinos.

FEEDING SIGNS A good look at the landscape soon reveals who had what for dinner. Elephant are the messiest of eaters: freshly broken branches, peeled strips of bark and tussocks of grass tossed across the track are all sure signs of their presence, as are deep holes dug in sandy riverbeds for fresh water. Big grazers such as hippo or rhino trim clearly defined and well-managed lawns. Giraffe prune thorn trees up to a height of 6m, creating a visible browse line, and leave glistening strings of saliva in overhead branches. Kudu leave bushes frayed and nibbled at head height, while black rhino will even munch thorny, poisonous euphorbias, sometimes demolishing them entirely. Many smaller animals also refashion the landscape in their search for food: bark stripped from the foot of a tree trunk is probably the work of porcupines; excavations at the base of an anthill show where an aardvark dug for termites; a hillside littered with overturned stones shows the methodical foraging of baboons for lizards and scorpions.

Predators usually leave evidence of their kills, though even a large carcass quickly disappears beneath an army of scavengers, as hyenas scatter the bones, vultures strip the skin, blowfly maggots consume the final shreds of flesh and ants clean the last drops of blood from the soil. Even the keratin of an antelope horn is food for the larvae of the horn-boring moth, which leaves strange tubular casts along its length. Leopards often cheat scavengers, at least for a while, by hoisting their kill into a tree, so look out for hooves overhead. A scattering of feathers may reveal the regular plucking post of a raptor – which tears out tough flight feathers individually, leaving small, V-shaped punctures on the shafts, whereas a mammalian predator rips them out in clumps, shearing right through the quills with its teeth. Owls and other birds of prey regurgitate pellets of undigested bones and fur, often found beneath their roosts, while some shrikes impale prey such as lizards and grasshoppers on acacia thorns and barbed-wire fences.

Appendix 2

Setswana is the national language of Botswana, while English is the official language. In practice, though many people speak other languages at home, most will be able to converse in Setswana. English will be spoken by those who have been to school, or who have been outside the country. In a country with a high level of education, this means most people, with the exception of the older generation in rural areas.

Learning to speak a little Setswana is easy and, even in educated circles, trying to speak a few words of the language will mark you out as showing respect for the country's culture. It will open many doors, and will really make a difference to how you are received. Carry the most important phrases on a slip of paper, and practise whenever you can.

PRONUNCIATION Setswana is not entirely phonetic, and some letters may not be pronounced. The only difficult sound is the g, usually pronounced like ch in the Scottish 'loch' or German 'ich'. If you have trouble with that, just say the g like an ordinary h. The r is often rolled, especially if it's written 'rr'. Vowels and other consonants are pronounced as follows:

a	like a in China	th	like t in table
e	like ay in day	u	like oo in too
i	like ee in see	x	like k in kite (also used
o	like o in go		to represent a click, as
ph	like p in put		in Nxai)

GREETINGS Greetings are relatively easy to master, as you can practise them with everyone you meet. They'll also get you instant results; using them is almost guaranteed to bring a smile to the face of those you greet – while sending out the message that you're not an arrogant foreigner who can't be bothered to learn a word of Setswana. So even if you never master anything else in Setswana, do learn the basic greetings and it'll make your trip so much easier and more pleasant.

English	Setswana
Words in underlined italics are optional	
Hello (literally 'Greetings Sir/Madam')	*Dumela Rra/Mma*
How did you rise?	*O tsogile jang?*
I have risen *well*	*Ke tsogile sentle*
How did you spend the day?	*O tlhotse jang?*
I spent the day *well*	*Ke tlhotse sentle*
How are you? (informal)	*O kae?*

I'm fine (lit, 'I'm here')	*Ke teng*
It's OK	*Go siame*
I am going	*Ke a tsamaya*
Stay well (said to someone staying)	*Sala sentle*
Go well (said to someone going)	*Tsamaya sentle*
Sleep well	*Robala sentle*

ESSENTIAL WORDS

Yes	*Ee*
No	*Nnyaa*
Thank you	*Ke aleboga, Ke itumetse* (lit, 'I am happy')
Excuse me!	*Sorry!*

BASIC QUESTIONS AND ANSWERS

What's your name? (formal)	*Leina la gago ke mang?*
My name is…	*Leina la me ke…*
Who are you? (informal)	*O mang?*
I'm…	*Ke…*
How goes it?	*Wa reng?*
It goes OK	*Ga ke bue*
Where are you (coming) from?	*O tswa kae?*
I'm (coming) from…	*Ke tswa kwa…*
Where are you going?	*O ya kae?*
I'm going to…	*Ke ya…*
What's the time?	*Nako ke mang?*
Where's the shop?	*Shopo e kae?*
What do you want?	*O batla eng?*
I want…	*Ke batla/kopa…*
There is none	*Ga go na*
How much?	*Ke bokae?*
It's expensive/cheap	*Go a tura/tshipi*
What is this *in Setswana*?	*Se ke eng ka <u>Setswana</u>?*
What do you do? (your job)	*O dira eng?*

NUMBERS Unusually, numbers are said in English.

FOOD AND DRINK

water	*metse*	sugar	*sukiri*
tea	*tee*	mealie meal	*dupr*
coffee	*kofee*	meat	*fnama*
milk	*mashi*		

OTHER USEFUL WORDS AND PHRASES

I don't know *Setswana*	*Ga ke itse <u>Setswana</u>*
It tastes good	*Go monate*
I'm satisfied (regarding food)	*Ke kgotshe*
Men/Women (written on toilets)	*Banna/Basadi*
Far/near	*Kgakala/gaufi*
I'm asking for money/tobacco	*Ke kopa madi/motsoko*
I have no money/tobacco	*Ga ke na madi/motsoko*

537

For more scientifically minded readers, here's a list of most of Botswana's main language groups, with their linguistic family roots and a few brief notes on where they're spoken. This tells you the history of that language, starting with the main group to which it belongs, and defining it more specifically; it is best read in conjunction with the whole section on social groups.

BANTU LANGUAGES

Setswana *Classification: Niger–Congo, Atlantic-Congo, Volta-Congo, Benue-Congo, Bantoid, Southern, Narrow Bantu, Central, S, Sotho-Tswana (S30), Tswana.* Around 70% of the population speak Setswana (also known as Tswana). Some official business is conducted in Setswana, the media often use English and Setswana interchangeably, and it's the lingua franca between different citizens who don't speak English.

Tswapong *Classification: Niger–Congo, Atlantic-Congo, Volta-Congo, Benue-Congo, Bantoid, Southern, Narrow Bantu, Central, S, Sotho-Tswana (S30), Tswapong.* Several thousand speakers, in the Central District and Mahalapye Sub-district.

Kagalagadi *Classification: Niger–Congo, Atlantic-Congo, Volta-Congo, Benue-Congo, Bantoid, Southern, Narrow Bantu, Central, S, Sotho-Tswana (S30), Kgalagadi.* Estimated total of about 35,000 speakers in Botswana.

Birwa *Classification: Niger–Congo, Atlantic-Congo, Volta-Congo, Benue-Congo, Bantoid, Southern, Narrow Bantu, Central, S, Sotho-Tswana (S30), Sotho.* Estimated total of about 10,000 speakers in Botswana.

Kalanga *Classification: Niger–Congo, Atlantic-Congo, Volta-Congo, Benue-Congo, Bantoid, Southern, Narrow Bantu, Central, S, Shona (S10).* Estimated total of about 160,000 speakers in Botswana.

Ndebele *Classification: Niger–Congo, Atlantic-Congo, Volta-Congo, Benue-Congo, Bantoid, Southern, Narrow Bantu, Central, S, Ngui.* Estimated total of about 10,000 speakers in the Northeast District, though this is the main language over the border in Zimbabwe's Matabele Province.

Herero *Classification: Niger–Congo, Atlantic-Congo, Volta-Congo, Benue-Congo, Bantoid, Southern, Narrow Bantu, Central, R, Herero.* Estimated total of about 31,000 speakers scattered among other ethnic groups in Botswana, often having their own area in towns and villages. This is one of Namibia's major ethnic groups.

Yeyi *Classification: Niger–Congo, Atlantic-Congo, Volta-Congo, Benue-Congo, Bantoid, Southern, Narrow Bantu, Central, R, Yeye.* Estimated total of about 27,000 speakers in Botswana, with probably another 20,000 ethnic Bayeyi who do not actually speak Yeyi.

Mbukushu *Classification: Niger–Congo, Atlantic-Congo, Volta-Congo, Benue-Congo, Bantoid, Southern, Narrow Bantu, Central, K, Kwangwa.* Estimated total of about 12,000 speakers in Botswana, located in the Northwest District, especially in Gumare and the villages to the north of there, and in the Okavango Delta.

Subiya *Classification: Niger–Congo, Atlantic-Congo, Volta-Congo, Benue-Congo, Bantoid, Southern, Narrow Bantu, Central, K, Subia (L50).* Estimated total of about 12,000 speakers in Botswana, mostly living in the Northwest and Chobe districts.

KHOISAN LANGUAGES

!Xoo *Classification: Khoisan, southern Africa, Southern, Hua.* There are between 3,000 and 4,000 speakers of this Khoisan language, and its related dialects, living in Botswana.

=/Hua *Classification: Khoisan, southern Africa, Southern, Hua.* Around 1,000–1,500 speakers, living mainly in the southern Kalahari Desert and the Kweneng District.

//Gana *Classification: Khoisan, southern Africa, Central Tshu-Khwe, Northwest.* Around 1,000 speakers living around the Ghanzi District, in villages and farms, and in the Central Kalahari Game Reserve. Speakers are also found in the Central District (Boteti Sub-district) and the cattle-posts south and west of Rakops.

/Anda *Classification: Khoisan, southern Africa, Central Tshu-Khwe, Northwest.* About 1,000 speakers live in the Northwest District, mostly around the Khwai River and Mababe Village areas.

Ksoe *Classification: Khoisan, southern Africa, Central Tshu-Khwe, Northwest.* Around 1,700–2,000 speakers, often known as the 'River Bushmen', live in and around the Northwest District, mainly in Gan, Cadikarauwe, Mohembo, Shakawe, Kaputura, /Ao-Kyao, Sikonkomboro, Ngarange, Sekanduko, Xongoa, Cauwe, Moxatce, Dungu, Seronga, Beyetca, Gudigoa, Sikokora, Geixa, /Qom-ca, Tobere, 0/Umbexa, Djaxo and Kangwara.

Deti *Classification: Khoisan, southern Africa, Central Tshu-Khwe, Central.* Spoken in the Central District, the Boteti Sub-district, and in the villages which are strung out along the Boteti River.

Nama *Classification: Khoisan, southern Africa, Central Tshu-Khwe, Central.* There are about 200–1,000 Nama speakers in Botswana, mostly in the Kgalagadi District around Tsabong, Makopong, Omaweneno and Tshane villages, and in the Ghanzi District, in the villages along the Ghanzi–Mamuno road. It's also spoken by a much larger population in Namibia.

Ganadi *Classification: Khoisan, southern Africa, Central Tshu-Khwe, North Central.* Spoken in the Northeastern area.

Shua *Classification: Khoisan, southern Africa, Central Tshu-Khwe, North Central.* Counted together with the Tshwa group, there are around 19,000 Shua speakers in Botswana, located in the Central District and Tutumi Sub-district.

//Gwi *Classification: Khoisan, southern Africa, Central, Tshu-Khwe, Southwest.* There are around 800 speakers in villages in the Kweneng and Ghanzi districts.

Naro *Classification: Khoisan, southern Africa, Central Tshu-Khwe, Southwest.* Botswana has an estimated 8,000 speakers of Naro.

Ju/'hoansi *Classification: Khoisan, southern Africa, Northern.* This is one of the larger Khoisan languages, with 4,000–8,000 speakers in Botswana, and many more in Namibia, around the Tsumkwe area.

=/Kx'au//'ein *Classification: Khoisan, southern Africa, Northern.* There are about 3,000 speakers in Botswana, mostly in the Ghanzi District, both in the villages and working on commercial farms.

EUROPEAN LANGUAGES
English *Classification: Indo-European, Germanic, West, English.* English is the official language in Botswana, the language of government and schools, although official work is increasingly being carried out in Setswana (Tswana).

Afrikaans *Classification: Indo-European, Germanic, West; Low Saxon-Low Franconian, Low Franconian.* There are some 20,000 people in Botswana whose native tongue is Afrikaans, mainly on the commercial farms in the Ghanzi District. Many of the white community with links to South Africa communicate in Afrikaans.

Appendix 3

BOOKS AND JOURNALS
Biography

Allison, Peter *Don't Run Whatever You Do: My Adventures as a Safari Guide* Nicholas Brealey Publishing, London, 2007. Light-hearted and easy reading, this behind-the-scenes series of anecdotes might just make you look at your safari guide in a new light.

Carruthers, Jane and Arnold, Marion *Life and Work of Thomas Baines* Fernwood Press, South Africa, 1995, reprinted 1996.

Davies, Caitlin *Place of Reeds: A True African Love Story* Simon & Schuster, London, 2006. Set in Maun in the early 1990s, this intensely personal and sometimes disturbing memoir is enriched by a very strong sense of place and a fascinating insight into the culture of northern Botswana.

Horton, Bernard *My Forever Heartache: Four Years of Discovery with the Kalahari Bushmen* Black Crake Books, Maun, 2013.

Owens, Mark and Delia *Cry of the Kalahari* HarperCollins, UK, 1986. A highly personal account of the authors' seven years in the Central Kalahari Game Reserve in the 1970s, during which time they conducted studies focusing largely on lions and brown hyena, and set up a conservation project.

Paton, Alan *Lost City of the Kalahari* University of KwaZulu Natal Press, South Africa, 2005. In 1886, the ruins of a 'lost city' in the Kalahari were described by G A Farin in *Through the Kalahari Desert*. Seventy years later, in 1956, seven adventurers set out in search of this mythical city, among them Alan Paton, author of *Cry, the Beloved Country*. This is the story of their expedition.

Slaughter, Carolyn *Before the Knife: Memories of an African Childhood* Doubleday, UK, 2002. For a young white girl, growing up in the British Protectorate of Bechuanaland was in itself unusual, but even in this context the author's childhood was outside the norm. Beyond her personal horror is pre-independence Botswana, described with both affection and, at times, a stark realism.

van der Post, Laurens *The Lost World of the Kalahari* Hogarth Press, London, 1958; many subsequent reprints by Penguin. Laurens van der Post's classic account of how he journeyed into the heart of the Kalahari Desert in search of a 'pure' Bushman group – eventually found at the Tsodilo Hills. His almost mystical description of the Bushmen is fascinating, so long as you can cope with the rather dated, turgid prose. You then need to read Robert J Gordon's very different book, *The Bushman Myth* (page 544), to put it in perspective.

Coffee-table picture books

Bailey, Adrian *Okavango: Africa's Wetland Wilderness* Struik Publishers, Cape Town, 1998. Bright colour plates and an informative text make this a good coffee-table overview of the Delta.

Balfour, Daryl and Sharna *Chobe: Africa's Untamed Wilderness* Southern Books, Johannesburg, 1997. An almost day-by-day account of a year that this renowned couple spent in Chobe and Selinda. Good pictures and a readable diary-format style give a fair picture of the changing seasons and the wildlife.

Forester, Bob, Murray-Hudson, Mike and Cherry, Lance *The Swamp Book: A View of the Okavango* Southern Books, Johannesburg, 1989. This interesting and quirky coffee-table book includes highly readable sections on the Okavango Delta and some of its more common flora and fauna, as well as comments on a few interesting historical accounts of travel there. Photographs include several taken underwater.

Gifford, James *Savute: Botswana's Wildlife Kingdom* HPH Publishing, South Africa, 2017. James Gifford's photographs capture both the drama and the wild beauty of the Savute region.

Lanting, Frans *Okavango: Africa's Last Eden* Chronicle Books, San Francisco, 1993. Probably the ultimate in coffee-table books includes minimal text but many impressive and beautiful images that were originally commissioned for *National Geographic* magazine.

McNutt, John and Boggs Ross, Lesley (text), Heldring, Hélène and Hamman, Dave (photography) *Running Wild: Dispelling the Myths of the African Wild Dog* Southern Books, Johannesburg, 1996. Some beautiful pictures of dogs in the Delta (the 'Mombo Pack' in the early 1990s) plus informative text about their behaviour and group dynamics – put into the context of observations made throughout northern Botswana.

Pickford, Peter and Beverly *The Miracle Rivers: The Okavango and Chobe of Botswana* Southern Books, Johannesburg, 1999. A coffee-table book with some colour plates and grainy black-and-white shots. The text is a mixture of quotes and travelogue with attention (and almost homage) paid to various hunting operations.

Ross, Karen *Okavango: Jewel of the Kalahari* BBC Enterprises Ltd, London, 1987. Written by Karen Ross in parallel with her research for a short series of films, produced by Partridge Films for the BBC. The film series is stunning, and certainly raised the UK's awareness of the Okavango Delta considerably when it was first shown. The book's also first class. Its photography is good, though not exceptional, but the depth of its text raises it well above the normal standard of coffee-table books. Though perhaps slightly dated now, it is still well worth getting hold of.

Walker, Clive *Savuti: The Vanishing River* Southern Books, Johannesburg, 1991. Using many simple line drawings, and just a sprinkling of generally impressive photographs, this is less pictorial than most coffee-table books. It concentrates mainly on Walker's personal experiences in Savuti, where he spent time with Lloyd Wilmot, among others, and witnessed the final drying out of the Savuti Channel. It's a good read, though too large to travel with easily.

Field guides

Although the choice of field guides continues to increase, those listed here are among the best. Top of your list should be Veronica Roodt's *Trees and Shrubs of the Okavango Delta*, even if you're not that interested in trees and shrubs. Serious birders should seek out *Birds of Botswana* while Richard Estes' *The Safari Companion* is a great general book on mammalian behaviour.

Butchart, Duncan *Wildlife of the Okavango: Common Animals and Plants* Struik Nature, Cape Town, 2000. Slim enough to take on a game drive, this handy guide with generally good photographs is an ideal first reference – albeit no substitute for a dedicated bird book.

Coates Palgrave, Keith and Coates Palgrave, Meg (eds) *Trees of Southern Africa* Struik, Cape Town, 3rd edn 2003. The definitive guide to the region's trees is a must-have for natural-history buffs.

Estes, Richard *The Safari Companion* Russell Friedman Books, South Africa, 1993 (co-published Tutorial Press, Zimbabwe and Chelsea Green Publishing, Vermont). While slightly too thick to be an ideal travelling companion, this is a real treasure chest of information on animal behaviour. It covers all the main animal species found in mainland Africa, from duikers and dwarf antelope to cats, dogs and the great apes. For each it includes a brief description of its social systems and forms of communication, along with helpful outlines of body postures and diagrams to explain typical forms of behaviour. If you've longed to decipher the language of animals, and have the time to stop and watch rather than simply tick game off a list, then you must bring this book.

Hancock, Peter and Randall, Richard *The Okavango Companion* Sandor Books, Maun, 2016. Covers most of the common animals and plants that you'll find in the Delta.

Hancock, Peter and Weiersbye, Ingrid *Birds of Botswana* Princeton University Press, New Jersey, 2016. A scholarly but very accessible field guide to Botswana's birds, with excellent illustrations. This is definitely the one for serious birders.

Newman, Kenneth *Newman's Birds of Southern Africa* Struik Publishers, South Africa, 2010. Republished numerous times since its first edition in 1988, Newman's has become one of the standard field guides to birds in southern Africa, south of the Kunene and Zambezi rivers. It also covers most species found in Zambia.

Roodt, Veronica *Common Wild Flowers of the Okavango Delta* Shell Oil Botswana, Gaborone, 1998. The second book in Shell's 'Field Guide' series is a little more specialist than the first book on trees, but still manages to comment on diverse topics from the formula for gunpowder to the treatment of scorpion stings. It's well worth getting, even for flower identification beyond the Delta.

Roodt, Veronica *Trees and Shrubs of the Okavango Delta* Shell Oil Botswana, Gaborone, 1998. This first book in Shell's 'Field Guide' series isn't just about trees or shrubs, and doesn't restrict its comments rigidly to the Okavango – but it is a masterpiece. Veronica Roodt has lived and worked in Moremi for many years, researching the plants of the area. This book is ostensibly just a field guide to slightly over 60 of the more common trees and shrubs in the area, but in reality it's a fascinating treatise on the insects and animals associated with all of them, plus the medicinal uses and local superstitions attached to each. It's well worth buying a copy even if you're not that interested in trees; it reads very well!

Roodt, Veronica *Wild Flowers, Waterplants and Grasses of the Okavango Delta and Kalahari* Veronica Roodt Publications, South Africa, 2011. Bringing together coverage of Chobe and the Makgadikgadi Pans as well as the Delta and the Kalahari, this field guide with excellent photographs is a must. There's also a companion volume, *Mammals of Botswana and Surrounding Areas.*

Sinclair, Ian, Ryan, Peter, Hockey, Phil and Tarboton, Warwick *Sasol Birds of Southern Africa* Struik, South Africa, 5th edn 2020. First published in 1993, so a more recent addition to the market than Newman's, this is particularly useful for the illustrations of birds at different stages of their development, and in flight.

Unwin, Mike *Southern African Wildlife* Bradt Guides, UK, 3rd edn 2022. A compact, single-volume guide to the habitats, identification and behavioural characteristics of the region's wildlife. A well-written text, which includes sections on tracks and signs, is matched by exceptionally good photographs.

Children's field guides I highly recommend The SASOL 'My first' guides series (Penguin Random House, South Africa) of A4 paperback books for young children (age 3–7) on safari. They are accurate, clearly organised, well illustrated and concisely written. The layout is good and the use of a graphic key means that even children who cannot read are able to decipher the pertinent points for each creature. Accompanying colouring books are available for many of the guides.

My First Book of Southern African Mammals 2008. 58 of the most common and popular African mammals with large colour illustrations, simple text and a key to the animals' size, tracks and diet.

My First Book of Southern African Animal Tracks 2014. A good tracking book with clear illustrations of the animal and its tracks, plus a scale to show the size of the tracks.

My First Book of Southern African Birds: Volume 1 2006. An excellent first reference book featuring the 56 most striking and commonly seen southern African bird species. Each page features a large illustration of each bird, with a small paragraph of information and a clear key to the food eaten, nesting style and the bird's track.

My First Book of Southern African Birds: Volume 2 2009. A further 58 birds.

My First Book of Southern African Creepy-Crawlies 2010. A companion to *Southern African Insects*, this showcases 58 spiders, snails, millipedes and other creepy crawlies. The key shows the creature's size, diet and when it is active.

My First Book of Southern African Insects 2009. Features 58 of the most common, colourful and unusual insects, from ants and dragonflies to beetles and bees.

My First Book of Southern African Snakes and Other Reptiles 2007. As well as 56 snakes, this covers other reptiles, from lizards to tortoises. It illustrates the reptile itself, with information about its home, diet, size, reproduction – and danger rating.

Newman, Kenneth *What's That Bird? A Starter's Guide to Birds of Southern Africa* Struik, South Africa, 3rd edn 2004. Written by the famous birder, Kenneth Newman, this is an excellent bird book for older children and adults new to African birdwatching. It's comprehensive and full of useful spotting tips: a great starter guide.

Health

Wilson-Howarth, Dr Jane *The Essential Guide to Travel Health: Don't Let Bugs Bites and Bowels Spoil Your Trip* Cadogan Books, London, 2009. Formerly simply *Bugs, Bites and Bowels*, this amusing and erudite overview of the hazards of tropical travel is small enough to take with you.

Wilson-Howarth, Dr Jane and Ellis, Dr Matthew *Your Child Abroad: A Travel Health Guide* Bradt Guides, UK, 3rd edn ebook 2014. Full of practical first-hand advice from two leading medical experts. An indispensable guide if you plan to travel abroad with young children.

Historical interest

Andersson, Charles John *Lake Ngami and the River Okavango* Originally published late 1850s; republished as a facsimile reprint by Struik, Cape Town, 1967. Records Namibia and Botswana in the 1850s through the eyes of one of the first traders and hunters in the area.

Baines, Thomas *Explorations in South-west Africa* London, 1864. Although linked more with the countries further east, the travels of Baines, as he accompanied Livingstone and others, makes good reading and is well illustrated by the author.

Bolaane, Dr Maitseo M M *Chiefs, Hunters and San in the Creation of the Moremi Game Reserve, Okavango Delta: Multiracial Interactions and Initiatives, 1956–1979* Botswana, 2013. A scholarly investigation into the social and political climate that underpinned the creation of Moremi Game Reserve in 1962.

Fawcus, Peter and Tilbury, Alan *Botswana: The Road to Independence* Co-publisher Botswana Society, Gaborone, 2000. The authors of this were two of Britain's most senior administrators during the final decade that led to Botswana's independence. Their book paints a rare picture (quite densely packed with detail) of a country's smooth transition from a colonial protectorate to an independent state – and has a particularly interesting foreword by Sir Ketumile Masire, one of Botswana's former presidents.

Gordon, Robert J *The Bushman Myth: The Making of a Namibian Underclass* Westview Press, Colorado and Oxford, 1992. If you, like me, had accepted the received wisdom that Bushmen are the last descendants of Stone Age man, then you must read this. It places the Bushmen in an accurate historical context and deconstructs many of the myths we have created about them. Despite being mainly about the San in Namibia, it's still well worth reading for an understanding of their position in contemporary Botswana.

Grant, Sandy *Botswana and its National Heritage* Melrose Books, Ely, 2012. This is as much a history of Botswana pre-independence than a dry record of its culture. Accessible text adds colour to many historical events and anecdotes, but it's the monochrome photographs from the archives that bring it to life. By the same author as *Botswana: An Historical Anthology*.

Head, Bessie *Serowe: Village of the Rain Wind* Heinemann, UK, 2008. This fascinating collection of oral-history transcripts records villagers' memories of their past, and especially the deeds of their enlightened leaders, Khama the Great, Tshekedi Khama and Sir Seretse Khama, who became first president of the independent Botswana.

Henk, Dan 'The Botswana Defence Force: Evolution of a Professional African Military', *African Security Review*, Volume 13, No 4, 2004.

Lane, Paul, Reid, Andrew and Segobya, Alinah (eds) *The Archaeology of Botswana* Co-publisher Botswana Society, Gaborone, 1998. This is a detailed and academic overview of the archaeology of Botswana, as well as how archaeology has progressed in the country to date. It's an excellent reference, but not a light read.

Livingstone, David *Missionary Travels and Researches in South Africa* John Murray, London, 1857. This classic is fascinating reading, over a century after it was written.

Reader, John *Africa: A Biography of the Continent* Penguin Books, London, 1997. Over 700 pages of highly readable history, interwoven with facts and statistics, to make a remarkable overview of Africa's past. Given that Botswana's boundaries were imposed from Europe, its history must be looked at from a pan-African context to be understood. This book can show you that wider view; it is compelling and essential reading. (Chapters 41 and 42 deal with the early settlers in the Cape, and are largely devoted to the Lozi people.)

Shortridge, G C *The Mammals of South West Africa* Heinemann, London, 1934. This is more of historical interest than a practical field guide.

Tlou, Thomas and Campbell, Alec *History of Botswana* Macmillan Botswana, Gaborone, 1997.

Williams, Susan *Colour Bar: The Triumph of Seretse Khama and His Nation* Penguin, UK, 2007. This recent book documents the impact of the marriage of Sir Seretse Khama and Lady Ruth Williams Khama.

Botswana Notes and Records
The Botswana Society has published an annual journal, *Botswana Notes and Records*, since 1969. It contains 'scientific, and semi-scientific articles and notes, written by amateur as well as professional experts on subjects of permanent interest relating to Botswana'. This is an amazing archive of reliable information, which I've only scratched the surface of here – it's a real treasure trove for anyone interested in Botswana. During my researches I've read many articles and made reference to some of them, including the main ones, which are mentioned here:

Andringa, J 'The Climate of Botswana in Histograms', Volume 16 (1984), pages 117–26.

Campbell, Alec 'A Comment on Kalahari Wildlife and the Khukhe Fence', Volume 13 (1981), pages 111–18.

Campbell, Alec 'The Riddle of the Stone Walls', Volume 23 (1991), pages 243–50.

Cooke, H J and Baillieul, T 'The Caves of Ngamiland: An Interim Report on Explorations and Fieldwork 1972–74', Volume 6 (1974), pages 147–56.

Cooper, Dr S M 'Clan Size of Spotted Hyenas in the Savuti Region of Chobe National Park, Botswana', Volume 21 (1989), pages 121–33.

Garner, R A and Ritter, R C 'Resurvey of Gcwihaba Cave and Exploration of the Aha Sinkhole Caves', Volume 26 (1994), pages 183–8.

Gieske, A 'Modelling of Surface Outflow from the Okavango Delta', Volume 28 (1996), pages 165–92.

Hitchcock, Robert 'A Chronology of Major Events Relating to the Central Kalahari Game Reserve', Volume 31 (1999), pages 105–17.

Mann, P M and Ritter, R C 'Further Exploration and Resurvey of !WaDoum Cave', Volume 27 (1995), pages 13–20.

Parsons, Q N 'Franz or Klikko, the Wild Dancing Bushman: A Case Study in Khoisan Stereotyping', Volume 20 (1989), pages 71–6.

Ramsay, Jeff 'Some Notes on the Colonial Era History of the Central Kalahari Game Reserve Region', Volume 20 (1989), pages 91–4.

Renew, Audrey 'Some Edible Wild Cucumbers of Botswana', Volume 1 (1968), pages 5–8.

Ritter, R C and Garner, R A 'Discovery and Preliminary Exploration of a New Cave in the Gcwihaba Valley', Volume 26 (1994), pages 55–65.

Ritter, Ron and Mann, Paul 'Discovery and Exploration of Two New Caves in the Northwest District', Volume 27 (1995), pages 1–12.

Robbins, L H and Campbell, A C 'The Depression Rock Shelter Site, Tsodilo Hills', Volume 20 (1989), pages 1–3.

Robbins, L H, Murphy, M L, Campbell, A C and Brook, G A 'Excavations at the Tsodilo Hills Rhino Cave', Volume 28 (1996), pages 23–45.

Robbins, Lawrence H 'The Middle Stone Age of Kudiakam Pan', Volume 20 (1989), pages 41–50.

Sommerlatte, M W L 'A Preliminary Report on the Number, Distribution and Movement of Elephants in the Chobe National Park with Notes on Browse Utilisation', Volume 7 (1975), pages 121–9.

Van der Post, Cornelius 'Putting the Bushmen on the Map of Botswana', Volume 32 (2000), pages 107–15.

Viljoen, P C 'New Locality Record for the Klipspinger', Volume 12 (1980), page 169.

Williamson, D T and J E 'An Assessment of the Impact of Fences on Large Herbivore Biomass in the Kalahari', Volume 13 (1981), pages 107–10.

Yellen, J E, Brooks, A S, Stuckenrath, R and Welbourne, R 'A Terminal Pleistocene Assemblage from Drotsky's Cave, Western Ngamiland', Volume 19 (1987), pages 1–6.

Language and culture

Davis, Ronald and researchers at Stanford University 'Y chromosome sequence variation and the history of human populations' *Nature Genetics,* November 2000.

Dunbar, R 'Why gossip is good for you' *New Scientist,* 21 November 1992, pages 28–31.

Rantao, Paul Mmolotsi *Setswana Culture and Tradition* Pentagon Publishers, Gaborone, 2006. A straightforward introduction to the traditional Setswana lifestyle, covering everything from social structure and daily rituals to religious beliefs and practices.

Novels

Dow, Unity *Far and Beyon'* Spinifex Press, Australia, 2000. Tackling the complex issues of the role of women in society, and the conflict of the traditional and modern world, this is the first of Unity Dow's novels. Botswana's first female high-court judge, she brings her experience of the legal profession to her deceptively simple stories. Later books, also published by Spinifex, are *The Screaming of the Innocent* (2002), *Juggling Truths* (2003), and *The Heavens May Fall* (2007).

Head, Bessie *Maru* Heinemann, UK, 1972. The uplifting story of a Masarwa orphan's experiences of racial prejudice at a time when the Bushmen were treated as slaves by the dominant peoples of Botswana. South African by birth, Bessie Head came to Botswana as a refugee and was granted citizenship after 15 years. Her other novels include *When Rain Clouds Gather* (1968) and *A Question of Power* (1974), both published by Heinemann.

McCall-Smith, Alexander *The No 1 Ladies' Detective Agency* Abacus, UK, 2003. Mma Precious Ramotswe and her detective agency have been taken to the hearts of readers worldwide, but her roots are firmly in Gaborone. McCall-Smith's gently humorous tales, of which this is the first, are set in the context of modern-day Botswana, and will enrich even the shortest visit to the country.

Children's novels

Botumile, Bontekanye *The Elephant Story* (2006), *Patterns in the Sky* (2007), *The Seed Children* (2008), Thari-e-Ntsho Storytellers, Maun (w botswanastories.com). This series of illustrated books for primary-school children combines Botswana legends with notes on topics such as traditional remedies.

McNeice, Angus, Maisie and Travers *The Lion Children* Orion Books Ltd, London, 2001. This entertaining scrapbook about life in the bush was written by three British children whose lives were transformed when their parents moved to the Okavango (around NG34) to research lions. While basically a children's book, it's a lot of fun to read and occasionally quite insightful.

Other useful guides

Bulpin, T V *Discovering Southern Africa* Discovering Southern Africa Productions, South Africa (distributed by Book Sales), 1992. Part guidebook and part history book, this covers mainly South Africa but also extends into Namibia and Zimbabwe. A weighty tome with useful background views and information, written from a South African perspective.

Campbell, Alec *The Guide to Botswana* Winchester Press, Johannesburg, first published 1968. Alec Campbell is perhaps the leading authority on Botswana's natural areas and history, having not only lived in Botswana for most of his life, but also held posts as the Director of National Parks and later as the Director of the National Museum of Botswana. There were several very substantial editions to this early guide which give insights into what Botswana was like decades ago. It's also fascinating to contrast and compare his guides with more contemporary guidebooks.

Campbell, Alec and Coulson, David *African Rock Art: Painting and Engraving on Stone* Abrams, New York, 2001. Campbell's informative text underpins some stunning photography, making this so much more than a coffee-table book.

Chittenden, Hugh (compiler) *Top Birding Spots of Southern Africa* Southern Book Publishers, South Africa, 1992. This useful, practical book details about 400 sites for keen birdwatchers, listing local specialities and endemic species with a checklist of key species for each site. Some of its simple maps are now out of date, though I'm not aware of it being reprinted in the last decade.

Dodwell, Christina *An Explorer's Handbook: Travel, Survival and Bush Cookery* Hodder and Stoughton, London, 1984. Over 170 pages of practical and amusing anecdotes, including chapters on 'unusual eatables', 'building an open fire' and 'tested exits from tight corners'. Practical advice for both possible and most unlikely eventualities – and it's a great read.

Gifford, James and Stockhall, Steven *Wildlife Photography in Botswana: A practical guide* Enlivened, Botswana, 2010. From technical know-how and equipment to where and how to photograph wildlife in Botswana, this is a helpful manual both for first-time photographers and those seeking more advanced skills – with some superb images.

Main, Mike *African Adventurer's Guide to Botswana* New Holland, UK, 2001. Mike Main is a leading authority on all things to do with Botswana, and especially its wilder areas. This book builds on the earlier *Visitor's Guide to Botswana*. It features route descriptions for some very offbeat 4x4 trips, including a few GPS points and schematic maps of the routes.

Main, Mike *Kalahari: Life's Variety in Dune and Delta* Macmillan, UK, 1988.

Rattray, Gordon *Access Africa* Bradt Guides, UK, 2009. An invaluable guide to Africa's major safari areas for travellers with limited mobility.

USEFUL WEBSITES For the websites of Botswana's most widely read newspapers, see page 150. A selection of the web's most interesting resources on Botswana include:

w **anthro.fullerton.edu/Okavango** A site by the Okavango anthropology researcher John Bock, which focuses on the peoples of the Okavango area.

w **bidpa.bw** Home for the Botswana Institute for Development Policy Analysis (BIDPA). It's a fairly dry NGO site but includes some quite detailed papers on Botswana's economic development.

w **botswanatourism.co.bw** The official website of the Botswana Tourism Board, complete with useful contacts, is both colourful and accessible.

w **clio.columbia.edu** and search 'Botswana'. Columbia University's Department of African Studies is a good starting place for information on Botswana, with basic summaries and lots of good links.

w **expertafrica.com** The home page for Expert Africa, run by this guide's author, incorporates interactive maps featuring many locations within Botswana and more lodge reviews than any other site apart from Tripadvisor.

w **gov.bw** The home page of Botswana's government. If you want to email a minister, download the customs regulations, apply for an e-visa or read the latest budget speech – this is the place.

w **library.stanford.edu/areas/african-collections** With a long page of links to sites relating to Botswana – some useful, others not – this is a helpful starting point if you're surfing around seeking information.

PHOTOGRAPHERS

Alamy.com: WorldFoto (WF/A); Ariadne Van Zandbergen (AVZ); Bob Hayne (BH); Charlotte McIntyre (ChaM); Chris McIntyre (CM); Dreamstime.com: Ben Mcrae (BM/D), Cezary Wojtkowski (CW/D), Charles Sichel-outcalt (CS/D), Daniel Smith (DS/D), Dietmar Temps (DT/D), Ecophoto (E/D), Hel080808 (H/D), Jennifer Pillingerr (JP/D), Kobus Peche (KP/D), Lucaar (L/D), Maniec/D (M/D), Ondřej Prosický (OP/D), Patrice Correia (PC/D), Rabor74 (R/D), Richard Isaacman (RI/D), Romitas (Ro/D), Rudmer Zwerver (RZ/D), Slowmotiongli (S/D), Stu Porter (SP/D); Wirestock (W/D); James Gifford (JG); James McIntyre (JM); Minden Pictures: Theo Allofs (TA/M); Shutterstock.com: 2630ben (26/S), Aboubakar Malipula (AM/S), Albie Venter (AV/S), bcampbell65 (B/S), Brian Stuart Nel (BSN/S), C_Schmittmann (CS/S), EcoPrint (E/S), Eugene Troskie (ET/S), Fotografie-Kuhlmann (FK/S), Gaston Piccinetti (GP/S), imageBROKER.com (IB/S), John Carnemolla (JC/S), John Peter Davies (JPD/S), Lars Royal (LR/S), Lookingforcats (L/S), LouieLea (LL/S), Lucian Coman (LC/S), Lukas Bischoff Photograph (LBP/S), Mark Dumbleton (M/S), Martin Mecnarowski (MM/S), Mary Angela Heys (MAH/S), Mike Dexter (MD/S), Ondřej Prosický (OP/S), Radek Borovka (RB/S), rebekkastutz (r/S), Robert Rusch (RR/S), Roger de La Harpe (RH/S), sasha_gerasimov (SG/S), Simon Eeman (SE/S), Snapped by Goose (SbG/S), SouWest Photography (SWP/S), Stacey Ann Alberts (SA/S), Stephan Roeger (SR/S), Stu Porter (SP/S), SW_Stock (SW/S), T. Wilbertz (TW/S), Thomas Retterath (TR/S), Tobie Oosthuizen (TO/S), Travelvolo (T/S), Trevor Fairbank (TF/S), Villiers Steyn (VS/S), Wirestock Creators (WC/S); SuperStock (SS); Tricia Hayne (TH)

Sixth edition published November 2024
First published 2003
Bradt Travel Guides Ltd
31a High Street, Chesham, Buckinghamshire, HP5 1BW, England
www.bradtguides.com
Print edition published in the USA by The Globe Pequot Press Inc,
PO Box 480, Guilford, Connecticut 06437-0480

Text copyright © Chris McIntyre, 2024
Maps copyright © Bradt Travel Guides Ltd, 2024; includes map data ©
OpenStreetMap contributors
Photographs copyright © Individual photographers (see below), 2024
Project Manager: Samantha Fletcher
Cover research: Pepi Bluck, Perfect Picture

ISBN: 9781804692233

British Library Cataloguing in Publication Data
A catalogue record for this book is available from the British Library

Photographs For photographer details, see page 547

Front cover Lion in Chobe National Park (TA/MP)
Back cover (clockwise from top left) Mokoro in the Okavango Delta (SR/S); carmine
bee-eater (OP/S); zebras (IB/S)
Title page (clockwise from top left) Leopard and cub (OP/S); elephant (MD/S); safari
in Moremi (OP/S)

Illustrations by Annabel Milne and Carole Vincer

Maps David McCutcheon FBCart.S. FRGS

Typeset by Ian Spick, Bradt Guides, and www.dataworks.co.in
Production managed by Gutenberg Press Ltd; printed in Malta
Digital conversion by www.dataworks.co.in

Paper used for this product comes from sustainably managed forests, and recycled
and controlled sources.

Acknowledgements

This sixth edition, like its predecessors, couldn't have been written without the help of many people and we're immensely grateful to them all. Our greatest thanks and recognition go to our children, James and Charlotte, who are without question the most engaging and entertaining travelling companions we could wish for. Their depth of knowledge about Africa's wildest corners, its birds and wildlife, is both impressive and heart-warming. It is our greatest pleasure to share these African adventures as a family.

At Expert Africa, we extend heartfelt thanks to our fantastically supportive team, notably Botswana specialists Anton Walker and Tom Morris, who not only provided great detail in researching sections of this edition, but offered invaluable insights into the country's safari industry and wildlife in general. Thanks also to the hundreds of Expert Africa's travellers who have helped with detailed feedback from their safaris and allowed us to publish their unedited feedback on w expertafrica. com; these online reports form an invaluable first-hand record of the country's better lodges and camps, from which we continually learn. These same Expert Africa travellers have also enthusiastically engaged in our fantastic citizen science project tracking Africa's key mammal species: w expertafrica.com/wildlife-surveys. With over 60,000 participants in the project already, we have built up an impressive picture of exactly where is best to see particular animals in the bush, and our extensive data is now being used by wildlife researchers too! We'd love you to join the project when you take your Botswana safari.

In Botswana, many individuals and companies have helped with the various editions of this guidebook and its predecessor, *Guide to Namibia & Botswana*, over the last few decades – and to them all, we owe thanks. I hope that those who aren't mentioned here will forgive the omissions, but those who have helped us most recently include Stuart Mackay and Michael Weyl at Mack Air; Hilton Walker, Tracy Bamber, Beverly Joubert and Dereck Joubert from Great Plains; Louis Mynhardt and Clive Millar of the Kwando team; Colin Bell and Dave van Smeerdijk from Natural Selection; Fran Hird at Ker & Downey Botswana; Alistair and Wendy Rankin, Richard Bennett, Shaun Malan and Ponche Whelpton at Machaba Safaris; Kate Holmes and Grant Truthe at Setari; Beks Ndlovu at African Bush Camps; Ralph Bousfield from Uncharted Africa; and Roberto Viviani and the Wilderness Safaris team, to whom we are also grateful for kind permission to borrow from their diagrams for the illustrations in Chapter 1.

In writing this, we're aware that there are many above who know much more about Botswana than we do. We'd particularly like to acknowledge Alec Campbell, Mike Main and the late, great Veronica Roodt. All have written amazing scholarly works on Botswana, which have been a real inspiration, and all kindly offered their help over the years. While we hope this guide introduces you to Botswana, do look up their erudite works (from page 540).

Finally, thanks to Samantha Fletcher, Susannah Lord and Claire Strange from Bradt. Their diligence and dedication to this guide have helped to make it the finest Botswana guide on the market and we're extremely proud to be part of the team.

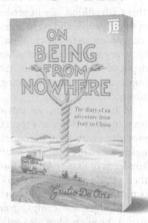

Index

Page numbers in **bold** indicate main entries; those in *italics* indicate maps.

aardvark **58**, 288, 385, 448, 455,
  464
aardwolf **34**, 288, 294, 385, 455
abseiling (Victoria Falls) 525
Abu Camp 364, 367
Abu Concession (NG 26) 363–6
acacia 16
accidents, road 126
accommodation 145–7
  costs 145–6
  tourism levy 145
  travellers with disabilities 122–3
  see also individual locations
Afrikaans 104, 539
agama **63**, 448
agriculture 87
Aha Campsite 440
Aha Hills 407, 420, 434–41, *435*
air travel
  charter flights 134, 144, 190
  deep vein thrombosis (DVT)
    157
  getting there and away 131–3
  internal flights 111–12, 132, 144
  luggage allowance 134
  scenic flights 210–11, 524
  travellers with disabilities 122
alcohol 148
Amber River Camp 390
Anantara Royal Livingstone 514
Andersson, Charles John 334, 422
anthrax 162
arrest 168
ATM machines 141
Atzaró Okavango Camp 390
Audi Camp 200–1
Avani Victoria Falls Resort 514

Babolaongwe people 104
baboon **37**, 259, 357, 448, 475
Baby Huey (elephant) 275
backpacking trips 121
  costs 138
  see also camping
Baines' Baobabs 451, 452, **459–60**
Baines' Baobabs campsites 458
Baines' Camp 390–1
Bakalanga people 101
Bakgwatheng people 104
Bakwena Lodge 122, 226–7
Balozi people 101, 102
Bamangwato people 75, 76, 78, 80,
  106, 108
Bana ba Letsatsi 208–9
Bangologa people 104
banks 141
Banoka people 102

Bantu languages 538
Bantu-speaking people 72, **73–4**,
  93, **101**
Baobab Safari Lodge 261
Baphaleng people 104
Bashaga people 104
basketry 103, 107, 205, 218, 420
Basubiya people **101–2**, 245, 270
bat 438
bat-eared fox **33**, 249, 288, 294,
  304, 463, 492
Batawana people 103, 301, 423
Bathoen, Chief 79
Batswana people 74–5, 79, 80,
  101
  white Batswana 104
Bayei people 101, 102, 107, 245
Bechuanaland, British Protectorate
  of 75, 78, **79–81**, 108, 260
Bechuanaland People's Party
  (BPP) 81
beers 148
Beetsha 335, 350
Big Five Chobe Lodge 227–8
bilharzia 161–2
binoculars **137**, 179
birds and birdwatching **66–9**
  Chobe riverfront 254–5
  highlights 66, 68, 115–16
  Impalila Island 239
  Kalahari 428, 438–9, 450–1,
    455–6, 464–5, 477, 493
  Kasane 235–6
  Kwando Concession 298
  Linyanti Concession 288
  migrants 66
  Moremi Game Reserve 305, 309,
    321, 323, 327, 330–1
  Ngwezumba Pans 269
  Okavango Delta 337, 344, 353,
    357, 361, 369, 374, 378–9,
    385–6, 389, 396, 400, 417,
    422–3
    see also Moremi Game
      Reserve; Panhandle
  Panhandle 404–6, 413
  Savuti 276
  Selinda Concession 294
  Victoria Falls 528–9
blackflies 159
boating
  Chobe River 236, 258–60, 261
  jet-boating 526
  mokoro **181–2**, 183, 211–12,
    236, 261, 333, 394
  Moremi Game Reserve 320–1,
    333

motorboats 181, **182**, 236, 252,
  342, 346, 359, 418
  Okavango Delta 211–12, 394
  Thamalakane River 210
  Victoria Falls 523
  wildlife hazards 182–3
  Zambezi River 257, 524
  see also canoeing
Bodumatau Lagoon 324, 325
border posts 133–4
Boro River 210, 211, 371, 373, 378,
  388, 389
Boteti River 114, 445, 474, 475,
  478
Boteti River Camp 478–9
Botswana Defence Force (BDF)
  21–2, 83, 84, 240–1, **242**
bribery 168
British South Africa Company
  (BSAC) 79, 80
budgeting 138–40
buffalo 25, **53**, 179–80, 275, 287,
  294, 298, 304, 329, 351, 352–3,
  378, 384–5, 396, 399
bungee jumping (Victoria Falls)
  525
bus travel 145
bush camping *see* camping
bush fires 116
bush, walking in *see* walking
  safaris
bushbaby **37**, 448, 455, 464
bushbuck **43**, 254, 352, 360, 475
Bushman Plains Camp 337
'Bushmen' 91
  see also San people
bushpig **54–5**, 288

cable swing/slide (Victoria Falls)
  525
Camp Kalahari 471
Camp Kuzuma 244
Camp Linyanti 281, 283
Camp Maru 391
Camp Moremi 317
Camp Okavango 348
Camp Savuti 277
Camp Xakanaxa 317–18
camping 173–7
  booking pitches 127–8
  campfires 174
  campsite facilities 128–9
  campsite operators and fees 128,
    139
  choosing a site 174
  equipment 136, 175–6, 206
  hygiene 183–4

INDEX OF ADVERTISERS

THE BRADT STORY

In the beginning

It all began in 1974 on an Amazon river barge. During an 18-month trip through South America, two adventurous young backpackers - Hilary Bradt and her then husband, George – decided to write about the hiking trails they had discovered through the Andes. *Backpacking Along Ancient Ways in Peru and Bolivia* included the very first descriptions of the Inca Trail. It was the start of a colourful journey to becoming one of the best-loved travel publishers in the world; you can read the full story on our website (**bradtguides. com/ourstory**).

Getting there first

Hilary quickly gained a reputation for being a true travel pioneer, and in the 1980s she started to focus on guides to places overlooked by other publishers. The Bradt Guides list became a roll call of guidebook 'firsts'. We published the first guide to Madagascar, followed by Mauritius, Czechoslovakia and Vietnam. The 1990s saw the beginning of our extensive coverage of Africa: Tanzania, Uganda, South Africa, and Eritrea. Later, post-conflict guides became a feature: Rwanda, Mozambique, Angola, and Sierra Leone, as well as the first standalone guides to the Baltic States following the fall of the Iron Curtain, and the first post-war guides to Bosnia, Kosovo and Albania.

Comprehensive – and with a conscience

Today, we are the world's largest independently owned travel publisher, with more than 200 titles. However, our ethos remains unchanged. Hilary is still keenly involved, and **we still get there first**: two-thirds of Bradt guides have no direct competition.

But we don't just get there first. Our guides are also known for being **more comprehensive** than any other series. We avoid templates and tick-lists. Each guide is a one-of-a-kind expression of an expert author's interests, knowledge and enthusiasm for telling it how it really is.

And a commitment to wildlife, conservation and respect for local communities has always been at the heart of our books. Bradt Guides was **championing sustainable travel** before any other guidebook publisher. We even have a series dedicated to Slow Travel in the UK, award-winning books that explore the country with a passion and depth you'll find nowhere else.

Thank you!

We can only do what we do because of the support of readers like you – people who value less-obvious experiences, less-visited places and a more thoughtful approach to travel. Those who, like us, take travel seriously.

TRAVEL TAKEN SERIOUSLY